T0190360

Communications in Computer and Information Science 1645

More information about this series at https://link.springer.com/bookseries/7899

Rocco Furferi · Lapo Governi · Yary Volpe ·
Kate Seymour · Anna Pelagotti ·
Francesco Gherardini (Eds.)

The Future of Heritage Science and Technologies

ICT and Digital Heritage

Third International Conference, Florence Heri-Tech 2022
Florence, Italy, May 16–18, 2022
Proceedings

 Springer

Editors
Rocco Furferi 🄳
University of Florence
Florence, Italy

Yary Volpe 🄳
University of Florence
Florence, Italy

Anna Pelagotti 🄳
European Research Council (ERC)
National Research Council of Italy (CNR)
Rome, Italy

Lapo Governi 🄳
University of Florence
Florence, Italy

Kate Seymour 🄳
Stichting Restauratie Atelier Limburg
Maastricht, The Netherlands

Francesco Gherardini 🄳
University of Modena and Reggio Emilia
Modena, Italy

ISSN 1865-0929   ISSN 1865-0937 (electronic)
Communications in Computer and Information Science
ISBN 978-3-031-20301-5   ISBN 978-3-031-20302-2 (eBook)
https://doi.org/10.1007/978-3-031-20302-2

This Springer imprint is published by the registered company Springer Nature Switzerland AG
The registered company address is: Gewerbestrasse 11, 6330 Cham, Switzerland

Preface

This book presents a selection of contributions, dealing with the application of ICT in the field of cultural heritage, presented at the 3rd Florence Heri-Tech International Conference (Florence Heri-Tech 2022) held during May 16–18, 2022, in Firenze, Italy.

Organized under the patronage of the University of Florence with the support of the Department of Industrial Engineering, Florence Heri-Tech 2022 gathered researchers and experts in the field of "heritage science and related technologies" to disseminate their recent research at an international level as well as to draw new inspiration. The conference was part of the 2022 Florence International Biennial for Art and Restoration, an international event attracting prestigious institutions and companies and creating a unique opportunity to bring together the academic world with industry.

The overarching goal of Florence Heri-Tech is to promote European mobility and cooperation among researchers, students, and practitioners, to further Europe's growth as a multi-cultural society, and to promote the idea that scientific-cultural research must be an important part of society. Furthermore, the conference aims to foster international networks between universities, training institutions, and businesses in order to foster long-term partnership prospects.

More than 80 experts, coordinated by the General Chairs and supported by a high-level Technical and Scientific Committee, were involved in the review process, which led to the selection of 32 papers (out of 101 papers submitted to the conference and 146 abstracts received by the Scientific Committee). The review process was double blind, with each submission receiving at least 3 reviews. The overall number of authors involved at the conference was 140. Contributions focused on multi-disciplinary and inter-disciplinary research concerning the use of innovative ICT-based methodologies and technologies for documenting, managing, preserving, and communicating cultural heritage.

The editors would like to personally thank everyone participating in the review process for their dedication and skill. Special appreciation goes to the members of the Technical and Scientific Committee who made it possible for the conference to take place.

The conference prestige was enhanced by the participation of the Honorary Chairs. The General Chairs also extend their thanks to all authors, speakers, and contributors whose labor, financial support, and encouragement made the Florence Heri-Tech 2022 event possible.

May 2022

Rocco Furferi
Lapo Governi
Yary Volpe
Kate Seymour
Anna Pelagotti
Francesco Gherardini

Organization

General Chairs

Rocco Furferi	University of Florence, Italy
Lapo Governi	University of Florence, Italy
Yary Volpe	University of Florence, Italy
Rodorico Giorgi	University of Florence, Italy
Anna Pelagotti	Executive Agency of the European Research Council, Italy
Kate Seymour	Stichting Restauratie Atelier Limburg (SRAL), The Netherlands

Organizing Committee

Elena Amodei	Salone Arte e Restauro di Firenze, Italy
Francesco Gherardini	University of Modena and Reggio Emilia, Italy
Rocco Furferi	University of Florence, Italy
Lucia Maranzana	Salone Arte e Restauro di Firenze, Italy

Honorary Chairs

Baglioni, Piero	University of Florence, Italy
Bonsanti, Giorgio	University of Florence, Italy
Cappellini, Vito	University of Florence, Italy
Cather, Sharon	The Courtauld Institute of Art, UK
Ciatti, Marco	Opificio delle Pietre Dure, Italy
Colombini Maria Perla	National Research Council of Italy - Institute for the Conservation and Valorization of Cultural Heritage (CNR-ICVBC), Italy
Dei, Luigi	University of Florence, Italy
Delgado Rodrigues, Jose	Laboratorio Nacional De Engenharia Civil, Portugal
Matteini, Mauro	National Research Council of Italy - Institute for the Conservation and Valorization of Cultural Heritage (CNR-ICVBC), Italy
Primicerio, Mario	University of Florence, Italy
Santos, Pedro	Fraunhofer Institute for Computer Graphics Research IGD, Germany
Sgamellotti, Antonio	University of Perugia, Italy

Technical and Scientific Committee

Al Huneidi, Hani M.	International Cultural Heritage Specialist, Jordan
Argenti, Fabrizio	University of Florence, Italy
Balocco, Carla	University of Florence, Italy
Berardi, Umberto	Ryerson University, Canada
Bianconi, Francesco	University of Perugia, Italy
Bici, Michele	Sapienza University of Rome, Italy
Buonamici, Francesco	University of Florence, Italy
Camilli, Andrea	Soprintendenza per i Beni Archeologici della Toscana, Italy
Cassar, JoAnn	University of Malta, Malta
Cavalieri, Duccio	University of Florence, Italy
Corallo, Angelo	University of Salento, Italy
Cheung, Sidney	The Chinese University of Hong Kong, Hong Kong
Del Bianco, Corinna	International Institute Life Beyond Tourism and Romualdo Del Bianco Foundation, Italy
Del Bimbo, Alberto	University of Florence, Italy
Di Angelo, Luca	University of L'Aquila, Italy
Bruno, Fabio	University of Calabria, Italy
Es Sebar, Leila	Politecnico di Torino, Italy
Fernandez, Federica	Istituto EuroMediterraneo di Scienza e Tecnologia, Italy
Ferrise, Francesco	Polytechnic of Milan, Italy
Fioravanti, Marco	University of Florence, Italy
Frischer, Bernard	Indiana University, USA
Garmendia Arrieta, Leire	University of the Basque Country (UPV/EHU), Spain
Gherardini, Francesco	University of Modena and Reggio Emilia, Italy
Goli, Giacomo	University of Florence, Italy
Guidi, Gabriele	Polytechnic of Milan, Italy
Hazan, Susan	Israel Consortium for Digital Heritage, Israel
Iadanza, Ernesto	University of Florence, Italy
Lanzoni, Luca	Polytechnical University of Cartagena, Spain
Lazoi, Mariangela	University of Salento, Italy
Macdonald, Susan	Getty Conservation Institute, USA
Markevicius, Tomas	University of Amsterdam, The Netherlands
Martín Lerones, Pedro	CARTIF Technology Center, Spain
Olsson, Nina	Art Conservation, LLC, USA
Patelli, Alessandro	University of Padua, Italy
Pavia, Anselmo	Federal University of Maranhão, Brazil
Pellicciari, Marcello	University of Modena and Reggio Emilia, Italy

Contents

3D Reconstruction of Tangible Cultural Heritage and Monitoring Devices

Digital Historical Pavia: 3D Modeling in Educational Context for Cultural Heritage Promotion

Virginio Cantoni$^{(\boxtimes)}$, Piercarlo Dondi , Alessio Gullotti, Luca Lombardi ,
Mauro Mosconi , Roberto Nour, and Alessandra Setti

Department of Electrical, Computer and Biomedical Engineering,
University of Pavia, Via A. Ferrata 5, 27100 Pavia, Italy
{virginio.cantoni,piercarlo.dondi,luca.lombardi,mauro.mosconi,
alessandra.setti}@unipv.it,
{alessio.gullotti01,roberto.nour01}@universitadipavia.it

Abstract. The "Digital Historical Pavia" project aims to prove the value of digital media technologies for enhancing promotion and accessibility of Cultural Heritage, while teaching students the basics of computer graphics. It integrates technology into attractive and meaningful presentations of local cultural assets of the $14^{th} - 16^{th}$ century when the city of Pavia experienced several transformations. This paper summarizes the main results of the project showing the outcomes of three case studies: (i) the setup of an educational and experiential room for the exhibition "1525–2015. Pavia, the Battle, the Future. Nothing was the same again"; (ii) the virtual reconstruction of the city of Pavia in the Renaissance, including a timelapse of the urban evolution of the city during the 16th century; (iii) the 3D modeling of the Ark of St. Augustine, a complex funerary monument of the second half of the 14th century, and the development of a related online serious game. All the 3D models were created by students of the master's degree in Computer Engineering of the University of Pavia, showing the potentiality of an experiential learning approach for teaching computer science and computer graphics concepts.

Keywords: Digital heritage · 3D modeling · Education

1 Introduction

Digital Humanities is an interdisciplinary research field that refers to the application of information technology instruments and methodologies for research, acquisition, analysis, annotation, and dissemination of knowledge of cultural assets [1–3]. The digitization of artworks is an effective way to answer the challenges they must face, such as, for example, destruction (targeted or for natural

R. Furferi et al. (Eds.): Florence Heri-Tech 2022, CCIS 1645, pp. 3–14, 2022.
https://doi.org/10.1007/978-3-031-20302-2_1

events), aging, fragility, accessibility issues, dissemination, and promotion. Digital contents allow access to remote audiences, enable new collaboration and interaction with content, supplement new methods to existing approaches, and create new knowledge.

In the last years, Europe has seen a significant investment in the digitization of its cultural assets. Different forms of digital publishing and new practices in the communication now empower the sector (e.g., the Europeana digital library [4]); and ensuring a wide use of digital technologies across the economy and society is one of the targets of the new EU funding program (2021–2027) "Digital Europe".

The "Digital Historical Pavia" project is born in this context to both enhancing the promotion and accessibility of historical buildings and monuments of the city of Pavia (Italy) and to teach students basic concepts of computer graphics in an engaging way. We applied a new teaching approach, *experiential learning* [5], that focuses on the realization of real projects improving the students' involvement. We assigned to students of the master's degree in Computer Engineering of the University of Pavia the 3D reproduction of many cultural assets, often not using straightforward direct digital acquisition, because prevented by different factors (no longer existing artifacts, fragility, difficult access), but instead using historical sources as references.

The project comprehends three case studies: (i) the setup of an educational and experiential room for the exhibition "1525–2015. Pavia, the Battle, the Future. Nothing was the same again" [6]; (ii) the virtual reconstruction of the city of Pavia in the Renaissance [7]; (iii) the 3D reconstruction of the Ark of St. Augustine, a complex funerary monument of the second half of the 14th century.

This work summarizes the main outcomes of these three case studies, focusing in particular on the latest results: a timelapse of the urban evolution of Pavia during the 16th century, the completion of the 3D model of the Ark of St. Augustine and the realization of a related online serious game, designed to teach historical information about the monument in an engaging way.

The remaining of the paper is structured as follows: Sect. 2 gives a brief overview about the use of 3D modeling in the Cultural Heritage field; Sect. 3 explains the structure of our teaching method; Sect. 4 describes the project and the obtained outcomes; finally, Sect. 5 draws the conclusions and proposes possible future steps.

2   3D Modeling in Cultural Heritage

Digital media can serve in preserving and promoting Cultural Heritage, granting permanent and easy access to artworks, by means of a transformation of an existing object into a virtual copy [3,8]. Notable examples include the digitization of statues [9,10], fresco fragments [11], archaeological sites [12,13] or even historical musical instruments [14].

In addition, when not applied to a mere conversion of existing resources into digital form, 3D modeling could be useful also for reconstruction or re-elaboration, for example to replace parts of a ruined relic [15] or to bring to new life lost masterpieces [16]. In this context, 3D printing is a crucial technology able to quickly produce replica of artworks (or of parts of them), that can be used both to substitute missing relics (e.g., due to temporary loans, stealing, or destruction), and to improve the accessibility of museums for blind or visually impaired visitors [17,18].

Nowadays, documenting and storing digitized cultural assets has become more affordable and reliable [19], and thus, museums are digitizing their collections not only for preservation or research purposes, but also for making them accessible to a larger audience in an attractive way, both online [20] or through virtual and augmented reality applications [21].

Different digitization approaches suit different classes of objects (according to size and type) and have different strengths and weaknesses. They can be implemented through active or passive 3D sensing techniques and so the creation of a content repository for 3D digitized relics must take into account the phases of data capture, modeling, storage and visualization [3].

Overall, 3D modeling has now a wide variety of potential uses in the Cultural Heritage field, such as: documentation and preservation; research analyses (e.g., morphological examination and comparison of fragile artifacts without risk of damaging them); re-contextualization (e.g., a statue now located in a museum, virtually placed where it was originally); virtual connection of artworks that are logically related but physically dispersed; virtual visit experiences (e.g., for temporary closed location, as in recent pandemic time, or to provide in advance the background needed to improve the comprehension of the on-site experience); replication (for the preservation of the original or for the recreation of stolen or lost artworks); restoration (e.g., add missing or broken parts); accessibility for people with disabilities (e.g., 3D printing with Braille annotations); improvement of cultural and scientific dissemination (e.g., through gaming, or virtual and augmented reality applications); and enhancement of the teaching experience.

These last two applications are the main goal of our project.

3   Teaching Method

In literature we can find many ways and approaches to properly teach computer graphics [22]. We chose an interactive method based on experiential learning [5], focusing in particular on the 3D modeling task. We employed it in a university-level course at the University of Pavia (Italy) for the master's degree in Computer Engineering, starting in the A.Y. 2014/15 until the A.Y. 2019/20. A complete description of the course organization can be found in [7], here we provide a summary of the main steps.

The course was structured on both theoretical (20 h) and practical lectures (40 h), followed by approximately 50 h of students' self-learning to complete their assigned task. The core idea was to boost self-motivated learning with Digital Humanities projects about the history of Pavia and its architecture. More precisely, we entrusted students with digital reconstructions of historical monuments, statues or buildings, using as reference various historical sources

Fig. 1. Some of the best 3D models made by the students. From top to bottom, left to right: the third order of the Ark of St. Augustine, front side; some architectural details of the Ark; the Collegio Borromeo; the fourth order of the Ark; the Visconti Castle; the 'Ponte Coperto' (covered bridge); the statue of the Authority; 'Piazza Grande' (now, Victory Square); the church of Santa Maria del Carmine; the church of San Francesco; the 'Pizzo in Giù' tower.

(paintings, drawings, frescoes) and/or photos for the still existing assets. No background in computer graphics or 3D modeling was requested; basic concepts have been provided with a series of introductory lectures. The practical lectures started "guided" and gradually became more "independent", giving the students the opportunity to try possible solutions by themselves, while the teachers acted only as supervisors. For their final assignment, the students were grouped into teams of two-three people, and each group had to model one or more objects (e.g., building, monuments, statues), depending on their dimension and complexity. As main 3D modeling software we initially adopted CINEMA 4D, and then we moved to Blender, a well-known open-source 3D creation suite. Other programs were occasionally used for specific sub-tasks (e.g., Mixamo Fuse Character Creator for base characters creation).

It is important to stress that the goal was not to obtain perfect reproductions of the original assets (like those achievable with laser scanners or photogrammetry), neither a professional 3D modeling, but rather to push the students to apply the methods learned during the theoretical lectures as well as to learn how to properly cooperate in group on a large project. The students modeled from scratch the assigned objects, trying to realize them as much similar as possible to the reference photos and drawings. They started applying standard modeling procedures, and then they searched and experimented by themselves the additional methods needed to complete the assigned tasks (e.g., some groups preferred to focus on texture, other on sculpting). Nevertheless, most of the students were able to produce 3D models very faithful to the original sources, in some cases far better than expected, considering their limited experience in 3D modeling (Fig. 1). Overall, only around 10% of the students produced models of insufficient quality, a reasonable percentage in view of the difficulty of the assigned tasks. The various editions of the course have been generally well received by the students (we obtained high scores in the evaluation questionnaires), as well as the experiential learning approach. We also assisted to an increase in the enrollments during the years.

4 Digital Historical Pavia

Between the 14th and the 16th centuries the city of Pavia experienced several transformations, with the construction of new buildings and monuments and the destruction of old ones. This project tries to integrate state-of-the-art computer graphics technologies into a more attractive and meaningful presentation of the historical local assets, while teaching students the basics of computer graphics.

As said in the Introduction, the project includes three case studies, each of them with different complexities. During the A.Y. 2014/15 the students created 3D models of the main characters and elements of seven famous tapestries depicting the Battle of Pavia of 1525, as part of an exhibition held at the Visconti Castle of Pavia, a side event of EXPO2015. This initial project was followed, during the A.Y. 2015/16 and 2016/17, by the reproduction of the city of Pavia as it was in the Renaissance. Finally, from the A.Y. 2017/18 to the A.Y. 2019/20, the students worked on the modeling of the Ark of St. Augustine, a big funeral monument made of hundreds of elements, mainly statues and bas-reliefs. The projects assigned to each group of students during the years were then merged and completed during a series of graduation theses, focused on the combination and refinement of the partial results (e.g., the completion of the city of Pavia starting from the main historical buildings, or the composition of the various levels of the Ark from the single statues and bas-reliefs).

In the following, we will describe in detail each project, focusing in particular on the most recent outcomes.

4.1 The Battle of Pavia Exhibition

At the end of 2014, our research group was entrusted by the municipality of Pavia to set up an educational and interactive room as part of the exhibition "1525–2015. Pavia, the Battle, the Future. Nothing was the same again", held at the Visconti Castle from June to November 2015. The exhibition was very successful with more than ten thousand tickets sold.

The realized installation (Fig. 2) included: 3D printed elements (six characters, a cannon, and two prints of the city of Pavia), a virtual avatar (one workstation); seven full-color tactile images for blind and partially sighted people; gesture interaction by means of a Kinect sensor (one workstation); and gaze-based interaction by means of eye trackers (three workstations) [6].

Fig. 2. Photos from the 2015 exhibition at the Visconti Castle [6]. On the left, from top to bottom: 3D printed characters and objects, tactile images of the tapestries, the gesture-based interactive system. On the right: a user tries the interactive avatar (top) and the gaze-based interactive application (bottom).

The part of the exhibition entrusted to the students was the 3D modeling of the main characters and items depicted in the tapestries, that were later 3D printed to be exposed. About thirty students (A.Y. 2014/2015) participated in the project, using CINEMA 4D and Mixamo Fuse Character Creator software tools. This was our first experiment of an experiential learning approach. The good results obtained by the students, as well as their positive feedback, convinced us to continue and refine this teaching method in the following years.

4.2   The City of Pavia in the Renaissance

During the A.Y. 2015/2016 and 2016/2017, we focused on a large-scale 3D reconstruction, the city of Pavia in the 16th century, that involved about seventy students [7]. As reference we used two main historical sources: a fresco attributed to Bernardino Lanzani, located in the church of San Teodoro in Pavia, dating back to 1522; and a city map, drawn in 1617 by Lodovico Corte, carved in 1654 by Cesare Bonacina and commissioned by Ottavio Ballada (and thus popularly known as the "Ballada map"), offering a view of the city from above, including areas not depicted in the fresco. Supplementary information was then gathered from specific drawings of various historical buildings, especially for those no longer existing. The data contained in the historical sources compared with the size of still existing buildings were enough to reasonably estimate the approximate dimensions of the missing buildings.

During these two years we refined our teaching approach that reached the final structure described in Sect. 3. This project was in fact far more complex than the previous one: it involved the modeling of elaborate buildings and monu-

Fig. 3. Sample frames of different "virtual tour" videos of 3D Renaissance Pavia.

Fig. 4. Sample frames from the timelapse of the evolution of Pavia during the 16th century. From top to bottom, left to right: destruction of the North side of the Visconti Castle, building of Collegio Ghislieri, of the Spanish walls and of Collegio Borromeo.

ments, sometimes rich of small details, as well as the proper managing of textures, shadows, and lights.

When the whole 3D model of the city was finished, some students designed a series of videos proposing different "virtual tours" around the main areas of the Renaissance Pavia and its most important buildings and monuments[1] (Fig. 3).

---

[1] Virtual tours available at: https://vision.unipv.it/research/Pavia-rinascimentale/.

Recently, a Computer Engineering Master's thesis project was dedicated to the creation of a timelapse[2] showing an animation of the urban evolution of the city of Pavia in the 16th century (Fig. 4). The timelapse focuses on the changes that affected the main buildings of the city: the destruction of the North side of the Visconti Castle; the building of the Monastery of San Felice; the destruction of the Medieval walls and the later building of the Spanish ones; the building of Palazzo Broletto, Collegio Borromeo, Collegio Ghislieri and of the complex of the church of Santa Maria di Canepanova. This work involves also a partial re-elaboration of the original 3D models, to adapt them at the need of the timelapse, namely, to be properly broken (to show the buildings destruction) or gradually grown (to show the buildings construction).

4.3   The Ark of St. Augustine

The last case study was the most complex one. The goal was the modeling of a very articulated funeral monument dated 1362, the Ark of St. Augustine [23], located in the church of San Pietro in Ciel d'Oro in Pavia. It is a big Gothic sculpture (3.07 m x 1.68 m x 3.93 m) in white Carrara marble, containing the remains of St. Augustine from Hippo. Originally conceived as a single artifact visible on all four sides, it is now located above the altar, making difficult to observe it (thus, a 3D reproduction will be useful also for promotion). Overall, it consists of 95 statues and 50 bas-reliefs, with a total of over 400 characters, as well as vegetation, objects, animals, and schematic representations of cities. The artwork is structured on four levels (or orders) of different heights and density of elements.

The complexity of the 3D reproduction of this sculpture was partly reduced by the only used material (without transparency, with reduced diffraction, fixed diffusion, and essential optics) and by the simplification in lighting management, which can be limited to the environment one. However, the monument is extremely detailed, far more than any of the other objects modeled in the previous years, with also a lot of curved and complex surfaces (e.g., the clothes of the statues or the decorations), very difficult to model from scratch and that cannot be substituted with simple textures. Furthermore, due to the current position of the Ark in the church, it is hard to acquire photos of all the parts of the monument, thus, for some areas, such as the sky over the statue of the saint, only old drawings were available as reference. Fortunately, we have detailed information about the dimensions of the monuments and of its single parts, that we used to reproduce the monument in scale.

For this project, more than one hundred students, from the A.Y. 2017/18 to the A.Y. 2019/2020, were involved. Despite the complexity of the subject, they were able to produce remarkable results, in most cases very faithful to the original objects (see some examples in Fig. 5, videos rendering is ongoing).

Following the completion of all the parts of the Ark, in the last year, we developed an online serious game to explore the whole 3D reconstruction. Seri-

---

[2] Timelapse video available at: https://www.youtube.com/watch?v=7EdjuLw-OWk.

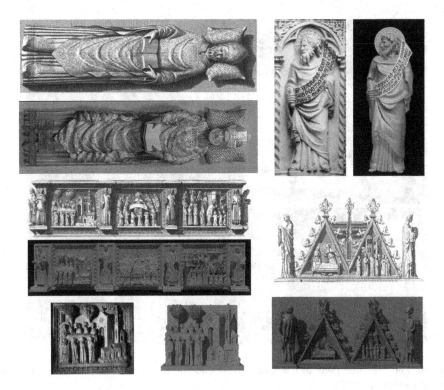

Fig. 5. 3D modeling of the Ark of St. Augustine: realized models of various statues and bas-reliefs next to the correspondent original objects (in photos or drawings). From top to bottom, left to right: St. Augustine; St. Andrew; third order, rear side; the funeral of St. Monica, mother of St. Augustine; fourth order, left side.

ous games are video games designed with educational purposes, and they are now commonly employed by museum and exhibits to attract visitors (especially younger ones) and to teach them historical and cultural contents in an engaging way [24,25]. In our case, the game is addressed to Italian students (other languages will be added later), who can virtually visit the monument and learn about it in a playful way, with fun and competitiveness. It simultaneously promotes both the knowledge of 3D modeling and of the monument itself.

The game (implemented in HTML, Javascript and PHP) follows a user centered design and focuses on the use of scoring and ranking. A simple and clear interface guides the user by means of animations and explanatory images.

In the welcome page (Fig. 6, top) the player can chose among various options: start playing; freely explore the sculpture and all its elements; check the ranking; run the tutorial; or close the application. During the game, the player is asked to answer a series of questions about the Ark. The game structure (Fig. 6, bottom) is inspired to that of the famous board game 'The Game of the Goose': there are several boxes (in correspondence of meaningful elements of the Ark) and four

Fig. 6. The welcome page of the game (top) and the four paths to be followed by the player (bottom).

paths, each one with an increasing level of difficulty and range of scores. The player moves around the track according to the throws of one dice and earns or loses points by correctly or wrongly answering questions related to the landing box. At the end of the game the player automatically enters in a global ranking whose position depends on the score obtained. The final purpose of the game is not to reach the endpoint, but to make as many points as possible, competing with other players or for self-improvement. The administrator can quickly update the game, changing the questions and the corresponding points through a simple interface. With regular update we can push players to retry the game multiple times and thus learn new information about the monument.

The product is still in a prototypical stage to which the necessary functional and aesthetic adjustments will be applied before to be made accessible online.

5   Conclusions

In this paper we presented the results of "Digital Historical Pavia", an educational project aimed to teach to university level students the basic of 3D modeling, and to present historical monuments and buildings of the city in an appealing and engaging way. During six academic years, more than 200 students of the master's degree in Computer Engineering of the University of Pavia were engaged in the project, realizing all the 3D models. The outcomes were remarkable, especially considering that, for most of the students, this was the first experience with computer graphics, proving the validity of an experiential learning approach.

As next step, we plan to enhance the 3D models adding animations (e.g., walking characters in the city, or talking statues in the Ark), and to complete and then release online the serious game about the Ark of St. Augustine.

Other initiatives for scientific and cultural dissemination, such as exhibitions or promotional books, will be considered, too.

Acknowledgments. We would like to thank all the students for their commitment in the realization of the project. Special thanks to Luigi Santangelo, the CINECA consortium, and the "Area Sistemi Informativi" of University of Pavia for the video renderings.

References

1. Sotirova, K., Peneva, J., Ivanov, S., Doneva, R., Dobreva, M.: Digitization of cultural heritage-standards, institutions, initiatives, pp. 23–68. Plovdiv University Publishing House "Paisii Hilendarski", Bulgaria (2012)
2. Bachi, V., Fresa, A., Pierotti, C., Prandoni, C.: The digitization age: mass culture is quality culture. challenges for cultural heritage and society. In: Ioannides, M., Magnenat-Thalmann, N., Fink, E., Žarnić, R., Yen, A.-Y., Quak, E. (eds.) EuroMed 2014. LNCS, vol. 8740, pp. 786–801. Springer, Cham (2014). https://doi.org/10.1007/978-3-319-13695-0_81
3. Guidi, G., Frischer, B.D.: 3D digitization of cultural heritage. In: Liu, Y., Pears, N., Rosin, P.L., Huber, P. (eds.) 3D Imaging, Analysis and Applications, pp. 631–697. Springer, Cham (2020). https://doi.org/10.1007/978-3-030-44070-1_13
4. Europeana digital library. https://www.europeana.eu/en. Accessed Nov 3 2021
5. Kokotsaki, D., Menzies, V., Wiggins, A.: Project-based learning: a review of the literature. Improv. Sch. **19**(3), 267–277 (2016). https://doi.org/10.1177/1365480216659733
6. Cantoni, V., Dondi, P., Lombardi, L., Nugrahaningsih, N., Porta, M., Setti, A.: A multi-sensory approach to cultural heritage: the battle of Pavia exhibition. In: IOP Conference Series: Materials Science and Engineering, vol. 364, p. 012039. IOP Publishing (2018). https://doi.org/10.1088/1757-899x/364/1/012039
7. Cantoni, V., Dondi, P., Lombardi, L., Setti, A.: Teaching computer graphics through a digital humanities project. IEEE Comput. Graphics Appl. **39**(2), 89–94 (2019). https://doi.org/10.1109/MCG.2019.2895487
8. Stanco, F., Battiato, S., Gallo, G.: Digital imaging for cultural heritage preservation: Analysis, restoration, and reconstruction of ancient artworks. CRC Press (2017). https://doi.org/10.1201/b11049
9. Levoy, M., et al.: The Digital Michelangelo Project: 3D Scanning of Large Statues. In: Proc. of the 27th Annual Conference on Computer Graphics and Interactive Techniques, SIGGRAPH '00, pp. 131–144. ACM Press/Addison-Wesley Publishing Co., USA (2000). https://doi.org/10.1145/344779.344849
10. Guidi, G., Beraldin, J.A., Atzeni, C.: High-accuracy 3D modeling of cultural heritage: the digitizing of Donatello's "Maddalena". IEEE Transactions on image processing **13**(3), 370–380 (2004). https://doi.org/10.1109/TIP.2003.822592

11. Brown, B.J., et al.: A system for high-volume acquisition and matching of fresco fragments: Reassembling Theran wall paintings. ACM Trans. Graph. (TOG) **27**(3), 1–9 (2008). https://doi.org/10.1145/1360612.1360683

12. Guidi, G., Russo, M., Angheleddu, D.: 3d survey and virtual reconstruction of archeological sites. Digit. Appl. Archaeol. Cult. Heritage **1**(2), 55–69 (2014). https://doi.org/10.1016/j.daach.2014.01.001

13. Quattrini, R., Pierdicca, R., Frontoni, E., Barcaglioni, R.: Virtual reconstruction of lost architectures: from the TLS survey to AR visualization. Int. Archives Photogramm. Remote Sensing Spatial Inform. Sci. **41**, 383–390 (2016). https://doi.org/10.5194/isprs-archives-XLI-B5-383-2016

14. Dondi, P., Lombardi, L., Malagodi, M., Licchelli, M.: 3D modelling and measurements of historical violins. Acta IMEKO **6**(3), 29–34 (2017). https://doi.org/10.21014/acta_imeko.v6i3.455

15. Arbace, L.: Innovative uses of 3d digital technologies to assist the restoration of a fragmented terracotta statue. J. Cult. Herit. **14**(4), 332–345 (2013). https://doi.org/10.1016/j.culher.2012.06.008

16. Charney, N.: The museum of lost art. Phaidon (2018)

17. Neumüller, M., Reichinger, A., Rist, F., Kern, C.: 3D printing for cultural heritage: Preservation, accessibility, research and education. In: 3D Research Challenges in Cultural Heritage, pp. 119–134. Springer, Berlin, Heidelberg (2014). https://doi.org/10.1007/978-3-662-44630-0_9

18. Ballarin, M., Balletti, C., Vernier, P.: Replicas in cultural heritage: 3D printing and the museum experience. International Archives of the Photogrammetry, Remote Sensing & Spatial Information Sciences **42**(2) (2018). https://doi.org/10.5194/isprs-archives-XLII-2-55-2018

19. Belhi, A., Foufou, S., Bouras, A., Sadka, A.H.: Digitization and preservation of cultural heritage products. In: IFIP International Conference on Product Lifecycle Management, pp. 241–253. Springer, Cham (2017). https://doi.org/10.1007/978-3-319-72905-3_22

20. Styliani, S., Fotis, L., Kostas, K., Petros, P.: Virtual museums, a survey and some issues for consideration. J. Cult. Herit. **10**(4), 520–528 (2009). https://doi.org/10.1016/j.culher.2009.03.003

21. Bekele, M.K., Pierdicca, R., Frontoni, E., Malinverni, E.S., Gain, J.: A survey of augmented, virtual, and mixed reality for cultural heritage. Journal on Computing and Cultural Heritage (JOCCH) **11**(2), 1–36 (2018). https://doi.org/10.1145/3145534

22. Suselo, T., Wünsche, B.C., Luxton-Reilly, A.: The journey to improve teaching computer graphics: A systematic review. In: Proceedings of the 25th International Conference Computer Educations, pp. 361–366 (2017)

23. Mazzilli Savini, M.T.: San Pietro in Ciel d'Oro a Pavia, mausoleo santuario di Agostino e Boezio: materiali antichi e problemi attuali. Comitato Pavia Città di Sant'Agostino (2013)

24. Anderson, E.F., McLoughlin, L., Liarokapis, F., Peters, C., Petridis, P., De Freitas, S.: Developing serious games for cultural heritage: a state-of-the-art review. Virtual Reality **14**(4), 255–275 (2010). https://doi.org/10.1007/s10055-010-0177-3

25. Mortara, M., Catalano, C.E., Bellotti, F., Fiucci, G., Houry-Panchetti, M., Petridis, P.: Learning cultural heritage by serious games. J. Cult. Herit. **15**(3), 318–325 (2014). https://doi.org/10.1016/j.culher.2013.04.004

3D Methods for the Anthropological Cultural Heritage

Alessandro Riga[1] , Tommaso Mori[1(✉)] , Fabio Di Vincenzo[2] ,
Filippo Pasquinelli[3], Roberto Carpi[3], and Jacopo Moggi-Cecchi[1]

[1] Department of Biology, University of Florence, 50122 Firenze, Italy
{alessandro.riga,tommaso.mori}@unifi.it
[2] Natural History Museum, University of Florence, 50122 Firenze, Italy
[3] Department of Radiology, Ospedale Santa Maria Nuova, Firenze, Italy

Abstract. Human remains can tell us the story of single individuals as well as entire populations, and they can be informative on cultural practices. Thus, they are part of our cultural heritage. The management of human remains as cultural heritage must consider the needs of preservation, research, and dissemination. The use of 3D technologies provides advantages in all these fields and helps in mitigating the conflicts among them.

While in research the use of 3D technologies is widespread, it is still under-exploited by anthropological and archaeological museums for preservation and dissemination purposes. The availability of virtual collections reduces the necessity of manipulation of the real objects by the researchers and it boosts research while improving preservation strategies.

A digital copy of a specimen would preserve the morphological information in case of destructive sampling, such as for molecular and biochemical analyses.

Moreover, 3D technologies can be helpful in resolving ethical issues related to the presentation of human remains, which brought many museums to avoid the exhibition of their anthropological collections. Recent releases of low-cost surface laser scanners can facilitate the spread of 3D technologies in the museums and could help in finding new ways of fruition for the anthropological collections, especially in periods of crisis such as those provoked by the recent pandemic events. Here, we present the case of the Museum of Anthropology and Ethnology from Florence in which different techniques (CT scan, laser scanning, photogrammetry) have been used and documented.

Keywords: Anthropology · Museum · Human remains · Ethics

1 The Anthropological Heritage and Virtual Anthropology (VA)

Human remains, such as skeletons and mummies, are open windows on the past of our species. Their study offers insights into the life and death of single individuals and entire populations [1]. They are the most prominent source of information on the evolution of our species and on the current and past human variability. Furthermore, they can inform on other bio-cultural aspects such as those related to the health of past populations,

R. Furferi et al. (Eds.): Florence Heri-Tech 2022, CCIS 1645, pp. 15–30, 2022.
https://doi.org/10.1007/978-3-031-20302-2_2

disease evolution, migrations, diet, funerary practices, interpersonal violence, surgery, and much more [2–10].

For these reasons, archaeological and paleontological human remains, as well as those hosted in museum collections, are part of our cultural heritage. Thus, they must be regarded as the rest of our cultural heritage and their management must consider different, and often conflicting, needs; 1) Conservation: the integrity of human remains must be preserved for the future. They are unique documents and the information they bear will be lost forever if destroyed; also, future development in technologies, methods, and theories could disclose new information currently out of reach. 2) Research: the value of human remains as cultural heritage is in the contribution they offer to the knowledge of our place in nature and our past. This knowledge can be reached only through the anthropological study of human remains. Research is the means by which human remains gain their status of cultural heritage. 3) Dissemination: the knowledge obtained by research must be shared with the community, to increase its awareness of our (natural) history. The management of cultural heritage should find the right balance between those aspects [11, 12]. For example, some research practices on anthropological specimens, such as ancient DNA (aDNA) sequencing and isotopic analysis, involve to some extent the destruction of skeletal remains, thus compromising its conservation and going against the scope of a Museum as a place to preserve our cultural heritage. Also, repeated manipulation by researchers can lead to the deterioration of the specimens. Even the exhibition of the collections, apart from the ethical issues concerning the exposition of human bodies, may cause the deterioration of the remains if the environment is not properly monitored.

3D technologies can help in resolving some of these issues and can mitigate some of the conflicts among research, conservation, and dissemination. The application of 3D technologies to anthropological remains is known as Virtual Anthropology (VA). VA anthropology is a multidisciplinary approach involving expertise from different domains such as anthropology, statistics, computer science, engineering [13, 14]. VA is widespread for research purposes, but its applications to conservation and dissemination are still limited.

Similar to what happened with other applications of 3D technologies, VA origins lie in the exceptional boost in computer technology and statistical methods that occurred in the 1990s. The development of computerized technologies based on X-rays, structured-light, and photogrammetry, allows us to acquire, record, and digitally process the morphology of remains [15–17]. These techniques are not only used on human remains, but also on cultural heritage objects such as coins [18], sculptures [19], frames, and decorated items [20].

Furthermore, analytical methods such as geometric morphometrics and multivariate statistical approaches, allowed new perspectives in the study of the shape and form of human remains [21, 22]. Such techniques allow us to operate in a totally virtual environment on unique and precious remains, without compromising their conservation or appreciation by a larger audience [23]. For example, the application of 3D technologies before sampling or casting a bone or a tooth, can reduce the risk of destroying the specimen [24] or can save morphological information in a digital model. Classically the traditional method of cast processing involves the production of a negative print of the specimen then used to obtain a positive cast by filling the inner cavity with plaster or plastic resins [25]. This is an invasive approach that can lead to physical damages and genetic contamination. A solution is 3D printing of the digital version of physical objects. 3D printing is one of the latest technologies which has made significant inroads in archaeology and in paleontology [26]. It is now possible to recreate duplicates of fossils, at different scales, without damaging sensitive collections and to virtually 'print' restored specimens [23, 27]. Replicas can be used both in scientific research as testing models and in dissemination activities. They can also play a crucial role as teaching support at different levels, especially for the visually impaired in hands-on experience [28–30]. Also, restoration of human remains from archeological context traditionally consisted in the reassembling of fragmented portions and their consolidation. Restoration of specimens in a physical manner therefore can cause additional physical and chemical stresses. On the contrary, by working on its digital models it is possible to restore a specimen virtually using different procedures more scientifically accurate, replicable, and reversible [31–38].

In the following decades, VA became perhaps the most dynamic topic in physical anthropology. Researchers in all the subfields of physical anthropology use the VA approach, with applications to paleoanthropology, bioarchaeology, functional morphology, dental anthropology, forensic anthropology [39–43]. Even if underexploited for conservation and dissemination purposes, VA is pivotal for the sharing of information, preservation, conservation, and dissemination [11, 24, 44, 45]. Thanks to technological advancements and cost reduction it is possible for many institutions to use such techniques and to find the best practice for their needs.

With the current worldwide pandemic situation visiting museums and traveling has been hard for scholars and tourists. Many museums, thus, developed new ways to entertain visitors and to "open" their collections. This exceptional situation boosts the interest of museums in the digitization of their cultural heritage and the importance of doing so.

The aim of this contribution is to review the application of 3D technologies to anthropological heritage and to discuss their benefits for conservation and dissemination. In doing so, we will present the experience of the Museum of Anthropology and Ethnology of the University of Florence and we will explore some possibilities for further developments.

2 The Experience at the Museum of Anthropology and Ethnology of the University of Florence

The Museum of Anthropology and Ethnology of Florence was founded in 1869 by Paolo Mantegazza, who also held the first chair of Anthropology in Italy. The purpose of the museum was to document the multifaceted aspects of the species *Homo sapiens* in all its diversity, both biological and cultural [46]. In the beginning, osteological collections were scarce, but in the late 19th century and the first half of the 20th century, they grew rapidly, thanks to the contribution of numerous naturalists and anthropologists (such as Mantegazza himself, E.H. Giglioli, T. Caruel, S. Sommier, E. Modigliani), to the donation from the hospitals (e.g. Ospedale di Santa Maria Nuova in Florence), to the acquisition of extra-european collection from explorers and scholars (e.g. O. Beccari).

Today, the Museum hosts the most important collection of skeletal remains of human populations in Italy, and certainly one of the most significant in the world, thanks to the presence of extremely rare specimens, such as the collection of skulls and skeletons of native people from the Tierra del Fuego (South America), a population now extinct for over a century [47].

For these reasons, the Museum of Anthropology and Ethnology of the University of Florence is the best candidate for experimenting with new approaches to the management of osteological collections. In the last years, the Museum, in collaboration with the Department of Biology of the University of Florence and the Department of Radiology of the Santa Maria Nuova Hospital in Florence, began to apply 3D technologies to the conservation of the osteological collections and to anthropological dissemination.

The availability of a virtual collection allows the Museum to reduce unnecessary manipulation of the object, thus improving their preservation. Any researcher willing to study the morphology of the skulls and the skeletons hosted at the museum, can ask for access to the digital models instead of the real specimens. This, beyond the positive impact on the preservation of the specimen, improves data sharing and research speed and reduces the travels of the researchers between countries.

The first step towards the building of a virtual collection is the digitization of the specimens. The choice of the technology to be used for the acquisition of the digital models depends on several factors: the accuracy needed, the interest in the inner structures of the specimen, the need for a texture or only for morphological information, and last but not least, the availability of equipment, fundings, and facilities. In the next section we will present the technologies that we applied to the osteological collections of the Museum. For each kind of 3D technology we will also present a brief case-study, to show how VA contributed to improving conservation strategies, research and dissemination in the anthropological field.

2.1 3D Modeling Through Photogrammetry

Photogrammetry is a technique that uses photos for measuring objects. It allows obtaining quantitative data on 3D objects from photos [48, 49]. This technique is used for processing image data and for 3D modeling. Photogrammetry is traditionally used in geodesy, cartography, and mapping and, more recently it is widely applied to cultural heritage [50–52]. Also, it has been successfully applied to the documentation of human remains for research purposes [43, 45, 53].

For obtaining three-dimensional information from photos, we need to take multiple pictures, partially overlapped, from different perspectives. A single photo gives information about the two-dimensional coordinates of the object. With two pictures, thanks to the principles of stereoscopic viewing, it is possible to extract information on the 3D coordinates of each point represented in both photos. In the practice, to obtain a 3D model of the desired object, the operator takes several pictures from different views, so that each point of the specimen, (in the anthropological field usually a skull, a bone, or a tooth) is present in at least two pictures. Once the operator has shot all the photos needed, the following step is the processing with dedicated software (e.g. Agisoft Metashape, COLMAP, Meshroom). The processing involves the removal of the background of each image, the alignment of the images, the generation of a point cloud, and, eventually, the building of a 3D mesh using a triangulation algorithm [45]. The use of a metric reference in one of the photos is needed because the 3D model obtained doesn't have a proper scale.

Photogrammetry offers some advantages. First, it can be done with simple and (relatively) cheap equipment: all that is needed is a camera and a good light for taking pictures. Furthermore, it allows the operator to obtain not only the morphological and shape information but also the texture of the specimen; this is of particular importance when the 3D model is aimed at dissemination – for example, a virtual exhibition of the skeletal collections. On the other hand, photogrammetry also has some cons. First, the processing of the images can be difficult and time-consuming. Second, photogrammetry can inform only on the external structure (the visible surface) of the object; inner structure and hidden portion of the specimen (such as trabecular bone, the pulp canal of the teeth, the cranial endocast etc.) cannot be investigated through this technique, and, therefore, they could be lost in the eventuality of a destructive analysis of a specimen.

3D Models of the Skulls of the Identified Collection. The Museum hosts an important collection of identified individuals, for whom sex, age at death, and other information are known. These kinds of collections are important for developing methodological works and for testing published methods [54–56]. In the framework of a study on sexual dimorphism in the frontal bone [43], 103 skulls of the Museum collections have been digitized using photogrammetry (Table 1).

Table 1. Digitization through photogrammetry of the crania belonging to the osteological collection of the Museum of Anthropology and Ethnology of the University of Florence. Composition of the sample.

Provenance	Males	Females	Tot
Florence	31	27	58
Sardinia	17	12	29
Siracusa	11	5	16
Tot	59	44	103

The interest of the work was to investigate the external shape and morphology of the frontal bone, thus photogrammetry was chosen as a proper technique to obtain the required data. 3D models were obtained for the entire skull, then only the frontal portion of the skull was used to explore how the frontal bone morphology varies between the sexes and which parts of the frontal bone are sexually dimorphic, using geometric morphometrics [43]. The digitization of these crania through photogrammetry increased the numbers of the virtual collection of the Museum. Moreover, this is an example of how important an anthropological collection can be today. Thanks to new technologies it is now possible to test hypotheses that were not testable without the help of a digital environment. Osteological collection of known sex and age at death are important sources of information also in light of the continuously growing machine learning and bioinformatic sector.

2.2 Laser Scanner

The laser scanner is a device that acquires reflections from a surface. The image of the physical object is acquired through a sensor and then is converted in a points cloud. Through the triangulation algorithm [57] multiple scans performed by different viewpoints allow the digital reconstruction of the physical object. Many laser scanners are built with a camera that can add color information about the object, the texture [58]. The colored specimen is therefore suitable for virtual exhibitions given their similarity to the original in all aspects: morphology and colors. Another advantage of a laser scanner is that the model is built at its original size and it is not required to correct the size of the digital object afterward. For research purposes and to be able to save as much information as possible from the physical object, the use of a high-resolution laser scanner is preferable, as many data can be obtained from small details of both shape and texture of

Fig. 1. Acquisition of the 3D model of the *Australopithecus africanus* skull STS-5 (Mrs. Ples) using a Revopoint POP 3D Laser scanner.

the objects (e.g. bones, fossils) [35, 38]. Today there are a plethora of different models and manufacturers which sell their scanners usually together with dedicated software (e.g. Artec, Revopoint, Breuckmann etc.)

In 2021 we acquired a low-cost laser scanner (Revopoint POP 3D Scanner) to test its applicability to research and scientific dissemination (Fig. 1). The POP 3D Scanner is a portable laser scanner, easy to use, and with user-friendly software for processing. Its accuracy (0.1 mm) allows obtaining good 3D models with color texture for teaching, dissemination, and virtual exhibitions.

3D Models of Paleoanthropological Specimens. The Museum hosts a collection of historical plaster casts of important paleoanthropological specimens. Among them are the casts of the Mauer mandible discovered in Germany in 1907, the calotte from the Neander valley near Feldhofer (Germany) discovered in 1856, and the fossils from Trinil (Java) discovered in 1891. Respectively, these fossils are the type specimens (i.e. the fossil used to describe a species the first time) of *H. heidelbergensis*, *H. neanderthalensis*, and *H. erectus*. Each cast has been donated to the Museum from the scholars who discovered and studied the specimens between the end of the 19th century and the beginning of the 20th century (Otto Schoetensack, Hermann Schaaffausen, Eugène Dubois). Thus, together with their scientific importance, the casts assumed an utmost historical value. The availability of a laser scanner allowed the Museum to build 3D models of some of the casts, to be used in dissemination and teaching. This also allows to avoid the handling of the fragile plaster casts.

The models obtained have a color texture that make them attractive for the general public. Also, when the dimensions of the files is opportunely reduced, the 3D model can be shared through dedicated portals such as Sketchfab.

In occasion of the bright night 2021, dedicated to the dissemination of the University research activities, we uploaded the 3D model of Mrs. Ples on Sketchfab and distributed a QR code for downloading the model on personal devices such as laptops and smartphones (Fig. 2).

The free availability of 3D models like these can also be useful for teaching purposes at different levels. At the University, during the lockdown periods in 2020 and 2021, when teaching was done via the internet, we experimented with success the use of 3D models for teaching skeletal anatomy without the availability of physical specimens. Moreover, these models can be useful in schools too, for example, printing 3D copies for use in classes during the lessons on human evolution allows a "hands-on" experience to the student giving them a deeper and more authentic learning experience.

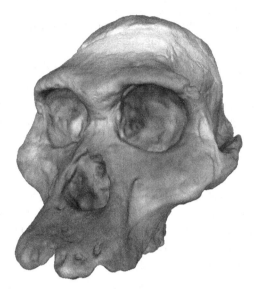

Fig. 2. Snapshot of the 3D model of the female *Australopithecus africanus* nicknamed Mrs. Ples (STS-5), obtained using the Revopoint POP 3D scanner. The model can be downloaded using the QR code on the right.

2.3 Computed Tomography (CT) Scans

3D scanners and photogrammetry are useful for building 3D models of the external surface of an object and for obtaining data on the texture. When the interest of the researcher is in the hidden portion of a bone or a tooth (for example the endocast of a cranium), one must rely on different technologies, based on X-rays. The first to use X-rays on anthropological remains was Gorjanović-Kramberger who, in 1906 published X-rays images of some Neandertal teeth from the Croatian site of Krapina [59]. From the 1980s, development in medical imaging led to a boost in X-rays technologies and the birth of Computer Tomography (CT). The functioning of a medical CT-scan is based on a X-ray source, mounted on a rotating ring and a line of detectors on the opposite side. A table with the object to be scanned moves along the rotation axis (Fig. 3). The source emits X-rays that pass through the object and are recorded by the detectors. The measure of the attenuation of the X-rays gives information on the density of the object, thus on the different tissues (and voids) that the rays pass through. Once the proper radio density range is set, it is possible to calculate a 3D model [38, 60].

This process leads to several slices spaced by an inter-slice distance, i.e. a series of equidistant 2D cross-sectional images. The resolution of the CT scan depends on the inter-slice distance and the resolution of each slice. The application of the Marching cubes algorithm allows the extraction of a polygonal mesh (isosurface) from a 3D-array [61].

The first application of 3D CT scans in combination with 3D digital technology in paleoanthropology was in 1984 [62, 63]. Since the early 1990s, the application of CT scans in paleoanthropology had a boost, with standard protocols and methods developed for the virtual reconstruction of fossil hominins [14, 64–67].

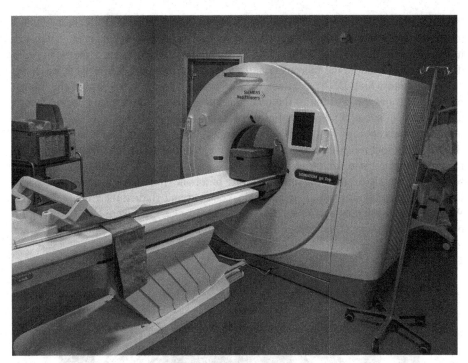

Fig. 3. Medical CT-scan at the Santa Maria Nuova Hospital in Florence, during a scanning section of anthropological material (in the box) from the Museum of Anthropology and Ethnology.

CT scan use is limited in dissemination and virtual exhibitions since no color information can be obtained. On the other hand, it is perhaps the most used 3D technology for research and conservation purposes in paleoanthropology, since it gives accurate information on the shape and morphology of the external surface as well as of the inner parts of a specimen. In the case of destructive sampling, a preliminary CT scan is often required in order to obtain a record of the morphological information. Sometimes, CT-scan also can help in mitigating the damages of destructive sampling, as we'll show in the next case-study.

Microsampling and 3D Technology. The osteological collections housed in the Museum are a database of morphological and genetic information about human variability. The study of Ancient DNA (aDNA) is a flourishing research sector. With the advent of new technologies and new sequencing techniques, it is possible to obtain the complete genomes of many individuals in a relatively short time [68–70]. However, genetic analyses are destructive and can compromise the integrity of the specimen. Moreover, recently, scholars are interested mainly in sampling the petrous bone. This skeletal district is part of the temporal bone, a bone of the skull. Its importance for scientists is related to the capacity of such a district to preserve very well genetic material. Unfortunately, it is also a very important bone for morphological studies [72–74]. The classical sampling strategy involves the disarticulation of the temporal bone from the skull by cutting it and once removed the petrous bone is cut in half in order to sample the inner portion of the bone where it is known there could be more genetic material [71]. Recently, thanks to the new technologies which required less and less material to make genetic analyses, it was proposed to use the Cranial Base Drilling Method [75]. Such a method used a drill to directly sample the petrous bone to reach the inner part rich in well preserved collagen (from which DNA is extracted). However, given the variability of the human petrous bone and the position of the inner ear, the method did not give as good results as the classical sampling strategy. For this reason, together with the colleagues of the molecular anthropology group of the Department of Biology, starting from the Cranial Base Drilling method, we focused on imaging techniques to find the best approach to reach this portion and sampling the petrous bone in a more accurate way. Using CT scans it is possible to study the inner structure of a bone. In this case, we CT scanned 8 isolated petrous bones from an archeological context and studied their inner structure. With the use of imaging software (Avizo, Thermo Fischer), we were able to detect the position of the inner ear and consequently to evaluate the best external position in order to reach it (Fig. 4).

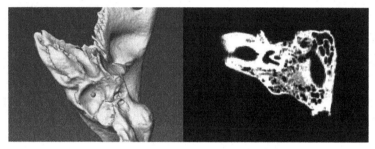

Fig. 4. 3D model of the petrous portion of the temporal bone (left), 2D slice from CT scan (right). The dot in the two figures represents the optimal point for the drilling.

Once we virtually established the best point on the surface to reach the inner ear, the correct location was reported on the physical specimen and with the use of a Dremel drill, we carried out the sampling (Fig. 5).

This approach allowed more precise localization of the drilling starting position. Results indicate that the sample extracted was of good quality [76] and, for this reason in the Museum we decided whenever possible to apply this sampling strategy. The first specimens housed in the Museum collection that were sampled using this technique were the human remains from Grotta dello Scoglietto (Grosseto, Italy). The specimens are dated around 4,422 years ago (on the border between the Eneolithic phase and the Bronze age). Genetic information about these individuals could be really useful in the understanding of the first peopling of the Italian peninsula but, on the other hand, these specimens are precious and destructive analysis should be limited as much as possible. Using the microsampling technique we were able to sample the specimens minimizing the impact of the procedure. Figure 6 shows one specimen after the sampling in which the hole left by the drill is visible. This damage is thus minimal when compared to the complete removal of the petrous bone and its cut in half.

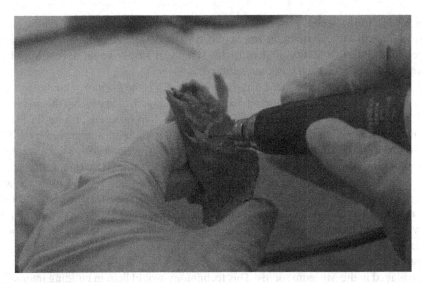

Fig. 5. Micro-sampling of a petrous bone for collagen extraction and ancient DNA analysis.

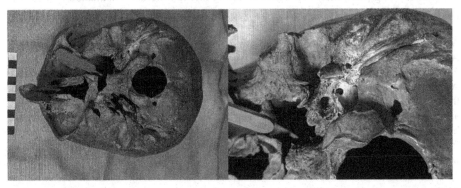

Fig. 6. Grotta dello Scoglietto, specimen N 6754. Inferior view of the specimen (left), detail of the petrous bone with a visible hole resulted from the sampling (right).

3 Further Developments for the Museum Activities

The application of 3D technologies to the management of the anthropological cultural heritage is just at the beginning and developments can occur in many directions. The first step must be the enlargement of the virtual collection, starting from the most important and requested series, such as the Fuegians and the identified collections. The best practice for building the virtual collection would be using CT-scans to obtain models of the external surface and of the inner structure. This would allow having all the necessary data for researchers working in morphology and morphometrics, drastically reducing the manipulation of the specimens and thus their deterioration. In addition, researchers may have remote access to the CT-scans, reducing unnecessary travels between countries. Moreover, remote sharing of CT-scans would be useful during periods of crisis such as those related to the recent pandemic events. In many cases, researchers had a forced stop in their activity because of the impossibility of traveling; the availability of a virtual collection and the possibility of sharing the 3D model's files would have allowed the researchers to carry on their work undisturbed.

Another issue that can be faced using a VA approach is the display of human remains to the public [77–79]. A long standing debate has developed, at least from the mid of the last Century, concerning the so-called culturally sensitive materials, primarily human remains. This debate has led to the formulation of the guidelines approved by ICOM for the proper exhibition of such materials. At present, human osteological remains are almost completely absent from the exhibit of the Museum. 3D virtual technologies become, in our view, essential to contextualize these materials by integrating a large amount of information to offer to the knowledge and to the correct enjoyment of the visitor. In this way it is possible to increase the sense of interest and respect that should always accompany the display of sensitive materials. A virtual collection of 3D models with color texture would allow the Museum to set up a virtual exhibition accessible by the internet. In addition, some models could be printed with 3D printing technologies and displayed in the Museum rooms. This technology would help in building interactive itineraries, where visitors can touch and interact with the specimens exposed. This would be an interesting possibility also for developing tactile itineraries dedicated to sightless people [80, 81].

Acknowledgments. This study was partially supported under the project grant "ANTINT: Antropologia Integrata: un approccio innovativo allo studio delle collezioni Museali" (POR FSE 2014 – 2020 Asse A Occupazione - Priorità di investimento A.2 – Obiettivo A.2.1 – Azione A.2.1.7 "ASSEGNI DI RICERCA IN AMBITO CULTURALE") financed by: Regione Toscana, the Museo di Storia Naturale dell'Università di Firenze, Fondazione Cassa di Risparmio di Firenze and from the Società Cooperativa "Opera d'Arte" (UNIFI_FSE2019). It was also partially funded by the project grant "DIVINA *DIgital and Virtual INnovative Anthropology*: tecniche avanzate di fruizione delle collezioni museali e ricadute applicative", financed by: Regione Toscana and the Museo di Storia Naturale dell'Università di Firenze (UNIFI_FSC2021).

References

1. Pearson, M.P., Pearson, M.P.: The Archaeology of Death and Burial. Phoenix Mill, Sutton (1999)
2. Sparacello, V.S., Dori, I., Rossi, S., Varalli, A., Riel-Salvatore, J., Gravel-Miguel, C., et al.: New human remains from the Late Epigravettian necropolis of Arene Candide (Liguria, northwestern Italy): direct radiocarbon evidence and inferences on the funerary use of the cave during the Younger Dryas. Quatern. Sci. Rev. **268**, 107131 (2021)
3. Posth, C., Zaro, V., Spyrou, M.A., Vai, S., Gnecchi-Ruscone, G.A., Modi, A., et al.: The origin and legacy of the Etruscans through a 2000-year archeogenomic time transect. Sci. Adv. **7**(39), 7673 (2021)
4. Riga, A., et al.: Is root exposure a good marker of periodontal disease? Bull. Int. Assoc. Paleodontol. **15**(1), 21–30 (2021)
5. Oxilia, G., Menghi Sartorio, J.C., Bortolini, E., Zampirolo, G., Papini, A., Boggioni, M., et al.: Exploring directional and fluctuating asymmetry in the human palate during growth. Am. J. Phys. Anthropol. **175**(4), 847–864 (2021)

6. Key, F.M., Posth, C., Esquivel-Gomez, L.R., Hübler, R., Spyrou, M.A., Neumann, G.U., et al.: Emergence of human-adapted Salmonella enterica is linked to the Neolithization process. Nat. Ecol. Evol. **4**(3), 324–333 (2020)
7. Varalli, A., Moggi-Cecchi, J., Moroni, A., Goude, G.: Dietary variability during Bronze Age in Central Italy: first results. Int. J. Osteoarchaeol. **26**(3), 431–446 (2016)
8. Riga, A., et al.: Human deciduous teeth from the middle Stone age layers of Sibudu cave (South Africa). J. Anthropol. Sci. **96**, 75–87 (2018)
9. Belcastro, M.G., Mariotti, V., Riga, A., Bonfiglioli, B., Frayer, D.W.: Tooth fractures in the Krapina Neandertals. J. Hum. Evol. **123**, 96–108 (2018)
10. Estabrook, V.H.: Violence and warfare in the European Mesolithic and Paleolithic. In: Allen, M.W., Jones, T.L. (ed.): Violence and Warfare among Hunter-Gatherers, pp. 49–69. Routledge, New York (2016)
11. LeCabec, A., Toussaint, M.: Impacts of curatorial and research practices on the preservation of fossil hominid remains. J. Anthropol. Sci. **95**, 1–28 (2017)
12. Baars, C.: Dare to prepare? the value of preparing and sampling historically important museum collections. Geological Curator **9**, 237–242 (2010)
13. Weber, G.W.: Virtual anthropology. Am. J. Phys. Anthropol. **156**, 22–42 (2015)
14. Weber, G.W., Recheis, W., Scholze, T., Seidler, H.: Virtual anthropology (VA): methodological aspects of linear and volume measurements—first results. Coll. Antropol. **22**, 575–584 (1998)
15. Bukreeva, I., et al.: Virtual unrolling and deciphering of herculaneum papyri by X-Ray phase-contrast tomography. Sci. Rep. **6**(1), 27227 (2016)
16. Micarelli, I., et al.: Survival to amputation in pre-antibiotic era: a case study from a longobard necropolis (6th-8th Centuries AD). J. Anthropol. Sci. **96**, 1–16 (2018)
17. Wilson, P., et al.: Utilizing X-Ray computed tomography for heritage conservation: the case of *Megalosaurus Bucklandii*. In: 2017 IEEE International Instrumentation and Measurement Technology Conference (I2MTC), Proceedings, pp. 1–5. IEEE (2017)
18. Zambanini, S., Schlapke, M., Hödlmoser, M., Kampel, M.: 3D acquisition of historical coins and its application area in numismatics. Comput. Vis. Image Anal. Art. Int. Soc. Optics Photonics **7531**, 1–8 (2010)
19. Guidi, G., Spinetti, A., Carosso, L., Atzeni, C.: Digital three-dimensional modelling of donatello's david by frequency-modulated laser radar. Stud. Conserv. **54**(1), 3–11 (2009)
20. Bruno, F., Bruno, S., De Sensi, G., Luchi, M.-L., Mancuso, S., Muzzupappa, M.: From 3D reconstruction to virtual reality: a complete methodology for digital archaeological exhibition. J. Cult. Herit. **11**, 42–49 (2009)
21. Rein, T.R., Harvati, K.: Geometric morphometrics and virtual anthropology: advances in human evolutionary studies. Anthropologischer Anzeiger; Bericht uber die biologisch-anthropologische Literatur **71**(1–2), 41–55 (2014)
22. Baab, K.L., McNulty, K.P., Rohlf, F.J.: The shape of human evolution: a geometric morphometrics perspective. Evol. Anthropol. Issues, News, Rev. **21**(4), 151–165 (2012)
23. Scopigno, R., Cignoni, P., Pietroni, N., Callieri, M., Dellepiane, M.: Digital fabrication techniques for cultural heritage: a survey. Comput. Graph. Forum **36**(1), 6–21 (2015)
24. O'Hara, M.C., LeCabec, A., Xing, S., Skinner, M.F., Guatelli-Steinberg, D.: Safe casting and reliable cusp reconstruction assisted by micro-computed tomographic scans of fossil teeth. Anat. Rec. **302**(9), 1516–1535 (2019)
25. Schoenemann, P.T., Gee, J., Avants, B., Holloway, R.L., Monge, J., Lewis, J.: Validation of plaster endocast morphology through 3D CT image analysis. Am. J. Phys. Anthropol. **132**(2), 183–192 (2007)
26. Leakey, L., Dzamabova, T.: Prehistoric collections and 3D printing for education. In: Canessa, E., Fonda, C., Zennaro, M. (ed.) Low-Cost 3D Printing for Science, Education and Sustainable Development, pp. 159–162. ICTP–The Abdus Salam International Centre for Theoretical Physics (2013)

27. Tembe, G., Siddiqui, S.: Applications of computed tomography to fossil conservation and education. Collection Forum **28**(1–2), 47–62 (2014)
28. Neumüller, M., Reichinger, A., Rist, F., Kern, C.: 3D printing for cultural heritage: preservation, accessibility, research and education. In: Ioannides, M., Quak, E. (eds.) 3D Research Challenges in Cultural Heritage. LNCS, vol. 8355, pp. 119–134. Springer, Heidelberg (2014). https://doi.org/10.1007/978-3-662-44630-0_9
29. Short, D.B.: Use of 3D printing by museums: educational exhibits, artifact education, and artifact restoration. 3D Print. Additive Manuf. **2**(4), 209–215 (2015)
30. Wilson, P.F., Stott, J., Warnett, J.M., Attridge, A., Smith, M.P., Williams, M.A.: Evaluation of touchable 3D-printed replicas in museums. Curator Museum J. **60**(4), 445–465 (2017)
31. Di Vincenzo, F., et al.: Digital reconstruction of the Ceprano Calvarium (Italy), and implications for its interpretation. Sci. Rep. **7**(1), 13974 (2017)
32. Schlager, S., Profico, A., Di Vincenzo, F., Manzi, G.: Retrodeformation of fossil specimens based on 3D bilateral semi-landmarks: implementation in the R package 'Morpho.' PLoS ONE **13**(3), e0194073 (2018)
33. Tallman, M., Amenta, N., Delson, E., Frost, S.R., Ghosh, D.: Evaluation of a new method of fossil retrodeformation by algorithmic symmetrization: crania of papionins (Primates, Cercopithecidae) as a test case. PLoS ONE **9**(7), e100833 (2014)
34. Zollikofer, C.P., et al.: Virtual cranial reconstruction of *Sahelanthropus tchadensis*. Nature **434**(7034), 755–759 (2005)
35. Friess, M.: Scratching the surface? the use of surface scanning in physical and paleoanthropology. J. Anthropol. Sci. **90**, 1–25 (2012)
36. Ni, X., Flynn, J.J., Wyss, A.R.: Imaging the inner ear in fossil mammals: high-resolution CT scanning and 3-D virtual reconstructions. Palaeontol. Electron. **15**(2), 1–10 (2012)
37. Veneziano, A., Landi, F., Profico, A.: Surface smoothing, decimation, and their effects on 3D biological specimens. Am. J. Phys. Anthropol. (2018)
38. Weber, G.W.: Virtual anthropology (VA): a call forglasnost in paleoanthropology. Anat. Rec. **265**(4), 193–201 (2001)
39. Benazzi, S., Kullmer, O., Grosse, I.R., Weber, G.W.: Using occlusal wear information and finite element analysis to investigate stress distributions in human molars. J. Anat. **219**(3), 259–272 (2011)
40. Gunz, P., Mitteroecker, P., Neubauer, S., Weber, G.W., Bookstein, F.L.: Principles for the virtual reconstruction of hominin crania. J. Hum. Evol. **57**(1), 48–62 (2009)
41. Buzi, C., et al.: Retrodeformation of the Steinheim cranium: insights into the evolution of Neanderthals. Symmetry **13**(9), 1611 (2021)
42. Mori, T., Profico, A., Reyes-Centeno, H., Harvati, K.: Frontal bone virtual reconstruction and geometric morphometric analysis of the mid-Pleistocene hominin KNM-OG 45500 (Olorgesailie, Kenya). J. Anthropol. Sci. **98**, 49–72 (2020)
43. Del Bove, A., Profico, A., Riga, A., Bucchi, A., Lorenzo, C.: A geometric morphometric approach to the study of sexual dimorphism in the modern human frontal bone. Am. J. Phys. Anthropol. **173**(4), 643–654 (2020)
44. Van den Akker, C., Legêne, S.: Museums in a Digital Culture. Amsterdam University Press, Amsterdam (2017)
45. Profico, A., et al.: Virtual anthropology and its application in cultural heritage studies. Stud. Conserv. **64**(6), 323–336 (2019)
46. Moggi-Cecchi, J., Stanyon, R.: Il Museo di Storia Naturale dell'Universitá degli Studi di Firenze: volume V: le collezioni antropologiche ed etnologiche. Firenze University Press, Firenze (2014)
47. Moggi-Cecchi, J.: Le Collezioni Antropologiche. In: Moggi-Cecchi, J., Stanyon, R. (ed.) Il Museo di Storia Naturale dell'Universitá degli Studi di Firenze: volume V: le collezioni antropologiche ed etnologiche, pp. 183–196. Firenze University Press, Firenze (2014)

48. Remondino, F.: Heritage recording and 3D modeling with photogrammetry and 3D scanning. Remote Sens. **3**(6), 1104–1138 (2011)
49. Linder, W.: Digital photogrammetry, Vol. 1. Springer, Berlin (2009)
50. Nicolae, C., Nocerino, E., Menna, F., Remondino, F.: Photogrammetry applied to problematic artefacts. Int. Arch. Photogrammetry Remote Sens. Spatial Inf. Sci. **40**(5), 451–456 (2014)
51. El-Hakim, S., et al.: Detailed 3D modelling of castles. Int. J. Archit. Comput. **5**, 199–220 (2007)
52. Yastikli, N.: Documentation of cultural heritage using digital photogrammetry and laser scanning. J. Cult. Herit. **8**(4), 423–427 (2007)
53. Buzi, C., et al.: Measuring the shape: performance evaluation of a photogrammetry improvement applied to the Neanderthal skull Saccopastore 1. Acta Imeko **7**(3), 79–85 (2018)
54. Milella, M., Belcastro, M.G., Mariotti, V., Nikita, E.: Estimation of adult age-at-death from entheseal robusticity: a test using an identified Italian skeletal collection. Am. J. Phys. Anthropol. **173**(1), 190–199 (2020)
55. Belcastro, M.G., Bonfiglioli, B., Pedrosi, M.E., Zuppello, M., Tanganelli, V., Mariotti, V.: The history and composition of the identified human skeletal collection of the certosa cemetery (Bologna, Italy, 19th–20th Century). Int. J. Osteoarchaeol. **27**, 912–925 (2017)
56. Radi, N., Mariotti, V., Riga, A., Zampetti, S., Villa, C., Belcastro, M.G.: Variation of the anterior aspect of the femoral head-neck junction in a modern human identified skeletal collection. Am. J. Phys. Anthropol. **152**, 261–272 (2013)
57. Pavlidis, G., Koutsoudis, A., Arnaoutoglou, F., Tsioukas, V., Chamzas, C.: Methods for 3D digitization of cultural heritage. J. Cult. Herit. **8**(1), 93–98 (2007)
58. Pieraccini, M., Guidi, G., Atzeni, C.: 3D Digitizing of cultural heritage. J. Cult. Herit. **2**(1), 63–70 (2001)
59. Gorjanović-Kramberger, D.: Der Diluviale Mensch von Krapina in Kroatien. Ein Beitrag Zur Paläoanthropologie. Studien Über Die Entwicklungsmechanik Des Primatenskelletes, Volume II. CW Kreidel, Wien (1906)
60. Livnat, Y., Shen, H.W., Johnson, C.R.: A Near optimal isosurface extraction algorithm using the span space. IEEE Trans. Visual Comput. Graphics **2**(1), 73–84 (1996)
61. Lorensen, W.E., Cline, H.E.: Marching cubes: a high resolution 3D surface construction algorithm. ACM SIGGRAPH Comput. Graph. **21**, 163–169 (1987)
62. Conroy, G.C., Vannier, M.V.: Noninvasive three-dimensional computer imaging of matrix-filled fossil skulls by high-resolution computed tomography. Science **226**(4673), 456–458 (1984)
63. Wind, J.: Computerized X-ray tomography of fossil hominid skulls. Am. J. Phys. Anthropol. **63**, 265–282 (1984)
64. Spoor, C.F., Zonneveld, F.W., Macho, G.A.: Linear measurements of cortical bone and dental enamel by computed tomography: applications and problems. Am. J. Phys. Anthropol. **91**(4), 469–484 (1993)
65. Weber, G.W., Bookstein, F.L., Strait, D.S.: Virtual anthropology meets biomechanics. J. Biomech. **44**, 1429–1432 (2011)
66. Zollikofer, C.P., Ponce de Leon, M.S., Martin, R.D., Stucki, P.: Neanderthal computer skulls. Nature **375**, 283–285 (1995)
67. Zollikofer, C.P., Ponce de Leon, M.S., Martin, R.D.: Computerassisted paleoanthropology. Evol. Anthropol. **6**, 41–54 (1998)
68. Dabney, J., et al.: Complete mitochondrial genome sequence of a Middle Pleistocene cave bear reconstructed from ultrashort DNA fragments. Proc. Natl. Acad. Sci. USA **110**, 15758–15763 (2013)
69. Rohland, N., Siedel, H., Hofreiter, M.: A rapid column-based ancient DNA extraction method for increased sample throughput. Mol. Ecol. Resour. **10**, 677–683 (2010)

70. Slatkin, M., Racimo, F.: Ancient DNA and human history. Proc. Natl. Acad. Sci. **113**(23), 6380–6387 (2016)
71. Pinhasi, R., et al.: Optimal ancient DNA yields from the inner ear part of the human petrous bone. PLOS ONE **10**(6), e0129102 (2015)
72. von Cramon-Taubadel, N.: Evolutionary insights into global patterns of human cranial diversity: population history, climatic and dietary effects. J. Anthropol. Sci. **92**(4), 43–77 (2014)
73. Reyes-Centeno, H., Ghirotto, S., Détroit, F., Grimaud-Hervé, D., Barbujani, G., Harvati, K.: Genomic and cranial phenotype data support multiple modern human dispersals from Africa and a southern route into Asia. Proc. Natl. Acad. Sci. **111**(20), 7248–7253 (2014)
74. Mori, T., Harvati, K.: Basicranial ontogeny comparison in *Pan troglodytes* and *Homo sapiens* and its use for developmental stage definition of KNM-ER 42700. Am. J. Phys. Anthropol. **170**(4), 579–594 (2019)
75. Sirak, K.A., et al.: A minimally-invasive method for sampling human petrous bones from the cranial base for ancient DNA analysis. Bio-Techiques **62**(6), 283–289 (2017)
76. Alabisio, V.: Analisi paleogenetica sui resti scheletrici umani del sito preistorico di Corna Nibbia (Brescia): micro campionamento delle rocche petrose e primi dati genetici. Master degree thesis, University of Florence (2020)
77. Swain, H.: Museum practice and the display of human remains. In: Willliams, H., Giles, M. (ed.) Archaeologists and The Dead: Mortuary Archaeology in Contemporary Society, pp. 169–183. Oxford University Press, Oxford (2016)
78. Lohman, J., Goodnow, K.J.: Human Remains & Museum Practice, vol. 918. Berghahn Books, New York (2006)
79. Kilminster, H.: Visitor perceptions of ancient Egyptian human remains in three United Kingdom museums. Papers Inst. Archaeol. **14**, 57–69 (2003)
80. Empler, T., Fusinetti, A.: Relief representation in museum itineraries. Diségno **6**, 169–178 (2020)
81. Hatwell, Y., Martinez-Sarrochi, F.: The tactile reading of maps and drawings, and the access of blind people to works of art. In: Hatwell, Y., Streri, A., Gentaz, E. (ed.) Touching for knowing: cognitive psychology of haptic manual perception, pp. 255–273. John Benjamins B.V., Amsterdam (2003)

Digitalizing the Artistic Heritage of Xoan Singing in Phú Thọ Province: Conservation and Promotion in Contemporary Cultural Life

Dinh Luong Khac[1] , Son Quang Van[2(✉)], Lam Nguyen Dinh[3] ,
Son Nguyen Truong[3] , and Ninh Ngo Hai[4]

[1] Faculty of Information Technology, Ha Long University, Quang Ninh, Vietnam
luongkhacdinh@daihochalong.edu.vn
[2] Instituteof Cultural Heritage and Development Studies, Van Lang University, Ho Chi Minh
City, Vietnam
son.qv@vlu.edu.vn
[3] VNU University of Social Sciences and Humanities, Hanoi, Vietnam
[4] Facultyof Culture, Ha Long University, Quang Ninh, Vietnam
ngohaininh@daihochalong.edu.vn

Abstract. Xoan singing is a type of ritual folk music in Vietnam, shaped and developed mainly in Phú Thọ province. Formed and developed for thousands of years, Xoan singing is closely associated with the custom of worshiping Hùng Vương, i.e. the early dynasties of the Vietnamese people BC. With 14 unique songs (quả cách) still preserved and promoted today, along with the principles of performing this heritage in the worship of Hùng Vương, Xoan singing has become a unique heritage separated from many other genres of Vietnamese folk songs. There have been many research works in the past decades, discovering outstanding values of this art form. We realize that, in the context of the industrial revolution 4.0, Xoan singing needs to be applied digitally to preserve, promote and introduce this heritage to international tourists and Vietnamese in many places other local people who have not directly come to enjoy Xoan singing. Applying information technology to protect Xoan singing will be a breakthrough approach to preserving and promoting intangible cultural heritage such as the performing arts of ethnic groups in Vietnam today. As a developing country, where many tangible and intangible cultural heritages are being invested by the government for restoration and development, the problem of applying high technology to digitize for developing tourism and economic growth for indigenous people is one of the solutions that need scientists' attention and research. The scope of the study will focus on identifying the unique values of the Xoan art and, at the same time, provide a model for applying digital technology to preserve and develop this unique heritage in the life of the country at present.

Keywords: Xoan singing · Digital technology application · Preserve and promote · Phú Thọ province · Vietnam

© The Author(s), under exclusive license to Springer Nature Switzerland AG 2022
R. Furferi et al. (Eds.): Florence Heri-Tech 2022, CCIS 1645, pp. 31–41, 2022.
https://doi.org/10.1007/978-3-031-20302-2_3

1 Introduction

In traditional Vietnamese music, each art form has its characteristics, reflected in its artistic performances, space, and function. Xoan singing is a type of folk song, ritual, and custom meant for worshiping gods and emperors with a multi-element art form, i.e., music, singing, and dancing. Usually, Xoan singing is performed in the early spring, and it is popular in Hùng Vương-Phú Thọ, a province in the midland region of Vietnam. While Quan họ singing, Trù singing, Tuồng, Chèo, and Cải Lương are more about their artistic and entertainment functions, Xoan singing in Phú Thọ has clear religious and belief functions.

Unlike many art forms serving a religious function, Xoan singing focuses on singing to worship the Hùng Kings and village lords who have made great contributions to Vietnam for thousands of years. However, as a traditional art form, Xoan singing is at risk of being lost as older artisans who practice Xoan singing become fewer. With the unique values of a ritual folk genre and the dangers of disappearing from contemporary society, on November 24, 2011, at the Sixth Conference of the Intergovernmental Commission on the Conservation of Intangible Cultural Heritage of UNESCO held in Bali, Indonesia, Vietnamese Xoan Singing of Phú Thọ has been registered as an Intangible Cultural Heritage of Humanity in need of urgent protection.

Historically, Xoan singing has been studied by domestic and foreign researchers such as [4, 7, 9, 10], and many others. The research focuses on the history, artistic characteristics, and other issues related to the art of Xoan singing. In several works, measures have been mentioned to preserve and promote Xoan singing in contemporary cultural life. Notably, the opinion of a leading music researcher in Vietnam – Nguyen Thuy Loan – states that we should prioritize preserving the inherent form of Xoan singing, including the space of Xoan singing in the communal houses and temples; as well as encourage the restoration of Xoan singing in the chamber and restore singing and competitions in the original Xoan villages [8]. However, in the current context, in addition to conservation and promotion of Xoan singing by traditional methods, such as introducing performances and bringing the art into schools, applying advanced technology to promote Xoan singing in domestic and international spaces is an important issue. This could also help support older artists in the regions where Xoan singing is performed.

Over the last few years, Vietnam's government has been promoting the conservation of cultural heritage through digital technology. Many tangible cultural heritages have been applied for conservation and promotion. However, regarding intangible cultural heritage, including Xoan singing, the creates a gap for interdisciplinary researchers of cultural heritage and technology, in which they need to work together to apply new technology in the preservation and promotion of Xoan singing and other arts in the contemporary world. This process is the main topic of this article. With today's advanced technologies, the application of digital technology to preserve and promote Xoan singing in Phú Thọ offers fascinating possibilities.

2   Research Methods

To conceptualize the application of information technology (IT) to preserve the art of Xoan singing, the author used an interdisciplinary research approach between ethnology and IT.

Firstly, within the approach of musical art and ethnography, the study conducted fieldwork to collect data related to the art of Xoan singing, from historical documents to materials related to the art, its forms, and performance spaces. This is a particularly important source of material for digitalizing the artistic heritage of Xoan singing. Along with that, the study approached the issue according to ethnographic methods, including in-depth interviews with Xoan practitioners in several localities. Within this approach, access to old and skilled artisans was one of the important resources. Further, the author conducted in-depth interviews with excellent artisans, recordings of Xoan singing programs, and detailed each song, as well as the vocal performance techniques and instruments used to accompany Xoan singing. These were important resources to identify the central values of Xoan singing in the community. In addition, the library information center of Phú Thọ province - one of the most important document centers where the art of Xoan singing was formed and developed - is also an important place for this study to exploit and use relevant reliable resources to the entire origin and history of the artistic heritage of Xoan singing. The Vietnam Music Research Institute and the Vietnam National Institute of Culture and Arts are also scientific centers specializing in Vietnamese culture and are also considered important places where we also conduct research and selection documents on the art of Xoan singing to ensure the accuracy of the source material for the digitization of this unique artistic heritage.

With technology, all advanced technologies are studied and used in this work. The digitization task begins with a detailed script, and the content being filmed, recorded, and digitized will be carried out according to a specific process. The source of filming material was identified as the most important for obtaining good image quality for product digitization with central digital technologies such as 360 degrees, slow motion, and 3D. This approach includes building modules and software to perform the overall digitalization of the entire Xoan singing performance program, including spaces and performance environments; building modules and software to digitalize each part – singing, performing musical instruments, and dancing in Xoan singing; and building software to digitalize the historical content of Xoan singing.

In this study, the technologies proposed to be applied to digitalize Xoan singing are identified as 3D technology, 360-degree, and slow-motion (Fig. 1).

Another important technological process is building a website to manage, preserve, introduce, and promote the art of Xoan singing in Phú Thọ. With this website, an electronic map can introduce the places at which Xoan singing is performed, helping domestic and international visitors to easily find such places and enjoy this unique art form.

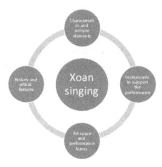

Fig. 1. Main contents relating to the art of Xoan singing

3   Basic Characteristics of the Art of Xoan Singing

The name Xoan singing, according to a survey conducted by a group of authors in 2009, comes from Xuan singing [3], i.e., Xoan singing is associated with rituals and customary singing that takes place at the beginning of spring. Later, in avoidance of the duplication of names and problems related to kings or gods in the villages where Xoan singing was performed, the word for Xuan singing was misread as Xoan singing. Thus, Xoan singing has been performed under this name, mainly in spring festivals in several wards and villages. At the beginning of spring, the elders in the village, along with young children and teenagers, will gather at the Hay Temple – the place to worship King Hung Vuong and the village gods – to hold festivals and sing Xoan together.

When it comes to Xoan singing, first of all, it is impossible not to mention the Xoan wards, i.e., villages at which Xoan singing is being performed. The Xoan wards are organized very closely and based on the connection of clans, families, and areas of residence. The number of people singing Xoan, as well as the organization of Xoan wards going to sing, includes 6–8 main performers, accompanied by other singers and a drummer. Dang Hoanh Loan added that, a Xoan ward's organization is very compact, and that the "Xoan peaches" (the girls who sing and dance Xoan) make up the majority [2]. According to Dang Dinh Thuan, people who sing Xoan often live in the same family or have "non-domestic and foreign" kinship relationships, as well as can live in the same villages and organize themselves into wards to teach each other [1]. This is also the reason why the singing technique of each Xoan ward often remains the secret of each ward. The head of a Xoan ward must be an older person and a man, with good morals and a professional reputation, called Trùm. A Trùm is an experienced and professional person who knows how to communicate and read Han-Nom characters, to sing and lead several songs that are written in this script. The members of the ward call the male performers (sons) Kép and the female (daughter) Đào. Each Xoan ward has about 15–18 people. Men wear a shirt (áo the), a turban (khăn xếp), white pants, and wooden clogs (guốc mộc). Women wear a five-body dress (áo ngũ thân), a raven-beak scarf (khan mỏ quả), a white blouse (áo cánh trắng), a bib (yếm điều), a bag belt (thắt lưng bao), a colorful bib strip (dải yếm các màu), silk pants (xà tích), and wooden clogs (guốc mộc). Villages, where people go to Xoan singing, are sworn in with the Xoan wards and these wards are also associated with each other. They consider each other as close as brothers, thus they are not allowed to marry young men and women of the village.

According to Tu Ngoc and Dang Dinh Thuan, a performance of Xoan singing must follow a uniformly prescribed sequence, including three stages (i.e., singing stages) [1]:

The first is the ritual singing step according to local folk beliefs, and includes the following songs:

Giáo trống,
Giáo pháo,
Thơ nhang,
Đóng đám.

The lyrics of these songs are prayers and wishes to the kings and gods to bless the villagers with peace and health. The ceremonial signing part is performed according to folk rituals in front of the hammock gate in the inner house (called the Cua communal house). These lyrics were carefully copied and preserved by the Trùm. Đào and Kép singers will alternate singing in response to each other, creating a sacred and reverent atmosphere before further participating in Xoan singing during such a festival.

The second step involves the 14 Guoqiao [10] (songs as a way of expression):

Kiều Giang Cách	Hạ Thời Cách
Nhàn Ngâm Cách	Thu thời Cách
Tràng Mai Cách	Đông thời Cách
Ngư Tiều Canh Mục Cách	Chơi Dâu Cách
Đối rẫy Cách	Tứ Mùa Cách
Xuân Thời Cách	Thuyền Chèo Cách
Hồi Liên Cách	Tứ Dân Cách

According to Dang Dinh Thuan, the content of the lyrics describes the life and activities of contemporaries in the countryside or praises the four seasons along with the changes of natural scenery through a year of farming, accompanied by ancient fairy tales. Each of these songzs has a clear three-part structure: interjection or opening (mở đầu), introduction or middle part (phần giữa), and ending (phần cuối) [10].

The third step is also known as Phu Ly singing. This part is lyrical, showcasing the relationship between men and women and reflecting the feelings and love that boys and girls have for each other in the form of reciprocal singing to show the improvisational talent of young people. This is also the most exciting, lively, and attractive part of Xoan singing in general. With this stage, the art of Xoan singing is unique and shows its characteristics.

One of the important elements of the art of Xoan singing is the music. According to Tu Ngoc, Xoan singing is mainly composed of 3-syllable and 4-tone scales (third or fourth interval [10]). According to Dang Dinh Thuan, Xoan wards in Phú Thọ province still preserve 31 Xoan songs in the following four ancient Xoan wards:

- An Thái Xoan singing village
- Thét Xoan singing village
- Phù Đức Xoan singing village
- Kim Đới Ward (or Kim Đái) Xoan singing village

These four Xoan wards all belong to Viet Tri-City. The head of each Xoan ward is the Trùm. In Xoan singing, the Kép (men) often perform the task of leading the vocals (lính xướng) and dances, as well as the accompaniment to the male and female drums. Meanwhile, the đào (women) often take the role of repeating the singing (hát nhắc lại), singing in response, and dancing. In addition, when Xoan performers are invited to perform elsewhere, there are also boys and girls representing the community of the host family [1].

Instruments in Xoan singing only use a small drum and two or three pairs of beats (phách instruments)[1] made of old bamboo. During the performance, double drums (kép drums) play a very important role in keeping the rhythm for the kép and đào to sing the whole song. Before starting to sing, the drums will beat for a while as an invitation and signal the start of the song, before continuing to maintain the rhythm for the song. When moving from one singing step to another, the double drum must always perform a transitional drumbeat.

In addition to these unique characteristics, when it comes to the art of Xoan singing, the lyrics play a crucial role. Since Xoan singing is rooted in the local people's worship of gods and kings, the lyrics are imbued with the local dialect of the midland region of Phú Thọ. Xoan lyrics are often expressed in the form of a poem, but with certain variations that are easy to memorize and sing.

Over thousands of years of formation and development, the art of Xoan singing is a heritage with a particularly important position and role in the cultural and religious life of the Vietnamese in Phú Thọ and Vinh Phuc provinces. The unique historical and artistic values in the art of Xoan singing and its functions need to be further promoted in contemporary cultural life. One of the important solutions to preserve and promote Xoan singing to the wider community and world is the application of digital technology. Digitalizing the art of Xoan singing not only helps provide information to those interested in this art but also helps those who love Xoan singing to learn this art through digitalized products.

4 Used Technology

Up to now, there have been no studies on digitalizing Xoan singing and creating technological products based on digitalization techniques with 3D, 360-degree, and slow-motion technologies. However, using such high-tech solutions to digitalize and preserve and promote Xoan singing for tourism development offers many advantages.

These technologies will help us to create products that directly provide information about the history, development, artistic characteristics, and the entire performance process, as well as performance spaces and environments. For instance, with 3D digital

---

[1] The diameter of the drum is 20 cm and its height is 25–30 cm, the two sides are covered with skin and the drum is made of jackfruit wood.

technology, we can digitalize objects such as the costumes of Xoan singers, the musical instruments, and some performance spaces including the setup of drums that are accompanying the singing.

With 360-degree technology, we can digitalize the performances of Xoan singing, as well as the process of reciprocal singing. The technology can also be applied to digitalize the process of learning Xoan singing, in which older artists can be recorded for younger people to learn Xoan singing.

With slow-motion technology, we can digitalize Xoan songs to help people learn the intricacies of Xoan singing during a performance, without having to learn directly from artists. Slow-motion technology can also be used to digitalize music, steps of making Xoan musical instruments, music melodies, and several other processes of Xoan singing.

Thus, the following technologies and software can be utilized for specific content in digitalizing Xoan singing:

- 3D technology can process and digitalize objects, including drums and props.
- Slow-motion technology can digitally process music melodies of songs, rhythms of drums, beats, and the like.
- 360-degree software can be used to digitalize the performance spaces of Xoan singing at different locations and in various forms (Fig. 2).

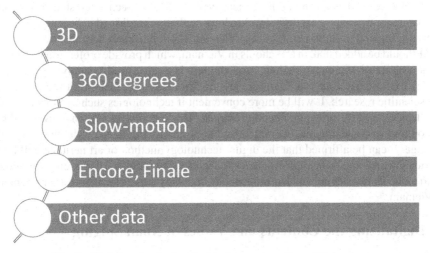

Fig. 2. Digital technologies used in the conservation of Xoan singing

- Encore and Finale recording software can digitalize and process music melodies in Xoan singing.
- Other software technologies will store historical and cultural resources of Xoan singing.

Thus, with the application of the above technologies, we can not only overcome the "dead heritages" sources of documents in libraries in the past decades in Vietnam but also make an important contribution to bringing living documents to life. Active and active about the entire heritage to promote in digital as well as electronic media.

The highlight of the technology application method is that the intangible values of the heritage are preserved, introduced, and promoted on the internet and digital websites. The folk songs of Xoan singing will be fully approached by people in many other localities of Vietnam or by tourists and art researchers in many other countries. Slow-motion technology, as mentioned above, will allow those who love the art of Xoan singing to learn to sing and practice this art, without having to come to learn directly from the artists in Phú Thọ.

It is interesting that the entire legacy of Xoan singing, through digital products, will help spread this legacy to other cultural regions. For example, now in Vietnam, there are dozens of places to worship King Hung, from the North, the Central to the South. These localities can learn and practice Xoan singing to serve performances during the Hung King's worshiping anniversaries - consider them as sacred ways that Vietnamese people in different regions can learn and practice, and perform to commemorate and honor the past King of their people. 3D and 360-degree technologies will help localities to restructure the performance space, performance form, and costumes, recreating the space and performance form as the traditional locality of Xoan singing existed.

3D technology also allows the digitization of music, which records the entire melody of Xoan songs, so that musicians in each locality of Vietnam can compose new songs based on folk tunes from Vietnam. These Xoan singing songs. The method based on folk melodies to develop modern musical works has also been interested in modern Vietnamese musicians. This digital technology method is confirmed to be a new method in preserving and promoting effectively Vietnam's folk music art heritage today.

It should be added that, in art schools in Vietnam, which provide professional training in the folk art of Vietnamese ethnic groups, there is a great need to apply digital technology to digitalize folk music, music, and traditional music, then put it into teaching and scientific research. It will be more convenient if technologies such as Slow motion, 360 degrees, and 3D are applied and promoted. This activity, as written above, will be a good way to create the most complete and high-quality digitized productions of each heritage. It can be affirmed that the digital technology method of art heritage will help shorten the time and bring high efficiency to lecturers, researchers, and even generations of art students in teaching and learning at the University's traditional art training centers in Vietnam.

5   Digitalizing the Contents and Values of Xoan Singing

After information and documents on the art of Xoan singing in Phú Thọ have been recorded and filmed, we can proceed to digitalizing and further processing these through the following steps.

First, all information related to the history of the formation and development of Xoan singing in Phú Thọ should be digitalized. This will help end-users learn about this unique genre of singing before switching to the pictures. Thus, relevant sources need to be fully digitalized to create a full product set.

Second, all three typical singing steps (i.e., stages – "chặng hát") of Xoan singing should be digitalized with the help of slow-motion, 360-degree, and 3D technology.

Third, the entire performance space of Xoan singing, including sacred spaces, communal houses, and festivals related to the practice of Xoan singing should be digitalized.

This source of the material is especially important for the researcher to fully and comprehensively recognize, analyze, and understand the art of Xoan singing and the practices and performances involved.

Fourth, all instruments used in Xoan singing, especially the drums, can be digitalized. With this, information about the size of the drum, the drum's performance process, and other technical details can be included.

Fifth, all costumes and performance props of Xoan singing can be digitalized. These are important sources to assert the overall and comprehensive art of Xoan singing.

In addition, several other advanced technologies will help describe the content, form, and movements of Xoan singing. Such digitalized products will then help viewers see every detail and be able to learn more about Xoan singing, without requiring the presence of an artisan. However, such advanced technology needs to be applied appropriately to create high-quality digital products.

Thus, the website will include a set of digitalized products detailing the entire tangible and intangible heritage related to the performing arts of Xoan singing, from costumes and performance spaces to the songs of Xoan singing performed by artists; as well as a software system for exploiting, using, and managing the art of Xoan singing that can serve both cultural managers, tourists, researchers, and other people interested in studying, enjoying, and wishing to learn Xoan singing (Fig. 3).

Finally, a website specializing in the art of Xoan singing should be implemented to serve as a central location for all created and published materials and digital products.

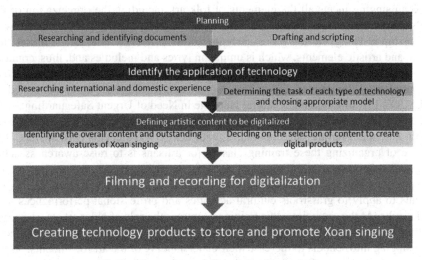

Fig. 3. The process of digitalizing Xoan singing

6 Conclusion

Xoan singing is a priceless heritage in the treasure trove of performing arts and folk music in Vietnam. The origin of Xoan singing lies in Phú Thọ province and then spread to the villages on both banks of the Lô and Red Rivers [5] through Vinh Phuc province. Four ancient wards – An Thái, Phu Đức, Kim Đới, and Thet located in the two communes of Kim Đức and Phượng Lâu (Phú Thọ) – are still preserving and maintaining Xoan singing in contemporary cultural and religious life.

Currently, according to a survey of Phú Thọ province, the number of Xoan singing artists is about 150 people. However, there are only about 10 people who can teach. Similarly, at present, the whole province of Phú Thọ has about 100 people participating in Xoan wards, but only about 50 people know how to sing. The relics, such as communal houses and shrines, where the Xoan singing activities take place, amount only to about 10 relics.

Xoan singing, since being included in UNESCO's Representative List of the Intangible Heritage of Humanity and List of Intangible Cultural Heritage in Need of Urgent Safeguarding, has been restored and returned to the contemporary cultural life of local people. Solutions to preserve and promote the heritage of Xoan singing has been mentioned by cultural and art researchers. However, applying digital technology to preserve Xoan singing remains a novum, which is why this article has proposed some digital solutions for the issue. The technologies proposed to be applied to create digitalized products of Xoan singing include 3D, 360-degree, and slow-motion technologies, as well as other related high-tech software and applications. The created digital products will be an important source of documentation for the conservation and promotion of the Xoan singing of Phú Thọ, actively contributing to bringing Xoan singing to the domestic and international public.

Xoan singing meets all the elements of folk art, including the organization of the wards, performances in a simple form of singing combined with dance, associated with the worship of Hùng Vương. It is a form of traditional music, combining cultural, historical, and artistic elements, which is unique in lyrics and melodies and, thus, contains many cultural values that have been preserved by the community for centuries. However, because of the low number of practitioners and teachers, the art is mentioned on UNESCO's List of Intangible Cultural Heritage in Need of Urgent Safeguarding.

From 2013 to 2014, Phú Thọ province held many successive artisan training classes in Kim Đức and Phương Lâu communes, with nearly 100 students participating. The purpose of organizing these training classes for artisans is to raise awareness about preserving and promoting the values of the Xoan singing heritage of Phú Thọ, as well as to provide basic knowledge and skills about the performing art of Xoan singing for students to apply to grassroots cultural activities and professional performances with good results. At the same time, this training promotes the role of older artists who teach and train the young generation to perform Xoan singing. Phú Thọ province has introduced Xoan singing into schools to increase their understanding of the art for students. Along with digital solutions and products, the teaching of Xoan singing to the next generation is a method that will help the art of Xoan singing thrive in contemporary cultural life.

Acknowledgement. The authors wish to express their gratitude to Van Lang University, Vietnam for funding this research.

References

1. Dang, D.T.: Phú Thọ Xoan singing – Distinctive features of organization and performance art. Website for supporting literary and artistic creation, Ministry of Culture, Sports, and Tourism (2018). Hanoi, Accessed 20 Sep 2021
2. Dang, H.L.: After fielding, I understand how to sing Xoan singing. Vietnamese Inst. Musicol. Hanoi Bull. **29**, 67–69 (2010)
3. Ministry of Culture, Sports and Tourism: National Profile of Xoan Singing in Phú Thọ. Library of Vietnamese Institute for Musicology, Hanoi (2009)
4. Ngo, V.B.: Journey to Xoan villages. Hanoi, Ethnographic Rev. **3** (1984)
5. Nguyen, K.X.: Discussing the Phú Thọ Xoan singing region. Vietnamese Inst. Musicol. Hanoi Bull. **29**, 62–65 (2010)
6. Nguyen, L.: Vinh Phu Xoan singing. Hanoi, Ethnograph. Rev. **3** (1974)
7. Nguyen, L.: Xoan Singing, Origins and Forms. Printed in Vinh Phuc Historical Issues, vol. 1, Vinh Phu Cultural Ty (1975)
8. Nguyen, T.L.: Method of preserving Xoan art – Practical basis and some highlights. Vietnamese Inst. Musicol. Hanoi Bull. **29**, 97–101 (2010)
9. Pham, T.T.: Similarities and differences between Xoan singing, Phú Thọ Ghẹo singing, and Quan họ singing in Bắc Ninh. Doctoral Thesis in Cultural Studies. Library of the Institute of Culture and Information, Hanoi (2005)
10. Tu, N.: Xoan Singing – Ritual Folk Songs – Customs. Publisher House Music, Hanoi (1997)

Analysis of a SLAM-Based Laser Scanner for the 3D Digitalization of Underground Heritage Structures. A Case Study in the Wineries of Baltanas (Palencia, Spain)

Javier Camiña[1] , Luis Javier Sánchez-Aparicio[1,2(✉)] ,
Cristina Mayo Corrochano[1] , David Sanz-Arauz[1] ,
and Diego González-Aguilera[2]

[1] Department of Construction and Technology in Architecture (DCTA),
Escuela Técnica Superior de Arquitectura de Madrid (ETSAM), Universidad Politécnica de
Madrid, Madrid, Spain
j.camina@alumnos.upm.es, lj.sanchez@upm.es,
cristina@estudiomayo.com, david.sanz.arauz@upm.com
[2] Department of Cartographic and Land Engineering, Higher Polytechnic School of Ávila,
University of Salamanca, Ávila, Spain
{luisj,daguilera}@usal.es

Abstract. This paper aims at evaluating the performance of a Wearable Mobile Mapping Solution (SLAM-based) for the 3D digitalization of underground heritage sites. This evaluation was carried out by using as study case one of the largest wineries of the underground complex of Baltanás. For its digitalization we have tested not only the standard protocol (based on the good practices) but also a proposed protocol on which the laser head is turned 45° with respect to the direction of advance. As the ground truth we have used a high accuracy 3D point cloud which was obtained with a static laser scanner. The results, after an in-depth statistical analysis, demonstrate that the proposed protocol outperforms the standard one, showing better accuracies with similar acquisition and processing times. Additionally, we have tested the influence of different SLAM parameters in the final 3D point cloud. The results of this work have revealed that the Wearable Mobile Mapping Solutions are suitable tools for the 3D digitalization of underground heritage sites, obtaining centimetric accuracy and reducing the time required for its data acquisition and processing, requiring just only the 8% of the time with respect to a TLS point cloud.

Keywords: Underground heritage · Geoinformatics · Wearable mobile mapping · 3D digitalization

1 Introduction

The 3D digitalization of Cultural Heritage (CH) has become widespread in recent years and has established itself as a useful practice for documentation, conservation, preservation, enhancement and visualization purposes [1]. Nowadays, although there are different

R. Furferi et al. (Eds.): Florence Heri-Tech 2022, CCIS 1645, pp. 42–56, 2022.
https://doi.org/10.1007/978-3-031-20302-2_4

ways of carrying out these digitalizations, it is necessary to adapt the different techniques to the specific situation, in this way the physical space in which the heritage is located has a great influence on its digitalization [1].

Within the different types of CH typologies, Underground Heritage (UH) is one of the most challenging typologies due to [2, 3]: i) the absence of proper light conditions which difficult the use of passive sensors (i.e. digital cameras); ii) presence of narrow, labyrinthine and irregular spaces; and iii) absence of GNSS signal. In accordance to Di Stefano et al. [1] a suitable sensor for digitalizing UH needs to be agile due to the presence of narrow spaces, easy to use, cost-effective and affordable due to the lack of resources for digitalizing this type of heritage. Among the 3D mapping solutions able to digitalize these environments we can find the terrestrial laser scanner (TLS). This sensor has been broadly used [4, 5] for obtaining high-resolution 3D point clouds. However, the characteristic of these spaces demands the use of a large number of scan stations and thus large time investments. In the last year, research community has been focused on evaluating more agile solutions such as the Mobile Mapping System (MMS) [6]. This type of sensors hybridized the laser scanning technologies with position systems such as the Inertial Measurement Unit (IMU) for generating 3D point clouds without being static/tripod mounted. This characteristic drastically reduces the working times [6] when we deal with the 3D documentation of heritage places. The main limitation of this sensors is the drift error that could appear during a data acquisition [7], making necessary to test additional acquisition protocol or even to understand the influence of the parameters in the final result.

Under the basis previously exposed, this work aims at evaluating the performance, in terms of accuracy and time, of an MMS for the digitalization of a specific type of UH: the wineries. More specifically, we have tested a wearable mobile mapping solution (WMMS) which could be carried in a small back-pack. The main novelty of this work, with respect to previous works [6, 7], lies on the extensive evaluation of the performance of this sensor in a challenging environment with "there and back" paths. Due to this we propose a cross protocol for the data acquisition. This protocol outperforms in terms of statistical indicators.

After this Introduction Sect. 2 will expose the materials and methods used. Section 3 will be devoted to show the experimental results, including and in-depth analysis. Section 4 will show the discussion arising from the experimental results. Finally, Sect. 5 summarizes the main conclusions as well as future works.

2 Materials and Methods

The equipment used to perform this study included two different LiDAR sensors: i) a wearable mobile mapping system (WMMS); and ii) a terrestrial laser scanner (TLS). In the following section it will be described in detail the specifications of each sensor as well as the approaches used for generating the 3D point cloud of the study case.

2.1 Wearable Mobile Mapping System

The WMMS used for the present study case was the Zeb-Revo mobile mapping system. This device is commercialized by the company GeoSLAM (https://geoslam.com/), integrating a 2D rotating laser scanner head (Hokuyo UTM-30LX-F) rigidly coupled to an Inertial Measurement Unit (IMU) on a rotary engine. The data captured by this set of sensors is stored in a small datalogger equipped within a backpack, being extremely portable (4.10 kg) and suitable for narrow spaces such as a winery (Fig. 1a). This system is able to capture 40,000 points per second with a nominal accuracy of 1–3 cm and a range that varies from 0.60 to 30 m indoor and 0.60 to 15 m outdoors. The autonomy of the equipment is about 4 h.

a)   b)

Fig. 1. Approaches used for the 3D digitalization: a) a WMMS and; b) a high-precision TLS.

The post-processing approach used for converting the 2D point cloud captured by the Hokuyo laser scanner and the data captured by the IMU was carried out by applying the Simultaneous Location and Mapping (SLAM) algorithm. This approach address with the problem of solving the position of a mobile system (such as the WMMS) inside an unknow environment, obtaining the 3D point cloud of the site. Among the different possibilities that exits today, the present work has applied the full SLAM approach due to its accuracy, being carried out off-line. Figure 2 shows a graphical workflow of a full SLAM approach. Data processing is an incremental and iterative procedure on which the environment is captured by segments (2D point clouds) which are registered one-by-one. The SLAM reconstruction starts when the laser head capture the first segment. Once it is captured, the algorithm evaluates its geometrical features (called surfels). After that, the algorithm considers the next segment by using the data captured by the IMU, calculating during this stage the surfels of the new segment. All these surfels (from the current segment and the previous one) are used to align the point cloud captured on each segment with respect to the previous one (see stage 3 of Fig. 2). Finally, this alignment is optimized by using a non-linear optimization on which the cost function is defined by the distance between surfels as well as by the IMU measurements.

Once all the data is property capture the SLAM algorithm pass to a global registration phase on which all the data is considered at the same time and the position of the laser head is refined globally. During this stage the algorithm could consider that the start and end points are the same (close loop solution), reducing the error accumulation of the local stage. For more details about this approach reader refers to di Fillipo et al. [6].

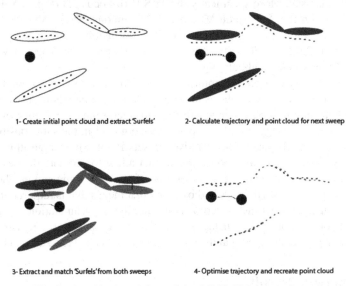

1- Create initial point cloud and extract 'Surfels'   2- Calculate trajectory and point cloud for next sweep

3- Extract and match 'Surfels' from both sweeps   4- Optimise trajectory and recreate point cloud

Fig. 2. Graphical workflow of the full SLAM approach used.

This approach was applied by using the Robotic Operative System (ROS) library [8] on which the following processing parameters were tested:

- *The convergence threshold (c):* this parameter defines the number of iterations for each processing stage during the local and global registration phases. This is useful when the drift effect appears. Range 0 to + 5, with a value of 0 by default.
- *Rigidity (r):* this parameter changes the influence of the IMU in the computation. The increase of this parameter makes that the SLAM algorithm will be more influenced by the IMU and less influenced by the laser point cloud. Range -5 to + 5, with a value of 0 by default.
- *The window size (w):* this parameter defines the size of the data samples during the local registration phase. Large values allow to match larger areas (more features). Range 0 to + 5 with a value of 0 by default.
- *Voxel density (v):* this parameter modifies the size of the voxels. Higher values increase the level of detail considered during the local registration at close range. Range -1 to + 3 with a default value of 0.
- *Prioritize planar surfaces (p):* this parameter prioritizes the matching of planar surfaces during the global registration phase.

Local parameters are used to solve most of the drift cases, global, instead, solves issues when the data capture method was inconsistent.

2.2 Terrestrial Laser Scanner

In order to evaluate the performance of the WMMS in terms of accuracy, a high-precision laser scanner was used. More specifically the TLS Faro Focus 3D (Fig. 1b). This laser scanner is based on the Amplitude Modulated Continuous Wave (AMCW) measure principle. This principle, highlights for its fast data acquisition and accuracy, allowing to capture from 122,000 to 976,000 points per second with a nominal accuracy of 2mm. The weight of the scanner is about 5 kg.

This sensor is only capable of capturing the data from a static position. Thus, it is required to station it in different places in order to digitalize the whole structure. Apart of this, each scan station is placed in an arbitrary local coordinate system, requiring the use of a registration strategy in order to place all the model in the same position. This procedure was carried by using the Iterative Closets Points (ICP) algorithm [9]. The ICP iteratively solves a minimization problem that allow to estimate the best Helmer transformation between two point clouds, one as reference or static and another one as mobile point cloud. This stage is applied by pairs, that means that is required to applied this algorithm at least n-1 times where n is the number of scan stations. Finally, the registration error is improved by using a network adjustment (global registration) on which the variables are the spatial and angular position of each scan station [10].

3   Experimental Results

3.1   The Wineries of Baltanás (Palencia, Spain)

The wineries of Baltanás are a group of 374 wineries located in Palencia. It is one of the most important peripheral excavated complexes in the province of Palencia and in the entire Autonomous Community of Castilla y León, not only for its number but also for its state of conservation. The cellars are arranged along the contour lines of the two hills that form them. It is worth mentioning that these wine cellars are distributed in depth in a total of six levels.

The complex dates back to the last third of the 9th century. It is believed that a medieval castle existed on the larger hill as a defensive base in the area during the Reconquest. This is consistent with the formation of other bodegas hills in the area. The first references to these other cellars date back to the 12th, 13th and 14th centuries in villages such as Astudillo and Dueñas. The castles were demolished as the Islamic threat diminished, and the previously occupied hills were used to excavate and build wine cellars. Félix Jové and José Luis Sainz have already published several works on the history of the village of Baltanás and its wine cellars [11, 12]. These publications refer to the first known reference to the wine cellars, which dates back to 1543, and although there is no exact date for the age of the wine cellars.

A very important wine-growing activity was soon generated on the slopes of the Villa, as the environmental conditions of the underground spaces, where the humidity and temperature are stable throughout the year, are favourable for the fermentation and conservation of the wine. Nowadays the location of this heritage within its underground condition makes really difficult its accessibility for tourism purposes, making necessary the digitalization of these buildings. However, the digitalization of these places entails important challenges such as: i) the large number of buildings (374); ii) the absence of proper light conditions; and iii) the presence of narrow spaces, similar to tunnels.

a)   b)

Fig. 3. Wineries of Baltanás: a) general view and; b) inner view of the winery digitalized during this work.

3.2   Digitalization of the Reference Winery

As it was stated previously, the main challenge of this study case relies on its extension and shape of this buildings. Thus, it is important to obtain a good compromise between accuracy and processing time. In order to study this question, it was chosen as study case the largest winery of Baltanás (Fig. 1 and 3a). This winery has a total extension of about 150 m^2 with a height (from the entrance to the lower point) of about 22 m.

WMMS Point Cloud
As stated di-Fillipo et al. [6], previously to the data acquisition with the WMMS device it is necessary to perform an on-site inspection. This inspection has the aim of designing the most proper data acquisition protocol in order to obtain the most favorable path for solving the SLAM problem This protocol requires to consider: i) the proper accessibility to all the winery (i.e. doors open); ii) the removal of obstacles along the way; ii) the planning of a closed-loop ring, trying to avoid "there and back" loops where the path simply doubles back on itself.

In accordance with the considerations previously showed, a total of two protocols were used for digitalizing the winery (Fig. 4): i) a standard protocol based on the good practices and on which the laser head is aligned with the direction of advance; and ii) a cross protocol (proposed by the authors) on which the laser is placed at 45° with respect to the direction of advance. The main limitation of the first protocol is the presence of a "there and back" loop on which the laser head capture the same scene from the same position. This limitation does not appear in the second acquisition protocol. The time spent for performing the path was 7:40 min and 7:30 min respectively.

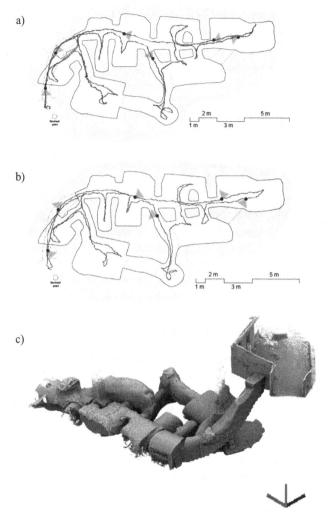

Fig. 4. Data acquisition and results obtained with the WMMS: a) standard protocol; b) cross protocol; and c) 3D point cloud obtained with the cross protocol with default parameters.

Once the data was acquired, a full 3D-SLAM approach was applied by considering the parameters defined in Sect. 2.1. With the aim of evaluating the impact of each parameter in the final result, a total of 38 SLAM solutions (19 for the standard protocol and 19 for the cross protocol) were obtained. In each one of this solution it was changed the value of one parameter according with Sect. 2.1. Figure 5 shows a graphical comparison of the times invested to solve each SLAM in an Intel Core 7 with 16 Gb of RAM. It is worth mentioning that both SLAM problems were not properly solved when it was chosen the maximum of the voxel size ($l/v/3$). For the standard protocol the winery was represented by a 3D point cloud made up by 12,966,501 points (31533 points/m^2). Meanwhile, the 3D point cloud obtained with the cross protocol was made up by 12,846,756 points (33697 points/m^2).

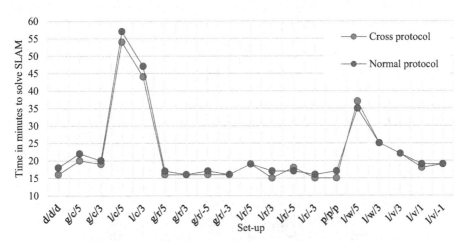

Fig. 5. Time invested per each SLAM solution. The notation is the following one: *a/b/c* where *a* represents if the parameter is applied at local or global stage; *b* is the parameter changed with respect to the default configuration in accordance with Sect. 2.1 and *c* is the value of this parameter. *d/d/d* represents the set-up with default paraments and *p/p/p* the set-up with prioritization to planar surfaces.

3.2.1 TLS Point Cloud

In addition to the WMMS point cloud, a TLS network was performed with the aim of obtaining a 3D point cloud of the winery with great accuracy. To this end a total of 22 scan stations were needed (Fig. 6). The alignment phase was carried out by using the procedure showed in Sect. 2.2, throwing an alignment error of 3 mm. Then the overlap areas between scan stations were decimated to 2mm (spatial filter), obtaining a 3D point cloud of the winery made up by 18,462,831 points and an average density of 53796 points/m2. The time required for performing this digitalization was about 3,00 h. Meanwhile the time required for the alignment of the data was about 2,30 h.

3.3 Evaluation of the WMMS Accuracy

This section complements the results obtained in Sect. 3.2 by evaluating the accuracy of each SLAM solution in comparison with the TLS point cloud. To this end the approach followed was: i) analysis of the discrepancies between the TLS and each WMMS point cloud; and ii) calculation of the main statistical indexes.

Computation of the Discrepancies Between the TLS and WMMS Point Cloud. The discrepancies between the TLS point cloud, that will act as ground truth, and the different WMMS point clouds was carried out by using the Multiscale Model to Model Cloud

a)

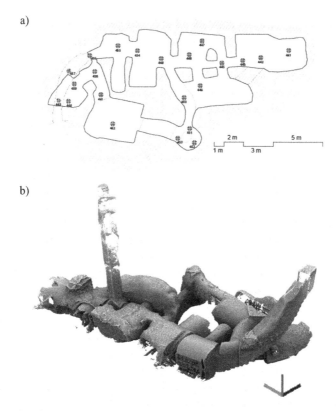

b)

Fig. 6. TLS point cloud: a) position of the scans during the data acquisition; and b) 3D view of the final one.

Comparison (M3C2) [13]. This algorithm outperforms other cloud to cloud algorithms by introducing the concept of signed distance and the multiscale normal estimation.

During the processing stage a total of two parameters were configured, namely: i) normal scale; and ii) projection scale. The first one defines the diameter of the sphere used for computing the normal. Meanwhile the second one defines the diameter of the cylinder used for searching the distance between point clouds. The first one was established as 25 times the average surface roughness of the TLS point cloud and the second was a diameter on which the cylinder is able to capture at least 20 points in the TLS/WMMS point cloud. The surface roughness of each point was calculated by using a plane fitting approach. In this method the roughness is estimated as the standard deviation between a set of points (the reference and its neighborhood) and the best fit plane. It is worth to mention that the normal orientation was computed by using the position of the TLS in each scan station. Both parameters, normal and projection scale, are in-line with the suggestions done by Lague et al. [13].

The analysis was carried out by using the open-source CloudCompare® (https://www.danielgm.net/cc/), obtaining two datasets, one for those point clouds obtained with the normal protocol and another one for those obtained with the cross protocol.

Each one of these datasets were made up by 19 point clouds on which are stored the signed distances (discrepancies) between the TLS and the WMMS point clouds. Figure 6 shows the results obtained over the point clouds obtained with the SLAM algorithm and the default parameters.

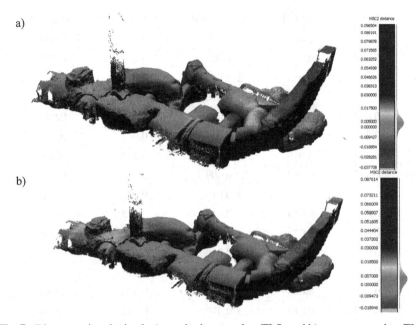

Fig. 7. Discrepancies obtained: a) standard protocol vs TLS; and b) cross protocol vs TLS.

Point Cloud Accuracy Assessment. Studies such as those carried out by Rodriguez-Martín et al. [14] demonstrated that in the accuracy assessment of laser scanner point clouds the hypothesis that discrepancies follow a Gaussian distribution is hardly verified due to the presence of points from non-overlapped areas or undesirable objects. In accordance to this, the normality of the dataset obtained in the previous section was verified by using the QQ-plots. In all the cases the population shows a non-normal distribution. Thus, its accuracy could not be measured by using the indices of a normal distribution (mean error and standard deviation). In these cases, the indices used where the median (m), the normalized median absolute deviation ($NMAD$) and the square root of the biweight midvariance ($BWMV$) [15]. It is worth mentioning that if the distribution does not show a symmetric distribution (like those obtained in this study), it is not possible to provide a plus-minus range. According to this, the percentile values at 2.5%, 25%, 75% and 97.5% were also calculated for computing the interpercentile range (IPR) at 50% and 95% of confidence level. Table 1 and Table 2 shows the results obtained in both datasets (standard and cross dataset).

Table 1. Results obtained during the evaluation of the different SLAM solutions with standard protocol. The notation is the following one: *a/b/c* where *a* represents if the parameter is applied at local or global stage; *b* is the parameter changed with respect to the default configuration in accordance with Sect. 2.1 and *c* is the value of this parameter. *d/d/d* represents the set-up with default paraments and *p/p/p* the set-up with prioritization to planar surfaces.

	Median	NMAD	Sqrt (BWMV)	IPR (50%)	IPR (95%)
d/d/d	0.007	0.012	± 0.010	0.012	0.049
g/c/5	0.007	0.012	± 0.010	0.012	0.045
g/c/3	0.007	0.013	± 0.010	0.012	0.049
l/c/5	0.007	0.013	± 0.010	0.012	0.046
l/c/3	0.007	0.013	± 0.010	0.012	0.049
g/r/5	0.007	0.045	± 0.039	0.042	0.182
g/r/3	0.007	0.016	± 0.013	0.015	0.059
g/r/-5	0.007	0.012	± 0.009	0.011	0.047
g/r/-3	0.007	0.012	± 0.010	0.011	0.048
l/r/5	0.007	0.014	± 0.011	0.013	0.051
l/r/3	0.007	0.012	± 0.010	0.012	0.046
l/r/-5	0.007	0.013	± 0.010	0.012	0.046
l/r/-3	0.007	0.013	± 0.011	0.012	0.052
p/p/p	0.008	0.024	± 0.019	0.022	0.086
l/w/5	0.007	0.012	± 0.010	0.011	0.050
l/w/3	0.007	0.012	± 0.010	0.012	0.046
l/v/3	-	-	-	-	-
l/v/1	0.007	0.012	± 0.010	0.012	0.046
l/v/-1	0.007	0.015	± 0.012	0.014	0.057

Table 2. Results obtained during the evaluation of the different SLAM solutions with cross protocol. The notation is the following one: *a/b/c* where *a* represents if the parameter is applied at local or global stage; *b* is the parameter changed with respect to the default configuration in accordance with Sect. 2.1 and *c* is the value of this parameter. *d/d/d* represents the set-up with default paraments and *p/p/p* the set-up with prioritization to planar surfaces.

	Median	NMAD	Sqrt (BWMV)	IPR (50%)	IPR (95%)
d/d/d	0.005	0.008	± 0.006	0.008	0.028
g/c/5	0.005	0.007	± 0.006	0.008	0.025
g/c/3	0.005	0.008	± 0.007	0.008	0.027

(continued)

Table 2. (*continued*)

	Median	NMAD	Sqrt (BWMV)	IPR (50%)	IPR (95%)
l/c/5	0.005	0.007	± 0.006	0.008	0.025
l/c/3	0.005	0.008	± 0.006	0.008	0.027
g/r/5	0.005	0.031	± 0.026	0.028	0.133
g/r/3	0.005	0.010	± 0.009	0.010	0.040
g/r/-5	0.005	0.007	± 0.006	0.007	0.025
g/r/-3	0.005	0.007	± 0.006	0.007	0.026
l/r/5	0.005	0.010	± 0.008	0.010	0.037
l/r/3	0.005	0.008	± 0.007	0.008	0.027
l/r/-5	0.005	0.008	± 0.007	0.008	0.030
l/r/-3	0.005	0.009	± 0.007	0.009	0.030
p/p/p	0.005	0.017	± 0.014	0.019	0.055
l/w/5	0.005	0.008	± 0.007	0.009	0.029
l/w/3	0.005	0.008	± 0.007	0.008	0.028
l/v/3	-	-	-	-	-
l/v/1	0.005	0.007	± 0.006	0.007	0.026
l/v/-1	0.005	0.009	± 0.008	0.010	0.033

4 Discussions

This section will be devoted to discuss the results obtained during the different analysis carried out. If we focus on the performance of the protocols, it is possible to extract the following conclusions according with the statistical analysis and the time invested:

- *Bias results:* the median in the standard protocol has an average value of 0.007 m (Table 1). Meanwhile the median in the cross protocol is 0.005 m (40% better) (Table 2). This discrepancy suggests that the point cloud of the standard protocol shows a higher overall deformation in comparison with the cross protocol due to the presence of more "there and back" areas. In both cases it is possible to observe a great stability in this value, being acceptable for digitalization purposes.
- *Dispersion results:* the use of the *NMAD, BWMV, IPR (50%)* and *IPR (95%)* have allowed the robust analysis of the discrepancies since the discrepancies of all the datasets do not show a normal distribution. In line with the bias, the standard protocol shows higher values of dispersion in comparison with the normal protocol (Table 1 and 2). These discrepancies are due to the weakness of the "there and back" areas that promote error in narrow spaces such as the entrance of the winery (Fig. 6). Regarding the *IPR (95%)*, the standard protocol with default parameters has a value near 0.05 m. Meanwhile, the *IPR (95%)* in the cross protocol has showed a value of 0.03 m (67% better).

- *Time consumption:* in both protocols the time required for solving the SLAM problem is identical, showing the same type of increments (Fig. 5).

With respect to the influence of each parameter inside each protocol it is possible to observe the following behavior (Table 1, Table 2, Fig. 5):

- *Convergence threshold*: incrementing the number of iterations, during the global and local phases, enhances the quality of the data. However, the time required for solving the problem is much higher. This question is especially relevant at the global phase on which the increment of times is about 400%.
- *Windows size*: the window size seems to improve the quality of the data if is not considered an extreme value. This issue is related with the fact that higher window values implies more detail to consider during the processing. In term of time this value does not increment the total time spent.
- *Voxel size*: higher values of voxel size slightly increment the quality of the data. However, if we use an extreme value the SLAM problem is not solved properly. In terms of time this value does not demand more time for solving the SLAM.
- *Rigidity*: prioritize the IMU data over the point cloud data does not contribute positively to the accuracy of the point cloud, especially in the extreme value on which the dispersion values increment in about 350%. It is possible to observe an enhancement of the accuracy if it prioritized the data of the laser scanner over the IMU. This behavior could be associated to the presence of a high number of geometrical features along the path. In all the cases the time required are similar to the default one.
- *Prioritization to planar surfaces*: this option does not improve the quality of the point cloud (two times worse). This is due to the absence of planar.

5   Conclusions

This work aims at evaluating the performance of a WMMS for the 3D digitalization of underground heritage, more specifically wineries. To this end it was chosen as study case the largest winery inside the complex of Baltanas. This site is specially challenging due to the presence of narrow spaces and adverse light conditions, being the unique feasible solution the use of active sensors. Within this context we have studied the use of a static laser scanner and a wearable mobile mapping solution. The first one is able to provide a high-accuracy point cloud with a density of about 53796 points/m^2 but requires a total of 5.30 h for obtain the 3D point cloud (about 3.6 min per m^2). The wearable mobile mapping solution is able to obtain the 3D point cloud in just only 23.30 min (8% of the time required by the static laser). In terms of quality we have proposed a cross protocol which outperforms the standard one based on the good-practices. This protocol shows a median and dispersion values 40% and 67% lower than the standard protocol, for which the 95% of the points are comprised in an error lower than 3 cm and the 50% of the points are lower than 8mm. Relative to the parameters of the SLAM approach it is possible to concluded that the rigidity, local convergence and voxel density could contribute to improve the quality of the final point cloud without incrementing notably the time for solving the SLAM problem.

Future works will be focused on evaluating the performance of different SLAM solutions when several parameters are modified. This question will demand another extensive statistical analysis but will allow us to better optimize the time/accuracy ratio of the WMMS in underground scenarios.

Acknowledgements. This activity was enclosed within the framework of the COST Action Undergroun4Value (CA18110) and in the EELISA (European Engineering Learning Innovation and Science Alliance) project. More specifically within the EELISA Sustainable BCC community.

References

1. Di Stefano, F., Torresani, A., Farella, E.M., Pierdicca, R., Menna, F., Remodino, F.: 3D surveying of undergroun built heritage: opportunities and challenges of mobile technologies. Sustainability **13**(23), 13289 (2021)
2. Toschi, I., et al.: The VAST project: valorisation of history and landscape from promoting the memory of WWI. In: 26th CIPA Symposium-Digital Workflows for Heritage Conservation, pp. 179–186. ISPRS. Ottawa (2017)
3. Pace, G., Salvarani, R.: Undergroun Built Heritage Valorisation. A Handbook. 1st edn. CNR, Rome (2021)
4. Fabbri, S., Sauro, F., Santagata, T., Rossi, G., De Waele, J.: High-resolution 3-D mapping using terrestrial laser scanning as a tool for geomorphological and speleogenetical studies in caves: an example from the LEssini mountains (Nort Italy). Geomorphology **280**, 16–29 (2017)
5. Gonzalez-Aguilera, D., Muñoz, A.L., Lahoz, J.G., Herrero, J.S., Corchón, M.S., García, E.: Recording and modeling Paleolithic caves through laser scanning. In: International Conference of Advanced Geographic Information Systems & Web Services. IEEE, Cancun (2009)
6. Farella, E., Menna, F., Nocerino, E., Morabito, D., Remondino, F., Campi, M. Knowledge and valorization of historical sites through 3D documentation and modeling. In: ISPRS Congress, pp. 255–262. ISPRS. Prague (2016)
7. Di Fillipo, A., Sánchez-Aparicio, L.J., Barba, S., Martín-Jiménez, J.A., Mora, R., González Aguilera, D.: Use of a wearable mobile laser system in seamless indoor 3D mapping of a complex historical site. Remote Sens. **10**(12), 1897 (2018)
8. Nocerino, E., Menna, F., Remondino, F., Toschi, I., Rodríguez-Gonzálvez, P.: Investigation of indoor and outdoor performance of two portable mobile mapping systems. In: Videometrics, Range Imaging, and Applications XIV, p. 103320I. International Society for Optics and Photonics. Munich (2017)
9. Quigley, M., et al.: ROS: an open-source Robot Operating System. In: ICRA workshop on open source software, 3–3.2 (2009)
10. Besl, P.J., McKay, N.D.: Method for registration of 3-D shapes. Int. Soc. Opt. Photonics **1611**, 586–606 (1992)
11. Santamaría, J., Cordón, O., Damas, S.: A comparative study of state-of-the-art evolutionary image registration methods for 3D modeling. Comput. Vis. Image Underst. **115**(9), 1340–1354 (2011)
12. Jové, F., Sáinz, J.L.: El barrio de bodegas de Baltanás. Caracterización del espacio excavado y su relación con el medio exterior. Congresos de Arquitectura de Tierra (2011)
13. Jové, F., Sáinz, J.L.: Arquitectura excavada. Las bodegas de Baltanás. Bien de interés cultural. Cátedra Juan de Villanueva, Valladolid (Spain) (2016)

14. Lague, D., Brodu, N., Lerous, J.: Accurate 3D comparison of complex topography with terrestrial laser scanner: application to the Rangitikei canyon (NZ). ISPRS J. Photogramm. Remote. Sens. **82**, 10–26 (2013)
15. Rodriguez-Martín, M., Rodríguez-Gonzálvez, P., Ruiz de Oña Crespo, E., González-Aguilera, D.: Validation of portable mobile mapping system for inspection tasks in thermal and fluid–mechanical facilities. Remote Sens. **11**(19), 2205 (2019)
16. Mood, A.M.: Introduction to the Theory of Stadistics. 3[rd]edn. McGraw Hill, England (1974)

A Portable Set up for Hyperspectral Imaging of Stained-Glass Panels

Agnese Babini[1]([✉]) [iD], Sony George[1] [iD], Tiziana Lombardo[2] [iD],
and Jon Yngve Hardeberg[1] [iD]

[1] Norwegian University of Science and Technology, Gjøvik,
Norway
{agnese.babini,sony.george,jon.hardeberg}@ntnu.no
[2] Collection Centre, Swiss National Museum, Affoltern am Albis, Switzerland
Tiziana.lombardo@nationalmuseum.ch

Abstract. In the past years, hyperspectral imaging has become a popular technique for the non-invasive investigation of works of art and has been extensively used for the analysis of pigments in paintings and manuscripts. The application of spectral imaging on stained glass however is very limited. Due to their transparency, imaging of stained glass presents some challenges, such as the necessity of a proper transmittance setup and the complex interaction between light and glass, which can affect the acquisition.

In this work, we present a portable setup for hyperspectral imaging of stained-glass panels. The setup has been designed for transmittance measurements, and in the current configuration, it can support panels with a maximum size of around 45×45 cm.

The portable setup has been tested at the facilities of the Swiss National Museum on 10 stained-glass panels belonging to the museum's collection, which were selected to be representative of different historical periods and glass-making techniques. Characteristics, advantages, and limitation of the system will be discussed, showing preliminary results on some of the case studies analyzed.

Keywords: Hyperspectral imaging · Stained glass · Transmittance imaging

1 Introduction

In the past years, hyperspectral imaging (HSI) has found many applications in the field of cultural heritage. This technique can be considered a combination of conventional imaging and spectroscopy; by acquiring many images across the electromagnetic spectrum, the spectral information can be obtained at each pixel. By analyzing the spectral data, it is possible to identify and map the materials that constitute the object under study. For this reason, spectral imaging has been successfully used for the non-invasive investigation of artworks, especially paintings and manuscripts [1]. The application of this technique on stained-glass windows however is still limited. The reason may lie in the fact that, due to the transparency/translucency of the glass, imaging of these objects presents some

R. Furferi et al. (Eds.): Florence Heri-Tech 2022, CCIS 1645, pp. 57–70, 2022.
https://doi.org/10.1007/978-3-031-20302-2_5

challenges, such as the necessity of a proper transmittance setup, the complex interaction occurring between light and glass, as well as degradation products present on the glass surface, which affect the image acquisition. At the best of the authors' knowledge, very few works have been published on the use of HSI on stained glass [2–4]. In these reported studies, the acquisition was performed exploiting the solar radiation as light source [3, 4]. Recently, we proposed a methodology for the acquisition of stained-glass panels (maximum size of 50 × 50 cm) in laboratory condition [5], using a translating stage and an illumination geometry similar to the study presented by Rebollo *et al.* [2].

In this work on the other hand, a *portable* setup for the hyperspectral imaging of stained-glass panels is presented. The setup has been designed for transmittance measurements, and in this current configuration, it can support glass panels with a maximum size of 45 × 45 cm. The characteristics of the system will be described, discussing design choices, advantages, and limitations.

The practical use of the system has been tested at the facilities of the Swiss National Museum on 10 selected stained-glass panels belonging to the museum's collection. The panels were selected after discussions with the museum conservators for their historical and artistic attributes. Preliminary results on some of the case studies will be shown to highlight some technical aspects regarding the system, as well as the image analysis performed on the acquired HSI data.

2 Materials and Methods

2.1 The Transmittance Setup

The acquisition was carried out using a push-broom hyperspectral camera HySpex VNIR-1800. The camera acquires 186 images in the visible and near infrared (VNIR) range (400–1000 nm), with a spectral sampling of 3.26 nm and a spatial resolution of 1800 pixels across the track. The camera lens has a fixed focus distance of 30 cm from the object, with a field of view of 17° and a pixel resolution of 50 μm.

For the measurements, the camera was mounted on a tripod equipped with a motorized rotating head. Scanning of this rotational stage is controlled from the computer and the movement is synchronized with the HSI acquisition parameters. The datacube is formed recording one line at a time, while the camera moves from left to right. Due to the rotating movement and the focus limit of the camera, it was possible to acquire only 1650 lines for a single acquisition, before significant geometric distortions and blurring occurred. These phenomena are usually visible at the edge of the image going toward the scanning direction (Fig. 1a).

The transmittance system has been designed in the laboratory, and later built using materials easily retrievable in common hardware stores and in conservation laboratories. This system consists of a wooden panel, which acts as support for the artworks, where a square-shaped area (25 × 25 cm^2) has been cut to accommodate a diffuser plate for the transmittance measurement. This diffuser is made of acrylic and has a thickness of 6 mm (Fig. 1c).

Two halogen lamps were used as light source to maximize the light distribution across the field of view. However, this solution had some drawbacks. Halogen lamps are usually the most used light sources for HSI, as they provide a continuous spectrum

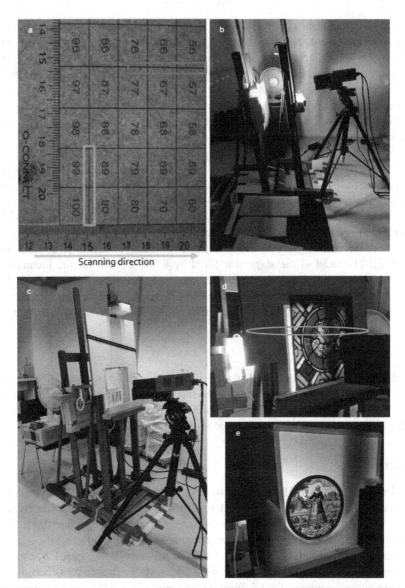

Fig. 1. Horizontal (in blue) and vertical (in red) distortions (a). Setup configuration at the Museum during acquisitions (b). Tentative set up before the beginning of acquisition campaign. The red circle highlights the metal L-shaped piece (a second one is hidden by the easel) that holds the thicker diffuser (c). Safety measures used to prevent the falling of the stained-glass panels during the acquisition: ethafoam sheets were used for the smaller panels (d) while strings were used to hold the bigger ones (e).

from UV up to Mid-IR [6]. However, they also generate a high amount of heat that can be harmful for the stained-glass; indeed, depending on the state of conservation of the object, high temperature could cause expansion of the different materials, as well as alteration and detachment of painted surfaces [7]. After discussions with the conservators at the museum, it was suggested that the temperature on the surface of the artwork should not exceed 25–30 °C during the acquisitions. To meet this requirement, the lamps were placed at around 30 cm beneath the diffuser area of the wooden panel; a second diffuser was placed between the lamps and the first diffuser. Differently from the first one, the second diffuser has a thickness of 8 mm and is made of glass, with a diffusing sheet applied in both sides. This diffuser is part of the laboratory set-up located at the NTNU Colorlab and was adapted for this acquisition campaign. Two L-shaped metal piece were used to hold the second diffuser. One side of the L-shape was nailed to the wooden pieces used to put the light sources at the necessary height, while the other side held the diffuser plate. This solution not only helped in reducing the exposure of the artwork to thermal radiation, but also improved the light distribution.

Two easels were used as support, one to hold the supporting wooden panel with the diffuser and the other to hold the light sources and the second diffusing plate (Fig. 2a). The safety of the stained-glass panels was ensured by using ethafoam pieces and strings (Fig. 2b, c). The head of the stage was tilted by 8° to account for the inclination of the easels. A cooling fan was also employed as an additional precaution to reduce the temperature. An integration time of 30000 μs was deemed good enough to obtain a good exposure and reduce the acquisition time and was kept fixed through all the campaign.

2.2 Case Studies

Stained Glass Panels. A total of 10 panels were acquired during the acquisition campaign. These case studies were selected to be representative of different historical periods and glass-making techniques. Information on the panels and acquisition details are reported in Table 1 for the case studies mentioned in the paper.

2.3 Methodology

Image Processing. The HSI datacubes were collected in raw format and corrected to radiance using the HySpex-RAD software provided by the camera manufacturer. Sensor corrections and dark current subtraction was done at this stage. After this step, the datacubes were processed using the open-source software Fiji [8].

In order to transform the radiance data into transmittance, the image of the object has to be divided by the image of a uniform transmitting surface. This task was performed by acquiring a reference image of the diffuser without any object in different moments of the day (morning, midday, afternoon, and evening), to account for any possible fluctuation of the intensity of the light source. A Gaussian blur filter was applied to the spatial dimensions of the reference image to reduce the artifacts caused by the dirt accumulated on the surface of the diffuser. The spectral dimension was not smoothed. This aspect will be discussed in detail in the result section. Lastly, all the spectra have been converted from transmittance to absorbance, to facilitate the observation of the characteristic peaks and an easier comparison with available literature.

Data Visualization. The first step to visualize a HSI datacube is to generate an RGB image, by extracting the representative red, green and blue bands. The default bands for red, green, and blue (642 nm, 549 nm, and 463 nm) are specified by the camera manufacturer and are usually stated in the header file associated to the datacube. In ImageJ, the RGB image can be built by selecting the three bands and arranging them to create a new image made of three separated channels. These selected bands are transformed into a color image.

Table 1. Information on some of the case studies analyzed during the acquisition campaign. Pic-tures courtesy of Swiss National Museum

	Panels information	Acquisition details
	ID: LM-12794 **Author:** N/A **Date:** 1322 **Dimension:** 31.2 x 31.6 cm	**N. of datacubes:** 12 **Total data size:** 12.4 Gb **Total acquisition time:** 2 h 20 m
	ID: AG-1170 **Author:** Karl van Egeri **Date:** 1551 **Dimension:** 36.5 x 27.2 cm	**N. of datacubes:** 12 **Total data size:** 12.4 Gb **Total acquisition time:** 1 h 50 m
	ID : LM-19635 **Author:** Auguste de Pourtales **Date:** 1633 **Dimension:** 14.33 cm Ø	**N. of datacubes:** 4 **Total data size:** 4.14 Gb **Total acquisition time:** 30 m
	ID: LM-167914 **Author:** Louis Halter **Date:** 1921 **Dimension:** 37.5 x 26 cm	**N. of datacubes:** 7 **Total data size:** 7.25 Gb **Total acquisition time:** 55 m
	ID: LM-167924 **Author:** Louis Halter **Date:** 1948-1950 **Dimension:** 42.1 x 35.5 cm	**N. of datacubes:** 15 **Total data size:** 15.5 Gb **Total acquisition time:** 2 h 30 m

A similar approach can be used to create false color images. This technique allows to distinguish materials with similar colors, but different spectral property and it is extensively used in the field of cultural heritage for preliminary discrimination of pigments with similar color [9, 10]. False color images are usually created by keeping the two bands related to red and green and selecting another band in the near-infrared region. Since there is no standard set for the choice of the infrared band, some trials were performed to understand which band provides most information. Once the bands were selected, the images were rearranged in a new image, putting the image related to infrared first, followed by images corresponding to red and green. The technique has been tested on a stained-glass panel in a paper we recently published [5], resulting particularly useful for distinction of green and blue glass.

Another form of visualization is color rendering, which converts the spectral data to RGB by means of color matching function and standard illuminants data. This task was performed in MATLAB using and adapting codes made available by Foster and Amano [11]. For the rendering, the CIE 1931–2° standard observer color matching function was used. The values of the D65 standard illuminant used for the color rendering were calculated using formulas retrieved from the Rochester Institute of Technology online repository of useful colorimetric data [12]. The values for the color matching function were obtained from the same repository.

3   Results and Discussion

Figure 2 shows the comparison between the high-resolution pictures provided by the museum (Fig. 2a), color rendered images (Fig. 2b) and band selection RGB images (Fig. 2c) for selected areas of the case studies LM-12794, AG-1170 and LM-167924. First of all, it is worthy of mention that the differences in the aspect ratio between the high-resolution images from the Museum and those created from HSI are due to the geometrical distortion mentioned previously. With respect to the band selection RGB images (Fig. 2c) the rendered images are able to provide a more accurate color representation (Fig. 2b), especially with regards to the visualization of darker glasses. Compared to the high-resolution images (Fig. 2a), the few differences are related to the fact that the rendering is solely based on the transmittance values of the stained-glass, without taking into account other phenomena such as specular reflection occurring on the glass surface. This is visible in areas with red glass, which appear more homogeneously colored in the rendered images from the HSI with respect to the high resolution one obtained with traditional imaging (Fig. 2a and b for the bottom part of case study AG-1170, see blue circle). In this case, the advantage of having a rendered image instead of the band selection images, is the possibility to have a faithful color image (alike the high-resolution images) of the same size of the HSI datacube, that can be exploited for the selection of spectra in regions of interest (Fig. 3). Indeed, due to the evident distortion, spectra selection using the high-resolution images as reference could lead to error.

Figures 3b and 4c represent false color images created by selecting two different bands in the infrared region, one at 811 nm (Fig. 3b) and one at 996 nm (Fig. 3c) compared to rendered images (Fig. 3a). The selection of the last available band in the NIR region in some cases allow a better distinction of green and blue glass. In fact, differently from red, yellow, and purple glass, most of blue and green glass show a different false color when selecting the 996 nm band, which can be related to the presence of another chromophore absorbing light farther in the NIR range, hinting at a different composition of the colored glass (Fig. 3b and c and Fig. 6). An example of this can be seen in Fig. 3c of AG-1170 (top), where the false color image with the band at 996 nm allow a better discrimination between the green glass employed for the arch (which display a dark blue appearance) and the fragment used in the left corner (purple, see red circled area).

By comparing the appearance in false color images of glass with similar color, as well as their spectral response, it is possible to make some preliminary hypotheses on the coloring agents used by the glassmakers.

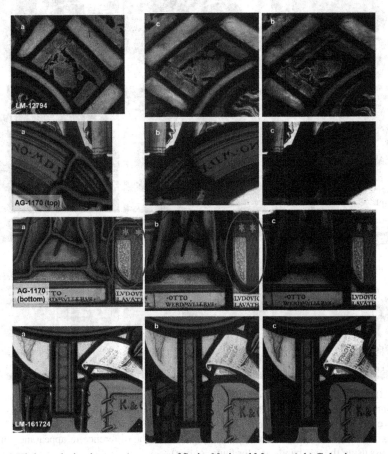

Fig. 2. a) High resolution images (courtesy of Swiss National Museum). b) Color images rendered using color matching function and standard illuminant D65. c) RGB images obtained by band selection. The blue circles show the different appearance of the red glass between the high-resolution image and the rendered one. Note that figure b) and c) for LM-12794 and AG-1170 (on top) are mirrored as those areas of the stained-glass panels were acquired from the back. (Color figure online)

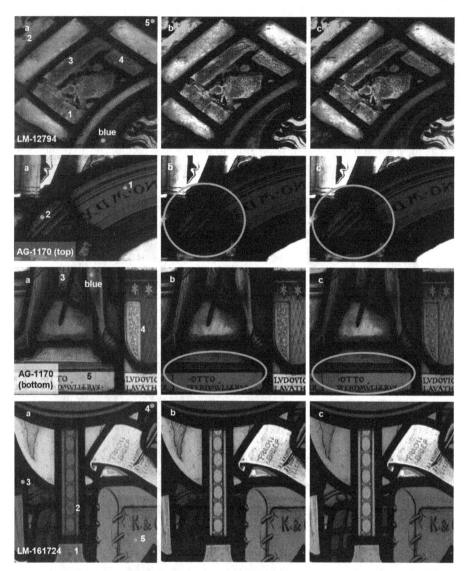

Fig. 3. a) Colored images rendered using color matching function and standard illuminant D65. The points indicate where the spectra were collected in the image for comparison in Fig. 4 and 6. b) False color image obtained by selecting the NIR band at 811 nm c) False color image obtained selecting the NIR band at 996 nm. The red circles show the difference in appearance of some green glass using the two bands. (Color figure online)

Comparing the spectra of red glass in Fig. 4 with the false color images in Fig. 3b, c, it is possible to notice that a lower intensity of the peak at 565 nm (well visible in Fig. 4 for LM-12794 pt. 1, LM-167924 pt. 1 and AG-1170, pt. 3), related to the surface plasmon resonance of copper nanoparticles (Cu^0) [13–15], generates a shift from a bright greenish yellow to orange (Fig. 3b and c, LM-12794).

Due to the strong absorption of the copper nanoparticle, this kind of red glass were traditionally produced by adding a thin red layer over a transparent one [14]; Bracci *et al.* [13] suggest that the changes in the shape of the spectrum could be related to a different roughness of the red layer, possibly caused by degradation. False color images can thus reveal interesting information on the conditions of the red layer in flashed red glass, even within the same sample, as well as help with the identification of other typology of red glass (Fig. 3 and 4, LM-167924, pt. 2).

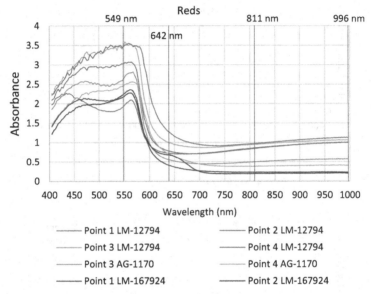

Fig. 4. Spectra of red glass collected on the three case studies. The four lines (one for green and blue and two for red) indicate the bands selected while the color of the lines indicate for which RGB channel are they used. The localization of the points is displayed in Fig. 2a.

The same hypotheses can be made for green glass pieces. By comparing the spectra with the false color images, two different behaviors can be noticed: glass pieces that appear dark blue in false color (Fig. 6a, pt.1 LM-12794, pt.2 AG-1170 top), in general seem to contain copper and iron as main chromophores, with a large absorption band centered at around 770–790 nm (Cu^{2+}) and a smaller one at 410–430 nm (Fe^{3+}) [2, 3, 13, 14]. The small absorption band around 675 nm in the spectrum of pt.4 LM-127924 suggest the presence of Cr^{3+} as well [2, 3]; however, since the absorption of copper seems more dominant, the false color of that green glass does not change significantly. On the other hand, a pinkish/purplish appearance (Fig. 6b), seems to be related to the presence of cobalt, in addition to other coloring agents. The reason behind this phenomenon depends on the fact that the two bands selected for the blue (549 nm) and the green channel (642 nm) fall in regions where characteristic absorbance bands of Co^{2+} [3, 14] can be observed. With regards to the NIR bands used for the red channel, the false color can shift toward a darker purple depending on the contribution of other chromophores (most probably Fe^{2+} for pt. 5 LM-167924 and Cu^{2+} in case of pt. 2 and 5 AG-1170 and pt. 3 LM-167924). This theory seems to be supported by the comparison of the spectra of cobalt containing green glass (point 2 in AG-1170 and pt. 5 and 3 in LM-167924), with blue glass containing the same chromophore, as well as with available literature [2, 3, 13, 14, 16]. In any case, further investigations, and additional analytical techniques, are needed to confirm these theories.

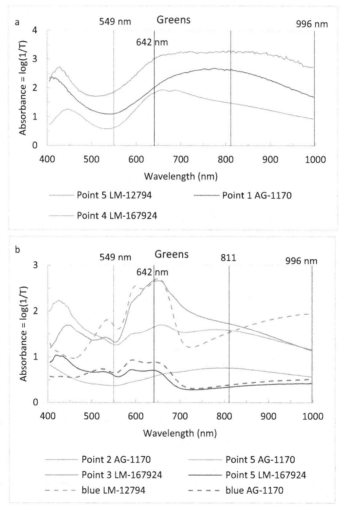

Fig. 5. Spectra of green glass collected on the three case studies. a) glass containing Cu^{2+} as main chromophore. b) glass containing Co^{2+}. Spectra of two blue glass containing cobalt have been added for comparison. The four lines (one for green and blue and two for the red) indicate the bands selected and for which RGB channel are they used. The localization of the points is displayed in Fig. 2a.

3.1   Limitation of the System

The use of a rotating stage instead of a linear translational system represents one of the biggest limitations of the setup. As already mentioned in the experimental section, the use of a rotational stage generates not only vertical distortion, which are related to the camera optics [17], but also horizontal distortion, caused by the rotation of the camera. If the resulting images are considered individually and used for the sole purpose of material identification, this aspect may be left aside. However, it can become an issue when attempting to stitch two images together. As shown in Fig. 1, the side opposite to the scanning direction results more elongated with respect to the other. If the overlapping part have been scanned in two different directions, the two images will not match, as the points taken as reference are shifted. This can be noticed for example by observing the two areas acquired from the panel AG-1170 (Fig. 2) where the two images seem stretched in two different directions. In addition, the movement of the camera causes the out of focus regions at the image edges, that can represent a distortion. From the spectral point of view, the out of focus does not hinder the quality of the spectral data collected (Fig. 7). However, it may become an issue during the stitching process, as the blurring reduces the quality of the final image. (Fig. 7c, d).

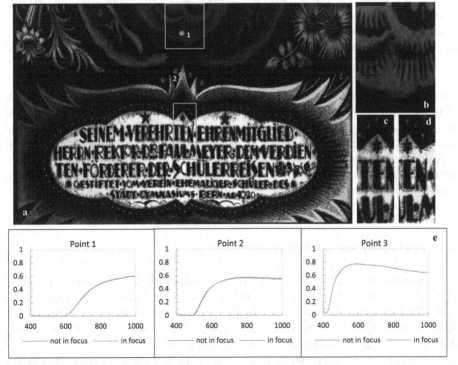

Fig. 6. a) Stitched image (RGB) of the lower part of LM-167914 obtained combining two datacubes. b) Detail of alignment error at the top of the image. c, d) Details of the overlapping areas, showing different focus due to the rotation movement of the camera. e) Comparison of the spectra collected from the overlapping area of the two datacubes.

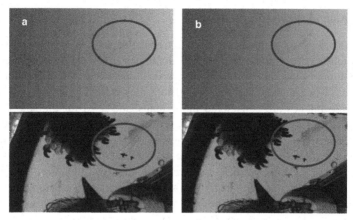

Fig. 7. Details of dirt particles on the diffuser (on top) and their effects on transparent glass (bottom) after flat fielding correction. Fig. b (bottom) show how the application of a Gaussian filter can slightly reduce the visual impact of the artifacts.

The material employed for the diffusing plate also play an important role. In this case, for the diffuser in contact with the artwork, an acrylic panel was preferred to a frosted glass one, as it was able to diffuse the light better. However, the electrostaticity of the acrylic attracts particles of dirt, that can accumulate on the surface despite constant cleaning. The presence of dirt on the diffuser surface can affect the flat fielding process, as the particles of dirt become artifacts in the corrected images.

These artifacts can be visible not only in areas with clean glass, but also in those with colored glass, when they are transparent to certain wavelengths. It was noticed that adding a Gaussian blur filter to the diffuser datacubes helped in reducing those artifacts. A sigma value of 3 was deemed enough for the purpose. The filter was not applied to the case studies datacube, to avoid the loss of details. Moreover, since the filter was applied only on the diffuser datacubes, it was decided to smooth only the spatial dimension, but not the spectral one, in order to avoid differences during the flat fielding process, where the object datacube must be divided by the diffuser one. Figure 8 shows the flat fielding results before and after adding the filter.

4 Conclusion and Perspectives

In this paper, a portable system for the hyperspectral imaging of stained-glass panels is presented, whose feasibility has been tested on selected set of stained-glass panels at the Swiss National Museum. At the moment, the system has some limitations, related to the necessity of using a rotational stage and to some design choices, such as the use of two diffusers, to reduce the heat coming from the light sources.

With regard to the first point, the issue of geometric distortions related to the rotation of the camera has been already discussed in the results section. Future works will be focused on addressing this aspect, by searching for solutions that can correct those distortions, especially in case image stitching is planned.

With regard to the second point, the advantages, or disadvantages of having two diffusers should be investigated more thoroughly. While this solution was helpful in reducing the heat, at the same time it was also limiting the light arriving to the artwork. These aspects can influence the acquisition, as compromises in choosing the right integration time must be done to avoid underexposure of dark glass, as well as a longer exposure time and consequent increase of noise. More efficient light sources should be explored so that the use of double diffuser could be avoided.

Despite these limitations, it was still possible to obtain a sufficiently good signal even for very dark glass and the quality of the data collected were satisfying. Regarding the image processing side, the use of false color images has been proved to be a useful tool for a preliminary identification of colored glass produced with different coloring agents. The comparison of these images with the spectra of the glass under study allowed to formulate some hypothesis, that could be confirmed in the future by complementary analysis.

An important aspect to stress is the constant collaboration with the Museum conservators and staff during the developing phase as well as during the acquisition. This collaboration has been fundamental to design the system in a way it could be possible to scan for a long period of time without damaging the panels. The use of such setup could be encouraged for documentation purposed during conservation treatments; the visualization of the data through rendered and false color imaging could be a fast tool for a first distinction of areas with possible restoration, without the need of complex classification algorithms.

Acknowledgements. This research was carried out as part of the CHANGE (Cultural Heritage Analysis for New Generation) Innovative Training Network project funded by the European Union's Horizon 2020 research and innovation programme under the Marie Skłodowska-Curie grant agreement No. 813789. The author would also like to thank the Swiss National Museum for giving access to the case studies and the Museum staff for the help and support before and during the acquisition campaign; Jan Cutajar and Deepshikha Sharma for helping in building the setup at the Museum; Federico Grillini and Irina Ciortan at NTNU and Silvia Russo for helping with logistic and shipping of the equipment to Switzerland and back.

References

1. Picollo, M., et al.: Hyper-spectral imaging technique in the cultural heritage field: new possible scenarios. Sensors **20**(10), 2843 (2020). https://doi.org/10.3390/s20102843
2. Rebollo, E., et al.: New trends in imaging spectroscopy: the non-invasive study of the Scrovegni Chapel stained glass windows. In: Proc. SPIE O3A: Optics for Arts, Architecture, and Archaeology III 8480 (2011). https://doi.org/10.1117/12.888839
3. Palomar, T., et al.: Analysis of chromophores in stained-glass windows using Visible Hyperspectral Imaging in-situ. Spectrochimica Acta Part A-Molecular and Biomolecular Spectroscopy 223 (2019). https://doi.org/10.1016/j.saa.2019.117378
4. Perri, A., et al.: Hyperspectral imaging with a TWINS birefringent interferometer. Opt. Express **27**(11), 15956–15967 (2019). https://doi.org/10.1364/OE.27.015956
5. Babini, A., George, S., Hardeberg, J.Y.: Hyperspectral imaging workflow for the acquisition and analysis of stained-glass panels. In: Proceeding SPIE O3A: Optics for Arts, Architecture, and Archaeology VIII 11784 (2021). https://doi.org/10.1117/12.2593735

6. Mandal, D.J., et al.: Influence of acquisition parameters on pigment classification using hyper-spectral imaging. J. Imaging Sci. Technol. **65**(5), 50406–1–50406–13 (2021). https://doi.org/10.2352/J.ImagingSci.Technol.2021.65.5.050406

7. Palomar, T., Agua, F., Gomez-Heras, M.: Comparative assessment of stained-glass windows materials by infrared thermography. Int. J. Appl. Glas. Sci. **9**(4), 530–539 (2018). https://doi.org/10.1111/ijag.12352

8. Schindelin, J., et al.: Fiji: an open-source platform for biological-image analysis. Nat. Methods **9**(7), 676–682 (2012). https://doi.org/10.1038/nmeth.2019

9. Hayem-Ghez, A., Ravaud, E., Boust, C., Bastian, G., Menu, M., Brodie-Linder, N.: Charac-terizing pigments with hyperspectral imaging variable false-color composites. Appl. Phys. A **121**(3), 939–947 (2015). https://doi.org/10.1007/s00339-015-9458-8

10. Buoso, M.C., Ceccato, D., Zafiropoulos, D.: False-color Infra Red Photography in the Iden-tification of Pigments Used for a late 13th Century Illuminated Manuscript, in LNL Annual Report, Applied and Interdisciplinary Physics Instrumentation (2009)

11. Foster, D.H., Amano, K.: Hyperspectral imaging in color vision research: tutorial. J. Opt. Soc. Am. A **36**(4), 606–627 (2019). https://doi.org/10.1364/JOSAA.36.000606

12. Rochester Institute of Technology Useful Color Data. https://www.rit.edu/science/munsell-color-science-lab-educational-resources#useful-color-data. Accessed 08 Dec 2021

13. Bracci, S., et al.: Integration of both non-invasive and micro-invasive techniques for the archaeometric study of the stained-glass window Apparizione degli Angeli in the basilica of Santa Croce in Florence. Italy. J. Cult. Heritage **44**, 307–316 (2020). https://doi.org/10.1016/j.culher.2020.02.006

14. Hunault, M.O.J.Y., et al.: Thirteenth-century stained glass windows of the Sainte-Chapelle in Paris: an insight into medieval glazing work practices. J. Archaeol. Sci. Rep. **35** (2021). https://doi.org/10.1016/j.jasrep.2020.102753

15. Palomar, T., et al.: Chemical degradation and chromophores of 18(th) century window glasses. Glass Technol. Eur. J. Glass Sci. Technol. Part A **52**(5), 145–153 (2011)

16. Green, L.R., Alan Hart, F.: Colour and chemical composition in ancient glass: an examination of some roman and wealden glass by means of ultraviolet-visible-infra-red spectrometry and electron microprobe analysis. J. Archaeol. Sci. **14**(3), 271–282 (1987). https://doi.org/10.1016/0305-4403(87)90015-X

17. Pillay, R., Hardeberg, J.Y., George, S.: Hyperspectral imaging of art: acquisition and cali-bration workflows. J. Am. Inst. Conserv. **58**(1–2), 3–15 (2019). https://doi.org/10.1080/01971360.2018.1549919

Hyperspectral Imaging of Artworks: A Custom Assembled Apparatus Endowed with an Open Source Software for Hypercube Analysis

Peppino Sapia[1](✉) ⓘ and Pasquale Barone[2]

[1] Department of Biology, Ecology and Earth Sciences, University of Calabria. Rende (CS), Calabria, Italy
peppino.sapia@unical.it
[2] Liceo "E. Medi" High School, Battipaglia (SA), Campania, Italy

Abstract. Hyperspectral imaging (HSI) techniques are widely used for fine arts diagnostics, in particular for pigments and binders identification. In fact, HSI allows to quickly obtain basic spectral reflectance information on large pictorial surfaces, which can then be further investigated by means of other more precise punctual techniques. HSI is usually performed by using ad hoc apparatuses (often expensive), equipped by proprietary software for the spectral analysis. However, it is possible to assemble custom devices, having the twofold advantage of being less expensive and more flexible than ad hoc apparatuses.

In this work we present both a custom assembled apparatus for HSI and the originally developed software application for analyzing HSI images, in order to extract local spectral information. The hyperspectral camera has been set up by using an LCD tunable band-pass filter together with a low noise scientific-grade camera. The software application for spectral analysis, developed in Wolfram Mathematica, features a very friendly user interface allowing to get the reflectance spectrum in a point of the image, by just clicking on that point.

Keywords: Hyperspectral imaging · Reflectance spectroscopy · Image processing · Artwork analysis

1 Introduction

Digital imaging of artworks represents a useful tool for repeatable inspection and research, and a basis for non-destructive analysis, that can also be carried out in times and places different form those of acquisition [1]. This claim is especially true for those techniques giving rise to images endowed with rich quantitative data set, such as hyperspectral imaging (HSI) [2, 3]. Extracting useful quantitative information from HSI images requires specific software tools, that are usually provided with the commercially available imaging devices. These dedicated devices are more or less costly, especially those able to extend the HSI hypercube (as defined in Sect. 2) to the SWIR spectral region. In this context, a convenient strategy for a typical laboratory of applied physics for cultural heritage (like ours) may be to assemble "at home" a relatively cheap

R. Furferi et al. (Eds.): Florence Heri-Tech 2022, CCIS 1645, pp. 71–81, 2022.
https://doi.org/10.1007/978-3-031-20302-2_6

HSI apparatus. This can be done using a scientific-level camera already supplied, while limiting the spectral extension of the hypercube to the NIR band, as regards the long wavelengths' region of the spectrum. Such on home-made apparatus needs a custom software tool for the qualitative analysis of HSI hypercube.

In this contribution, we describe the custom assembled HSI camera and a software tool we have developed using Wolfram's Mathematica programming language [4], that allows extracting from the HIS hypercube the spectrum in a given spatial region by just clicking on it. The paper is arranged as follows: *i)* in Sect. 2 the fundamentals of HSI are briefly summarized, in order to make the work self-consistent even for readers who are not familiar with this technique; *ii)* in Sect. 3 our custom assembled apparatus for HSI is described and the main points pertaining its calibration are discussed; *iii)* Sect. 4 presents the general architecture of the software application we have developed for the HSI spectral analysis, and some practical examples are presented in order to validate the apparatus equipped with our processing software; finally, conclusions are drawn in section iv*)*.

2 Hyperspectral Imaging

For the sake of completeness, we briefly recall the basic facts about HSI, an imaging technique based on the acquisition of various spectral sections of the same subject [2, 3]. The number of sections can vary, from some units (in this case the term "multi-spectral" is used instead) to several tens or hundreds. Spectral sections are obtained through various techniques, mainly based on interference bandpass filters, either discrete (filter wheels) or continuously tunable: the latter is the case for the filter we employ in our device and will be described in the next section. Some newer hyperspectral cameras are based on a color dispersive optical element directly integrated in the CMOS sensor during the fabrication process [5].

A typical HSI acquisition produces a 3-D matrix of data in the base-space (x, y, λ), known as *hypercube* (see Fig. 1). In this space, the first two coordinates refer to the spatial position in the plane of the image, while λ is the center wavelength of the given spectral section, i.e., the center of the corresponding band-pass filter. In other words, to each spatial pixel (x, y) of the image is associated a vector quantity (sometime named *voxel* [2]), whose N components are the intensities of the given pixel at the different N wavelength bands. The voxel encodes the spectral signature of the pixel. As we will see in Sect. 4, extracting a given voxel from the hypercube is the main task to be accomplished by a software for hyperspectral analysis.

HSI is currently applied in many different contexts, including: biomedicine [6, 7], Earth remote sensing [8], food quality control [9] and cultural heritage conservation [3, 10, 11].

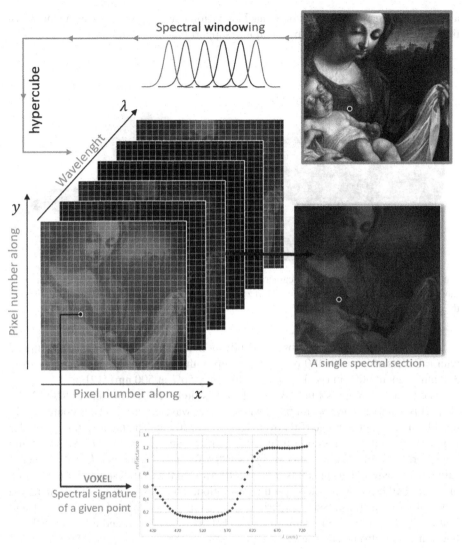

Fig. 1. Hyperspectral imaging consists in the acquisition of many "monochromatic" pictures of the same subject, each taken in a (more or less narrow) spectral window. The acquisition results in a 3D matrix in the (x, y, λ) space, containing the intensity values of the reflected light from the (x, y) region in the λ-centered spectral window. Processing such a matrix allows obtaining a spatial map of the spectral reflectance. The image used in this illustration is a detail from the 18th century painting "Rest on the flight into Egypt" kept at the Diocesan Museum of Santa Severina, KR, Italy.

3   Custom Assembled Apparatus for HSI

The customized apparatus is shown in Fig. 2, where letter A to D explaining the hardware are the cited reference in the text. It consists of a scientific grade monochrome camera, a tunable bandpass filter and a zoom machine vision lens, assembled by using their own threading, furtherly supported by an *ad hoc* support bracket (D in Fig. 1).

Fig. 2. The custom assembled HSI camera. A) low-noise monochrome camera; B) Liquid crystal tunable band-bass filter; C) Machine vision zoom lens; D) Support bracket. Details are given in the main text.

The camera (A) is a Thorlabs 340M-GE monochrome scientific camera equipped with a CCD sensor (640x480 pixel resolution) with a spectral response ranging from 370 nm to about 900 nm (peak quantum efficiency 50% at 500 nm) [12].

The tunable bandpass filter (B) is a Thorlabs liquid-crystal model KURIOS-WL1 [13]. This is a fixed band-width filter, whose center wavelength (CWL) is continuously tunable in the spectral range (SR) from 420 nm to 730 nm. The manufacturer provides a typical spectral transmission function of the filter sampled (across the SR) at 25 nm steps, corresponding to the mean FWHM (see "Performance plots" in ref. [13]). To better calibrate our assembled apparatus, we have determined the overall spectral transmission of the KURIOS, at 5 nm step spectral resolution. This has been accomplished by a classical spectral transmission experiment, by using: a wideband Laser Driven Light Source (LDLS), model Energetiq EQ-99X [14], as light source, and a Horiba VS-140 linear array spectrometer as detector. Figure 3 shows the obtained spectral transmission curve.

The machine vision zoom lens (C) is a Navitar C-mount lens 18–108 mm focal length, distributed by Thorlabs under the code MVL7000, featuring a maximum numerical aperture F = 2.5. As a zoom lens, this model has a fixed overall length when the focal length is varied: this is an indispensable feature for the type of use described, since the distance between the camera and the KURIOS filter must be constant. This requirement, in turns, descent from the need to use a metal bracket (D in Fig. 2) to secure the filter to the camera body, due to the high overall weight of the lens/filter block, with the consequently high mechanical stress on the camera threading.

In order to have a complete spectral characterization of the apparatus, also the spectral transmission curve of the lens has been experimentally determined, by using the same method as for the KURIOS filter, based on the LDLS and the Horiba spectrometer. The corresponding spectral transmission curve is shown in Fig. 4.

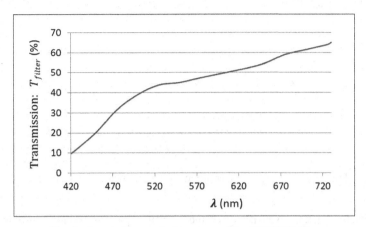

Fig. 3. Spectral transmission curve of the KURIOS filter

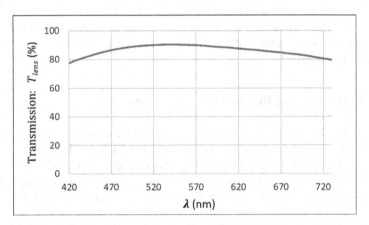

Fig. 4. Spectral transmission curve of the MVL7000 zoom lens.

Using the spectral dependence of the camera quantum efficiency $Q(\lambda)$ [12], the overall spectral sensitivity of our HSI apparatus can be expressed as:

$$S(\lambda) = Q(\lambda) \times T_{filter}(\lambda) \times T_{lens}(\lambda) \qquad (1)$$

where T_{filter} and T_{lens} are respectively defined in Fig. 3 and Fig. 4. A plot of $S(\lambda)$ expressed in arbitrary units is given in Fig. 5.

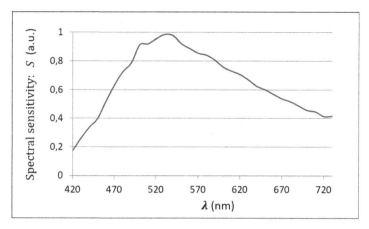

Fig. 5. Relative spectral sensitivity of the assembled HSI apparatus.

The relative spectral sensitivity of the overall apparatus is indispensable to find the spectral reflectance of a specimen. However, in many practical cases concerning the characterization of pictorial pigments in the visible or NIR range, one can avoid complications arising from considering the precise form of $S(\lambda)$, by including in the field of view of the HSI a white diffuse reflectance standard (WDRS) [15]. In the example given in this paper, we use a sheet of high-quality white paper as an approximate substitute for the reference standard.

4   The Software Application for HSI Analysis

As seen in Sect. 2, the hyperspectral imaging of a sample consists of a stack of images (hypercube) generated by measuring the diffuse reflected radiation by the sample surface illuminated with a broadband light source [3]. Each image of the stack, corresponding to a single spectral window, actually is a 2D intensity map (grayscale image). In other words, the hypercube consists of a set of N matrices, each having n rows and m columns, where N is the number of spectral bands and $n \times m$ is the pixel resolution of the digital images corresponding to each band. Then, the hypercube can be represented by a matrix function of the wavelength as:

$$H_{i,j,k} = I_{i,j}(\lambda_k); i = 1, \ldots, n; j = 1, \ldots, m; k = 1, \ldots, N; \tag{2}$$

where $H_{i,j,k}$ is the intesity I recorded by the (i, j)-pixel of the camera sensor, in the spectral band centered around λ_k. The quantity of interest in order to determine the spectral reflectance of the surface under investigation is the intensity radiated in the spectral band λ_k, from the physical region of the surface which is mapped (through the imaging process) onto the (i, j)-pixel: Let's indicate this quantity with the symbol $R_{i,j,k}$. The relationship between the *recorded* and the *radiated* intensities is:

$$R_{i,j,k} = \frac{I_{i,j}(\lambda_k)}{S(\lambda_k)} \tag{3}$$

The spectral reflectance $\rho_{i,j}(\lambda_k)$ of the (i, j)-region of the physical surface is then given by the formula:

$$\rho_{i,j}(\lambda_k) = \frac{R_{i,j,k}}{L(\lambda_k)} = \frac{I_{i,j}(\lambda_k)}{L(\lambda_k) \times S(\lambda_k)} \tag{4}$$

where the function $L(\lambda)$ is the spectral composition of the light source used to illuminate the sample surface [3].

In many practical cases (as that illustrated in the following as an example), where a WDRS specimen can be included in the field of view of the camera, we can usefully consider for the reflectance characterization of the surface under investigation, its relative reflectance with respect to that of the WDRS:

$$r_{i,j}(\lambda_k) = \frac{\rho_{i,j}(\lambda_k)}{\rho_{i,j}^{WDRS}(\lambda_k)} \tag{5}$$

It's easy to show that this relative reflectance is both independent of the apparatus spectral sensitivity $S(\lambda)$, and of the spectral composition of the light source. This last statement is only true for wideband light sources not to different among them, as are the C- and D-type CIE daylight illuminants [16]. Under these conditions the relative spectral reflectance is simply given by:

$$r_{i,j}(\lambda_k) = \frac{I_{i,j}(\lambda_k)}{I^{WDRS}(\lambda_k)} \tag{6}$$

where $I^{WDRS}(\lambda_k)$ is the intensity recorded by the camera sensor in correspondence of the WDRS region of the image at the given band centered around λ_k. .

The software application we have developed processes the N grayscale images acquired by the HSI apparatus, in order to calculate the relative reflectance of the (i, j)-region of the physical surface, by just mouse-clicking on the (i, j)-pixel of the surface image. In the rest of this section we describe the general aspects of the software implementation, as well as some application examples, aimed at validating the correct functioning of both the hardware apparatus and the data processing.

The symbolic architecture of the Wolfram Mathematica language permits treating images just like any other kind of digital objects, for example as regards: applying functions to them, displaying and inputting them in notebooks (*notebooks* constitute the standard GUI of Mathematica), including them directly in the program code. Moreover, the language provides an efficient collection of functions for basic image manipulation, fully integrated with more advanced processing tools [17].

The logic workflow of the processing tool we have developed is as follows (referring to Fig. 6). As the application starts, the N grayscale images recorded in the corresponding spectral windows (see Fig. 1) are loaded in the vector-image variable named "λimage" (code-box B). Then, the user chooses a point of interest (POI) on the painting by clicking on its visible RGB image (code-box A); subsequently, a circular portion of the image, centered on the POI, is trimmed out from each of the N grayscale components of "λimage" and the portions are stored in the vector variable named "imagetemp" (code-box B), which is then passed as an argument to the Mathematica object "ImageMeasurements" (code-box C). This object is a very powerful one, able to return a wide range of properties of the images, including the mean value of the intensity of a monochromatic image in a given area. The N values returned by "ImageMeasurements" after clicking on the (i, j)-POI are the spectral components $I_{i,j}(\lambda_k)$ in Eq. (6). By repeating the same routine, the software obtains the $I^{WDRS}(\lambda_k)$ values present in the same equation, and then calculates the relative reflectance by using Eq. (6).

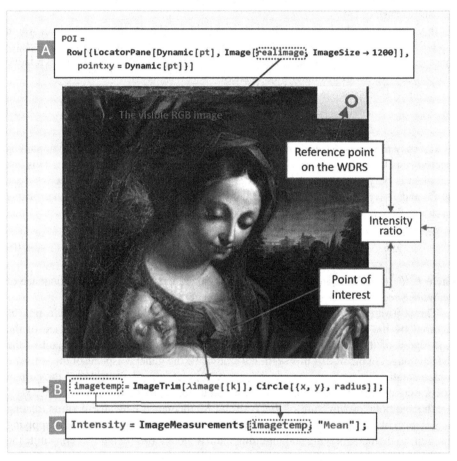

Fig. 6. Overview of the software structure (the sample image is from the same painting referenced in Fig. 1). The rectangle in the top right corner of the painting is the withe paper used as a WDRS. The color highlighted circles are the areas on which the mean intensities are measured for, respectively: the point of interest (yellow circle) and the reference white (red circle). The letter-labeled boxes show relevant portion of the Mathematica code, discussed in the main text.

The hardware apparatus and the software procedure have been put to the test on some commercial sample of pictorial pigments [18], by comparing the spectra obtained with the HSI procedure to those obtained with a classical Fiber Optics Reflectance Spectroscopy (FORS) setup, based on the wideband lamp LDLS and on the spectrometer, both described in Sect.2. Some test results are given in Fig. 7, showing that the HSI

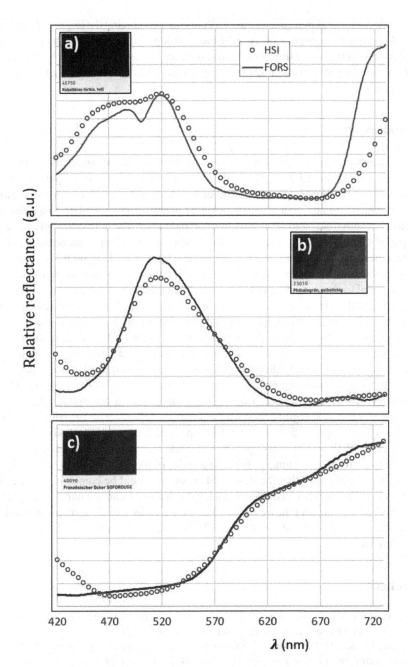

Fig. 7. Comparison of the HSI relative spectral reflectance (red circles) with the FORS-determined spectral reflectance for three KREMER pigment samples: a) Cobalt blue turquoise light (cod. K45570), b) Phthalo green yellowish (cod. K23010), c) French ochre soforouge (cod. 40090). (Color figure online)

spectral reflectance well agrees with the FORS one in reproducing the large-scale spectral details. A systematic tendency of the HSI methodology (also suggested by other tests, not shown here) is the overestimate of relative reflectance at short wavelength. We are not yet able to satisfactorily explain this systematic discrepancy, so that further researches are underway.

5   Conclusions

In this contribution we have presented both: a custom assembled apparatus for HSI, set up by using a λ-tunable LCD bandpass filter, and an original software application that permits analyzing the HSI hypercube, in order to extract spectral reflectance information on the sample. The main characteristics of the apparatus are described to a sufficient extent to allow possible interested users to build their own. The software application for the hypercube analysis, developed in Wolfram Mathematica language, permits getting the reflectance spectrum in any point of the image, by just clicking on it. The principal features of the software application are described, paying particular attention to some powerful digital tools, available in Mathematica, that render very simple the quantitative analysis of digital images. Such tools could be of interest for those readers (also outside the specific HSI users), who employ digital imaging methods as diagnostic tools for fine arts, and who could usefully develop their own customized analysis software. The apparatus has been tested, both in its hardware and software aspects, by comparing, for an extended palette of KREMER color samples, the HSI spectral reflectance character-ization with the corresponding characterization obtained by the well-established FORS methodology. Tests feature a good behavior of the apparatus in determining the spectral reflectance in the visible region, except a systematic discrepancy at the edge of the UV band. The software application we have developed for the hypercube analysis can also be used for the SWIR region of the spectrum, provided that both, an extended sensitivity camera and a corresponding tunable filter (or a series of fixed band filters), are available. Last, it is worth observing that the described apparatus could be employed for the HSI analysis of non-flat surfaces, provided that a lens with narrow enough numerical aperture is available (F16 or higher); however, in such a case further calibration are needed, in order to account for possible stereo-optical effects with respect to the usually flat WDRS white reference.

References

1. MacDonald, F., et al.: Assessment of multispectral and hyperspectral imaging systems for digitisation of a Russian icon. Heritage Sci. 5(41), 1–16 (2017)
2. ElMasry, G., Sun, D.-W.: Principles of hyperspectral imaging technology. In: Sun, D.-W. (ed.) Hyperspectral Imaging for Food Quality Analysis and Control, pp. 3–43. Academic Press, Elsevier, London, Burlington, San Diego (2010)
3. Striova, J., Dal Fovo, A., Fontana, R.: Reflectance imaging spectroscopy in heritage science. La Rivista del Nuovo Cimento 43(10), 515–566 (2020). https://doi.org/10.1007/s40766-020-00011-6
4. The entry point is the dedicated web page at the URL: https://www.wolfram.com/language/

5. He, X., et al.: A single sensor based multispectral imaging camera using a narrow spectral band color mosaic integrated on the monochrome CMOS image sensor. APL Photon **5**, 046104–046110 (2020)
6. Offerhaus, H.L., Bohndiek, S.E., Harvey, A.R.: Hyperspectral imaging in biomedical applications. J. Opt. **21**, 010202–010203 (2019)
7. Lu, G., Fei, B.: Medical hyperspectral imaging: a review. J. Biomed. Opt. **19**(1), 010901–010923 (2014)
8. Manolakis, D., Lockwood, R., Cooley, T.: Hyperspectral Imaging Remote Sensing, 1st edn. Cambridge University Press, Cambridge UK (2016)
9. Basantia, N.C., Nollet, L.M.L., Kamruzzaman, M.: Hyperspectral Imaging Analysis and Applications for Food Quality. CRC Press, Boca Raton, FL (2019)
10. Liang, H.: Advances in multispectral and hyperspectral imaging for archaeology and art conservation. Appl. Fis. A **106**, 309–323 (2012)
11. Grabowski, B., Masarczyk, W., Głomb, P., Mendis, A.: Automatic pigment identification from hyperspectral data. J. Cult. Herit. **31**, 1–12 (2018)
12. Manufacturer web page 340M-GE, https://www.thorlabs.com/thorproduct.cfm?partnumber=340M-GE
13. Manufacturer web page for KURIOS-WL1, https://www.thorlabs.com/newgrouppage9.cfm?objectgroup_id=3488
14. Manufacturer web page, https://www.energetiq.com/eq99x-high-brightness-broadband-light-source?hsLang=en
15. Wen, B.J.: Reflectance standards. In: Luo, M.R. (eds,) Encyclopedia of Color Science and Technology. Springer, New York, NY (2016)
16. Kránicz, B.: Daylight illuminants. In: Luo, M.R. (eds.) Encyclopedia of Color Science and Technology. Springer, New York, NY (2016)
17. "Basic Image Manipulation" entry of the Wolfram Language Documentation Center: https://reference.wolfram.com/language/guide/BasicImageManipulation.html
18. The sample used for checking are pigments color charts from KREMER: https://shop.kremerpigments.com/us/shop/books-color-charts/

Survey of the State of Conservation of Detached Wall Paintings by Digital and IR Techniques. The Case Study of Verde Cloister in the Church of Santa Maria Novella, Firenze

Sofia Brizzi[1,2]([✉]) [iD], Anastasia Cottini[2] [iD], Rachele Manganelli Del Fà[1] [iD], Alberto Felici[3] [iD], Stefano Bertocci[2] [iD], and Cristiano Riminesi[1] [iD]

[1] National Research Council of Italy – Institute of Heritage Science (CNR-ISPC), Via Madonna del Piano 10, Sesto Fiorentino (FI), Tuscany, Italy
sofia.brizzi@ispc.cnr.it

[2] Department of Architecture (DIDA), University of Florence, Via della Mattonaia 8, Tuscany, Florence, Italy

[3] Soprintendenza Archeologia, Belle Arti e Paesaggio (SABAP), Tuscany, Florence, Pistoia and Prato, Italy

Abstract. The detachment of wall paintings was one of the most widely used techniques to preserve frescoes and discover the underlying drawings (sinopia) during the second half of the XX century. Today, their conservation is a challenge for restorers and scientists mainly due to the combination of two problems: the natural decay of the original parts (painted and preparation layers) and the decay of the support. These problems are related, but in practice conservation is often focused only on the painted part, while the support is disregarded. In this contribution, the authors highlight the problems related to the support and how these can reflect on the integrity of the painted surface. This problem is studied in the real case of the wall paintings of the Verde cloister, in the church of Santa Maria Novella - painted by Paolo Uccello in the 15th century - using the technique of IR thermography, laser scanner and photogrammetric surveys. The first stage of the conservation proces is the diagnosis of the structural integrity of the support. The recognition of the type of support (Masonite - wood and monolayer - fibreglass) can be achieved with a combination of IR thermographic survey and visual inspection. The structural integrity was completed by the investigation of deformations and loss of flatness through a laser scanner combined with photogrammetric survey. The analysis of the results allows the classification of the detached wall paintings with respect to the type of support, their deformation and structural stability (also the anchoring defect). This classification will be useful for planning an effective conservation programme.

Keywords: Laser scanner · SfM photogrammetry · IR Thermography passive modality · Monitoring · Preventive conservation

© The Author(s), under exclusive license to Springer Nature Switzerland AG 2022
R. Furferi et al. (Eds.): Florence Heri-Tech 2022, CCIS 1645, pp. 82–93, 2022.
https://doi.org/10.1007/978-3-031-20302-2_7

1 Introduction

The conservation of the detached wall paintings on mobile support represents an important issue in relation to lots of critical aspects [1–3]. Depending on different constituent materials, the type of structure and different exposure to environmental factors, the support presents different characteristics and different vulnerability. In this research, the authors wish to highlight the importance of the conservation of the support to preserve the work of art as a whole through a non-destructive approach based on remote sensing techniques. The study began in Verde cloister in the church of Santa Maria Novella (Firenze), where there are many detached wall paintings, including paintings of Paolo Uccello. These frescoes were restored and detached by the Central Institute for Restoration in 1942, and detached again in 1954 by Leonetto Tintori for the final bonding on Masonite support [4]. Today, the detached wall paintings of Paolo Uccello are recovered in the Museum of Santa Maria Novella in the refectory room, whereas the others are still located in the original lunettes of the cloister. They exhibit various types of decay, such as deformations, cracks, and decohesion of the painted layer. An interdisciplinary study has been carried out in this research project using non-destructive techniques based on remote sensing approach, including IR Thermography, 3D laser-scanner survey, and Structure from Motion photogrammetry (SfM).

The wall paintings of Verde cloister have a long conservation history. The eastern side was painted by Paolo Uccello in 1425–1430. During the centuries, they underwent some restoration due to the several factors of decay, in particular loss of superficial cohesion. In 1853 Gaetano Bianchi cleaned the frescoes and prevented material loss by applying an egg-based protective layer known as "beverone". In 1907–1910 a detachment campaign began: Domenico Fiscali removed some scenes painted by Paolo Uccello probably using the detachment technique called "stacco", with the application of linen fiber. He used a galvanized wire mesh reinforced with calcium caseinate and gypsum. This method, however, involves the loss of the underlying drawing *sinopia*. In 1930–1943, Amedeo Benini done a restoration using casein and an egg-based solution to consolidate the painted surface on the detached wall paintings on the eastern side. Over time this caused the painting deterioration. In 1942 the Central Restauration Institute (ICR) continued the detachment work in the east cloister side, but they used the "strappo" technique, which allows the *sinopias* to be discovered. In 1952–1954, Leonetto Tintori restored again the scenes detached by the ICR. He transported all frescoes of the South and West side of the cloister on a timbered Masonite supports. In 1966 the tragic flood in Florence swarmed the cloister and damaged all the scenes in the lower part. A team of restorers performed urgently *in situ* intervention to remove mud, fuel oil, and rubbish from the frescoes before their removal by the restoration laboratory. In 1983 after spending years in the Sopraintendences's storage factory, the entire cycle of painting was replaced in Verde cloister. Since 2005, the paintings were monitored with datalogger sensors to evaluate the moisture exchange between the paintings and the environment, a crucial factor in determining the condition for sulfation phenomena. In 2011–2014 a new campaign restoration took place. The Opificio delle Pietre Dure removed the paintings in the first four lunettes of the east cloister side. The initial survey revealed that the detached wall paintings presented different problems according to their conservation history, so specific operations were planned for each fresco [5, 6]. Finally, the frescoes of the east side, except for a fragment present in the last lunette, were moved to the refectory in the Museum of Santa Maria Novella, where they are still located today. All the remaining frescoes are still *in situ* and they are located on the South and West sides of the cloister as shown in Fig. 1.

Fig. 1. The 3D model obtained via laser scanner of the Verde cloister in the church of Santa Maria Novella. The axonometric cross-section highlights the wall paintings of the South and West sides.

The cloister is an open space and it can be classified as semi-confined, therefore the exposure to the environmental conditions (changes in temperature and humidity, wind, solar radiation, dust and pollution) can be just mitigated but it's not fully avoidable. The observed decay phenomena are fundamentally bounded to the anchoring fault combined with environmental factors. This contribution describes the first step of the conservation activity which aims to assess the state of conservation of detached wall paintings and their sources of decay.

The proposed interdisciplinary approach is a continuation of the authors' preliminary study on this topic [7] and in particular, it has accomplished two fundamental targets:

- a procedure for a rapid relief on the state of conservation of the detached wall paintings based on completely non-destructive methods;
- a simple procedure for planning the restoration woks with compliance the criterion of the preventive conservation.

2   Materials and Methods

Every lunette hosts two detached paintings, each one on its support - upper and lower. Each support, composed by several panels anchored one to each other, is anchored to the wall by screws and wall plugs. The frescoes still present in 1954 were detached by Leonetto Tintori and applied on a timbered Masonite support. It consists of three layers, in which the outer panels are made of single layers of Masonite, whereas the internal layer is a frame made of Masonite (see Fig. 2).

Fig. 2. Structure of the timbered Masonite support used for the frescoes of the South and West side of the cloister.

With regards to the frescoes in the Refectory, the frescoes "Ebrezza di Noé" was transported on fiberglass support, while the frescoes "La cacciata dal paradiso terrestre ed il lavoro dei progenitori" was transported in a galvanized wire mesh by Domenico Fiscali. For the other scenes on the east side, Tintori used supports made of a single Masonite panel applied on a gridded structure in wood. However, during the last restoration campaign (2011 by Opificio delle Pietre Dure), the supports located at the East side were restored and the original Masonite support was reinforced with carbon fiber and epoxy resin. Furthermore, old frames were removed and replaced by new support in aerolam, which are considerably lighter, thinner, and easy to peel away [8].

2.1 The Digital Survey Techniques

The recognition on the support in the Verde cloister was carried out by integrating digital techniques and IR thermography (IRT) in passive mode. The integration of results allows to achieve the research goals.

The digital surveys inside the Verde cloister have been carried out with laser-scanner and photographic instrumentation, in order to integrate the two different data and obtain a three-dimensional coloured model as complete as possible of the spaces of the cloister. The survey was performed by the FARO Focus M70 laser-scanner system (accuracy of 3 mm) with an integrated camera. Scans were carried out in 24 different locations inside the cloister see Fig. 3.

Each scan produced a three-dimensional point-cloud with a resolution of 6.1 mm/10 m - the recording of all scans with Leica Cyclone software allowed to obtain a colored point-cloud in 1:1 scale with an overall error of 2–3 mm. The point-cloud can be used as a reliable reference for the drawing of 2D technical drawings such as plants and cross-sections, that are used to contextualize the frescoes and their supports within the architectural complex. Elevation maps can be generated from the point cloud referred to the set plan [9]. Elevation maps are useful to check the status of the frescoes and their supports, or to verify the presence of deformations on the surfaces, in the specific case with a range of 3 mm.

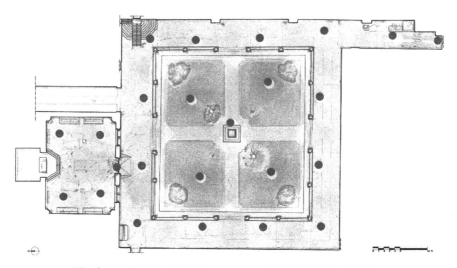

Fig. 3. Positioning of the laser-scanner station inside the cloister.

At the same time, a photographic campaign was carried out to obtain a three-dimensional model of the detached paintings by the Structure from Motion (SfM) technique (Fig. 4). SfM is a range imaging technique, based on photogrammetric principles, that allows us to reconstruct three-dimensional models starting from points extrapolated from two-dimensional images. Starting from a properly set of photographic images by Agisoft Metashape, a 3D model was extracted. All the photos were taken by using a digital reflex camera Nikon D5300 equipped with a 18 mm lens. In this preliminary phase, no illuminators were used, however, given the need to obtain reliable data also from the point of view of the color profile of the frescoes, this instrumentation will be used in subsequent investigations.

These 3D models of the panels were scaled by recognizing homologous points that could be identified both on the point cloud of the laser scanner and on the photogrammetric one. Finally, the photogrammetric models were used to build the orthomosaic of the panels.

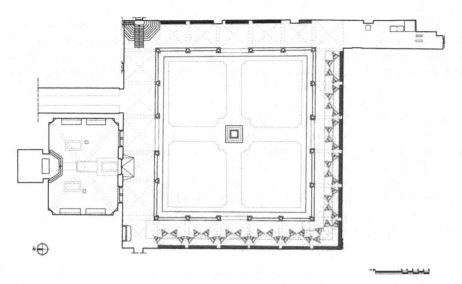

Fig. 4. In red the shooting points for structure from motion photogrammetry. The support in timbered Masonite are highlighted in green, whilst yellow is indicated the original position of the Paolo Uccello's detached paintings. (Color figure online)

2.2 IR Thermography Survey

The East and the West side of the cloister were investigated by the passive IRT technique. The IRT survey aims were to find detachments from walls, water infiltrations/leaks, rising damp phenomena and to discover the different types of supports, without the need to remove the entire fresco.

The device used for the IRT survey is the FLIR infrared camera T540, with a resolution of 464 × 348 pixels, the thermal sensibility of (NETD) < 30 Mk a 30 °C (optic lens of 42°) of 50 mK, temperature range from −20 °C to + 350 °C, and accuracy of ± 2%. The thermal image was elaborated by FLIR software and the mosaic reconstruction was performed by Adobe Photoshop software.

3   Results

The acquired data integrated into superimposed two-dimensional graphics allowed a preliminary assessment of the state of conservation of the detached paintings, so to correlate their deformation to the type of support. Thanks to these results, an assessment of the condition of the support was carried out and, consequently, a preliminary evaluation of the structural safety of detached paintings located in the cloister.

3.1   Integration of the Digital Survey

The survey was performed on 12 painted lunettes (the detached painting of the Crucifixion, located on the last lunette on the West side, is not on-site because under restoration).

The elevation maps were generated using Leica Cyclone software using the point-cloud model obtained by the laser-scanner survey. These maps are a graphical representation of the point-cloud by a chosen color's palette. A metric scale is associated with the palette and a color scheme. The elevation map is referred to the reference plane set by selecting a line on the portion of wall below the lower paintings. The color palette range is coded with Multi-Hue/Rainbow code color, and it corresponds to a metric variation up to 9 cm with a resolution of 3 mm. The colors that describe the worst cases, attributed to greater variations from the reference plane, are coded in red and blue respectively for positive and negative distance. Instead, the green color represents an area that is almost aligned with the reference plane (about zero distance).

The contour lines (i.e., points at the same quota), were plotted on the elevation map as well, using Cloud Compare software with an inter-distance of 3 mm.

In Fig. 5 the merging of the elevation maps and contour lines for both the sides of the cloister, West and South sides, for each lunette, are reported.

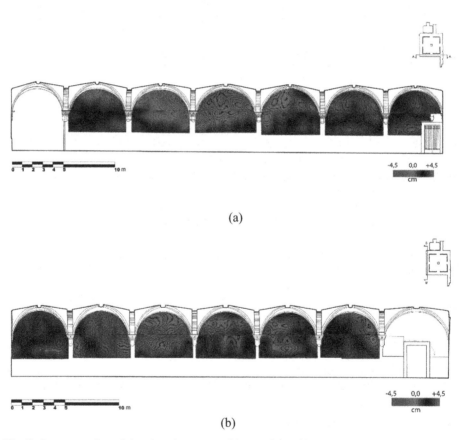

(a)

(b)

Fig. 5. Representation of the elevation maps with superimposition of the contour lines. (a) the South side, (b) the West side.

The areas mainly affected by deformations are located on the lower panel. The peak on the elevation map, in red, is identified in correspondence with falling screws from the wall plug.

The deformations also affect the upper panels on the West side of the cloister (Fig. 5b).

The photogrammetric survey with SfM technique has been carried out on the same lunettes. For each panel, 4 photos from the ground plane were taken, using a tripod and maintaining the same distance from the object. An example of a orthomosaic obtained photogrammetry on a single lunette is shown in Fig. 6.

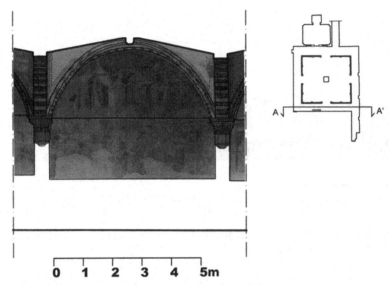

Fig. 6. Orthomosaic of the fourth lunette on the South side of the cloister (section A-A'). In green line the location of the lunette. (Color figure online)

3.2 Infrared Thermography Survey

The IRT survey has been performed on each lunette on the South side and the West side. A single IR image is not enough to cover the whole lunette so a mosaic reconstruction by the Adobe Photoshop elaboration program was carried out. Figure 7 shows the results obtained after the mosaic reconstruction. The survey was conducted on each lunette, from the ceiling up to the floor.

From the observation of the processed IR images, it is possible to acquire different information such as:

- The type of the support and its internal composition was detected without any contact with the target (non-destructive approach). The differences within the frame of timbered Masonite were also highlighted. In Fig. 8a is reported the cloister layout with the position of the different types of support.

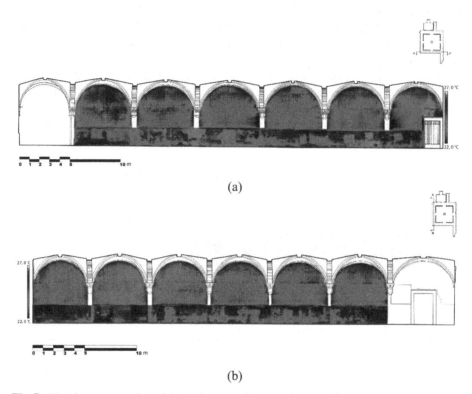

Fig. 7. Mosaic reconstruction of the IR images of the paintings and the masonry below that. (a) the South side, (b) the West side.

- The localization of areas with different gradient temperature can indicate the presence of some anomalies inside the structure of the support, for example, air gaps among the internal layers or between the back of the support and the walls. The temperature variations seem to correspond to the major deformations detected by the digital survey (see Fig. 5). These temperature anomalies could also be due to wall/masonry defects that reflect their presence, through temperature transmission, on the painted surface.
- The presence of infilled elements on masonry with regular shapes (rectangular) at different temperature (lower temperature, Fig. 7) could be recognized by stratigraphic essay. Their origin is under study, even if the presence of possible ancient graves cannot be excluded, as the South and West sides of the cloister are the only ones with floor graves.

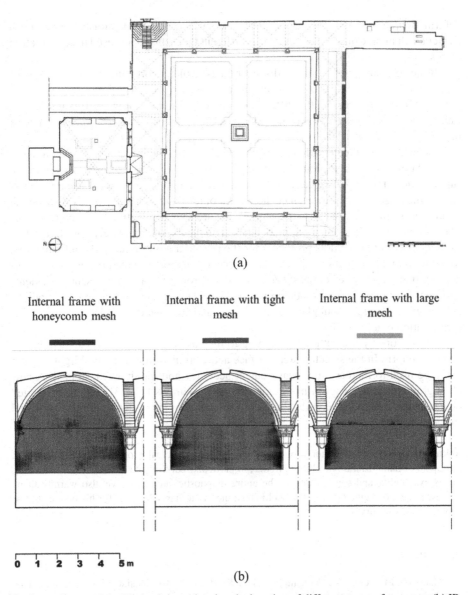

Internal frame with honeycomb mesh

Internal frame with tight mesh

Internal frame with large mesh

0 1 2 3 4 5 m

(b)

Fig. 8. (a) layout of the Verde cloister showing the location of different types of supports; (b) IR images of the three types of supports present in the cloister (timbered Masonite with large, tight and honeycomb grid).

4 Discussion and Conclusion

The aim of this research was a non-destructive tool based on digital and IR survey techniques for a preliminary assessment of the state of conservation of the detached wall paintings, with particular focus to the correlation between the importance of the deformation and the type of support. The case study of the Verde cloister represents a particular challenge due to the presence of different types of support used in conservation works.

IR thermography allowed us to discover the type of support without any sampling of the materials overcoming the limitation due to visual inspection. All the supports are in timbered Masonite (Fig. 2), the differences found are in the size in the frame grid (see Fig. 8): large (grid size about 20 cm), tight (grid size about 10 cm), and honeycomb with the cell size of about 10 cm.

The analysis of the elevation maps obtained through the integration of digital techniques, laser-scanner and photogrammetry, showed the presence of deformation in the support due to the loss of efficacy of the anchoring system. The anchors have lost adherence to the masonry, therefore, since the weight of the panel is not uniformly distributed, it induces asymmetric forces on the support that are a source of stress and deformations. The proposed interdisciplinary approach based on the use of completely non-destructive techniques could be used as protocols for the preservation of detached wall paintings, for a preliminary evaluation of the reliability of the support and the presence of support deformations. The survey of the surfaces using the proposed tool provides measurements with high accuracy without touching the artifacts. This means that these investigations are suitable for carrying out planned monitoring and are a good candidate for preventive conservation practices.

Future work by the authors is ongoing to increase the accuracy of data acquisition and data return. In the selected area, surface acquisition with a structured light scanner could be used to increase the measurement accuracy and monitor cracks [10]. A new photogrammetric acquisition using color balance methods [11–13] could be repeated on a selected area to increase the amount of information in terms of color variation and surface roughness.

Acknowledgments. The authors would like to thank the Municipality of Firenze, the Museum of the Opera of Santa Maria Novella in Firenze, in particular Dr. Silvia Colucci (museum director) for its availability and support during the entire diagnostic campaign. We also warmly thank the researcher colleague Giorgio Pocobelli (Institute of Heritage Science) for his help using the photogrammetric survey.

References

1. Calmanti, M., Felici, A., Manganelli Del Fà, R., Pizzo, B., Riminesi, C.: La conservazione di dipinti murali strappati applicati su masonite: Il caso applicativo della Crocifissione e santi nel Chiostro Verde di Santa Maria Novella, Kermes: la rivista del restauro. Ed. Nardini Editore **116**, 50–54 (2019)
2. Mariotti, P.I.: Supporti impiegati per il distacco e lo strappo delle pitture murali. In sostituzione dell'originale, dalle origini ad oggi. Ricerca tecnica sui materiali e sui metodi di impiego. Letture di comportamento, Opificio delle Pietre Dure e Laboratori di Restauro, Firenze (1983)
3. Shashoua, Y.: Conservation of Plastics, Material Science: Degradation and Preservation. Routledge (2012)
4. Tintori, L., Del Serra, A.: Nuove metodologie nel distacco degli affreschi, Atti del Convegno sul restauro delle opere d'arte, Firenze, 2–7 novembre 1976, pp. 157–159 441–443. Edizioni Polistampa, Firenze (1981)

5. Bandini, F., Felici, A., Frosinini, C., Vigna, A.: Stato di avanzamento dei lavori nel restauro dei dipinti murali distaccati del lato orientale del Chiostro Verde di Santa Maria Novella a Firenze, OPD Restauro, N. 25, (2013)
6. Vigna, A.: I restauri dell'Opificio delle Pietre Dure al Chiostro Verde (2005–2019), Paolo Uccello in Santa Maria Novella. Restauri e studi sulla tecnica in terraverde, a cura di Cecilia Frosinini, pp. 183–240, Firenze (2021)
7. Salvadori, B., Manganelli Del Fà, R., Riminesi, C.: Proposta per un approccio interdisciplinare di monitoraggio dei dipinti murali strappati, Kermes: la rivista del restauro. Ed. Nardini Editore **116**, 75–82 (2019)
8. Felici, A., Pini, S., Vigna, A.: Il Chiostro Verde nel complesso di Santa Maria Novella a Firenze: storia e restauri, OPD Restauro n. 19-2007, Firenze, (2008)
9. Arrighetti, A.: Registering and documenting the stratification of disruptions and restorations in historical edifices. Contrib. Archaeoseismology Archit. **23**, 243–251 (2019). https://doi.org/10.1016/j.jasrep.2018.10.028
10. Felici, A., Vigna, A.: Le scelte metodologiche e la descrizione dell'intervento di restauro sui supporti dei dipinti murali del lato orientale. Paolo Uccello in Santa Maria Novella. Restauri e studi sulla tecnica in terraverde, a cura di Cecilia Frosinini, pp. 345–352, Firenze (2021)
11. Degrigny, C., Boochs, F., Raddatz, L., Veller, J., Justus, C., Pinette, M.: Use of imaging techniques as a support for the preventive conservation strategy of wall paintings: application to the Medieval Decors of the Château de Germolles. In: El Moataz, A., Mammass, D., Mansouri, A., Nouboud, F. (eds.) ICISP 2020. LNCS, vol. 12119, pp. 24–34. Springer, Cham (2020). https://doi.org/10.1007/978-3-030-51935-3_3
12. Elkhuizen, W.S., et al.: Comparison of three 3D scanning techniques for paintings, as applied to Vermeer's 'Girl with a Pearl Earring.' Heritage Science **7**(1), 1–22 (2019). https://doi.org/10.1186/s40494-019-0331-5
13. Jackson, M.K.: Color Management in 3D Fine-Art Painting Reproduction, Color and Imaging Conference, 396 (2018). https://doi.org/10.2352/ISSN.2169-2629.2018.26.396

IA and AR/VR Based Methods
and Applications for CH

Machine Learning Tools to Improve the Quality of Imperfect Keywords

Maria Teresa Artese[iD] and Isabella Gagliardi[(✉)] [iD]

IMATI - CNR (National Research Council), Milan, Italy
{teresa,isabella}@mi.imati.cnr.it

Abstract. The availability of keywords that describe the content of a text or document certainly is essential for effective and efficient content-based retrieval. But their quality, the presence of spelling variants, synonyms, near-synonyms, and spelling errors make their use less effective. Here we present a set of tools we are developing for the management of tags. These tools are intended to be used to improve the quality of textual features and to enhance traditional ways of searching and browsing data on the web. This approach integrates different methods: word embedding models, able to capture the semantics of words and their context, clustering algorithms, able to identify/group semantically related terms, and methods able to calculate the syntactic similarity between strings. The work is still under development, and the paper will present some preliminary qualitative results that demonstrate the feasibility of our approach.

Keywords: Semantic relatedness · Syntactic similarity · Clustering · Multilingual tags · Content based retrieval · Natural language processing · Word embedding models · Quality of data

1 Introduction

The possibility to create and manage archives to be used on the net has become a reality, thanks also to the cloud and "prefabricated" tools. In addition, the spread of linked open data offers new horizons in the fruition of information.

Now, the real challenge to be overcome concerns the quality of the data and the user's satisfaction in being able to find the data and information he is really interested in.

This paper will propose supervised and unsupervised tools based on natural language processing using machine learning approaches to improve the quality of textual data. The tools are intended also to be used to enhance traditional ways of searching and browsing data on the web and offer multimodal search and visualization tools.

The information we speak of is not only simple text but also tags or keywords to allow a faster and more efficient search.

The main problems that tag present are: i) the use of different terms to express (more or less) the same concept, or spelling variants, ii) the presence of tags expressed in different languages, iii) the extreme specialization of the terms used, iv) the lack of context and v) sometimes even syntactically/semantically inaccurate or wrong.

R. Furferi et al. (Eds.): Florence Heri-Tech 2022, CCIS 1645, pp. 97–111, 2022.
https://doi.org/10.1007/978-3-031-20302-2_8

The approach addresses automatic detection of the language in which a text is written, in our case very short, the automatic detection of spelling errors and syntactic/semantic relatedness. The main feature of this approach is the integration of several methods that have yielded interesting results:

- machine learning classification methods, both to identify the language of the tags and the presence of misspellings,
- word embedding models, such as Word2Vec or GloVe capable of capturing the semantics of words and their context,
- clustering algorithms for identifying/grouping semantically related terms
- methods capable of calculating the similarity between strings.

The tools we are developing have been tested on datasets of tags associated with scientific articles produced by researchers in a research institution, thus giving rise to all the problems previously outlined.

Being the datasets too small to be used to train machine learning methods, we train the models using different datasets found on the net that share common characteristics with the starting dataset. Moreover, to overcome the lack of context, which characterizes the problem addressed by this paper, two possible solutions have been analyzed and evaluated: on the one hand, using pre-trained models on Wikipedia, Google, or other generic datasets, in different languages, and on the other hand using a large dataset that is close to the content of tags: in this case study it is the entire content of ArXiv.org [1].

The paper is structured as follows: in Sect. 2, the related works are outlined quickly, then our approach is described in detail. In Sect. 4, the experimentation is presented on the dataset of tags related to scientific papers, in two languages, Italian and English, with some preliminary results and a brief discussion to comment on them, including a comparison between the two different word embedding models used, pre-trained and trained on ArXiv. Conclusions and future work complete the paper.

2 State of the Art

This paper deals with the definition and development of supervised and unsupervised tools that allow tags, already defined and associated with data, to be exploited at their best, unifying them, harmonizing them, integrating methods to assess their syntactic or semantic similarity. We do not deal with defining methods and models to extract keywords or tags, either automatically or in a supervised way.

In [2], the authors introduce a general framework of syntactic similarity measures for matching short text. The purpose of [3] is a learning-based approach for automatic construction of domain glossary from source code and software documentation, using word-embedding models integrated with lexical similarity. The integration of word embedding models with clustering algorithms is now being studied by different research groups, mainly for classification purposes and/or in specific contexts (for example, [4, 5]) due to its ability in extracting semantic and discriminative keywords.

In the literature, there are cluster-based methods capable of extracting terms, grouping them into clusters based on their semantic relationship using Wikipedia and/or other co-occurrence similarity measures, and selecting sentences that contain one or more cluster centroids. Examples are KeyCluster [6] and SemCluster [7].

3   Our Approach

Catalogers/researchers often use very specific keywords, to make searches "precision" oriented [8] - in the sense of information retrieval, limiting the set of results to only highly relevant items. But sometimes, web users are interested in the topic in a broader sense aiming to retrieve specific information and other elements around it. In this case, we can speak of a system that operates in a "recall" oriented way.

Our overall purpose is to define tools to improve the use of online catalogs, making the keywords, associated by the catalogers more incisive, inclusive, discriminating, relevant and purposeful.

The approach presented in the paper consists of many steps (see Fig. 1), which offer different types of similarities between tags, both syntactic and semantic. Specifically, these steps are:

- Preprocessing
- Language identification
- Misspelling identification
- Syntactic relatedness
- Semantic relatedness: used in two ways

  – Clustering
  – Similarity measures (cosine similarity)

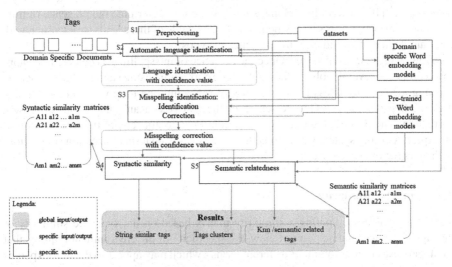

Fig. 1. Schema of the proposed approach

3.1 Preprocessing

Usually, in natural language processing (NLP) tasks such as keyword extraction or automatic summarization, the purpose of the pre-processing phase is cleaning, lemmatizing, stemming, and pos tagging of the text. The result is a set of terms, single or compound words, which will then be processed. In our case, the dataset is already composed only of simple or compound terms, so the pre-processing step is very light: only lemmatization and pos tagging could be performed.

3.2 Automatic Language Detection

Keywords associated with collections of items are generally in the same language as the item itself. Therefore, when we deal with multilingual collections, for example, books and magazines of a library or scientific production of a university, the tags can be indifferently in English, Italian, French, etc.

Automatic identification of the language, using statistical techniques or Machine Learning methods, is therefore required [9]. In the following, a more detailed description of this step is given.

3.3 Misspelling Identification and Correction

This work is designed specifically for specialized keywords in research areas, such as scientific libraries, books, journals, articles, or research activities. Thus, tags can be very specialized and fall outside of common lexicons. Therefore, catalogers/researchers, due to the extreme specialization of terms and their continuous updating, cannot choose terms from predefined vocabularies or lists and thus may include misspellings.

How to identify misspelling? The mere use of standard methods such as presence in WordNet[1] [10] or term lists alone is not sufficient to determine the presence of misspellings. This work uses several methods: the ensemble of these leads to detecting, with a certain degree of confidence, the presence of typos.

How to suggest corrections? Once the presence of misspellings is detected, the approach proposes several tools for their automatic correction, using statistical and Machine learning methods to assess the probability of replacing one term with another. It also uses the first results of a Google search or the "do you mean" function to propose a correction. The proposed automatic correction tools do not require the intervention of an expert. A voting system was defined that associates each term (correction suggestion) with a degree of confidence.

3.4 Syntactic Similarity

This step involves computing a similarity matrix based on the syntactic similarity of the tags. From a semantic point of view, the specificity of the environment requires that catalogers use singular/plural or different terms - which may appear to the non-expert as

---

[1] https://wordnet.princeton.edu/.

synonyms. When using a web search engine, the system must be able to propose, clearly and visibly, a syntactic grouping for terms that share a large number of letters.

In literature, several methods of calculating similarity are presented [2], such as Levenshtein, Damerau, Jaro, Jaro-Winkler … In this paper, after a series of tests, we chose the Jaro-Winkler algorithm, which measures the difference between 2 strings, then normalizes it, with values ranging from 1 (when two strings are identical) to 0 when they are completely dissimilar. The choice of this measure is due to the ease of understanding the results and the fact that it gives results in the same range as semantic similarity, described later, and therefore seamlessly integrable.

3.5 Semantic Relatedness

Catalogers/researchers may choose terms that are similar to others while making use of different words. This may be due to the need to differentiate concepts, or to the different background of the catalogers/researchers who uses distinct languages and jargon. On the one hand, it is correct not to replace or suggest changes to tags, on the other hand, it is critical that during search and visualization, the search engine can retrieve all items that are semantically related.

The semantic relatedness of terms is based both on the term itself and on the context in which this term is used. Several approaches for calculating the semantic correlation of terms are presented in the literature. Here we provide a method to compute semantic correlation based on word embedding. The word embedding technique is one of the most popular ways to represent terms, where words with similar meanings have a similar representation, being able to capture the context of a word in a document, its semantic and syntactic similarity, the relationship with other words, etc. Each word is represented as a real-valued vector in a predefined vector space, and the vector values are learned in a way that resembles a neural network, so the technique is often included in the field of deep learning.

Several models have been developed since 2013 when the first models appeared: here we use word2vec, which is one of the most widely used techniques for learning word embedding using a shallow neural network [11, 12].

Particular attention has been paid to compound tags, which are not present in the compound form in the word embedding model, but as individual components. In this case, a new vector is computed as the average of the composing vectors.

In this work, we are interested in the semantic correlation between tags, in a broad sense. So, we did not investigate the type of correlation, e.g. synonyms, and antonyms, see also [13], being interested in all, without the need for distinction, using the cosine between the vectors representing the tags as a similarity measure.

Semantic correlation of terms is used in two ways: the first involves clustering all terms using standard algorithms, while the second calculates, for each term, the most similar tags, using cosine similarity, as explained more fully later.

Clustering aims to assign objects into groups such that objects in the same cluster are more similar to each other than any object in any other cluster [14]. In this paper, we use three widely used clustering algorithms: affinity propagation, k-means, and hierarchical clustering to group embedded vectors into semantically equivalent clusters.

Affinity Propagation (AP) is a clustering algorithm that identifies a set of "exemplars" representing the dataset [15]. The number of clusters is computed by the algorithm, without the need to assign it a priori, using trial and error methods. The number of clusters identified by the affinity propagation algorithm is also used by the other algorithms used in the experiments in the paper.

K-means clustering (KM) is one of the simplest and most popular unsupervised machine learning algorithms [16] that aims to cluster similar data points and discover the underlying patterns.

Hierarchical clustering (AC) is a cluster analysis method that attempts to construct a hierarchy of clusters. Hierarchical clustering can be created by following a bottom-up or a top-down approach.

The most similar terms for a given tag are suggested based on cosine similarity, a standard measure in these cases. Web users have become accustomed to having suggestions to keep exploring. Cosine similarity gives us a measure of how similar two vectors are by measuring the angle between vectors, then calculating the cosine. Other possible measures are Euclidean distance, Manhattan distance, etc.

4 Experimentation

The method depicted in Fig. 1 has been implemented, according to the steps described in depth in their computational aspects.

4.1 Datasets and Models

The data on which we tested our approach is composed of scientific articles produced by researchers in a research institution. It contains 4000 scientific papers in the Italian or English language, to which 7000 different keywords, single or compound, have been associated. This dataset is called PAPERS1. Being too small to use statistical methods or train machine learning methods, we used different datasets, found on the net and eventually further processed, that share common characteristics with the starting dataset.

- For language identification, the starting dataset is composed of the title and abstract of Wikipedia articles, as stored in the dumps of 20210801, in the different languages considered. In this case, Italian and English. Two experiments were done:

  - for each language, all the words (in the title and abstract) in the annotated dataset for that language were kept. This implied that the same word could appear annotated in multiple languages (WIKITXT);
  - from WIKITXT dataset have been eliminated those terms not present in the pretrained models of word2vec (WIKI_NOOOV).

- For the evaluation of the presence of term misspellings in English, the dataset of all articles stored in the ArXiv repository was used (about 1,700,000 papers). The aim was to ensure the presence of specialized scientific terms that might be excluded from a standard vocabulary. The papers of our dataset were also added.

- For the terms identified as Italian, we used the same dataset used for the language identification: the Italian Wikipedia[2], containing more than one million articles. Again, we decided to keep only the title and abstract of each Wikipedia article.

To help in overcoming the lack of context, different word embedding models have been tested, and the results are reported here:

- Word2Vec pre-trained on Wikipedia[3]: both Italian and English versions have been trained on a Wikipedia version of April 2018.
- ARXIV dataset has been used to train a model more closely matching the data in use, adding the parameter (leaving others the same)

  - min_word_count = 2: minimum number of occurrences.

This is to get a larger number of terms, and thus cover as much as possible the lexicon used in the experiment. In Table 1, the dimension of the trained word embedding models used is shown.

Table 1. Dimensions of trained models used

Model	Italian	English
W2v wiki	1.721.340	4.530.030
ArXiv		272.064

We applied two misspelling algorithms mimicking the most frequent errors that are introduced when writing, to ARXIV and PAPER1 datasets:

- changes to a word, such as a deletion (removing a letter), a transposition (swapping two adjacent letters), a substitution (changing one letter for another), or an insertion (adding a letter). This algorithm is called EDIT1 and is based on the correction algorithm of Peter Norvig[4]
- replacement of a letter with another nearby on the keyboard or deletion of a letter: this algorithm is called NEARBY.

4.2 Preprocessing

No preprocessing was done in this experiment. The tags, exactly as entered by the catalogers/researchers, were used. For compound tags, the set of terms was enriched by breaking them up into individual words, useful during the typos identification and correction phase.

---

[2] https://dumps.wikimedia.org/backup-index.html.

[3] https://wikipedia2vec.github.io/wikipedia2vec/pretrained/.

[4] http://norvig.com/spell-correct.html.

4.3 Language Identification

The data used in this experiment are in Italian or English. The language of the tag is not necessarily the same as the title or abstract of the article. For language identification, we implemented two machine learning classification methods (Logistic regression and multinomial Naive Bayes classifier), using those features that better characterize our data:

– single words (1-g) and
– character n-grams which are sets of n consecutive characters: in this case n = 3. This is a similar approach to a bag-of-words model except we are using characters and not words.

Classifiers as implemented in scikit-learn[5] were used, with standard parameters.

Tests were done with a different maximum number of features, to confirm the intuitive idea that more data leads to greater accuracy. Table (2 and 3) reports results for logistic regression and Naïve Bayes classifiers trained on wikitxt and wiki_noov datasets using single words (1-g) or char 3-g with 400, 800 and 1200 features.

It can be seen that the results obtained with the trained model on wikitxt are vastly worse than those obtained using cleaner data. Also char 3-g get better results than whole words, and regardless of the training set, words feature generalizes worse than 3-g.

4.4 Language Identification

Due to the specific scope of the experiment, identifying misspelled words was a particularly difficult task due to:

– different languages;
– very specialized scientific terms;
– the presence of proper nouns/project names.

Therefore, several identification strategies were fielded - to be integrated - since individually none proved sufficient in the specific case. All these strategies indicate hints of the correctness of the tags:

- the presence of the tag in the word embedding models adopted;
- the presence of "as is" tags (both compound and as single components) in the title/abstract of the articles and the ArXiv dataset;
- the presence "as is" in the first results of Google or the title/abstract/content of Wikipedia (Italian or English);
- the presence in synsets of WordNet/MultiWordNet (the multilingual version of WN).

In case the indicators suggest with a high confidence value that the term is misspelled, automatic corrections are suggested:

---

[5] https://scikit-learn.org/stable/index.html.

1. automatic correction of the error, due to the inversion of two characters, the substitution of two close characters in the keyboard, etc.;
2. Google search first n results, those strings having a syntactic similarity higher than 0.95, with n = 2 or 3.

Table 2. Results for the classifiers trained on the wikitxt dataset

Feature	Training dataset	No. features	Features extracted	Dataset	Accuracy (logreg/naïve bayes)
Trigrams	Wikitxt	1200	1736	Train	0.883/0.844
				Test	0.872/0.845
				Papers1	0.689/0.743
		600	894	Train	0.872/0.840
				Test	0.867/0.841
				Papers1	0.687/0.715
		400	618	Train	0.855/0.834
				Test	0.851/0.834
				Papers1	0.643/0.676
Words	Wikitxt	1200	2310	Train	0.843/0.838
				Test	0.840/0.839
				Papers1	0.328/0.394
		600	1551	Train	0.833/0.830
				Test	0.831/0.831
				Papers1	0.285/0.324
		400	784	Train	0.821/0.820
				Test	0.819/0.819
				Papers1	0.203/0.211

The starting point is to check the presence of individual terms in the vocabulary of the word embedding models. The oov (out-of-vocabulary) tags are those not present in the model. Three different models were considered, two for English and one for Italian. We report here the values for the two models for English.

In the PAPERS1 dataset, 165 tags are oov for the pre-trained model: analyzing the data we can see that they belong to two categories: i) proper names of projects and persons, ii) misspelled tags.

Using the word embedding model trained on ArXiv, oov tags, 105, are of the following types: i) those extremely rare terms (occurring only 1 time in the whole dataset) ii) tags in Italian, therefore not present in ArXiv (only in the added papers) iii) project names, iv) misspelled.

Table 3. Results for the classifiers trained on the wiki_noov dataset

Feature	Training dataset	No. features	Features extracted	Dataset	Accuracy
Trigrams	Wiki_nooov	1200	1612	Train	0.969/0.957
				Test	0.963/0.918
				Papers1	0,856/0.767
		800	1098	Train	0.949/0.904
				Test	0.945/0.904
				Papers1	0.819/0.739
		400	570	Train	0.916/0.87
				Test	0,916/0.88
				Papers1	0,950/0.945
Words	Wiki_nooov	1200	2400	Train	0.796/0.796
				Test	0.754/0.754
				Papers1	0.184/0.184
		800	1600	Train	0.778/0.778
				Test	0.746/0.746
				Papers1	0.177/0.177
		400	800	Train	0.758/0.758
				Test	0.738/0.738
				Papers1	0.177/0.177

These last ones, for both models, are the object of the automatic correction procedure. The presence of the tags in the title or abstract of the articles and/or in the ArXiv dataset or Google, Wikipedia, or WordNet helps to understand if they are errors or rare terms. Most errors are corrected through the automatic procedure that looks like Google's "do you mean?" which swaps adjacent characters or deletes doubles. The automatic misspelling correction suggestion is calculated on the probability that a (corrected) term has a given wording, based on the frequency of that term in the ArXiv dataset.

In other cases, the similarity - using Jaro-Winkler above a certain threshold, in this case very high (see below for more details) - with the first Google answers gives good results. A voting system (ensemble) has been defined, which associates with each term (suggestion of correction) a degree of confidence. Table 4 reports the results for each step of the automatic correction tools and the final ensemble (in grey) accuracy values.

Table 4. Accuracy values for ML approach for misspelling correction

	Nearby Misspelling algorithm			Edit1 Misspelling algorithm		
Datasets	ArXiv & Papers1	ArXiv	Papers1	ArXiv & Papers1	ArXiv	Papers1
Presence as is	0.249	0.266	0.226	0.256	0.266	0.233
Autom. correction	0.794	0.723	0.863	0.822	0.741	0.906
Google first result	0.180	0.145	0.219	0.234	0.204	0.269
Ensemble	0.881	0.872	0.893	0.919	0.903	0.928

Due to the method used to introduce errors, the edit1 misspelling algorithm yields better results than those nearby.

4.5 Syntactic Similarity

The syntactic similarity between the two terms implies that these terms share many characters in common. Two strings have a very high similarity when they are virtually identical: it can be the same singular/plural tag or the presence of an extra or substituted letter. To calculate syntactic similarity, we used the Jaro-Winkler algorithm (using the Jellyfish python package) with a minimum similarity value. In this case, strings with a similarity greater than 0.84 were considered related and stored in a syntactic similarity matrix. For example, a web user interested in *"a_posteriori_error_analysis"* should also be suggested *"a_posteriori_error_estimators"*, *"a_posteriori_error_estimates"*, and *"a_posteriori_error_estimate"*, all with similarity values greater than 0.91. Figure 2 shows the syntactic similarity graph for *"a_posteriori_error_analysis"*.

4.6 Semantic Relatedness

The semantic relatedness has been used in two ways: firstly, the tags were clustered using Affinity Propagation, K-means, and Spectral clustering. These algorithms have been applied to the similarity matrices and/or directly to word2vec models, related to the terms (and their vectors) of the tags, using cosine similarity as criteria of similarity. K-means and hierarchical clustering algorithms require the number of clusters as input: therefore, the number of clusters obtained by the AP has been inserted in these cases. Different results are obtained with the two models in English. The number of terms in the model is 3099 and 3128 for the w2vec pre-trained wiki and ArXiv model, respectively. The clusters using the wiki model are 351, with an average number of terms of 8 tags per cluster, from as low as 1 tag per cluster up to 15. Using the ArXiv model, the number of clusters decreases to 335, from 2 up to a maximum of 52. These results lead to some considerations:

1. the different number of clusters and the elements of each cluster are related to the vectors representing the tags. The model trained on ArXiv (and on the same papers to which the tags are associated) is able to produce vectors that best represent the semantic content of the tag and its context;

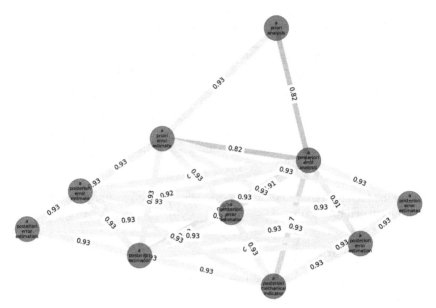

Fig. 2. Syntactic similarity graph for "*a_posteriori_error_analysis*"

2. since the ArXiv dataset contains sentences in Italian and English, which are the vast majority, some clusters are composed of tags in Italian only. These tags are not necessarily also semantically similar;
3. by choice, the number of clusters is defined by what is identified by AP. The various clustering algorithms produce different clusters, both in composition and number of elements. In the case of AP, the algorithm chooses an "exemplar" of the data as its centroid, and in the other cases, for each cluster, the element that is closest to its centroid is chosen.

The second use of semantic relatedness is the suggestion of tags to web users to allow them to continue their exploration according to content-based browsing.

For cosine similarity, similarity values of 0.5, 0.6, 0.7, 0,75,0.8, 0.85 and 0.90 were tested. In the end, 0.75 was chosen as a reasonable trade-off between a too low number of similar tags and the retrieval of elements that are not too closely related. The same value was adopted for both word2vec models. By analyzing the semantically related results, it can be seen that using the model trained on ArXiv, the similarities between the terms are more useful in the specific context. Figure 3 shows the tags most similar to a_posteriori_error_analysis using the pre-trained or ArXiv trained model, above and below respectively.

The experimental setup has been implemented in Python 3.7, using standard packages like Numpy, Matplotlib, Pandas and other more specific ones for processing of textual data such as NLTK, Treetagger, Gensim, Scikit-learn, jellyfish together with some experimental packages in GitHub.

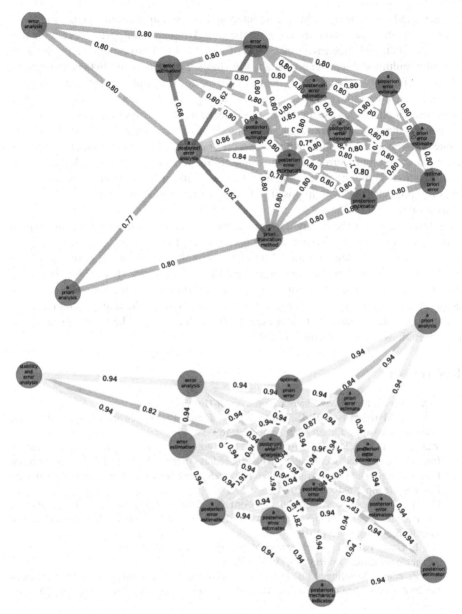

Fig. 3. Semantic relatedness graph for *a_posteriori_error_analysis*, pretrained or ArXiv trained model, above and below respectively

5   Conclusion and Future Works

We presented a new approach for automated management of multilingual tags associated with text or cards: namely supervised correction of misspelling and unsupervised syntactic and semantic relatedness computation. It aims to improve the quality of textual features and the search and browsing on the web. We plan to integrate these tools into web catalogs to enhance traditional ways of searching and browsing data on the web, and offer multimodal search and visualization tools. The work is still in the development phase. Preliminary qualitative results have proved to be useful to identify and suggest an automatic correction in misspellings and to organize and make tags more effective in the search phases: analyzing the results, according to our experience and sensibility, we can say that indeed proposing a search mode based on cluster results can be of great value to a web user, integrated with other more standard ones. Some issues have already emerged in automatic error detection, dataset creation to train the model, and cluster identification. There are cases, mainly when tags refer to very specific instances, e.g. ongoing projects, that it is impossible to automatically determine whether the tag is correct or not.

Clustering using the ArXiv dataset (which also contains some articles in Italian) automatically produces a division of the tags according to languages. The use of different word embedding models or a model trained on a multilingual dataset poses a problem when computing similarities between tags in different languages. This needs to be further investigated to evaluate the results and fully exploit them in the research phase. In addition, we intend to evaluate the results of these tools by conducting questionnaires on general users and researchers to understand if for both user types the results are adequate to expectations and by the content of the research.

References

1. ArXiv dataset. https://www.kaggle.com/Cornell-University/arxiv
2. Gali, N., Mariescu-Istodor, R., Hostettler, D., Fränti, P.: Framework for syntactic string similarity measures. Expert Syst. Appl. **129**, 169–185 (2019)
3. Wang, C., et al.: A learning-based approach for automatic construction of domain glossary from source code and documentation. In: Proceedings of the 2019 27th ACM Joint Meeting on European Software Engineering Conference and Symposium on the Foundations of Software Engineering, pp. 97–108 (2019)
4. Comito, C., Forestiero, A., Pizzuti, C.: Word embedding based clustering to detect topics in social media. In: Proceedings of the 2019 IEEE/WIC/ACM International Conference on Web Intelligence (WI). IEEE (2019)
5. Hu, J., et al.: Patent keyword extraction algorithm based on distributed representation for patent classification. Entropy **20**(2), 104 (2018)
6. Liu, Z., et al.: Clustering to find exemplar terms for keyphrase extraction. In: Proceedings of the 2009 Conference on Empirical Methods in Natural Language Processing, pp. 257–266 (2009)
7. Alrehamy, H.H., Walker, C.: SemCluster: unsupervised automatic keyphrase extraction using affinity propagation. In: Chao, F., Schockaert, S., Zhang, Q. (eds.) UKCI 2017. AISC, vol. 650, pp. 222–235. Springer, Cham (2018). https://doi.org/10.1007/978-3-319-66939-7_19
8. Schütze, H., Manning, C.D., Raghavan, P.: Introduction to information retrieval. Cambridge University Press, Cambridge (2008)
9. Jauhiainen, T., Lui, M., Zampieri, M., Baldwin, T., Lindén, K.: Automatic language identification in texts: a survey. J. Artif. Intell. Res. **65**, 675–782 (2019)
10. Fellbaum, C.: WordNet. In: Theory and Applications of Ontology: Computer Applications, pp. 231–243. Springer, Dordrecht (2010). https://doi.org/10.1007/978-90-481-8847-5_10

11. Mikolov, T., Sutskever, I., Chen, K., Corrado, G.S., Dean, J.: Distributed representations of words and phrases and their compositionality. In: Proceedings of the Advances in Neural Information Processing Systems, vol. 26, pp. 3111–3119 (2013)

12. Mikolov, T., Chen, K., Corrado, G., Dean, J., Sutskever, L., Zweig, G.: Tool for computing continuous distributed representations of words: word2vec. https://code.google.com/p/word2vec. Accessed 27 Mar 2020

13. Mohammed, N.: Extracting word synonyms from text using neural approaches. Int. Arab J. Inf. Technol. **17**(1), 45–51 (2020)

14. Aggarwal, C.C., Zhai, C.: A survey of text clustering algorithms In: Mining Text Data, pp. 77–128. Springer Boston, MA (2012). https://doi.org/10.1007/978-1-4614-3223-4_4

15. Frey, B.J., Dueck, D.: Clustering by passing messages between data points. Science **315**(5814), 972–976 (2007)

16. MacQueen, J.: Some methods for classification and analysis of multivariate observations. In: Proceedings of the Fifth Berkeley Symposium on Mathematical Statistics and Probability, vol. 1, no. 14, pp. 281–297 (1967)

An Augmented Reality Application for the Frescoes of the Basilica of Saint Catherine in Galatina

Valerio De Luca[1] , Laura Corchia[2] , Carola Gatto[2] , Giovanna Ilenia Paladini[1],
and Lucio Tommaso De Paolis[1(✉)]

[1] Department of Engineering for Innovation, University of Salento, Lecce, Italy
{valerio.deluca,ilenia.paladini,lucio.depaolis}@unisalento.it
[2] Department of Cultural Heritage, University of Salento, Lecce, Italy
{laura.corchia1,carola.gatto}@unisalento.it

Abstract. Recent developments in IT technologies have enabled new forms of enhancement and dissemination of cultural heritage. In particular, augmented reality is increasingly emerging as a valuable tool to enrich the visitor experience by providing contextually relevant information. This work presents a mobile augmented reality application developed to support the fruition of the Basilica of Saint Catherine in Galatina: it guides the user through eleven points of interest, where it is possible to frame portions of the frescoes with a tablet to access multimedia content that helps understand the story and meaning behind the images.

Experimental tests were conducted to evaluate the application: data collected through the questionnaires filled in by the users revealed a good level of usability and acceptance.

Keywords: Augmented reality · Digital storytelling · Mobile application · User experience

1 Introduction

In recent years, alongside the traditional forms of enjoyment of cultural heritage, tools linked to new technologies have emerged, capable of narrating a territory or an asset of historical-artistic interest in an increasingly innovative and interactive way. Augmented Reality (AR) is one of the most widely used technological tools in the field of education and dissemination as it enriches the reality surrounding the user with multimedia content without distancing him from it and allowing him to perceive it as dominant [1]. This happens thanks to a software that recognises the scene framed by a device and enriches it with virtual contents, giving the perception of a coexistence of real and multimedia elements, with which it is also possible to interact. If well designed, an application based on Augmented Reality is useful in overcoming the mistrust that the field of cultural heritage has towards new technologies because it is useful in conveying information related to a work of art or an archaeological artefact, fully satisfying the educational purpose that museums aim to pursue, transforming them from places of "collection" to places of "narration". This technology allows cultural heritage to be told to users in a completely new way, based on a communicative impact based on emotion and involvement, making it stimulating, immediate, intuitive and easily accessible through the use of mobile devices.

Museums and exhibitions can use four forms of storytelling [2]:

1. Outdoor guides and explorers, based on 3D models of situations and contexts that are no longer visible on site and designed for outdoor use; this type of application is also particularly useful for advancing reconstructive hypotheses in the field of Virtual Restoration [3];
2. Interpretative mediation, which add multimedia information to the work observed;
3. New forms of art and sculpture, as in the case of artist Jeff Koons who, in 2017, started a collaboration with Snapchat by building lenses inspired by some of his most famous works.
4. Virtual Exhibition, i.e., the creation and implementation of virtual exhibitions that merge with those in the real world the moment they are framed by a smartphone or tablet.

As highlighted in [4], Virtual and Augmented Reality technologies need to be accompanied by a solid storytelling that starts from the study of the cultural context for an appropriate design of the user experience. The exploitation of these technologies represents a new paradigm of innovation for storytelling needs. The physical presence of the visitor in cultural places, such as churches and museums, is certainly encouraged when this can be done in total safety, but it is necessary to prepare other tools of fruition, able to extend the museum space and intercept new targets.

This work focuses on the development of a mobile augmented reality application designed to accompany thematic tours of the frescoes inside the Basilica of Santa Caterina in Galatina [5], facilitating the understanding of the contents and telling the story behind them.

The rest of the paper is organised as follows: Sect. 2 reports a short survey on other augmented reality based applications for the promotion of cultural heritage; Sect. 3 introduces the Basilica of St Catherine of Alexandria in Galatina, which is the case study considered in this paper; Sect. 4 describes the development of the mobile AR application; Sect. 5 reports the experimental results on the use of the application; Sect. 6 briefly discusses the result of the work; Sect. 7 concludes the paper and hints at possible future developments.

2 Related Work

In recent years, there has been an increase in AR applications aimed at improving the experience of visitors to exhibitions, museums and cultural venues [6]. Already in 2009, the Museum of London was open to new technologies and proposed Streetmuseum, an app for iOS devices that exploited the user's geolocation to report points of interest in the city by clicking on the "3D View" button [7]. In Italy too, several tourism and museum projects have been developed which, by exploiting the potential of ICT (Information and Communication Technology), enhance the territory and the collections, making the visit more interesting and engaging. In Apulia, the application Puglia Reality +, in addition to returning points of interest with respect to the user's geographical location, provides various itineraries and makes available 350 audio and video guides [7]. In the archaeological field, several virtual reconstructions have been proposed for some ancient cities such as Egnathia, Herdonia, Canosa, Roca Vecchia and Faragola. Augmented Reality has also been used in the urban environment, with the aim of enhancing small villages and bringing to light some'little treasures'. This is the case in villages such as Ostuni, Gallipoli, Vieste, Polignano a Mare and Locorotondo, which, using this new technology, have organised treasure hunts in the alleys of their historic centres which, in addition to highlighting historical and artistic beauty, provide information on crafts, events and news. A mobile AR application [8], developed for the archaeological site of the "Castello di Alceste" Diffuse Museum in San Vito dei Normanni (Brindisi) and the early Christian complex of "Fondo Giuliano" (Vaste, Lecce), shows 3D models and other contextual information when an aerial photo is framed by a smartphone. Another application based on AR and aimed at the valorization of sites of archaeological interest is based on the superimposition of information on images taken from an aerial perspective with Unmanned Aerial Vehicles (UAV) [9].

In the field of art, the Città Ideale AR application inspired by the famous painting 'The Ideal City' (painted between 1470 and 1490 and housed in the Galleria Nazionale delle Marche in Urbino) allows users to view the work in HD, take a virtual tour of the rooms of the Ducal Palace and share the contents on the main social networks [10].

Contemporary art has also benefited from the contributions of new technologies, as in the case of the MAUA - Museum of Augmented Urban Art [11], a widespread museum present in Turin, Milan, Palermo and Waterford, whose exhibition includes a series of street art works that, once framed by the camera of mobile devices, come to life and turn into works of digital art.

Similarly, a mobile AR application, developed to facilitate the understanding of Leonardo Da Vinci's sketches, shows animated 3D models superimposed on the drawings framed by the camera of a smartphone [12].

A possibility for on-site exploration is provided by virtual portals, displayed by mobile mixed reality applications at specific points of interest, which allow the user to visit a virtually reconstructed past reality by simply walking through them [13]. A combination of virtual and mixed reality technologies [14] was adopted for an underground oil mill to overcome place accessibility issues and promote itineraries and rural heritage.

3   The Case Study: The Basilica of St Catherine of Alexandria in Galatina

3.1   Historical Background

The Basilica of Saint Catherine of Alexandria was built on the outskirts of the ancient centre of Galatina, a modest rural settlement that belonged to the county of Soleto and is located between Otranto and Gallipoli. Built at the behest of Raimondo (known as Raimondello) Orsini del Balzo between 1383–85 and 1391, together with the cloister and the adjacent hospital, the building is located in an area that, until then, had been of Greek observance and is configured as a temple of the Latin rite, whose officiating was entrusted to the Friars Minor [15]. The decision to dedicate the church to St Catherine of Alexandria was due to the fulfilment of a vow made by the patron on the tomb of the martyr. In fact, when he went to the monastery on Mount Sinai where the tomb is still located, he is said to have bitten off the finger of the saint and taken it to Galatina [16], where it is kept in a precious reliquary [17].

In 1385, Raimondello succeeded in obtaining the County of Lecce thanks to his marriage with Maria d'Enghien. Work had to continue until 1391, when Pope Boniface IX issued a bull entrusting the church and adjoining convent to the Observant Franciscans of the Vicariate of Bosnia. In that year, the basilica was probably completed, as expected from the date engraved on the architrave of the left portal.

After the death of the patron in 1406, Maria d'Enghien married King Ladislaus of Durazzo and became Queen of Naples. She did not return to her feuds until 1416 and commissioned the pictorial decoration of the building.

After this first construction and decorative phase, the work was continued by her son Giovanni Antonio, who built the polygonal choir covered by a ribbed vault.

In 1494 the church was entrusted to the Benedictines of the congregation of Santa Maria del Monte Oliveto and assumed the title of Royal Basilica. The Renaissance altars and furnishings sculpted by the artist Nuzzo Barba belong to this phase. At the end of the 16th century, the complex passed into the hands of the Reformed Fathers and, during the following century, the cloisters were decorated with frescoes by Friar Giuseppe da Gravina. Since 1992 the church has been a Pontifical Minor Basilica [18].

3.2 Exterior of the Basilica

The basilica of St Catherine of Alexandria stands on a pre-existing structure of Greek-Byzantine rite and today faces a small square named after Raimondello Orsini. The façade is divided vertically into three sections, with the central one almost twice as high as the lateral ones. The tricuspidate crowning is emphasised by a series of hanging arches and the presence of three acroters depicting the Cross (centre), St Paul the Apostle (left) and St Francis (right). The surface is divided horizontally by a string-course cornice that makes the lower order more projecting than the upper one. At the top, the curtain is illuminated by the central rose window with twelve rays converging towards a circular polychrome stained-glass window on which the coat of arms of the D'Anjou Durazzo and d'Enghien-Brienne families stands out, while at the bottom there are three access portals. The main portal, larger than the side ones, is characterised by a prothyrum resting on two columns supported by lions and surmounted by headless griffins. The three stone bands framing the portal are richly sculpted with anthropomorphic and zoomorphic figures, intertwined leaves and phytomorphic elements. On the architrave is a relief depicting Christ among the twelve apostles holding a scroll with the inscription 'Ego vos elegi ut eatis' (I have chosen you so that you may go). The lintel of the left minor portal bears an inscription with the date'1391' in Roman numerals: A.D. MCCCLXXXXI. On the left, however, there is an inscription which, due to abrasion caused by weathering and the passage of time, is hardly visible today. If the left side of the basilica is occupied by the conventual rooms and is characterised by the soaring geometric volume of the bell tower, the right side, flanked by what is now Via Cavour, allows a glimpse of the three-lobed hanging arches and, at the end of the road, the octagonal choir wanted by Giovanni Antonio to, as the scholar Antonio Antonaci says, give "a head to this stone giant" [19].

3.3 Interior of the Basilica

Internally, the church is characterized by its solemn longitudinal arrangement of the three naves, whose walls are entirely covered with frescoes. The nave, with three cross-vaulted bays, is higher than the side bays and is connected to them by three lowered pointed arches giving access to two vaulted ambulatories. Each of these spaces corresponds to a small central rose window that provides light to the rooms, but which, on the façade, is asymmetrical with respect to the cusps, a clear sign of interventions that have disrupted its appearance.

Along the wall of the right aisle is a small apse, probably belonging to the original chapel dedicated to the Virgin Mary, which was later incorporated into the new basilica.

The pictorial decoration covers all the wall surfaces: in the first bay of the nave, the walls host the cycle dedicated to the Apocalypse of John, while the vault is painted with the Virtues. In the second bay are frescoes depicting the Stories of Genesis, dominated at the top by the representation of the Seven Sacraments; the walls of the third bay contain stories from the Gospel, while the angelic hosts are painted at the top. The story of St Catherine of Alexandria is narrated in the presbytery, dominated by the figures of the Evangelists and Doctors of the Church.

According to the most recent studies, the frescoes were painted by three main personalities who were probably each the head of a workshop: the stories of St. Catherine of Alexandria, the figures at the top, the angelic hosts and the scenes depicting the Seven Sacraments were painted by a master with an elegant style; the one who painted the stories from the Gospel appears to be more expressive. Both are clearly influenced by the Veneto and Padua in particular [20]. Finally, there is a third painter in the first span who seems to be familiar with Neapolitan painting and, in particular, with the two panels now in Stuttgart and inspired by Giotto's cycle in Santa Chiara in Naples [16].

Local craftsmen are active in the cycle in the side aisle, depicting the Life of Mary and Childhood of Christ. This part of the pictorial decoration must have been carried out between 1415 and 1425, as attested by the coats of arms painted on the vault. The painter of these stories appears to be more inclined towards anecdotal narration, as shown by the rich depictions of interiors that linger on small details and represent an important repertoire of customs, clothing, landscapes, domestic interiors, animals and plants.

Finally, in the low portions of the wall there is a succession of figures of saints that would date back to the earliest phase of the pictorial decoration, carried out at the time when the construction of the church was completed (1391).

4 Development of the Mobile Application

4.1 Objectives

The development of a mobile application was born from the need to provide a tool that can complement the traditional guided tour and enrich the cultural offer through thematic routes based on a compelling storytelling that can facilitate the reading of the valuable pictorial cycles. The application is based on Augmented Reality [21], a technology that allows multimedia content to be conveyed easily, intuitively and at relatively low cost because it uses users' mobile devices with no need for additional hardware.

4.2 Data Collection

At the same time as assessing the technology, it was necessary to carry out an in-depth bibliographic and archive study in order to identify the most interesting pictorial parts within the fresco cycles. The aim of the research was to delve into the history of the building and its patrons and to understand the iconographic significance of the cycles in order to select the pictorial portions to be included in the itinerary. The choice of the scenes to be rendered in Augmented Reality was therefore based on the historical-critical solidity of the contents to be conveyed, on their coherence within the itinerary and, finally, on certain technical requirements necessary for the application to function correctly (height of the paintings to be framed by the camera of the devices, correct and adequate lighting of the rooms, absence of light reflections that could in fact prevent correct recognition of the frescoes).

4.3 Content Choice, Creation and Implementation

The pictorial cycles on the walls of the Basilica of Saint Catherine of Alexandria are characterised by the extreme heterogeneity of the contents narrated and the presence of several workshops that executed them. They are still studied by scholars and art historians today. Because of this, the choice of the pictorial portions to be included in the itinerary, taking into account the technical requirements already mentioned, was aimed at selecting some of the most emblematic narrative episodes, highlighting historical, executive and stylistic peculiarities little known to most visitors. Once inside the church, the user is guided through eleven points of interest located in the main nave and the right-side aisle. The audio guide is impersonated by Pietro Cavoti (1819–1890), an artist from Galatina who spent years studying the Basilica, making many pencil and watercolor studies, sometimes accompanied by interesting stylistic notes, preserved at the Civic Museum Cavoti and useful to better frame his artistic activity. Some of the artist's notes, drawings and watercolours acquired photographically were included in an introductory video which can be viewed at point 1.

After a bibliographical and archival research, the work proceeded with the graphic design of the logo and user interface, taking into account the usability and target characteristics of the final product and aiming at an immediate comprehension by the user.

The design of the user interface has been oriented towards the principles of effectiveness, efficiency and simplicity of use by even inexperienced users. A homepage gives access to a screen containing instructions and shows the plan of the building and the clickable points of interest while the user can continue navigating in the scene (Fig. 1). Every time the visitor gets in front of the chosen point of interest, he selects it and accesses a preview screen that shows him which fresco to frame through a photographic reproduction, the title of the work and information about the cycle to which it belongs

(Fig. 2). The camera-shaped button at the bottom right gives access to the AR scenes: the visitor frames the fresco and sees a series of icons appear on his device that allow him to listen to the audio guide or to enjoy other multimedia content (for example, virtual restoration hypotheses or the sound of some of the medieval instruments depicted in the cycles).

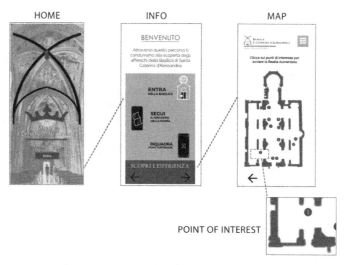

Fig. 1. Application interface: Home, Info and Map sheets

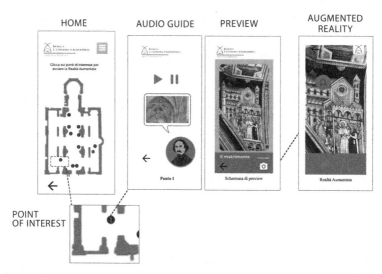

Fig. 2. Application interface: Home, Audio Guide, Preview and Augmented Reality sheets

As already mentioned, the itinerary is divided into eleven points: at point 1, Pietro Cavoti's narrative voice welcomes the visitor, tells him about his activity inside the

Basilica and invites him to continue the tour. Point 2 concerns the noble coats of arms placed on the counter-façade, an opportunity to narrate the history of the patronage. Point 3 corresponds to the 'Chastisement of Babylon' scene on the counter façade, in which the cycle of paintings to which it belongs, the 'Apocalypse of John', is described. Point 4 shows the 'Construction of the Tower of Babel', an opportunity to describe the workings of a medieval building site. The tour continues at point 5 where the 'End of the Flood' is depicted and here Cavoti's narrative focuses on the anecdotal description of bloated bodies floating in the water. Point 6, located on the cross vault of the second bay, bears the "Marriage" scene, an opportunity to return to the story of the patrons and to tell of the union between Maria d'Enghien and Ladislaus of Durazzo. At point 7, the 'Baptism of Christ', the guide reveals a little-known detail to the visitor: the young man in green clothes painted in the scene is, according to the critics, Giovanni Antonio del Balzo Orsini. Point 8, with the 'Resurrection of Lazarus' and, further down, the 'Judgement of Pilate', offer the opportunity to describe the grotesque style of the painter and to propose a hypothesis of virtual restoration aimed at reconstructing some lost pictorial parts. Point 9, located in the third bay of the main nave, features a sinopia depicting the 'Ascent to Calvary', an opportunity for Cavoti to illustrate how a fresco was created in medieval times. The last two points of interest are located in the Orsini Chapel (right aisle): "The Coronation of the Virgin" (point 10) allows the user to access a section of the application in which it is possible to listen to the sound of some medieval musical instruments; "The Birth of Mary" (point 11) reveals some anecdotal details related to the narration and iconography.

The application also has a drop-down menu in the scene showing the plan of the Basilica (Fig. 3), which allows access to some textual details (Historical notes, Painting cycles, Museum and Credits).

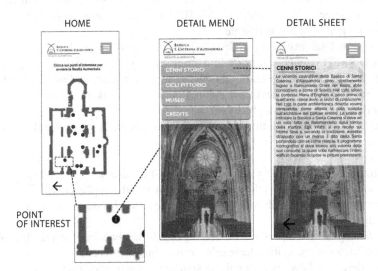

Fig. 3. Application interface: Home, Detail Menu and Detail sheets

4.4 Implementation and Technological Details

The first step towards the conception and development of the application consisted in several inspections inside the Basilica of St Catherine of Alexandria in order to assess the position of the frescoes and the lighting conditions. The photographic material used to perform the preliminary tests and the subsequent implementation was acquired with a FujiFilm X-T20 mirrorless digital camera and an iPhone 11 Pro. A post-production process was carried out on the frames using Photoshop to improve the quality of the images by increasing chromatic contrast and reducing their weight within the maximum limit of 2 MB imposed by Vuforia [22], the software development kit (SDK) that allows the recognition of images in real time and the correct positioning of multimedia elements in the framing space. The 2018 4.12f1 version of the Unity game engine [23] was adopted as the development environment.

5 Experimental Tests

The test of the application involved 41 users aged between 23 and 77 (31.7% male and 68.3% female) who were asked to fill in a questionnaire about their impressions of the experience. The questionnaire was composed by combining items from NASA-TLX [24], SUS [25] and UEQ [26] standard questionnaires.

The NASA Task Load Index (NASA-TLX) [24] is made up of 6 items dealing with the workload experienced by the user when performing a task. *Physical demand* and *temporal demand* were discarded, as the use of the application does not require any particular physical activity and tasks have no time constraints. On the other hand, *mental demand*, *performance* (the ability to complete tasks), *effort* (how hard the user had to work to achieve a certain level of performance) and *frustration* were included in the overall questionnaire. For each NASA-TLX item, users were requested to express their opinion on a 7-point Likert scale.

The System Usability Scale (SUS) [25] consists of 10 items that can be grouped in two factors [27], namely *usability* in a strict sense and *learnability*, i.e., the ability of quickly and independently learning how to use the application. For each SUS item, users were requested to express their opinion on a 5-point Likert scale ranging from 1 (Strongly disagree) to 5 (Strongly agree).

The User Experience Questionnaire (UEQ) is made up of 26 items, rated on a 7-point Likert scale, that can be grouped into 6 components [26]:

- *Attractiveness*, which is the general impression of the users;
- *Efficiency*, which represents the ability to quickly use the application;
- *Perspicuity*, which describes how quickly the user becomes familiar with the application;
- *Dependability*, which represents the feeling of effectively controlling the interaction;
- *Stimulation*, which describes the user's motivation and interest;
- *Novelty*, describes how appealing the design of the application is perceived.

Table 1 shows the mean values, standard deviations and coefficients of variation of the factor scores of the three questionnaires considered in this study.

Table 1. Mean values, standard deviation and coefficient of variations of the scores of mental demand, usability and user experience factors.

Questionnaire	Factor	Mean	Standard deviation	Coefficient of variation
NASA-TLX	Mental demand	3,415	2,085	0,611
	Performance	4,122	2,410	0,585
	Effort	1,951	1,516	0,777
	Frustration	0,561	1,184	2,111
SUS	Learnability	3,134	0,949	0,303
	Usability	3,479	0,449	0,129
UEQ	Attractiveness	5,618	0,718	0,128
	Perspicuity	5,390	0,762	0,141
	Efficiency	5,366	0,872	0,162
	Dependability	5,098	0,827	0,177
	Stimulation	5,610	0,740	0,132
	Novelty	5,390	0,835	0,155

The scores of NASA-TLX items and of UEQ components are expressed on a 0–6 scale, while the scores of SUS factors are expressed on a 0–4 scale.

The coefficients of variation (i.e., the ratios between standard deviations and mean values) give an indication of the level of variability of the scores.

The density ridgeline plots in Fig. 4 represent the density estimates obtained for the factors of the NASA-TLX, SUS and UEQ questionnaires. Among NASA-TLX items, *performance* is the highest scoring item, as suggested by the waveform promontory near score 6. The *mental demand* waveform does not exhibit any particularly evident hump, suggesting that there is no clear dominance of a particular score. The high coefficient of variation also suggests great variability between *mental demand* scores. *Effort* also has a fairly wide variability, but it only includes values between 0 and 3, leaving out the higher values. The *frustration* waveform has a single very high promontory around a value just above 0, which denotes a low level of frustration for almost all the users. Nevertheless, *frustration* has the highest coefficient of variation, which makes the range of variability quite wide in relation to the mean of the scores for this factor.

The *usability* and *learnability* waveforms partially reflect the weak correlation that is typically expected between the two SUS factors, even though the density wave of learnability suggests a higher variability in users' opinions, confirmed by the higher coefficient of variation. In particular, while *usability* has a single fairly pronounced peak just below the maximum score of 4, the trend of the *learnability* waveform is more undulatory and presents in particular two medium-pronounced humps around scores 3 and 4, suggesting the presence of two possible clusters in the users' opinions regarding this aspect. This is probably due to a different level of familiarity and prior experience that various users had with information technology.

The six user experience factors, assessed with the UEQ questionnaire, earned rather high average scores (greater than 5 on a scale of 0 to 6). In particular, the highest scores are those of *attractiveness* and *stimulation*, while the lowest is that of dependability. In general, the *dependability* waveform is devoid of any particular peaks and lies in a wider range that includes values even below 5, while all the other waveforms have a more or less pronounced peak just below 6. In particular, similar waveforms suggest a correlation between *attractiveness* and *stimulation*: motivation and interest thus seem

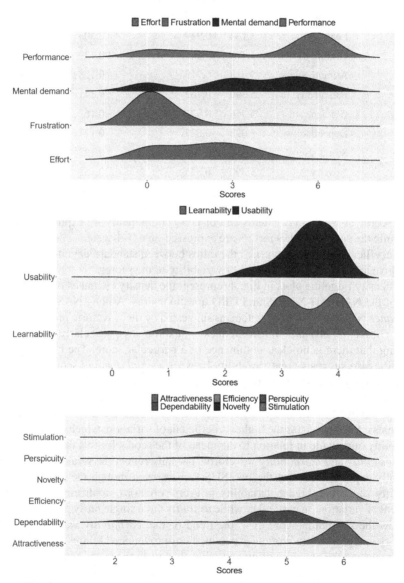

Fig. 4. Distribution of the scores for the NASA-TLX, SUS and UEQ factors

to be the factors that most influence the overall impression of the user. Any problems (albeit minor) that some users may have had in controlling the interaction (suggested by the slightly lower *dependability* scores) do not seem to have negatively influenced the interest and extremely positive opinions towards the application, probably because the fascination of augmented reality prevailed over some slight difficulties.

6   Discussion

The present research was carried out thanks to the contribution of different skills. Its objective was to provide an innovative tool to narrate the history of the Basilica and to describe its remarkable decorative cycles. The considered path is only one example of the countless thematic approaches that could be proposed to tell the visitor about a multifaceted monument. Therefore, its implementation should be considered as a starting point, capable of welcoming new thematic paths and different narrative ideas. From the very first approach, the work has tried to convey the idea of an open book on the history and peculiarities of an architectural work which contains a treasure chest of historical, stylistic and anecdotal information. The visitor can draw on it with both hands, personalising his experience and enriching it with information on all aspects of the pictorial cycles. Each painted scene is a story within a story, a book whose pages tell of the customs, lifestyles and spirituality of people who seem so far removed from our time but who still have much to tell.

7   Conclusions and Future Work

An augmented reality application was presented, developed to accompany visitors in their discovery of the frescoes in the Basilica of Santa Caterina, facilitating the understanding and interpretation of the pictorial cycles and telling the story behind them.

The experimental tests showed a good level of usability of the application and good performance in the user experience also in terms of mental load.

As a future development of the application, in addition to enriching the path with new points of interest, the possibility of adding gamification elements will be considered. Finally, a further test scenario could evaluate the effectiveness of the application in educational terms.

References

1. Bimber, O., Raskar, R.: Spatial Augmented Reality: Merging Real and Virtual Worlds. A K Peters/CRC Press (2005)
2. Solima, L.: Management per l'impresa culturale. Studi superiori (Carocci editore).: Economia, Carocci (2018)
3. Limoncelli, M., Schepis, L., Germinario, C., Metcalf, G.: Virtual Restoration 1. Paintings and Mosaics. L'Erma di Bretschneider (2017)

4. Gatto, C., D'Errico, G., Paladini, G.I., De Paolis, L.T.: Virtual reality in Italian museums: a brief discussion. In: De Paolis, L.T., Arpaia, P., Bourdot, P. (eds.) AVR 2021. LNCS, vol. 12980, pp. 306–314. Springer, Cham (2021). https://doi.org/10.1007/978-3-030-87595-4_22

5. Cisternino, D., et al.: Augmented reality applications to support the promotion of cultural heritage. J. Comput. Cult. Heritage **14**(4), 1–30 (2021)

6. Bekele, M.K., Pierdicca, R., Frontoni, E., Malinverni, E.S., Gain, J.: A survey of augmented, virtual, and mixed reality for cultural heritage. J. Comput. Cult. Heritage **11**(2), 1–36 (2018)

7. Bonacini, E.: La realtà aumentata e le app culturali in Italia: storie da un matrimonio in mobilità/Augmented reality and cultural apps in Italy: stories on a marriage in mobility. IL CAPITALE CULTURALE. Studies on the Value of Cultural Heritage **0**(9), 89–121 (2014). http://riviste.unimc.it/index.php/cap-cult/article/view/740

8. Cisternino, D., Gatto, C., De Paolis, L.T.: Augmented reality for the enhancement of Apulian archaeological areas. In: De Paolis, L.T., Bourdot, P. (eds.) AVR 2018. LNCS, vol. 10851, pp. 370–382. Springer, Cham (2018). https://doi.org/10.1007/978-3-319-95282-6_27

9. Botrugno, M.C., D'Errico, G., De Paolis, L.T.: Augmented reality and UAVs in archaeology: development of a location-based AR application. In: De Paolis, L.T., Bourdot, P., Mongelli, A. (eds.) AVR 2017. LNCS, vol. 10325, pp. 261–270. Springer, Cham (2017). https://doi.org/10.1007/978-3-319-60928-7_23

10. Quattrini, R., Pierdicca, R., Frontoni, E., Clini, P.: Mobile e realtà aumentata al Palazzo Ducale di Urbino: il Museo è digitale. Archeomatica **6**(1) (2015)

11. MAUA Museum: (2021). https://mauamuseum.com/

12. De Paolis, L.T., De Luca, V., D'Errico, G.: Augmented reality to understand the Leonardo's machines. In: De Paolis, L.T., Bourdot, P. (eds.) AVR 2018. LNCS, vol. 10851, pp. 320–331. Springer, Cham (2018). https://doi.org/10.1007/978-3-319-95282-6_24

13. Cisternino, D., et al.: Virtual portals for a smart fruition of historical and archaeological contexts. In: De Paolis, L.T., Bourdot, P. (eds.) AVR 2019. LNCS, vol. 11614, pp. 264–273. Springer, Cham (2019). https://doi.org/10.1007/978-3-030-25999-0_23

14. De Paolis, L.T., Chiarello, S., D'Errico, G., Gatto, C., Nuzzo, B.L., Sumerano, G.: Mobile extended reality for the enhancement of an underground oil mill: a preliminary discussion. In: De Paolis, L.T., Arpaia, P., Bourdot, P. (eds.) AVR 2021. LNCS, vol. 12980, pp. 326–335. Springer, Cham (2021). https://doi.org/10.1007/978-3-030-87595-4_24

15. Massaro, C.: Economia e società in una "quasi città" del Mezzogiorno tardomedievale: San Pietro in Galatina. VETERE - CASSIANO (2006)

16. Casciaro, R.: La Basilica di Santa Caterina d'Alessandria in Galatina. Mario Congedo Editore, Galatina. English and Italian edition (2019)

17. Specchia, D.: Basilica di Santa Caterina d'Alessandria - Galatina (Le). Il Tesoro: problematiche storiche religiose artistiche. Editrice Salentina, Galatina (2001)

18. Russo, F.: La parola si fa immagine. Storia e restauro della basilica di S. Caterina a Galatina. Marsilio (2005)

19. Antonaci, A.: Galatina storia & Arte. Panico (1999)

20. Cuciniello, A.: D'agli intendenti ammirata. La decorazione pittorica. Ortese, S. (2014)

21. Azuma, R.T.: A survey of augmented reality. Presence Teleop. Virt. **6**(4), 355–385 (1997)

22. PTC: Vuforia (2021). ptc.com/en/products/vuforia

23. Unity Technologies: Unity (2021). https://unity.com/

24. Nasa, N.A., Administration, S.: NASA TLX: Task Load Index. Planta Medica (2010)

25. Brooke, J.: SUS - A quick and dirty usability scale (1996)

26. Laugwitz, B., Held, T., Schrepp, M.: Construction and evaluation of a user experience questionnaire. In: Holzinger, A. (ed.) USAB 2008. LNCS, vol. 5298, pp. 63–76. Springer, Heidelberg (2008). https://doi.org/10.1007/978-3-540-89350-9_6

27. Lewis, J.R., Sauro, J.: The factor structure of the system usability scale. In: Kurosu, M. (ed.) Human Centered Design. Lecture Notes in Computer Science, pp. 94–103. Springer, Berlin, Heidelberg (2009)

Ancient Egyptian Hieroglyphs Segmentation and Classification with Convolutional Neural Networks

Andrea Barucci[1]([✉]) [iD], Chiara Canfailla[1,2], Costanza Cucci[1] [iD], Matteo Forasassi[2], Massimiliano Franci[3], Guido Guarducci[3], Tommaso Guidi[1,2], Marco Loschiavo[2], Marcello Picollo[1] [iD], Roberto Pini[1] [iD], Lorenzo Python[2], Stefano Valentini[3], and Fabrizio Argenti[2] [iD]

[1] Institute of Applied Physics "Nello Carrara", IFAC-CNR, Via Madonna del Piano, Sesto Fiorentino, 10 – 50019 Florence, Italy
a.barucci@ifac.cnr.it
[2] Department of Information Engineering, University of Florence, Via di Santa Marta, 3 – 50139 Florence, Italy
[3] Center for Ancient Mediterranean and Near Eastern Studies, CAMNES, Via del Giglio, 15 – 50123 Florence, Italy

Abstract. Deep Learning is expanding in every domain of knowledge, allowing specialists to build tools to support their work in fields apparently unrelated to information technology. In this study, we exploit this opportunity by focusing on ancient Egyptian hieroglyphic texts and inscriptions. We investigate the ability of several convolutional neural networks (CNNs) to segment glyphs and classify images of ancient Egyptian hieroglyphs derived from various image datasets. Three well-known CNN architectures (ResNet-50, Inception-v3, and Xception) were considered for classification and trained on the supplied pictures using both the transfer learning and training from scratch paradigms. Furthermore, we constructed a specifically devoted CNN, termed Glyphnet, by changing the architecture of one of the prior networks and customizing its complexity to our classification goal. The suggested Glyphnet outperformed the others in terms of performance, ease of training, and computational savings, as judged by established measures. The ancient hieroglyphs segmentation was faced in parallel, using a deep neural network architecture known as Mask-RCNN. This network was trained to segment the glyphs, identifying the bounding box, which will be the input to a network for classification. Even though we focus here on single hieroglyph segmentation and classification tasks, the application of Deep Learning techniques in the Egyptological field opens up new and beneficial opportunities. In this light, the proposed work can be viewed as a jumping-off point for much more complex goals such as hieroglyphic sign coding, recognition, and transliteration; toposyntax of hieroglyphic signs combined to form words; linguistics analysis of hieroglyphic texts; recognition of corrupt, rewritten, and erased signs, and even identification of the scribe's "hand" or sculptor's school. This work shows how the ancient Egyptian hieroglyphs identification task can be supported by the Deep.
Learning paradigm, laying the foundation for developing novel information tools for automatic documents recognition, classification and, most importantly, the language translation task.

R. Furferi et al. (Eds.): Florence Heri-Tech 2022, CCIS 1645, pp. 126–139, 2022.
https://doi.org/10.1007/978-3-031-20302-2_10

Keywords: Deep learning · Convolutional neural networks · Image recognition and classification · Ancient Egyptian hieroglyphs · Cultural heritage

1 Introduction

Artificial Intelligence (AI) applications are getting more and more popular in a wide range of fields [1], from fundamental physics to natural language processing and health, with significant implications for our daily lives [2–8], despite some concerns (for example related to privacy or algorithm fairness, explainability, accountability and trustworthiness) associated to its use have been raising [9–11].

Even though AI's true role has yet to be thoroughly researched and understood, it is beginning to pervade fields such as Cultural Heritage [12, 13], archaeology [14, 15], philology [16, 17] and human sciences [18], very different from the "hard science" where these applications were born and first applied.

Actually, nowadays, scientific literature begins to show the diffusion of applications of this new technologies to the classification of ideograms belonging to ancient or no more used languages. In [19, 20], for example, the KuroNet network, based on a Unet architecture, is proposed to recognize the old Kuzushiji Japanese writing style, while in [21], autoencoders are used to characterize local regions of complex shapes and are applied to indexing a collection of hieroglyphs from the ancient Maya civilization.

In this work we address the problem of ancient Egyptian hieroglyphs recognition and classification, taking advantage of the results in the field of patterns recognition, where such AI methods have strong and deep roots.

The classification task we focused on is that of single hieroglyph identification, starting from three well-known CNNs and testing them on a specifically built dataset, either by using the transfer learning paradigm or by training from scratch. Inspired by the architecture of one of the previous networks, a new CNN - referred to in the following as Glyphnet - specifically tailored to the complexity of the classification problem at hand, was also developed. Experimental classification tests were performed to compare the classical CNNs and the new proposed one, showing extremely good results in terms of classification rates, with Glyphnet outperforming the other tested CNNs. Furthermore, promising results were achieved from the implementation of a different deep learning architecture, known as Fully Convolutional Network (FCNs), able to obtain the segmentation of any single hieroglyph in a picture [22–26].

In our opinion, time has come to trace the path of AI applications in the fields of Cultural Heritage and Archaeology, not forgetting that the major ambition of AI is not only automating human tasks, but also improving human understanding.

2 The Egyptian Hieroglyphic Writing System

According to the Sausserian definition, the Egyptian word is a linguistic sign with a signifier and a signified [27]. The first component is a graphic representation of the external aspect, which can be made up of one or several hieroglyphics. The second is the internal structure, which is primarily linguistics. A semagram (or ideogram) and a phonogram make up an Egyptian hieroglyph, which is a complicated sign made up of these two parts. A semagram is a graphic symbol that represents a relationship with an idea. A semagram can have two different values, depending on its function in the word: the proper semagram, which means the represented object indicating directly a word, and the determinative, a sign with a purely semantic and no phonetic value, whose function is to express the lexical field to which the word belongs. The "phonogram" can also play two roles: the proper phonogram, which only indicates the phonetic value of the sign and metaphonically the sound (or phonetic sequence); and the phonetic complement, which is a specific set of signs that expresses the sound of the sign to which they are accompanied in a redundant way Fig. 1.

Hieroglyphs are represented by a vast range of ideograms, which are composed to give words and sounds and are generally divisible into around 26 categories [28]. They might be written in a many of styles, including monumental or cursive, and on a variety of materials, including papyrus, wood, and stones. A civilisation that lasted nearly 5000 years has left a significant number of papers that must still be acquired, translated, and interpreted. This is where AI comes into play, assisting in the classification and translation of ideograms. Given its complexity, the hieroglyphic symbol shows to be an ideal candidate for applying a deep learning method to recognition and classification.

2.1 The AI - Egyptian Hieroglyphs Connection

The field of investigation at the intersection between deep learning and the ancient egyptian hieroglyphs writing system can be clearly fruitful from different points of view, ranging from Egyptology to computer science, neural networking engineering, computational analysis. Given the complexity of the Egyptian language in all its components, integrating the AI tools for its analysis is of paramount importance. The advantages of such an analysis can be numerous also for the Egyptian philology, both at the synchronic and diachronic level [27]: the graphemic evolutions and hieroglyphics palaeography, the recognition of variants, the calculation of the logographic, syllabic and alphabetic percentage of hieroglyphic writing system, to name a few.

2.2 State of the Art

The subject of ancient Egyptian language retrieval and categorization has been tackled in numerous publications, each with a distinct objective. Image descriptors and image matching algorithms were developed at [29] to classify a database of over 4000 hieroglyphs [30]. Computer vision algorithms are employed in [31] to identify hieroglyphs in pieces of Egyptian cartouches with the goal of designing a museum navigation system. In [32], computer vision approaches for hieroglyph recognition are also applied. The study in [33] proposes a text information retrieval system that is meant to operate with Egyptian hieroglyphic manuscripts. In addition, [34, 35] propose the identification and transliteration of the signs. The Google team [36, 37] has recently shown interest in the field of hieroglyphics recognition.

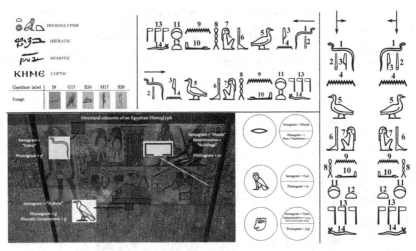

Fig. 1. The writing systems of ancient Egypt. Top left: ancient Egyptian script systems and Gardiner signs list examples. Middle and Right: writing systems directions. Bottom panels: the structural elements of hieroglyphs.

3   Architectures for Hieroglyph Classification

3.1   Architectures for Image Classification

Three classical CNNs - ResNet [38], Inception-v3 [39], Xception [40] - developed for image classification were used in our experimental tests (Table 1).

Table 1. CNNs architectures for hieroglyph classification.

Architecture	Parameters	Image input-size
Resnet50	∼ 25.6 million	224 × 224
Xception	∼ 23.8 million	299 × 299
InceptionV3	∼ 22.9 million	299 × 299
Glyphnet	∼ 499.000	100 × 100

3.2   Glyphnet

Glyphnet [41] was inspired by the networks discussed previously. The core idea is that by focusing on and customizing the network to the specific aim of hieroglyph recognition, the complexity and overfitting issues can be solved without losing performance.

Glyphnet Architecture. The separable convolutional layers, which are also present in the Xception network, provide the foundation of our model. The network's overall structure is divided into six blocks, as shown in the Fig. 2.

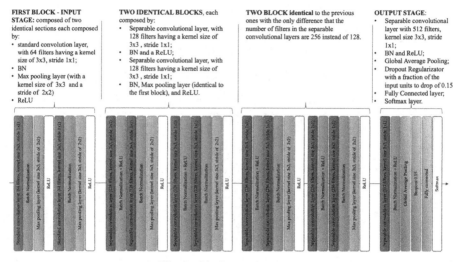

Fig. 2. Glyphnet architecture

The input image dimensions have been chosen to 100×100 pixels, which is a sufficiently compact size that allows humans to easily detect the features of the hieroglyphic while reducing the computational burden without impacting classification results. Moreover, thanks to a reduced number of filters and layers compared to the architectures described in Sect. 3.1, Glyphnet has a much lower number of parameters (Table 1). Glyphnet hyperparameters optimization details can be found in [41], while the model is available in the public repository [42].

3.3   Transfer Learning

In this study pre-trained models described in Sects. 3.1 were employed, leveraging on the textittransfer learning [43] paradigm. The the last output layers were replaced with new fully connected layers and trained using our dataset, utilizing most of the bottom layers

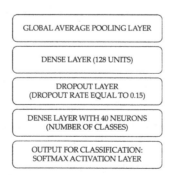

Fig. 3. Top layers applied to the ResNet50

of the original architectures with frozen weights. An example of the new top layers used for ResNet50 is shown in Fig. 3.

The InceptionV3 and Xception networks employed similar layers with minor differences. In the following part, the results of transfer learning will be given for comparison.

3.4 Classification Results

Image Datasets for Classification. Two separate image datasets were employed in the classification investigation, referred to as D_1 and D_2 respectively. The first is publicly accessible [29] and contains labelled photos of Egyptian hieroglyphs discovered in the Pyramid of Unas, while the second comprises photographs chosen and labelled by the authors, representing hieroglyphs on various supports. The hieroglyphs in the photos are labeled using the Gardiner sign list [28].

Original Datasets. The first dataset [29], D_1, contains 4310 grayscale images of hieroglyphs collected from photos of the walls within the pyramid of Unas [44]. Each graphic is 75×50 pixels in size and represents a single hieroglyph. There are 172 different hieroglyphs included in this dataset.

The second dataset, D_2, consists of 1310 tagged color (RGB format) images of varied dimensions, each representing a single element from one of 48 potential hieroglyphs. These photos, unlike those in the first collection, come from a variety of texts, written by a variety of hands and systems (sculpted, drawn, etc.) and spanning different periods of Egyptian history.

This choice improves the recognition's generalizability. The photos in the D_2 dataset were treated to uniform their dimensions, and the color information was transformed to grayscale for consistency with the D_1 dataset.

Because images were cut from scanned photos, producing an irregular con- tour, the final image were obtained by filling its rectangular bounding box with a white background. To produce a consistent format, each image was inscribed into a square without changing the aspect ratio of the original data; after that, the fake white background was removed and replaced with a pseudorandom Gaussian texture that matched the original background around the hieroglyph. The photographs were eventually resized to a size of 100×100 pixels. Details of the preprocessing procedure described above can be found in [41].

Merged Dataset. The images in D_1 appear to be pretty uniform since they share the same physical support, whereas the images in D_2 are obtained from various supports (papyrus, stone, wood) and appear to be rather dissimilar. Machine learning methods require heterogeneous datasets to attain high generalization capacity. As a result, the original D_1 and D_2 datasets were merged into a single dataset, which will be referred to as D from now on.

The combined dataset contains only images from classes (i.e. hieroglyphs) in both datasets. After this process, the final dataset D consisted of 4309 photos divided into 40 classes. The photos in the $D1$ dataset were enlarged to 75×75 pixels (with some background) before being magnified to 100×100 pixels. At the end, however, the dataset D results quite unbalanced.

Data Augmentation and Dataset Balancing. In order to train a deep learning model, a dataset must be partitioned into training, validation, and test subsets; in our study, the distribution of the full dataset into these subsets was 70%, 15%, and 15%, in that order. Data augmentation was performed on the training data in order to mitigate the unbalanced dataset issue while also seeking to improve the CNN's performance and lessen the overfitting problem [45]. New items were then added to poorly populated classes, whereas images from classes with an excessive amount of instances were removed.

We employed random translation (maximum 10 pixels) in both the horizontal and vertical axes, as well as modest random rotations ($pm10$ degrees) and random zooming (factor from 0.95 to 1.05). After that, because hieroglyphs can be orientated left or right (without changing their meaning), augmentation included horizontal flipping as well. Finally, the maximum number of training images in a class is set to two times the average number of images per label. The total number of images in the training set is 3014, which increases to 3670 after data augmentation and downsampling, and 7340 after flipping.

Classification Results. All of the networks' performance was calculated using the dataset D, with data augmentation applied to the training set. The computation times were also compared for both training and prediction.

Tables 2 reports the performance metrics when either training from scratch or transfer learning were used. Results show that the standard networks works better when trained from scratch. Moreover, Glyphnet yields, with reference to all the metrics, the best performance.

Table 2. Networks performance.

	Training from scratch				Transfer learning architecture			
	Accuracy	Precision	Recall	F1-Score	Accuracy	Precision	Recall	F1-Score
Resnet50	0.945	0.919	0.905	0.903	0.906	0.882	0.825	0.840
Xception	0.956	0.919	0.930	0.919	0.834	0.715	0.720	0.703
InceptionV3	0.948	0.917	0.904	0.900	0.864	0.730	0.737	0.717
Glyphnet	**0.976**	**0.975**	**0.965**	**0.968**				

A deeper discussion about robustness test (based on stratified 5-fold cross-validation), influence of data augmentation and computational time can be found in [41]. An example of the output of the different layers in Glyphnet during the hieroglyph classification is shown in Fig. 4.

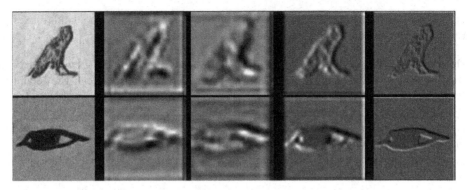

Fig. 4. An example of the output of different layers in Glyphnet.

4 Hieroglyph Segmentation

4.1 Architectures for Hieroglyph Segmentation

Besides to the recognition of a single hieroglyph, we focused also on identifying Deep
Learning algorithms able to perform instance segmentation of the hieroglyphs in a picture. For this purpose, we used the Mask R-CNN structure [22] by the Detectron2
platform [25, 46], developed by the Facebook AI Research Group. Mask R-CNN is an
extension of an already existing structure built for classification tasks, Faster R-CNN
[23], that integrates CNN based classification algorithms with a Region Proposal Network (RPN), also based on convolution and responsible for detecting regions of the
image that are likely to contain an object of interest (Regions of Interest, RoI). Faster
R-CNN is composed by two modules working as a single net. The first one is the RPN,
which basically is an FCN that returns the RoIs as bounding-boxes as well as, for each
of them, an "objectiveness score", i.e., an index related to the confidence of finding
an object in that window. The second module operates on each detected RoI and is in
charge of refining the final bounding-box and assigning the actual classification score. It's
important to underline that finding bounding-boxes and providing classification scores
are the outputs of two parallel branches and that such operations are independent. To
speed up the training process, however, both the RPN and the classifier share the first
convolutional layers, reducing the amount of parameters that need to be learnt by the
network.

Mask R-CNN. Mask R-CNN adds a third branch, responsible for segmentation mask's
generation, to the structure of the Faster R-CNN. The RPN is preserved, whereas changes
are made to the classifier. In particular, the RoI Pooling operation is replaced by RoI
Align, which uses bilinear interpolation to prevent quantization: this could lead to a
little misalignment (of the order of some pixels) between the features and the RoI,
which is completely negligible for classification tasks, but might have negative effects
in the prediction of pixel-accurate masks. The branch responsible for mask generation
is a simple FCN, able to output a precise segmentation mask of the object within the
RoI, corresponding to the required instance segmentation. Again, the masking branch

is independent from the other ones, so that the results obtained for bounding-boxes regression, classification and segmentation are unrelated.

Detectron2's API. In this work, a Python code was developed to interact with Detectron2's [38] API as shown in the Colab notebook provided by the developers. The default backbone used by Detectron2 is the ResNet50 [38] with a Feature Pyramid Network (FPN [47]) used to extract multiscale features. Detectron's API let the user set a large variety of parameters, in order to fully customize the network to find the most suitable one for each application. For demonstration purposes only, we tested only a few of these parameters, changing the number of iterations in the learning process and the threshold used to discard instances.

4.2 Dataset for Image Segmentation

For the training of the segmentation network, we used a different dataset w.r.t. the one used for classification. In this dataset, images containing multiple hieroglyphs were used in order to implement the ability of extracting single in- stances of the objects. More specifically, we used 100 images of papyri and stelae, split into train (59), validation (14), test (27) subsets; training and validation datasets were integrated with ground-truth masks, that is the (manually drawn) polygonal containing the single hieroglyph. To annotate the train and validation datasets we used VGG Image Annotator (VIA) [48, 49], which allowed us to create polygonal masks on the images (Fig. 5) and save their vertices in a .json file. We totally annotated 2198 instances for the training set and 564 for the validation one. Performance was evaluated by using standard metrics for segmentation such as average precision (AP) and Intersection over Union (IoU).

Fig. 5. Manual segmentation using VGG Image Annotator [48, 49] (Left). Deep Learning segmentation on a specific hieroglyph (Right), showing performance increasing with the number of iterations.

4.3 Experimental Results

We tested the performances of our model using a picture that was completely different from the ones used during training. The results were obtained leveraging on transfer learning, loading a model pre-trained on the COCO dataset [50] and fine-tuning its last layers. Training from scratch was also tested.

The major parameters that were changed in the experimental validation were the number of iterations of the network training and the threshold applied to detect the hieroglyph instances. In Figures 6, 7, and 8, segmentation results varying with the number of iterations and the value of the threshold are shown. More specifically, Figure 6 presents the results with the same number of iterations (300) and different values of the thresholds (0.5 and 0.7). Figure 7 presents the results with the same threshold (0.5) and a different number of iterations (300 and 500); the same in Figure 8, where, however the threshold is 0.7 and the number of iterations is either 300 or 500. The effects in the number of instances detected and accuracy deriving from the choice of the threshold and from the number of iterations is evident. Figure 9 shows an example of the results obtained from the network trained from scratch, which demonstrate only minor improvements with respect to using transfer learning.

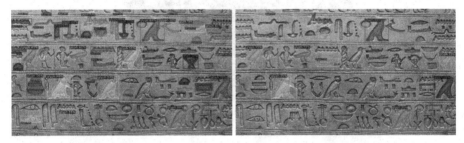

Fig. 6. Detectron2 results after 300 iterations with a threshold of 0.5 (left) and 0.7 (right).

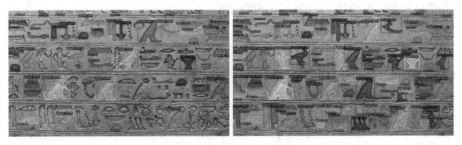

Fig. 7. Detectron2 results achieved training the net for 500 iterations (right) instead of 300 (left), using for both images the same threshold value of 0.5.

A quantitative assessment of the segmentation performance is obtained by using the precision at a given IoU value, computed on the validation dataset and comparing the predictions made by the networks with the ground-truth masks drawn with VIA. Table 3 summarizes such results, showing the precision of our algorithm in the operation of bounding-box regression and the masking process. Again, the effect of the number of iterations on the achievable performance is clearly appreciable.

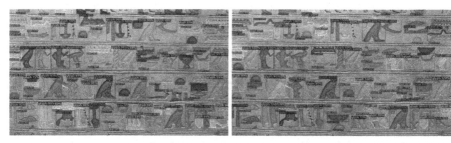

Fig. 8. Detectron2 results achieved training the net for 1000 (left) and 3000 (right) iterations, using for both images the same threshold value of 0.7.

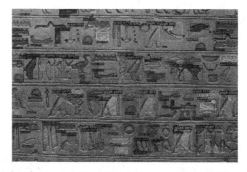

Fig. 9. Detectron2 results obtained with training from scratch (3000 iterations, thresh- old equal to 0.7).

Table 3. Average Precision (AP) of the segmentation algorithm. AP50 and AP75 refer to the AP with an index IoU equal to 50% and 75% respectively.

Number of iterations	Bounding-box regression			Masking process		
	AP	AP50	AP75	AP	AP50	AP75
300	50.980	81.989	55.963	41.080	77.801	37.792
500	65.479	90.426	77.312	49.379	86.812	51.351
1000	70.513	93.067	83.281	54.862	91.794	59.038
3000	71.728	93.383	85.038	56.029	91.228	65.764

5   Conclusions

In this paper, we investigated the capabilities of deep learning techniques to deal with the challenge of Egyptian hieroglyphs classification and segmentation. Three image recognition networks were analysed, and a new one – Glyphnet - developed and tailored for the specific purpose at hand, outperforming the standard networks in terms of performance, ease of training, and computational savings. The Detectron2 network was also tested for the problem of hieroglyphs segmentation, showing very promising results again.

The application of deep learning techniques in the subject of Egyptology opens up new and profitable perspectives. In this light, this study might be viewed as a springboard for achieving far more difficult objectives. In fact, the proposed approach could help with a number of open issues, including coding, recognition, and transliteration of hieroglyphic signs; recognition of determinatives and their semantic field; toposyntax of hieroglyphic signs combined to form words; linguistics analysis of hieroglyphic texts; recognition of corrupt, rewritten, and erased signs, and even identification of the scribe's "hand" or sculptor's school.

References

1. Alber, M., et al.: Integrating machine learning and multiscale modeling—perspectives, challenges, and opportunities in the biological, biomedical, and behavioral sciences. NPJ Digital Med. **2**(1), 1–11 (2019)
2. Goodfellow, I., Bengio, Y., Courville, A.: Deep Learning. MIT Press (2016). http://www.dee plearningbook.org
3. Carleo, G., Cirac, I., Cranmer, K., Daudet, L., Schuld, M., Tishby, N., Vogt-Maranto, L., Zdeborov´a, L.: Machine learning and the physical sciences. Rev. Mod. Phys. **91**, 045002 (2019). https://doi.org/10.1103/RevModPhys.91.045002
4. Reichstein, M., Camps-Valls, G., Stevens, B., Jung, M., Denzler, J., Carvalhais, N.: Deep learning and process understanding for data-driven earth system science. Nature **566**(7743), 195–204 (2019)
5. Yu, K., Beam, A., Kohane, I.: Artificial intelligence in healthcare. Nat. Biomed. Eng. **2**(10), 719–731 (2018)
6. Barucci, A., et al.: Label-free SERS detection of proteins based on machine learning classification of chemo-structural determinants. Analyst **146**(2), 674–682 (2021)
7. Scapicchio, C., Gabelloni, M., Barucci, A., Cioni, D., Saba, L., Neri, E.: A deep look into radiomics. Radiol. Med. (Torino) **126**(10), 1296–1311 (2021). https://doi.org/10.1007/s11 547-021-01389-x
8. Avanzo, M., et al.: Artificial intelligence applications in medical imaging: a review of the medical physics research in Italy. Physica Med. **83**, 221–241 (2021)
9. Barucci, A., Neri, E.: Adversarial radiomics: the rising of potential risks in medical imaging from adversarial learning. Eur. J. Nucl. Med. Mol. Imaging **47**(13), 2941–2943 (2020). https://doi.org/10.1007/s00259-020-04879-8
10. Shneiderman, B.: Human-centered artificial intelligence: reliable, safe & trust-worthy. Int. J. Hum.-Comput. Interact. **36**, 495–504 (2020)
11. Chatila, R., Dignum, V., Fisher, M., Giannotti, F., Morik, K., Russell, S., Yeung, K.: Trustworthy AI. In: Braunschweig, B., Ghallab, M. (eds.) Reflections on Artificial Intelligence for Humanity. LNCS (LNAI), vol. 12600, pp. 13–39. Springer, Cham (2021). https://doi.org/10.1007/978-3-030-69128-8_2
12. Cucci, C., Barucci, A., Stefani, L., Picollo, M., Jiménez-Garnica, R., Fuster-Lopez, L.: Reflectance hyperspectral data processing on a set of picasso paintings: which algorithm provides what? a comparative analysis of multivariate, statistical and artificial intelligence methods. In: Optics for Arts, Architecture, and Archaeology VIII, vol. 11784. International Society for Optics and Photonics (2021)
13. Michelin, A., Pottier, F., Andraud, C.: 2D macro-XRF to reveal redacted sections of French queen Marie-Antoinette secret correspondence with Swedish count Axel Von Fersen. Sci. Adv. **7**(40), eabg4266 (2021)

14. Bickler, S.H.: Machine learning arrives in archaeology. Adv. Archaeol. Pract. **9**(2), 186–191 (2021)
15. Mantovan, L., Nanni, L.: The computerization of archaeology: survey on artificial intelligence techniques. SN Comput. Sci. **1**(5), 1–32 (2020)
16. Crane, G.: Beyond translation: language hacking and philology. Harvard Data Sci. Rev. **1**(2), 11 (2019). https://hdsr.mitpress.mit.edu/pub/owxwohyz
17. Church, K., Liberman, M.: The future of computational linguistics: on beyond alchemy. Front. Artif. Intell. **4**, 10 (2021)
18. Grimmer, J., Roberts, M.E., Stewart, B.M.: Machine learning for social science: an agnostic approach. Annu. Rev. Polit. Sci. **24**, 395–419 (2021)
19. T. Clanuwat, A. Lamb, and A. Kitamoto, "Kuronet: Pre-modern japanese kuzushiji character recognition with deep learning. In: 15th International Conference on Document Analysis and Recognition (ICDAR), pp. 607–614, Sydney, Australia (2019)
20. Lamb, A., Clanuwat, T., Kitamoto, A.: Kuronet: regularized residual u-nets for end-to-end Kuzushiji character recognition. SN Comput. Sci. **1**(3), 1–15 (2020). https://doi.org/10.1007/s42979-020-00186-z
21. Roman-Rangel, E., Marchand-Maillet, S.: Indexing mayan hieroglyphs with neural codes. In: 2016 23rd International Conference on Pattern Recognition (ICPR), pp. 253–258 (2016)
22. He, K., Gkioxari, G., Dollár, P., Girshick, R.: Mask r-cnn. In: Proceedings of the IEEE International Conference on Computer Vision, pp. 2961–2969 (2017)
23. Ren, S., He, K., Girshick, R., Sun, J.: Faster r-cnn: towards real-time object detection with region proposal networks. Adv. Neural. Inf. Process. Syst. **28**, 91–99 (2015)
24. Girshick, R.: Fast r-cnn. In: Proceedings of the IEEE International Conference on Computer Vision, pp. 1440–1448 (2015)
25. GitHub. https://github.com/facebookresearch/detectron2
26. GitHub. https://detectron2.readthedocs.io/en/latest/index.html
27. de Saussure, F.: Course in General Linguistics. Meisel, P., Saussy, H. (eds) Columbia University Press, New York (2011)
28. Gardiner, A.: Egyptian Grammar. Griffith Institute (1957)
29. Franken, M., van Gemert, J.: Automatic egyptian hieroglyph recognition by retrieving images as texts. In: Proceedings of the 21st ACM International Conference on Multimedia. Association for Computing Machinery, p. 765–768, New York, NY, USA (2013). https://doi.org/10.1145/2502081.2502199
30. Franken, M.: Glyphreader. GitHub (2017). https://github.com/morrisfranken/glyphreader
31. Duque-Domingo, J., Herrera, P., Valero, E., Cerrada, C.: Deciphering Egyptian Hieroglyphs: towards a new strategy for navigation in museums. Sensors **17**(3), 589 (2017). https://www.mdpi.com/1424-8220/17/3/589
32. Elnabawy, R., Elias, R., Salem, M.: Image based hieroglyphic character recognition. In: 2018 14th International Conference on Signal-Image Technology Internet-Based Systems (SITIS), pp. 32–39 (2018)
33. Iglesias-Franjo, E., Vilares, J.: TIR over Egyptian hieroglyphs. In: 2016 27th International Workshop on Database and Expert Systems Applications (DEXA), pp. 198–203 (2016)
34. Rosmorduc, S.: Automated transliteration of Egyptian hieroglyphs. In: Information Technology and Egyptology in 2008: Proceedings of the Meeting of the Computer Working Group of the International Association of Egyptologists, pp. 167–183. Gorgias Press, Piscataway, Wien, NJ (2008)
35. Nederhof, M.: OCR of handwritten transcriptions of ancient Egyptian hieroglyphic text. In: Berti, M., (eds) Proceedings of the Altertumswissenschaften in a Digital Age: Egyptology, Papyrology and Beyond (DHEgypt15). Leipzig, Germany (2015)
36. https://blog.google/outreach-initiatives/arts-culture/unravel-symbols-ancient-egypt

37. https://artsexperiments.withgoogle.com/fabricius/en
38. He, K., Zhang, X., Ren, S., Sun, J.: Deep residual learning for image recognition. In: IEEE Conference on Computer Vision and Pattern Recognition (CVPR) 2016, pp. 770–778 (2016)
39. Szegedy, C., Vanhoucke, V., Ioffe, S., Shlens, J., Wojna, Z.: Rethinking the inception architecture for computer vision. In: IEEE Conference on Computer Vision and Pattern Recognition (CVPR) 2016, pp. 2818–2826 (2016)
40. Chollet, F.: Xception: deep learning with depthwise separable convolutions. In: Proceedings of the IEEE Conference on Computer Vision and Pattern Recognition (CVPR) 2017, pp. 1800–1807 (2017)
41. Barucci, A., Cucci, C., Franci, M., Loschiavo, M., Argenti, F.: A deep learning approach to ancient egyptian hieroglyphs classification. IEEE Access **9**, 123438–123447 (2021)
42. Barucci, A., Guidi, T., Loschiavo, M., Marzi, C., Argenti, F.: Glyphnet github (2017). https://github.com/GAIA-IFAC-CNR/Glyphnet.git. Accessed 12 Apr 2022
43. Yosinski, J., Clune, J., Bengio, Y., Lipson, H.: How transferable are features in deep neural networks?. In: Proceedings of the 27th International Conference on Neural Information Processing Systems - Volume 2, NIPS 2014, pp. 3320–3328. MIT Press, Cambridge, MA, USA (2014)
44. Piankoff, A.: The pyramid of Unas. Bollingen series. Princeton University Press, Princeton, NJ (1969)
45. Shorten, C., Khoshgoftaar, T.: A survey on image data augmentation for deep learning. J. Big Data **6**(1), 60 (2019)
46. Wu, Y., Kirillov, A., Massa, F., Lo, W.-Y., Girshick, R.: Detectron2. https://github.com/facebookresearch/detectron2 (2019)
47. Lin, T.-Y., Doll´ar, P., Girshick, R., He, K., Hariharan, B., Belongie, S.: Feature pyramid networks for object detection. In: Proceedings of the IEEE Conference on Computer Vision and Pattern Recognition, pp. 2117–2125 (2017)
48. Dutta, A., Gupta, A., Zissermann, A.: VGG image annotator (VIA). http://www.robots.ox.ac.uk/vgg/software/via/ (2016)
49. Dutta, A., Zisserman, A.: The VIA annotation software for images, audio and video. In: Proceedings of the 27th ACM International Conference on Multimedia 2019. ACM, New York, NY, USA (2019). https://doi.org/10.1145/3343031.3350535
50. https://cocodataset.org/#home

Exploiting CLIP-Based Multi-modal Approach for Artwork Classification and Retrieval

Alberto Baldrati[1,2], Marco Bertini[1(✉)] ⓘ, Tiberio Uricchio[1],
and Alberto Del Bimbo[1] ⓘ

[1] Università degli Studi di Firenze - MICC, Florence, Italy
{alberto.baldrati,marco.bertini,tiberio.uricchio,
alberto.delbimbo}@unifi.it
[2] Università di Pisa, Pisa, Italy

Abstract. Given the recent advantages in multimodal image pretraining where visual models trained with semantically dense textual super- vision tend to have better generalization capabilities than those trained using categorical attributes or through unsupervised techniques, in this work we investigate how recent CLIP model can be applied in several tasks in artwork domain. We perform exhaustive experiments on the NoisyArt dataset which is a collection of artwork images collected from public resources on the web. On such dataset CLIP achieve impressive results on (zero-shot) classification and promising results in both artwork-to-artwork and description-to-artwork domain.

Keywords: Image retrieval · Zero-shot classification · Artwork · CLIP

1 Introduction

Image Classification and Content-Based Image Retrieval (CBIR) are fundamental tasks for many domains, and have been thoroughly studied by the multimedia and computer vision communities. In cultural heritage domain, these tasks allow to simplify the management of large collections of images, allowing to annotate, search and explore them more easily and with lower costs.

In the latest years neural networks have proved to outperform engineered features in both tasks. These networks are typically used in an unimodal fashion, i.e. only one media is used to train and use a network. This may limit the types of application that can be developed and may also reduce the performance of the networks. Several recent works are showing how using multi-modal approaches may improve the performance in several tasks related to visual information. In [14] it has been shown that CLIP, a model trained using an image-caption objective alignment on a giant dataset made of 400 million (image, text) pairs, obtain impressive results on several downstream tasks. The authors pointed out that, using only textual supervision, CLIP model learns to perform a wide set of tasks during pre-training including OCR, geo-localization, action recognition and many others. This task learning can be leveraged via natural language prompting to enable zero-shot transfer to many existing dataset.

R. Furferi et al. (Eds.): Florence Heri-Tech 2022, CCIS 1645, pp. 140–149, 2022.
https://doi.org/10.1007/978-3-031-20302-2_11

In this work we try to exploit the zero-shot capabilities of CLIP in the artworks domain, in particular we focus on the NoisyArt [2] dataset which is originally designed to support research on webly-supervised recognition of artworks and Zero-Shot Learning (ZSL). Webly-supervised learning is interesting since it allows to greatly reduce annotation costs required to train deep neural networks, thus allowing cultural institutions to train and develop deep learning methods while keeping their budgets for the curation of their collections rather than the curation of training datasets. In Zero-Shot Learning approaches visual categories are acquired without any training samples, exploiting the alignment of semantic and visual information learned on some training dataset. ZSL in artwork recognition is a problem of instance recognition, unlike the other common ZSL problems that address class recognition. Zero-shot recognition is particularly appealing for cultural heritage and artwork recognition, although it is an extremely challenging problem, since it can be reasonably expected that museums have a set of curated description paired with artworks in their collections.

To get a better idea of how CLIP behaves in the artworks domain we started with a classification task using a shallow classifier and CLIP as the backbone. Subsequently, thanks to the descriptions of the artworks in the dataset, we performed experiments in the field of zero-shot classification where CLIP was able to demonstrate its abilities in this task. Finally, we performed experiments on the tasks of artwork-to-artwork and description-to-artwork retrieval obtaining very promising results and superior performance to a ResNet-50 pre-trained on ImageNet [16].

2 Related Works

Regarding CBIR, after the introduction of the successful Bag-of-Visual-Words model in [19] that use engineered visual features such as SIFT points, many works have improved the performance addressing different aspects such as approximating local descriptors [7], learning improved codebooks [11], improving local features aggregation [4, 8, 12]. In the last years, following the success obtained using Convolutional Neural Networks (CNN) to address the problem of image classification [10], CNN-based features have started to be used also for image retrieval tasks. A complete survey that compares SIFT-based and CNN-based methods for instance-based image retrieval is presented in [22]. Commonly used backbone networks are VGG [18] and ResNet [6], typically pretrained on ImageNet and then fine tuned for a specific domain. CNN features have been pooled using techniques like Regional maximum activation of convolutions (R- MAC) [20]. R-MAC considers a set of fixed squared regions at different scales, collecting the maximum response in each channel and then sum-pooling them to create the final R-MAC descriptor. More recent works follow an end-to-end approach: in [1] has been proposed a layer called NetVLAD, pluggable in any CNN architecture and trainable through backpropagation, that allows to train end-to-end a network using an aggregation of VGG16 convolutional activations. Multi-scale pooling of CNN features followed by NetVLAD has been proposed in [21], obtaining state-of-the-art results using VGG16. In [13] a trainable pooling layer called Generalized-Mean (GeM) has been proposed, along with learning whitening, for short representations. In this work a two stream Siamese network is trained using contrastive loss. The authors use up to 5 image scales to extract features.

3   Dataset

NoisyArt [2] is a collection of artwork images collected using articulated queries to metadata repositories and image search engines on the web. According to the creators of the dataset, the goal of NoisyArt is to support research on webly-supervised artwork recognition for cultural heritage applications.

In Table 1 the characteristics of the NoisyArt dataset are summarized.

Table 1. Characteristics of the NoisyArt dataset

	(Webly images)			(Verified images)
	Classes	Training	Validation	Test
	2,920	65,759	17,368	0
	200	4,715	1,253	1,355
Totals	3,120	70,474	18,621	1,355

NoisyArt is a complex dataset which can be used on a wide variety of automated recognition problems. The dataset is particularly well suited to webly supervised instance recognition as a weakly-supervised extension of fully-supervised learning. In the dataset, for testing purposes, a subset of classes with manually verified test images is provided (*i.e.* with no label noise).

The NoisyArt dataset is collected from numerous public resources available on the web. These resources are DBpedia (where also the metadata are retrieved), Google Images and Flickr. Figure 1 shows some examples of artworks with their respective sources.

From these sources the authors collected 89,095 images divided into 3,120 classes. Each class contains a minimum of 20 images and a maximum of 33. To make sure to have a non-noisy and more reliable test set the authors decided to create a supervised test set using a small subset of the original classes: 200 classes containing more than 1,300 images taken from the web or from personal photos. This test set is not balanced: for some classes we have few images, and some others have up to 12. The different method of collecting training and test sets also raises the issue of a strong domain shift between these images and those in the training set. Finally, each artwork has a description and metadata retrieved from DBpedia, from which a single textual document was created for each class. These descriptions are included in the dataset to support research on zero-shot learning and other multi-modal approaches to learning over weakly supervised data.

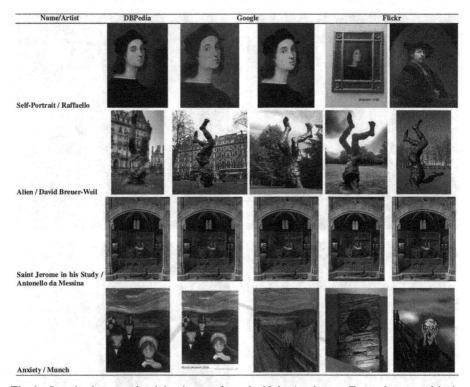

Name/Artist	DBPedia	Google		Flickr	

Self-Portrait / Raffaello

Alien / David Breuer-Weil

Saint Jerome in his Study / Antonello da Messina

Anxiety / Munch

Fig. 1. Sample classes and training images from the NoisyArt dataset. For each art- work/artist pair we show the seed image obtained from DBpedia, the first two Google Image search results, and first two Flickr search. Image taken from [2]

3.1 GradCAM Visualization

In order to have a better idea of the portions of the image that CLIP considers most important when it associates a text with an image, before moving on to the quantitative experiments, we carried out some qualitative tests using the well-know visualization technique gradCAM [17]. The technique we used is a generalization of gradCAM, where, instead of computing gradients with respect to an output class, gradients are computed with respect to textual features computed with CLIP's text encoder from the description. This approach makes each heat-map calculated by gradCAM dependent on the individual description, showing us the portions of the image that CLIP most closely associates with it. As a common practice the *saliency layer* used is the last convolutional layer of CLIP's visual encoder.

Figure 2 shows four examples of gradCAM visualization. We can see how, using the descriptions in the dataset, CLIP places attention to the most significant portions of the image. This fact made us confident that CLIP would work very well in the domain of artwork.

Fig. 2. Examples of gradCAM visualization on NoisyArt computing the gradients respect to the description CLIP text features

4 Experiments

4.1 Webly-Supervised Classification

To test the performance of CLIP in the art domain, following the experimental setup followed by the authors of the dataset, we performed a webly-supervised classification on the 200 classes that are also available in the test set.

Experimental Setup. Given an input image x, we extract a feature vector using only the CLIP image encoder and then we pass it through a shallow classifier, consisting of a single hidden layer and an output layer that estimates class probabilities $p(c\;x)$. The hidden layer is followed by an L^2-normalization layer which, as noted in [3], helps to create similar representations for image with different visual characteristics because the magnitude of features is ignored by the final classification layer. Such normalization is therefore useful to alleviate the effects of the domain shift between training and test set.

The structure of the shallow classifier is basically the same of [2, 9]. This choice was made intentionally to analyze the effects of using the CLIP image encoder instead of a convolutional backbone trained on ImageNet. For mitigating and identifying label noise during training in [2] several techniques like Labelflip noise, entropy scaling for Outlier Mitigation and Gradual Bootstrapping are used. In our experiments however, following [3], we only use the L^2-normalization layer after the hidden layer.

We trained such shallow classifier for 300 epochs with a batch size of 64, the learning rate used was $1e\,4$. We used the CLIP model which has as convolutional backbone a slightly modified version of the ResNet-50. The hidden layer has an input dimension of 1024 (CLIP output dimension) and and output dimension of 4096.

Table 2. Recognition accuracy (acc) and mean Average Precision (mAP) on NoisyArt dataset

Model	Test		Validation	
	acc	mAP	acc	mAP
RN50 BL [2]	64.80	51.69	76.14	63.08
RN50 BS [2]	68.27	57.44	75.98	62.83
RN50 $\alpha = 0.4$ [3]	74.89	62.86	77.14	63.71
CLIP RN50	86.63	77.88	83.56	72.23

Experimental Results. Table 2 summarizes the experimental results we obtained in this classification setting. In the table *BL* refers to the baseline network [2] without any sort of label mitigating approach, *BS* refers to the noisy mitigating approach of [2] and *RN50* $\alpha = 0.4$ refers to the normalization approach of [3] where the L^2-normalization is scaled by α.

From the table it is immediately evident that with the use of CLIP as a backbone it is possible to obtain very significant improvements both on the test and the validation set. It is very interesting to see that [2, 3] have better results on validation than on the test set. In our case, however, the situation is reversed by having comparable and slightly better results on the test set. This demonstrates how CLIP is quite robust to domain shift being it able to extract the semantic of an image regardless of its raw content.

4.2 Zero-Shot Classification

The availability of descriptions associated with artwork made it possible to perform experiments in the area of zero-shot classification by exploiting CLIP's ability to assign a similarity score between text and images.

Experimental Results. Table 3 shows the immense potential in the zero-shot classification domain of CLIP. As a matter of fact, comparing the results with those found in the literature, we notice that by using CLIP, improvements of over 20% can be achieved.

Table 3. Zero-shot recognition accuracy (acc) and mean Average Precision (mAP) on NoisyArt dataset

Model	Acc	mAP
DEVISE RN50 [5]	24.79	31.90
EsZSL RN50 [15]	25.63	29.89
COS + NLL + L2 RN50 [3]	34.93	45.53
CLIP RN50	60.27	69.23

It is also worth noting that the results we have compared ours with have been achieved through a training process that uses a three-fold cross validation where the 200 verified classes are divided into 150 for training/validation and 50 for zero-shot test classes. On our side we used CLIP out-of-the-box without any training on NoisyArt dataset.

In order to make a complete argument, it is also necessary to mention that since the data on which CLIP was actually trained is not public, we do not know if any images from this dataset were used in its training process. If so we would have some sort of leak of information that would make the comparison less fair.

4.3 Image Retrieval

Seeing the excellent behavior of CLIP in the (zero-shot) classification of artwork, we decided to perform some experiments in image retrieval.

In all the experiments that we are going to present, the images contained in the validation set (1253 images belonging to the 200 verified classes) were used as queries, while those of the test set (1379 images of the same 200 classes) were used as index images.

Experimental Setup. We have conducted numerous experiments to make sure that we have a complete idea of how CLIP performs in this task on the NoisyArt dataset. As in classification experiments he CLIP model which has as visual backbone a modified version of the ResNet-50 is used.

The most natural way to use CLIP in retrieval is obviously to use the output of the visual encoder as global descriptor comparing only the visual features, that is exactly what we did initially as a first experiment.

To take advantage of the CLIP textual encoder and of its goodness in zero- shot classification, we then reinterpreted the image-to-image retrieval task as zero-shot classification followed by text-to-image retrieval. This reinterpretation was made possible by the description and the metadata associated to each class. Thus given a query, zero-shot classification of that image was performed as first phase, by exploiting CLIP's ability to link images and texts. We therefore used CLIP to assign a similarity score to each possible (query image, artwork description) pair using the description with the highest score in the second phase. The second phase consists in comparing the description chosen at the end of the first one with all the images in the dataset, assigning a similarity score to each possible (query description, index image). For a complete comparison in the results we have also reported an experiment where the first part of classification is bypassed and the correct monument is always used in the text-to-image retrieval phase.

Another setup we experimented with consists in adding to the zero-shot classification followed by text-to-image retrieval experiment as a re-ranking phase where the first 100 retrieved images are re-ordered using the similarity of the visual features.

Finally, the CLIP network was fine-tuned for adapting to this task. The fine-tuning process was done by inserting a shallow classifier composed of two linear layers at the output of the visual encoder. The learning rate was set to $1e\,7$ for the CLIP encoder (keeping the normalization layers frozen) and $1e\,4$ for the shallow classifier. For ease of use, a classification loss (categorical cross-entropy) was used during this fine-tuning process. We fine-tuned the model for 30 epochs using the 2,920 classes not included in the test set.

Experimental Results. Before commenting on the results obtained we summarize the experimental setups:

- RN50 image features: We compare the image features extracted with a ResNet-50 pretrained on ImageNet
- CLIP image features: We compare the image features extracted with the CLIP image encoder
- CLIP class + text-to-image: We perform a zero-shot classification of the query followed by a text-to-image retrieval using CLIP text and visual encoder
- CLIP class + text-to-image + visual re-ranking: We perform a visual re-ranking of the first 100 retrieved results after CLIP zero-shot classification and text-to-image retrieval
- Oracle + CLIP text-to-image: We perform only the text-to-image retrieval using the ground-truth class for the description
- CLIP fine-tuned image features: We compare the image features extracted with the CLIP image encoder after fine-tuning

Table 4. Retrieval results on NoisyArt dataset using as queries the validation set and as index images the test set.

Experimental setup	mAP
RN50 image features	36.32
CLIP image features	46.40
CLIP class + text-to-image	40.54
CLIP class + text-to-image + visual re-ranking	47.41
Oracle + CLIP text-to-image	54.21
CLIP fine-tuned image features	69.60

Table 4 summarizes the results of the experiments performed in the image retrieval setting previously described. It can be seen that CLIP visual features perform better than features extracted with a ResNet-50 pre-trained on ImageNet. It is interesting to note that the re-ranking process makes the retrieval process performed by a zero-shot classification followed by a text-to-image retrieval operation more performing than the approach which uses only the visual features pre fine-tuning. This fact is obviously made possible by CLIP's good results in zero-shot classification illustrated in previous section. It is also worth mentioning that using the ground-truth class and performing the text-to-image retrieval operation yields surprisingly good results: this confirms the goodness of CLIP in the text-to-image retrieval task. These results are even greater, by a significant margin, than those obtained using only visual features pre fine-tuning. This is probably due to the domain shift between validation and test set the visual features are more subject to. Finally, we can see that CLIP fine-tuning was very successful, bringing a very significant performance boost and achieving better results than all other approaches.

5   Conclusions

In this paper we propose to use the zero-shot capabilities of CLIP in the artworks domain, showing how this approach can greatly improve over competing state-of-the-art approaches in the challenging NoisyArt dataset. Experiments show that in addition to zero-shot classification, the proposed approach can be used for content-based image retrieval, again outperforming by a large margin other competing approaches. A benefit of using the proposed method is that it can be trained using very small datasets, thanks to the extensive pretraining of CLIP, and thus the method can be deployed also to be used on relatively small collections like those of small and medium-sized museums.

Acknowledgments. This work was partially supported by the European Commission under European Horizon 2020 Programme, grant number 101004545 - ReInHerit.

Bibliography

1. Arandjelovic, R., Gronat, P., Torii, A., Pajdla, T., Sivic, J.: NetVLAD: CNN architecture for weakly supervised place recognition. In: Proceedings of the CVPR (2016)
2. Del Chiaro, R., Bagdanov, A.D., Del Bimbo, A.: Noisyart: a dataset for webly-supervised artwork recognition. In: VISIGRAPP (4: VISAPP), pp. 467–475 (2019)
3. Del Chiaro, R., Bagdanov, A.D., Del Bimbo, A.: Webly-supervised zero-shot learning for artwork instance recognition. Pattern Recogn. Lett. **128**, 420–426 (2019). ISSN 0167–8655. https://doi.org/10.1016/j.patrec.2019.09.027. https://www.sciencedirect.com/science/article/pii/S0167865519302739
4. Delhumeau, J., Gosselin, P.-H., Jégou, H., Pérez, P.: Revisiting the VLAD image representation. In: Proceedings of the ACM MM (2013)
5. Frome, A., et al.: Devise: a deep visual-semantic embedding model. In: Burges, C.J.C., Bottou, L., Welling, M., Ghahramani, Z., Weinberger, K.Q. (eds) Advances in Neural Information Processing Systems, vol. 26. Curran Associates, Inc. (2013). https://proceedings.neurips.cc/paper/2013/file/7cce53cf90577442771720a370c3c723-Paper.pdf

6. He, K., Zhang, X., Ren, S., Sun, J.: Deep residual learning for image recognition. In: Proceedings of the CVPR, pp. 770–778 (2016). https://doi.org/10.1109/CVPR.2016.90
7. Jégou, H., Douze, M., Schmid, C.: Improving bag-of-features for large scale image search. Int. J. Comput. Vis. **87**(3), 316–336 (2010). https://doi.org/10.1007/s11263-009-0285-2
8. Jégou, H., Perronnin, F., Douze, M., Sánchez, J., Pérez, P., Schmid, C.: Aggregating local image descriptors into compact codes. IEEE Trans. Pattern Anal. Mach. Intell. **34**(9), 1704–1716 (2012). ISSN 1939–3539. https://doi.org/10.1109/TPAMI.2011.235
9. Kalantidis, Y., Mellina, C., Osindero, S.: Cross-dimensional weighting for aggregated deep convolutional features (2016). https://doi.org/10.1007/978-3-319-46604-0_48
10. Krizhevsky, A., Sutskever, I., Hinton, G.E.: Imagenet classification with deep convolutional neural networks. In: Proceedings of the NIPS (2012)
11. Mikulik, A., Perdoch, M., Chum, O., Matas, J.: Learning vocabularies over a fine quantization. Int. J. Comput. Vision **103**(1), 163–175 (2013)
12. Perronnin, F., Sánchez, J., Mensink, T.: Improving the fisher kernel for large-scale image classification. In: Daniilidis, K., Maragos, P., Paragios, N. (eds.) ECCV 2010. LNCS, vol. 6314, pp. 143–156. Springer, Heidelberg (2010). https://doi.org/10.1007/978-3-642-15561-1_11
13. Radenovic, F., Tolias, G., Chum, O.: Fine-tuning CNN image retrieval with no human annotation. IEEE Trans. Pattern Anal. Mach. Intell. **41**(7), 1655–1668 (2019). https://doi.org/10.1109/TPAMI.2018.2846566
14. Radford, A., et al: Learning transferable visual models from natural language supervision (2021). https://doi.org/10.1007/978-3-319-46604-0_48
15. Romera-Paredes, B., Torr, P.: An embarrassingly simple approach to zero-shot learning. In: Bach, F., Blei, D. (eds) Proceedings of the 32nd International Conference on Machine Learning, volume 37 of Proceedings of Machine Learning Research, pp. 2152–2161, Lille, France. PMLR (2015). https://proceedings.mlr.press/v37/romera-paredes15.html
16. Russakovsky, O., et al.: Imagenet large scale visual recognition challenge (2015). https://doi.org/10.1007/s11263-015-0816-y
17. Selvaraju, R.R., Cogswell, M., Das, A., Vedantam, R., Parikh, D., Batra, D.: Grad-cam: visual explanations from deep networks via gradient- based localization. Int. J. Comput. Vis. **128**(2), 336359 (2019). ISSN 1573–1405. https://doi.org/10.1007/s11263-019-01228-7
18. Simonyan, K., Zisserman, A.: Very deep convolutional networks for large-scale image recognition. arXiv:1409.1556 (2014)
19. Sivic, J., Zisserman, A.: Video google: a text retrieval approach to object matching in videos. In: Proceedings of the ICCV (2003). https://doi.org/10.1109/ICCV.2003.1238663
20. Tolias, G., Sicre, R., J´egou, H.: Particular object retrieval with integral max-pooling of CNN activations. In: Proceedings of the ICLR (2016)
21. Vaccaro, F., Bertini, M., Uricchio, T., Del Bimbo, A.: Image retrieval using multi-scale CNN features pooling (2020)
22. Zheng, L., Yang, Y., Tian, Q.: Sift meets cnn: a decade survey of instance retrieval (2017)

Multi-scale Painter Classification

Irina Mihaela Ciortan[1](✉)(iD), Yoko Arteaga[1,2](iD), Sony George[1](iD),
and Jon Yngve Hardeberg[1](iD)

[1] NTNU - Norwegian University of Science and Technology, 2815 Gjøvik, Norway
irina-mihaela.ciortan@ntnu.no
[2] C2RMF - Center for Research and Restoration of the Museums of France,
Paris, France

Abstract. The characterization of a painter's style is useful for a series
of applications, such as documenting art history, planning style-aware
conservation and restoration, and discarding forgery attempts. In this
work, we propose a method to assign paintings to the right artist with two
strategies: traditional machine learning and deep learning. In particular,
we quantify the visual characteristics of a painting at multiple scales,
covering low-level as well as mid-level features (pyramid of histogram
of oriented gradients, residual convolutional neural network features).
We focus on coeval artists, representing Impressionism, Expressionism
and Cubism art periods. Our results are consistent with state-of-the-art
findings in art and computer vision literature.

Keywords: Art attribution · Multi-scale classification · Machine
learning · Pyramid of histogram of oriented gradients · Residual neural
network

1 Introduction

In the field of art history, the identification of artists, and moreover the attribution of a disputed artwork to a particular artist is a complex task with well-recognised challenges. Specialised art historians and curators would usually consult a number of sources in an attempt to discern between artworks. First-hand, they would recur to visual examination to appreciate the stylistic coherence of the paintings themselves, but also to historical archives to verify provenance. Analytical methods from conservation science are carried out in order to obtain a more detailed, evidence-based understanding of artists' materials, artworks' age and execution, stylistic technique, and any changes the artworks may have undergone [8].

In the light of the digital era, "computational connoisseurship" [11] has gained stronger credibility as there have been more and more cases where computational tools have aided art attribution. To name only a few: automation of canvas thread count and weave pattern analysis of Vermeer paintings [23], watermark identification in Rembrandt's etchings, and photographic paper classification [11].

R. Furferi et al. (Eds.): Florence Heri-Tech 2022, CCIS 1645, pp. 150–162, 2022.
https://doi.org/10.1007/978-3-031-20302-2_12

2   Related Work

Painter identification has been addressed through computational digital image analysis in many scientific works over the last two decades [7]. While the first attempts were designing handcrafted features in a traditional machine learning setting, the take off and increasing accessibility of convolutional neural networks (CNN) has greatly enabled the application of deep learning for artworks analysis.

Machine Learning Approaches. As one of the earliest works on painter identification, Keren [18] trained a Naive Bayes classifier to identify 5 different painters (Rembrandt, van Gogh, Picasso, Magritte, and Dali). They used discrete cosine transform (DCT) coefficients as features and obtained 86% of accuracy. In another work, Widjaja et al. [29] conducted an artist identification for Nude paintings. They exploited skin color as feature and support vector machines (SVM) as classifier to attribute paintings to Rubens, Michelangelo, Ingres, and Botticelli. Wavelets derived with a multi-resolution hidden Markov model (HMM) have been used in Li and Wang's research [22] on grayscale images of traditional Chinese ink paintings to recognize between 5 artists.

In the attempt to identify 5 artists (Cezanne, Van Gogh, Monet, Picasso, Dali), Blessing and Wen [5] tested 15 simple and advanced features, including color histograms, histogram of oriented gradients (HOG) [9], local binary patterns (LBP), and Dense SIFT (for the full list please refer to the paper). The features were employed to assign paintings to one of two artists (binary classification), as well as one out of all 5 artists (multi-class classification). For both classification tasks, the highest performance was given by HOG features. In the binary case, the accuracy ranges from 90.2% (Picasso/Cezanne) to 95.9% (Van Gogh/Cezanne), while in the multi-categorical case, the average overall accuracy was 82%. With higher number of classes, the accuracy given the same feature, decreases due to increased complexity and variation.

Keshvari and Chalechale [19] use traditional machine learning to classify 5 Iranian painters in binary and multi-class fashion. In total, 6 features are defined: 256-bin histogram, 18-bin histogram, 16-bin histogram, Gabor filter, HOG, LBP, concatenated HOG and LBP. For the binary classification, the HOG features were the most discriminative, while for the multi-class task, LBP was overall outperforming HOG. Moreover, two models, namely SVM and K-nearest neighbor (KNN) are compared, SVM giving the best accuracy.

In brief, as mentioned in [7], comparing these identification methods is not an easy task, as different datasets are used. It can be concluded that most of the features and descriptors in these studies are mainly low level features (color histograms, edge histograms and texture descriptors). Particularly, HOG has been found to have a good discerning power [5, 19]. Furthermore, in these studies, multiple classifiers are tested out.

Deep Learning Approaches. Towards recognizing 91 painters based on multi-class image classification, Bianco et al. [4] propose a network that is sensitive to multi-scale features by training in parallel 3 branches that have 3 different inputs, as follows: two random crops of 227×227 pixels extracted after resizing the original image to 512×512 resolution and another 227×227 crop after resizing the original image to 256×256. The network is formed by residual blocks, similar to those of Residual Neural Network (ResNet) [12], with an inversion in the order of the batch normalization layers and the summation of the skip connection layer. The model achieves a 78.8% accuracy as the average of a 10-fold classification experiment. In line with the findings of [27], the authors of [4] confirm that the highest confusion happens for contemporaneous and coeval artists. Viswanathan [28] compared 3 CNN designs based on their accuracy in assigning unseen painting to 57 artists: a simple CNN with only 2 convolutional layers trained from scratch, the Residual Neural Network architecture with 18 convolutional layers (ResNet18), trained from scratch on the painting images and ResNet18 pretrained on ImageNet dataset [25] fine tuned on the artworks images. The fine tuning experiment outperformed the train-from-scratch designs, reaching a top-1 accuracy of 77% and a top-3 accuracy of 89.8% on the test images. With the intention of mapping art periods and style in a coherent and automatic manner using CNN features, Elgammal et al. [10] compare the suitability of state-of-the-art deep learning architectures (AlexNet [21], VGG [26] and ResNet [12]), in a transfer learning setup and a train-from-scratch setup. The overall best performance is given by the transfer learning methodology, where the highest accuracy (63.7%) is given by ResNet152. Bai et al. [2] proposed a Multi-layer Feature Fusion DenseNet [13] to combine shallow features with deep features. They trained the system for 23 painters and reached a multi-categorical classification accuracy of 86.83%. Within the Kaggle platform, a solution was proposed to recognize artists from a subset of the "Best Artworks of All Time" using ResNet50, reporting a multi-class accuracy of 84% on the validation set [17] for artists broadly spread over various historical periods.

As in the case of traditional machine learning approaches, the inconsistency of the studied datasets, makes it difficult to compare all the above described deep learning methods on a one-to-one correspondence basis. A common finding is that fine tuning outperforms learning from scratch methodologies. The reason for this is the comparatively small number of images of artworks to the datasets available for natural images. In addition to the dataset dimensionality, there also seems to be a lack of a unique, standardized and holistic image test-bed for paintings. Complexity of multi-class painter identification, especially if the painters represent similar art periods, is a challenge repeatedly pointed out in the literature for both machine learning and deep learning techniques. Another agreed upon intuition is that multi-scale analysis provides a more thorough understanding of the visual characteristics of a certain artist [2,4,14].

3   Method

In this work, we have addressed painter identification as a digital image classification task solved using traditional machine learning and deep learning. Following the insights from the literature review, we opted to deepen the analysis on HOG features and fine tuning ResNet, by testing both approaches at multiple scales.

3.1 Pyramid of Histograms of Oriented Gradients

In the first approach, a conventional machine learning approach is exploited where several statistics are extracted from Pyramid of Histograms of Oriented Gradients (PHOG) descriptors and multiple different classifiers are used to identify the painter. PHOG [6] computes HOG features at various sub-regions of an image that follow a pyramidal distribution. At each level, the image is split into 4^L sub-regions, where L is the level . Thus, level 0 corresponds to the initial image, level 1 corresponds to the initial image split into 4 sub-regions, level 2 to 16 sub-regions and so on and so forth. For each sub-region, HOG is computed on its gradient representation and then all the HOG vectors are concatenated into a single array, namely PHOG.

Based on PHOG features, several statistics were proposed by Amirshahi et al. [1] to assess the aesthetic quality of natural images and artworks: weighted self-similarity, complexity and anisotropy. Self-similarity is based on the notion that natural scenes, as well as artworks have a self-similar structure (fractal-like) in the Fourier domain.

To measure self similarity, first the the histogram intersection kernel HIK is computed:

$$HIK(h, h') = \Sigma_{i=1}^{m} min(h(i), h(i'))$$ (1)

where $h(i)$ and $h(i')$ represent the HOG features of two sub-regions in an image. HIK is unity for identical histograms.

From HIK, the self-similarity $SefS$ of an image I can be calculated with respect to the level at which HOG is being assessed, L:

$$SefS(I, L) = median(HIK(h(S), h(Ref(S))))$$ (2)

where $h(S)$ is the HOG vector of a sub-region S in the image I at level L and $h(Ref(S))$ corresponds to the HOG vector of the reference region that the sub-region is compared to. The formula 2 outputs a number that assesses the self-similarity of an image at a certain level - the higher the number, the higher the self-similarity. However, the concept of self-similarity should take into account various levels of resolutions in order to verify for the fractal-like properties of natural images [1]. Hence, the weighted self-similarity was proposed, which balances the importance of scale for the self-similarity of an image:

$$WSefS(I) = \frac{1 - \sigma(SefS(I))}{\sum_{L=1}^{l} \frac{1}{L}} \cdot \sum_{L=1}^{l} \frac{1}{L} \cdot SefS(I, L)$$ (3)

where l is the total number of levels in the PHOG pyramid, $SefS(I)$ is the vector that concatenates the self-similarities for all levels $L = 1, ..., l$, and σ represents the standard deviation. The weighted self-similarity assigns greater importance to lower levels in the pyramid.

Anisotropy refers to the heterogeneity of an image across its orientations and it was found to be a property coherent among certain image categories [20]. Mathematically, the anisotropy of an image is given by the variance of the gradient strength in the HOG vector across its bin entries [1]:

$$AnI(L) = \sigma^2(H(L)) \tag{4}$$

AnI represents the anisotropy in the image at level L, where $H(L)$ corresponds to the concatenated HOG vector at level L in the PHOG pyramid, and σ^2 is the variance. In aesthetical studies, complexity was identified by psychologist Berlyne [3] as crucial for the appreciation of artworks: there is a certain threshold of complexity up to which images are considered puzzling enough. While an image that is too simple might induce boredom in an observer, a highly complex image might lead to frustration and difficulty to interpreting its meaning. The complexity Co of an image can be computed as the mean of the image gradient G across all orientations in the x, y directions [1].

$$Co(I) = \frac{1}{N \cdot M} \sum_{x=1}^{M} \sum_{y=1}^{N} G(x, y) \tag{5}$$

In this equation, N and M are the height and width of the gradient G of an image I. Since image gradients represent the changes of lightness in an image, it is assumed that calculating the mean gradient over the luminance channel will give a good prediction of image complexity. The higher the mean absolute gradient, the more complex an image is. As opposed to weighted self-similarity and anisotropy, the complexity of an image is a global measure, extracted for the full image resolution and doesn't take sub-regions into account.

3.2   Residual Neural Network

As mentioned in the literature review, ResNet, pretrained on ImageNet dataset [25], has shown a good performance for artist identification tasks in a transfer learning setup. The ResNet architecture [12] contains modules of residual blocks, where each block is composed of convolutional layers, batch normalization layers and non-linear activation (ReLu) function layers. The most innovative component of the ResNet architecture is the use of skip connections that solves the problem of vanishing gradients in deep convolutional neural networks. The way a residual connection (also known as skip or shortcut connections) works is that it jumps over some layers, facilitating the forward propagation of the input through the network and thus, allowing for deeper architecture without placing a high burden on the training speed.

ResNet comes in shallower and deeper configurations according to the cardinality of the convolutional layers, leading to ResNetX series, where X stands for the number of core layers: ResNet18, ResNet50, ResNet101, etc. A higher cardinality of layers is proportional to the level of features that the networks is learning. Since we are interested in characterizing the artists' style and not in recognizing high-level semantics in the paintings, we assume that low-level and mid-level features are sufficient for our classification tasks. For this reason and in order to mitigate overfitting, we don't choose very deep architectures of ResNet.

4 Experimental Design

4.1 Dataset

As far as dataset is concerned, the collection of previous works show a heterogeneity of number of painters, where some painters are over-represented and others, under-represented. For example, none of the works include the Norwegian painter Edvard Munch. In our formulation of artist recognition, we narrowed down the search to late 19th century to first half of the 20th century art periods: Symbolism, Impressionim, Expressionism, Cubism; and to 8 famous representatives: Alfred Sisley (259 images), Edgar Degas (702 images), Edward Munch (382 images), Marc Chagall (239 images), Pablo Picasso (439 images), Paul Gauguin (311 images), Pierre-Auguste Renoir (336 images) and Vincent Van Gogh (877 images). Some of these painters have inspired each other and might have reiterated the same themes, which adds complexity to the task of differentiating among them. Most of the images were taken from the Kaggle dataset "Best Artworks of All Time" [16], but because there were few images for Edward Munch in this dataset, additional images of his paintings were downloaded from Wiki-Commons.

Given the sparsity of artist identification works in the literature that consider the Norwegian painter Edvard Munch into account, we have defined two classification experiments: binary classification between Munch and all the other painters, and multi-category classification on all painters against all painters. To the best of our knowledge, Edward Munch is underrepresented in most of the previous classification works and it is for this reason that we chose to revolve the binary categorization around Munch/not Munch.

Table 1. Test set accuracy for the Munch vs Others and All vs All classification tasks based on anisotropy, complexity, parent and ground self-similarity for multiscale PHOG pyramid, trained with SVM and KNN classifiers. While for the binary task, there are models that achieve an accuracy higher than 50%, in the multiclass case, the models have a rather poor performance.There is an overall slight improvement when splitting the image into 5 levels instead of 3.

		Fine KNN	Medium KNN	Coarse KNN	Cosine KNN	Cubic KNN	Weighted KNN	Linear SVM	Quadratic SVM	Fine Gaussian SVM	Medium Gaussian SVM	Coarse Gaussian SVM
PHOG 3 levels	Binary	**85.00%**	76.60%	65.70%	69.10%	77.10%	70.90%	61.70%	67.80%	**73.10%**	64.50 %	63.90%
	Multiclass	27.10%	**31.60%**	28.20%	29.10%	31.20%	29.80%	33.60%	34.50%	33.80%	**36.90%**	32.20%
PHOG 4 levels	Binary	**84.50%**	73.40%	65.90%	70.00%	73.90%	67.30%	62.00%	57.60%	**73.20 %**	65.20 %	64.60%
	Multiclass	30.10%	31.40%	30.20%	31.10%	**33.20%**	29.90%	34.60%	38.10%	37.30%	**39.40%**	33.90%
PHOG 5 levels	Binary	**85.70%**	75.50%	65.60%	70.50%	76.10%	69.90%	61.60%	63.10%	**74.30%**	64.90%	64.40%
	Multiclass	32.90%	33.50%	29.80%	31.80%	**34.30%**	31.20%	33.50%	38.60%	37.10%	**39.00%**	33.90%

4.2   Specifications of Classification Experiments

We split our dataset into 80% training set and 20% test set, where 20% of the training data was held out for validation.

In the handcrafted classification approach, PHOG-based features (self-similarity, complexity and anisotropy) were calculated for the whole dataset using a Matlab implementation [24]. We compute anisotropy and self-similarity for 3 different scales of the PHOG pyramid (3, 4, 5). We extract the self-similarity with respect to the ground image, as well as the parent region and compute its average over the studied levels according to Eq. 3. This process results into a 4-feature vector for each level. Then, using the Matlab Classification Learner toolbox, SVM and KNN classifiers are trained with these features as input.

For the deep learning approach, we fine-tuned 3 configurations of ResNet, all pretrained on the ImageNet dataset. Even though our deep learning approach is similar to [17], we would like to clarify that we implemented different training strategies (freezing the pre-trained weights in a one-stage training process), we applied multi-scale analysis, we selected different painters for comparison, who were contemporaneous and similar in their styles, and we reported the results for the test instead of the validation set as in [17]. Given the rather small number of images in our dataset, we took several measures to prevent overfitting. Firstly, we didn't choose the very deep configurations of ResNetX, selecting ResNet18, ResNet34 and ResNet50, since higher layer depths leverage the risk of overfitting. Secondly, we tried different data augmentation options: random horizontal flip and zoom-in effect up to 20% so that we get a slight variation in scale without losing meaning and semantics of the image. However, horizontal flip was decreasing the performance of the trained models and we believe it is due to the fact that the horizontal orientations are idiosyncrasies of the painters' techniques, an insight confirmed as well by [27]. Nonetheless, we preserved the zoom-in factor, since it adds multi-scale variation that we try to account for in our work. Thirdly, for all three ResNet configurations, we froze the pretrained weights for all convolutional layers. Conversely, the fully connected layer was trained to match our data, where each class had different weights proportional to the number of available images, as a way to compensate for the unbalanced dataset. Lastly, we trained the network using Adam optimizer for a maximum number of 50 epochs, with early stop option (patience 20 epochs) and learning rate of 10^{-4} (that decays with a factor of 10^{-1} if the cross-entropy loss on the validation set has stopped improving for 5 epochs). We set up the deep learning experiments in Python programming language, using Tensorflow and Keras libraries on a CUDA-enabled GPU machine.

4.3   Discussion of Results

In agreement with the findings of previous works in the literature, our classification methods give overall higher accuracy for the binary task than for the multi-categorical task. Tables 1 and 2 summarize our results. The accuracy values show that the deep learning approach outperforms the handcrafted features

Table 2. Test set accuracy for the Munch vs Others and All vs All classification tasks based on fine-tuned ResNet of depths. While it seems that the highest layer depth brings the highest accuracy, the difference is not higher than 2 units.

	ResNet18	ResNet34	ResNet50
Binary	93.66 %	93.79 %	**95.72 %**
Multi-class	78.93 %	77.39 %	**79.07 %**

based on PHOG representation. As a matter of fact, in the multi-class experiment, the trained machine learning models don't converge, as they don't achieve an accuracy higher than 50%. It is noteworthy to mention that the SVM and KNN classifiers were trained separately on the handcrafted features extracted for different levels (3,4,5) in the pyramid, and the highest accuracy was obtained by level 5, even though the difference among the layers is rather small (in some cases less than unit). This might be due to the fact that the higher level encompasses all the previous lower levels. Nonetheless, the outperformance of level 5 PHOG features suggests that including a larger range of scales covers more thoroughly the visual characteristics of an image.

Aiming for features at various scales seem to impact the performance of the pretrained ResNet as well. The highest accuracy is given by the 50-layer configuration, with the mention that the differences between various layer configurations do not exceed 2 units. ResNet50 manages to correctly distinguish Munch from other artists in 73% of the cases, leaving a 27% false negative rate. Figure 1 highlights 4 randomly picked test images along with their predictions. The two Munch paintings containing human poses are correctly identified, while the landscape painting is a false negative. This could be related to the painting theme itself (natural scenery are sometimes more commonly depicted in arts) that makes the artists be more similar in some cases (natural scenery) than others (portraits), resulting in similar features as processed by the classification models. Moreover, in their early career, it is common that most artists start painting in a classic rendition, before defining their own style signature.

The confusion matrix of the multi-categorical classification with ResNet50, shown in Fig. 2 displays no red off-diagonal values, meaning that in average, the painters get correctly attributed with a rate of more than 50%. However the shades of lighter blue in the first column (corresponding to Van Gogh) indicate that many painters get misattributed to Van Gogh. A possible reason for this could be the unbalanced dataset (where Van Gogh has the highest number of training images), that the prior class weights didn't manage to fully account for. Several randomly selected images are illustrated in Fig. 3 and they represent correct predictions. Chagall is mistaken for Picasso with a false negative rate of 19% (see Fig. 4). Munch is confused 12% of the cases with Van Gogh and 8%

Fig. 1. Munch vs Others predictions by fine-tuned ResNet50. While the two paintings containing human poses get correctly identified as Munch, the landscape painting gets misattributed to Van Gogh with 92% probability.

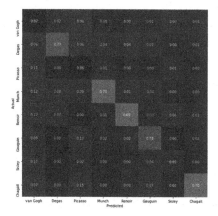

Fig. 2. All vs All: confusion matrix on the fine-tuned ResNet50. Van Gogh is recognized with the highest true positive rate (87%), while Munch and Chagall are accurately identified in 70% of the cases.

of the cases with Degas. Interestingly, the similarities between Munch and Van Gogh have been previously emphasized in the world of art [15], meaning that our model is able to detect an acknowledged resemblance. Figure 5 illustrates 4 Munch vs Others predictions by fine-tuned ResNet50. While the two paintings containing human characters get correctly identified as Munch, the landscape painting gets misattributed to Others (Van Gogh) with 92% probability. These similarities are also in agreement with the PHOG-based features. All the 3 features (ground self-similarity, anisotropy and complexity) are more similar among the two artists for the landscape rendition than they are for the human portrayal.

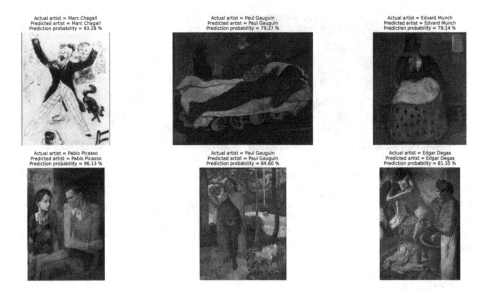

Fig. 3. Examples of correct artist attributions, as predicted by fine-tuned ResNet50.

Fig. 4. Examples of wrong artist attributions, as predicted by fine-tuned ResNet50.

Fig. 5. The self-portraits get correctly classified, while the landscapes get misattributed by the finetuned ResNet50 binary model. This complies with PHOG-based features. From left to right, weighted ground self-similarity, anisotropy, complexity at level 5: a) A portrait by Edward Munch: 0.85, 12.36, $0.92 \cdot 10^{-5}$; b) A portrait by Vincent Van Gogh: 0.64, 14.57, $2.38 \cdot 10^{-5}$; c) A landscape by Munch: 0.73, $11.27, 2.24 \cdot 10^{-5}$; d)A landscape by Van Gogh: 0.71, 12.91, $2.94 \cdot 10^{-5}$

5   Conclusion

This article shows how computer vision learning-based techniques, using multi-scale pyramid of histogram of oriented gradients and pretrained residual neural network features, are able to distinguish coeval painters who adopted similar art styles. Even though many computer vision methods have been designed for art attribution, the problem has not yet converged to a fully optimized solution that, as of now, offers full credibility stand-alone. Nonetheless, classification procedures can be a valuable clue as long as they are supported by other art forensic methods.

Acknowledgments. This paper is a spin-off of the group project deliverable submitted for the DT8121 Colour Imaging course, completed in December 2020 at NTNU. Thus, we would like to acknowledge the other members of the group: Majid Ansari-Asl, Agnese Babini and Jan Cutajar.

References

1. Amirshahi, S.A., Koch, M., Denzler, J., Redies, C.: PHOG analysis of self-similarity in aesthetic images. In: Rogowitz, B.E., Pappas, T.N., Ridder, H.D., (eds.) Human Vision and Electronic Imaging XVII, vol. 8291, pp. 450–459. International Society for Optics and Photonics, SPIE (2012)
2. Bai, R., Ling, H., Kai, Z., Qi, D., Wang, Q.: Author recognition of fine-art paintings. In 2019 Chinese Control Conference (CCC), pp. 8513–8518. IEEE (2019)
3. Berlyne, D.E.: Studies in the new experimental aesthetics: Steps toward an objective psychology of aesthetic appreciation. Hemisphere (1974)
4. Bianco, S., Mazzini, D., Schettini, R.: Deep multibranch neural network for painting categorization. In: Battiato, S., Gallo, G., Schettini, R., Stanco, F. (eds.) ICIAP 2017. LNCS, vol. 10484, pp. 414–423. Springer, Cham (2017). https://doi.org/10.1007/978-3-319-68560-1_37

5. Blessing, A., Wen, K.: Using machine learning for identification of art paintings. Technical report (2010)
6. Bosch, A., Zisserman, A., Munoz, X.: Representing shape with a spatial pyramid kernel. In: Proceedings of the 6th ACM international conference on Image and video retrieval, pp. 401–408 (2007)
7. Brachmann, A., Redies, C.: Computational and experimental approaches to visual aesthetics. Front. Comput. Neurosci. **11**, 102 (2017)
8. Craddock, P.: Scientific investigation of copies, fakes and forgeries. Routledge (2009)
9. Dalal, N., Triggs, B.: Histograms of oriented gradients for human detection. In: 2005 IEEE computer society conference on computer vision and pattern recognition (CVPR'05), vol. 1, pp. 886–893. IEEE (2005)
10. Elgammal, A., Liu, B., Kim, D., Elhoseiny, M., Mazzone, M.: The shape of art history in the eyes of the machine. In: Proceedings of the AAAI Conference on Artificial Intelligence, vol. 32 (2018)
11. Ellis, M.H., Johnson, C.R.: Computational connoisseurship: Enhanced examination using automated image analysis. Visual Res. **35**(1–2), 125–140 (2019)
12. He, K., Zhang, X., Ren, S., Sun, J.: Deep residual learning for image recognition. In: Proceedings of the IEEE Conference on Computer Vision and Pattern Recognition, pp. 770–778 (2016)
13. Huang, G., Liu, Z., Van Der Maaten, L., Weinberger, K.Q.: Densely connected convolutional networks. In Proceedings of the IEEE conference on computer vision and pattern recognition, pp. 4700–4708 (2017)
14. Johnson, C.R., et al.: Image processing for artist identification. IEEE Signal Process. Mag. **25**(4), 37–48 (2008)
15. Jones, J.: Side by side, Edvard Munch and Vincent van Gogh scream the birth of expressionism. The Guardian (2015)
16. Kaggle.: Collection of Paintings of the 50 Most Influential Artists of All Time (2020). https://kaggle.com/ikarus777/best-artworks-of-all-time
17. Kaggle. Explore and run machine learning code with Kaggle Notebooks — Using data from Best Artworks of All Time (2020). https://kaggle.com/supratimhaldar/deepartist-identify-artist-from-art
18. Keren, D.: Painter identification using local features and naive Bayes. In Object recognition supported by user interaction for service robots, volume 2, pp. 474–477. IEEE (2002)
19. Keshvari, S., Chalechale, A.: Stylometry of Painting Using Histogram of Oriented Gradients (HOG) and Local Binary Patterns (LBP). Tabriz J. Electr. Eng. **47**(3), 1195–1204 (2017)
20. Koch, M., Denzler, J., Redies, C.: 1/f2 characteristics and isotropy in the fourier power spectra of visual art, cartoons, comics, mangas, and different categories of photographs. PLoS ONE **5**(8), e12268 (2010)
21. Krizhevsky, A., Sutskever, I., Hinton, G.E.: Imagenet classification with deep convolutional neural networks. Adv. Neural Inform. Process. Syst. **25** 1097–1105 (2012)
22. Jia Li and James Ze Wang: Studying digital imagery of ancient paintings by mixtures of stochastic models. IEEE Trans. Image Process. **13**(3), 340–353 (2004)
23. Liedtke, W., Johnson, C.R., Johnson, D.H.: Canvas Matches in Vermeer: A Case Study in the Computer Analysis of Fabric Supports. Metropolitan Mus. J. **47** 101–108 (2012)
24. Redies, C.: Matlab code to calculate PHOG self-similarity, complexity and anisotropy (2020). https://osf.io/csvta/

25. Russakovsky, O., et al.: Imagenet large scale visual recognition challenge. Int. J. Comput. Vision **115**(3), 211–252 (2015)
26. Simonyan, K., Zisserman, A.: Very deep convolutional networks for large-scale image recognition. arXiv preprint arXiv:1409.1556 (2014)
27. van Noord, N., Hendriks, E., Postma, E.: Toward discovery of the artist's style: Learning to recognize artists by their artworks. IEEE Signal Process. Mag. **32**(4), 46–54 (2015)
28. Viswanathan, N.: Artist identification with convolutional neural networks. Standford193CS231N Report (2017)
29. Widjaja, I., Leow, W.K., Wu, F.-C.: Identifying painters from color profiles of skin patches in painting images. In: Proceedings 2003 International Conference on Image Processing (Cat. No. 03CH37429), vol. 1, pp. I-845. IEEE (2003)

PH-Remix. Enhancing Cataloguing and Promotion of Film Heritage Through Video Remix and Artificial Intelligence

Giovanni Grasso, Chiara Mannari[✉], and Davide Italo Serramazza

University of Pisa, Pisa, Italy
{giovanni.grasso,chiara.mannari,
davide.serramazza}@fileli.unipi.it

Abstract. PH-Remix is a prototype of a web platform based on artificial intelligence that enables the uploading, cataloguing, search, consultation, extraction and remix of multimedia content. The platform was developed with the aim of creating an innovative tool to complement the classic methodologies of research and study of sources by providing easy access and the possibility to reuse a large number of primary filmic sources.

Paying particular attention to the challenges and critical issues that may arise during the development of such a tool, this paper aims to present: - The remix prototype and some possible practical applications in the context of public history arising from the possibility of creating new contributions/multimedia contents; - The machine learning techniques used to extract information from audiovisual works.

Keywords: Cinema and history · Remix culture · Artificial Intelligence · Audiovisual archives · Digital public history

1 Introduction

The platform PH-Remix (Public History Remix)[1] is a prototype based on artificial intelligence (AI) developed in the context of a two year research project led by the Laboratory of Digital Culture of the University of Pisa, in collaboration with Festival dei Popoli and Fondazione Mediateca Toscana (the latter has been a member of FIAF - International Federation of Film Archives - since 2011).

The archive collection of the Festival dei Popoli represents the case study for the realisation of the project and the development of the prototype. It consists of a collection of documentary films stored in several different supports (16 and 35 mms, VHS, U-matic, DVDs): more than 25.000 titles collected in over 60 festival editions and represents a continuously growing cultural heritage, as its content is constantly increasing, with around 1600 new entries per year. Starting to collect films of various genres, styles and themes from the very first edition of the festival in 1959, the Festival dei Popoli

---

[1] http://www.labcd.unipi.it/ph-remix, last accessed 2022/01/10.

© The Author(s), under exclusive license to Springer Nature Switzerland AG 2022
R. Furferi et al. (Eds.): Florence Heri-Tech 2022, CCIS 1645, pp. 163–177, 2022.
https://doi.org/10.1007/978-3-031-20302-2_13

archive reflects the evolution of documentary cinema over the years. The covered topics include the principal categories of documentary cinema: from the most traditional such as anthropology and social science, to the more contemporary including history of art, music, dance, costume, architecture, new media, contemporary history, current events and politics.

The data of the archive are managed in the platform both through traditional metadata, by importing the cataloguing files produced as part of the parallel project to digitise the archive, and by using AI techniques that allow the automatic extraction of numerous significant video segments of varying length (clips). To this end, several machine learning algorithms specialised in extracting information from audiovisual content were used, such as: object recognition, subtitle extraction by an Optical Character Recognition (OCR), segmentation into frames labelled according to the dominant colour.

Finally, a web interface accessible to end users has been developed to provide access to the index of clips, preview them and create remixes through a video editing tool.

As described in detail in the chapters below, the working prototype enables scholars coming from different fields a series of direct evaluations made possible by direct experimentation in the platform. The principal innovations brought by such a tool are related to the use of artificial intelligence for treating audiovisual archives along with the practice of video remix with the double objective of creating new content for didactic aims and enhancing the Festival dei Popoli archive.

2   The Platform

Starting from the materials produced by the digitization of the Festival dei Popoli archive, PH-Remix platform aims to join the great potential of the recent algorithms based on AI with the possibilities offered from the modern web technologies. While machine learning techniques allow the development of powerful algorithms capable of automatically extracting a huge amount of information contained in multimedia formats, the adoption of modern web standards for video management, such as media fragment, html5 video and JavaScript frameworks enables a component based approach development, that makes it possible the creation of dynamic complex applications that not only allow users to view multimedia contents but also to manipulate them. PH-Remix is thus a complex platform based on a microservices architecture. Microservices is a modern modular approach for building software: each application is a suite of small services developed individually and devoted to a specific function. In this kind of framework each single component communicates with the other services through APIs (application programming interfaces). The biggest advantage of this approach is that each service can be improved independently, even in subsequent stages of development, choosing the programming language and system requirements most suitable for each task. A similar structure is particularly indicated for complex platforms characterised by highly specialised services and multiple user interfaces. The schema of PH-Remix platform is represented in Fig. 1 and each service is described below.

Films, already available in a digital format, are uploaded to the platform through a web interface. The interface is accessible only to authorised users that are allowed to upload the video files on the server in charge of the automatic extraction. During the

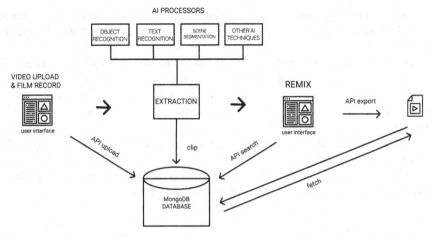

Fig. 1. PH-Remix platform diagram

extraction process each film is analysed by different processors based on AI algorithms that give as a result a large amount of clips of varying duration containing all the extracted information. The different processors that have been developed include: visual analysis for object detection (object recognition), the extraction of subtitles through OCR and scene segmentation based on dominant colour. Detailed information about the extraction process and processors are given in the next chapter of this paper. In parallel to the extraction phase, it is possible for the authorised users to create a record with data related to the film uploaded. Both the manually uploaded data, and the ones coming from the extraction process are recorded in a document oriented database that enables the storage and querying of large quantities of data. The use of a semi-structured database represents an alternative solution to the fixed structure typical of relational databases that are far more common for storing archival data. This choice represents a further innovative element in the panorama of such archives, not only meeting the need for high performances to query a very large database made of hundreds of thousands of records, but also providing a minimalist and user-friendly interface to search into a wide index of resources in a way of interaction similar to search engines and social networks, as described in the final part of this paragraph. The system requires a small set of metadata that are necessary for the submission and remix interfaces and an unlimited number of additional custom fields. Mandatory fields are: title, director, year, country and archive number. Regarding additional fields, in the framework of PH-Remix project it is adopted the standard promoted by the already mentioned FIAF with the import of the cataloguing records compiled for the catalogue of Mediateca Toscana digital archive. Furthermore, the platform supports flexible metadata schemas, allowing the user to easily add custom fields and choose different metadata standards in order to do advanced searches and share information. Leaving to the final user the possibility to add fields in a flexible way, the platform is designed to potentially support any metadata schema. Metadata inserted by the users are related to the films uploaded but thanks to the hierarchical structure of the database tables these data can be easily extended to the clips extracted automatically, enriching each video fragment with punctual information obtained from traditional cataloguing. These metadata are particularly important also for study purposes because linking each clip to the film it was extracted from, allow scholars to treat the clips as sources.

The extracted clips and all the related metadata are then accessible to final users in the remix environment, a potentially publicly accessible single page web application through which it is possible to search, view, edit and export videos. A modular approach similar to the microservices structure of the platform has been adopted for the remix interface that is developed with the JavaScript component based framework LitElement. The interface components interact with the server side scripts through the REST API responsible for the search in the index of clips, the video streaming and the video editing. Starting from a modular structure like that it is easier to develop a complex front-end software with the improvement and reuse of single components.

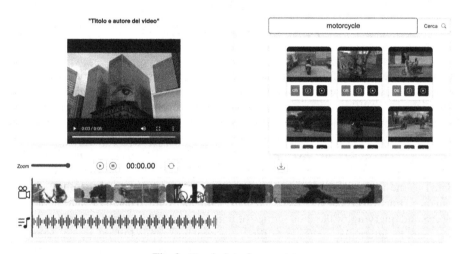

Fig. 2. Remix interface prototype

Figure 2 represents the structure of the remix interface. The top right area of the screen is the access point to the index of clips. The user inserts one or more keywords in a text field and launches the search in the database of clips through a call to the search API. The server side search module searches for the key inserted by the user in the table of clips. For example, by performing the search of the word "flag" the system returns all the clips containing an object recognised as a flag by the object recognition algorithm or containing the word "flag" in the subtitle imprinted on the frames and detected by the OCR processor; by performing the search of the word "red" the system returns all the clips containing the word "red" in the subtitles or the scenes in which the dominant colour is red, as detected from the scenes segmentation processor. A query language based on prefixes has been developed to perform searches filtering by people, places, nationalities and film titles. Thanks to these filters it is possible to search for an object or a text contained in a particular film or search for a scene in a film directed by a specific person or acted or produced by a specific actor, producer or technician. The search engine developed constitutes a significant expansion of the traditional catalogue. By the use of automatic techniques, the platform indexes huge quantities of video fragments otherwise impossible to treat with manual video analysis. It also provides direct reference to the full bibliographical records on the online catalogue of Mediateca Toscana. Resulting clips returned by the system can be browsed through an infinite scroll in the area under the search form. For each clip it is possible to watch a preview that appears in the preview area on the left of the screen or open a lightbox with a minimal set of metadata related to the film the clip was extracted from: film title, director, year, country of production and archival number. The latter provides the direct connection to the full bibliographical record in the Mediateca Toscana online catalogue.

In addition to search and preview, the most innovative functionality of the interface is the remix with the video editor. Through drag and drop operations it is possible to add clips to the timeline on the lower area of the screen, resize their duration, and add audio tracks. At any time users can play the video editing preview and once the remix is completed, launch the server side export process that is responsible for the assemblage of the clips in *mp4* format. A download link to the final file is then made available to the author of the remix. Besides the clips, the final video contains audio tracks and credits with information about the author, title and date of the remix and data about the films the clips are extracted from. Future versions of the video editor could include additional features like multitrack support, video effects, transitions, textual levels for captions support, the possibility to register voice over video track, upload file from user's pc and a reserved area for registered users to save the created remixes and searched clips.

3 Contribution of the AI

The kind of heritage we treat is primarily composed of audiovisual content. In the scientific literature, more in detail in the *Machine Learning* field, are published many works describing models and algorithms dealing with this kind of content. Generally speaking, all these algorithms extract *information* of different nature from the content they analyse. Our aim is to select, among the available ones, the models that are closer to our purposes and apply the modification required to adapt to the needs of the project.

Referring to the *pipeline* the documentaries are subjected to, once uploaded, each film will be analysed from different algorithms (in the following referred to as *processors*) which split them into **clips.** We can define the clips as continuous and *homogeneous* film fragments. Indeed the processors, using their ability to detect some specific characteristics in the video, divide the original films into shorter segments, having the necessary length (ranging from tens of second to a whole minute) to be used in the remix platform as the base content to define remixes. Once a clip is detected, it is isolated from the rest of the film and indexed assigning to it, along with other data, a **label** that represents the specific information/feature extracted for the clip. These labels are the keys to retrieve the clips in the remix platform: the clips can be queried using the labels attached to them and, as described in the previous section, the clips can be *reused* from the platform users to create new video remixes. To be more concrete, we are now going to give more details about the three processors used in our project. Specifically, we detail how they work and how they were modified to adapt them to the necessity of the project.

The first processor is TransNet V2 (Souček et al. 2020), a model for *shot segmentation,* namely the task of dividing a video into the framing composing it. Thus using this model the extracted fragments from a film correspond to the different framings. As it is, this algorithm results in a split of the film but the detected fragments do not have any label on them thus they can not be queried in the remix platform. To this end, the modification made to this algorithm was to implement a second module that analyses each extracted clip labeling them with their dominant colours. The other two processors instead were originally born for still-images, thus the modifications mostly concern the change of operating domain from images to videos.

The second processor is RetinaNet (Lin et al. 2017), a model for object detection (in Fig. 3 there is an example). To remark that object detection is a misleading name since it is also possible to detect humans, animals, etc. It relies on ResNet (He et al. 2015) to extract image features, specifically on ResNet 101 (composed of 101 layers). In the paper it was proposed the performances of its architecture were tested training the model on the popular dataset for image msCoco (Lin et al. 2014). The version used in our project instead relies on ResNet152 to extract features and it is trained on Open Image (Kuznetsova et al. 2018) a dataset recently released. This choice was made since this last dataset is arguably one of the richer in terms of different output categories indeed it has 500 different categories while msCoco has just 91. The obvious result is that using the model trained on the second dataset there is a wider range of possible recognized objects from the analysed film. This model gives as *output* a sequence of *prediction* (detected object) and *confidence* (the probability the model puts in its prediction) pairs regarding different subsections of the whole frame. To adapt the processor to work with videos rather than still images, we use this processor as follows: each frame of the film is fed to the model giving as output a sequence of prediction and confidence for each frame. From the list of predictions of all frames, the video segments extracted as clips are the ones for which a specific object is detected (with a confidence higher than a fixed threshold) in more than one consecutive frame. Thus the results of this processor are portions of films in which a specific object is present. For instance, if an object O appears in the film at time tl for s seconds a clip labelled with O starting at time tl of the film with durations s second is extracted. Moreover, this processor is the only one that is capable of extracting more than one clip with different labels from the same video portion: in fact, it might happen that in the same video portion, two different objects O_1 and O_2 are detected. In this case, the clips extracted are two even if they partially/totally share the same frames, the first one with label O_1 while other one with label O_2.

The last processor to mention has the purpose to extract the subtitles imprinted in the video frames (in Fig. 4 there is an example). It operates thanks to the concatenation of two models: the first one is EAST (Zhou et al. 2017) that has the task of detecting the portion of the frames in which there is text. The second model is the popular library *tesseract* that receives as input the frame portion for which EAST detects the appearance of text. This pipeline is applied to all frames in the films resulting in a list of textual elements, specifically at most once for each frame of the video (some frames might have no subtitles).

Remembering our goal that is to extract clips, for each text in this list two handcrafted metrics are computed. The first one measures the difference from the text extracted from a frame compared to what was extracted from the previous one: this metric is used to isolate the set of frames F for which the same subtitle is shown. On the other hand, the second metric is used to give a measure of how likely is for the transcription to be a well-formed sentence: it is used to select among all the transcription in F (that not necessary are every time equals due to possible error in the OCR among different frames) which one is the more likely to be the true transcription and thus which one should become the label of the clip.

Thus from this last processor, the extracted clips are the video portion in which a single subtitle appears and they are labelled with the detected transcript.

Using just these three processors it is possible to achieve the following goals: on one hand it is possible to analyse in detail each video that is submitted to the platform (a task that is unfeasible with this level of detail with human cataloguing due to the amount of work to be done). On the other hand, thanks to machine learning algorithms, it is possible to achieve a *semantic* split in clips: as explained above, the films are divided using criteria thus resulting in clips suitable to be used in remixes. This process of automatic extraction and labelling of clips is integrated with the manual cataloguing of the films. As said before, each film is paired with a richer set of metadata describing it. In the query of a segment it is possible to define some filters based on these metadata, for instance it is possible to query the database for clips containing a specific colour, object or transcript coming from films having in the toponym some specific field or directed from specific directors, etc. This combination of automatic and manual extracted information allows querying the datastore even deeper, exploring the films submitted to the platform with a fine-grain.

Lastly, the microservices based architecture of the platform allows for adopting a modular approach also in the processors development: thanks to this architecture it is very simple to add some other processors which perform different analyses on the films or to modify a processor that is already present. This last opportunity is particularly important

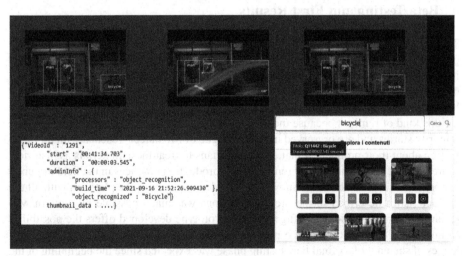

Fig. 3. A segment extracted by object detection. On top, three frames from the extracted clip (the red rectangles and names of the recognized objects are for illustrative purposes only). On the bottom left corner, the item inserted in the database, and on the right bottom corner a screenshot of the remix platform retrieving the segment by typing "bicycle" into the search field.

in a still-developing field, as machine learning is, to update the models/algorithms used when a new model substantially improves the performances.

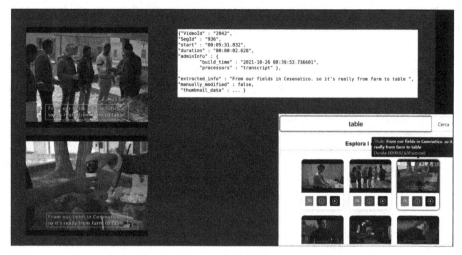

Fig. 4. A segment extracted by the OCR processor. On the left, two frames from the extracted clips (the red rectangles surrounding the subtitles are for illustrative purposes). On the top right corner, the item inserted in the database, and on the right bottom corner a screenshot of the remix platform retrieving the segment by typing "table" into the search field.

4   Beta Testing and First Results

The prototype was developed in the framework of public history, an academic discipline whose aim is to make use of the same ways of interaction used by the public and involve people in the creation of historical contents through the use of the methodology of history, first of all the correct treatment of the sources and rigorous ways to publish historical products. The filmic heritage of Festival dei Popoli is particularly suitable for this kind of remixes because the documentaries tell historical events, social causes, minority stories and are preserved in the catalogue of Mediateca Toscana with all information about their production that allow historians to treat these materials as historical sources. The experimentation of remix culture production practices in the field of public history represents an absolute innovation. The development of the platform with all the characteristics described in the previous sections was made possible by modern web technologies and Artificial Intelligence. The prototype developed offers the possibility to final users to interact with the platform for directly estimating strenghts and challenges of such a tool. A final beta testing phase was expected since the beginning of the project and considered extremely useful for the continuation of the project and a future publication of the platform.

During the initial phases of the project some examples of remixes were created with traditional video editing software to define a model of public history remix[2]. This model contributed to establish the principal requirements for all the video remixes generated through the platform: each remix starts with an intro containing essential data like title, author and date of the creation of the remix along with logos of the institutions taking part in the project. After the intro it is displayed the sequence of video and audio clips as arranged by the user during the video editing in the remix interface (as described in paragraph 2). Each clip has an overlay text with title and director of the film it was extracted from. As shown in Fig. 5, the remix is closed by an outro with automatically generated credits: a list of all the films that appear in the remix with additional info about the production and the reference to trace the documentary in the Festival dei Popoli section of Mediateca Toscana archive[3].

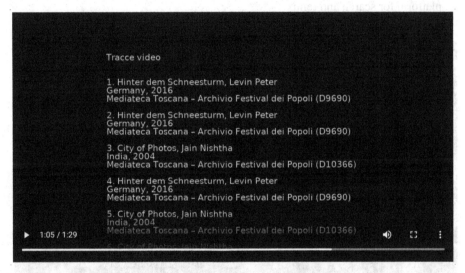

Fig. 5. Video credits automatically generated by the export script are displayed at the end of the remixes. This screen is taken from the remix "Foto, lettere, tracce" created during the beta testing http://www.labcd.unipi.it/wp-content/uploads/2022/04/Foto-lettere-tracce.mp4.

The model of public history remix included additional features that will be developed in future versions of the platform, e.g. the possibility to upload audio, video or even images from user's local; additional layers on clips with custom text to support captions, filters and transitions, multiple traces to support advanced edits like picture in picture

---

[2] These examples were presented at the University of Pisa on 12 May 2021 during the seminar of Digital Culture entitled "Remix Culture". The seminar can be watched at the link https://www.labcd.unipi.it/seminari/chiara-mannari-remix-culture/. The model of public history remix is presented at 1'17". Video remix examples are also available at these links: https://www.labcd.unipi.it/remix-culture/#/6/2 and https://www.labcd.unipi.it/remix-culture/#/6/3

[3] An examples of remix can be watched at the link: http://www.labcd.unipi.it/wp-content/uploads/2022/04/celebrate-earth-day.mp4

and much more. All these functionalities will give users the possibility to create more complex remixes to satisfy all the requirements emerging from public history practice.

After the release of a first version of the prototype, another fundamental objective of the project consisted of the testing of the platform with users.

Testers were given the possibility to access the prototype with credentials, performing searches and creating remixes. The infographic in Fig. 6 summarises some of the most important quantitative results of the project at the time the prototype was firstly released: 408 films, all from the Festival dei Popoli archive, were processed by the three AI algorithms described above. These films, corresponding to 402 hours of video, have 60 different countries of production and present 116 different themes from the catalogue. Finally, more than 1.1 million clips were extracted from these films, specifically 183,000 from the shot segmentation processor, 180,000 from the transcription processor and 740,000 from the object recognition processor. The clips extracted are all available in the platform for search and remix.

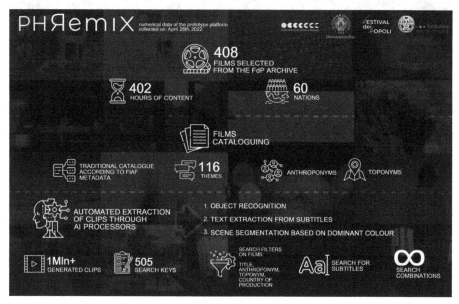

Fig. 6. Poster summarising quantitative information of the project: 408 films, from 60 different countries, corresponding in total to 402 h of content, were processed by the three processors. From these films, the number of clips extracted was over 1.1 million.

The beta testing involved a group of people composed by: research fellows from the Department of Philology, Literature and Linguistics at the University of Pisa who were directly involved in the project, students of Digital Humanities at the University of Pisa that had previously taken part to the project contributing to the development of the platform and public historians from the Master's Degree Course in Public & Digital History at the University of Modena and Reggio Emilia. In line with public history methodology the tests with end users represent not only an occasion to collect feedbacks on the functionalities of the remix interface, but also an opportunity for a wider public made of scholars, academics, teachers and students to interact with an innovative tool for the creation of new historical contents through the manipulation of significant fragments of archival materials.

Testers were asked to evaluate the prototype mainly focusing on search and remix of content of historical relevance. The documentaries of the FdP archive contain several testimonies of news events, recent history and political facts. The challenge consisted of finding keywords useful to bring out historical contents. Figure 7 shows an example of search for the object "flag" returning over 1000 results. Flags represent symbols for public events witnessing the main historical facts that involve masses. Starting from this simple search it is possible to investigate the main historical events treated in documentaries having the opportunity to watch and reuse video clips related to these main events[4].

Other examples include the search of historical characters within particular documentaries[5], specific testimonies of facts narrated[6], antroponyms or proper nouns[7].

The final phase of beta testing enabled some initial results to be obtained by broadening the audience of possible users of the tool and defining a format for subsequent tests[8]. After the direct interaction with the platform, users were asked to answer a questionnaire giving feedback not only about their experience with the prototype but also providing suggestions on how a similar platform could be used in the framework of public history studies. The point of view of experts in digital humanities is particularly important at this moment to evolve the prototype into a user friendly tool suitable for public history aims. The main suggestions received deal with the proposal to make clips timing adjustable

---

[4] E.g.the clip http://remix.unipi.it:3000/api/0.1/videos/2244/segment/2567 that is extracted from the documentary Maidan (a film directed by Sergei Loznitsa. Ukraina, Netherlands 2014), contains scenes from the protest against the pro-Russian Yanukovich regime in Maidan square in Kiev between end 2013 and 2014. More information about the documentary can be found on the Mediateca catalogue: https://www.mediatecatoscana.it/catalogo/vedi_pub.php?lista=046921

[5] The clip http://www.labcd.unipi.it/wp-content/uploads/2022/04/che-guevara.mp4 extracted from the documentary Ruta del Che (directed by Yvonne Ruechel-Aebersold, Philip Koch.Germany, 2009) contains the image of Che Guevara on his deathbed. The clip was found by searching for the object "humanface" within the documentary Ruta del Che.

[6] The clip http://www.labcd.unipi.it/wp-content/uploads/2022/04/baloon-andree.mp4 extracted from the documentary Desert 79°: 3 Journeys Beyond the Known World (directed by Anna Abrahams, Netherlands, 2010) contains the image of the ballon that the Swedish explorer Andree used during his polar expedition in 1897. The clip was found by searching for the object "balloon" within the documentaries.

[7] By searching "Moby Prince" within the index of clips it is returned the clip http://www.labcd. unipi.it/wp-content/uploads/2022/05/moby-prince.mp4 containing the Moby Prince ferry that was involved in the fire accident in Livorno arbour in 1991. The clip was retrieved by the system because the subtitles printed on the frames contain the word "Moby Prince".

[8] A recording of the first online meeting of the test group with the explanation of the prototype, some examples of remixes generated by users and feedback received have been published at the link: https://www.labcd.unipi.it/ph-remix/aiph-award (contents and recordings are in Italian). This page contains also a general presentation of the project and some examples of historical contents that can be retrieved by the search engine of clips and was realized in occasion of the participation to the contest organized by AIPH (Associazione Italiana di Public History) for the best public history project developed between 2021 and 2022.

Fig. 7. Search result for "flag" returning over 1000 clips. The system returns all the clips that contain the object flag as recognized by AI object recognition processor or the word flag in the subtitles.

giving users the possibility to enlarge the clips automatically extracted by AI to catch the context of a single scene, in fact in many cases single clips last few seconds, just the time for an object or a word to appear on the screen, while for extrapolating the context of a scene it would be useful to enlarge this duration watching the frames immediately preceding or following the initial result. Other shared proposals were to add the functionality for uploading resources from the user local to enlarge the possibilities of creation of remixes with custom materials or being able to save on the server the video editing session in order to back to the video editing of the remix at a later time, creating so longer and more elaborated remixes. Another idea emerging from beta tests was to enrich data extracted by AI through social tagging, that is giving final users the possibility to add custom tags to clips individuating people, places or even abstract concepts, supplying additional information that at the state of the art it is not possible to detect by means of AI techniques (cf. Previous chapter). The social tagging could be organized as a public or didactic initiative intended for secondary and university students with a double aim: on one hand to circulate the documentaries of the archive, contributing to spread the knowledge of Festival dei Popoli and its themes with the public, on the other hand to enrich the great amount of automatically generated data with more refined information that in a future could be used as a set for the training of even more sophisticated machine learning algorithms. In the end users agreed that the Festival dei Popoli multimedia heritage is an extremely interesting case study and the platform is useful for exploring documentaries through new perspectives and creating connections between the stories narrated. The possibility to access and reuse fragments of films contributes to spread the knowledge of the archive and to promote documentaries that even if they are preserved in the archive they do not have the visibility that they would deserve for the importance of the images and facts they contain. Another possible evolution could be to gather in the platform a multitude of audiovisual archives evolving the prototype to a huge data store of clips in a way similar to the main social network services. The architecture developed, as explained in chapters 2 and 3 supports this kind of upgrade.

The experimentation of video remix in the field of education, along with the use of a search engine that returns as a result a potentially infinite list of clips automatically extracted from AI processors, represent the two main challenges of PH-Remix project with influence in the whole panorama of digital humanities. The main issue related to making such a tool freely available to the public is concerned with copyright. All data processed by the platform are subject to copyright and an explicit consent by the copyright owners formulated through licenses following the model of Creative Commons seemed the best solution for making available the contents in the platform. But a complex rights chain that includes producers, authors and all the actors who took part in the films makes this license based solution difficult to adopt. An evaluation with law experts is underway within the project to find solutions for publishing materials, taking into account the transposition from Italy of the EU Directive on Copyright[9] that at the time of writing is in the final stages. The new copyright law legitimates the data mining and the publication of fragments of copyrighted materials for non commercial aims in the framework of limited access networks reserved to educational institutions.

5   Conclusion

The web platform belongs to the domain of remix culture, an artistic production practice that is based on the reuse of pre-existing contents coming from different sources. This practice was born in the music panorama but nowadays it is widely spread also in video

---

[9] Directive (EU) 2019/790 of the European Parliament and of the Council of 17 April 2019 on copyright and related rights in the Digital Single Market and amending Directives 96/9/EC and 2001/29/EC http://data.europa.eu/eli/dir/2019/790/oj, last accessed 2022/01/10.

production and many websites and social media allow users to create and share remix works: the action of copying, transforming and re-elaborating[10] is legitimised by the production practices typical of the web, which are based on the sharing of content that is now part of mass culture. The PH-Remix platform was created as part of a public history project whose aim is to make use of widespread ways of interaction to involve end users in the development of historical content through the use of documentary cinema.

As planned in the final phase of the project and in a future with the continuation of the project with the testing of the prototype with a wide audience characterised by scholars for the production of new teaching materials and students of different school orders for the use and remix of multimedia content of historical nature, it is intended to create remix products aimed at reinforcing the public history remix model and to evolve the initial reflection on the challenges and potential of such a tool. Firstly, the challenge of introducing into academia a research tool based on artificial intelligence algorithms and capable of producing and returning large quantities of fragmented multimedia documents, and secondly the actual possibility of putting archival audiovisual materials online in compliance with current copyright laws. As regards the potentialities, in addition to the aforementioned advantages for end users, it is worth highlighting how the availability of an online platform allowing the visualisation and re-use of clips extracted from thousands of digitised, filed and indexed films in a systematic way thanks to the contribution of artificial intelligence, triggers a mechanism of re-launch and revalorisation of film funds, contributing to the dissemination of the knowledge of the archive.

References

Bell, D.: Documentary film and the poetics of history. J. Media Pract. **12**(1), 3–25 (2011)

Burrough, X., Gallagher, O., Navas, E.: Forking paths in new media art practices: investigating remix. media-N. J. New Media Caucus, **17**(1) (2021)

De Luna, G.: Le nuove frontiere della storia. Il cinema come documento storico. In: Le fonti - audiovisive per la storia e la didattica, Annali AAMOD n. 16, Roma (2013)

Fairbairn, N., Pimpinelli M. A., Ross, T.: The FIAF Moving Image Cataloguing Manual. Indiana University press, Indiana (2016)

Gallagher, O.: Reclaiming Critical Remix: the Role of Sampling in Transformative Works. Routledge (2018)

He, K., Zhang, X., Ren, S., Sun, J.: Deep Residual Learning for Image Recognition. arXiv preprint arXiv:1512.03385 (2015)

Kuznetsova, A., Rom, H., Alldrin, N., Uijlings, J., Krasin, I., PontTuset, J., et al.: The open images dataset v4: Unified image classification, object detection, and visual relationship detection at scale. arXiv:1811.00982 (2018)

Lagny, M.: Il cinema come fonte di storia. In: Brunetta G. P. (eds.), Storia del cinema mondiale, vol. 5 Teorie, strumenti, memorie, Einaudi, Torino (2001)

Lin, T.-Y., et al.: Microsoft COCO: common objects in context. In: Fleet, D., Pajdla, T., Schiele, B., Tuytelaars, T. (eds.) ECCV 2014. LNCS, vol. 8693, pp. 740–755. Springer, Cham (2014). https://doi.org/10.1007/978-3-319-10602-1_48

Lin, T., Goyal, P., Girshick, R., He, K., Dollár, P.: Focal Loss for Dense Object Detection. arXiv: 1708.02002. (2017)

---

[10] Kirby Ferguson "Everything is a Remix".https://www.everythingisaremix.info/watch-the-ser ies/, last accessed 2022/01/10.

Navas, E.: Remix Theory. Springer, The aesthetics of sampling (2012)

Salvatori, E.: Digital (public) history: the new road of an ancient discipline. RiMe Rivista dell'Istituto di Storia dell'Europa Mediterranea 1(1), 57–94 (2017)

Sorlin, P.: L'immagine e l'evento. L'uso storico delle fonti audiovisive, Paravia, Torino (1999)

Sorlin, P.: Una premessa. Scuola, storia, mezzi audiovisivi nell'era digitale». Le fonti - audiovisive per la storia e la didattica, Annali AAMOD n. 16 (2013)

Souček, T., Lokoč, J.: Transnet v2: An effective deep net-work architecture for fast shot transition detection, arXiv preprint arXiv:2008.04838 (2020)

Zhou, X., et al.: East: an efficient and accurate scene text detector. In: Proceedings of the IEEE Conference on Computer Vision and Pattern Recognition, pp. 5551–5560 (2017)

A Pipeline for the Implementation of Immersive Experience in Cultural Heritage Sites in Sicily

Roberto Barbera[1] , Francesca Condorelli[2] , Giuseppe Di Gregorio[2] ,
Giuseppe Di Piazza[5], Mariella Farella[3,4,5] , Giosué Lo Bosco[3,5] ,
Andrey Megvinov[5], Daniele Pirrone[5], Daniele Schicchi[3,5(✉)] ,
and Antonino Zora[5]

[1] Department of Physics and Astronomy, "E. Maiorana", University of Catania,
Piazza Università 2, 95131 Catania, Italy
`roberto.barbera@ct.infn.it`
[2] Department of Civil Engineering and Architecture, University of Catania,
Piazza Università 2, 95131 Catania, Italy
`condorelli@darc.unict.it, giuseppe.digregorio@unict.it`
[3] Department of Computer Science, University of Palermo, Via Archirafi 34,
90123 Palermo, Italy
`{mariella.farella,giosue.lobosco,daniele.schicchi}@unipa.it`
[4] National Research Council of Italy - Institute for Educational Technology,
Via Ugo La Malfa 153, 90146 Palermo, Italy
`mariella.farella@itd.cnr.it`
[5] Department of Sciences for Technological Innovation, Euro-Mediterranean Institute
of Science and Technology, Via Michele Miraglia, 20, 90133 Palermo, Italy
`{giuseppedipiazza,andreymegvinov,danielepirrone,antoninozora}@iemest.eu`

Abstract. Modern digital technologies allow potentially to explore Cultural Heritage sites in immersive virtual environments. This is surely an advantage for the users that can better experiment and understand a specific site, also before a real visit. This specific approach has gained increasing attention during the extreme conditions of the recent COVID-19 pandemic. In this work, we present the processes that lead to the implementation of an immersive app for different kinds of low and high-cost devices, which have been attained in the context of the 3dLab-Sicilia project. 3dLab-Sicilia's main objective is to sponsor the creation, development, and validation of a sustainable infrastructure that interconnects three main Sicilian centres specialized in augmented and virtual reality. The project gives great importance to the cultural heritage, as well as to the tourism-related areas. Despite the presentation of the case study of the Santa Maria La Vetere church, the process of the final app implementation guided by the general pipeline here presented is general and can be applied to other cultural heritage sites.

Keywords: Virtual reality · Cultural heritage · CAVE · VR-headset · Virtual heritage

1 Introduction

The digital revolution has brought the development of innovative technologies capable of revolutionizing the engagement of users during the digital experience. Virtual Reality (VR) [1], Augmented Reality (AR) [4] and Mixed Reality (MR) [27] are means to either project a user into a virtual world or to include digital elements into the real world to interact with. AR/VR and MR enable the user to achieve an *immersive* experience, that is the perception of being part of a non-physical world, fostering the focus on the main activity to carry on avoiding distractions. Research on immersive technologies is ongoing and worthy to be more investigated since they provide fertile ground for supporting several application domains related to culture [12,23], medicine [2,3,14], education [13,17] and much more.

In particular, Virtual Reality is a human-computer interface that simulates a realistic environment [29]. In the virtual environment, the user can act according to the project specification in a 3D environment. For instance, in the virtual representation of a house, the user may behave like he would do in the real world, for example, by moving around and grabbing objects. The user does not need to use classical input devices like a mouse and keyboard for inputting commands, but the interactions with the environment can happen by body-related devices. A VR experience can be joined by several devices. The most common are mobile devices that, if combined with cardboard helmets (e.g. Google Cardboard), can offer a low-cost and widely accessible immersive experience. A better experience can be provided through the VR headsets (e.g. Oculus Quest2) capable of tracking the head and eyes movements, recording voices and output sounds. Generally, VR headsets are equipped with specifically made physical controllers that improve the interactivity with the virtual world.

Finally, the Cave Automatic Virtual Environment (CAVE) [19] is a technology created for providing immersive experiences to people without using headsets. It is a cube-shaped room whose walls act as displays for rear projections. The CAVE creates a virtual environment in which the user can experience immersivity. Often, the user is equipped with special glasses useful for tracking the movements inside the room.

The above-mentioned devices need proper implementations in order to be usable. There are nowadays several possibilities to implement immersive VR applications [28], yet there are two engines that are dominating the development market: Unity3D and Unreal Engine 4. Both of them are used to realize 3D games and are open source solutions. Unity3D was first released in 2005 and nowadays is broadly adopted for AR/VR content and mobile games. This is also motivated by the fact that it is highly multiplatform. Unreal Engine has a long history starting in 1998. Most of the biggest Video Game Companies provided their top titles using this engine, but it is not due to superiority over others. The platform compatibility of Unreal is reduced compared to Unity. For the specific case the VR development, what is very useful is the possibility to dispose of the so-called assets, i.e. virtual objects that represent a real or imaginary world.

Both Unity and Unreal Engine have assets markets, with the first providing 3 times more assets than the latter (30.000 vs 10.000).

The aim of this paper is to present the processes and the results in support of cultural heritage which have been attained in the context of the 3dLab-Sicilia[1] project. 3dLab-Sicilia's main objective is to sponsor the creation, development, and validation of a sustainable infrastructure that interconnects three main Sicilian centres specialized in augmented and virtual reality. The project gives great importance to the cultural heritage, as well as to the tourism-related areas. Thus, our principal contribution is to make virtually explorable an iconic Sicilian monument, Santa Maria La Vetere church, by presenting a state of the art pipeline suitable for the development of multi-platform applications. The church is located in Militello in Val di Catania. It was built by the Normans around 1090, after having taken these lands from the Muslim rule. Destroyed and rebuilt several times over the centuries, in increasingly large and monumental, the last suffered partial destruction due to the earthquake of 1693. The church, stripped of many architectural elements, was adapted to the cult thanks to the plugging of the arches of the only surviving aisle.

The paper is organized as follows: in Sect. 2 are presented some correlated research useful to understand the state-of-the-art and current direction of this research topic; in Sect. 3 is presented the pipeline used to develop VR applications in the domain of cultural heritage; in Sects. 4 and 5 will be discussed the 3D scanning techniques used for the acquisition of cultural assets and then for creating a 3D model; in Sect. 6 will be shown how the model is made accessible through virtual reality devices and CAVE. Finally, conclusions are given.

2   Related Works

The literature shows several examples of successful applications of VR systems in support of cultural heritage. According to [8], such applications can be classified on the basis of their purposes. Some of them are specifically developed for *education* aims such as helping the users to learn more about historical details of tangible and eventually non-tangible heritage assets. *Exhibition* enhancement addresses the visitor experience by enriching it with virtual elements (e.g. maps, virtual tour guide). VR has been shown useful also for *exploration* purposes, in which tangible heritage assets are made viewable and manipulable. Often, cultural heritage assets that have existed only in the past are made explorable by VR systems after a *reconstruction* process. Finally, Virtual museums applications aim at proposing the experience of visiting physical museums virtually, including their tangible and intangible assets.

In [24] is presented a gesture-based system created to educate people about the cultural heritage. The system acts as a vehicle to make people capable of interacting by body movements with the virtual representation of tangible and intangible assets. It has been shown capable of improving the engagement of the public in the ancient Maya archaeology context. Authors of [20] present a solution

---

[1] https://www.3dlab-sicilia.it.

to improve immersitivy in a VR context based on mobile devices and exploitable in several applications. Their approach addresses the problem of lacking controls during the usage of such devices mixed with Google cardboard. The solution provides a system based on two smartphones in which one of them is used as the main display and the second one as a controller for implementing functions such as rotation and scale. In [5], HBIM and VR have been combined to virtually create the Unesco World Heritage site of Lombardy known as *Santa Maria Delle Grazie*. Moreover, the paper presents a new methodology for creating intangible parts of monuments that have been lost through time.

In [22], *Villa Ad Gallinas Albas*, an ancient Roman villa, has been made accessible by creating a VR application that leveraged both Unity3D and reconstruction technologies. The application provides mid-air gestures that the visitor can use to explore the villa. Alongside the mere exploration, it is made possible to enjoy an innovative storytelling approach combining several media, that make the experience instructive. Virtual tours of the historical town centre of Mons in Belgium are proposed in [20]. The description of cultural assets is made by a storytelling approach, in which the user is informed about the historical value of the building that is going to be visited. In the same direction, in [16] a historical graveyard (i.e. *Salla World War II graveyard*) placed in a remote area between Russia and Finland is made available to visitors by using VR headsets. The application provides a high-quality representation of the site, including the possibility of acting as in the real world such as turning on candles.

To the best of our knowledge, there are few similar works that have supported the cultural heritage of Sicily, an island that is well-known to be rich in tangible and intangible cultural assets. In [10] is proposed a virtual diving system, created for educational purposes. It allows the user to explore *Cala Minnola*, an underwater archaeological site located near Levanzo (Aegadian Islands). For similar purposes, a virtual reconstruction of the archaeological site of Ancient Noto, a city located in the East part of Sicily is proposed in [7]. The work has been done in the context of the EFIAN project that aims at valorizing the ancient Noto by meeting the principles of the Italian Code for Cultural Heritage and Landscape. In [9], an approach based on high-resolution photo-realistic texture mapping onto 3D models has been exploited to make virtually accessible the temple C of Selinunte, one of the foremost Greek colonies in Sicily.

Authors have presented in [6] three applications that allow the user to virtually explore the SS. Crocifisso al Calvario, a church that is located in the municipality of Militello in Val di Catania. A small demo of the work is made available here[2].

3   The Pipeline

This section describes the sequence of steps, hereinafter pipeline, that have led to the creation of the immersive scenarios. The pipeline is made according to

---

[2] https://www.3dlab-sicilia.it/en/demo-della-chiesa-del-calvario/.

the state of the art, but it focuses on the development of multi-platform applications. Indeed, the pipeline shows the steps to create the 3D model, which is
then made explorable via several VR devices. As shown in Fig. 1, the first step
of the pipeline is the digital acquisition of a cultural site through specific 3D
scanners. The output obtained from the scanning process is then processed by
3D modelling software to arrange a *point cloud* as a 3D model. To do so, main
components such as norms, meshes and textures are computed to compose such
a model then stored as *obj* format. The model is imported in Unity3D, that
is the software utilized to implement the applications deployed to VR devices
– i.e. smartphones in combination with cardboard (Sect. 6.1), Oculus Quest 2
(Sect. 6.2) – and CAVE (Sect. 6.3).

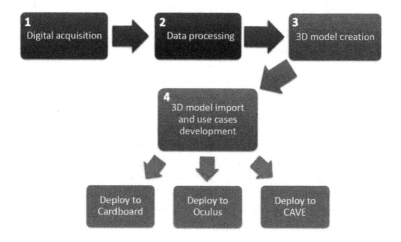

Fig. 1. The proposed pipeline

4 Digital Acquisition and Data-Processing

The object of the surveys described in this paper is a church located in the
municipality of Militello in Val di Catania: Santa Maria la Vetere Church. The
data acquisition described below has been obtained by different instruments
(SFM with terrestrial and drone photos), but we focus in particular on the point
clouds created with the Faro Focus 350S laser scanner. The surveys were carried
out for this church both outside and inside using white reflective spheres to
improve the subsequent orientation and alignment in the joining and registration
phase. These spheres were positioned in order to be clearly visible from each
station point. In Santa Maria la Vetere Church (Fig. 2) the external surveys are
applied to the remains of the right aisle (the only persisted in the south) and of
the central portico (open to the west), to the surroundings: the stone churchyard
in front of the Church with baptismal font, the pit tombs below the missing aisles
and a Norman turret located at the northeast of the site (Fig. 3(a)).

Fig. 2. Santa Maria la Vetere Church - Militello in Val di Catania

The station points for the outside survey are 49 and 9 for the inside; also in this case many of the points have been chosen for the connection between inside and outside and to take care of the connection between the nave and the chapel located behind the altar (Fig. 3 (b)). The correct alignment of the clouds has been obtained thanks to the spheres but even by evaluating the homologous points and planes in the different clouds and considering them as constraints.

(a) Survey of outside: point of station

(b) Survey of inside: point of station

Fig. 3. Distance between one station point and another

The church has required a quite long processing time to obtain the union and registration of the clouds in a resulting 3D model with very dense points (Fig. 4). The transition from the cloud (namely from the discrete model) to the mesh (namely the surfaces resting on the points of the cloud) has instead created considerable problems both for the very high number of points and for the size of the files (about 100 GB).

(a) Union and registration of point cloud

(b) Overall view of point cloud: Santa Maria la Vetere Church

Fig. 4. Point cloud

5   Models Creation

During the process of creating a 3D model for cultural heritage related to religious architecture, the level of detail of the formal elements requires special care. For the Mesh and Texture processing phase, different kinds of software were used to then compare the results, including Faro Scene, Meshlab, Cloud Compare, and Zephyr by 3DFlow. The amount of scans and data does not allow to arrive at an acceptable mesh processing with standard procedures, in which it is possible to appreciate the details. For the creation of navigable VR models with standalone viewers and with smartphone viewers, the amount of data is an already known criticality, from which studies and research for the segmentation of clouds have derived, the state of affairs in this sector is still in evolution.

There is extensive literature on the subject, by way of example, recent works may be used as a reference [21], but other works have also shown the complexity of the problem [15,18], most felt for religious architecture. The visual experience is linked to the quality of details in virtual reality, therefore conflicts with the amount of data. Automatic procedures do not solve the problem of the different concentrations of points in the areas with more details. The problems described have manifested themselves in different ways, both in the case of use illustrated and in others of the same project.

In relation to the model of the Church of Santa Maria La Vetere (Fig. 5), among the detailed scale elements of considerable visual impact, we can mention the altar, the two internal portals and the external porch with low reliefs. The first overall elaborations of the meshes gave a low-quality visual result where it was not possible to appreciate the detail of the formal elements (Fig. 6).

Then the point clouds of the various internal parts of the church have been disassembled into their constituent elements: the altar (Fig. 7), the two portals separately, the floor, the ceiling, the walls, the space behind the altar, the cross vault behind the altar. Different processing modes and different software

Fig. 5. Santa Maria La Vetere Church, union of the clouds in the area in the ruins of the aisles that collapsed in 1693

Fig. 6. Santa Maria La Vetere Church, mesh elaboration of the surviving aisle

for creating meshes were followed, the two results that provided better visual quality saw the use of Meshlab and the mixed one of Faro Scene and Meshlab. The pipeline with Meshlab had the following steps: importing the cloud of Scene software into Meshlab, simplification through decimation algorithms, normal calculation, and mesh calculation. The processing with Faro Scene combined with Meshlab was handled as follows: the processing of the mesh of the individual elements through Faro Scene, then the point cloud from the laser scanner

Fig. 7. Santa Maria La Vetere Church, the individual elaborations of the altar, the arch and the portals

was imported into MeshLab and simplified through decimation procedures, the individual meshes, previously processed with Scenes, have been relocated to the cloud previously loaded in MeshLab. An overall model has been defined with a differentiated detail for the various formal elements. The external model acquired by the laser scanner was then combined with the photogrammetric model of the aerial shots of the drone.

6   Use Case Development

After the creation of the 3D model as described in Sect. 4, we proceeded to implement the applications for Virtual Reality devices and the CAVE. The application has been developed by exploiting *Unity*, a game engine cross-platform that enables the development of VR applications by providing effective tools and a handy visual development environment. The application behaviour can be defined programmatically by using the C# programming language.

Below, we will discuss the development phases that have led to the creation of an application, compatible with smartphones combined with Cardboard, Oculus Quest2 and CAVE (Fig. 8), that allows the user to visit Santa Maria la Vetere church. A brief demo of our work can be found here[3].

---

[3] https://www.3dlab-sicilia.it/en/demo-della-chiesa-di-s-maria-la-vetere/.

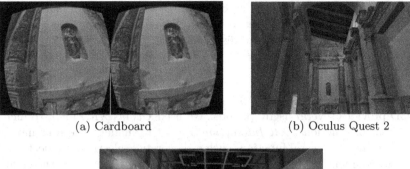

(a) Cardboard   (b) Oculus Quest 2

(c) CAVE

Fig. 8. Virtual exploration of the Santa Maria La Vetere Church

6.1 Smartphone with Cardboard

The application development addressing smartphones has leveraged Unity version 2020.3.x alongside plugins to simplify the whole process. In particular, XRPlugin Management and Cardboard XR Plugin have been used.

XRPlugin Management was used to manage, load and initialize Extended Reality (XR) plugins useful for developing VR/AR and MR systems. The second plugin, Cardboard XR Plugin, has allowed us the management and the creation of a stereoscopic VR system for Google Cardboard. It supports base VR features like motion tracking and stereoscopic rendering simplifying the creation of the user interface. To allow the user movements within the virtual environment, "trigger points" have been implemented. Trigger points are located in several different places in the environment. They are utilized as means for teleporting the user towards a different area of the environment. Therefore, if the user looks at one of the trigger points (e.g. a floor's point) for a specific interval of time, the user's position will be set up nearby such a point.

In terms of optimization, various elements have been considered. Lights have been pre-compiled and shadows have been managed in such a way to make it possible to run the application even for smartphones with limited computational resources, that otherwise, would not be capable of providing a fluid experience.

Regarding the computational complexity of the system, it depends on the texture resolution. The correct resolution choice provides optimal model navigation including a good detail level. In fact, providing a high-level experience avoid the user to run into VR sickness or Cybersickness [11], that is the sensations of lightheadedness, disorientation or sickness caused by the delay in latency[4]. This delay can produce a dissonance between body movements and actions in a virtual environment, generating a sense of disorientation.

6.2   Oculus Quest2

To develop VR applications for VR headsets, in particular for Oculus Quest2, Unity3D provides several useful plugins. We used *Oculus XR Plugin* to include motion control functions; *XR Interaction Toolkit* to manage the user interface since it implements several functions such as hover and selection of objects in the virtual environment; and *XRPlugin Management* that was used for the creation and management of the XR plugin.

The above plugins help to control the player's movements within the environment and manage the interactions with other objects. As for the development of VR systems on smartphones, the set of optimizations related to 3D models and the virtual system has been considered. Such a process allows the user of experiencing optimal navigation by Oculus devices (see Sect. 6.1).

6.3   CAVE

For what concerns the VR application for the CAVE, the use case was designed for a 3-wall CAVE composed of a front wall, a left side wall, and a right sidewall. Leveraging on Unity3D 2019.4.x version, the *Mirror* library was used to implement the communication among the CAVE's walls through the network. This library serves for managing and synchronizing two workstations. The first workstation is dedicated to managing the front wall and the second one manages the two side walls. The network components make it possible to synchronize the player's position and the virtual objects in the CAVE.

For the real-time management of the controllers and the user position in the CAVE, the *UVRPN* plugin (VRPN wrapper for Unity3D[5]) has been used. It simplifies the management of the tracking data sent by the worn devices and acquired through the VRPN technology. Thus, the user can move around, and in real-time, the virtual environment can be arranged in respect of the user's actions.

Regarding the optimization of the models, the use of dedicated hardware has made it possible to choose a higher 3d-model texture resolution if compared to the ones of the previous systems (Sect. 6.1 and Sect. 6.2). Moreover, both lights and shadows rendering are computed in real-time.

7   Conclusions

The pipeline here presented has been used for the development of the virtual exploration of the Santa Maria La Vetere church. The Oculus Quest2 head-

---

[4] the time gap between the moment in which the command input is sent to the system and the moment in which it is outputted.

[5] https://github.com/hendrik-schulte/UVRPN.

set gives the most immersive effect, due to the specific nature of the device because the viewer hides the real-world perception. In terms of resolution, the Cave implementation is the best, but with quite low immersivity with respect to the headset. The cardboard version is the worse in terms of resolution and interactions capabilities, despite representing a very efficient low-cost alternative. Following the presented pipeline we are working on the implementation of new apps related to new Sicilian sites, making more evident the potentiality of VR devices and outlining the value of cultural assets in Sicily. Moreover, Virtual Assistants to embed in the virtual tour are being developed exploiting cutting edge methodologies known as Graph Neural Networks and Text Simplification [25, 26].

Acknowledgements. The following paper has been supported by the project "Creazione di una rete regionale per l'erogazione di servizi innovativi basati su tecnologie avanzate di visualizzazione" (3DLab-Sicilia), Grant No. 08CT4669990220, funded by Operational Program 2014–2020 of the European Regional Development Fund (ERDF) of the Sicilian Region.

Daniele Schicchi acknowledges funding from the European Union PON project Ricerca e Innovazione 2014–2020, DM 1062/2021.

References

1. Anthes, C., García-Hernández, R.J., Wiedemann, M., Kranzlmüller, D.: State of the art of virtual reality technology. In: IEEE Aerospace Conference, pp. 1–19. IEEE (2016)
2. Argo, A., et al.: Augmented reality gamification for human anatomy. In: Gentile, M., Allegra, M., Söbke, H. (eds.) GALA 2018. LNCS, vol. 11385, pp. 409–413. Springer, Cham (2019). https://doi.org/10.1007/978-3-030-11548-7_38
3. Arrigo, M., et al.: Heart mobile learning. In: 10th Annual International Conference on Education and New Learning Technologies, EDULEARN 18, IATED Academy, pp. 10899–10905 (2018)
4. Azuma, R.T.: A survey of augmented reality. Presence: Teleoperat. Virt. Environ. **6**(4), pp. 355–385 (1997)
5. Banfi, F., Bolognesi, C.: Virtual reality for cultural heritage: new levels of computer-generated simulation of a UNESCO world heritage site. In: From Building Information Modelling to Mixed Reality, pp. 47–64. Springer (2021). https://doi.org/10.1007/978-3-030-49278-6_4
6. Barbera, R., et al.: A case study for the design and implementation of immersive experiences in support of Sicilian cultural heritage. In: Proceedings of the 2nd International Workshop on Fine Art Pattern Extraction and Recognition (2022). (in press)
7. Barone, Z., Nuccio, G.: For a conscious fruition of the cultural heritage of ancient NOTO (Sicily) - EFIAN project as opportunity for valorisation. Int. Arch. Photogramm. Remote Sens. Spatial Inf. Sci. **42** (2017)
8. Bekele, M.K., Pierdicca, R., Frontoni, E., Malinverni, E.S., Gain, J.: A survey of augmented, virtual, and mixed reality for cultural heritage. J. Comput. Cult. Herit. **11**(2) (2018)

9. Beraldin, J.A., et al.: Virtual heritage: the cases of the byzantine Cript of Santa Cristina and temple c of Selinunte. In: Proceedings of 10th International Conference on Virtual Systems and Multimedia (2004)

10. Bruno, F., et al.: Virtual reality technologies for the exploitation of underwater cultural heritage. Volume: Latest Developments in Reality-Based 3D Surveying and Modelling, pp. 220–236 (2018)

11. Chang, E., Kim, H.T., Yoo, B.: Virtual reality sickness: a review of causes and measurements. Int. J. Hum.-Comput. Interact. **36**(17), 1658–1682 (2020)

12. Donghui, C., Guanfa, L., Wensheng, Z., Qiyuan, L., Shuping, B., Xiaokang, L.: Virtual reality technology applied in digitalization of cultural heritage. Cluster Comput. **22**(4), 10063–10074 (2019)

13. Farella, M., Arrigo, M., Taibi, D., Todaro, G., Chiazzese, G., Fulantelli, G.: ARLectio: an augmented reality platform to support teachers in producing educational resources. In: Proceedings of 12th International Conference on Computer Supported Education, pp. 469–475 (2020)

14. Goo, H.W., Park, S.J., Yoo, S.J.: Advanced medical use of three-dimensional imaging in congenital heart disease: augmented reality, mixed reality, virtual reality, and three-dimensional printing. Korean J. Radiol. **21**(2), 133–145 (2020)

15. Griffiths, D., Boehm, J.: A review on deep learning techniques for 3D sensed data classification. Remote Sens. **11**(12), 1499 (2019)

16. Häkkilä, J., et al.: Visiting a virtual graveyard: designing virtual reality cultural heritage experiences. In: Proceedings of the 18th International Conference on Mobile and Ubiquitous Multimedia. MUM 2019, New York, NY, USA. Association for Computing Machinery (2019)

17. Maas, M.J., Hughes, J.M.: Virtual, augmented and mixed reality in k-12 education: a review of the literature. Technol. Pedagogy Educ. **29**(2), 231–249 (2020)

18. Matrone, F., Lingua, A.: Tecniche di deep learning per la segmentazione semantica di nuvole di punti del patrimonio architettonico

19. Muhanna, M.A.: Virtual reality and the cave: taxonomy, interaction challenges and research directions. J. King Saud Univ.-Comput. Inf. Sci. **27**(3), 344–361 (2015)

20. Papaefthymiou, M., Plelis, K., Mavromatis, D., Papagiannakis, G.: Mobile virtual reality featuring a six degrees of freedom interaction paradigm in a virtual museum application. Institute of Computer Science, December 2015

21. Pierdicca, R., et al.: Point cloud semantic segmentation using a deep learning framework for cultural heritage. Remote Sens. **12**(6), 1005 (2020)

22. Pietroni, E., Forlani, M., Rufa, C.: Livia's villa reloaded: an example of re-use and update of a pre-existing virtual museum, following a novel approach in storytelling inside virtual reality environments. In: Digital Heritage, vol. 2, pp. 511–518. IEEE (2015)

23. Plecher, D.A., Wandinger, M., Klinker, G.: Mixed reality for cultural heritage. In: IEEE Conference on Virtual Reality and 3D User Interfaces (VR), pp. 1618–1622. IEEE (2019)

24. Richards-Rissetto, H., Robertsson, J., von Schwerin, J., Agugiaro, G., Remondino, F., Girardi, G.: Geospatial virtual heritage: a gesture-based 3D GIS to engage the public with ancient Maya Archaeology. In: Archaeology in the Digital Era. Amsterdam University Press, pp. 118–130 (2014)

25. Schicchi, D., Pilato, G., Lo Bosco, G.: Attention-based model for evaluating the complexity of sentences in English language. In: Proceedings of 20th IEEE Mediterranean Electrotechnical Conference, MELECON 2020, pp. 221–225 (2020)

26. Schicchi, D., Pilato, G., Lo Bosco, G.: Deep neural attention-based model for the evaluation of Italian sentences complexity. In: Proceedings of 14th IEEE International Conference on Semantic Computing, ICSC 2020, pp. 253–256 (2020)
27. Speicher, M., Hall, B.D., Nebeling, M.: What is mixed reality? In: Proceedings of the 2019 CHI Conference on Human Factors in Computing Systems, pp. 1–15 (2019)
28. Voštinár, P., Horváthová, D., Mitter, M., Bako, M.: The look at the various uses of VR. Open Comput. Sci. **11**(1), 241–250 (2021)
29. Zheng, J., Chan, K., Gibson, I.: Virtual reality. IEEE Potent. **17**(2), 20–23 (1998)

Methods and Systems for Enhancing Heritage Fruition and Storytelling

Sustainable Well-Lighting Design for Cultural Heritage. Natural Light Control by Biological Elements and Digital Technologies

Carla Balocco[1]([☒]) [iD] and Simona Carbone[2]

[1] Department of Architecture, DiDA, University of Florence, Firenze, Italy
carla.balocco@unifi.it
[2] Freelance Engineering Cooperating with DiDA, University of Florence, Firenze, Italy

Abstract. The aim of our research was to define a methodological approach useful for sustainable lighting design, vision and perception quality, new visual paths and perceptive emotional experiences, in historic building. Ermanno Scervino's boutique in Florence was the case study. LED systems integrated with control devices for dynamic regulation were custom designed using COB and DALI with minimal invasiveness, in accordance with protection and preventive conservation requirements of building and exhibited artefacts/fabrics. A biological system collocation allowed the dynamic control of natural light for thermal and luminous aspects. Information communication technologies (ICT) were connected to the dynamic control systems for natural and artificial light, and Gaze system allowing a new lighting project for museum and exhibition, fruition and sale, respecting the physical distancing, but recovering the historical philological value of the space and offering completely new visual, perceptive and emotional experiences.

Keywords: Well-Lighting · Sustainability · Cultural heritage · Digital technology · Natural lighting design · Visuo-perceptive path

1 Introduction

The first Historic and more generally cultural heritage buildings, are subjected to external impulses, anthropic and natural changes, new digital technology, IOT and ICT applications, but also to virtual reality and robot design, new forms-modalities and, as the case may be, flows of user/customer/visitor and then changes in technology and people behaviour [1–4].

The climate change, functional transformations, mass tourism, growing demand for high levels of comfort and safety, consumption control and energy efficiency are just some of the current challenges to be faced and which lead us to a basic reflection on how to deal with, rationalize, make strategic and stimulating these transformations [2–5]. Designing light and with light for cultural heritage buildings means conveying information, communicating and enhancing spaces and artworks, improving vision and perception and finally recovering their historical memory, in accordance with the green and digital transitions [3]. On the one hand, this choice represents the necessity for

© The Author(s), under exclusive license to Springer Nature Switzerland AG 2022
R. Furferi et al. (Eds.): Florence Heri-Tech 2022, CCIS 1645, pp. 195–206, 2022.
https://doi.org/10.1007/978-3-031-20302-2_15

enhancing particular environment; on the other, it is a challenge for the designer, who must use light to adapt environments, originally designed for specific uses, to new and very different ones.

In Italy many existing, historic and cultural heritage buildings are used as retail spaces, shops and boutiques. Retail transformation is a wide and complex process that started before the covid-19 pandemic [5–8]. The great development and diffusion of digital technologies, communication systems, artificial intelligence applications, machine learning, big data, virtual reality, neurosciences and deep-sciences application, mobile apps, have strongly changed retail places, in-store systems, back-end operations, supply-inventory-delivery systems, business models, but also the shopping ways, behaviour, choices and preferences of customer [5–10]. Therefore, due to these big and also dramatic changes, lighting design must be reimagined, rethought and transformed, adapting over time and space the application of new digital technologies for a well-lighting, green (natural-biological), adaptive/sustainable, environmental conscious design [10–13].

In this present research, the proposed lighting project takes into account the multi-disciplinary aspects that lighting technology today requires, because light quantity and quality are the key components of well-lighting, understood as vision and perception quality, environmental quality, sustainability, comfort, i.e. people health and well-being. Dynamic light control and design allowed to reorganize spaces and create paths that suggest information contents and new perceptions to the user/visitor/customer, telling about the critical and dramatic period we are experiencing, drive with prospective optimism, along new proximity paths, with defined but creative distances. The new light, rhythmic over time for quantity and quality, enhances the historical retail space and the exclusive sartorial art, marks dynamic paths of vision that make the (indoor) space, a place of light (outdoor), connecting it to the itineraries for visiting the city and the surrounding museums. The proposed lighting based on advanced control systems integrated with natural elements (i.e. plants that filter it and transform it) and with digital techniques, creates a visual and perceptive frame where the purchase becomes a new proximal and emotional experience.

2 Methods and Materials

2.1 Settings

In this section, fundamental architectural and historical features of the Scervino boutique, the case study, are provided. The boutique housed in a historic building, was designed by Ermanno Daelli and Toni Scervino, overlooks via Dei Pescioni and via Degli Strozzi, in the inner centre in Florence. It is spread over two levels of 150 m^2 each. It is a portion of the nineteenth-century Palazzo Mosca, designed by architect Riccardo Mazzanti, a building built with four floors in neo-sixteenth-century form that houses the Hotel Helvetia & Bristol, founded by the hotelier Giacomo Mosca in 1883 (Fig. 1).

Fig. 1. Photo: West shop-window (left); internal view of the South-East shop-window (centre); South shop-window (right).

All the rooms at the ground floor, have been used for a long time by the Neuber store, one of the oldest stores in Florence, just as a symbol of Florentine elegance with slightly English tones. Scervino boutique is a space of historical and cultural value, but also an exhibition space for exclusive sartorial art. The boutique design combines tradition and modernity, bringing together antique furnishings and late nineteenth-century decorations (industrial cement), used for floor and those walls on which inlaid frames with gold accents stand out. The particular staircase, that leads to the basement, is made by exposed reinforced concrete with a parapet in shaded red glass with LED illumination. The environment at the ground floor mainly represents the entrance volume to the boutique, frames the sub-volumes dedicated to the exhibition. It is the only space where natural light is present. It was read by means of light, as a light space to a light place (Fig. 1). The fine wood in briar is the dominant material in the environment, of the original shelves, tables, shop windows and furnishings with gilded finishes. The shelves surmounted by large mirrors, covered with precious fabrics and illuminated with strips LEDs, constitute unique display niches of equally unique and precious accessories. Four chandeliers, belonging to the original historical furnishings, are on the ceiling framed by stucco, now equipped with the integrated LED systems. Many adjustable/pivotable LED spotlights illuminate all of the shop-windows.

3 Designing New Effective Lighting Solutions. ICT with Green Integration

Results and validated simulation models of our recent study were used [14]. All the simulations were carried out under precautionary conditions, i.e. with the maximum solar radiation value, varying the extreme luminance conditions of the sky. The hourly climatic data of direct and diffuse solar radiation, sky conditions, sunshine index, illuminance and UV values, provided by the Environmental Monitoring and Modelling Laboratory for sustainable development (LAMMA CNR IBIMET), were used.

In our present research, light was designed for presenting products, creating an atmosphere, communicating the identity of the retail space. The existing luminous climate assessment provided important findings for a new lighting proposal oriented to enhance the aesthetic quality of the store, people/customers perception and vision, increasing the sensorial experience and interaction with its surroundings, but also guaranteeing energy consumption reduction and preventive conservation fundamental conditions [15–17]. The total space of the boutique was redesigned, better highlighting its functions and features spread over the two floors of the building (i.e. ground floor and basement). The ground floor, reception area and main entrance, was reorganized because it is the only environment with natural light presence: the doorway into the shop is a critical zone, because the customer has to decide whether or not to continue into the shop and take a look around. Light was designed to balance cold and warm shadows, together with the exact distribution of lighting points to create an inviting environment that appeals to and stimulates the sense of comfort, security and familiarity in a potential customer. The different zones of the boutique's ground floor, e.g. shelves and exhibition cases, were highlighted by a carefully planned LED lighting installation, combined with backlighting and track lighting, and in some cases by wall-mounted lights. Tables 1 and 2 show the new LEDs used for the ground floor and basement, that were selected depending on the primary and secondary optics with emissive and elliptical glass, respectively for basic and accent lighting. Taking into account the conversion of the photopic (visual) parameters into melanopic (biological-circadiano stimulus) parameters, in Table 2 the Melanopic Natural Efficacy Ratio (MNER), Melanopic Daylight Efficacy Ratio (MDER) and Melanopic Equal-energy Efficacy Ratio (MEER) are also provided for each LED according to [18, 20].

Table 1. Photometric characteristics of ground floor light sources

Name	n°	Typology	Representation	Absorbed power	Luminous flux	Efficiency	Color temperature	Ra	MNER	MDER	MEER
Semi-recessed spotlight	36	LED		14.5W	825 lm	57 lm/W	3000K	80	/	/	/
Flexible strip	33	LED		11.9 W	454 lm	39 lm/W	2339K	13	/	/	/
Antique chandelier with 4 lamps*	4	LED		23 W	3156 lm	138 lm/W	/	/	/	/	/
Spotlight	33	LED		9 W	682 lm	75 lm/W	3000K	>90	1.04	0.55	0.60

The new lighting was connected to the dynamic visual paths that are controlled, modified and adapted to the quality of vision and perception by means of the Gaze system installation. Gaze allowed to detect the user behaviour within the environment during any visit (i.e. position, tracking, gaze, age, gender, emotional state). In particular, the new light provided: basic light that comes from the illuminated and grazing ceiling on the basis of the wall-washing principle, goes downwards diffused mainly obtained with crossed beams; accent light for shelves and showcases with higher intensity obtained with collimated directional beams. The light paths were obtained, referring to the visual mapping technique, to identify dynamic light corridors that varies in intensity and direction with the people passage. Catadriotic tapes (i.e. phosphorescent and reflective light-grey adhesive fabric well suited to the colour of the floor) were placed on the ground and basement floor.

Table 2. Photometric characteristics of ground floor light sources

Name	n°	Typology	Representation	Absorbed power	Luminous flux	Efficiency	Color temperature	Ra	MNER	MDER	MEER
Linear system	23	LED	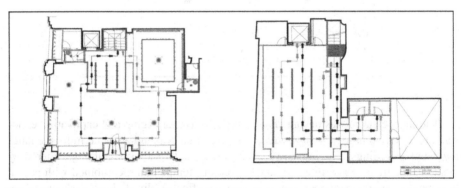	12.3W	647 lm	53 lm/W	3000K	>90	1.04	0.55	0.60
Track lights	49	COB LED		9 W	815 lm	90.5 lm/W	3000K	>90	1.04	0.55	0.60

The study of the paths dynamics and geometry, in reference to a recent work [21], provided the choice for a circulation layout based on a linear system. This type of layout ensures an optimal people distribution inside the space, because it was designed according to the three-dimensionality and temporality of the environment, decreasing crowding, but increasing levels of curiosity and desire for exploration by the user. This linear circulation system was linked to the light dynamic distribution by means of the ICT connection used for COB and DALI control/regulation systems (Fig. 2).

Fig. 2. Linear circulation layout for the inlet and outlet at the ground floor (left) and basement (right)

Two lighting scenarios were identified, but for the first the natural lighting control was provided by integration between digital techniques and natural-biological system [14, 22–26]. Three groups of large-leaved tropical plants were used referring to their height and leaf area, arranged in subsequent layers, with the intention of controlling, shielding and absorb solar radiation in the shop-window zones. The first group includes: Palma Areca, Bamboo and Strelizia Nicolai with 4 m average height and 1–1.5 m^3 average green volume; the second group includes Philodendron, Ficus and Banana with 2.5–3 m average height and 1 m^3 average green volume; the third group with Alocasia, Strelizia Reginae and intertwined Ficus of 1.5–2 m height and 1.5 m^3 green volume. By comparing some relevant literature results [25, 26], it was deduced that the amount of solar radiation on average absorbed by a tropical plant leaf can be 50% of the incident one (early in the morning and at the end of the evening the absorption drops to 40%). Although the only 50% of solar radiation is photosynthetically active, as much as 85% of it is absorbed by the leaves. During cloudy days the average absorption can increase up to 59% due to spectral distribution of light that takes place entirely in the ultraviolet and visible wavelengths, where leaves have maximum absorption. The shielding effect of solar radiation on shop windows, i.e. the amount of radiation intercepted by plants, is related to the parameter LAI (Leaf Area Index) which represents the bioclimatic efficiency of the shielding effect generally expressed as a percentage of radiation intercepted (or transmitted) in the different seasons and is especially valid for broad-leaved plants, such as the chosen tropical ones. Therefore, taking into account the average surface index and thickness of the leaves, the average value of the absorption and reflection coefficient obtained, were used for all the three groups, respectively equal to 80–85% and 20–15%. Table 3 shows the Photosynthetically Active Radiation (PAR) index for each plants' layer.

Table 3. Photosynthetically active radiation (PAR) for each plants' layer

	PAR Incident (W·m^{-2})	PAR Riflected (W·m^{-2})	PAR Transmitted (W·m^{-2})	PAR Absorbed (W·m^{-2})
Layer 1	200	20	20	160
Layer 2	20	2	2	16
Layer 3	2	0.2	0.2	1.6
Total				177.6
%				88.8

The first scenario was designed as follows: active, engaging and captivating exposure and sale/purchase, obtained with a mixture of natural and artificial light, the latter regulated according to the intensity of the external solar radiation although filtered by plants; basic light of low intensity and low colour temperature, combined with accent light with high colour temperature to obtain the effect of dim-light to darkness in the surroundings. It has been demonstrated that this effect pushes to purchase with greater freedom of choice, concentration and satisfaction [27, 28]. Therefore, accent lighting is activated together with visual walking, that is the paths marked with artificial light.

In the absence of natural light or for very low values of its intensity, this scenario is guaranteed by the dynamic control of the LED sources. The second scenario concerns the museum visit, which must be immersive, activate reflection, memory, mental processing and representation, and is achieved with only the adaptable and dynamic base light provided by the LED luminaires. This lighting system takes place during the closing times of the sale, but open to evening visits in conjunction with those of the adjacent city museums (e.g. Palazzo Strozzi and Ferragamo Museum).

The new light broadens the visual/perceptive path from space to place, or rather to the urban historical-artistic context. Also for this scenario there are linear visual-walking paths.

4 Results and Discussion

In this section lighting simulation results of the project proposal are shown and discussed. The lighting scenario for the ground floor (i.e. sale and visit to the boutique) was obtained on the basis of the combination of natural light filtered by the system of tropical-plant layers with accent lighting on the shelves, adjusting, in relation to the amount of natural light, the pointing angle and the light beam opening up to a max of 45°. The results of the average value of the maximum illuminance values do not exceed 500 lx (Fig. 3a). This scenario was simulated at two conditions corresponding to two critical days: the first is representative of the worst summer condition, with clear sky, maximum levels of illumination and total solar radiation (i.e. 06/07/2018 at 13:00); the second is representative of the worst winter conditions with overcast sky, minimum levels of illumination and total solar radiation (i.e. 05/01/2018 at 11:30 am). In the first condition, it is evident that the mix of natural and artificial light leads to higher illuminance values than those due to only artificial light.

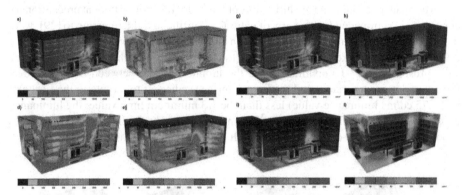

Fig. 3. Illuminance (lx; left) and luminance (cd/m^2; right) distribution at the ground floor

This happens near the windows facing South where at h 13,00 the illuminance value is 2 klx (Fig. 3b). In the shelving area, the illuminance values, due to the accent lighting, never exceed 500 lx. Tropical plants not only allow solar radiation control, but also a good and balanced illuminance distribution without any glare phenomena risk (Fig. 3h). For the winter condition with overcast sky, the illuminance values are more homogeneous, of 454 lx average value comparable with those due to only artificial lighting (Fig. 3c).

In this condition, the luminance balance guarantees the absence of any glare phenomena (Fig. 3i). The lighting scenario, that concerns the museum visit and which was simulated without natural light, produces homogeneous and low illuminance values of 329 lx (Fig. 3d). The wall-washer lighting technique conceived for this scenario was obtained by varying the positioning and aiming of some spotlights, placed near the shop-windows. In particular, for each of the two groups of 10 spotlights on the South wall, two of them were directed perpendicular to the horizontal with a rotation angle of 60° on the vertical plane. These same angular coordinates were used for 2 of all the 6 spotlights that make up the group in correspondence with the North-West shop-window.

For the group of spotlights in the South-West showcase, no change was considered to avoid interference phenomena due to the light coming from the South Wall. For the basement, the scenario proposed for nocturnal museum visit, involved calibration and variation of the pointing angles, light beam opening and positioning of all the spotlights housed on 8 electrified tracks suspended in the centre of the room. These variations (about 45°), were alternatively carried out on spotlights with diffusing glass optics. At the same time, for each electrified track, 6 groups of all the 10 suspended spotlights, were switched off and adjusted for a 50% luminous flux reduction. The obtained results showed a very homogenous illuminance distribution in the whole environment with 200 lx maximum values (Fig. 4f). The uniform distribution of very low luminance values guaranteed the absence of any type of glare (direct, indirect or veil; [29]) as shown in Fig. 4n. For the lighting scenario designed for sale at the basement, obtained through the installation of fixed spotlights and linear systems along the room perimeter, transient simulation results performed during the whole day, showed higher illuminance values that only in some areas slightly exceed 500 lx (Fig. 4e). It should be noted the important effect of luminance balance and uniformity (Fig. 4m).

In particular, the luminance ratio results obtained for the ground floor at precautionary conditions in summer and with a mix of natural and artificial light, referring to [29], were the following: the luminance ratio between the visual task (worktop with luminance 80 cd/m^2) and the darker surfaces adjacent to it (East shelves with 38 cd/m^2 luminance value) respects the 3/1 maximum limit; the luminance ratio between the visual task (80 cd/m^2 luminance value) and the lighter surfaces adjacent to it (path to the East exit with 275 cd/m^2 luminance value) less than the 1/3 minimum limit value; the luminance ratio between the visual task (70 cd/m^2 luminance value) and the lighter distant surfaces (South wall with 1500 cd/m^2 luminance value) respects the 1/20 minimum limit value.

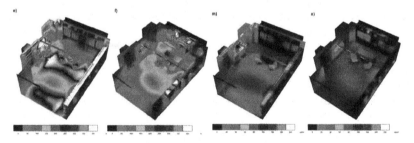

Fig. 4. Illuminance (lx; left) and luminance (cd/m^2; right) distribution at the basement

The luminance ratios at the basement, in the presence of artificial light only for day and night hours, were calculated taking into account the regulation/control of all the LED systems according to the intensity of the emitted flux, beam opening, and specular/diffuse reflections on different surfaces.

In particular, the results for the daytime scenario including the accent lighting are the following: the luminance ratio between the visual task (work surface with 10 cd/m^2 luminance value) and the adjacent lighter surfaces (East wall with 30 cd/m^2 luminance value) falls within the 1/3minimum limit value. For the evening scenario including basic lighting and museum visit, the luminance ratio between the floor (6,53 cd/m^2 luminance value) and the adjacent darker surfaces (North wall with 1,75 cd/m^2 luminance value) falls within the 3/1maximum limit value.

The maximum annual light dose values were also calculated and compared with the limits imposed by [15–17, 30] for the categories of photosensitivity to which the generally exposed fine fabrics correspond (e.g. silk, cotton, velvet, linen, wool with silk yarns, lace and damask).

Taking into account that the display of the artefacts, both in the shop-windows and shelves, is usually carried out with exposure times for shifts of up to 15 days, the hours corresponding to this time range, were used for the calculation. For the shop-windows, an exposure of 24 h/day to artificial light was considered, i.e. 15h/day to natural light in summer conditions and 10h/day in winter conditions; for shelving, the duration of exposure to artificial light alone corresponds to the opening hours of the boutique, i.e. 9h/day. For all the lighting scenarios, at the ground floor and basement, it can be deduced that: only for the summer conditions in the presence of both natural and artificial light, the annual light dose values are slightly higher for the very high photosensitivity category (South wall 5,8 klx/h year, West wall 6,27 klx/h year), while for all other scenarios, including natural light in winter conditions and covered skies, the values are within the maximum limits set for all the categories.

As a matter of fact, the differentiation of lighting groups between day and night scenarios, considerably reduces the quantity of lux emitted, thus avoiding the risk due to photodegradation for the different types of fabrics/materials exposed.

The new design structured on two dynamic lighting scenarios, for day and evening/night, on the one hand involved a general increase in the hours of the LEDs switching on, but customization with control groups, adaptation/regulation to the intensity of natural light access at the ground floor, number of luminaires reduction, dynamic adjustment of the luminous flux and light colour of each LED, provided significant reductions in energy consumption and of the LENI index value [31] for each scenario more than 60% compared to the existing condition (Table 4).

Table 4. Energy consumption and LENI value comparison between the new lighting proposal and the existing state

	New lighting proposal Ground floor		Existingstate Ground floor	New lighting proposal Basement		Existing state Basement
	Day	Night		Day	Night	
LENI kWh/(m^{2}year)	12.47	13.55	42.92	23.66	10.37	66.16
Total energy kWh/year	551.26	599.40	1898.11	1182.73	518.40	3307.21
LENI %variation	70.95%	68.43%		64.29%	84.33%	

5   Conclusions

What was proposed is not a closed definitive solution, a single answer to the application of ICT connected to natural-biological elements and digital technologies for a sustainable well-lighting design. Rather, it stands as a new integrated methodological approach and a strong perspective for new questions, new research and developments. The natural biological system for dynamic control of natural light linked to ICT was used to manage all the LED systems (i.e. dynamic regulation and custom design with COB and DALI), but also by means of GAZE application, to acquire information on space/place vision and perception, and communicate to the manager/owner about post-processed results (e.g. the most used path, the average age of visitors, which object arouses the most interest, how many visitors in certain time slots, Fig. 5). The new lighting has minimal invasiveness, reversibility and adaptivity, in accordance with protection and preventive conservation requirements of both the building and the exhibited artefacts/fabrics. The new lighting marks the physical spaces, conveying information on the historical and philological content, exclusivity and prestige of the artefacts, and triggering interpretative and perceptive, creative and stimulating processes providing an optimistic perspective and ensuring health protection of the artworks and visitors/operators, especially during the dramatic time which we are experiencing (Fig. 5). Results obtained from this study, concerning the lighting system integration with natural elements (plants) for light control and filtering and transformation in effective data, but also an important energy consumption reduction, can be a support for lighting design aimed to visual quality and cultural heritage protection improving daylight penetration and uniform light distribution by means of the best combination between biological elements and digital technologies.

Fig. 5. Rendering: the new lighting for the ground floor with the first luminous scenario (active, engaging and captivating exposure and sale/purchase; left) and basement with the second luminous scenario (the museum visit; right)

Acknowledgements. The authors thank LUCE 5 company in Arezzo, Italy (https://www.luce5. it/it/); Dr. Cosimo Morganti, Brand Project Manager of the Ermanno Scervino boutique and all his staff; Dr. Luca Fibbi, Environmental Monitoring and Modelling Laboratory for sustainable development (LAMMA CNR IBIMET) of Sesto Fiorentino (Florence, Italy).

References

1. Camuffo, D., Pagan, E., Bernardi, A., Becherini, F.: The impact of heating, lighting and people in reusing historical buildings: a case study. J. Cult. Herit. **5**(4), 409–416 (2004)

2. Esther, H.K., Chan, E.H.W.: Implementation challenges to the adaptive reuse of heritage buildings: towards 1, the goals of sustainable, low carbon cities. Habit. Int. **36**(3), 352–361 (2012)
3. EU Leeuwarden Declaration 2018 Adaptive re-use of the built heritage (https://europa.eu/regions-andcities/programme/sessions/475_en). Accessed 10 Feb 2020
4. Al-Sallal, K.A., AbouElhamd, A.R., Dalmouk, M.B.:UAE heritage buildings converted into museums: evaluation of daylighting effectiveness and potential risks on artifacts and visual comfort. Energy Build. **176**, 333–359 (2018). https://doi.org/10.1016/j.enbuild.2018.06.067
5. Grewal, D., Kauri, D.K., Roggeveen, A.L., Sethuraman, R.: Strategizing retailing in the new technology Era. In. J. Retail. **97**(1), 6–12 (2021) https://doi.org/10.1016/j.jretai.2021.02.004
6. Biswas, D.: Sensory aspects of retailing: theoretical and practical implications. Int. J. Retail. **95**(4), 111–115 (2019)
7. Jayakumar, J., Suresh, M.: Assessment of physical enablers of retail store environment using fuzzy logic approach. Mater. Today Proc. in press (2021)
8. Laski, J., Brunault, C.A., Schmidt, R., Ryu, S.C.: An exploratory study of retail lighting with continuous modulation of color rendering properties to influence shoppers' spatial range of browsing. J. Bus. Res. **111**, 148–162 (2020) https://doi.org/10.1016/j.jbusres.2018.10.032
9. Ampenbergera, A., Staggla, S., Pohl, W. Attention guidance, perceived brightness and energy demand in retail lighting. In: 8th International Conference on Sustainability in Energy and Buildings, SEB-16, 11–13 September 2016, Turin (IT) Energy Procedia, vol. 111 (2017). http://creativecommons.org/licenses/by-nc-nd/4.0/
10. Piccablotto, C., Aghemo, C., Pellegrino, A., Iacomussi, P., Radis, M.: Study on conservation aspects using LED technology for museum lighting. Energy Procedia **78**, 1347–1352 (2015) https://doi.org/10.1016/j.egypro.2015.11.152
11. Tantanatewin, W., Inkarojrit, V.: Effects of color and lighting on retail impression and identity. J. Environ. Psychol. **46**, 197–205 (2016) https://doi.org/10.1016/j.ijresmar.2017.12.005
12. Deepika, J., Neeraja, T.: Lighting impact on consumer's shopping behaviour in retail cloth stores Int. J. Sci. Res. **3**(11), 933–938 (2014)
13. Nie, J., et al.: Investigation on entraining and enhancing human circadian rhythm in closed environments using daylight-like LED mixed lighting. Sci. Total Environ. **732**, 139334 (2020) https://doi.org/10.1016/j.scitotenv.2020.139334
14. Balocco, C., Carbone, S.: Light intensity and quality for the enhancement of historic places, susttainability and helath in their proximity. The Scervino space in Florence. LUCE 335 (2021)
15. CEN/TS 16163–2014 Conservation of Cultural Heritage-Guidelines and Procedures for Choosing Appropriate Lighting for Indoor Exhibitions; EU: Brussels, Belgium
16. UNI 11630–2016 Light and Lighting-Criteria for the Preparation of the Lighting Design; EU: Brussels, Belgium
17. I.E.S. Lighting Handbook: The Standard Lighting Guide; Illuminating Engineering Society of North America (Classic reprint): New York, NY, USA (2018)
18. CIE S026-E2008 System for metrology of optical radiation for iprgc-influenced responses to light. https://doi.org/10.25039/S026.2018
19. DIN SPEC 5031/100–2015 Optical radiation physics and illuminating engineering - Part 100: Melanopic effects of ocular light on human beings - Quantities, symbols and action spectra
20. ANSI/IES TM-30–2018 IES Method for Evaluating Light Source Color Rendition; Washington, USA
21. Park, S., Zhang, S.: A pilot study of circulation layout based on perceived retail crowding. J. Retail. Cons. Serv. **49**, 305–315 (2019) https://doi.org/10.1016/j.jretconser.2019.04.008
22. Bringslimark, T., Hartig, T., Patil, G.G.: The psychological benefits of indoor plants: a critical review of the experimental literature J. Environ. Psychol. **29**(4), 422–433 (2009)

23. Jumeno, D., Matsumoto, H.: The effects of indoor foliage plants on perceived air quality, mood, attention, and productivity J. Health.com **3**(4), 1359–1370 (2016)
24. Lohr, V.I., Pearson-Mims, C.H., Goodwin, G.K.: Interior plants may improve worker productivity and reduce stress in a windowless environment J. Environ. Hortic. **14**(2), 97-100 (1996)
25. Larsen, L., Adams, J., Deal, B., Kweon, B.S., Tyler, E.: Plants in the workplace the effects of plant density on productivity, attitudes, and perceptions Environ. Behav. **30** (3), 261–281 (1998)
26. Debattista, R., Tidy, H., Clark, M.: Investigating the effect photodegradation has on natural fibres at a microscopic level. Int. J. Sci. Justice (2019). https://doi.org/10.1016/j.scijus.2019.04.002
27. Huang, I.X., Dong, P., Labroo, A.A.: Feeling disconnected from others: The effects of ambient darkness on hedonic choice Int. J. Res. Mark. **35**(1), 144–153 (2018). https://doi.org/10.1016/j.ijresmar.2017.12.005
28. Estekya, S., Wootenb, D.B., Bos, M.W.: Illuminating illumination: Understanding the influence of ambient lighting on prosocial behaviors J. Environ. Psychol. **68** (2020) https://doi.org/10.1016/j.jenvp.2020.101405
29. UNI EN 12464–1–2011. Light and lighting - Workplace lighting Part 1: Indoor workplaces
30. MiBact, D.: Lgs. n.112/98 art. 150 comma 6. Ministry for Cultural Heritage and Activities - Act of address on technical-scientific criteria and on the functioning and development standards of museums (in Italian)
31. UNI EN 15193–1–2017 Energy Performance of Buildings-Energy Requirements for Lighting-Part 1: Specifications, Module M9; EU: Brussels, Belgium

Reuse, a Challenge for the Preservation of 20th Century Heritage. The Royal Bank of Canada, Santo Domingo, Dominican Republic

Esteban Prieto-Vicioso[1]([⊠]) [iD], Virginia Flores-Sasso[2] [iD],
and Gabriela Fernández-Flores[2] [iD]

[1] Universidad Nacional Pedro Henríquez Ureña (UNPHU), Santo Domingo,
Dominican Republic
eprieto@unphu.edu.do
[2] Pontificia Universidad Católica Madre y Maestra (PUCMM), Santiago de los Caballeros,
Dominican Republic
virginiaflores@pucmm.edu.do, ga.fernandez@ce.pucmm.edu.do

Abstract. Preserving the architectural heritage of the 20th century remains a challenge even though it has been protected for the last decades. The lack of recognition of its value, the absence of a legal framework for its protection and the limited research on their construction systems, structural performance and materials has caused the loss of many places and buildings of the world. It still presents many conservation challenges, including adaptation to new uses, technologies, performance criteria, structural safety requirements and the high cost of repair and adaptation. For this reason, the aim of this paper is to present the methodology used and the results obtained from the rehabilitation of a 20th century neoclassical style building in Santo Domingo, Dominican Republic. The building was constructed for the Royal Bank of Canada in 1914, then abandoned for many years and in 2019 was restored to establish a restaurant. The preservation work included the recognition of its construction system, the recovery of interior and exterior decorative elements, the finishes, the original polychromy of its walls, part of the hydraulic mosaics of the floors, its windows, staircase, and other elements. In addition, the historical research revealed that the building was designed and built by the American firm Purdy & Henderson, one of a prestige firm, which built almost all the buildings for Royal Bank of Canada in the early 20th century. This building is an example of 1920s American architecture abroad.

Keywords: Reuse · 20th century heritage · Neoclassical style · American architecture · Dominican Republic'

1 Introduction

Built form is subject to various types of obsolesces in the course of time especially the functional, taking place as an outcome of the advance of technology, changing modes of living, production, and consumption. It's common to see how 20th century architecture

R. Furferi et al. (Eds.): Florence Heri-Tech 2022, CCIS 1645, pp. 207–222, 2022.
https://doi.org/10.1007/978-3-031-20302-2_16

and modern building change with the development of the city. When heritage buildings can no longer fit the functions needed for urban development and change, they have a high probability of being destroyed. However, Architects have found reuse potential in almost any type of building, rejuvenating these heritage sites. Adaptive reuse helps cities develop space more efficiently for their citizens and businesses, while preserving the built environment's and is a solution to avoiding the obsolescence of buildings in urban development. It is beneficial for the city, for the culture, for the environment, and for the building itself [1]. Adaptive reuse projects involve not only alterations of an existing building but also radical changes and transformations in the urban space.

Since the 1970s, a concern for 20th century architecture and how to give a new use to many abandoned buildings began. In 1975, architect Sherban Cantacuzino published a book where documenting projects around Europe in which an old building was used differently inside but maintained on the exterior similarly to original appearance [2], and in 1989 published another one [3]. Also, Weaver (1975) examines some of the opportunities and challenges around the issues of reuse of older buildings with short features on four types of building [4]. Highfield published in 1987 a small booklet 'The rehabilitation and reuse of old buildings' in which he first expounds the advantages of rehabilitation, making a distinction between domestic and nondomestic buildings.

Van Cayseele and Van Meerbeeck (2001) argued that the behavior of a monument owner influences the expected costs of restoration and said that Governments should consider this behavior to implement efficient restoration policies [5]. Smith (2006) published a book stating that heritage value is self-evident and have an inherent position. Also demonstrates that heritage value is not inherent in physical objects or places, but rather that these objects and places are used to give tangibility to the values that underpin different communities and to assert and affirm these values [6]. Koslow (2009) said that the most sustainable type of real estate development is the adaptive reuse of an existing building. Adaptive reuse of inner-city buildings is an opportunity to return underutilized to improve the environmental impact of buildings, and to provide robust rates of return which compensate developers for the higher risk inherent in this type of development [7].

In 2009 started a project to develop a "Critical encyclopedia of restoration and reuse of 20th century architecture", opening possibilities for inter-regional collaboration between different institutions. The Charter for Conservation of Places of Cultural Heritage Value (among others), notes that the new function should be compatible with the original because the new function should be compatible with the cultural values of the place, so that its authenticity and integrity are not adversely affected. It is also emphasized that the intervention should not dominate the original form and structure [8].

In the 2010s, a great interest in 20th century heritage emerged. The Getty Conservation Institute, with ICOMOS, DOCOMOMO and other institutions celebrated many meetings and published documents to examine the current state of the field and identify areas of outstanding need to develop actions to advance practice in this area of conservation. In 2011, was celebrated *Developing an Historic Thematic Framework to Assess the Significance of Twentieth-Century Cultural Heritage*, in 2013, the *Colloquium to Advance the Practice of Conserving Modern Heritage* [9] and *Conserving Twentieth*

Century Built Heritage: A Bibliography as a resource for conservation practitioners working with twentieth century-built heritage [10], just to mention a few.

The U.S. Department of the Interior's National Park Service published in 1995 a book about building materials, as part of 20th century heritage conservation efforts, which have often been hampered by a lack of technical information about the materials used in their structures. In 2014, this guide is reissued and included manufacturing processes and uses of a wide range of materials [11]. However, sometimes modern interior space receives secondary consideration and is important that the architects also find skillful solutions that achieve the preservation of those values that preliminary analysis has identified as being essential [12].

In 2011, Plevoets and Van Cleempoel concluded within our review of literature on adaptive reuse we have distinguished three contemporary approaches: the typological approach, the technical approach, and the strategic approach [13]. Also, some authors explored the social dimensions of heritage conservation [14] and included the adaptative reused as a goal of sustainable, low carbon cities [15].

In 2014, concerned about the conservation conditions of modern buildings, the Universidade do Minho, Portugal celebrated a seminar "Modern Building Reuse: Documentation, Maintenance, Recovery and Renewal" where the need to disseminate research methodologies and best intervention practices applicable to the material and cultural conservation of modern buildings, whether classified as heritage or simply as common places in our daily lives, was recognized [16].

Zhang and Dong (2021) provide a model for an architectural heritage conservation strategy, guidance regarding the decision-making process and offer a model to find the minimum intervention for a heritage building [17].

The growing number of adaptive reused experiences in different geographical contexts shows the global diffusion of this transformation strategy in the last decades, obviously with some essential differences depending on the local conditions. For that reason, the aim of this research is to present the methodology used and the results obtained from the rehabilitation of a 20th century neoclassical style building in Santo Domingo, Dominican Republic.

2 Exporting of American Architecture

The late 19th and early 20th century were a period of transition architecturally, because was the beginning of forward-looking architectural design, using new materials and techniques, because of the new industrial needs, but with a mixt of style and with new styles not based on previous building forms. This moment marked the entrance into a new era of building and changes in construction techniques. Two principal characteristics distinguish 19th-century architecture: the use of a variety of historical styles and the development of new materials and structural methods [18].

The development of the steel frame, which became a crucial aspect at that moment. Windows became larger and cladding thinner. The non-load-bearing walls came to be known as curtain walls because they hung on their frames. Steel frames also allowed for considerable flexibility of plan, with steel beams and girders allowing for the creation of wide interior spaces. The architects were adapted to the new technologies of the early modern age and approaching design from a functionalist approach that resulted in buildings perfectly suited for their intended use, without unnecessary detail or extraneous decoration.

The export of American architecture began in the mid-19th century with the export of wooden building components, prefabricated structures, metal and wooden decorative details, and the complete building such as houses, churches, and mills. Beginning in 1864, books and construction guides were published and sold favored the export of American architecture [19]. Between 1876 and 1914, many businessmen, engineers, planners, contractors, and architects lured abroad by new kinds of clients or propelled overseas by their US based headquarters began to export wood, iron, steel, and concrete architecture. However, it was not until the waning gasp of the nineteenth century that Americans awoke more fully to the possibilities of exporting their construction knowledge to commercial and cultural contexts so much further afield [20].

Cody said that some Engineering firms such as Purdy and Henderson also exemplified how American designers were attracted to the commercial possibilities opened by the Cuban-US political connection that emerged from 1901 when Purdy & Henderson established an office in Empedrado Street, in Havana [20]. In Cuba they built important buildings as the National Capitol, Centro Gallego, Centro Asturiano, Hotel Nacional, Hotel Plaza, Lonja del Comercio, Habana Yatch Club, Santiago de Cuba Customs Office, La Metropolitana, Radiocentro and all the Royal Bank of Canada (RBC) buildings as well as other landmark structures. In addition, the firm imported building materials and equipment needed on the Island. All these buildings show a marked influence of the fashionable style and use the predominant construction system at that time in the United States based on steel and concrete structures [20].

The 1920s in the United States witnessed rapid growth in production and an increase in consumption that consolidated the upper and middle classes, generating great optimism and security among entrepreneurs who began to do business abroad, including those related to construction. Between 1920–1945, life, the city model and American architecture became the paradigm of progress. The export of American products increased, including construction materials and systems.

Cuba seems to be the first country in the Spanish Caribbean to have used concrete block as a building material with the establishment of a Cuban branch of the New York firm of Purdy & Henderson. Amongst their earliest projects using this building material were several steel frame and concrete block structures in La Habana built as early as 1901 and in 1904 the National Bank of Cuba, establish a Havana branch, [21]. Cuba was the first country to produce cement in the Caribbean, Fábrica Cuba, which started production on July 7, 1895. This cement factory added the production of hydraulic mosaics to its company, naming it "La Cubana", with 200 employees producing 100,000 hydraulic mosaics per week [22]. In 1903 La Cubana was announced by the press of the time as the largest hydraulic mosaic factory in the world. It belonged to Ladislao Diaz, Ramón Planiol and Agapito Cagiga, and was about Luyano, in Havana. Its advantage over other industries was the use of modern tools and mine sands, completely siliceous and free of salts, which favored the fidelity of the colors. It also stood out because many of its employees were former workers of the Escofet, Orsola and Butsems houses, considered among the best in Barcelona.

Original historic documents of the first buildings constructed with concrete block in Cuba by the North American firm of Purdy & Henderson were important finds. In a 1910 article published in the local magazine, *Sociedad Cubana de Ingenieros* it was reported that blocks (were) fabricated in the city of La Habana by Purdy Henderson, with 1 part Portland cement, 2 ½ (parts) limestone sand and 2 ½ (parts) siliceous rock, after 55 days from fabrication…75 kgm [23].

3 Historical Context

The concrete arrives in the Dominican Republic in late nineteenth century. The first used was mass concrete cast in-situ with no internal reinforcement. These structures were built using imported Portland cement products and/or reinforced concrete following models brought by the U.S. Government. The first evidence about the use of concrete in the country dates from 1891 when the railroad begins to be built and made a few bases of bridge and piles foundations [18] also some irrigation channels were constructed in the late 19th and early 20th century, and some dams, reservoirs, maritime structures. These concrete structures became the pioneer in the use of reinforced concrete and incorporated innovative designs, inclusive became used as piles on house.

From 1905–1911, the largest amount of cement came from the USA with a total of 8,230,900 barrels. Also, having been imported from Germany about 3,014,734 barrels, and for other countries like Belgium, England, France, Denmark, and Spain [18].

At the beginning of the 20th century, some cities in the Dominican Republic began to build with decorative concrete elements such as columns and verandas, extending quickly to the rest of the country.

The first house to be built in the city of Santo Domingo entirely of concrete, including slabs and beams, was in 1905, according to a newspaper report [24]. This house had only one level. In previous years only reinforced concrete slabs had been built in narrow areas of galleries, as well as some prefabricated elements such as columns, capitals, and balusters.

At the beginning of the 20th century, the Dominican Republic had an important economic growth due to the rise of sugar cane prices that increased exponentially reaching unprecedented values, which caused a commercial boom and the consolidation of a middle and upper social class. Immediately all kinds of foreign companies began to arrive to the Caribbean, including commercial banks, among them the Royal Bank of Canada, that had already been established in Santiago, Cuba, since 1903 when bought Banco de Oriente and in 1904 bought Banco del Comercio de La Habana and by the mid-1920s, RBC had 65 branches in Cuba and is the largest bank in the country. In 1907, the Royal Bank opened a branch in San Juan, Puerto Rico, and a few years later other branches in Mayagüez and Ponce. In 1912, RBC purchased the Bank of British Honduras, incorporated in 1902 by U.S. citizens from Mobile.

The first foreign banking institution to be in the Dominican Republic, was Royal Bank of Canada, established in the city of Sanchez in the north of the island, in 1912, directed by Mr. L. J. McCarthy. Two years later, in 1914, another branch began to be built in the city of Santo Domingo directed by Mr. T. B. O'Connell, later in San Pedro de Macoris directed by Mr. Juan Moll, La Romana directed by Mr. M. W. Newell, Santiago directed by Mr. T. J. Reardon, and Puerto Plata. In 1985, RBC started to withdraw from the Caribbean. Sold its 12 branches in the Dominican Republic to Banco de Comercio Dominicano.

Since the end of the 19th century, the sugar trade was in the hands of Cuban and North American businessmen, and the influence of both nations was reflected in many areas, especially in the architecture and infrastructure they built. In the Dominican Republic, North American architecture and materials began to be imported, some of them arrived through Cuba, because many North American construction companies had offices there.

3.1 Description of the Building

The Royal Bank of Canada building was designed and built by the firm Purdy & Henderson and located on Isabel la Católica and Las Mercedes Streets, in Colonial City of Santo Domingo, declared a World Cultural Heritage Site by UNESCO in 1990. This building, with a marked neoclassical style, was built in 1914 with a structure of columns and beams of metal profiles, embedded in concrete, known as ferroconcrete. (Fig. 1).

Fig. 1. Royal Bank of Canada, build in Santo Domingo in 1914 (Archivo General de la Nación)

It has two levels of great height. On the lower level were the bank's offices and on the upper level the manager's apartment, which was accessed directly from Isabel la Católica Street, through a small vestibule and an elegant marble staircase with wrought iron railings.

The ground floor, with a height of 5.70 m, is accessed from the corner, through a high door crowned by a cornice supported by two Ionic brackets. On the corner there is a chamfer. Above the door is a large window with an arch that leads to the social area of the house, on the upper floor. The lower level has a free plan with six freestanding rough-hewn columns on pedestals, supporting beams that follow a somewhat radial design.

The upper level, with a height of 5.40 m, was divided by brick partitions to form the different rooms of the house, with a pavement of hydraulic cement mosaic tiles, stamped, built in Havana.

On the facades there is a continuous cushioning on a plinth and an upper cornice in flight, supported by simple modillions between which there are some coffers. A parapet serves as a crown, where there is a high relief with the date in Roman numerals of the beginning of the construction of the building. The lower level has windows supported on the plinth, while the upper level has balconies with wrought iron railings.

3.2 Purdy and Henderson Firm

The firm Purdy & Henderson founded by Engineer Corydon Tyler Purdy (1859–1944), known as father of the structural engineering profession, and Engineer Lightner Henderson (1866–1916), one of the great structural engineers of that moment. The firm was established in 1893 to 1944. Originally was in Chicago and then opened a branch office in New York, in midtown Manhattan in 1894 and moved its base of operations to that city by about 1896, because the projects in the Eastern United States became so lucrative that they soon decided made New York his headquarters and center of operations. This New York office designed some of the most notable buildings and skyscrapers in the Western Hemisphere, that included the 700-foot-tall Metropolitan Life Tower, the world's tallest building from 1909 to 1913 [25]; the structural scheme for the Waldorf-Astoria Hotel in New York, designed by Schultze and Weaver, Architects, which was completed in 1931, the world's tallest hotel from 1931 to 1963 [26] and the structural design of the Main Branch of The Royal Bank's British Columbia District, that was the Vancouver's first bank skyscraper from 1931 to 1973 [27].

Also, in 1899, Purdy supervised the start-up of a New York office for Fuller Company, a firm owner of his friend, architect George Fuller, and by 1900 had obtained consulting work all over the U.S. and in several foreign countries, most notably in Cuba [28], where produced important buildings including El Capitolio and the Hotel Nacional. They formally incorporated in 1901 and after that, Henderson became the President of the concern from 1901 to 1915.

By 1910, the office had in addition to its New York office, four branches including Havana, Cuba, Boston, MA, Chicago, IL, and Seattle, WA. Purdy & Henderson designed the Metropolitan Life Insurance Company Tower's footing and skeletal frame, an office building that was built from 1907 until 1909 and was the tallest in the world from 1909 to 1913. Purdy & Henderson designed the tower's footing and skeletal frame. The firm spanned all North America predominantly provided professional services and in foreign countries like Canada, Cuba (Fig. 2), Puerto Rico and Dominican Republic where included contracting, and construction management as well as designing. During his career, he was involved in the design of more skyscrapers than anyone else in the world, by far. The Purdy and Henderson firm closed shortly after Purdy's death in 1944 [25].

Fig. 2. Purdy & Henderson Co. Advertising in El Libro de Cuba, La Habana 1925 (Del Cueto 2018)

4 Methodology

The preservation methodology for the Royal Bank of Canada building includes three stages: 1) Detailed inspection; 2) Analysis and 3) Proposal of intervention. In the first stage, to be able to make decisions and to use the resources, was made: historical documentation, survey, pathologic processes, and identify the construction system of the building. In the second phase, an analysis was done, which includes a material characterization, determinate the causes of damage present in the building, and a diagnosis and assessment. After analyzing the data collected, the third stage includes an intervention proposal which cover a minimal intervention defined according to the needs of the building, to finish was made a maintenance plan. (Fig. 3).

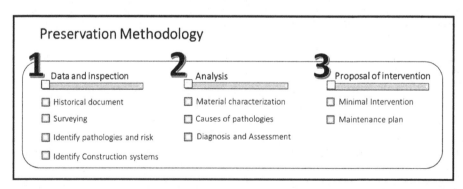

Fig. 3. Preservation methodology (Source: Flores and Prieto)

4.1 Data and Inspection

The process began with a historical documentary research in the *Archivo General de la Nación* and other bibliographic sources, where old photographs, letters and advertisements in newspapers and magazines were found where the original building could be seen inside and outside. In the early 60 s, the Royal Bank building was abandoned and in the 80's was bought by a Dominican bank that installed a branch office there. At that moment the façade and the interior spaces was modified with the aim of modernizing the building (Fig. 4).

Fig. 4. Exterior of modified building (Prieto Vicioso)

The upper cornice and the wooden doors were eliminated, and the exterior walls were covered with ceramic tiles. Also, the window at the corner was closed with concrete blocks. The pedestal and the columns bases were demolished, and a false ceiling was installed to conceal the chapiters and beams. Also, the brick walls of the dwelling were removed to add the upper floor to the commercial area.

In 2018, the building was renovated to install a restaurant and lounge. After a historical study, the owner and architects decide to give the original appearance like was in 1914. This decision to adapt the building to its new use involved the construction of new toilets on both floors, a kitchen, and other facilities. The bank's security vault was converted into a wine cellar.

In San Pedro de Macorís, a city 60 km east of Santo Domingo, a similar building was built in the same year 1914 that has remained practically unaltered, which served as a model for the recovery of the one in Santo Domingo. There it was possible to take measurements of all the elements and details that had disappeared in the other building (Fig. 5). With all this information it was possible to prepare the project for the reintegration of the building and present it to the authorities for their approval.

Fig. 5. Details of the building constructed in San Pedro de Macorís (Prieto Vicioso)

The survey was carried out and through it was possible to determine some differences in the widths of the walls, which upon review were found to be the original walls. When the false ceilings were removed and the original beams were exposed, it was determined that they were prefabricated metal profiles covered with concrete (Fig. 6). The same could be determined in the columns. The walls were made of concrete blocks while the first story and the roof are concrete slabs. Everything, including the metallic elements, was imported by the Purdy firm from Havana, where they had a materials factory. The floors were hydraulic mosaic tiles, very popular at that time.

Fig. 6. Prefabricated metal profiles covered with concrete (Prieto Vicioso)

4.2 Analysis

The analysis of the building began with the identification of the construction materials of the different elements, which at first glance appeared to be reinforced concrete. When analyzing one of the columns on the ground floor, it was found that it had a metal I-profile embedded in concrete. When removing a plafond, it could be observed that the beams were also metal profiles covered with concrete. In both cases the metal profiles were in very good condition and showed no signs of corrosion. Precisely the role of the concrete covering the steel profile, in the case of ferroconcrete type members, is that it protects the metal, increases its buckling capacity and its fire resistance.

The building did not show any cracks or fissures in its structural elements, the walls and columns were plumb, and no subsidence was observed in the floors. Being a building that was already one hundred and five years old, it showed an excellent state of conservation, which is not usual in other constructions of the same period, where the concrete has been losing its faculties.

The interior, non-load-bearing walls were constructed of mud bricks. On the second level, which was originally intended for housing, the brick walls had been removed when the bank extended its office area to the upper floor. The second level of the building retained its 20 by 20 cm hydraulic cement tile floors, with several different designs, which were manufactured in Havana, Cuba by the Fábrica La Cubana (Fig. 7). The wall surfaces were investigated to observe the original colors and select the color to be applied.

Fig. 7. Hydraulic mosaic and traces of it in the cement (Prieto Vicioso)

4.3 Description of Intervention

It was decided to make the minimum intervention. The ceramic covering of the facades was removed and found evidence of the elements that had undergone transformations appeared, which helped in the interpretation of the building. An interesting finding was part of the original staircase which had been mutilated and completely hidden (Fig. 8). The stairwell was closed at the top with a concrete slab and the first flight of stairs was removed. The metal structure of the building, covered with concrete, was also visible.

Fig. 8. Part of the original staircase found (Prieto Vicioso)

On the first floor, the pedestals and bases of the columns were reintegrated, the staircase was freed and the section that had been lost was rebuilt, using a marble like the one found, and the railing was completed following the same original design. The wall that formed the vestibule of the dwelling on the first floor was not reconstructed, remaining integrated to the first level. On the upper level, the free floor plan was maintained, and a hydraulic mosaic pavement was installed, but with a different design from the existing ones. The bank security vault was converted into a wine cellar.

The metal window and balcony railings were reconstructed following the original designs new doors and windows were made in mahogany, also following the original design, but replacing the wooden lattices with fixed glass. The design of the new cornices was simplified and built-in foam, covered with cement plaster. The facades were complemented with ambient lighting.

5   Results and Discussion

The restoration project of the old Royal Bank of Canada's building in Santo Domingo emphasized the recovery of the original façade (Fig. 9), which was fully modified, eliminating all the decorative elements it had, such as cornices, moldings, corbels, and cushioning on the exterior wall. Inside, the bases of the columns and the elegant marble staircase that had been mutilated and hidden were rescued (Fig. 10).

The building needed modern services as new electrical installations, ambient lighting, fiber optic cables, new air conditioning system without visible ducts, new sanitary installations, and security system. All doors and windows were built in wood and glass following their original design, which could be seen in old photographs, eliminating the aluminum windows that had been installed in the previous intervention. For the flooring, hydraulic mosaic tiles or pressed cement were used, like the original ones, thus maintaining the character of the interior spaces.

Fig. 9. Façades of the building restored in 2019 (Prieto Vicioso)

Fig. 10. Ground floor restored in 2019 (Prieto Vicioso)

An industrial kitchen was incorporated because the new use of the building is for a restaurant. Also, a bar with all the necessary services, a storage and garbage storage were added. In all the works carried out, respect for the original building prevailed, without preventing the necessary modifications and adaptations for the development of this new use.

6 Conclusions

An important contribution of this research is that it was determined that the Royal Bank of Canada building in 1914 is the first important building constructed with reinforced concrete in the city of Santo Domingo, with the particularity of having steel profiles embedded in the concrete, which were imported by the construction firm Purdy & Henderson, as well as the steel used in the concrete slabs, Portland cement and hydraulic mosaics.

This paper highlighted the processes related to the adaptive reuse of architectural heritage and including the principles of sustainable development and the creation of cities friendly to inhabitants and the environment. The most important thing is to introduce changes that will be satisfactory for contemporary society and at the same time will not exclude the future understanding and perception of the artefact as a testimony of the past. Introducing new functions, values and meanings into old buildings/sites is a clear example of adaptive reuse.

One of the goals of this intervention is to protect this building which preserves the historical and cultural memory of the city and its community, and to ensure the long-term sustainable uses of the building which are often very different from the original ones. The rescue and reuse of the Royal Bank of Canada's building in Santo Domingo, has a relevant impact on the daily life of the inhabitants and the users of the area.

The methodology was based on the juxtaposition of historical documentation, characterization and analysis of the materials and structure, to produce the conservation strategy and maintenance plan. With this research we want to contribute a methodology of architectural heritage conservation. We understand that to introduction of a new function in architectural heritage is not only an important impulse for the tangible regeneration of urban tissue, but can also help to reconstruct the memory, image, and identity of a city.

References

1. Zhang, Y.: 20-Century Building Adaptive-Reuse: Office Buildings Con-verted to Apartments. Thesis of Historic Preservation **697** (2020). https://repository.upenn.edu/hp_theses/697
2. Cantacuzino, S.: New Uses for Old Buildings. Architectural Press, London (1975)
3. Cantacuzino, S.: Re-Architecture: Old Buildings - New Uses (1989)
4. Weaver, M.E.: Reviewed work: new uses for old buildings by Sherban Cantacuzino. Bull. Assoc. Preserv. Technol. **7**(3), 90–91 (1975). doi.org/10.2307/1493507
5. Van Cayseele, P., Van Meerbeeck, W.: Reusing old buildings: protected monuments in Belgium. J. Arch. Conserv. **7**(2), 64–79 (2001). https://doi.org/10.1080/13556207.2001.107 85295

6. Smith, L.: Uses of Heritage. Routledge, UK (2006)
7. Koslow, J.: Opportunities and Challenges in Whole-Building Retrofits, in Engineering (2009)
8. Cizler, J.: The role of creative and civil initiatives in transforming post-industrial landscapes: a case study of industrial heritage re-use in the Czech Republic. Archit. Civ. Eng. **12**, 207–219 (2014)
9. Normandin, K.C., Macdonald, S.A.: Colloquium to Advance the Practice of Conserving Modern Heritage: March 6–7: Meeting Report. Los Angeles: The Getty Conservation Institute (2013). http://hdl.handle.net/10020/gci_pubs/colloquium_report
10. Macdonald, S, Ostergren, G.: Conserving Twentieth Century Built Heritage: A Bibliography, 2nd ed. Los Angeles, CA: Getty Conservation Institute (2013). http://hdl.handle.net/10020/gci_pubs/twentieth_centruy_built_heritage
11. Jester, T.C.: Twentieth-Century Building Materials: History and Conservation. Los Angeles: Getty Conservation Institute (2014). http://hdl.handle.net/10020/gci_pubs_20th_cent_building_materials
12. Grignolo, R., Reichlin, B.: Lo spazio interno moderno come oggetto di salvaguardia/Modern Interior Space as an Object of Preservation, Mendrisio Academy Press-Silvana Editoriale (2012)
13. Plevoets, B., Van Cleempoel, K.: Adaptive reuse as a strategy towards conservation of cultural heritage: a literature review, in structural repairs and maintenance of heritage architecture. Trans. Built Environ. **118**, 155–164 (2011). https://doi.org/10.2495/STR110131
14. Angel, V.: Exploring the social dimensions of heritage conservation. In: Proceedings - heritage conservation 20/20: Hindsight and foresight, (eds) Cameron, C, and Herrmann, J, pp. 136–145 (2012)
15. Yung, E.H., Chan, E.H.: Implementation challenges to the adaptive reuse of heritage buildings: towards the goals of sustainable, low carbon cities. Habitat Int. **36**(3), 352–361 (2012). https://doi.org/10.1016/j.habitatint.2011.11.001
16. Riso, V. (ed.): Modern Building Reuse: Documentation. Recovery and Renewal, Escola de Arquitectura da Universidade do Minho, Maintenance (2014)
17. Zhang, Y., Dong, W.: Determining minimum intervention in the preservation of heritage buildings. Int. J. Arch. Heritage **15**(5), 698–712 (2021). https://doi.org/10.1080/15583058.2019.1645237
18. Flores-Sasso, V., Prieto-Vicioso, E., Garcia de Miguel, J.: Physico-chemical analysis of historic concrete structures in the Caribbean. In: RE-HABEND 2020, Construction Pathology, Rehabilitation Technology and Heritage Management, Granada, Spain, pp. 539–553 (2020)
19. Flores-Sasso, V.: Timbers, palm board and construction materials of eighteenth and nineteenth century's architecture in dominican republic. In: Campbell, J., et al. (eds.) Further Studies in the History of Construction: The Proceedings of the Third Annual Conference of the Construction History Society, (ed), pp. 333–356 (2016)
20. Cody, J.W.: Exporting American Architecture 1870–2000, Taylor & Francis Group (2003)
21. Del Cueto, B.: Los mosaicos hidráulicos y los bloques de concreto en el trópico caribeño: su origen, historia y conservación. In: Actas del Noveno Congreso Nacional y el Primer Congreso Internacional Hispanoamericano de Historia de la Construcción, pp. 509–519 (2015)
22. De las Cuevas-Toraya, J.: 500 Años de Construcciones en Cuba. La Habana: Chavín, Servicios Gráficos y Editoriales, S.I (2001)
23. Joynt, A.: Cuban Mortar Tiles. International Cooperation and Regeneration through Rediscovery of a Lost Craft, independent research supported by The British Academy in London: chapter 5 (2009)
24. Penson, E.: Arquitectura dominicana. 1906–1950. Laboratorio de Ingenieria, Santo Domingo (2005)
25. Weingardt, R.G.: Corydon tyler purdy. Leadersh. Manag. Eng. **10**(3), 124–130 (2010). https://doi.org/10.1061/(ASCE)LM.1943-5630.0000067

26. Cashman, S.: America in the Age of the Titans: The Progressive Era and World War I. New York University Press (1988)
27. VHF West Hastings Map Guide, Vancouver Heritage Inventory Phase II 1986 Summary Report, RBC Royal Bank. A Brief History
28. Del Cueto, B.: An American Design and Construction Firm in Cuba at the end of the 19th century: Purdy & Henderson, New York (2018)

The Interdisciplinary Role of Archaeoacoustics and Its Applications

Paolo Croce[1](✉) [ID], Francesco Leccese[1] [ID], Giacomo Salvadori[1] [ID], and Umberto Berardi[2] [ID]

[1] University of Pisa, 56126 Pisa, PI, Italy
paolo.croce@phd.unipi.it, {francesco.leccese,
giacomo.salvadori}@unipi.it
[2] Ryerson University, Toronto, ON M5B 2K3, Canada
uberardi@ryerson.ca

Abstract. In the last two decades, a new discipline called archaeoacoustics has begun to emerge seeking to use modern acoustic methodologies to understand and analyze historical artifacts from a new perspective. The interdisciplinary nature of this subject makes it a fertile ground for archaeologists, anthropologists, psychologists and acousticians. Among the objectives of archaeoacoustics, there are to virtually reconstruct lost atmospheres with the help of virtual reality devices and auralization software, to understand the real form or function of historical sites, to understand how sound can interact with the psychological and spiritual aspects of past civilizations, to study the choices that led to the morphological evolution of theatrical buildings as a function of different acoustics, and so on. It is here considered that the real potential of this discipline is to understand the biunivocal relationship that binds the history and the acoustics of ancient environments. Rediscovering how the humankind in the past have selected or built places for sacred and recreational functions can help to complete our current knowledge on the topic. This article aims to present the different connotations of this discipline and their fields of applications.

Keywords: Archaeoacoustics · Acoustics · Historical sites · Cultural heritage

1 Introduction

Archaeoacoustics, born at the beginning of this century as an interdisciplinary subject, is presented as an evolution of what was called music archaeology, a subject that explored the music of past eras through archaeological evidence and related findings [1]. Thanks to the growth and establishment of new technologies and methodologies in the field of acoustics, began to emerge studies extended to the concept of sound itself.

Those who are considered among the first pioneers [1] of this new discipline, although there were also similar previous contributions [2, 3], were Watson and Keating, an archaeologist and an expert in acoustics, who in 1999 began to study the acoustics of Stonehenge [4] realizing that the possible discovery of the acoustics of an archaeological site could provide additional information on what activities could take place within it and what degree of intentionality there was in its construction.

A few years later, from a conference held at the Mac-Donald Institute at Cambridge University in 2003, the first book on archaeoacoustics was published in 2006, edited by Chris Scarre and Graeme Lawson [5], which already began to outline what were the possible fields of study and what the possible big questions of this emerging discipline.

Even after about twenty years, archaeoacoustics manages to embrace disciplines such as archaeology, acoustics, engineering, architecture, anthropology, neurosciences and many other fields, as demonstrated by the publications of successive conferences organized by the OTS Foundation, a United State of America not-for-profit educational institution, held on the subject in 2014 in Malta [6], in 2015 in Istanbul [7] and in 2017 in Portugal [8].

The lack of a common methodology, due to the great heterogeneity of topics, and the number of possible approaches that this subject allows, however, lead to a dispersion of information and efforts that do not allow a clear view of the whole. For this reason, some of the research that has been carried out on different types of buildings and sites has been considered here: rock art caves [9, 10], Stonehenge [11, 12], the places of prayer of the Christian cult [13, 14], Mesoamerican architecture [15, 16], hypogeums [17], musical instruments found [18] and those that are still part of modern culture [19], mythological places of Ancient Greece [20], catacombs [21], Islamic religious buildings [22], and theaters [23, 24].

This large mosaic of research (Fig. 1) forms the basis on which to define the field of application of archaeoacoustics. The presence of very different techniques and methodologies demonstrates the interdisciplinary nature of this field of research. Regardless of the location and type of site, archaeoacoustic research requires the collaboration of scholars such as the sound engineer, the architect, the archaeologist, the ethnomusicologist, etc. This is because the figure of the archaeoacoustician has not yet been defined [25].

What will be done in this article will be to describe most of the research areas present in the field of archaeoacoustics in order to analyze the different approaches. Finally, it will be proposed to unify some of the methodologies presented in past conferences and research on the external and internal environments of archaeoacoustic sites. The final aim is to stimulate future interest in creating the necessary and coherent methodological approach that has long been called for [7].

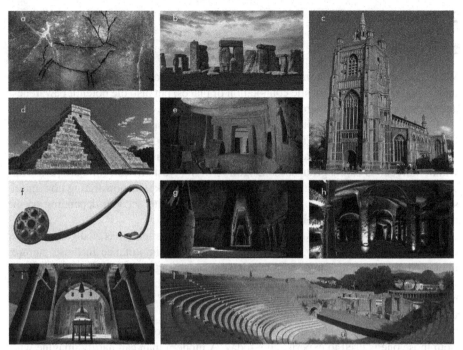

Fig. 1. a) Painting of a stag from Las Chimeneas cave in Spain, a small chamber with a powerful low frequency response [9]; b) Stonehenge monument in England, whose stones differentially filter high and low-frequency sound [12]; c) Church of St Peter Mancroft in Norwich, whose choir has a space under the floor with acoustic vessels [13]; d) Mayan-Toltec stepped pyramid temple called the Castillo at Chichen Itza in Yucatan, Mexico. A percussive sound made in a certain area to the north of the Castillo results in a curious 'chirped echo' (*la cola del Quetzal*) that sounds like the call of the Quetzal, a bird of colourful plumage sacred to the Maya [16]; e) The Main Hall of the Ħal Saflieni Hypogeum in Malta, characterized by powerful resonances and a reverberation time up to 16 s at low frequencies (63 Hz) [17]; f) A pair of "lurs" or "bronze-age lurs", instruments horn-shaped in cross section dated to the late Bronz Age, probably blown by the player as a brass or lip-reed instrument [18]; g) Cumaean Sibyl cave at the north west of the Gulf of Naples, Italy. The acoustic characteristics are compatible with the myth according to which a visitor walking along the corridor to reach the Sibyl was guided by an unintelligible voice that became clearer once they got closer [20]; h) The catacombs of San Gennaro in Naples, whose reverberation time is longer (over 2.0 s) at low frequencies (63 Hz), but decreases at high frequencies without compromising speech intelligibility. These characteristics are compatible with the use of the site for religious functions [21]; i) Sultan-Barquq complex in Cairo, Egypt, acoustically characterized in [22]; l) Theater of Pompeii in Italy, whose original acoustics is penalized by the partial loss of the *scenae frons*, a reflective surface that contributed to the correct diffusion of sound [23].

2 Research Areas

2.1 Origin

What gave rise to the first areas of research in archaeoacoustics was the attempt to understand not only the acoustic connotation of places, but also the potential awareness and intentionality of those who once built and lived there.

Culturally, there is the belief that the primary sense is sight, because it is the primary focus of the contemporary way of experiencing the world, but this thought cannot be translated to all civilizations and all historical periods. This is demonstrated even today within indigenous ethnic groups: the Dogon of Mali (West Africa), for example, 'hear' smells and classify words according to the smell they make, demonstrating how multisensory or synesthetic possibilities must also be taken into account depending on the type of archaeological site being analyzed [12].

Moreover, the contemporary perception of sound and silence has changed a lot over time. Sound and the activity of listening were of vital importance in those cultures immersed in potentially dangerous environments or strongly characterized by activities such as hunting. This aspect was probably the reason why sound took on magical or metamorphic characteristics: wind became the whisper of the gods, echoes became the voices of spirits [16].

The characteristics of the environments generally took on connotations very different from those one is used to experiencing today. A modern man can hardly imagine what it must be like to live an entire life in an atmosphere in which the background noise is incredibly low, in which the sounds of nature surround and overwhelm the listener [26].

This kind of difference in perception also inevitably leads to new, more modern ways of experiencing historical spaces. For example, in [27], it is pointed out how indeed the acoustics in cathedrals have an effect on the human subconscious, but how this has become completely distorted over time. While cathedrals were built for people immersed in silence, who found echoes and reverberations that suggested the presence of the divine, they are now experienced by people immersed in noise, who find in these places atmospheres of peace and silence. In this context, not only the subjective aspect of the sound experience is of particular importance, but also the conditioning due to the context. For this reason, it is considered necessary to include ethnographic information in the study of archaeological sites [28].

In the specific case of man-made structures with particular acoustic characteristics, a first distinction must be made about the intentionality of those who designed and the awareness of those who visited the site. The specific acoustical effects could be:

- Integral part of the design (as in the case of Stonehenge [16], in which the stones used were chosen from an area so far away that their use suggests that the builders were aware of their proprieties);
- An accidental by-product of the design, which was recognized and used (as in the Whispering Gallery at St Paul's Cathedral [29]);
- An accidental by-product of the design, which was never used intentionally (as in the main chambers of the great Pyramid in Egypt [30]).

In any case it should be noted that any structure or environment will have acoustic characteristics and that the absence of specific elements cannot exclude the possibility that sound had a particular function in that place [29].

2.2 Research Areas Identification

The British researcher and main editor of *Time & Mind – the Journal of Archaeology, Consciousness and Culture* Paul Devereux highlights in [16] four areas of research in the field of archaeoacoustics:

- Cataloguing the correlation between rock arts and musical natural features;
- Searching for acoustic symbolism at sites of interest and interpreting them;
- Studying anthropology to identify the importance of sound within different cultures;
- Studying the effects of archaeoacoustic phenomena on the human brain using EEG monitoring (In more recent research, TRV Cameras and FUTURA Cameras have been combined with EEG monitoring for the same purposes [31, 32]).

In addition to these, the following research areas can be identified:

- Studying and improving procedures for measuring sound and acoustic parameters in the archaeoacoustic field;
- Studying sound effects that are considered 'undesirable phenomena' in modern room acoustics, such as echoes, flutter echoes, filters or partial sound-occlusions that can lead to auditory illusions that were enhanced and sought after in many environments of archaeological interest [26];
- Studying, improving and using tools for the virtual reconstruction of the environments and their possible acoustic simulation [33, 34];
- Cataloguing the acoustic characteristics of buildings of the same type in order to compare them with their evolution of materials and forms (as was done in [35] with the acoustics of theaters);
- Studying documents concerning acoustics and their treaties (as was done in [36] for the acoustic vessels present in the *Problémata XI 8* of Pseudo-Aristotle and in Vitruvius' treatise *De Architectura*, not found so often inside ancient theaters, but very similar to the acoustic earth-enware pots found in later churches [30]);
- Studying contemporary sound perception of environments through auralization [37] and other subjective analysis techniques (as was done, for example, in [27] using binaural microphones, observation and Interviews and Questionnaires);
- Studying Aural Architecture [37] to build environments that allow one to relive and understand atmospheres similar to those found in sites.

These are the main fields of research that have been proposed here among those found in the literature. However, one cannot exclude the possibility that these fields will intermingle, divide, evolve, or disappear as knowledge and study technologies advance.

3   Methodologies Found in Literature

3.1   Preliminary Analysis

The presence of numerous areas of research covering every place, material and historical period does not make it easy to identify a uniform methodology. This does not preclude the possibility of being able to identify common methods to refer to in the preliminary phase, to be then characterized with respect to the specific case.

An element to be taken into account is the frequency range of interest. This data has a great impact in practical research, even considering that the range of audible goes from about 20 Hz to 20 kHz.

Generally, in modern architectural acoustics, the number of octave bands (or thirds of an octave) that is considered is closely related to the intended use of the building, often distinguishing macroscopically in use for speech or music. In the archaeological context, on the other hand, not considering a particular range of the sound spectrum could lead to incorrect assessments. At some sites, a characteristic enhancement of specific frequencies, often around 110 Hz, has been found to result in regional brain effects [38]. Having to analyze a wide range of frequencies brings practical issues both in measurement and in acoustic simulations.

Currently, there are two main categories of acoustic simulations: geometric acoustics (raytracing methods for example), which is more accurate and more suitable for simulating sound at high frequencies; wave acoustics (FEM and BEM for example), which is more accurate and more suitable for simulating sound at low frequencies, but much more computationally heavy and almost impractical for environments with large volumes or particular geometries.

Once the frequency range to be considered has been established, the actual field measurement phase should not be neglected. Modern techniques for measuring acoustic parameters (described in ISO 3382–1 [39]) are often ineffective in the field of archaeoacoustics because they mimic a condition in which the audience is focused on someone speaking or playing, whereas in many archaeoacoustic contexts, especially ritual or religious ones, collective sound production and listening activities were conducted [26].

In the case of cramped environments or complex geometry, an additional problem could be not being able to place sources and receivers at adequate distances, both from each other's positions and from reflective surfaces, limiting the location and number of measurements. Even the choice of parameters and reference values is not easy. All the optimum values found in the literature are strongly conditioned by contemporary acoustic taste, making objective acoustic analysis difficult. For example, the use of average values could be very little useful for the characterization of the environment, often requiring a more in-depth analysis of the parameters found for individual positions.

Finally, elements that are generally considered disturbance phenomena in architectural acoustics are important in archaeoacoustics. Examples are echoes, flutter-echoes, resonances, filter phenomena and partial sound occlusion. In fact, the presence of acoustic illusions without visual correlation can have an enormous suggestive power, as if the sound sources resided exclusively in the acoustic domain [26].

3.2   Detail Analysis

Several methodologies proposed by different authors in articles concerning archaeoacoustics have been here selected and put together.

Coherently with what has been done for the research areas, it is possible to start from Paul Devereux's summary in [40] of the three main methods that have been used in recent years to study the behavior of sound within archaeological sites:

- Staging modern performances at sites to test their acoustic properties;
- Using electronic monitoring equipment to measure acoustic parameters;
- Listening to the natural sounds occurring at a site.

The first point summarizes the methodologies used in both research on auralization of environments [41, 42] and research on evaluating human interaction with the site [27], through the use of questionnaires or observation of how visitors move through the space.

Between the first and the second point, Iegor Reznikoff points out the necessity to explore with a trained ear the acoustic behavior of the site [43]. He argues that the instrumentation provides only partial results to be analyzed later in the study and that its use in a space that has not been explored by a human ear may lead to incomplete or false results.

The method he calls the "musical approach" consists of making vocal sounds - homogenous sounds of around 70–80 dB (and 90 dB for echoes), during 1–2 s. - and measuring:

- Time with a chronometer (e.g. a good watch),
- Pitch with a tuning fork (usually tuned on A = 440 Hz),
- Intensity with a sonometer,
- Richness of the resonance by the number of echoes.

The second point summarizes all the various methodologies used for the actual measurement of acoustic parameters, whose possibilities and criticalities have been analyzed by Ian Cross and Aaron Watson in [26].

The third point includes all that concerns the sounds that make up the atmosphere of a place whether they come from the structure itself or from environmental factors such as flowing water, wind, rain. This point concerns both the subjective aspect of the sound atmosphere in which the site is immersed and its objective interaction with the element to be analyzed. In this regard, the useful distinction of acoustics to be analyzed proposed by Zorana Đorđević in [44] is introduced here, which distinguishes the sound studied within archaeoacoustic research into:

- Live sound (based on the still living, more or less intact soundscapes and religious practice);
- Harmonic sound (based on the inaudible relation of acoustic principles and the geometry and proportions of architecture);
- Impulse response (based on in situ measurements or virtual model examination in specialized software).

Among the different types of sound, the most problematic to analyze is here considered to be the "live sound", which is strongly influenced by the drastic change in environmental noise that has occurred throughout history and by the possible lack or paucity of information we have about the activities that were taking place at certain sites.

4 Proposal of a Comprehensive Methodology

From the analysis and combination of the methodologies presented here, the outline of a methodological approach for the sound analysis of archaeoacoustic sites was proposed (Fig. 2).

In order to better understand the effectiveness of this method, the Roman Theatre of Volterra, Italy, will be taken as a hypothetical practical example (Fig. 3).

The first thing to do, once arrived on site, is to preliminarily evaluate the acoustics and the space through the musical approach, using vocal sounds or impulsive sources (in a large open space like the theater of Volterra the simple clap of hands may not be sufficient).

Once it has been established which are the main acoustic characteristics of the place, the possible points of interest and the possible presence of acoustic phenomena, the analysis of the three sound categories is carried out.

Starting from the live sound, both the environmental noise and the acoustic effect of the performance must be evaluated. In the case of the theater of Volterra, unfortunately, the background conditions have been completely disrupted by the intense human activity and the close proximity to busy roads, making it necessary to study documents that can suggest what the sound conditions were. In the absence of further information a plausible scenario will be considered.

Regarding the performance, the theater, having lost most of the steps and most of the scenae frons, must necessarily be reconstructed in a virtual environment. Subsequently will be recorded in anechoic chamber the extract of a Roman drama coeval to the period of use and then auralized. Finally, this will be submitted to a group of individuals to be evaluated subjectively. The shapes, proportions and materials of the theatre will be studied for what has been called Harmonic Sound. The aim is to find out whether the design was acoustically conscious. In the case of theatres this is very likely, but it can still be interesting to see any similarities and differences with similar buildings. Another element of study is the possible presence of acoustic devices or traces of them, also considering that Vitruvius himself speaks of the need to introduce inside the theaters acoustic vessels.

Once all these considerations have been made, it is finally possible to move on to measurements. Since the site is not perfectly preserved, an acoustic simulation is carried out. Subsequently, acoustic measurements can be performed within the theater to validate and/or compare the results. In the case of theaters, measurements can be conducted according to the guidelines of ISO 3382–1 [39], but always paying attention to the possible presence of significant points. If the measures should reveal the presence of acoustic phenomena, the effect of these on the human brain can be studied by EEG monitoring and TRV Cameras.

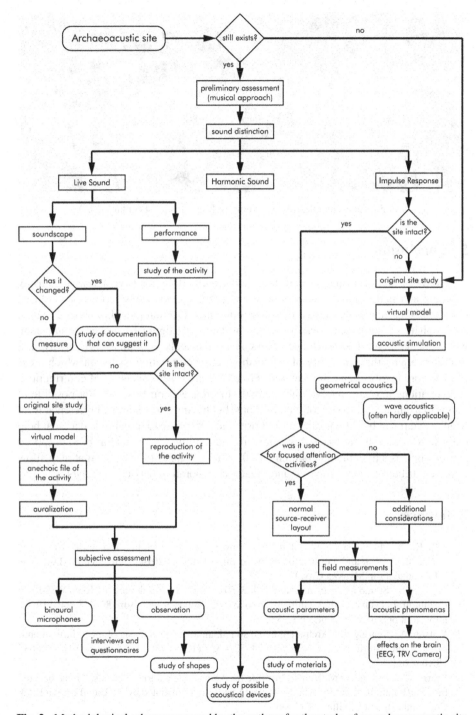

Fig. 2. Methodological scheme proposed by the authors for the study of an archaeoacoustic site

Fig. 3. The roman theater of Volterra in Italy (dated 1st century B.C.)

5   Conclusions

The study of archaeoacoustics and its possible methodologies have shown increasing cohesion across disciplines. What until a few years ago was considered as a confused mass of disorganized contributions, is becoming now a coherent and organized matter. Although it is difficult the appearance in the short term of a figure, the archaeoacoustician, who can contain all the knowledge necessary for the analysis of all aspects involved, it is still emerging the possibility of establishing clear correlations between which areas can be more involved and in what way. Given the great heterogeneity of contributions and situations that are involved in the study of archaeoacoustics, it is not possible to establish a unique succession of interventions, but having some points of reference from which to start can be a great support to those who contribute to research and a great help to those who want to approach this innovative field of interest. What has been proposed in this article is a hypothetical planning of the various stages of research that may allow future contributions more focused and greater collaboration between scholars.

References

1. Till, R.: Sound archaeology: an interdisciplinary perspective. In: Archaeoacoustics: the Archaeology of Sound. Publication of Proceedings from the 2014 Conference in Malta. The OTS Foundation, Myakka City, FL (2014)
2. Waller, S.J.: Sound and rock art. Nature **363**, 501 (1993). https://doi.org/10.1038/363501a0
3. Reznikoff, I., Dauvois, M.: La dimension sonore desgrottes ornées. bspf. **85**, 238–246 (1988). https://doi.org/10.3406/bspf.1988.9349
4. Watson, A., Keating, D.: Architecture and sound: an acoustic analysis of mega-lithic monuments in prehistoric Britain. Antiquity **73**, 325–336 (1999). https://doi.org/10.1017/S0003598X00088281
5. Scarre, C., Lawson, G.: McDonald Institute for Archaeological Research eds: Archaeoacoustics. McDonald Institute for Archaeological Research, Distributed by the David Brown Book Co, Cambridge : Oakville, CT (2006)
6. Eneix, L.C., ed: Archaeoacoustics: The Archaeology of Sound; Publication of Proceedings from the 2014 Conference in Malta. The OTS Foundation, Myakka City, FL (2014)

7. Eneix, L.C. ed: Archaeoacoustics II In: The Archaeology of Sound: Publication of Proceedings from the 2015 Conference in Istanbul. The OTS Foundation, Myakka City, FL (2016)
8. Eneix, L.C., Ragussa, M. eds: Archaeoacoustics III: the Archaeology of Sound : Publication of Proceedings from the 2017 Conference in Portugal : Third International Multidisciplinary Conference on Archaeoacoustics. OTS Foundation, Myakka City, FL (2018)
9. Till, R.: Sound archaeology: a study of the acoustics of three world heritage sites, Spanish prehistoric painted caves, stonehenge, and paphos theatre. Acoustics. 1, 661–692 (2019). https://doi.org/10.3390/acoustics1030039
10. Díaz-Andreu, M., García Benito, C., Lazarich, M.: The sound of rock art. the acoustics of the rock art of Southern Andalusia (Spain): the sound of Rock art. the acoustics of the rock art of Southern Andalusia. Oxford J. Archaeol. 33, 1–18 (2014). https://doi.org/10.1111/ojoa.12024
11. Fazenda, B., Drumm, I.: Recreating the sound of stonehenge. Acta Acust. Acust. 99, 110–117 (2013). https://doi.org/10.3813/AAA.918594
12. Watson, A.: (Un)intentional sound? acoustics and neolithic monuments. In: Archaeoacoustics. McDonald Institute for Archaeological Research ; Distributed by the David Brown Book Co, pp. 11–22. Cambridge : Oakville, CT (2006)
13. Lawson, G.: Large scale-small scale: medieval stone buildings, early medieval timber halls and the problem of the lyre. In: Archaeoacoustics, McDonald Institute for Archaeological Research ; Distributed by the David Brown Book Co, Cambridge, Oakville, CT, pp. 85–94 (2006)
14. Duran, S., Chambers, M., Kanellopoulos, I.: An archaeoacoustics investigation of the Beaulieu Abbey. In: Reproduced Sound 2020. Institute of Acoustics, Virtual (2020). https://doi.org/10.25144/13373
15. Ramos-Amézquita, A.: Mesoamerican archaeoacoustics. In: Archaeoacoustics: the Archaeology of Sound; Publication of Proceedings from the 2014 Conference in Malta, pp. 179–184. The OTS Foundation, Myakka City, FL (2014)
16. Devereux, P.: Ears & years: aspects of acoustics and intentionality in antiquity. In: Archaeoacoustics McDonald Institute for Archaeological Research ; Distributed by the David Brown Book Co, Cambridge Oakville, CT, pp. 23–30 (2006)
17. Stroud, K.: Ħal Saflieni hypogeum: an introduction to the site and its acoustics. In: Archaeoacoustics III: the Archaeology of Sound : Publication of Proceedings from the 2017 Conference in Portugal : Third International Multidisciplinary Conference on Archaeoacoustics, pp. 191–198. The OTS Foundation, Myakka City, FL (2018)
18. Holmes, P.: The scandinavian Bronze lurs: accident or intent? In: Archaeoacoustics. McDonald Institute for Archaeological Research; Distributed by the David Brown Book Co, Cambridge, Oakville, CT, pp. 59–69 (2006)
19. Leccese, F., Salvadori, G., Bernardini, G., Bernardini, P.: The bowed string instruments: acoustic characterization of unique pieces from the Italian lutherie. In: IOP Conference Series: Materials Science and Engineering, vol. 364, no. 1, p. 012022 (2018). https://doi.org/10.1088/1757-899X/364/1/012022
20. Iannace, G., Berardi, U.: The acoustic of cumaean sibyl. In: Presented at the 173rd Meeting of Acoustical Society of America and 8th Forum Acusticum, vol. 30, no. 1, p. 015010. Boston, Massachusetts (2017). https://doi.org/10.1121/2.0000606
21. Ciaburro, G., Berardi, U., Iannace, G., Trematerra, A., Puyana-Romero, V.: The acoustics of ancient catacombs in Southern Italy. Build. Acoust. 28, 411–422 (2021). https://doi.org/10.1177/1351010X20967571
22. Omar, N.M., Al-Sayad, Z.M., Maarouf, I.S., Al-Hagla, K.S.: The documentation of archaeoacoustics identity of Sultan-Barquq complex. Alex. Eng. J. 59, 4159–4169 (2020). https://doi.org/10.1016/j.aej.2020.07.022

23. Berardi, U., Iannace, G.: The acoustic of Roman theatres in Southern Italy and some reflections for their modern uses. Appl. Acoust. **170**, 107530 (2020). https://doi.org/10.1016/j.apacoust.2020.107530
24. Weinzierl, S., Sanvito, P., Schultz, F., Büttner, C.: The acoustics of renaissance theatres in Italy. Acta Acust. Acust. **101**, 632–641 (2015). https://doi.org/10.3813/AAA.918858
25. Zubrow, E.B.W.: The silence of sound: a prologue. In: Archaeoacoustics: the Archaeology of Sound; Publication of Proceedings from the 2014 Conference in Malta. the OTS Foundation, Myakka City, FL (2014)
26. Cross, I., Watson, A.: Acoustics and the human experience of socially-organized sound. Archaeoacoustics, 107–116. McDonald Institute for Archaeological Research; Distributed by the David Brown Book Co, Cambridge, Oakville, CT (2006)
27. Harvey, K.: How do the acoustics in cathedrals affect the human subconscious? In: Archaeoacoustics III: the Archaeology of Sound : Publication of Proceedings from the 2017 Conference in Portugal : Third International Multidisciplinary Conference on Archaeoacoustics, pp. 85–95. The OTS Foundation, Myakka City, FL (2018)
28. Waller, S.J.: Can we hear the sounds of archaeological sites the way our ancestors heard them? In: Archaeoacoustics III: the Archaeology of Sound : Publication of Proceedings from the 2017 Conference in Portugal : Third International Multidisciplinary Conference on Archaeoacoustics, pp. 249–256. The OTS Foundation, Myakka City, FL (2018)
29. Scarre, C.: Sound, place and space: towards an archaeology of acoustics. Archaeoacoustics, 1–10. McDonald Institute for Archaeological Research; Distributed by the David Brown Book Co, Cambridge: Oakville, CT (2006)
30. Reznikoff, I.: The evidence of the use of sound resonance from paleolithic to medieval times. Archaeoacoustics, 77–84. McDonald Institute for Archaeological Research; Distributed by the David Brown Book Co, Cambridge Oak-ville, CT (2006)
31. Debertolis, P., Richeldi, F.: Archaeoacoustic analysis of an ancient hypogeum using new TRV camera (Variable Resonance Camera) technology. In: Proceedings of the 2nd International Virtual Conference on Advanced Scientific Results (SCIECONF 2014), pp. 323–329 (2014)
32. Debertolis, P.: New technologies of analysis in archaeoacoustics. In: Archaeo-acoustics II: the Archaeology of Sound: Publication of Proceedings from the 2015 Conference in Istanbul, pp. 33–50. The OTS Foundation, Myakka City, FL (2016)
33. Iannace, G., Berardi, U.: Acoustic virtual reconstruction of the Roman theater of Posillipo, Naples. In: Presented at the 173rd Meeting of Acoustical Society of America and 8th Forum Acusticum, vol. 30, no. 1, p. 015011. Boston, Massachusetts (2017). https://doi.org/10.1121/2.0000607
34. D'Orazio, D., Fratoni, G., Rossi, E., Garai, M.: Understanding the acoustics of St. John's Baptistery in Pisa through a virtual approach. J. Build. Perform. Simul. **13**, 320–333 (2020). https://doi.org/10.1080/19401493.2020.1728382
35. Chourmouziadou, K., Kang, J.: Acoustic evolution of ancient Greek and Roman theatres. Appl. Acoust. **69**, 514–529 (2008). https://doi.org/10.1016/j.apacoust.2006.12.009
36. Rocconi, E.: Theatres and theatre design in the graeco-roman world: theoretical and empirical approaches. In: Archaeoacoustics, McDonald Institute for Archaeological Research ; Distributed by the David Brown Book Co, Cambridge. Oakville, CT, pp. 71–76 (2006)
37. Martinho, C.: Exploring aural architecture: experience, resonance, attunement. In: Archaeoacoustics III: the Archaeology of Sound : Publication of Proceedings from the 2017 Conference in Portugal : Third International Multidisciplinary Conference on Archaeoacoustics, pp. 127–137. The OTS Foundation, Myakka City, FL (2018)
38. Cook, I.A., Pajot, S.K., Leuchter, A.F.: Ancient architectural acoustic resonance patterns and regional brain activity. Time Mind. **1**, 95–104 (2008). https://doi.org/10.2752/175169608783489099

39. ISO International Organization for Standardization: Acoustics — Measurement of room acoustic parameters — Part 1: Performance spaces (EN ISO 3382–1), Switzerland (2009)
40. Devereux, P.: When the ancient world got a soundtrack. In: Archaeoacoustics III: the Archaeology of Sound : Publication of Proceedings from the 2017 Conference in Portugal: Third International Multidisciplinary Conference on Archaeo-acoustics, pp. 7–8. The OTS Foundation, Myakka City, FL (2018)
41. Manzetti, M.C.: Experiencing an ancient performance in a roman theatre. In: Archaeoacoustics III: the Archaeology of Sound: Publication of Proceedings from the 2017 Conference in Portugal : Third International Multidisciplinary Conference on Archaeoacoustics, pp. 122–126. The OTS Foundation, Myakka City, FL (2018)
42. Rindel, J.H.: Roman theatres and revival of their acoustics in the ERATO project. Acta Acust. Acust. **99**, 21–29 (2013). https://doi.org/10.3813/AAA.918584
43. Reznikoff, I.: On foundations of archaeoacoustics. In: Archaeoacoustics III: the Archaeology of Sound : Publication of Proceedings from the 2017 Conference in Portugal : Third International Multidisciplinary Conference on Archaeoacoustics, pp. 155–166. The OTS Foundation, Myakka City, FL (2018)
44. Đorđević, Z.: Acoustics of medieval architectural heritage - research methodology. In: Archaeoacoustics III: the Archaeology of Sound : Publication of Proceedings from the 2017 Conference in Portugal : Third International Multidisciplinary Conference on Archaeoacoustics, pp. 45–53. The OTS Foundation, Myakka City, FL (2018)

Darker Inks in 14th-Century Norway

Þorgeir Sigurðsson[1](✉) (iD), Tor Weidling[2], Haukur Þorgeirsson[3],
and Jon Yngve Hardeberg[1]

[1] NTNU, Norwegian University of Science and Technology, 2815 Gjøvik, Norway
Ths185@hi.is
[2] National Archives of Norway, 0862 Oslo, Norway
[3] Árni Magnússon Institute for Icelandic Studies, 102 Reykjavik, Iceland
https://uni.hi.is/ths185/articles/

Abstract. This article demonstrates a transition in 14th-century Norway to the use of darker inks, visualized with low-cost digital photographs in 950 nm infrared light (IR). In these photographs, the transition manifests itself in increased contrast, on average, in 101 Norwegian dated documents (charters) written immediately after the year 1400, as compared to 56 charters written at the beginning of the 14th century. Similar results were obtained from Iceland by a more subjective method of visually inspecting IR pictures of 64 charters from the period 1300–1450. These results may assist in detecting incorrectly dated manuscripts in Norway and Iceland.

Keywords: Iron-gall ink · Infrared imaging · Cultural heritage

1 Introduction

Long before Old Norse writing began in the 12th century, the Catholic Church replaced carbon inks with the more sophisticated iron-gall inks. Consequently, we would expect iron-gall inks to have been used for the writing of Old Norse in Norway and Iceland. No information from medieval times does, however, exist on the sources or manufacture of Norse inks. Icelandic scholars have speculated that the inks were domestically produced. Manuscript experts at the Árni Magnússon Institute have noted some common properties of the inks. Ólafur Halldórsson [1] in 1967 notes that the ink integrated itself firmly into the parchment and was very resilient to wear and tear. He states that some parchment-books, especially in the 15th century, had a black and reflective ink that appeared to be thick. Unfortunately, Ólafur gave no examples of manuscripts with this ink. Sigurgeir Steingrímsson in 1994 [2], at the same institute, notes the fine quality and durability of the traditional ink. He and Ólafur, entertained the thought that it had been produced using a formula known from the 17th century, based on the boiling of *sortulyng* (Arctostaphylos uva-ursi), but Sigurgeir concludes from testing by Per M. Boll [3], that this formula appeared not to produce ink of the same quality. In Norway, Knut Johannessen [4] notes that ink was traded as powder in the 16th century to be mixed with water. Low concentration could lead to pale, gray-brown writing. He gives some ink recipes from the first half of the 18th century (from Åker, a farm in Hedmark) and from Kristiania in 1821.

In preparation for a PhD study that involved the fourteenth-century manuscript Möðruvallabók, Þorgeir Sigurðsson noticed that it had two types of inks when viewed in the near infrared range (950 nm). One was nearly invisible, as expected for iron-gall inks (or plant inks with no iron), while the other ink reflected little light (was black), as expected for carbon inks, or iron-gall inks with carbon added. In passing, he reported on the two types of inks in Möðruvallabók in an article in 2018 [5] and suggested that the darker ink had been domestically produced.

To investigate if the blacker ink was a newcomer in the 14th century, Þorgeir, together with Haukur Þorgeirsson at the Árni Magnússon Institute in Reykjavík, took infrared photographs of dated charters at the institute (with shelf names beginning with AM). This unpublished work was done in 2014, but in 2021 they added charters, mainly from the beginning of the 14th century, from the Icelandic National Archives, see Table 1.

Table 1. Appearance of inks on dated Icelandic charters.

Years	Extant	Inspected	Light	Unclear	Dark
1300–1349	23	14[1]	14	0	0
1350–1399	72	26[2]	23	0	3
1400–1449	212	24[3]	8	5	11

The three charters with dark ink in the 14th century were all from its last decade, AM Dipl. Isl. Fasc V 5 (1393), V 20 (1397), and AM V 21 (1397). Only exceptionally is it possible to date other manuscripts than charters accurately. A chronicle in AM 420 a 4to is, however, known to have been written in 1362 or 1363 and it has the new type of ink as seen in Fig. 1. It is written with the same unknown hand that introduced the new ink into Möðruvallabók.

This investigation had some shortcomings: The number of charters in Iceland is low and the ink classification was subjective, without a numerical measure, and it was not

---

[1] These are: AM Dipl. Isl. Fasc. I 1, I 3, I 4, LXIV 1, LXIV 2, LXIV 3, I 6, I 7, I 8, I 9, I 9 ad, I 11, I 12 (light, at the National Archives) and AM Dipl. Isl. Fasc. I 12 (light, at the Árni Magnússon Institute).

[2] These are: AM Dipl. Isl. Fasc. II 2, II 3, II 4, II 6 (light, at the National Archives) and AM Dipl. Isl. Fasc. II 8, II 13, II 19, III 1, III 13, III 10, IV 4, IV 5, IV 11, IV 14, IV 19, V 25, IV 18, V 1, V 3, V 12, V 14, V 11, V 22 (light, at the Árni Magnússon Institute) and AM Dipl. Isl. Fasc. V 5, V 20, V 21 (dark, at the Árni Magnússon Institute).

[3] These are (all at the Árni Magnússon Institute): AM Dipl. Isl. Fasc. V 28, VI 10, VI 26, VI 30, VII 4 a, VII 7, VII 20, VII 30 (light), AM Dipl. Isl. Fasc. VI 16, VII 5, VII 8, VII 11, VII 27 (ambiguous) and AM Dipl. Isl. Fasc. VI 2 a, VI 2 b, VI 4, VI 12, VI 11, VII 12, VII 18, VII 19, VII 28, VII 22, XI 19 (dark).

possible to classify all charters with confidence. Nevertheless, it seemed clear that a blacker type of ink came into use in 14th-century Iceland.

The data in Table 1 was obtained at different times in different locations, using IR illumination from different lamps, normally with classical OSRAM light bulbs. Figures 1 and 2 illustrate the big difference we could observe in normal light and in infrared light at ca. 950 nm. These figures show the oldest dated document with the black ink that we came across in Iceland (the chronicle discussed earlier).

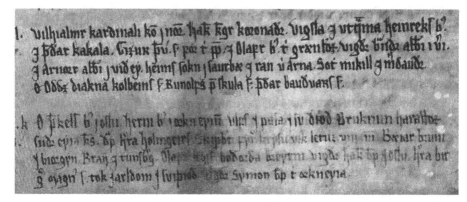

Fig. 1.   From a chronicle in AM 420 a 4to, the manuscript dates from 1362 or 1363. The paragraph on top has the old traditional ink. The second paragraph (an entry for the year 1248) is more faded but may have been darker originally. The picture is from handrit.is. The manuscript is at the Árni Magnússon Institute in Iceland.

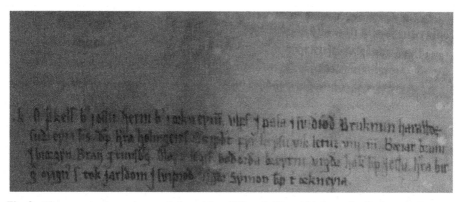

Fig. 2.   The same text seen in near infrared (ca. 950 nm). The old ink nearly disappears. See next section on how this picture was taken.

To find out whether the darker ink was an Icelandic peculiarity or not, and using a better methodology, Norwegian charters were inspected together with Tor Weidling, at *Riksarkivet*, The National Archives of Norway in Oslo. The charters examined were from the first 20 years of the fourteenth century (1300–1319) and from the first 5 years of the fifteenth century (1400–1404). This article reports on our approach and the finding that darker inks were also introduced in Norway in the 14th century.

It has not been noted before that both Iceland and Norway introduced a black ink for use on legal documents in the 14th century. It remains to be investigated if this also happened elsewhere in Europe and if this can be used to detect incorrectly dated manuscripts in a simple and inexpensive manner.

2 Method

For the initial study of Icelandic manuscripts, pictures (as in Fig. 2) were taken with a Canon Rebel Xti camera with the standard infrared (IR) filter removed. A 950 nm IR filter from NEEWER was used in its place (that only allows IR light to pass). The objects were lit by a classic incandescent bulb, which is rich in near infrared radiation. Because the camera is only sensitive up to ca. 1000 nm, the pictures obtained are close to being ca. 950 nm images.

For the new study in 2021, a Dino-lite USB microscope (model AM4113T) with a built-in 950 nm light source was used. The choice of this microscope was motivated by G. Nehring *et al.* [6] who demonstrated its use for non-destructive classification of inks with different reflectance values in the infrared range, as described for instance by Mrusek *et al.* [7]. Iron-carbon inks and plant inks become increasingly more reflective (become lighter) in longer wavelengths, while inks with carbon, (carbon inks and inks blended with carbon) remain non-reflective (dark). The longer the wavelength, the greater the distinction is between the two types of inks. Light with 950 nm wavelength is near the limit of detectability by the CMOS sensors of ordinary cameras.

In addition to a 950 nm light source, the Dino-lite model has a 395 nm blue/UV light source that may assist in identifying inks with tannin through their effect on fluorescence. Nehring *et al.* used what they called a standard BAM protocol to classify inks, which involves an initial reflectographic screening (in IR and UV light) followed by spectroscopic analysis (Rabin *et al.* 2012 [8]). Nehring *et al.* described methods for classifying historical inks, but our aim in this study is more modest. We only wish to demonstrate that a change took place towards less reflective (darker) inks. We do this by showing that the contrast in IR pictures of Norwegian charters increased during the 14th century.

We compute the contrast (Weber contrast, C_w) by calculating $(I_b\text{-}I)/I_b$, where I_b is the light intensity reflected from the parchment and I is the intensity reflected from the ink. We estimate the light intensity by the average pixel value. Assuming that pixel values are proportional to the number of photons received, they are also proportional to the intensity. The relation between pixel values and light intensity can be adjusted in pictures from the Dino-lite camera with a so-called gamma value. The default value is 1, which should give a linear relationship, but our measurements showed that this was only approximately true. For pixel values from 0–255, the relationship was nearly linear up to ca. 100. For greater intensities this relationship breaks down. When exposure time was doubled the pixel value only increased by ca. 50% (instead of 100%). The four pictures below illustrate this. They were all taken in the same light intensity, but the exposure time of the camera increased from 1/1000 s, 1/500 s, 1/250 s, to 1/125 s.

Fig. 3. Four IR-pictures. The word "Iron" written with iron-gall ink (Diamine registrar's blue-black ink) on new parchment, using four shutter speeds. The dark stroke in the upper right corner is carbon ink (Diamine India ink).

The average pixel values for the parchment in the above pictures should double from left to right. This applies approximately for the first three, but not the fourth. The values are: 29, 57, 108, and 161. These values are displayed in Fig. 4.

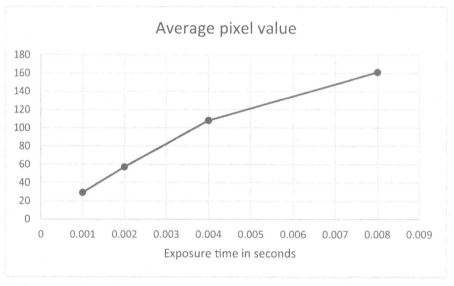

Fig. 4. Average pixel value from a square (c 35000 pixels) near the center between r and o in Fig. 3.

By default, Dino-lite adjusts its exposure intensity to avoid saturation and to maximize the dynamic range. In our experience, as seen in Figs. 7, 8 and 9 this means that all parchments will appear with similar levels of gray with pixel values well above 100. The contrast values (C_w) calculated at this level will be underestimates, because the pixels values underestimate the intensity of strong light, as revealed by Fig. 4. We can, however, assume that by using the same setup, we get comparable C_w values within this study.

Figure 5 shows the setup with a white calibration patch instead of a manuscript or a charter. The Dino-lite camera is on a flexible arm. It has a black extension cap (shown to the right) with a small piece of a reference parchment glued to its end. The distance from the LED light sources to the reference parchment is 35 mm. Because we did not allow the instrument to touch the objects being measured, some millimeters are added that slightly decrease the reflected light (as compared to the reference parchment).

Fig. 5. The setup. The Dino-lite is connected to a lap-top via a USB port.

3   Charters in the First 20 Years of the 14th Century

IR pictures of 56 Norwegian charters in the national archives in Oslo are in Fig. 6; their shelf number is written under each of them. The charters are from the series RA-perg, which is by far the largest [9]. They are here in a chronological order from the years 1300 to 1319; no charter from this series was intentionally omitted. Only a handful of charters exist that are older, while many undated manuscripts do.

The pictures in Fig. 6 were all taken on the 7th of December 2021 by Þorgeir Sigurðsson and Tor Weidling at the Norwegian National Achieves, Oslo. The contrast in all of them is clearly very low.In normal light, these charters are easy to read, but most of them cannot be read in IR.

To get a numerical measure of how low the contrast is in these images, we select those charters that clearly have the highest contrast and calculate a contrast number for them. These are (C_w number is in parenthesis): RN III 139 (0.04), RN III 496 (0.14), RN III 550 (0.14), and RN III 768 (0.13). We look closer at RN III 496 in Fig. 7.

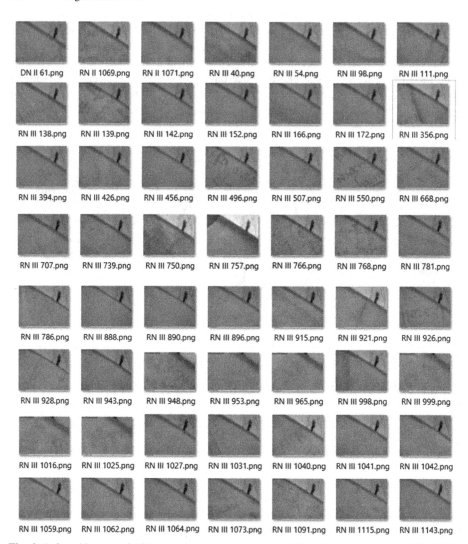

Fig. 6. Infrared images of 56 Norwegian charters written in 1300–1319. For charters RN III 948, RN III 953, RN III 965, RN III 999, RN III 1016, RN, and RN III 1025, a 2X zoom was used inadvertently.

The rectangles in Fig. 7 show the areas, within which we calculated the average pixel values, using the analyze/histogram-feature in the ImageJ software. As must be clear from this picture, different C_w values could be obtained for each image. By choosing a letter that appears lighter, a lower value could be obtained. In general, we tried to draw the rectangles near the center of the images (where the auto-exposure of Dino-lite normally made the parchments similarly gray) in areas that seemed representable for the charter.

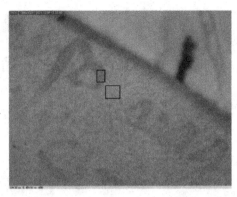

Fig. 7. Charter RN III 496. The reference parchment (top right) is not in focus because the camera does not touch the charter. The black stroke is drawn with a Diamine India ink (a carbon ink).

From the above it seems that a C_w higher than 0.15 is abnormal. To stay on the safe side, we claim that charters in this group are characterized by a C_w below 0.20 (rather than 0.15).

4   Charters in the First Five Years of the 15th Century

Figure 8 displays the first 56 charters dated to the 15th century (1400–1402) in the series RA perg in the National archives in Oslo, photographed 7th of December 2021, for comparison with charters in Fig. 6. The pictures in Fig. 8 were taken earlier in the same day as the pictures in Fig. 6.

The group of charters in Fig. 8 are different from those in Fig. 6. It has many charters that have more contrast than any of the older charters. Some charters, however, have invisible inks like most of the old charters. Most are in-between.

To get a numerical measure of the change, we estimate how large a percentage of the charters in Fig. 8 have a C_w above 0.20. To do this, we calculate a C_w value for those charters that obviously have a high contrast and for the borderline cases as well. The following are those that we found above 0.20: RN VIII 814 (0.37), RN VIII 833 (0.26), RN VIII 836 (0.23), RN VIII 841 (0.56), RN VIII 847 (0.73), RN VIII 873 (0.27), RN VIII 884 (0.24), RN VIII 886 (0.29), RN VIII 925 (0.30), RN VIII 982 (0.37), RN VIII 1000 (0.23), RN VIII 1024 (0.28), RN VIII 1034 (0.29), RN VIII 1044 (0.35), RN VIII 1073 (0.22), RN VIII 1074 (0.21), RN VIII 1089 (0.22), RN VIII 1097 (0.21), and RN VIII 1100 (0.40). These are 19 charters that constitute 34% of the charters, or one third.

In Fig. 6, most of the charters appear similar in reflectance as the reference parchment. This is not true for Fig. 8. The reference parchment appears lighter in most of the images. This is because there is greater distance between the parchment and the camera. The automatic exposure control of Dino-lite has compensated for this by increasing the light intensity. That the distance is greater, is clear from the wider shadow cast by the reference parchment. This need not have had any effect on the C_w values, but it is nevertheless fortunate that we tested for that possibility by continuing with the 45 charters displayed

Fig. 8. Fifty-six charters dated to the beginning of the 15th century (until summer of 1402).

in Fig. 9, which have a smaller size of the gap (as seen by the width of the shadow in Fig. 9).

These charters are in chronological order from the summer of 1402, until the end of year 1404. The pictures of these charters were taken immediately after the pictures in Fig. 8 and before the pictures in Fig. 6. All are from the series RA-perg.

Fig. 9. 45 additional charters from the beginning of the 15th century (until 1404).

For this set of charters, 15, or one third, have a Weber fraction (contrast) larger than 0.20. This is the same proportion as previously. These are: RN VIII 1147 (0.27), RN VIII 1182 (0.30), RN VIII 1190 (0.41), RN VIII 1197 (0.25), RN VIII 1198 (0.26), RN VIII 1203 (0.24), RN VIII 1204 (0.28), RN VIII 1217 (0.36), RN VIII 1222 (0.53), RN VIII 1227 (0.32), RN VIII 1241 (0.22), RN VIII 1279 (0.31), RN VIII 1293 (0.30), RN VIII 1323 (0.26), and RN VIII 1324 (0.61).

We conclude that the difference that we observe between charters from the beginning to the end of the 14th century is real and not due to a flaw in our method.

5 It was not the Plague

What led to the introduction of darker inks is not obvious. The traditional inks had the valuable property of binding themselves firmly to the parchment, which made them resistant to removal. For legal documents (charters), this is very useful, but it is useful for saga books as well, because they tolerated wear and tear very well (as observed by Óskar Halldórsson, see the Introduction). At least some of the new inks were not as tolerant, as witnessed by Figs 1 and 2. It is natural to ask why the scribes would want to change their proven ink formulas.

One possible explanation could be that the Black Death in the middle of the century stopped all import by sea and might have forced Norwegians (and later Icelanders) to use a domestically produced ink. Carbon inks are easy to produce, but the inks that were formerly used may have been imported. The blacker inks would have been used out of necessity. This theory can, however, be proven wrong, by noting that dark inks appear in some documents before the winter of 1349–1350 when the plague invaded Norway. We have noted this for RN V 1030 (15th of March 1348), RN V 1133 (23rd of March 1349), and RN V 1137 (27th of March 1349). Additionally, we note that one of the early users of the dark ink was Chancellor Pétr Eiríksson, the highest official of King Hákon VI. Three charters exist that are written in his hand [10]. One of them states that he sealed and wrote it, and we observe that the other two have the same hand. RN VI 893 is from 22nd of February 1363, RN VI 592 is from 5th of August 1359, and RN VI 483 is from 22nd of February 1358. RN VI 592 has a very dark ink, but the other two appear to have ink of the traditional type (Fig. 10).

Fig. 10. Charter RN VIII 592 from 1359 written by Chancellor Pétr Eiríksson on behalf of King Hákon VI.

6 Conclusions

With no evidence to the contrary, it is natural to assume that inks in both Norway and Iceland were of the iron-gall type, like elsewhere in Europe, with varying amount of iron (with no iron they were plant inks), but little or no carbon, otherwise some charters with contrast above 0.20 would have shown up in charters at the beginning of the 14th century.

We can ascertain that during the 14th century a change took place that manifests itself in darker inks on extant charters. It is unlikely that this change is caused by a different storage condition for new and old charters. Such a difference for even a large proportion of the charters would not have removed all charters with dark inks from the beginning of the 14th century. It is also unlikely that the Black Death or poverty played a role, since dark inks appeared some years before the plague arrived and both rich and poor used the dark ink.

If darker inks were not used out of necessity, they must have had a property that was desirable. This property might have been a better contrast in the visual range. It might have been especially welcome in the winter darkness at northern latitudes and possibly it allowed darker parchments to be used. More research is needed to test whether a similar development took place elsewhere in Europe and whether our finding is useful in detecting incorrectly dated documents.

Acknowledgements. We thank the institutes that enabled this work. These are: the Árni Magnússon Institute in Iceland, the Norwegian National Archives, and the Icelandic National Archives. We also thank ERCIM for providing a post-doc funding for Þorgeir Sigurðsson with NTNU in Gjøvik as a host institute.

References

1. Halldórsson, Ó.: Sögur úr Skarðsbók. Almenna bókafélagið, Reykjavik, pp. 9–10 (1967)
2. Steingrímsson, S.: The care of the manuscripts in the Árni Magnússon institute in Reykjavík. In: Fellows-Jensen, G., Springborg, P. (eds.) Proceedings of the First International Seminar on the Care and Conservation of Manuscripts held at the University of Copenhagen, 25–26 April 1994, pp. 53–59 (1994)
3. Boll, P.M.: Sagaernes blæk. Naturens Verden, pp. 433–499 (1994)
4. Johannessen, K.: Den glemte skriften. Gotisk håndskrift i Norge. Riksarkivaren skriftserie 28, pp. 48–49. Universitetsforlaget, Oslo (2007)
5. Sigurðsson, Þ: Hví skal eigi drepa Egil? Són **16**, 13–33 (2018)
6. Nehring, G., Bonnerot, O., Gerhardt, M., Krutzsch, M., Rabin, I.: Looking for the missing link in the evolution of black inks. Archaeol. Anthropol. Sci. **13**(4), 1 (2021). https://doi.org/10.1007/s12520-021-01320-5
7. Mrusek, R., Fuchs, R., Oltrogge, D.: Spektrale Fenster zur Vergangenheit. Ein neues Reflektographieverfahren zur Untersuchung von Buchmalerei und historischem Schriftgut. Sci Nat **82** (2), 68–79 (1995)
8. Rabin, I., et al.: Identification and classification of historical writing inks in spectroscopy: a methodological overview. COMSt Newslett. **3**, 26–30 (2012)
9. Charters from the RA-pergs series at the Norwegian National Archives with pictures of their front and back at: media.digitalarkivet.no/db/contents/72085. Accessed 10 Jan 2022
10. The text for each Norwegian charter: (from *Diplomatarium Norvegicum*). www.dokpro.uio.no/dipl_norv/diplom_felt.html#Innstillinger. Accessed 10 Jan 2022

Digital Manufacturing for the Enhancement of Heritage. The Case of Spazio Geco

Marianna Belvedere[✉], Simone Burton, Maria Emanuela Oddo, Sergio Camici, Laura Benedetti, and Luca de Sanctis

Spazio Geco Società Cooperativa, 27100 Pavia, Italy
marianna.b@spaziogeco.it

Abstract. This article presents and disserts the multiple activities carried out by Spazio Geco to innovate museum exhibits and made them more interactive and effective. A number of projects aimed at improving in various Italian museums the exploration and fruition by the visitor of the exhibited cultural heritage have been set up in Spazio Geco. These projects are based on advanced interactive methods and augmented reality systems specifically developed for virtual exploration and fruition of cultural heritage and are thoroughly described and illustrated with many pictures in the present paper. In perspective, the group of young and creative Geco researchers and collaborators intend to take advantage of the skills acquired in the last five years to kick off new projects aiming at further development and implementation of the interactive multimedia communication forms within Italian as well as foreign museums.

Keywords: Fablab · Digital manufacturing · Enhancement · Museums · Fruition

1 Introduction

Spazio Geco - Geco Fab Lab is a space of innovation and creativity where professionals from different fields can collectively combine their skill sets to create and develop innovative and technological projects. Founded in 2013, we created an environment where like-minded people can work together on pioneering projects that not only bring value to the territory but also bring new ways of designing and using new digital tools and platforms so as to push boundaries and provide original digital content aligning with the needs and demands in today's digital society.

In Geco Fab Lab fully integrated fabricating work space is equipped with cutting edge technology and equipment that allows us to focus on modernizing the field of cultural heritage. In 2015, we earned our first project i.e. the interactive installations for the museum path of the civic museum of Pavia. The success of such project prompted us to work for obtaining the entrusting of further interactive and multimedia installations projects in different regions. Over the years, our portfolio of projects and achievements grew considerably and in 2018 the company won an important call named "Funder35", a grant given to young creative companies which gave us the opportunity to add a new media lab, make grow our team providing them with training both on the technical IT and the design side. Moreover, the communication and the fundamentally humanistic side of the cultural heritage world could be enhanced.

Our aim is to deliver awe-inspiring, high-quality technically demanding projects and interactive installations with a focus on enhancing the cultural heritage world. We believe that the experience and the ability to interact with the world of cultural heritage is in fact an added value that only those who are able to deal with the contents of heritage can carry forward. Technology and culture run parallel, therefore museums and places of culture will evolve over time, changing the way the public will interact with them [1–3]. Therefore, the projects in the field of Cultural Tourism & Travel Applications that we have worked on in recent years make use of Interactive methods and augmented reality for virtual exploration and fruition of cultural heritage and of advanced methods and systems for enhancing heritage fruition and storytelling, as well as Archaeological Analysis and Interpretive Design.

With the use of digital manufacturing [4, 5] and open source technologies, the "geckos" of Pavia have created numerous interventions for museums and places of culture aiming at the enhancement of cultural heritage of the territory in which they were born (Pavia) and beyond. The Group is made up of individuals with different professional backgrounds: engineers who are well experienced in automation, programmers, architects, designers, communication experts. In addition, there are individuals who bring a "humanistic component" to the group: art historians, archaeologists, naturalists and didactic experts. These individuals are able to relate with competence and intuition with the world of cultural and environmental heritage. This is a key-point for Spazio Geco because we believe that heritage education and fruition is in a period of strong evolution and the company intends to be in charge of this change paying great attention to the needs of the operators.

The Fab Lab is equipped with additive and subtractive digital manufacturing machinery. Among the most valuable: high precision large and medium format 3d printers, CNC laser machinery and a large format cnc router of $2500 \times 1300 \times 200$ mm working volume for wood, plastics and composites. We also possess power tools for iron and wood and have a sector dedicated to casts and molds in various two-component materials including silicones and epoxy resins. Another sector is dedicated to technologies related to 3D scanning and stereophotogrammetry. In addition to these, we have a Medialab in which we work using different softwares (ict area). Lastly, we are equipped with various vr viewers and working systems based on touch screen video projection and Hololens for the innovation and new media department.

2 Accomplished Projects

2.1 Museum of Electrical Technology of Pavia University

One of our most notable and accomplished projects was the intervention linked to the needs of the Museum of Electrical Technology of the Museum System for the University of Pavia. The aim of this project was to improve and enhance the fruibility of a very big opera not easy to be interpreted and appreciated by the public, namely a work of industrial archeology dating back to the second half of the nineteenth century. Indeed, the Museum intended to highlight the stator of the Bertini hydroelectric power plant in Paderno D'Adda and part of its rotor. Bertini plant is the oldest hydroelectric power station of the Edison group and one of the oldest in Italy [6]. When it was inaugurated in September 1898, it was the most impressive electric plant in Europe and the second in the world. The plant was built mainly with the aim of producing sufficient power and energy to proceed with the electrification of the Milan tramway network, which Edison group had taken over from the Municipality. Such enterprise sparked the beginning of the Italian electrical industry and at the onset of the second Industrial Revolution. The stator (Fig. 1A and 1B) kept in the Museum over the years was part of an old alternator of the power station that allowed to transform the water energy into mechanical energy and, later, into electricity. In fact, inside the stator and outside the rotor, whose movement was fed by the force of the river Adda, there were isolated copper windings which, by rubbing together, produced electricity. The stator is exposed separately from its rotor, of which only a part remains. For this reason, it was difficult for those visiting the museum to imagine and understand the functioning of the two devices, especially if they were not experts in the field.

The curators welcomed the Geco team and led them to make a careful visit of the collections, highlighting the key steps and elaborating the most suitable fitting solutions for the enhancement of the heritage they wanted to propose to the public in an interactive and communicatively more effective way. Together with the curator of the collection, the geckos thus questioned how to solve the problem and the solution was found in using the Augmented reality. Indeed, outside its original context, in the hangar that houses the interesting collection of Pavia, the enormous contraption, obviously immobile, was not very understandable in its operation, thus entailing This a huge challenge. Therefore, the idea of geckos was to implement the possibility of enriching human sensory perception through information that was manipulated and conveyed electronically through a mobile device (in our case a tablet). This produced a result that proved to be particularly successful from a communicative point of view. A 3D simulation of the rotor (Fig. 1C) was in fact created and positioned inside the original stator, in order to show the "in motion" operation for the production of electric energy. The simulation is activated by the framing of a target represented by the reproduction of an ancient photograph of the stator itself in its original location at the Lombard power station, positioned on a pedestal in the immediate vicinity of the work. The dissemination effect was of great impact on the public and the visitor's tours (either guided or not) greatly benefited.

From a technical point of view: this work was realized with Unity and Vuforia [7]. With the first software we created augmented reality starting from 3D modeling on a photographic base. The A/R application allows the animated function to start through the framing of a 2d target, represented by the historical photograph of the hydroelectric power plant. Vuforia has allowed the export to the tablets supplied by the museum. It is possible to visualize on the device the ensemble or the parts of the stator and modify its speed and other parameters from a control menu.

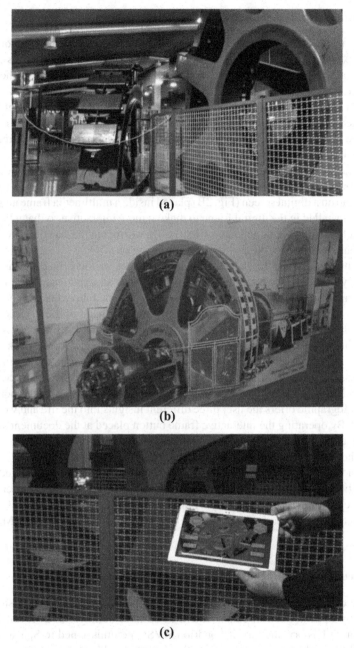

Fig. 1. A. The Bertini plant stator. **B.** Stator ancient pic. **C.** Augmented Reality set up by Spazio Geco.

2.2 Museo Martinitt e Stelline of Milan

In 2017 Spazio Geco was commissioned by the Museo Martinitt e Stelline of Milan to create an exhibition inside the Milan State Archive for the celebration of its 250 years since the death of the benefactor Prince Antonio Tolomeo Trivulzio [8]. Together with the curators, Geco team realized that the best communicative and divulgative idea was that of enclosing a lot of information, photographs, documents, prints and images of historical assets linked to the life of the Prince. Such interactive "portrait" represents a convenient reply to the questions of the public and so may result engaging and fascinating.

Spazio Geco team designed a path in which the visitor, walking through the exhibition, is attracted by the portrait of an elegant and beautiful benefactor, Prince Antonio Tolomeo Trivulzio. The image of the pictorial portrait of this prince is in fact presented to the visitors on a digital screen (Fig. 2B) placed inside a multimedia frame and a special sensor was installed in the digital frame to make it more interactive so that when visitors pass through the frame, they activate a slight call, a whisper in the ears of visitors inviting them to pause and inspect the picture before moving on.

In addition, the team brought to life some images of the prince by installing an introductory button that when pressed by visitor starts an experience of "interaction" with the Prince himself. The team installed what they called the wink which causes the appearance of a blinking in correspondence with the left hand of the Prince indicating an invitation to operate the button placed at the same height on the frame. Pressing such button, visitors will thus find themselves in front of the home base of the work: a view of the desk of the prince seen from above. On the shelf, in random order, the original writing instruments, scattered and bound documents, the shoulders and the "parruccata" head of the Prince intent on arranging his cards in three piles (Fig. 2C). In correspondence of these, an infographic offers the user three different insights into the life and works of the benefactor. By operating the interactive frame button placed at the document stacks, the visitor can then enjoy the multimedia contents inserted in a short video clip, and then return to the home screen of the whispering portrait.

From a technical point of view: the installation consists of a camouflaged monitor with an antiqued frame in order to simulate a painting. Three buttons are inserted in the frame and everything is controlled by a miniPC.

Today, the work is part of the exhibition of the Martinitt and Stelline Museum in Milan.

2.3 Museum of Valtellinese History and Art of Sondrio (Italy)

The above described project is not the only example of interactive use of storytelling [9] made by Spazio Geco in enhancement of cultural heritage: in 2019 the Museum of Valtellinese History and Art of Sondrio (MVSa) commissioned to Spazio Geco the creation of the multimedia installation called "what is hidden behind a fragment". The need for the curatorship was to communicate the difference between an archaeological findings coming from excavation, which is normally not very aesthetically appreciable but full of information, and the findings coming from a private collection or an occasional discovery, which are often more precious and beautiful, but without context and historical information. The idea born during the meetings between Geco team and the Valtellina

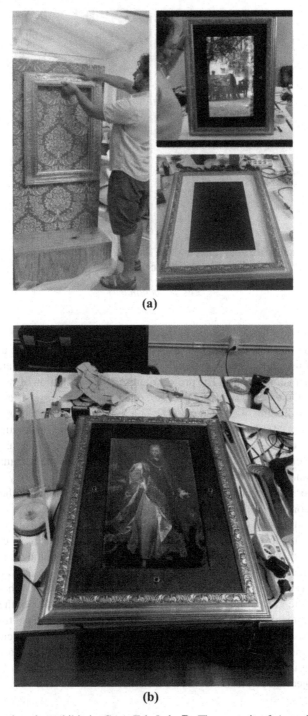

(a)

(b)

Fig. 2. **A.** Preparing the exhibit in Geco Fab Lab. **B.** The portrait of Antonio Tolomeo. **C.** Screenshots of the installation home page.

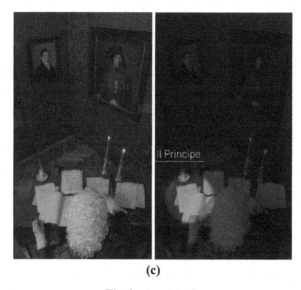

(c)

Fig. 2. (*continued*)

Museum curatorship was to include in the installation two symbolic objects, one from excavation and one from a casual discovery that supply visitors with an understandable explanation of the significant contextual and museological difference and at the same time involve them emotionally. The project required the installation of two columns that were placed inside a niche: in one of them we decided to propose an artefact originating from a fortuitous finding of a "gold coin" and on the other column an "ugly" excavation fragment (see Fig. 3). Through the movement of sensors, the installation is activated when the audience passes: the lights go out and only the gold coin remains illuminated. When this happens a 20–30 s video in wire frame style presents the information available on the finding and it highlights the place of discovery and the chronology of the findings. After the video is completed, the lights go down again leaving only the column with the fragment coming from the excavation illuminated. Then a longer video 1–2 min long appears with much richer information that can be obtained from the highlighted fragment. The display is very interactive and the whole fragment is combined with different whole shapes, until you find the right one, at this point, the fragment becomes a small pitcher, from which pollen is extracted and analyzed so as to reconstruct its contents, i.e. everything that was found together with the fragment. These will fill the pitcher so that the visitor can eventually analyze them and reconstruct the findings.

From a technical point of view: the installation consists of a control system that includes a wide-range sensor and two minipcs connected to two projectors. When the sensor detects the presence of a visitor, the system activates the first projection and, in sync with what is narrated, turns on the first display case. At the end of this narration the second projection begins on a wall on the side.

Fig. 3. The Sondrio exhibit.

2.4 Museo delle Grigne in Esino Lario (Como, Italy)

Another work completed during 2019 was carried out in the small Museo delle Grigne in Esino Lario (Como). On this occasion, the client's wishes were various: first they wanted to create a guide which allows visitors to see the museum independently, without the help of a tour guide; then they wanted to implement a digital platform in the museum where the public can make an own digital experience, and finally they intended to make the museum more "alive" through gamification by integrating game mechanism into the visit so as to encourage participation.

This project required the team to create a video guide [10, 11] that was set up on different tablets that would be given to groups of visitors (especially school classes) during their visit (Fig. 4A). In video creation process required us to create four different characters (see an example in Fig. 4B) that guided people through the different tracks in the museum with each character covering the exhibition in a pre-established order which also helped the circulation of the public in the rather small environments. It is an app developed with Construct3 software [12].

The four characters created were: the "Wikipediana" - Esino Lario was the site of an important congress of Wikipedia in recent years, so it was important to implement this as one of the features; the second character was a "child of 100 years ago", the third character was a Celtic warrior and the fourth was a paleontologist from the early '900. Each character welcomes visitors and invites them to follow him along a historical journey, while stimulating some form of digital interaction with them. For example, to show that visitors arrived at the point indicated by the character, the visitor must insert a code (a particular date or an inventory number) which he must find inside the particular findings he is viewing; after insertion of the code, the character continues the interaction with the user proposing a more deepening and challenging game to solve. Some features of the games can include dividing ancient goods from the modern ones in a series of works taken from those that are kept in the windows; to solve these games correctly the visitor has to focus on the exhibited assets and apply the knowledge derived from

Fig. 4. A. The game on the tablet. **B.** The "Paleontologa" character.

the historic information presented on the route in the museum that the visitor is going through.

2.5   Egyptian Corner at the Archaeological Collection of Pavia University (Italy)

In 2017 the Egyptian Corner [13] was inaugurated at the Archaeological Collection of the University System of Pavia. Such realization is the final result of a valorization project called "Mummy Project" that involved our laboratory with the realization of a particular didactic support in 1: 1 scale with the Mummy at the center of the exhibition itself. The Egyptian mummy was donated in 1842 to the Human Anatomy Cabinet of the University of Pavia directly from Cairo. In 1933 the mummy passed to the Museum of Natural History and then in the 1960s it was placed in a tower of the Castello Visconteo of Pavia, where it remained until its transfer to the archaeological collections of the University. The specimen, without bandages and in good condition, was not kept in a sarcophagus but in a nineteenth-century case with an enigmatic lid that reads: "Egyptian mummy of a woman who died 810 years before the vulgar era. Gift of S. Giorgiani of Cairo of 1824". In order to prepare and design the right approach for this project, the Spazio Geco team undertook a careful research to charachterize the mummy anthropological profile. For this purpose, the most modern medical and forensic investigation techniques were employed thanks also to a number of collaborations with various institutes, including the IRCCS Policlinico San Matteo Foundation in Pavia. So, it was ascertained that the mummy belonged indeed to a woman about 20–22 years old, 1.42–1.48 cm tall, who lived approximately in the third century BC. The mummy was then restored, scanned and enhanced with the help of the above cited involved collaborators.

Spazio Geco's proposal was to provide the typical tools of digital manufacturing for the creation of a scale reproduction that would allow the public to take a tactile approach, particularly interesting and decidedly avant-garde in the setting up and museographic context for various users partially sighted, but also for the ordinary public, children and all the users who would be finally free to "touch" the works exhibited in the usually intransigent way in the rooms of a traditional museum. To achieve this, the teams involved decided that they would have to implement the use of some specific digital fabrication techniques such as advanced 3D printers, large format 2d laser cuts and CNC milling machines. It was then possible to make a great contribution to the realization of this type of project [4, 5]. In particular, the use of the advanced 3D portable scanning technology made it possible to grasp with great precision the architectural and archaeological elements. Then, these can be digitally managed so as to rebuild in scale or full size the components that can be effectively implemented in 3D by the digital fabrication machines.

The realization of the replica of the mummy in a 1:1 scale is the result of the assembly of the scanned layers of sections of the original object (Fig. 5A), which in this way was digitally "recreated". Thanks to the laser cutting, the digitally driven incision of wooden material (4MM plywood) could be carried out allowing the "duplication" of the mummy. The work involved a first phase of acquisition of the file from high-precision 3d scans with "EVA" Artec 3D tools [14], and then we moved on to the "cleaning" phase of the file until obtaining the stl type 3d file, using Autodesk's 12d design software [15]. In the modeling phase, grooves were created within the file that could guarantee the seats for housing an internal structure consisting of housings for metal pipes, useful for supporting the entire structure (Fig. 5B and 5C).

Subsequently, we proceeded to create the slicing part with dedicated software and the layout and creation of the numerous panels of plywood or cardboard by laser cutting. The last phase involved the assembly and insertion of the internal supports in the appropriate housings. At the end of the assembly process, canvases covering the genital areas and minor adjustments to the "cut" slices were recreated, to guarantee a reproduction faithful to the original. The final result (Fig. 5D), very realistic, is daily touched by hundreds of hands since the day the permanent installation is opened to the public.

2.6   Laus Pompeia Museum in Lodi Vecchio (Lodi, Italy) and Museo degli Studi Patri in Gallarate (Varese, Italy)

Remaining in the archaeological field, in the last few years Spazio Geco has carried out work in Lombardy on various enhancement fronts: two interesting examples character-ized by a strong component of interpretative design were created for the "Laus Pompeia Museum" in Lodi Vecchio and the "Museo degli Studi Patri" in Gallarate.

Laus Pompeia Museum: The curatorship wanted to expose in a suitable manner a helmet of the Roman era found in an excavation of the territory. The solution found by Spazio Geco was to produce a human head shape tailored to the helmet itself (Fig. 6A and 6B) through the already experimented approach adopted for the "Mummy Pavese" project, using the same method of overlapping slices, this time made of plexiglass. In particular, we used an open source 3D model of an ancient Roman "type" found online. On this base we modified sizes and small sections working on the 3d file via Rhino [16], to ensure a safe and easy casing for the helmet. We then carried out a plane of parallel sections with constant pitch, the same pitch as the plexiglass we used, to define gradual and parallel cutting sections.

After the realization of a first prototype, we created the final model by aligning the slices cut by the CNC milling machine in slots prepared ad hoc. After the assembly and gluing, the anthropomorphic head was ready to welcome the helmet from Lodi. The end result was very much appreciated by the client and by the public that is now better able to contextualize the archaeological find.

As regards Museo degli Studi Patri, the curatorship wanted a mirror from the Longo-bardian era to be reconstructed and then exhibited on a support. Working in the respect of particular parameters and following the indications of an extensive bibliographic search, the gekcos team was able to reconstruct with the use of plexiglass a very plau-sible hypothesis of a whole outline of the fragmentary Gallaratese finding. The outline was engraved in additional plexiglass (Fig. 6C) customized with the use of the laser cutting techniques implemented in our lab. We made the design of the digital outline using the Adobe tools Photoshop and Illustrator [17]. The ancient mirror is now exposed (Fig. 6D) overlapping the engraved shape with excellent informative result with respect to the reconstruction of its original shape.

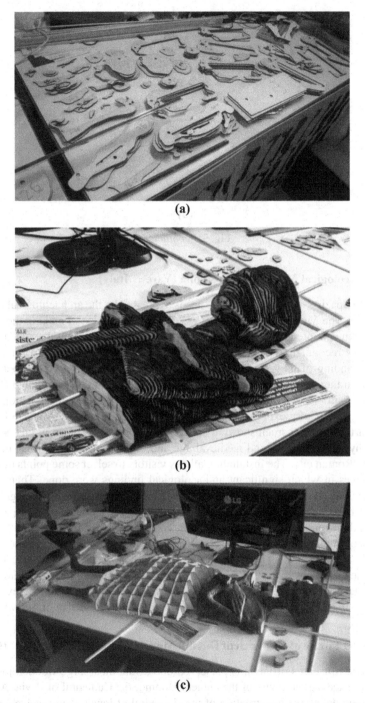

(a)

(b)

(c)

Fig. 5. **A.** The slices just cut. **B and C.** The two steps of the slicing composition. **D.** The final exhibit.

(d)

Fig. 5. (*continued*)

2.7 Archaeological Museum of Cremona (Varese, Italy)

In 2018 the Spazio Geco confronted the needs expressed by the archaeological Museum of Cremona. The Museum direction expressed a strong interest in making the museum more modern and interactive through the creation of interactive digital installations that would allow recognizing the archaeological presence on the territory while allowing the understanding of its geographical location with respect to the contemporary city. Spazio Geco thus created an interactive "Forma Urbis", a multimedia table (Fig. 7A) that allows visitors to interact with the map of the city and put them in a position suitable to explore their territory, explore the aspects of major interest and understand its historical depth. Starting from a screen showing the city as it is today, one can in fact access the cartography of the modern and medieval age and, finally the "form Urbis" that is the plan of the Roman city. The installation allows visitors to select some points of interest, mostly places in which significant archaeological findings were done. Then they can activate textual and visual contents of the findings. It is also possible to highlight the paleo riverbed of the Po River and the route of the Via Postumia with respect to the ancient and current urban map. Finally, the visitor can build itineraries that connect the points of interest underlined in the map and send the relative contents to their email address, to continue the visit even outside the museum. The results of the project (Fig. 7B) allowed the numerous schools that visit the rooms of the museum to dive into the past and the interactive and multimedia use allows them to have a pleasant digital experience, certainly in line with the way "digital natives" assimilate knowledge of the world [18].

2.8 The 3D Puzzle of the Ancient Duomo Model in Musei Civici Pavesi (Italy)

At the Civic Museums of Pavia is preserved one of the most large wooden models of the Renaissance age: a model of the ancient Duomo, the Cathedral of Pavia. Although recently remodeled, the construction of the Cathedral of Pavia begun in 1488 and was interrupted several times, but was finally completed in 1933; to date, it is certainly useful to study and fully reconstruct the various phases of the church building. The complex

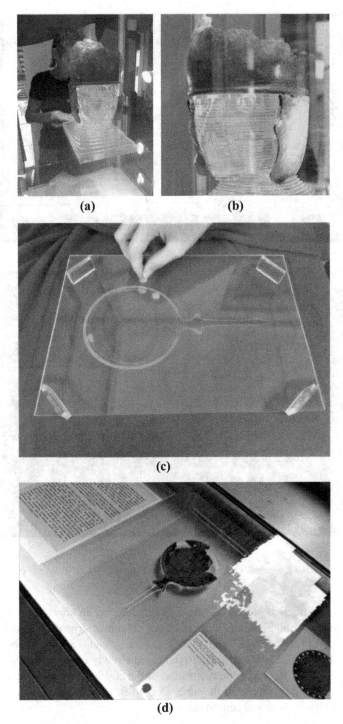

Fig. 6. **A and B.** The The Laus Pomepeia digital manufact for the helmet. **C.** The support for the Longobard mirror in Gallarate Museum. **D.** The final exhibit in Gallarate Museum.

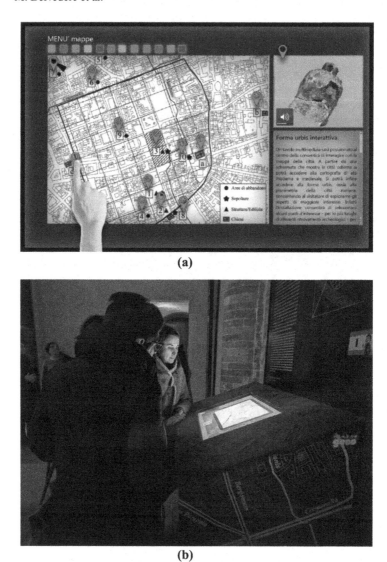

Fig. 7. A. The Cremona's ancient map on the digital table. **B.** The final exhibit.

history of the construction of the cathedral of Pavia sees the architect Giovanni Antonio Amadeo from Pavia and his fellow citizen master carpenter Cristoforo Rocchi engaged in the first project between 1487 and 1488. Cardinal Ascanio Sforza, Bishop of Pavia and brother of Ludovico il Moro, was also engaged already from the laying of the first stone (29 June 1488). However, the realization of the building required the intervention of one of the greatest architects of the time, Donato Bramante, who prepared a second project with a Greek cross and central dome.

The completely rearranged model of the Cathedral of Pavia is being displayed now in the Civic Museums imposing itself on the visitor in all its overbearing presence. It concretely conveys the idea of the grandeur designed at the time for the Pavia cathedral. This wooden model was built with a complex and very interesting construction method: without nails or unifying elements of materials other than wood, it was entirely created with an interlocking system, thus being completely disassemblable and reassemblable. However, this beautiful and ancient prototype does not really allow the visitors to realize and understand the evolution pattern of the project of the cathedral over the centuries. Therefore, in the frame of a reorganization project of the museum hall, it was proposed to create a model that addresses these issues. So, Spazio Geco was commissioned in 2021 to create a 3D puzzle of the model for educational purposes. The modeling was made from scratch based on photographs of the original using Rhino [16] (Fig. 8A). Scanning was not performed.

The idea was not to create a copy but an educational object typologically and formally conforming to the original. It is in fact a simplification of the elaborate original composition, also by virtue of a reduction in scale. We proceeded by creating construction systems and parts of the model that could be assembled together. We produced the various linear parts of the puzzle with CNC milling systems according to interlocking design logics. The components were designed to be inserted into specific "holes" on a wooden base aimed at supporting the entire product. Each element (especially the 4 main fronts) was equipped with bas-relief decorations carved from solid in 20 mm plywood, then dark walnut was impregnated against wear and for better cleaning. The double-curved or highly complex parts (such as the dome, drum and apses and side domes) were 3D printed in PLA, then cleaned, plastered and finished (Fig. 8B). These elements fit perfectly with the rest of the blocks obtained and assembled with screws that are not completely visible and joints in the base. The creation of the gcode took place with proprietary and open source such as Pre form or Slicer [19].

Spazio Geco's goal was to create a playful artifact that could achieve the fundamental purpose but also provide specific educational information that would spark a certain type of interest inducing in the visitor the wish of composing and reassembling the puzzle. In particular, this could provide children with a more elaborate and deeper awareness of the artifact, a goal that every museum in our opinion should pursue. The model of the Cathedral of Pavia is not an exact replica of the cathedral, but it is a construction tool, an object of study and reasoning, transportable if necessary and therefore completely dismantlable and reassemblable. Even if a single child, after having carried out the dismantling and reassembly of the puzzle, will have understood something more about the design essence of the model of the Duomo in the center of the room, then as operators in the world of heritage enhancement, we would have achieved an important goal.

In summary, the newly renovated room in the Cathedral of Pavia was recently unveiled to the public and the educational game developed by the Geckos is being considered by the Museums as a teaching tool to be manipulated into numerous classes and workshop groups (Fig. 8C, 8D).

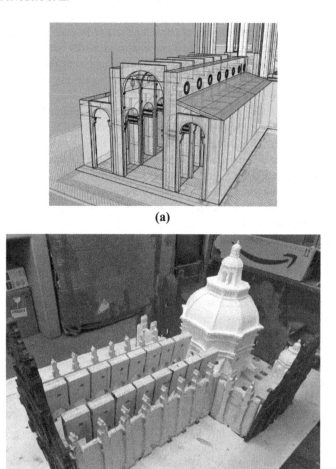

(a)

(b)

Fig. 8. A. The digital composition of 3D puzzle. **B.** One step of the set up. **C.** The 3D puzzle during a whorkshop with kids. **D.** The 3D puzzle in the final exhibit.

(c)

(d)

Fig. 8. (*continued*)

3 Conclusion

In conclusion, this paper brings to reader's knowledge the most interesting and successful projects carried out or under construction at the Geco Fab Lab of Pavia in the course of 2015–2021. In the meantime, many other job and growth opportunities have emerged in the field of the enhancement of the Italian cultural heritage through the use of innovative technologies. So, our group of young and creative researchers and collaborators are well determined to take advantage of the training, and of the growth of their technical knowledge and managerial skills and in general of the skills acquired in these five years to kick off new projects aiming at further development and implementation of the interactive multimedia communication within Italian as well as foreign museums.

Taking into account that today seems the right moment for entrepreneurial initiatives in the field of cultural heritage defense and of the improvement of its fruition, it seems there are good opportunities for a further growth of Geco Fab Lab itself with obvious positive consequences for its achievements quality and its competitiveness.

References

1. Freedman, G.: The changing nature of museums. Curator Mus. J. **43**(4), 295–306 (2010)
2. Peacock, D.: Making ways for change: Museums, disruptive technologies and organisational change. Mus. Manag. Curatorsh. **23**(4), 333–351 (2018)
3. Parry, R.: Recording the Museum: Digital Heritage and the Technologies of Change. Routledge, London (2010)
4. Scopigno, R., Cignoni, P., Pietroni, N., Callieri, M., Dellepiane, M.: Digital fabrication techniques for Cultural Heritage: a survey. Comput. Graph. Forum **36**(1), 6–21 (2017)
5. Short, D.B.: Digital fabrication techniques for cultural heritage: a survey. 3D Print. Addit. Manuf. **2**(4), 209–215 (2017)
6. Edison homepage. https://www.edison.it/it/la-centrale-idroelettrica-angelo-bertini-di-paderno-mi
7. The softwares homepage. https://unity.com/, https://developer.vuforia.com/
8. Cenedella C., Belvedere M.: La storia va in scena: appunti di museologia dal percorso di realizzazione del Museo Martinitt e stelline di Milano. Sondrio, Ramponi Arti Grafiche (2012)
9. Wyman, B., Smith, S., Meyers, D., Godfrey, M.: Digital storytelling in museums: observations and best practices. Mus. J. **54**(4), 461–468 (2011)
10. Cesário, V.: Guidelines for combining storytelling and gamification: which features would teenagers desire to have a more enjoyable museum experience? In: CHI EA 19, pp. 1–6 (2019)
11. Roussou, M., Pujol, L., Katifori, A., Chrysanthi, A., Perry, S., Vayanou, M.: The museum as digital storyteller: collaborative participatory creation of interactive digital experiences. In: MW 2015: Museums and the Web (2015)
12. Constructor 3 homepage. https://www.construct.net/en
13. De Pietri, M.: Tra il Nilo e il Ticino: la collezione egizia del Museo Archeologico dell'Università degli Studi di Pavia Gilgameš **2**(2), 85–93 (2018)
14. The device homepage. https://www.artec3d.com/
15. The software homepage. https://www.12d.com/
16. The software homepage. https://www.rhino3d.com/
17. The software homepage. https://www.adobe.com/it/

18. Radeta, M., Cesario, V., Matos, S., Nisi, V.: Gaming versus storytelling: understanding children's interactive experiences in a museum setting. In: Nunes, N., Oakley, I., Nisi, V. (eds.) ICIDS 2017. LNCS, vol. 10690, pp. 163–178. Springer, Cham (2017). https://doi.org/10.1007/978-3-319-71027-3_14
19. The softwares homepage. https://formlabs.com/software/ and https://www.slicer.org/

The Presentation of Linguistic Works on the Bulgarian Language in the World Slavic Bibliography 'Rocznik Slawistyczny' (1908): A Digital Resource Study

Velislava Stoykova(✉) 🄳

Institute for the Bulgarian Language "Prof. Lyubomir Andreychin", Bulgarian
Academy of Sciences, 52, Shipchensky proh. blvd, bl. 17, 1113 Sofia, Bulgaria
vstoykova@yahoo.com
http://www.ibl.bas.bg

Abstract. The paper offers the first analysis of the Bulgarian language
linguistic works which are included and presented in the first world bibliography on Slavic linguistics 'Rocznik Slawistyczny (Revue slavistique)'
(1908) published in Krakow, Poland. The analysis is based on the digital resource of the bibliography offered by the Wielkopolska Biblioteka
Cyfrowa (Great Polish Digital Library) and includes an overview of the
principles, structure, and content of the bibliography as well as a description and comments on the Bulgarian language sources with attention to
the specific features of its content presented as a part of the national
cultural heritage.

Keywords: ICT and Digital Heritage · Digital humanities · Digital
resources applications · Slavic studies · Bibliographic resources

1 Introduction

Nowadays more libraries and research centers are digitizing and offering their
printed resources in order to be accessible online to the wider research communities. Especially, some collections from the old archives contain rare printed
editions that are very valuable sources for researchers from all over the world
since most of them are unique and is hard to be found in printed version [8].

The main process of digitization needs to offer the printed resources in a
manner such, that they can be accessible for the online search. Thus, it requires
restructuring the printed source (or archive) in order to transform it into an
online database by using a related meta-data scheme that allows search procedures, and different libraries are using their own approaches for accessibility and
metadata-extraction functionalities to improve the search of their online digital
resources [7].

However, the study of the main printed resource with its original structuring
gives invaluable information about the time it was created, related cultural facts,
and its impact on the field. Further, we are going to present the first analysis

R. Furferi et al. (Eds.): Florence Heri-Tech 2022, CCIS 1645, pp. 268–276, 2022.
https://doi.org/10.1007/978-3-031-20302-2_20

of the content and the presentation of Bulgarian language linguistic works in the first world Slavic linguistic bibliography 'Rocznik Slawistyczny (Revue slavistique)' published by G. Gebethner i Spolka in 1908 in Krakow, Poland based on its digital resource.

2   'Rocznik Slawistyczny (Revue Slavistique)', Part II, 1908

The first world Slavic linguistic bibliography 'Rocznik Slawistyczny (Revue slavistique)', 1908 (Fig. 1) was published as a separate part (Czesc II Przeglad Bibljograficzny na rok 1907 (Part II Review of Bibliography for 1907)) (Fig. 2) of the

Fig. 1. The title page of 'Rocznik Slawistyczny (Revue slavistique)' (1908). (https://www.wbc.poznan.pl/dlibra/publication/137125/edition/148724?language=pl)

journal, which introduction was both in Polish and French language. Thus, from its early beginning, the bibliography was aimed to be issued periodically, systematically, and with attention to analyzing the presented linguistic works which differ from the related works at that time.

The main editors of the journal 'Rocznik Slawistyczny (Revue slavistique)' (1908), J. Los, L. Mankowski, K. Nitsch, and J. Rozwadowski started that bibliographic review, as they pointed out in the introduction, aimed to present an informative and critical review of the work in the area of Slavic linguistics. Also, they pointed out that the bibliography is going to be continuing and systematic, and offer related analysis, summaries, reviews, and critical overviews but without taking into account ethnic-linguistic subdivisions of Slavic languages typology since the accepted classification is given taking into account the historical considerations [2].

2.1 Principles, Structure, and Content

As it was pointed out, the first world bibliography on Slavic linguistics was the first attempt to present a multilingual, continuing (published annually), commented and analysed exhaustive presentation of all published works in the area of Slavic languages which continue to be issued for more than a hundred years [9], updated and offered to the academic audience nowadays.

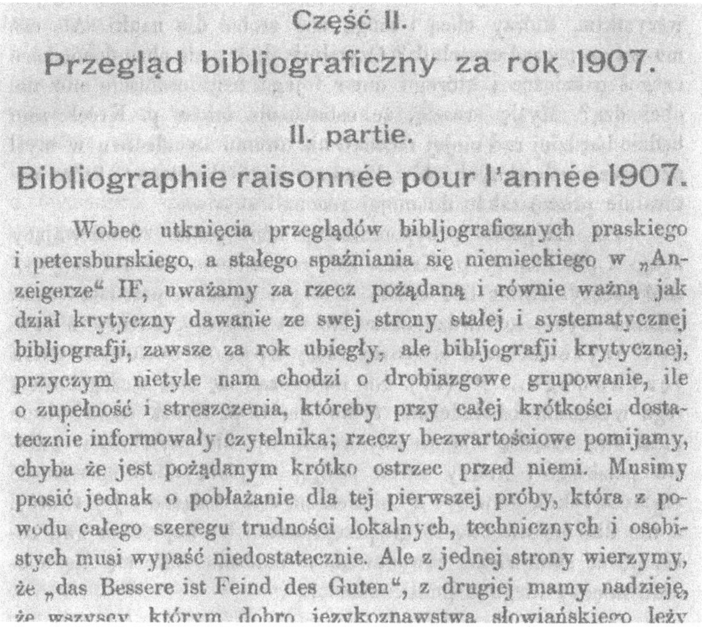
Część II.

Przegląd bibljograficzny za rok 1907.

II. partie.

Bibliographie raisonnée pour l'année 1907.

Wobec utknięcia przeglądów bibljograficznych praskiego i petersburskiego, a stałego spaźniania się niemieckiego w „Anzeigerze" IF, uważamy za rzecz pożądaną i równie ważną jak dział krytyczny dawanie ze swej strony stałej i systematycznej bibljografji, zawsze za rok ubiegły, ale bibljografji krytycznej, przyczym nietyle nam chodzi o drobiazgowe grupowanie, ile o zupełność i streszczenia, któreby przy całej krótkości dostatecznie informowały czytelnika; rzeczy bezwartościowe pomijamy, chyba że jest pożądanym krótko ostrzec przed niemi. Musimy prosić jednak o pobłażanie dla tej pierwszej próby, która z powodu całego szeregu trudności lokalnych, technicznych i osobistych musi wypaść niedostatecznie. Ale z jednej strony wierzymy, że „das Bessere ist Feind des Guten", z drugiej mamy nadzieję, że wszyscy którym dobro językoznawstwa słowiańskiego leży

Fig. 2. The title page of the bibliography 'Czesc II Przeglad Bibljograficzny na rok 1907' (EN – Part II Review of Bibliography for 1907). (https://www.wbc.poznan.pl/dlibra/publication/137125/edition/148724?language=pl)

The reviewers were the main editors of the journal 'Rocznik Slawistyczny (Revue slavistique)' (1908) which abbreviations are given at the end of the introduction as well as at the end of the reviewed title. The main source of the bibliography is the list of previously selected periodically published academic editions (Fig. 3) in the area of Slavic linguistics of most notable European universities which are the source of the presented overviews and summaries of related authors and titles.

The bibliography contains 271 titles which are alphabetically ordered, numbered, subsumed, and analysed (each of which) according to the Slavic language that relates to, i.e. the dividing principle is the accepted Slavic languages classification which includes: (i) General linguistics, (ii) Old Church Slavonic language, (iii) Group Bulgaro-Macedonian, (iv) Group Serbo-Croatian, (v) Slovene, (vi) Group Czech-Slovak, (vii) Group Luzyck, (viii) Group Lechitic, (ix) Group Russian. Accordingly, for every included title a full bibliographic description is given including author, title, source edition, pages, and optional review, summary, or abstract signed at the end by the reviewer. That last commentary part of the bibliographic information description was elaborated with the time and was accepted as an important part of its contemporary electronic version [1,5,6].

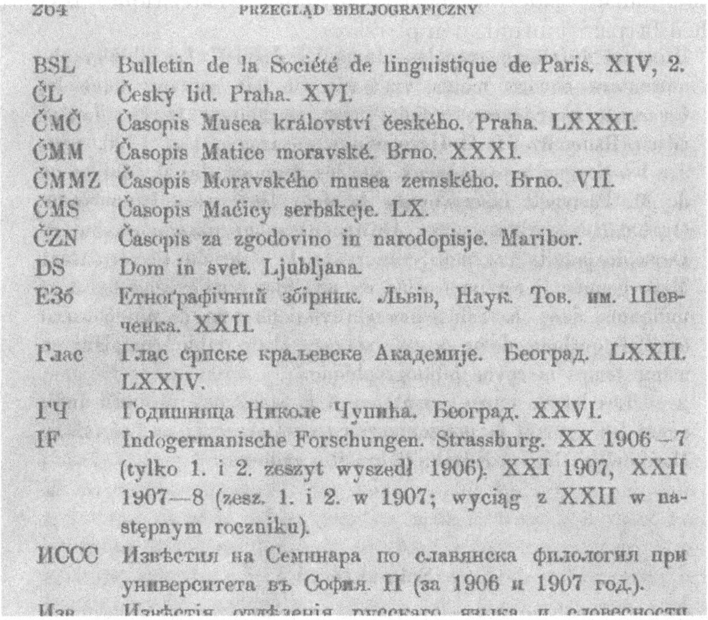
204 PRZEGLĄD BIBLJOGRAFICZNY

BSL	Bulletin de la Société de linguistique de Paris. XIV, 2.
ČL	Český lid. Praha. XVI.
ČMČ	Časopis Musea království českého. Praha. LXXXI.
ČMM	Časopis Matice moravské. Brno. XXXI.
ČMMZ	Časopis Moravského musea zemského. Brno. VII.
ČMS	Časopis Maćicy serbskeje. LX.
ČZN	Časopis za zgodovino in narodopisje. Maribor.
DS	Dom in svet. Ljubljana.
Е36	Етноґрафічний збірник. Львів, Наук. Тов. им. Шевченка. XXII.
Глас	Глас српске краљевске Академије. Београд. LXXII. LXXIV.
ГЧ	Годишница Николе Чупића. Београд. XXVI.
IF	Indogermanische Forschungen. Strassburg. XX 1906 – 7 (tylko 1. i 2. zeszyt wyszedł 1906). XXI 1907, XXII 1907—8 (zesz. 1. i 2. w 1907; wyciąg z XXII w następnym roczniku).
ИССС	Извѣстия на Семинара по славянска филология при университета въ София. II (за 1906 и 1907 год.).

Fig. 3. The list of source editions of the bibliography that are abbreviated, signate, and alphabetically ordered. (https://www.wbc.poznan.pl/dlibra/publication/137125/edition/148724?language=pl)

2.2 Digital Resources

From 2007 onward, the world bibliography on Slavic linguistics is offered as an online and annually updated electronic web-based search system iSybislaw [4] which still maintains the main structure of its original, i.e. is multilingual (offers the bibliographic information in all Slavic languages), is based on hierarchical Slavic languages classification and linguistic terms classification (keywords), contains also titles abstracts, summaries, and optional reviews.

Volume II of the journal 'Rocznik Slawistyczny (Revue slavistique)' (1908) is publicly available in the catalogs of the major Polish libraries but in the digitized format, is offered from two official sources:

(i) Wielkopolska Biblioteka Cyfrowa (Great Polish Digital Library), Digital resource from the Collection of the Biblioteka Kórnicka, PAN: https://www.wbc.poznan.pl/dlibra/publication/137125/edition/148724?language=pl
(ii) Internet Archive Books, Digital resource from the Collection of the University of Michigan: https://archive.org/details/rocznikslawisty00sogoog/page/n5/mode/2up.

The main journal 'Rocznik Slawistyczny (Revue slavistique)' is continuing to be published https://journals.pan.pl/rslaw.

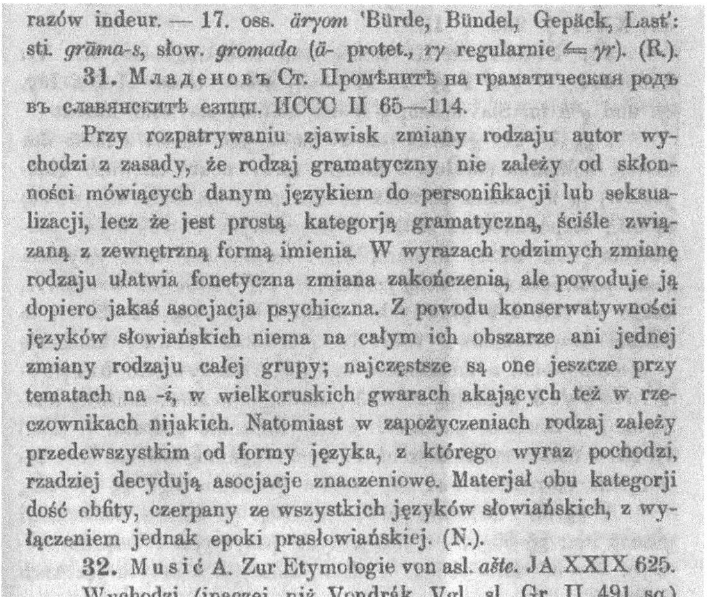
razów indeur. — 17. oss. *ärγom* 'Bürde, Bündel, Gepäck, Last': sti. *grāma-s*, słow. *gromada* (*ă-* protet., *rγ* regularnie ⇐ *γr*). (R.).

31. Младеновъ Ст. Промѣнитѣ на граматическия родъ въ славянскитѣ езици. ИССС II 65—114.

Przy rozpatrywaniu zjawisk zmiany rodzaju autor wychodzi z zasady, że rodzaj gramatyczny nie zależy od skłonności mówiących danym językiem do personifikacji lub seksualizacji, lecz że jest prostą kategorją gramatyczną, ściśle związaną z zewnętrzną formą imienia. W wyrazach rodzimych zmianę rodzaju ułatwia fonetyczna zmiana zakończenia, ale powoduje ją dopiero jakaś asocjacja psychiczna. Z powodu konserwatywności języków słowiańskich niema na całym ich obszarze ani jednej zmiany rodzaju całej grupy; najczęstsze są one jeszcze przy tematach na *-ĭ*, w wielkoruskich gwarach akających też w rzeczownikach nijakich. Natomiast w zapożyczeniach rodzaj zależy przedewszystkim od formy języka, z którego wyraz pochodzi, rzadziej decydują asocjacje znaczeniowe. Materjał obu kategorji dość obfity, czerpany ze wszystkich języków słowiańskich, z wyłączeniem jednak epoki prasłowiańskiej. (N.).

32. Musić A. Zur Etymologie von asl. *ašte*. JA XXIX 625. Wychodzi (inaczej niż Vondrák Vgl. sl. Gr. II 491 sq.)

Fig. 4. The Bulgarian language source (№ 31.) from section (i) General linguistics of the bibliography. (https://www.wbc.poznan.pl/dlibra/publication/137125/edition/148724?language=pl)

Further, we are going to present the first analysis of the linguistic works on the Bulgarian language included in 'Rocznik Slawistyczny (Revue slavistique)' (1908) on the base of the first digital resource.

3 Linguistic Works on the Bulgarian Language in 'Rocznik Slawistyczny' (1908)

The linguistic works of the Bulgarian language are presented in four sections of the 'Rocznik Slawistyczny (Revue slavistique)' (1908). First, they are included in the alphabetical list of the observed source editions (Fig. 3). There are three main sources in the Bulgarian language included in the bibliography (two proceedings and one journal) all of which are issued periodically.

In section (i) General linguistics (containing 60 items) – there is only one title in Bulgarian language (Fig. 4) – № 31. (EN - Mladenov, St. The Changes of Grammatical Gender in Slavic Languages). The title is accompanied by the related commented summary written by the journal's editor K. Nitsch.

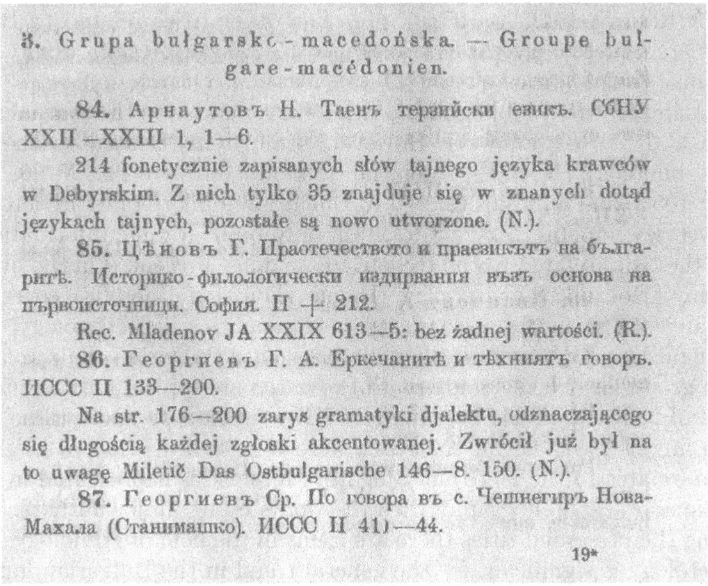

3. Grupa bułgarsko-macedońska. — Groupe bulgare-macédonien.

84. Арнаутовъ Н. Таенъ теранйски езикъ. СбНУ XXII–XXIII 1, 1—6.

214 fonetycznie zapisanych słów tajnego języka krawców w Debyrskim. Z nich tylko 35 znajduje się w znanych dotąd językach tajnych, pozostałe są nowo utworzone. (N.).

85. Цѣновъ Г. Праотечеството и праезикътъ на българитѣ. Историко-филологически издирвания възъ основа на първоизточници. София. II + 212.

Rec. Mladenov JA XXIX 613—5: bez żadnej wartości. (R.).

86. Георгиевъ Г. А. Еркечанитѣ и тѣхниятъ говоръ. ИССС II 133—200.

Na str. 176—200 zarys gramatyki djalektu, odznaczającego się długością każdej zgłoski akcentowanej. Zwrócił już był na to uwagę Miletič Das Ostbulgarische 146—8. 150. (N.).

87. Георгиевъ Ср. По говора въ с. Чешнегиръ Нова-Махала (Станимашко). ИССС II 41)—44.

19*

Fig. 5. The beginning of the (iii) Group Bulgaro-Macedonian of the bibliography. (https://www.wbc.poznan.pl/dlibra/publication/137125/edition/148724?language=pl)

However, in section (ii) Old Church Slavonic language there are two titles in the Bulgarian language – № 64. presenting the published manuscript of (EN - The Royal Charter of King Ioan Alexander from 1348). The title is reviewed by the journal's editor J. Rozwadowski. The second title – № 71. (EN - Oreshkov, P. The

Relation of Old Bulgarian Manuscripts toward the Epenthetic 'l') presents the analysis of Old Bulgarian language's manuscripts with respect to the epenthetic consonant 'l'. The title is reviewed by the journal's editor K. Nitsch.

Also, in the section are included two titles that are written by Russian authors but relate to the Old Bulgarian language. The first - № 68. presents the analysis of published by the Ministry of Education in Sofia the Old Bulgarian manuscript from the town of Ohrid (EN - The Ohrid's Manuscript of the Acts of the Apostle) from the end of XII c. The commentaries to it are written by the journal's editor K. Nitsch. The second title - № 74. describes the study on the Bulgarian manuscripts in Skopje's Metropolia (EN - Notes on the Manuscripts from the Bulgarian Metropolia in Skopje).

The section (iii) Group Bulgaro-Macedonian (Fig. 5) contains 23 titles 2 of which are not written in the Bulgarian language but relate to it – the title № 93. is written in the Russian language but relates to Bulgarian dialectology, and the title № 106. which is written in the German language but relates to Bulgarian grammar (Weigand, G. Bulgarische Grammatik, Leipzig, 1907).

The other titles are written in the Bulgarian language and contribute to the fields of Bulgarian ethnology (№ 85., № 95., № 102.), Bulgarian folklore genres: tales (№ 92., № 97.), proverbs (№ 89.), songs (№ 90., № 92., № 94., № 96., № 101., № 103., № 104., № 105.,), etc. The other titles related to Bulgarian linguistics are dialectology (№ 84., № 86., № 87., № 88., № 98., № 99., № 100.), and grammar (№ 91.), etc.

Almost all presented bibliographic titles are reviewed by the journal's editors K. Nitsch and J. Rozwadowski. However, some items related to the field of Bulgarian ethnology (№ 102.), Bulgarian folklore songs (№ 92., № 96., № 101., № 103., № 105.), and all items related to Bulgarian folklore tales are left without review, overview, or summary and contain only bibliographic information.

Thus, the titles related to the Bulgarian language presented in the first world bibliography 'Rocznik Slawistyczny (Revue slavistique)' (1908) cover a wide range of areas of scientific research in the humanities like ethnology, folklore, general linguistics, Old Church Slavonic language, Bulgarian dialectology, and Bulgarian grammar. The related areas of research are typical for the humanities of the end of XIX c. and the beginning of XX c. in Europe and outline that the Bulgarian linguistic studies at that time were very well developed.

It, also, relates to the fact that Bulgarian linguistics is presented in the first three sections of the bibliography with the works by its major authors. The fact that among the presented titles there are items in the field of ethnology, folklore, and dialectology is significant for the general trend in the Bulgarian humanities of that time, i.e. forming the fundamentals of national identities by relating the national humanity studies to the national cultural heritage.

Additionally, the fact that the section (i) General linguistics contains 60 titles and is the most numerous leads to the conclusion that at the time the bibliography was published the comparative studies were the most active field in Slavic linguistics research.

4   Conclusions

The publication of the first world bibliography on Slavic linguistics in 'Rocznik Slawistyczny (Revue slavistique)' (1908) is significant for the scientific research in the field. The main bibliography uses mostly academic editions as a source of the included titles as well as a scientific principle for the organization of the information included, which lead to the conclusion that at that time Slavic studies were a well-developed area of research. The fact that the bibliography is digitized and offered publicly and free for online access by two sources is important for its significance and allows more researchers to analyse its titles in the new cultural and scientific context nowadays.

The first analysis of Bulgarian language sources and related included titles points out the fact that the Bulgarian linguistics received good coverage in the bibliography and is presented by showing its specific trends of research relating to Bulgarian ethnology and folklore by connecting them to the national cultural heritage.

A   Online Resources

The digital sources are available via

- https://www.wbc.poznan.pl/dlibra/publication/137125/edition/148724?language=pl Rocznik Slawistyczny, 1908, Wielkopolska Biblioteka Cyfrowa, Digital resource from the Collection of the Biblioteka Kórnicka, PAN
- https://archive.org/details/rocznikslawisty00sogoog/page/n5/mode/2up Rocznik Slawistyczny, 1908, Internet Archive Books, Digital resource from the Collection of the University of Michigan,
- https://journals.pan.pl/rslaw Rocznik Slawistyczny.

References

1. Kowalski, P.: Abstrakt i adnotacja jako element opisu dokumentu w bazie iSybislaw, Studia z Filologii Polskiej i Slowianskiej, vol. 49, pp. 88–98 (2014). Instytut Slawistyki PAN, Fundacja Slawistyczna, Warszawa, Poland, ISSN 0081–7090
2. Los, J., Mankowski, L., Nitsch, K., Rozwadowski, J.: Rocznik Slawistyczny (Revue slavistique), vol. 1. G. Gebethner i Spolka, Krakow, Poland (1908)
3. Petkova, E., Banasiak, J.: Presentation of Some Systematic Relationships between Terms Keywords in the iSybislaw System, Russian Studies without Borders, vol. 4, 1, pp. 39–47 (2020). Sofia, Bulgaria, ISSN 2535–0390
4. Rudnik-Karwatowa, Z., Banasiak, J., Mikos, Z.: Jezykowe problemy optymalizacji wyszukiwania informacji w systemie iSybislaw, Slavia Orientalis **62**(4), 631–646 (2013). Panstwowe Wydawnictwo Naukowe, Polska Akademia Nauk, Warszawa, Poland. https://journals.pan.pl/dlibra/publication/96616/edition/83364/content
5. Sekowska, E.: Rozwoj recenzji jezykoznawczej na przelomie XIX i XX wieku (na przykladzie „Prac Filologicznych" i „Rocznika Slawistycznego"), Konferencja "Akt mowy - tekst - gatunek wypowiedzi", Bialystok, 29–30 czerwca 2012 2013, pp. 335–350, Wydawnictwo Uniwersytetu w Bialymstoku, Bialystok, Poland, ISBN 978-83-7431-393-3. http://hdl.handle.net/11320/9786

6. Sekowska, E.: Z historii stylu naukowego: poczatki recenzji jezykoznawczej, Poradnik Jezykowy (The Linguistic Guide), vol. 7, pp. 21–30 (2013). Towarzystwa kultury jezyka, ELIPSA, Warszawa, Poland, ISSN 0051–5343
7. Stoykova, V.: Digitization of Bulgarian Natural Science School Books Published in Belgrade During the Period of National Revival (1806–1878), Review of the National Center for Digitization, 31, pp. 18–24 (2017). Belgrade, Serbia, ISSN 1820–0109. http://www.ncd.matf.bg.ac.rs/issues/31/NCD31018.pdf
8. Stoykova, V.: The Digitized Old Books: First Grammar to Teach Romanian Language for Bulgarians, Florence Heri-Tech - The Future of Heritage Science and Technologies 16–18 May 2018, IOP Conference Series: Materials Science and Engineering, 2018, vol. 364, pp. 012049, Florence, Italy, IOP Publishing Ltd, ISSN 1757–8981. https://iopscience.iop.org/article/10.1088/1757-899X/364/1/012049
9. Wojtyla–Swierzowska, M.: W stulecie Rocznika Slawistycznego: Rocznik Slawistyczny, Krakow 1908–2008 (2010). Polska Akademia Umiejetnosci, Krakow, Poland. ISBN 978-83-7676-077-3

Towards a Cultural Ecosystem: Museum Narration Meets Conservation Issues

Laura Baratin[ID], Veronica Tronconi[✉][ID], and Francesca Gasparetto[ID]

School of Conservation and Restoration of Cultural Heritage, University of Urbino, 61029
Urbino, PU, Italy
{laura.baratin,francesca.gasparetto}@uniurb.it,
v.tronconi@campus.uniurb.it

Abstract. This contribution starts from the most recent theories in the field of communication sciences regarding narrative ecosystems and hypothesizes their application in the cultural and museum field, creating a sort of "cultural ecosystem" through the use of ICT. In particular, this study starts analysing an initiative designed by the National Gallery of London entitled "Jan van Huysum Visits": during 2021, the painting "Flowers in a Terracotta Vase" travelled to six different regions in the UK and it was exhibited in unusual locations, to bring the less accustomed public closer to visiting museums, also designing recreational activities related to the artwork, and collaboration with local institutions. Although virtuous from the point of view of creating truly extended experiences around the museum collections, these projects risk not keeping in the right mind the theme of conservation of the artworks, which can be compromised by continuous movements or exhibitions in places that are not suitable from the microclimatic point of view. This study presents some applications to propose a practical solution, replicable and able of combining the conservation needs of works of art with the new narrative and ecosystemic perspectives that we hope for museum use. This goal can be achieved using digital technologies, which allow the reproduction of the physicality of artworks and different insights into diverse content. Referring to new information architecture and documentation systems, we can develop a new concept of sustainable digital heritage also creating some ad hoc digital platforms for the narration of all aspects of conservation.

Keywords: Narrative ecosystem · Cultural ecosystem · Information architecture · Extended experience · Museums · Conservation

1 Introduction

From the 1960s until today, the continuous increase in the use of new technologies in daily life has progressively determined the creation of complex media systems, up to the most recent theories about the existence of real "narrative ecosystems", which are claimed to redefine the traditional methods of communication and to trigger up to now unprecedented processes of participation by the public. By definition, a narrative ecosystem is a transmedia and extended product, endowed with a life of its own, characterized by coherence and resilience, able to extend over time and space and to stimulate unusual interactions with users. To study such a product, it is necessary to rely on the conceptual models of biology, systems and complexity theories, and information architecture. In our current increasingly digitalized context, the creation of extended narratives in the form of ecosystems could also concern museum use. Thus, starting from the definition of narrative ecosystems and analysing their characteristics, as they are outlined by Media Studies, this contribution intends to highlight how even in the cultural and museum environment we are starting to apply some practices related to the concept of ecosystem, creating the so-called "cultural ecosystems". Taking into account the state of the art and the first museum experiments for the creation of extended narratives in the form of ecosystems, the project carried out by the National Gallery of London in 2021 entitled "Jan van Huysum Visits" will be analyzed in detail. The project, although innovative and truly valuable from a narrative point of view, however, has the defect of not taking into account the conservation needs of an original work of art. The study, therefore, takes into consideration some digital experiments developed by large international organizations and a small example of "digital conservation" designed in the context of the School of Conservation and Restoration of the University of Urbino. The proposed working hypotheses, through the digitization of works and the use of ICT, allow creating true extended narratives without subjecting the works to movements or continuous microclimatic variations that could compromise their conservation.

2   The Concept of "Narrative Ecosystem" in Media Studies

The concept of narrative ecosystem was born around the Sixties within the studies on mass media, which were born as a result of the increase in new technologies. The great impact from the cognitive, linguistic, cultural and social point of view that the new means of communication were making led Postman, between 1960 and 1970, to theorize the concept of "media ecology", which is the study of mass media as ecosystems, using an approach of analysis of scientific disciplines and in particular to biology. A few years later McLuhan highlighted how technologies interact with individuals in such a way as to create a holistic system with a certain internal resilience (or, using a technical term derived from ecology, homeostasis), in which the single parts are interconnected in multiple and complex ways [1]. The ecological approach - or, as evidenced by Heise, the metaphor of the ecosystem [2] - took more and more ground up to the most recent elaborations, which are attributable in the Italian context to the contributions of the research group formed by Innocenti, Pescatore and Rosati. Today, the narrative ecosystem assumes the connotation of an adequate heuristic tool for studying the main characteristics of the contemporary mediascape, with particular reference to television and serial narrative production [3]. By definition, therefore, a narrative ecosystem is a narration extended in time (which can therefore last for many years while keeping some fundamental contents unaltered) and in space (so that it can expand into a multiplicity of means, giving rise to a large number of diversified textual objects). It is precisely for this extension that it is difficult to analyze it with the tools used for traditional narratives. For its analysis, therefore, the biological metaphor is used, comparing these types of narratives to real ecosystems, endowed with their own life and independence, built in a transmedia way, characterized by high levels of openness, internal coherence, resilience, interconnection, balance, content, nonprocedural, the coexistence of biotic and abiotic elements and finally able to stimulate unprecedented interactions with the public. To study these products, which possess the complexity and the degree of unpredictability of real living organisms, it is necessary to refer to the conceptual models not only of biology, as already mentioned but also of the systems and complexity theories and information architecture. Considering both this definition with the most relevant aspects of current media production and, more specifically, of serial narrative forms, it seems obvious that the current mediascape requires us to abandon in every field the traditional "medium-specific" model, in favour of a holistic point of view [4, 5].

3   Towards a Cultural Ecosystem: The State of the Art

Even more recent than the theories on narrative ecosystems in the field of Media Studies are the hypotheses about their application in the cultural sphere, and above all in the museum environment. In a conference on Media Studies in 2001, eloquently entitled "Media Mutations", an intervention by Mandelli underlined how museums and cultural institutions in general, from fixed systems firmly anchored to traditional methods of communication to the public, were expanding towards digital solutions and applying an ecosystemic perspective [6]. The first experimental digitizations of museum collections date back to the same years. These experimentations aimed to extend the viewing experience even outside the actual exhibition halls, paving the way for the conceptual transition from "museum as a building" to "museum as extended information architecture" and initiating the processes of re-appropriation of art objects and their meanings by the public. At the same time as the processes of mere digitization of the collections (on which, however, the Italian context has come with a considerable delay compared to the British and American examples), museum institutions have begun to reflect on the various strategies to be implemented to make museum visits more and more suitable to different types of public and different needs. For this reason, as Mandelli points out, museums have begun to rely on information architecture to create physical and digital information systems capable of adapting to the different information needs of the public, thus creating complex structures with the support of the network, capable of offering different entry points for visitors, which is one of the founding characteristics of ecosystems [7]. The concept of cultural ecosystem has been resumed a few years later, analyzing, in particular, the Italian situation of "diffused heritage" and using an economic perspective. From this point of view, the cultural ecosystem is described as a cultural organizational network that is not limited in space to a specific administrative region, province or municipality, but rather creates an organization that considers the real distribution of the widespread cultural heritage and the characteristics of the territory [8]. The territorial ecosystem approach could, according to the authors, unlock the economic potential of the different areas, positively exploiting the dimension of social capital, including the involvement of citizens and creating links between the local community and creative and cultural enterprises, for the creation of value and the identity recognition of tangible and intangible assets at all levels of society. Even this "diffused" approach, which is expanded in space, which closely follows the Italian cultural reality, represents a characteristic of an ecosystem [9]. Finally, it is necessary to underline that due to the recent pandemic situation, also at the Italian level, the network of museums and cultural institutions both at the national and local level has implemented a capillary plan of technological and digital innovation capable of implementing the ecosystemic complexity. In particular, the data acquired by the Osservatorio Innovazione Digitale per i Beni e Attività Culturali of the Politecnico di Milano highlighted that between 2019 and 2020 the role of the digital in the user experience in Italian museums and cultural institutions went through a period of profound rethinking towards a model of true integration between the online visit experience and the physical one, which was defined as "onsite" [10]. Also in this case, the concept of the integration of different media represents for this contribution a fundamental characteristic for the definition of a true cultural ecosystem. In the second report of 2021 carried out by the Osservatorio, and with the eloquent name "Extended experience: the challenge for the cultural ecosystem", Michela Arnaboldi, referring to the growing of the online and social presence of museums, states: "Thanks to the digital, we have the opportunity to rethink the relationship with the user as an experience extended in time and space, as it is not confined to the place and time of the on-site experience, but potentially it is continuous and accessible from any place and any time" [11]. In particular, the most interesting data found here is that 83% of Italian museums have at least one official social network account, and in particular, an increase in the use of the Instagram platform is registered, thanks to its greater representative and narrative potential compared to other social networks. The creation of ad hoc digital content offered by museums, in the conclusions of the report, seems to demonstrate how physical and digital should not be mutually exclusive but rather, always following an ecosystemic approach that includes both of them, they should always be in a complementary relationship [12]. It would therefore be desirable to produce some ad hoc online and onsite content created and managed through specific professionals and through a long-term strategic plan, which includes an overall physical and digital design. Once again, the extension of the cultural experience in time and space achieved also thanks to digital support is attested: in the Italian context, the achievement of the ecosystem approach, at least for the most important cultural institutions, seems complete [13, 14].

4   An Exemplary Case of Ecosystem: The "Jan Van Huysum Visits" Experience

As highlighted in the previous paragraph (which in any case does not want to be an exhaustive state of the art on the subject but rather to outline the main points of the transition towards the ecosystem approach in the cultural field) a cultural ecosystem, to be so intended, has to present some key features. The extension of the museum visit experience over time and space, the integration between digital and physical, the use of different media and platforms, a diversified offer capable of offering multiple entry points for the user, a significant level of initial planning to guarantee a high internal coherence of the system but at the same time an openness to participation and a certain level of unpredictability such as to stimulate unexpected interactions with the public, are some of the founding traits that allow us to deal with museums and cultural institutions as real ecosystems. Taking these characteristics into consideration, we have to move to the Anglo-Saxon environment where we can find the most exemplary experimentations.

Although some italian cultural institutions in the last year have also tried to move towards the ecosystem approach for museum narration, the English experience we are about to talk embodies so many ecosystemic characteristics that it seems necessary to take it as an example and analyze it in all its features. For this reason, it seems here emblematic to analyze a project created by the National Gallery in London in the last year and entitled "Jan Van Huysum Visits". The project was based on a previous experiment carried out in 2019 and called "Artemisia visits", in which the self-portrait of Artemisia Gentileschi as Saint Catherine of Alexandria, restored in 2018, left the rooms of the Gallery throughout 2019 to be exhibited in some unusual places on British soil, including a school, a clinic and a prison (Fig. 1). The "Jan Van Huysum visits" project wanted to take a step forward compared to "Artemisia visits": during the summer of 2021 Jan Van Huysum's painting called "Flowers in a terracotta vase" was subjected to a real six-stage tour throughout the British territory, and exhibited in a series of unusual and unexpected locations, which were non-museum venues, such as a food bank and community library, a covered market, a former department store and community centres. The reasons for the tour were not connected to a recent restoration, as in the case of Artemisia Gentileschi's painting, but to the recent pandemic situation and to the negative effects on mental health that the lockdown period had entailed for some sections of the population. The tour, therefore, aimed to show how art and culture can support the well-being of a community and reach the public who was affected the most by the pandemic situation. At each destination, this first-of-its-kind exhibition explored six different "Ways to Wellbeing": Connect, Be Active, Take Notice, Keep Learning, Give, and Care (for the Planet). The organizers of the initiative worked closely with the exhibition sites, as well as with local museums and galleries to ensure that as many people as possible could interact with the painting and bring it to life in new and different ways, carrying out recreational and educational activities linked to the themes listed above. As expected, in addition to these six physical "happenings", the project was enriched with the creation of some ad hoc content for the online public, in particular on the official website of the National Gallery and the Instagram page, to combine the vision of the painting or some details with meditative activities connected to the six ways of wellbeing [15]. It seems that, more than any other example, the "Jan Van Huysum Visits" project embraces many of the characteristics of an ecosystem: the derivation from a minor project but of which it shares the outline; a true extension of the user experience in the space outside the museum venues; an extension of the visit over time, thanks to the online content that can be used at different levels; a real integration between digital and physical, with contents and events created differently for the two spaces; the use of different media and platforms; a diversified offer in space with multiple entry points for users; a high level of initial planning and an equally high level of openness to the participation of the communities involved, seeking remediations and recreations of meaning by users through the creative activities proposed. Despite the large number of features that make it the perfect example of an ecosystem, the "Jan Van Huysum visits" project has, in our opinion, one major flaw. Considering the continuous movements to which the work is constantly subjected, it seems that it's not taking into account the conservation needs of such an artefact, a delicate oil painting on canvas, whose microclimatic conditions of exposure are essential to ensure correct long-term preservation.

Fig. 1. The Jan Van Huysum's painting first visit in Norfolk, inside a shopping centre. Photo courtesy of The National Gallery, Jan Van Husum project (https://www.nationalgallery.org.uk/whats-on/jan-van-huysum-visits)

5   When Storytelling Considers Conservation Issues

There are various possibilities to approach the model of the "Jan Van Huysum Visits" project differently. If it tries to explore this kind of content with the eyes of restorers, it is easy to identify the reasons why they seem to have difficulty in accepting heritage fruition without considering the conservative aspects. On the other hand, it is nothing new. The role of conservation in communicative initiatives was often hidden following the idea that the topic was too technical. Unfortunately, our historical culture tends to focus on the historical story about the object rather than engagement with the physicality of the objects themselves. But almost ten years ago, a conference held in 2011 in the USA, grappled with some experiences about the issues of conservation in the public eye and the conservation outreach. The meeting was entitled "Playing to the Galleries and Engaging new Audiences: the Public Face of Conservation". The conference sought different papers submissions that focused on communicating conservation and on educational initiatives. The result was a collection of experiences in which conservation had earned a prominent place in museums and exhibitions. In some way, the American conference demonstrates the important role in communicating the activities of artefacts preservation and it brings the knowledge obtained through conservative processes into the public domain. To bring the audience behind-the-scenes to attract attention to the role of conservation in maintaining collections and our global heritage. According to Mary Brooks, in the eyes of the audience significance and accessibility need to be valued as much as preservation [16]. For these reasons, we should rethink the storytelling content approaching heritage communication. We should involve conservators and restorers with a multi-level system of documentation to design a new form of outreach starting from the technical data they produce in restoration work. As a strategy to help raise awareness of the importance of preservation, a procedural workflow of documentation could be provided, depending on the activity designed by the conservator. In other words, to bring the public ever closer to the conservative experience it is necessary to capture technical data as they evolve and translate them in an accessible manner [17]. Visitors, in fact, do not need to see conservators in uncomfortable positions, during boring activities or repetitive tasks. They want an intimate experience with the object, a proximity achieved with more clear information [18]. In this sense, the ecosystem design approach can help in achieving this goal. The practice of conservation and restoration is a complex process, which requires collaboration between different professionals and the production of a large amount of data of different nature. These data are often created on different analog and digital supports, such as to suggest different communicative outputs and different narrative strands, not necessarily orderable according to a univocal logic [19]. These characteristics lead to the ones listed for the narrative ecosystems: high level of internal coherence due to a unique subject; narration designed on different media; implementation of both onsite and online content; different narrative strands offering different entry points to the users. The ecosystem approach can really be a fertile ground to talk about conservation! In this way, digital tools which are now at our disposal offer still little experimented ways of ordering data and making them narrative and coherent with each other, in order to create a multimedia communication plan for the public. The increased funding for digital technologies applied to heritage education and fruition makes our times a particularly fruitful moment for innovative initiatives [20, 21]. But we need to put conservation's issues in a central framework for teaching applied science concepts to a wider audience [22].

6   ICT for Conservation: Digital Documentation and Digital Representation for Communicating Heritage

ICTs are becoming support for various processes in different contexts of our life. In multiple ways they are transforming the forms of communication and social interaction, affecting how we interact with cultural experiences as well. Cultural knowledge is accessed easier and transferred through multi-channel information in multiple formats, creating immersive outreaching experiences open to a wider public [23]. Involving conservation data and information from restoration work, we launch a sort of new entry-point in the evolving cultural ecosystem and we generate a new space of knowledge. E-tools can contribute significantly in creating this kind of content, by integrating the use of technologies and allowing the generation of new digital heritage, and they can make these content more accessible for the citizens to use [24]. Take the example of Google Arts & Culture that features content from over 2000 leading museums and archives, opening different kinds of content for online visitors. Browsing the website, one can find the experience "Restoring the Globes". Here, the whole intervention is explained, from diagnostic aspects to practical tasks, and it is possible to focus some technical aspects on a 3D model of a historical globe. In this case, technologies were used to produce the 3D globe and to enjoy the set of data [25]. The internet and digital technology can create important new opportunities for exhibitions and heritage fruition, considering that the web offers them a great possibility to improve the space in which they can develop their content and in the way they can reach participation and access to the heritage of a growing number of virtual visitors [26]. The ever-changing nature of digital can indeed be disorienting. In this sense, the efforts of the scientific community around this topic shall address identifying tangible methodologies as support for steady content creation [27]. The solution could be a documental system that challenges current scientific communication of conservation activities, creating a high-content ground for a transmedial communication system. As a research group born inside the Conservation and Restoration School of the University of Urbino, we are now experimenting with a standardized workflow for the organization and management of conservation and restoration data, capable of creating a documental system and a communication strategy with an ecosystem perspective. The contents thus created are progressively inserted into an online platform called Open Restoration, connected to an Instagram page. In the future, we hope to be able to increase the digital experience with physical events, such as visits to the School's restoration laboratories or information paths within the exhibition places of the restored works of art. This would offer different entry points for users, a high coherence between the contents and a diversified offer between digital and physical experiences, providing enriched information on the works of art and different ways of use and fruition, without subjecting them to movements or stress (Fig. 2).

Fig. 2. The Open Restoration website (www.openrestoration.uniurb.it)

7   Conclusions

With all the considerations and the different experiences listed so far, it is now clear that through the use of ICT and digital technology applied to cultural experiences we can radically change the traditional models of cultural fruition and even the museum narration [28]. The most recent experiences on media mutations and the reports of the last two years on the Italian museum situation drawn up by the Osservatorio on Digital

Innovation of Polytechnic of Milano demonstrate that many projects performed in the cultural field fall fully within the definition of an ecosystem. In particular, the example analyzed "Jan Van Huysum Visits" demonstrates how many ecosystem features can be positively included in a single project. However, this contribution aimed to demonstrate how the ecosystem approach should also take into account the conservation needs of works of art. Conservation needs are not only an aspect to be taken into consideration, but can indeed offer further possibilities for ecosystemic coherence (i.e. different entry points for the artwork fruition, enriched data and information, extension over time of the visitor experience, extension over space with the support of digital content). We must also take greater account that our pandemic era is accelerating the digital change and digital technologies in the museum and cultural contexts as well, enabling them to interact with communities more efficiently and attract new public. According to what we said, the research around conservative issues should focus on new ecosystemic models, considering digital language as an opportunity for interdisciplinary competencies. This theoretical scenario led us to experiment with an open and documentative system in which technical data are the starting point for building accessible content about conservation. Indeed, the preservation of our heritage depends on accurate documentation. Starting from this basic principle we can design cultural storytelling from conservation issues and use the data produced by conservation processes in a useful way. In this sense, the current digital challenges allow conservative practices to conform with the adoption of ecosystemic approaches, using a standard workflow to manage different data. And it's exactly what we are evaluating with the practical experience of the Open Restoration website. Conservation should include a process that passes through preventive work, constant maintenance up to restoration, if necessary. The way how information is managed before arriving at conservative decisions has a strong ecosystemic character that must be introduced and made explicit also in professional practice, starting with the training of new generations of conservators – restorers [29], in terms of communication strategies to the public.

References

1. Carpentier, N.: Contextualising author-audience convergences. "New" technologies' claims to increased participation, novelty and uniqueness. Cult. Stud. 25, 517–533 (2011)
2. Heise, U.K.: Unnatural ecologies: the metaphor of the environment in media theory. Configurations 10, 149–168 (2002)
3. Bisoni, C., Pescatore, G., Innocenti, V.: Il concetto di ecosistema e i media studies: un'introduzione. Media Mutations. Gli ecosistemi narrativi nello scenario mediale contemporaneo. Spazi, modelli, usi sociali, pp. 11–26. Modena, Mucchi Editore (2013)
4. Innocenti, V., Pescatore, G., Rosati, L.: Converging universes and media niches in serial narratives: an approach through information architecture. In: Lugmayr, A., Dal Zotto, C. (eds.) Media convergences Handbook. Media Business and Innovation, vol. 2, pp. 137–152. Springer, Heidelberg (2016). https://doi.org/10.1007/978-3-642-54487-3_8
5. Pescatore, G.: Ecosistemi narrativi. Dal fumetto alle serie tv, Carocci Editore (2018)
6. Mandelli, E.: Il museo come ecosistema narrativo: nuovi media e valorizzazione del patrimonio culturale. In: Innocenti, V. (ed.) Media Mutations 3. Ecosistemi narrativi: spazi, strumenti, modelli, Bologna, 24–25 maggio 2011 (2011)

7. Mandelli, E.: Architettura dell'informazione e design museale. Tafter Journal. Tecno-scenari (2011)
8. Borin, E., Donato, F.: Unlocking the potential of IC in Italian cultural ecosystems. J. Intellect. Cap. **16**(2), 285–304 (2015)
9. Borin, E.: Patrimonio culturale e ecosistemi imprenditoriali del settore culturale e creativo. Paesaggio Urbano. Urban Des. **2**, 102–109 (2018)
10. Osservatorio Innovazione Digitale per i Beni e Attività Culturali, Dall'emergenza nuovi paradigmi per la cultura (2020)
11. Osservatorio Innovazione Digitale per i Beni e Attività Culturali, Extended experience: la sfida per l'ecosistema culturale (2021)
12. Osservatorio Innovazione Digitale per i Beni e Attività Culturali, La reputazione online di musei, parchi archeologici, istituti e luoghi della cultura italiani, report di sintesi (2020)
13. Cicerchia, A., Solima, L.: The show must go on...line. Museums and their audiences during the lockdown in Italy. SCIRESit **11**(1), 35–44 (2021)
14. Resta, G., Dicuonzo, F., Karacan, E., Pastore, D.: The impact of virtual tours on museum exhibitions after the onset of Covid-19 restrictions: visitor engagement and long term perspectives. SCIRESit **11**(1), 151–166 (2021)
15. Jan Van Huysum Visits project. https://www.nationalgallery.org.uk/whats-on/jan-van-huy sum-visits. Accessed 04 Apr 2022
16. Williams, E.: The Public Face of Conservation. Archetype Publications, London (2011)
17. Baratin, L., Gasparetto, F.: La documentazione per una conservazione "sostenibile": come il digital può integrare il lavoro dei restauratori. In: Scicolone, G. (ed.) Nuovi polimeri per il restauro - La sperimentazione MIUR/Smart cities, pp. 151–176. Nardini Editore (2020)
18. Crutcher, M.: Engaging visitors with conservation: the key to museum sustainability (2019). https://dsc.duq.edu/gsrs/2019/Proceedings/7
19. Pugliese, M., Ferriani, B., Ratti, I.: Materiality and immateriality in Lucio Fontana's environments: from documentary research to the reproduction of lost artworks. Stud. Conserv. **61**(sup2), 188–192 (2016)
20. Garlandini, A.: Museums and Heritage in the digital age. The challenge of cultural change and technological innovation. SCIRESit **11**(1), 11–18 (2021)
21. Valzano, V., Mannino, K.: Cultural heritage communication and digital resources: three examples from Messapian Archaeolog. SCIRESit **10**(2), 1–18 (2020)
22. Valzano, V.: Open Science: new models of scientific communication and research evaluation. SCIRESit **10**(Special Issue), 5–12 (2020)
23. Economou, M.: Heritage in the digital age. In: Logan, W., Craith, M.N., Kockel, U. (eds.) A Companion to Heritage Studies, 1st edn. Wiley, New York (2016)
24. Vargas Arteaga, J., Gravini-Donado, M.L., Zanello Riva, L.D.: Digital technologies for heritage teaching: trend analysis in new realities. Int. J. Emerg. Technol. Learn. (iJET) **16**(21), 132–148 (2021)
25. Restoring the Globes project. In: Google Arts and Culture project. https://artsandculture.goo gle.com/story/vAWRCEij3wT2YQ. Accessed 04 Apr 2022
26. ARUP Foresight + Research + Innovation, Museums in the digital age (2013)
27. European Commission: Implementation of Commission Recommendations on the digitization and online accessibility of cultural material and digital preservation, Consolidated progress report 2015–2017
28. Kyi, C., Tse, N., Khazam, S.: The potential role of citizen conservation in re-shaping approaches to murals in an urban context. Stud. Conserv. **61**(sup2), 98–103 (2016)
29. Hess, M., Schlieder, C., Schnier, V., Troi, A.: M.Sc. in Digital Technologies in Heritage Conservation. Sustainable mission for education in heritage. IOP Conf. Ser. Earth Environ. Sci. **863**, 012035 (2021)

Pandemic-Driven Digital Innovation in Latvian Museums: Diversity, Diffusion, and Role in Sustainable Development

Elina Vikmane$^{(\boxtimes)}$ (iD) and Ance Kristala (iD)

Institute of Arts and Cultural Studies, Latvian Academy of Culture, Riga, Latvia
elina.vikmane@lka.edu.lv

Abstract. The paper aims to propose the first-ever critical review of digital innovation in Latvian museums, focusing on its diversity, diffusion and role in museum efforts towards sustainability whilst testing the applicability of Rogers' *diffusion of innovation* model, where diffusion is defined as a process whereby alteration occurs in the functions of a social system – the accredited museum sector in this case. The study rests on a quantitative strategy. The sample includes 92% (n = 102) of all Latvia's accredited museums (N = 111). Data on the attitudes to the importance of digital tools and various digital technologies towards cultural and social sustainability in the museum sector, such as (1) access to collections, (2) digital technologies to enhance visitor experience, (3) digital tools for scientific communication, and (4) digital communication and audience engagement, was collected, covering all basic museum functions – preservation, research, and communication.

Latvian museums have developed a wide range of digital tools during the pandemic. Most digital innovations have been focused on giving access to educational content, improving visitor experiences online and planning ahead for when they will return to exhibition halls, and continuing the digitalisation of museum collections towards cultural sustainability. Nevertheless, digital innovation, whose actual purpose is to solve problems with digital tools, connect and empower communities by giving them partial control over their cultural heritage, in the case of Latvian museums remains a largely underused opportunity towards social sustainability.

Keywords: Museums · Digital innovation · Digital technologies · Diffusion of innovation · Sustainability

1 Introduction

Over the last fifteen years, the number of internet users worldwide has increased from roughly one billion to almost five billion [1]. As Klaus Schwab, founder of the World Economic Forum, said in his 2016 address [2]:

'The speed of current breakthroughs has no historical precedent. The Fourth [industrial revolution] is disrupting almost every industry in every country. And the breadth and depth of change heralds a transformation of entire systems.'

R. Furferi et al. (Eds.): Florence Heri-Tech 2022, CCIS 1645, pp. 287–302, 2022.
https://doi.org/10.1007/978-3-031-20302-2_22

By the third industrial revolution, we mean the arrival of digital technologies in the past century. The fourth industrial revolution refers to the fundamental changes in people's lives brought by the latest wave of technological advances – a time when technology convergence could help to increase the quality of life and enhance accessibility, but also raises concerns regarding inequality because of growing gap in wealth.

Since we are living in an increasingly technological and digital world, with numerous services that provide innovative user experiences and greater customer involvement, museums must invent original and brand-new ways to communicate their stories and engage with their public [3]. To this end, museums want to explore new communication tools and means and use digital innovation to improve their relationship with stakeholders. This can be interpreted as a reaction to the numerous technological advancements of today.

This paper aims to propose the first-ever critical review of digital innovation in Latvian museums, concentrating on its diversity, diffusion, and role in museum efforts towards their sustainability priorities, primarily focusing on the digital breakthrough of 2020 and 2021 whilst testing the applicability of Rogers' [4] *diffusion of innovation* theory as a conceptual and methodological framework in museum research. The research objectives include (1) performing a critical analysis of relevant literature about the forms of digital innovation and its role in museum work; (2) identifying digital innovation and its diffusion across Latvian museums, with a focus on digital innovation priorities during the pandemic, and (3) tracing the role of digital innovation towards cultural and social sustainability in the museum sector.

2 Theoretical Framework

In 2015, cybermuseology, previously treated as a knowledge-driven practice [5], was defined as 'an area of museological discussions about changes, problems, and challenges in the relationship between museums and their visitors caused by the implementation of digital technologies' [6]. In some sources, the two terms, 'cyber' and 'digital', are referred to as twin or overlapping concepts. Thus, research on autoethnography refers to cyber or digital autoethnography [7]. Others distinguish 'digital' from 'cyber', for instance, in the security sector [8].

What is innovation? In his *diffusion of innovation* model, Rogers [4] defines innovation as 'an idea, practice or object that is perceived as new by a unit of adoption', whereas diffusion is seen as 'a kind of social change, defined as the process by which alteration occurs in the structure and function of a social system'. Innovation is adopted by the unit in a manner that suggests various degrees of resistance to the new idea, so the cumulative number of adopters across time has been shown to follow an S curve, with adoption beginning slowly, followed by a period of rapid growth in adoption, and ending with the remaining members of a social system slowly adopting the innovation to complete the diffusion process. Since the first edition of Rogers' Diffusion of Innovation [9], researchers have used it as a framework to study the acceptance and spread of all sorts of ideas and practices worldwide. Despite being a well-established model, *diffusion of innovation* does have its limits. Rogers [4] has openly acknowledged and agreed with the primary criticism levelled against his theory – its pro-innovation bias or the assumption that most innovations are worthwhile, and their adoption is in everybody's best interest. He also admits the inclusion of time as a variable in diffusion research is both a strength, as it can be used to identify the earliness/lateness with which an innovation is adopted compared to other members of the system, and a risk for research, as the perception of time depends on the respondent's ability to recall past events. Nevertheless, the *diffusion of innovation* theory has gained widespread popularity because it provides a basis to understand how social change occurs through adoption of new ideas [10]. Moreover, the relevance of Rogers' life's work has not diminished, as theoretical debates on the development, influences, empirical approaches, and limitations of the concept continue in various research fields across social sciences [11–13].

Digital technologies have shaped the necessary condition for digital innovation [14], creating not only new techniques but also cultural breakthroughs [15]. Due to continuous developments in modern technologies and the enthusiasm surrounding the advent of the digitalisation era, the traditional way of working in museums is changing, driving heritage institutions to revolutionise their public role. Museum tasks and technologies have been in the focus of on-going debate ever since museums entered the digital age, but now the question is whether they should be fundamentally redefined as institutions and if so, how [16]. The continuous drive of museums to undertake increasingly innovative activities translates into their capacity to perform in a more tenable, engaging, and interactive manner, not only towards their public but to all the society in its entirety [17], because new and interactive social technologies have dramatically transformed the daily habits of all people, fundamentally changing how individuals approach reality. Parry [18] argues that digitality has 'helped to support a realignment of museography that was taking place, from an object-centred to an experience-centred design'. Innovative tools have a central role as the chief determinants of this on-going and forthcoming transformation that encompasses all cultural heritage institutions [19], otherwise there is a high risk of them becoming marginalised [20].

The current pandemic has brought technological innovations into centre stage, so it is reasonable to expect significant breakthroughs within the field, addressing various sustainability aspects such as education, research, engagement, accessibility, inclusion and many more, strengthening the means of implementing sustainable practices [21]. When digital innovation is implemented purposefully, it can drive sustainable action and create value for all stakeholders. For instance, contributions to social and cultural sustainability include heritage preservation and protection, encouraging new skills or reaching out to vulnerable groups, thus eliminating exclusionary practices, creating tailor-made experiences, helping engage audiences, increasing accessibility, developing new ways of marketing, creating networks, becoming more socially or community-oriented and more inclusive. Multiple pan-European digitalisation projects have played a part in the key strategies towards a knowledge economy enabled by 'unrestricted, sustainable and reliable digital access to Europe's cultural and scientific knowledge' [22, 23], to re-organise public service innovation and delivery in ways that reduce costs and increase quality, proactivity and citizen-centricity [24]. While the social expectations of heritage content in sustainable development discourse grow increasingly louder, some argue that 'there is little known about the extent to which heritage organisations are able to innovate' [23] or that the cultural heritage organisations might 'not being able to fully adopt digital technologies to fit the information economy' [25]. This study proposes to apply Rogers' *diffusion of innovation* model as a framework in museum research to analyse digital innovation implementation in different dimensions of museum work over time and across the system to stay or become relevant and sustainable.

3 Data and Methodology

This study is the first known attempt to use Rogers' *diffusion of innovation* concept, where diffusion is seen as a kind of social change, when innovation (which is any new idea for the members of a particular system) is accepted by the majority, across the entire museum sector (which is seen as a social system), where digital innovation towards cultural and social sustainability is diffused over time among its members. It is important to note that since the survey was part of a larger project, the authors here focus on quantitative data on attitudes towards the importance of digital tools for reaching overall museum objectives and combine them with data on various digital technologies towards cultural and social sustainability, such as (1) access to collection, (2) digital technologies to enhance visitor experience, (3) digital tools for scientific communication, and (4) digital communication and audience engagement. The data was categorised according to museum functions – work with the collection, research, educating through exhibitions, displays and public programmes, and communication.

A quantitative study was conducted using an online survey for data collection to identify digital innovation priorities and diffusion over time and across Latvia's museum sector. The survey form was compiled with the LimeSurvey online tool and included 33 closed and open questions. It was piloted in 5 museums and adjusted in the process. Total population sampling was selected as the most suitable approach since the total population consists of 111 units of Latvia's state-accredited museums. Information about the units was retrieved from the national Accredited Museums Registry [26]. Museum heads and directors were addressed by e-mail. Researchers identified themselves as representatives of the LAC Research Centre and received assistance from the Latvian Museum Association and the Ministry of Culture Department of Museums, Libraries and Archives in the form of reminders and encouragements sent to museum representatives to fill in the questionnaire, which helped increase the response rate. 178 responses were received between 3 September and 24 September 2021. 110 of them contained answers to all the mandatory questions. The final sample was narrowed down to 102 units, excluding repeated or duplicated entries from the same institution to secure statistical equity.

Although data collection was not anonymous due to the reason explained above, all respondents were made aware that the data would be analysed and published in aggregated form to secure anonymity. With the confidence interval at 3%, the final sample of 102 units is representative, meaning that the findings analysed below can be generalised to the entire population. In 95% of the cases, the survey form was filled in by the highest-ranking official – museum head or director, acting director or deputy director. The identified locations, staff numbers, funding amounts and legal terms correspond to the situation in the sector as a whole. The extent of a museum's financial resources depends on the degree to which it is funded by the founder – for instance, if the museum provides free admission and is 100% funded by the municipality, its financial resources might remain the same. Given that heritage institutions could participate in several state-funded support programmes during the pandemic, including one focused on introducing digital tools and targeted work with visitors with disabilities, their financial resources could even have increased. 11% of the respondents admitted this had been the case since the start of the Covid-19 pandemic, for 40%, the amount had not changed, and another 47% reported a drop in available funding, while 2% struggled to answer the question.

4 Results and Discussion

Sustainable development principles and goals are described in numerous international commitments [27–29]. Although the potential of cultural heritage institutions such as museums towards sustainable development goals seems to have been convincingly outlined in the last decade, a relevant shift in museography or museum practice seems not to be progressing at the same rate. Studies on museum work in Britain suggest that this theoretical framework has failed to change traditional museum practices to a full extent – the current trend seems to expose museums as deficient in the inclusion and representation of all social groups [30]. Digital innovation can produce helpful tools for solutions towards greater sustainability.

Latvian museums (Fig. 1) see digital technologies primarily as a tool to stay relevant and popular in the community. The overwhelming majority sees digital development as an image builder but also as means to protect and manage cultural heritage, diversify the content and forms of interaction with the public and attract new audiences. To a lesser extent, technologies are seen as a tool to increase cooperation and do audience research. The findings also suggest that museums see technologies as detrimental to their financial sustainability or reduce environmental impact.

4.1 Access to Collection

The digitalisation of museums' collections signals an important shift in the museum experience that mirrors the overall shift in digital culture, from the physical to the digital and from private to public space [31]. Collection digitalisation and online publication can be seen as an indicator of innovation potential according to Borowiecky and Navarrete [23]. In other words, museums that are able to adopt technology to manage the collection digitally will be able to innovate regarding information services.

The survey results suggest (Fig. 2) that the situation with the digitalisation of museum collections in Latvia is ambiguous – only 5% of the museums had digitalised more than 90% of their collections by the time of the study. 31% of the respondents had digitalised 50 to 89%. 50% of the respondents had digitalised their collections up to the 10–49% mark, and only 6% had digitalised less than 6% of their collections. It should be noted that accredited museums in Latvia are mandated to digitalise their collections for storage in the National Museum Collections Catalogue – an online database of museum collections run by the Cultural Information Systems Centre, a government agency in charge of information management for Latvia's cultural sector.

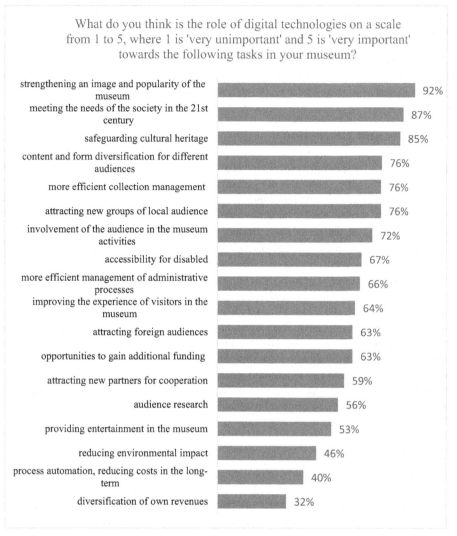

Fig. 1. Importance of digital technologies towards museum tasks. Answers 'very important' and 'important' combined (*n = 102*)

However, the Latvian museum sector still uses other collection management software, both internet-connected and not, as well as Google Sheet and Microsoft Excel. Although the online Catalogue of the National Museum Collections aims to provide access to the 95% of museum objects currently unavailable on-site in permanent exhibitions and displays, digitalisation of museum collections does not automatically imply public access.

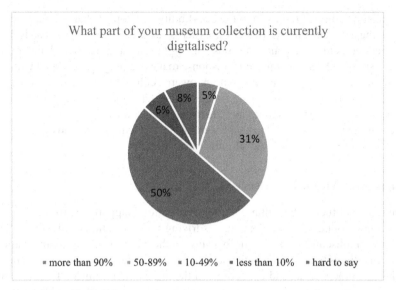

Fig. 2. Digitalisation rates of Latvia's museum collections (*n = 102*)

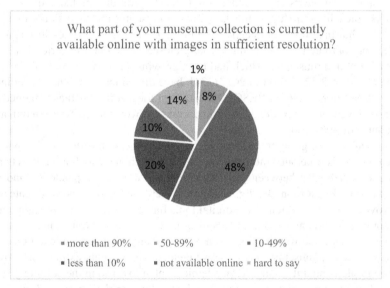

Fig. 3. Museum collections availability online with images in sufficient resolution (*n = 102*)

Survey results (Fig. 3) suggest that 30% of the respondents (or 31 museums) have zero to 9% of their collections online. Another 14% of the respondents struggled to answer this question. 10 to 49% of the collection is accessible with 48% of respondents. Only 9% of the museums provide more than 50% of the collections online with high-resolution images. In addition, problems related to system usage, such as technical glitches in the search function, further reduce public accessibility. On top of that, 'the quantity and quality of the metadata on each object varies across the field (…). Object type is the only fully structured field (…),' concludes museum digitalisation researcher Maija Spurina in her recent study [32]. Some museums' response to the challenges associated with public access to museum objects as a contribution towards cultural and social sustainability is to duplicate platforms, that is, create or use other platforms to make their collections available online. These alternatives include the museums' own platforms, Google Arts & Culture, Europeana or others. This approach further stretches the already thin resources of museum staff and increases the administrative burden.

4.2 Improving Visitor Experience

The environment fuelled by cultural heritage collections supports the formation of genuine breeding grounds [33], fundamental to driving soft innovation in all sectors [23]. To study Latvian museums as a system, focusing on the adoption of digital innovations, it was essential for us to analyse how the pandemic has affected different forms of museum activities and practices around collections in the digital environment. Therefore, many questions had a temporal dimension, tracing the situation before and during the pandemic (up to the moment of the survey) and exploring the respondents' expectations for the coming few years. The pandemic has had a profound global impact and has changed people's lives, including the daily lives of museums and their staff – firstly, due to museums shutting down completely in March 2020 and having to re-close again at a later stage or continue to operate in a partially closed mode due to restrictions. Visitor numbers to Latvian museums, which had been growing steadily every year (from 1.54 million in 2001 to 3.72 million in 2017) [34], have dramatically fallen. This coincides with the overall trend in the UNESCO report: even for institutions that remained open with sanitary measures in place, the drastic decrease in world tourism resulted in a drop in attendance of 70% [35].

As museums were going through such a major change and were forced to go partly or fully digital, this watershed moment was strong enough in the authors' minds to allow museums to distinguish between projects introduced during the pandemic and those launched before. In addition, the digital practices were analysed across three categories: (1) improving visitor experience, (2) digital tools for scientific communication, and (3) digital communication and visitor engagement in the digital environment.

The only digital innovation (Fig. 4) introduced before the pandemics in more than half of the country's museums is interactive elements in museum exhibitions. Another 25% have implemented it during the pandemic or plan to do so in the coming years.

Digital innovations related to educational activities, on the other hand, were most frequently introduced during the pandemic (by the time the survey was completed in September 2021). Online educational activities have been done by 32% of the respondents and are planned by another 34% in the coming few years, compared to just 2% before the pandemic. Other digital tools for educational purposes, such as educational games, quizzes, worksheets, etc., were used by 33% of the respondents during the pandemic, and another 21% of respondents plan to use them in the coming years, compared to just 3% before COVID.

Several activities around visitor experience are also emerging as near-future innovations and trends. These have been relatively rare in museums in the period leading up to the pandemic but are planned for the coming years, mostly related to 'pandemic safe' remote or individual access to museum content. Introducing such tools takes time and financial resources, so we are currently seeing diffusion trends for the coming years in Latvian museums. Some of the strongest examples are audio guides in multiple languages on the visitor's device (37%), 360-degree digital tours (19%), interactive elements in the exhibition (20%), QR codes for additional information (29%), mobile apps for museums or exhibitions (28%).

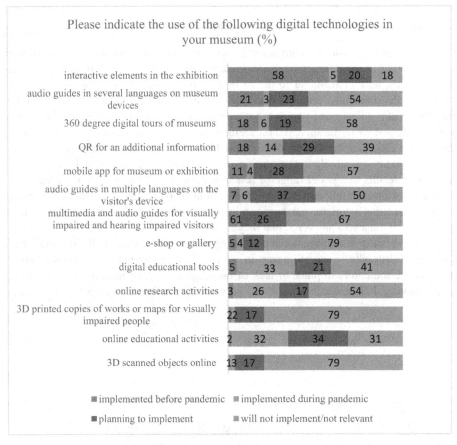

Fig. 4. Digital technologies in museums (n = *102)*

However, digital innovations to reach, enhance or diversify visitor experience that Latvian museums have most often decided not to introduce or considered irrelevant to the museum include 3D-printed copies of works or maps on the premises for visually impaired visitors and 3D-scanned objects available online (79%), setting up an e-shop or e-gallery (79%), adapting multimedia and audio guides for visually impaired and hearing-impaired visitors (67%) and creating mobile apps for museum exhibitions (57%).

A previous study on Latvian museums [32], focusing on their strategic documents, found that the country's most popular museums prioritise access to knowledge through providing accurate and research-based information with their activities, educational programmes and information materials as their effort towards social sustainability. This study confirms that prioritising the educational function applies to the whole sector. At the same time, museum reluctance to improve their work with visually and hearing-impaired visitors and introduce multilingualism to improve access to content is a cause for concern with regard to social sustainability.

4.3   Digital Tools for Scientific Communication

The most popular pandemic innovation in research communication (Fig. 4) is online research activities (conferences, seminars, etc.) – 26% had already done it by the time of the survey, and 17% intend to do so in the coming few years, compared to just 3% before the pandemic. Another important issue for Latvian museums is the online availability of publications by museum researchers (Fig. 5) on their websites, in digital archives, etc. – 43% of the surveyed museums gave access to these before the pandemic, another 9% did it during the pandemic, and 11% of the surveyed institutions plan to make publications available in the coming years. Overall, publication and accessibility of research results to a wider range of researchers or stakeholders were identified as a missed opportunity. Publications are available online in international academic databases in 3% of museums before the pandemic and will be made available in 11% in the coming years. 87% of museums answered that they had not considered it or struggled to answer, which may suggest that international publishing seemed not relevant to the museum they represented. But why? Lack of interest in sharing, lack of international communication performance indicators in place or lack of language skills? Besides, museums are not used to sharing their research data either – publishing their data in open-access databases

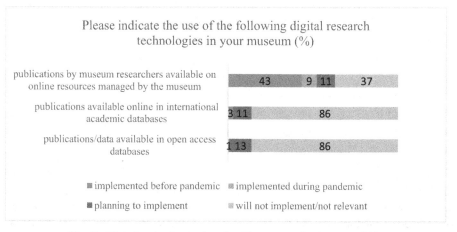

Fig. 5.   Digital technologies in scientific communication *(n = 102)*

was practised in 1% of museums before the pandemics and 13% plan to share their data in the coming years. However, neither publications in international academic databases nor research data available for other researchers have been a priority for a single respondent, or else the highest-ranking officials at the museums were not aware of it.

While museum activity to make their research findings locally available is commendable, the hesitation of Latvian museum researchers to share their knowledge more intensively in the international scientific arena is troubling. Access to knowledge, best practices, discoveries, and methodological developments are critical for protecting cultural heritage, creating institutional networks and partnerships, and interpreting museum efforts towards cultural and social sustainability.

4.4 Digital Communication and Audience Engagement

In contrast to scientific communication, the introduction of technologies in Latvian museums has been much more dynamic in the field of communication with visitors (Fig. 6).

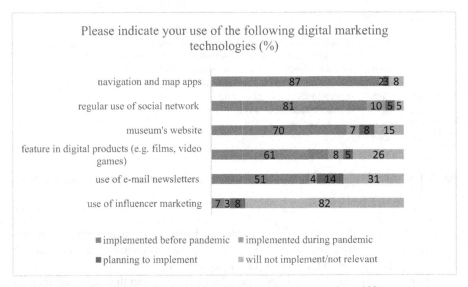

Fig. 6. Digital marketing technologies in museums (*n = 102*)

For example, 70% of museums had a website before the pandemic, and 81% regularly used at least one social media platform in their communication. 87% of museums are found in navigation and map applications, 61% have had their objects or spaces used in third-party digital products such as films, TV shows, video games, etc. 51% used email newsletters before the pandemic. Influencer marketing has been identified as an innovation in museum practices: 7% of museums used it before the pandemic, 3% and 8% plan to use it during the pandemic or in the coming years, while 82% of museums have not considered introducing it, struggle to answer or consider it irrelevant to their museum.

The most popular social media platform for communication with stakeholders (Fig. 7) among Latvian museums is Facebook (used by 82% of museums at the time of the survey), followed by Youtube and Whatsapp with 67% each and Instagram with 62%, which is in line with the popularity trends of social media worldwide [36]. Meanwhile, the lesser-used communication platforms in Latvian museums are Pinterest and Telegram (not used by 83% of museums), followed by Snapchat (81%), Clubhouse and Tumblr (80%), TikTok (78%), Linkedin (77%) and Twitter (52%). Given that Instagram, Snapchat and TikTok are especially popular among young adults under 30 [37], Latvian museums are currently at a crossroads – to increase their presence on these platforms in the coming years to reach younger audiences or risk long-term problems with finding a common language and workable forms of interaction with younger audiences.

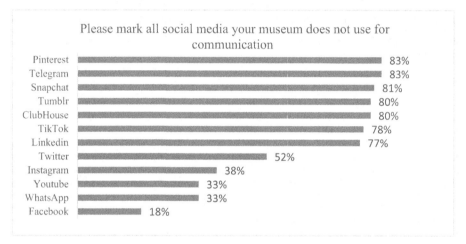

Fig. 7. Lesser-used social media platforms in museum communication. Multiple choice question. (*n = 102*)

A different picture emerges when we analyse visitor engagement in the digital environment. In all responses in this category, innovations have been introduced most rapidly during the pandemic up to the time of the survey (Fig. 8).

Among Latvian museums, the most popular (still low given that 82% said they use Facebook) form of interaction with visitors in Latvian museums is inviting the audience to share their museum experience online. This was done by 28% of museums before the pandemic, with 15% practising it during the pandemic and 16% planning it in the coming years. The second most popular activity is inviting audiences to use metadata or hashtags on social media – 28% of museums have done it before the pandemic, 6% have been doing it during the pandemic and 14% plan it for the coming years. The types of interaction that most Latvian museums have decided not to implement, have not thought about, struggle to answer or consider irrelevant to their institution are audience engagement in donation campaigns (73%), opportunities to create individual object selections or exhibitions (64%), social media content (61%), audience involvement in exhibitions/displays (58%). This reluctance has kept museum audiences away from co-creation and may have been motivated by fear to lose control of the story.

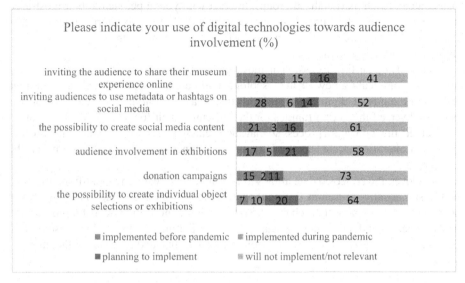

Fig. 8. Digital technologies towards audience involvement *(n = 102)*

Rogge et al. [38] found that social interaction is an important criterion contributing to social sustainability. Langlais [5] stresses that interactivity gives audiences a chance to create more 'freely' their representation of knowledge and heritage, while for museums, it is an opportunity for emergent and discordant voices to be heard besides the dominant discourse. Such interaction or feedback is not only a way to ensure participation and improve museum services and basic performance but also an important tool to closely observe various audiences and communities easier than ever before to identify emergent and otherwise muted voices and plan new potential interactions for the future. It is missed by more than half of Latvian museums.

5   Conclusion

Introduction of new digital technologies is recognised as an essential part of Latvian museum work to boost heritage institutions' overall image and popularity, preserve their collections, and meet public needs – all massive cultural and social sustainability commitments for any museum.

During the pandemic, Latvian museums have developed numerous digital tools that have allowed them to innovate locally, especially in educational services, and improve visitor experience online and onsite once they return to the premises. Nevertheless, digital innovation, whose fundamental purpose is to solve problems and foster change through digital tools, connect people, support knowledge and information exchange and empower communities by giving them partial control over their cultural heritage, in the case of Latvian museums, remains a largely undeveloped area. Even with external pressure from the global pandemic and the whole world going digital, Latvian museums are struggling to make their collections available online with high-resolution images and rich content, reach marginalised groups, interact with young people on their most-used social media, make their presence more prominently felt in the international research community and truly co-create with audiences online, giving them an actual say in how museums work and communicate.

The study opens the discussion on the *diffusion of innovation* concept as a theoretical and methodological framework in museological research, while empirical data identifies the overall status of digital innovation diffusion across Latvia's museum sector and exposes diverse future opportunities for the museums, their founders and policy makers to complete the innovation process so that social change or, as Rogers puts it, the process by which alteration occurs in the structure and function of a social system, can be completed.

Moreover, the collected data allows to continue the research by identifying the most and least innovative museums (from innovators to laggards, according to Rogers) in this social system to explore their characteristics, trace the innovation decision process and analyse success and failure determinants, thus contributing to a broader interdisciplinary discussion on *diffusion of innovation* from the perspective and specifics of the museum sector.

Acknowledgment. The study is funded by the Latvian Ministry of Culture through the project No. VPP-KM-LKRVA-2020/1-000 – Cultural Capital as a Resource for Sustainable Development of Latvia/CARD.

References

1. Statista. https://www.statista.com/statistics/273018/number-of-internet-users-worldwide/. Accessed 02 Feb 2021
2. World Economic Forum. https://www.weforum.org/agenda/2016/01/the-fourth-industrial-revolution-what-it-means-and-how-to-respond/. Accessed 28 Nov 2021
3. Bahkshi, H., Throsby, D.: Culture of Innovation: an Economic Analysis of Innovation in Arts and Cultural Organisations. National Endowment for Science, Technology and the Arts, NESTA, London (2010)
4. Rogers, E.: Diffusion of Innovation, 5th edn. Free Press, New York (2003)
5. Langlais, D.: Cybermuseology and intangible heritage, pp. 72–81 (2005). http://www.yorku.ca/etopia/docs/conference/Langlais.pdf. Accessed 02 June 2022
6. Leshchenko, A.: Digital dimensions of the museum: defining cybermuseology's subject of study. ICOFOM Stud. Ser. **43**(a), 237–241 (2015)
7. Atay, A.: What is cyber or digital autoethnography? Int. Rev. Qual. Res. (2020). https://doi.org/10.1177/1940844720934373
8. OECD. https://www.oecd.org/sti/ieconomy/digital-security/. Accessed 02 June 2022
9. Rogers, E.: Diffusion of Innovation. Free Press, New York (1962)
10. Singhal, A.: Everett M. Rogers, an intercultural life: from Iowa farm boy to global intellectual. Int. J. Intercult. Relat. **36**, 848–856 (2012)
11. Srivastava, J., Moreland, J.: Diffusion of innovations: communication evolution and influences. Commun. Rev. **15**(4), 294–312 (2012)

12. Dearing, J., Singhal, A.: New directions for diffusion of innovations research: dissemination, implementation, and positive deviance. Hum. Behav. Emerg. Technol. **2**, 307–313 (2020)
13. MacVaugh, J., Schiavone, F.: Limits to the diffusion of innovation: a literature review and integrative model. Eur. J. Innov. Manag. **13**, 197–221 (2010)
14. Yoo, Y., et al.: The new organising logic of digital innovation: an agenda for information systems research. Inf. Syst. Res. **21**, 724–735 (2010)
15. Schmitt, E., Cohen, J.: The New Digital Age. Reshaping the Future of People. Nations and Business. John Murray, London (2013)
16. Parry, R. (ed.): Museums in a Digital Age. Routledge, London, New York (2010)
17. Mulgan, G., et al.: Social Innovation: What It Is, Why It Matters and How It Can Be Accelerated. The Basingstoke Press, London (2007)
18. Parry, R.: Recoding the Museum: Cultural Heritage and the Technologies of Change. Routledge, London (2007)
19. Hempell, T., et al.: ICT, innovation and business performances in services: evidence for Germany and the Netherlands. In: The Economic Impact of ICT: Measurement, Evidence, and Implications, pp. 131–152. OECD Publications Service (2004)
20. Wayne Clough, G.: Best of Both Worlds: Museums, Libraries, and Archives in a Digital Age (2013). https://doi.org/10.5479/si.9780981950013
21. Vikmane, E., Lake, A.: Critical review of sustainability priorities in the heritage sector: evidence from Latvia's most visited museums. Eur. Integr. Stud. **1**, 95–110 (2021)
22. Navarette, T.: Becoming digital: a Dutch heritage perspective. J. Arts Manag. Law Soc. **44**(3), 153–168 (2014)
23. Borowiecki, K., Navarrete, T.: Digitisation of heritage collections as indicator of innovation. Econ. Innov. New Technol. **26**(1), 1–20 (2016)
24. Digiser Inception Report. https://www.espon.eu/DIGISER. Accessed 01 Apr 2022
25. Borowiecki, K., Navarrete, T.: Digitisation of heritage collections as indicator of innovation. Econ. Innov. New Technol. **26**(3), 227–246 (2017)
26. Ministry of Culture Republic of Latvia: The Registry of Accredited Museums. https://www.km.gov.lv/lv/media/11319/download. Accessed 02 June 2022
27. UN, Report of the United Nations Conference on Environment and Development. https://www.un.org/en/development/desa/population/migration/generalassembly/docs/globalcompact/A_CONF.151_26_Vol.I_Declaration.pdf. Accessed 02 June 2022
28. UNESCO, Convention for the Safeguarding of the Intangible Cultural Heritage. https://ich.unesco.org/en/convention. Accessed 13 Jan 2022
29. United Nations, Transforming our world: The 2030Agenda for Sustainable Development. https://sustainabledevelopment.un.org/content/documents/21252030%20Agenda%20for%20Sustainable%20Development%20web.pdf. Accessed 13 Jan 2022
30. McCall, V., Gray, C.: Museums and the 'new museology': theory, practice and organisational change. Mus. Manag. Curatorsh. **29**(1), 19–35 (2014)
31. Culture Action Europe. https://cultureactioneurope.org/news/museums-in-the-digital-era-mu-sa-project-mooc. Accessed 13 Jan 2022
32. Spurina, M.: Shape of storage memory: a digital analysis of the museum storages of Northeast Europe (2021). https://doi.org/10.13140/RG.2.2.31884.03207
33. Neil, L., Rodríguez-Pose, A.: Creativity, cities, and innovation. Environ. Plan. **46**, 1139–1159 (2014)
34. Latvian Academy of Culture. https://lka.edu.lv/lv/aktuali/jaunumi/latvijas-kulturas-akademija-isteno-nozimigu-petijumu-par-muzejiem-un-auditoriju/kult. Accessed 01 Apr 2022
35. UNESCO. https://unesdoc.unesco.org/ark:/48223/pf0000373530. Accessed 01 Apr 2022

36. Statista. https://www.statista.com/statistics/272014/global-social-networks-ranked-by-num ber-of-users/. Accessed 01 Apr 2022
37. Pew Research Centre, Social Media Use in 2021. https://www.pewresearch.org/internet/2021/ 04/07/social-media-use-in-2021/. Accessed 01 Apr 2022
38. Rogge, N., et al.: Social sustainability through social interaction—a national survey on community gardens in Germany. Sustainability **10**(4), 1085 (2018)

Practical and Digital Proposals for Restoration of the Main Apse of the Basilica of Santa Maria Assunta in Torcello

Jovan Djordjevic[(✉)] [ID] and Diego Calaon [ID]

Università Ca Foscari, Dorsoduro, 3246 Venice, VE, Italy
jovandjordjevic44@gmail.com, calaon@unive.it

Abstract. One of the recent developments in the digital domain is its application to the preservation and presentation of cultural heritage. Although a lot has been done on describing and improving the technical aspect of it, insufficient attention has been given to its theoretical aspect. Especially to the part that concerns the relation between the practical philosophical and ethical postulates of contemporary conservation and restoration practice and the sphere of digital restoration. The case study on which the whole research is applied is the basilica of Santa Maria Assunta on the island of Torcello, located in the northern part of the Venetian lagoon. More precisely, the aim of this paper is to offer possible solutions for both the digital and practical restoration practice regarding the main apse of the church, with its two-layered fresco and mosaic strata.

Keywords: Digital · Virtual · Restoration · Torcello · Medieval art · Cultural heritage

1 Introduction

The basilica of Santa Maria Assunta on the island of Torcello is one of the oldest and historically most important monuments in the Venetian lagoon. Its fame stems from the beautiful mosaic and sculptural decoration that attracts tourists. However, the church has several issues that require interventions with the aim of conserving the architectural structure and the works of art that are housed in it.

In this paper, the focus will be on the two-layered wall decoration of the main apse. The main idea is to present the proposals for future conservation that will be carried out in near future. All the proposals are based and argued on the postulates and concepts previously exhibited in this paper using the multidisciplinary and transdisciplinary approach. A particularly innovative approach is in the use of digital technologies, mainly VR, that will compensate for the consequences of practical restoration. The aim is to stress the connection between physical and virtual practice and to pay attention to the possible consequences of seductive properties of digital tools.

R. Furferi et al. (Eds.): Florence Heri-Tech 2022, CCIS 1645, pp. 303–316, 2022.
https://doi.org/10.1007/978-3-031-20302-2_23

2 History of the Basilica of Torcello

The island of Torcello is located in the northern part of the Venetian lagoon. The basilica of Santa Maria Assunta is its main monument that has dominated the island for centuries. Thanks to the recent archeological excavations, the real history, and development of architecture can be reimagined.

Due to economic development and the flourishing urban character of the new settlement [1], in 639 the construction of the first cathedral in Torcello was started during the reign of Byzantine emperor Heraclitus. It was dedicated to Santa Maria Genetrix [2]. The church had two subsequent changes that led to its current appearance: in the 9th century during Deusdedit II, and in the 11th century during the Orseolo rule [3]; as well as a heavy restoration in the 19th century.

2.1 Santa Maria Assunta

The *Chronicon Venetum* which is hypothetically ascribed to Giovanni Diacono [4] (John the deacon) is the main document that describes all the construction phases of the basilica [5]. According to it, the biggest transformation occurred in the 11th century when the bishops were Orso (1008–1012) and his brother Vitale III (1012–1047), the sons of doge Pietro II Orseolo [5]. Archaeological excavations have managed to shed light on certain parts and confirm the statements in the chronicle. The focus will be solely on the 11th century because the main apse was reconstructed and decorated in that period.

This is understandable since the 11th century is described as a period in which "Europe cloaked itself in the robes of the new basilicas or reconstructed old ones" [6]. According to Giovanni Diacono, the whole church has been refurbished [5]. This reconstruction included arched collonades that divided the nave into three parts, the relocation of the bodily remains of St Heliodorus under the main altar, creating a new set of the mosaic floor decoration, and the mosaic decoration of the interior walls [5]. The Byzantine workshops were brought to execute the mosaic decorations as well as the sculptural ones with motives imported from the East [7].

The frescoes are, according to Trevisan, dated to the 11th century [3]. The synthronon slightly covers the frescoes meaning that it was added after their execution.[1] The mosaic decoration was done after these two additions, covering the frescoes.

2.2 Internal Decoration

Today, the basilica in Torcello is considered one of the artistic peaks of medieval art in the lagoon, right after the church of San Marco. Visitors are usually struck by the beauty and complexity of the *sectile* floor, as well as by the monumental golden mosaics covering the entrance wall and the main apse with *diaconicon* (Fig. 1).

The fresco fragments are described by A. Niero as being in the Benedictine style similar to that of the frescoes from the crypt in Aquileia [8]. The Benedictine monastic

---

[1] Regarding the frescoes, they were discovered in the 1930s and at that period were dated to the 7th century. However, in the 1980s they were proved originate from the 11th century. (La Cripta, 3).

order had a strong presence on the island. When the synthronon has been created in the 11th century, probably during the reign of bishop Vitale III, the frescoes were covered with marble slabs, and a mosaic showing the twelve apostles and the Virgin Mary with baby Jesus has been put [7].

In the middle of the synthronon is a *cathedra* where the bishop would sit. Above it is a bust-length depiction of St Heliodorus, the first bishop of Altino. On both, his left and right are the twelve apostles standing on a grass field with flowers that can be found in the lagoon. Behind them is a typical golden background. In the upper part, occupying the whole semidome is the standing figure of the Virgin Mary holding baby Jesus. The effect of this mosaic is nicely described by Niero, saying that it serves as a reminder that "the space that surrounds us, the time in which we live, is a foretaste of eternity" [8]. This interpretation is reasonable when one considers that art, in our notion of the word, served, through beauty as a tie between "this world and the higher, earth and the sky, and the man and God" [6]. In the corners above the apse is the scene of Annunciation which is typically positioned there in Eastern churches [8].

Comparing the mosaics and the technique of their production as well as stylistic components with other contemporary examples, Andreescu concluded that they were all done "somewhere in the eleventh century" [9].

Fig. 1. The synthronon in the main apse with the marble slabs and the mosaic. The fresco fragments can be seen on the left where the slabs are missing.

3   Virtual Restoration: Theory and Practice

Before going into the definition of virtual restoration, the digital object itself must be defined first. "It can be a reproduction of a physical artifact, or it can be natively digital. The digital object, if limited to the reproduction of a real object, becomes a replica, if it is obtained through criteria and methodologies that guarantee fidelity and accuracy both at the topological/metric level and at the surface properties level. In this sense, the digital replica becomes a transmitter of information and allows the preservation of the knowledge of the object, even if the real original is lost" [10]. This definition given by E. Pietroni and D. Ferdani encompasses all the key aspects: reproduction or natively digital (model), based on information accumulated within the object as a document, transmission of information, creating knowledge, and creating a digital testimony/patrimony. All of these characteristics of the digital object should be kept in mind for further discussion.

The idea behind digital heritage is not just to document and keep objects of cultural heritage in a repository of information, but to contextualize it. That is why the term virtual, understood as a recontextualization of an object is highly applicable here. According to R. Deloche, virtualization is understood as "the process of transitioning into the problem, decontextualization or manipulation of the artifact" [11]. In other words, it "allows the transition of the given problem...into other possible solutions" [11]. When a digital version of an object is made, it allows for innumerable changes to be made, in contrast with the one in the material reality, that, when once altered, permanently remains as such.

However, the point is not just to digitize something, but to create "a parallel testimony" between the material original and the virtual copy. As nice as this might sound, there is another theoretical problem of understanding the virtual. These equivalents that are paradoxically unequal to the starting material object are actually self-referent images, or at least have a tendency to become. The real danger of the virtualization of an object used in a museum context (bear in mind the educational aspect) is the annihilation of the referential aspect, leading to a simulacrum. As a consequence, the parallel testimony is lost [12].

Thus, when put into this new situation, a digital model can serve for representing abstract ideas and concepts that help recreate the past and present it to the viewer. In this way, the goal of obtaining knowledge and disseminating it is achieved. "Hence, the goal of a virtual process is to increase perceptual and cognitive levels, reactivating spatial-temporal relationships and meanings of the cultural object. The virtual dimension facilitates the mental process of imagination, giving shape to an abstract concept (a vanished ancient context cannot be perceived and experienced), making legible and recognizable what the visitor is often unable to "decode," identify, and contextualize" [10]. VR serves as the best illustration of this description.

There are two main charters that regulate the use of digital tools in heritage conservation. The London Charter emphasized the importance of documentation, not just the one used in creating a virtual model, but also to try and document the process of model production. "Sufficient information should be documented and disseminated to allow computer-based visualization methods and outcomes to be understood and evaluated in relation to the contexts and purposes for which they are deployed." It was followed by the Principles of Seville that deal with the authenticity and scientific transparency. The former one stresses the need to distinguish the "real, genuine, or authentic" from the additions and reconstructions. The latter addresses the same issue by pointing out the need to "gather and present transparently the entire work process" [10].

4 Restoration Proposal for the Main Apse

This chapter deals with the practical approach as suggestions to be applied in the case of the conservation issues in the main apse of the basilica of Santa Maria Assunta in Torcello. It is based on the contemporary postulates in conservation, museological theory, and the knowledge of the virtual.

Before addressing the main issues, it is important to stress that Santa Maria Assunta is the church in the cult [13], that exhibits its objects and works of art in a museum-like context with the aim of preserving its sanctity. Therefore, all of the interventions made need to take into account the importance of the objects themselves, their place within the church, the importance of the church for the island and its local community, and finally, the role of the island of Torcello in the lagoon of Venice. The logic of this approach is based on the micro-macro principle. This follows the value-based approach in which "conservation professionals" are "supervising the stakeholder groups" [14].

"In the case of entire 'sites', i.e. complex works of man and nature than combine both tangible and intangible assets, insofar as these areas are still associated with a 'living' religious tradition and, thus, are still functioning as 'sacral' places, their legal approach, and therefore their management, involves delicate issues of cultural, spiritual and natural maintenance. Hence, when approaching such sites, one must keep a balance between heritage preservation, cultural management, tourism development, and 'active' practices of faith" [15]. A very important point related to the church as a museum space is the preservation of sacral character. B. Deloche, when quoting Malraux says that any museum has the function of preserving the sacred [11]. In the case of Torcello, and its potential virtual tools, it plays the main role of narrating the "time, people, context of life, and knowledge" [13]. The beginning of this kind of preservation begins with the conservation of the material, especially of that which by Brandi is termed "aspect," as it is the bearer of the artistic meaning [16]. This is achieved when the tangible is viewed in the wider context, the intangible one [15].

As for the virtual counterpart, it should be noted that the use of technology, however appealing it may be, should not lead to fetishizing it [17]. On the other hand, the cybernetic approach and the digital heritage have become an almost inseparable part of the museum and exhibition practice. Digitalization and virtualization allow for new ways of presenting and understanding the past. This is made possible because virtualization transports the given problem into other possible solutions [11]. These solutions are visualizations in the form of a movie, VR, augmented reality (AR) or mixed reality (MR), 3D models, or 2D reproductions. Whichever of these is chosen as an adequate tool for the solution to the problem, two important questions must be answered: 1. "Is the use of this tool in a digital form adding value to the project that is balanced by the ethics of its use?" [18] 2. For whom is the model made i.e. who is the group that the model is meant for? [10] Only when both of these questions are provided with satisfactory answers, one can proceed to make digital models.

4.1 Fine or Applied Art?

Despite the interventions from a later date, the apse must be treated as an original medieval setting. Speaking of medieval art, a very important question should be posed and answered in order to decide how to treat the restoration problem. Should the mosaics and the synthronon be treated by today's understanding of art, or according to the medieval notion? To reformulate it, should it be viewed as fine or applied art?

Personally, I am more for the option of treating it in its original meaning because that is the only way we can truly respect this work of art. The purpose of an image, whether a fresco, an icon, or a mosaic, was to openly and directly spread Christian messages onto the faithful. "The notion of sacredness is intertwined with the notion of functionality" [15]. In the Middle Ages, the meaning and its bearer are the same [6]. This is most evident during the religious service. At that moment, the functionality of an artwork reaches its peak. In the *Dialogues* of Gregory the Great, he states that during the service "the heavens are opened and choirs of angels are presented at the mystery of Jesus Christ, that the lowest is united with the most sublime, earth is joined to the heavens, the visible and the invisible become one" [19]. Therefore, the role of art was to help the believer overcome the material and reach the divine. Hence, if we view the apse as a masterpiece of medieval art, we neglect its non-artistic intangible properties which were the main reason for adorning it in the first place. It is very important to note that these objects that constitute the interior decoration of the apse incorporate in themselves "specific ideas, beliefs, and theological doctrines" [15]. This goes hand in hand with the UNESCO Convention on the Safeguarding of the Intangible Cultural Heritage that treated religious "practices, representations, expressions, knowledge, skills—as well as the instruments, objects, artifacts and cultural spaces associated therewith" [15] as part of religious heritage and should not be separated from its material counterpart.

In conclusion, it can be said that for the sake of preserving the religious intangible properties embedded in the material, the decoration of the apse should be viewed, understood, and conserved/restored as a work of applied art (by today's notion).

4.2 Proposal for Practical Restoration

Since the apse is viewed as applied art, before going into proposals for practical restoration, we should turn to Cesare Brandi. He differs the work of art from an industrial object. In the case of the latter, restoration tends to bring back its functionality. When it comes to the works of art that have a functional purpose, such as architecture or objects of applied arts, restoring their functionality, according to Brandi, is only secondary [16]. However, when the functionality is what gives meaning to the object, especially that of a religious function that is inexplicably tied to the interior of an architectural space, restoring it should not be of secondary importance. Medieval art is a special case because its utility is realized through its aesthetics. The best unity between the concept of beauty and functionality is realized in the interior decoration of the church, in this case, the apse.

The next question is addressed to the newly discovered frescoes that adorned the walls of the apse at the beginning of the 11th century. If they remain visible, how does that affect the overall aesthetic unity and readability of them, of the mosaics, and of the apse as a whole? The first part of the frescoes was discovered at the end of the 30s of the previous century [7]. They were restored and the marble slabs that covered them have been removed. The apse looked like that ever since. However, the new ones are in a very bad state. Most of the mortar is gone, and only a few figures are recognizable (the ones on the far left and far right). On top of that, the upper parts are covered with the mosaic, so it is impossible to identify who is represented. If they are cleaned, conserved, and restored, they would still remain fragments that would be hard to read and understand, especially for the tourists who are often not educated in the history of art. In Brandi's terminology, this is defined as a "ruin," i.e. an artifact that remains in such a poor condition that it is impossible to return it to its former potential unity without making a forgery [16]. However, a ruin or a fragment is still transmitted from one reality, the past, into another reality, the present. As such, it is understood as a document by using imaginative mechanisms [12]. Hence, these frescoes, or rather what remains of them, cannot be disregarded. On the other hand, if the bishops remain visible, they would add to the confusion making the decoration harder to understand. This leads to two possible solutions: return the marble slabs completely, or return the slabs partially revealing the fragments that were discovered in the 30s and the ones that have been recently discovered.

In the first case, the aesthetical unity would be fully achieved. The role of marble slabs in Byzantine art is a symbolic one as they represent the element of water or the Holy Spirit. Having them returned partially will result in partial unity of the decoration. The support for this is found in Brandi's theory of restoration. The second principle of restoration states that it should tend to reestablish the potential unity of a work of art without making a forgery, and without canceling every trace of the passage of time that is visible in the work of art [16]. At first, this might seem like an argument for keeping the parts of fresco fragments visible since they are evidence of the past times before the mosaic decoration. However, it should be noted that they originally were not meant to be seen and they are not evidence of the passage of time on the mosaic, rather they are considered an autonomous and separate work of art. Furthermore, Brandi often stated that the aesthetical principle always has priority over the historical [16]. On top of this, he states the importance of understanding the space based on the paintings exhibited in it and their relation to it. By this, he is not referring to interior design, rather to the interpretation of space [16]. This is fully compatible with the functionality of medieval architecture, its separation of the sacred from the profane, and the role of art as the bearer of intangible religious beliefs and doctrines. By returning all of the marble slabs to their place, the restorers will put the "tangible religious heritage in its wider (intangible) context" [15]. Another argument pro returning of marble slabs stems from the medieval notion of art and symmetry as one of its main attributes. Even though medieval art is rather spontaneous and diverse, the idea of symmetry and balance is omnipresent [20]. Therefore, if the slabs are returned unequally, the apse loses its symmetry, and consequentially, its aesthetics is diminished.

The cons of this practical solution are seen in the loss of a historical narrative. Neither the public nor the experts would have the access to these fragments. If the philosophy of heritage is understood as selected memory that is crucial for preserving an identity [12], we can say that this approach would mean an open cancelation of one part of the basilica's historic narrative. However, this could be overcome, at least in the case of the expert audience, by cleaning, conserving, and making detailed documentation of the fragments before returning the marble slabs.

On the other hand, the partial return of the slabs would only partially re-establish the visual unity in the Byzantine aesthetic. The pros of this situation are that the best-looking or most easily-readable fragments remain accessible to the public. According to a different interpretation of Brandi's second law of restoration, the historical interventions, however bad they might have been, should be exposed because they too are the documents of the past [16]. Every action in the domain of preservation and exhibition of heritage has a documentary duality. On one side it tends to extract and communicate the ideas embedded in the object, on the other, it is a document of its own time and practice. As a consequence, the aesthetic unity that is crucial for the functionality of medieval art is only partially realized, while the historic narrative is reconstructed more easily.

Where, then, is the solution to this problem? I would opt for the total return of the marble slabs because the importance is given to the aesthetic principle and medieval unity. The loss of the narrative can be overcome by the use of digital tools.

If one insists on making a compromised solution between the first two proposals, it can be done by borrowing the logic used in the church of Santa Maria Novella in Florence. In it, movable mechanisms hold the paintings in the 16th-century frames. From time to time, these paintings are "opened" to exhibit the remains of frescoes dated before Vasari's renovation. A similar thing can be done in Santa Maria Assunta, where the first set of slabs on both sides of the apse can be made movable and occasionally opened to allow for the observers to peak behind them.

The last issue addressed here regarding the apse is the bishop's throne. There are strong indications that the so-called "Throne of Attila" was the cathedra of the bishop and adorned the top of the synthronon. Returning it to its original place would complete the visual/aesthetical unity of the apse that was argued before, but it would deprive the island of Torcello of its famous symbol. The solution to this problem is a rather simple one. A 1:1 scale 3D material copy of Attila's throne can be made and put in its current place in front of Santa Fosca, while the original is returned to its former place.

4.3 Virtual Proposals and Solutions

Unlike in the previous case, there are several solutions here that will be presented, giving their pros and cons. It should be noted that they all depend on what the officials who are responsible for the church intend to do. The virtual solutions, especially the elaborate ones such as virtual reality require a proper team, a significant amount of time, and, naturally, a lot of resources.

The dynamic history of renovations and interventions should be narrated before presenting the problem of the apse to visitors. One of the possibilities is to make material 3D models. However, these consume a lot of space. An even bigger problem is that they require more information. In the case of the first two architectural phases of the church, as well as the fresco decoration of the apse, virtually no information remains. Therefore, a lot of reinventing should be done, which leads to the forging of history. Instead, schematic 3D models that are deprived of details should be used. In this way, the architectural and artistic evolution is easier to understand, both for the professional and non-professional audience. A new question that opens up is this: how and where should these models be presented?

Fig. 2. Usage of flat screens and information panels for educational purposes

There are two options: the first one is on a screen; the second one is on panels (Fig. 2). There is a common problem for both. "Positioned physical means, like information boards [, screens,] and plaques, may be helpful in providing explanations and interpretations close to the object, but they can never furnish the object with rich and deep contextual information and knowledge without cluttering the environment and thus disturb the cultural experience one initially intends to improve" [21]. What is meant by this is that they often seclude parts of the historical environment. Indeed, putting large-scale panels or flatscreens inside a church does seem a bit strange. The solution to the problem can be to put these in a side chamber that has no function and is of no importance for understanding, experiencing, and enjoying the religious structure. In the case of Santa Maria Assunta, this can be, perhaps, in one of the rooms in the so-called fourth isle, that is currently used as storage. It is immensely important for the digital objects to be close to the original structure because in the perception of the visitors, the value or the importance of the virtual stems from the authority of the material original [22]. There is another reason that confirms this idea. It stems from the understanding of religious art that the common visitors often lack. T. Tsivolas noted that only "someone familiar with the conventions can understand the significance of the symbols" [15]. In the domain of education, it is more useful if the object one just heard or learned about can be experienced immediately, especially if the person is not familiar with the language of the symbols, as is often the case with religious heritage and art. "It will often be completely impossible for the visiting layman to understand their original shape, use, and significance" [21].

Indirect Augmented Reality (IAR) might be another helpful tool for visitors to use. "A large array of video cameras and other sensors that would capture, in real-time, the real environment and permit a perfect reconstruction of that environment, in real-time, as seen from any arbitrary viewpoint" [21]. As a consequence, if a viewer aims his/her phone towards the apse, he/she would see a corresponding virtual reconstruction on the screen. The practical use of IAR so far was mostly limited to outdoor sites and archaeology. It is a complex technique that brings us back to one of the starting questions: how is this tool adding value to the project? In the case of the apse of the basilica in Torcello, not much.

The reconstructions that would be viewed on the screen of the phone are appealing but they can be viewed, on a much smaller budget on a flat-screen in the annex chamber with other digital models. Using the IAR for the sake of its attractiveness would be fetishizing technology. Another risk, that is applied also to VR, is that a certain percentage of users would focus "on the process of using the technology, rather than on the content" [23].

If, however, one wants to invest in high-tech equipment that enhances the experience of visitors, a far superior tool is a Virtual Reality model. Before any further elaboration of its usage, it should be noted that VR involves the space around the observer. As such, it is often not acceptable in museum spaces, especially in a church. It also often threatens to become the protagonist instead of the real object [23]. This can be overcome by placing it in a separate room that has no historic importance and is deprived of any artifacts. As proposed earlier, the one in the adjacent part of the church would suit this purpose nicely.

Fig. 3. An illustration of the potential VR reconstruction of a service held in the 11th century in the basilica of Torcello

Where does VR's advantage lay? It lies in its use of the screen as a phenomenon. In the case of IAR, the visitor holds the device that allows for a visual overlap. However, the edges, or rather the limit of the screen are clearly visible allowing for a perfect distinction between the real and the virtual. In the case of VR, the dynamic screen covers the whole field of view canceling all visual/mental connections that its consumer has with his/her surrounding [24]. Instead, the viewer is instantly and mentally transported into the domain of the virtual [25], allowing for a fuller experience that satiates the visual (and other) sense in a more comprehensive way.

The proposal for use of VR would be the presence in a sequence of a virtual medieval service (Fig. 3). This is envisioned following the concept of "electrification of imagination" that allows the viewer to experience the past and "cross centuries" [26]. The inspiration for this idea came from the (at that time) groundbreaking VR pilgrimage in the Cluny Abbey that was presented in 1993 [27] and became one of the most revolutionary innovations in the application of new technologies in cultural heritage.

The religious aspect can be further enhanced by stimulating the original use of the object, i.e. holding services in the basilica. However, since this probably will not be an option, a ritual aspect can be simulated through the use of VR. It "can include various non-material aspects such as symbolism, ideology, and ritual; a concern with the social and abstract dimensions of heritage, ceremony, and the creative use of aesthetic objects and spaces" [28]. Through a stimulating setting like this, it can allow for a more personal relationship between the visitor and the represented object. "Given the idiom 'seeing is believing,' the realism achieved by modern visualization systems could lead the users to perceive the virtual model as 'truth' instead of as the result of interpretation" [10]. This is unlikely in the case of Torcello because with the return of the slabs in the apse, the visual difference between the virtual and the real would be a matter of atmosphere, not the artistic aesthetic. The viewer would experience something that is otherwise inaccessible, something for which the apse with its synthronon, mosaic, and marble slabs would serve as a scenography. The idea is that a description of a medieval service, that is today completely abandoned in the sense of its atmosphere, no longer needs to be just a written description. These vivid descriptions of medieval religious service, such as that of Gregory of Nyssa [29] can become even more vivid through the use of VR. In real life in the 21st century, no church is going to light hundreds of candles to illuminate its interior. In the case of Santa Maria Assunta, it is unlikely that a large congregation of believers would gather to attend the mass. On the contrary, this can be accurately reproduced and visualized in the virtual domain. I reiterate, there is no fear of virtual competing with the real, as it would be clearly presented as a didactic tool with the aim of compensating for the lack of possible experience. This is because "in a simulation environment, presence and excitement are privileged over the reflection and contemplation associated with direct experience at the monument" [28]. The contemplating part can be done in direct contact with the work of art in its original setting, i.e. the central nave of the church. The "excitement" is reserved for the VR domain in the adjacent room.

4.4 Remarks Regarding the Use of VR

There are, however, a few important remarks that can be said about the use of virtual reality in cultural heritage: 1. The immersion into the virtual does not equal knowledge gaining; 2. Realism can act as a distractor from the content; 3. VR eliminates the communication within a group; 4. VR imposes its own narrative on the viewer.

Regarding the first problem, the "users needed to have the representation codes of the original knowledge domain, otherwise, the immersive application would become another source of problems, added to those which arise while trying to understand the content" [23]. Basically, the same problem as with viewing a work of art without any previous knowledge. To overcome this, the use of a VR headset would be assisted by a staff member or a plaque explaining its purpose and content.

One particular characteristic of VR is its alluring realism and the ability to accurately reproduce physical reality. According to certain studies, a more detailed version of virtual reality is not necessarily better. On the contrary, it can distract the user from the point of the content. "Simplified or abstract representations can be more effective" [23]. In the case of the common audience, as mentioned above, details often distract resulting in a lack of obtained knowledge. When it comes to professionals, the abundance of details is not important since they "can work with increased levels of abstraction." In the case of my proposal, the context justifies the details. I would deliberately focus on a more detailed simulation because the purpose of it is the experience. The educational part is done by the digital models and other visual tools before a user reaches the headset.

The third remark is a valid one and cannot be countered. It is in most part the fault of technology as it often prevents a group from collectively enjoying a simulation.

The fourth and the final remark is made towards the persuasiveness of VR. "Certainly, a compelling visualization can make itself 'easy to love and difficult to doubt'" [17]. Because of this, it needs to be clearly stated that virtual reality is a hypothetical simulation or a visual interpretation of certain data. One can indeed make a remark about how the guided tour leaves more space for imagination, and it would be fully valid. However, imagination is highly personal, and not everyone has the ability to mentally recreate an 11th-century religious service. Also, the usage of VR technology is not mandatory. Those who prefer to stroll around and absorb the current atmosphere of the church are fully encouraged to do so.

5   Conclusion

In conclusion, the marble slabs and the throne of Attila should be put back as an aim to restore the aesthetic unity of the apse. It would further contribute to its functionality in the religious interior. The fresco fragments that would be covered by the marble slabs would be visible in digital reconstructions. In the adjacent chamber, information panels or screens should be put. They would demonstrate the architectural narrative of the church through 3D models while providing the necessary information to the visitors. Instead of using AR, MR, or IAR, it is better to invest in a VR version of the apse, that would help the viewer to experience, and through it understand the purpose and function of art in the Middle Ages by being present in an 11th-century service.

The main outcome of this paper is the importance of connection and dependence of the digital restoration on the physical one, both in terms of theory and practice.

References

1. Calaon, D.: Quando Torcello era abitata. Regione del Veneto, Venice (2013)
2. Andreescu-Treadgold, I.: A Ninth-Century Chapel in the Basilica's Crypt at Torcello. In: Per l'Arte da Venezia all'Europa, Studi in Onore di Giuseppe Maria Pilo, ARTE, pp. 55–66. Edizioni della Laguna, Venice (2001)

3. Trevisan, G.: Il rinnovamento architettonico degli edifice religiosi a Torcello, Aquileia e Venezia nella prima meta del secolo XI. In: Cantarella, G., Calzona, A. (eds.) La reliquia del Sangue di Cristo: Mantova, l'Italia e l'Europa al tempo di Leone IX, Atti del Convegno internazionale, Mantova, 23–26 novembre 2011. Scripta, Verona, pp. 479–504 (2012)
4. Gasparri, S.: The formation of an early medieval community: Venice between provincial and urban identity. In: West-Harling, V. (ed.) Three Empires, Three Cities: Identity, Material Culture and Legitimacy in Venice, Ravenna and Rome, 750-1000, An International Workshop organized by All Souls College of University of Oxford, 20–22 March 2014, pp. 35–51. Brepols, Turnhout (2015)
5. Zanetto, S.: Tradizione Costruttive nell'alto e medio Adriatico (secoli VII-XI): Eredita e innovazione nell'alto Medioevo, All'Insegna del Giglio, Sesto Fiorentino (2017)
6. ***   Асунто, Розарио. Тоерија о Лепом у Средњем Веку, прев.*** Г. Ерњаковић, Српска*** Књижевна Задруга, Београд(1975)
7. Fabbri, L.: La cripta di Santa Maria Assunta a Torcello: il richiamo a Bisanzio all'interno della politica di legittimazione orseoliana. In: Citazioni, modelli e tipologie nella produzione dell'opera d'arte. Atti delle Giornate di studio, Padova, 29–30 maggio 2008, pp. 3–10 (2011)
8. Niero, A.: Die Basilika von Torcello und Santa Fosca, Ardo/Edizioni d'Arte, Venezia (1963)
9. Andreescu-Treadgold, I.: The mosaics of venice and venetian lagoon: thirty-five years of research at Torcello. In: Arte Medievale, Sapienza Universita di Roma, Rome, pp. 193–207 (2013)
10. Pietroni, E., Ferdani, D.: Virtual restoration and virtual reconstruction in cultural heritage: terminology, methodologies, visual representation techniques, and cognitive models. Information 12, 167 (2021). https://doi.org/10.3390/info12040167
11. Deloš, B.: Virtuelni Muzej, prev. V. Pavlović. Clio, Beograd (2006)
12. Popadić, M.: Čiji je Mikelandjelov David? Baština u Svakodnevnom Životu, ur. D. Bulatović, Centar za muzeologiju i heritologiju Filozofskog fakulteta Univerziteta u Beogradu, Beograd (2012)
13. Maroević, I.: Uvod u Muzeologiju, Zavod za informacijske studije Odsjeka za informacijske znanosti Filozofskog fakulteta Sveučilišta u Zagrebu, Zagreb (1993)
14. Poulios, I.: Discussing strategy in heritage conservation: living heritage approach as an example of strategic innovation. J. Cult. Herit. Manag. Sustain. Dev. 4(1), 16–34 (2014)
15. Tsivolas, T.: Law and Religious Cultural Heritage in Europe. Springer, London (2014). https://doi.org/10.1007/978-3-319-07932-5
16. ***   Бранди, Чезаре. Теорија Рестаурације, ур. и прев. *** Б. Шекарић, Италијанска *** кооперација, Београд*** (2007)
17. Watterson, A.: Beyond digital dwelling: re-thinking interpretive visualization in archaeology. Open Archaeol. 1, 119–130 (2015). https://doi.org/10.1515/opar-2015-0006
18. Dennis, L.M.: Digital archaeological ethics: successes and failures in disciplinary attention. J. Comput. Appl. Archaeol. 3(1), 210–218 (2020). https://doi.org/10.5334/jcaa.24
19. Wingfield, K.B.: Networks of knowledge: inventing theology in the Stanza della Segnatura. Stud. Iconogr 38, 174–221 (2017)
20. Gilbert, K.E., Kun, H.: Istorija estetike, Transl. D. Puhalo. Kultura, Beograd (1969)
21. Liestøl, G., Hadjidaki, E.: Quasi–mixed reality in digital cultural heritage. combining 3d reconstructions with real structures on location—the case of Ancient Phalasarna. In: Kremers, H. (ed.) Digital Cultural Heritage, pp. 423–433. Springer, Cham (2020). https://doi.org/10.1007/978-3-030-15200-0_29
22. Cameron, F.: Beyond the cult of the replicant – museums and historical digital objects: traditional concerns, new discourses. In: Cameron, F., Kenderdine, S. (eds.) Theorizing Digital Cultural Heritage, pp. 49–77. MIT Press, Cambridge (2007)

23. Economou, M., Pujol-Tost, L.: Educational tool or expensive toy? Evaluating VR evaluation and its relevance for virtual heritage. In: Kalay, Y.E., Kvan, T., Affleck, J. (eds.) New Heritage: New Media and Cultural Heritage, pp. 242–261. Routledge, New York (2008)
24. Manovič, L.: Metamediji. Centar za savremenu umetnost, Beograd (2001)
25. Grau, O.: Virtual Art: From Illusion to Immersion, trans. G. Custance. MIT Press, London (2003)
26. Thwaites, H.: Digital heritage: what happens when we digitize everything? In: Ch'ng, E., Gaffney, V., Chapman, H. (eds.) Visual Heritage in the Digital Age, pp. 327–349. Springer, London (2013). https://doi.org/10.1007/978-1-4471-5535-5_17
27. Boniface, P.: Managing Quality Cultural Tourism. Routledge, New York (2003)
28. Flynn, B.: The morphology of space in virtual heritage. In: Cameron, F., Kenderdine, S. (eds.) Theorizing Digital Cultural Heritage, pp. 349–369. MIT Press, Cambridge (2007)
29. Iozzia, D.: Aesthetic Themes in Pagan and Christian Neoplatonism: From Plotinus to Gregory of Nyssa. Bloomsbury, London (2015)

"Un Convivio Che Offre a Chi Ha Desiderio Di Conoscenza Una Difficile Vivanda" (Dante, Convivio)

The Role of the Scientific Research and Its Restitution to the Public by Digital Technology

Anna Cipparrone[(✉)]

Attilio and Elena Giuliani Foundation, Villa Rendano, Via Triglio 21, 87100 Cosenza, Italy
direzione@consentiaitinera.com

Abstract. The paper intends to clarify the value of digital technology applied in the museum field in the transfer and communication of scientific contents to the community, despite the variety of audiences and their respective cultural backgrounds, through the case study of the multimedia Museum Consentia Itinera. ICOM institutional member and recognized by the regional museum system, it is located in Villa Rendano, the famous home of the musician Alfonso, inventor of the third pedal of the piano and undisputed talent in the European field.

From a synthetic rereading of the ancient sources (Ovidio, Euripide, Strabone etc.) and of the specialized studies about the history of Cosenza, the Multimedia immersive paths (Consentia Itinera and Genius loci) and their emotional storytelling, intercept the collective memory and link the individual with his most remote past.

Aware of the social impact of heritage in the global era and of the role of museums especially in the so-called "minor" contexts in which the relational approach of these institutions is evident, the contribution will focus on heritage education and legality projects with TPC Command aimed at to confirm that the museums of the 21st century are places of cultural democracy. Digital technology makes it possible by offering "a difficult meal to those who thirst for knowledge" making museums inclusive, accessible, places of emotional contact, well-being and active training.

Keywords: Scientific research · Digital storytelling · Legality · Educational

1 The Attilio and Elena Giuliani Foundation

The Attilio and Elena Giuliani Foundation was established in Rome in 2010 thanks to the donation of the founder Sergio Giuliani. The name recalls some of the best known and most appreciated entrepreneur figures in Cosenza for the innovative spirit with which they made their company, in the furniture sector, a successful reality even outside the borders of Calabria. The commitment shown with Villa Rendano, which has undergone a radical restoration since 2012 in collaboration with the Superintendence for Architectural and

R. Furferi et al. (Eds.): Florence Heri-Tech 2022, CCIS 1645, pp. 317–339, 2022.
https://doi.org/10.1007/978-3-031-20302-2_24

Landscape Heritage of Cosenza, represented the beginning of an ambitious journey that the Foundation has set itself, but above all has allowed to return to the city of Cosenza one of its most beautiful buildings, unjustly subtracted for a long time from the use and even from the knowledge of the community. In the early years of its existence, the Foundation conceived and implemented the Villa Rendano (Fig. 1). From the beginning, Villa Rendano has been configured as a center for advanced training and research on energy and environmental issues and, from today, as a multimedia museum space and as a place for cultural and tourist experiences.

Fig. 1. Villa Rendano, Cosenza

A multidirectional path, that of the first 4 years, however, gave way, in 2016, to the identification of a clear mission of the Attilio and Elena Giuliani Foundation of Villa Rendano: the identity project consigned at the Museum. Villa Rendano, from the house of ideas, assumed the facies of a place of connection between citizens and the city, acquiring in 2019 the claim or unique value proposition of "city in the center", or house of citizens. From 2016 onwards, all the initiatives, institutional commitments, projects, relations with professionals and other local realities have contributed to the definition and implementation of an ambitious project aimed, on the one hand, at the rediscovery of values and identity elements of the city through the philological recovery of the millenary history of Cosenza and, on the other hand, to strengthen the knowledge, the sense of belonging and the participation of citizens in the cultural and social life of this small but indisputably active reality, choosing digital technology as privileged instrument of connection and communication. Still in an embryonic way and yet already characterized by initiatives of great artistic and cultural quality, the commitment of the Giuliani Foundation since 2016 has been expressed by undertaking some important lines of research: identity (of the city, of the territory, of ethnic minorities), technologies digital, urban regeneration, legality, musical and theatrical entertainment, etc. therefore Villa Rendano was increasingly becoming a place for sharing, exchanging ideas and culture.

The Giuliani Foundation has progressively identified and circumscribed the objective and the institutional mission by interacting - in a very simple and easy path - with multiple professionals, each of which has contributed to determining the genesis of the multimedia proposal which in November 2017 was fully completed with the inauguration of Consentia Itinera. Multimedia itineraries in the history of the city of Cosenza entrusted to the ETT company[1].

The Foundation intended to transform Villa Rendano into a propulsive center of ideas and projects destined for the territory and, above all, for the enhancement of the historic center of Cosenza, starting from a highly qualified and innovative initiative that is a precise and multidisciplinary investigation into the history of the translated city in an immersive multimedia journey. A nineteenth century building that became more and more concretely an engine aimed at technological innovation and internationalization through the common thread of the identity project. The famous Villa of the musician Alfonso Rendano, from a place without reputation, from a building that remained privately owned for decades without ever having a relationship with the community (it was considered the place where gas bills were paid), from a place enveloped in an aura of mystery reinforced by the historical evidence relating to its well-known inhabitant, inventor of the third pedal of the piano, a personality of absolute importance in the European cultural milieu of the second half of the 19th century, from an institution without any relationship with the territory it intended to rise, according to the will of the Giuliani Foundation , an institute of the story, an open museum and space for the territory. Since the inauguration of Consentia Itinera - November 7, 2017 - Villa Rendano has been transformed into a cultural institution in which citizens and tourists can experience the absences that characterize the history of the city by living as a protagonist, through a captivating and inclusive storytelling, suitable for all ages and cultural backgrounds, the progressive evolution of Cosenza.

Thanks to the combination of scientific research and digital technologies, Villa Rendano became a privileged gateway for knowledge and visits to the city, highlighting that thanks to digital technology it is now possible to reactivate interest in history, return literary sources to diversified audiences, narrating specialist studies and research to the community with emotion and involvement, intercepting the sense of belonging and collective memory. The intention of the Foundation was therefore to return to the community a property left for decades in private ownership and therefore unknown to most and, moreover, to make the historic center of Cosenza and its millenary history and deep stratification, the center of interests and projects of an institute created in response to the constitutional provision of article 118 focused on the issue of subsidiarity. By establishing the Multimedia Museum, which in a short time obtained the 2018 mark - *European Year of Cultural Heritage*, it became ICOM member and it received the recognition of a Museum of Regional Interest, the Foundation wanted to reposition the millennial history of the city and the evocative, albeit degraded places of the historic center, in the heart of the inhabitants through a non-trivial story, not aimed at mere spectacle but focused on the recovery of studies and sources and with a faithful and engaging digital rendering (Fig. 2) (Cipparrone 2021a, 2021b; La Fondazione Attilio ed Elena Giuliani 2016–2020 2021; Cipparrone 2018, 2019, 2020).

---

[1] https://www.youtube.com/watch?v=hZQoBtEchWc.

Fig. 2. The mark European Year of Cultural Heritage received thanks to the Museum project

2 "Un Convivio Che Offre a Chi Ha Desiderio Di Conoscenza Una Difficile Vivanda"

"A banquet that offers a difficult meal to those with a desire for knowledge" - declares Dante in the Convivio. Unworthily assuming this statement and transferring it from the question of language to that of humanistic and digital studies, addressing the case study of the Consentia Itinera Museum, it is the intention of this contribution to clarify the value of technology in the museum field in the transfer and communication of scientific contents to the community, despite the variety of audiences and their respective cultural backgrounds (Greco 2019; Modena 2019; Mascheroni 2008, 2016, 2019, 2021; Cipparrone 2021a, 2021b; Incerti et al. 2018; Greco et al. 2020; Parry 2010; Colombo 2020; Dal Maso 2018).

Immersion and identification in the histories since the antiquity pass through the great decorations arriving to the digital experience in the global Era. The concept of immersion and the storytelling (Bonacini 2020; Halbwachs 1950; Kadoyama 2018; Arnaldo 2021; Damone 2019; D'Orazio 2017; Branchesi et al. 2016; Bodo 2003) have their roots in antiquity (Mattei 1996; Lughi 2015a, 2015b, 2015c, 2018, 2019, 2020a, 2020b, 2021; Cataldo 2011; Bonacini 2021). From the Greek *bythízomai* and from the Latin *mergere*, immersion always presupposes a change of state and above all, even today in the world of digital culture, so-called immersive experiences always take place in presence, that is, they are physical and not virtual experiences, remotely (Miller 2014; Schachtner 2020; Bianco 2019; D'Acunto 2020; Biscioni 2017; Gambaro and Vannicola 2015; Salvarani 2013). They are created with digital tools and solutions within museum spaces, in contact with works of art, in real digital landscapes based on enveloping visual and sound effects. If we look back, in history, man has always felt the need to feel enveloped and therefore involved, denouncing the need to immerse himself in order to feel legitimized by his own existence

In the antiquity, emblematic is the example of the Rock Paintings of Lascaux, one of the best-known examples of prehistoric art that represent a great variety of wild animals. The Rock Paintings of the Lascaux cave date back to 18,000–16,500 years ago and are found in France, Dordogne, Montigna (Bataille 1992; Laval 1950). The images of animals of the time are distributed within different environments and painted on the rock walls. Various species appear such as horses, deer, bison, bears, birds, rhinos. There are also images of an extinct species of bovine called Uro. Among others, a human figure is recognized. In 1979, UNESCO added the cave complex to the list of places considered a World Heritage Site. On 12 September 1940 four French boys, Marcel Ravidat (1922–1995), Jacques Marsal (1926–1989), Georges Agnel (1924–2012) and Simon Coencas, discovered the cave complex. The authorities thus opened the town to tourist visits after the Second World War. Equally significant is the case of the decorative programs of the noble residences and of the architectural spaces better known as the Galleria and Studiolo, through which the client - immersing himself in the lives of the characters he asked to portray - self-celebrated himself (Prinz 1988; Liebenwein 1977).

Equally immersive are Fontana's spatial settings (Celant 2012; Studio azzurro 1992). Once the space age began, a new dimension took shape in which science and technology have become tools of knowledge of space. The "Space Movement" investigated the relationship between man and the space that surrounds him; Fontana wrote of the art "there is only a spatial concept of art", the theoretical assumption that inspired his "Spatial environments" (the first ever environments in the history of contemporary art), staged as early as 1949 at the Galleria del Naviglio and in 1951 at the IX Triennale in Milan. The first manifesto of the movement is an unsigned leaflet entitled "Spaziali" (1947): others followed, but the official drafting is dated November 26, 1951, five years after the movement broke up. At the end of the 1950s, Fontana's perforated canvases and "Spatial Concepts" opened up new perspectives to contemporary art, changing our relationship with space, anticipating fashions of the virtual and the dematerialization of objects, even in his quest for enhancement of traditional materials such as ceramics, earth, glass, stones, pastel colors, ink, iron, zinc, copper, canvas, paper.

In the 1980s, Studio Azzurro created sensitive environments and experiences that combined interactivity and storytelling. Also in the 1980s, Electrosonic ltd in London was experimenting with new forms. Immersivity has therefore always been an action that involves a change of state, emotional, physical and attitude. The spectator, in the immersive project, from observer becomes the protagonist of the works. The so-called experiences are an emblematic example carried out by important studies on which we discuss and will discuss because if in some ways they allow you to live within a work of art (and there are numerous studies on the behavior of people in immersive experiences), on the other hand they are criticized for the total absence of methodological rigor and for the excessive authorship of the projects that become almost entirely filmic, cinematic, sensational and spectacular. In immersive projects - although real immersion continues to be discussed as it should presuppose the involvement of all the senses and the loss of space-time references - the visitor is in any case placed at the center of the questions of those who produce culture.

In our century was born a new digital art way: the immersive art experience. Those projects (such as Van Gogh Experience, Klimt Experience, Inside Magritte, Caravaggio experience, Monet and so on) aren't only digital exhibit realized in order to show masterpieces in high definition, but they are digital art productions in architectural places entirely projected that have a specific language, style and aesthetic. In the digital art experience, the visitor is the main character of the space in which he results entirely enveloped[2]. From the antiquities of Lascaux to the "studiolo" and "gallerie" of the Renaissance until the spacial environment, we arrive in the XXI century to the digital productions in architectural spaces aimed to the immersion of the visitor in the master-pieces or in the life of the important artists of the past. An immersion originated by the union among images in very high definition, textual elements, musical effects and the maximum freedom of the visitor to move and to understand the history.

"Each masterpiece is the result of its time and mother of our sentiments. Every cultural age expresses its art production that, probably, don't repeat again" -says Kandinsky in 1912; digital art experiences are digital productions of our century and global Era that produce desire, inspiration, knowledge, curiosity generated thanks the develop of digital technologies and thanks the software evolution in graphic computer. Those multimedia exhibitions show important social and emotional implications that here have place for the strong relevance with the main topic of this paper: the case history of the Multimedia Museum Consentia Itinera aimed to share the storytelling of the local identity and to construct and reinforce, starting by digital immersive path, the relationship among people and cultural heritage, among community and historical center of Cosenza. The case history explains the role of digital technologies to stimulate a change of status caused by the emotional and educative involvement that the multimedia storytelling produces.

The concepts of digital culture and digital immersion - briefly announced so far - allow us to reach the focus of the contribution or the case study of the Consentia itinera Museum. In the first instance, it leads us to reflect on the theme, role and types of storytelling used today by Museums, well investigated by Elisa Bonacini in her volume "Museums and the forms of digital storytelling" (Bonacini 2021): Oral, written, video storytelling, storytelling visual, animated, interactive, immersive, social media storytelling, participatory storytelling, generative, geo-storytelling, multimedia mobile storytelling, cross-media storytelling, transmedia storytelling, the types of narrative methodology known as storytelling. Furthermore, by classifying it on the basis of a user experience, digital storytelling can be divided into 5 categories: collaborative, mobile/rental, transmedia, immersive and generative.

Materializing the story or restoring the past through the narration of facts, events and people (storytelling, in fact) is something that has always existed but is realized in the Consentia Itinera Museum which tool to restore value to ancient sources and specialized studies and to reposition the city in the heart of its inhabitants with the path "Consentia Itinera" as well as motivate it in an awareness and in the removal of the barriers of indifference towards the deterioration of the historic center, with the digital exhibition "Genius Loci" (Figs. 3 and 4).

---

[2] http://thefakefactory.com.

Fig. 3. The multimedia museum Consentia Itinera, an immersive path

Fig. 4. Digital solutions in the multimedia Museum Consentia Itinera

Telling the territory, exploring its events and returning them to the local public and external visitors, is the goal of the multimedia museum Consentia itinera and it is a desirable intent for those institutions which, like Villa Rendano, decide to act as a hinge between citizens and cities. Between people and assets throughout the national territory. Calabria, thanks to the variety and fragmentation of its identity elements, as well as in order to strengthen skills and human capital with knowledge of the past and a perspective of the future, deserves more places to narrate and tell the history of the territory from an integrated perspective.

But how did Consentia Itinera's digital storytelling come about and what is it for? From a synthetic reinterpretation of the ancient sources and the specialist studies consulted for the realization of the immersive path, it was considered that digital technology could represent the instrument of restitution and of emotional involvement of communities, as well as the "place" in which to build a relationship and an introspective bond - which passes through the heart of each individual - between goods and people, between cultural heritage and care, between conservation and safeguarding.

3   Una Ricerca Scientifica in Costante Evoluzione, Narrata Attraverso Le Tecnologie Digitali. Il Progetto Identitario

Consentia Itinera is a tale, an uninterrupted continuum in the flow of time in which, while providing the coordinates of the so-called "historical periodization" limited to the case of Cosenza, it aspires to provide that interpretation more intimately corresponding to the emotion towards the city, which surprises for its millenary history and its suggestive charm. By reading and visiting the Consentia Itinera Museum we intend to return, through several thematic-chronological explorations, the fascinating history of the city, perhaps helping to putting back in the citizen's heart Cosenza and to proudly present it to travelers. It is not an essay, but rather a narration and a concrete mediation between the past and the present of the city in perfect harmony and correspondence with the performance of the seven rooms of the multimedia museum Consentia Itinera.

The selection of the facts, of the historical events, of the personalities who contributed to the constitution of the image of our city, correspond with the intent to identify the so-called "identity markers" that characterize its heritage; this selection was made on the basis of documentary and iconographic sources, studies, suggestions, ancient chronicles in a seductive synthesis that can be appreciated by both the educated reader and the curious.

The Museum's aim is therefore to allow the realignment of the thousand-year history of Cosenza with the most famous paths of national and international history, from Greek and Roman colonization to the Middle Ages, from the Renaissance to the Risorgimento up to the present day, reuniting personalities related to this only apparently peripheral area of the nation with the most flourishing centers of art, politics and culture of the past.

Through a story that is rather an easy and inclusive tool, absolutely not specialized or difficult while making use of research and studies of different pertinence which on the contrary are, it will be clear the absolute certainty that Cosenza was not extraneous to that complex cultural phenomenology, art and politics that characterized the liveliness and uniqueness of Italy in past centuries but, on the contrary, the role played by the city in important and delicate historical conjunctures will be highlighted.

In any case, each episode extrapolated from the timeline has been investigated and explored in order to be returned to the reader/visitor as the bearer of an "other world", of a tangible and recognizable reality, the result of links and correlations between artistic phenomena, historical, social, political and economic which, precisely because of its manifest breadth and complexity, may perhaps arouse the emotion of the reader, both of the citizen and of the traveler.

Writing the history of a city is only apparently a simple activity. The thriving bibliography on the history of Cosenza, a beloved and in many respects complicated city, provides copious information of a historical, archaeological, anthropological, cartographic, artistic and architectural nature and yet what Consentia itinera - a long and complex research merged into a multimedia museum - intends being an unveiling, an epiphany of relationships, not a mere re-reading of the episodes.

Writing the history of Cosenza as Consentia itinera aims, means penetrating into the deepest depths of its existence starting from when the waters of the seas bathed this strip of land and nothing else could be seen around it. Imagining the intertwining of events and letting the reader's imagination to run free, helping to strengthen the knowledge of the city's history and to fuel the love for its millenary story, will ensure that this suggestive passage of time is not abstract, but as the fruit of a slow and consecutive progression of facts, as the result of exchanges and contaminations, the effect of the contention of wars and conflicts; the furrow determined by the passage of various and distant peoples, the theater of ideals and exceptional intellects. But above all Cosenza will emerge as a felix land, rich in resources, quality, crossroads of cultures that have left tangible traces in its cultural heritage and in those numerous "absences" that this story of ours tries to evoke.

Writing the history of a city describing what exists is in fact something already done; therefore, the ambition of this Museum is to unveil and narrate what cannot be seen and what is not there, or to narrate and mediate between past and present, shedding light on those pieces of micro and macro history that led to generate our large monuments or the choices of sovereigns, guiding urban growth and development.

And it is for this reason that in the continuum of history, in that fascinating flow that is life with its contrasts and its magic, with its difficulties and its unrepeatable uniqueness, we will try to restore value to those events, often invisible because intangible, which however have profoundly marked the story of Cosenza.

The first citations relating to the site on which Cosenza stands, so gently lying on its Pancrazio hill, are related to the Crati river and it is from here that our story will begin... Consentia itinera. Paths/Routes in the history of the city of Cosenza. Driven by the continuous flow of river waters, events and characters will shed light on the extraordinary beauty of Cosenza, placing it back in the hearts of its inhabitants and proudly presenting it to external visitors.

The old town center is monumental and alive at the same time but almost unreachable for many citizens who a priori exclude it from their itineraries. The historic center is a soul, to be investigated, discovered, admired, understood, praised... to be protected.

Consentia Itinera was born from unconditional, though sometimes critical, love for the city. The narrative ductus of the Consentia Itinera Museum includes a physical and chronological trend, forward.

Here are the chapters, or immersive rooms, of the digital exhibition on the historical periodization of the city[3]:

---

[3] The immersive path about the history of Cosenza and its cultural heritage it was possible thanks a multidisciplinar scientific research from the ancient sources until the contemporary specialistic studies.

Sala 1 "I primordi"

- Città sui fiumi. La magia delle acque fluviali nelle antiche fonti sulla città
- Le fonti antiche sul fiume Crati
- La poesia di Eliano e l'etimologia del nome Crati
- La metropoli dei Brettii. Cosenza donna e guerriera
- Il Gran bosco della Sila

Sala 2 "La fase romana"

- Consentia dai Brettii ai Romani. Le guerre puniche e la romanizzazione del Bruttium
- Le terme romane nell'antica città di Cosenza
- Importanza di Cosentia in epoca romana dai riscontri cartografici: via Popilia, Lapis Pollae, Tabula Peutigeriana e Itinerario Antonini

Sala 3 "Alarico e Cosenza"

- Una sottile linea congiunge ancora Roma e Cosenza. Il Sacco del 410 d.C. e il viaggio di Alarico verso il Sud
- Morte di Alarico e seppellimento nel letto del fiume Busento
- La città dal V secolo all'XI: da Consentia a Costantia

Sala 4 "Il Medioevo a Cosenza"

- Cosenza. Città medievale dal passato brettio e romano
- Funesto e terribile fu il terremoto del 1184
- Storia architettonica del castello di Cosenza
- Ambienti del castello e saloni regi
- Patrimonio artistico medievale
- La regina di Francia Isabella d'Aragona ed il suo monumento funebre nella cattedrale di Cosenza
- Un prezioso dono per la città di Cosenza: la Stauroteca di Federico II
- La cappella della Madonna del Pilerio nella Cattedrale di Cosenza

Sala 5 "Il Rinascimento a Cosenza"

- Cosenza, città di Bernardino Telesio e dell'Accademia cosentina
- Tra humanae litterae e politica: la felicissima entrata di Carlo V a Cosenza nel 1535
- Arte a Cosenza nel Rinascimento
- I palazzi della città demaniale Cosenza nel Rinascimento
- Fonti e opere d'arte del Rinascimento a Cosenza
- Citazioni letterarie della città e dei fiumi nel Rinascimento
- Citazioni letterarie della città e dei fiumi nel Seicento

Sala 6 "L'Ottocento a Cosenza"

- I moti del Risorgimento
- I Sovrani in visita a Cosenza dopo l'Unità d'Italia
- Il palazzo del Governo nella piazza XV Marzo
- Il teatro comunale di Cosenza dalle sue origini
- La vicenda del sipario del Teatro comunale "Alfonso Rendano"
- I viaggiatori del Grand Tour alla scoperta di Cosenza. Vedute e racconti
- Descrizioni letterarie della città di Cosenza nell'800

Sala 7 "Cosenza nel contemporaneo"

- Descrizioni letterarie di Cosenza dal '900 ai giorni nostri
- Enrico Salfi, artista cosentino del Novecento
- Evidenze culturali della Cosenza novecentesca: la Biblioteca Civica, la Biblioteca nazionale e l'Archivio di Stato
- Cassa di Risparmio di Calabria e di Lucania
- I bombardamenti del 1943
- Alfonso Rendano e Villa Rendano

4   The Immersive Path into the Museum of Villa Rendano

The Consentia Itinera Museum does not have a collection of material assets but has made the study and enhancement of the historic center of Cosenza the central theme of its interests and cultural actions. Digital exhibitions, educational projects, conference initiatives, participatory programming and a communication plan constitute the poles of a project that aspires to philologically reconstruct the places and assets of the old city and to reposition it in the government actions of the institutions and in the daily actions of citizens.

4.1   Consentia Itinera, the First Digital Exhibition that Can Be Used Permanently at Villa Rendano

The tour, divided into 7 rooms dedicated to the history of Cosenza, thanks to a skilful work of digital storytelling, tells the history of the city of Cosenza through immersive projections, digital animations and sound suggestions, trying to give the visitor a vision of the events that you satisfy the soul and at the same time stimulate the desire for knowledge (Fig. 5). The visitor will retrace the history of Cosenza from the beginnings to the contemporary age, concluding his journey with a 360° flight over the city through VR viewers (Fig. 6).

4.2   Genius Loci. Un Viaggio Nel Cuore Del Centro Storico, Cuore Della Città

An immersive path created with a topological criterion that is added to the cultural offer of the multimedia Museum Consentia Itinera, narrates the current state of the city in 7 rooms, stimulating a greater care and protection of the material heritage and the spirit of the places and leaving room for new proposals and plans for the future. Genius

Fig. 5. The seven rooms of the multimedia museum Consentia itinera in the digital exhibition about the history of Cosenza

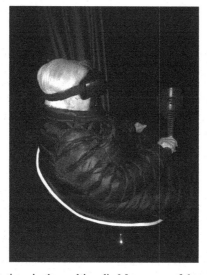

Fig. 6. Digital solutions in the multimedia Museum useful to adults and children

Loci through the skilful combination of audio, video, photos and interviews of citizens who have put the old city back at the center of their existence - by living there or by transferring their work there - mends a deep tear that has lasted for too many years and shows Cosenza Vecchia to citizens in its suggestiveness and uniqueness but also in its current state of decay and impoverishment (Figs. 7 and 8).

A museum that lives fully immersed in its community; an Institute that is the result of a donation act such as Villa Rendano and the Giuliani Foundation cannot ignore the events and it is for this reason that in the month of May 2022, on the occasion of the

Fig. 7. Another immersive path of the multimedia Museum: Genius loci, in order to protect the historical center of Cosenza

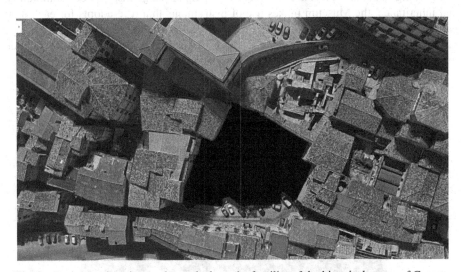

Fig. 8. Genius Loci, an immersive path about the fragility of the historical center of Cosenza

celebrations for the 800th anniversary of the Cathedral of Cosenza, a new digital project dedicated to the building consecrated in 1222 in the presence of Emperor Frederick II of Swabia who donated the precious Stauroteca (Fig. 9).

Informed by the evident intention of achieving economic sustainability, since it is a project for which the resources invested are exclusively those of the founder Sergio Giuliani[4] with the exception of some funding relating to regional tenders and the MUR, but also environmental sustainability without having to constantly renew its own digital

---

[4] After the death of the founder Giuliani, in the new deal of the Foundation, the economic resources are used also to sustain the "I Calabresi" editorial project wanted by the current President.

Fig. 9. The third immersive path about the 800 years of the local Cathedral and its architectonical and artistic history

instruments, the Museum foresees the reuse of the rooms and the related digital tools for each new immersive path.

Therefore, aimed at the narration of heritage and contexts and at the construction, from the digital, of a direct relationship between people and goods, between community and inheritance, the Museum makes use of instruments that it re-adopts for each new narration. In this case there are video projections, touch interfaces, video-mapping, virtual reality and, at the end of the path, a mobile App that leads the visitor to discover the places of the city. A tablet activates the immersive path (Fig. 10).

Fig. 10. The director of the Museum always in the first line to involve community and create relationship between people and cultural heritage starting by digital tecnologies

But despite being a multimedia and immersive museum, conceived for a narration in which the visitor can experience the stories that happened in the past as a protagonist and reunite with his own deepest identity by intercepting his own memory and a collective one, Consentia Itinera assigns great importance to cultural mediation, for this reason each visitor is introduced by a cultural operator to the route and, after it, to the history and extraordinary beauty of the city and its heritage.

So, digital purposes in the Multimedia Museum Consentia Itinera are:

- To valorize the ancient sources and the scientific studies about the city. To promote the humanities involving visitors regardless of the individual background.
- To catch the collective memory in order to allow into the people a vision of the future.
- To promote protective behaviors towards to the historical center and cultural heritage with digital exhibit pointed at the heart of the people.
- To encourage the younger to be protagonist of the change (educational projects, internship by university students, formative paths and other project as #vicinidimuseo or #villarendanoambassador).
- To ensure well-being and active participation of the special publics (we made special program with parkinson, about blind accessibility ecc.
- To become familiar with the past to empathize with it, with himself and with others.
- To share the knowledge about using of digital technologies in the Museums.
- To disseminate, with an original and inclusive language, the scientific studies about cultural heritage of the territory increasing care and protection, as the real interest, toward it.
- To be a special storytelling place of the land enforcing the relationship and the dialog with others institutions.

The Multimedia Museum Consentia Itinera revolution: from digital technologies as communication and involvement language to a real relationship between community and cultural heritage; from the reconstruction and presentation of the history to the creation of the authentic connection of care and protection of cultural heritage.

5   Digital Museum to Encourage the Real Relationship with People and Cultural Heritage and Its Care and Protection

The methodology adopted by the Multimedia Museum and its individual temporary and permanent immersive paths provides a deep anchoring to the rigor of scientific research and is expressed with an inclusive and emotional storytelling capable of intercepting the collective memory and reuniting the individual with his most remote past. Not only. Sustainable behaviors are promoted thanks the new Museums role in the Global Era and in this case, from the digital storytelling the Museum Consentia Itinera aims to ensure involvement and emotion reinforcing the relationship with the Cultural Heritage. Aware of the social impact of heritage in the global era and sure of the role of museums especially in the so-called minor contexts in which the relational approach of these institutions is evident, the contribution will focus on heritage education and legality projects aimed at to confirm that the museums of the 21st century are places of cultural democracy and that respect for the environment, fairness and care for the cultural heritage are inevitable in the education of contemporary man.

«Into the art-history Books those histories there aren't» declare the General of Carabinieri Roberto Riccardi in his book "Detective dell'arte. Dai monuments men ai carabinieri della cultura». So, the Multimedia Consentia Itinera Museum knows that Cultural Heritage is constantly at risk of dispersion and disappearance both for natural reasons and for destruction and for the unlawfulness committed by man. Answering at its social role, the Museum works for the dissemination of the care and respect towards to the cultural heritage and to construct a sustainable future, coherent with Agenda 2030 Goals.

The greatest risk that our cultural heritage runs is destruction but let's not forget that one of the causes of loss of cultural heritage is oblivion, the lack of knowledge and care on the part of the communities themselves. Heritage is always in danger despite the commitment of people and institutions. Over the centuries, the deliberate attack on cultural heritage and the destructive intent of the symbols of some civilizations of the past has been profound. Ideologies, religious reasons, ethnic-identity struggle, etc. are the main causes. The Second World War recorded destruction and disappearance but also in the nineties of the last century in the territories of the former Yugoslavia the destruction of mosques and churches was tragic or, in Afghanistan just as violent was the destruction of the monumental statues of the Buddha carved in the rock 1800 Years ago. Numerous other devastations suffered the material heritage of Kabul but also the National Museum of Iraq, sacked during the occupation of Baghdad in 2003 (L'arte di salvare l'arte 2019; La tutela del patrimonio culturale 2019; Greco and Christillin 2021). Multiple terrorist attacks that destroyed those assets that testify to the passage of ancient civilizations and many scares suffered from the landscape. In addition to these reasons, the penetration of the illegal art market is very serious, a reason for theft and illicit circulation of historical goods in which it is often unsuspecting citizens who happen to be involved.

The history of art theft is plentiful; the interest and deep link between the mafia and cultural heritage is noteworthy. Fugitives, bosses have often been found in possession of precious works of art both because they were kidnapped by the intense beauty and wanted to enjoy them for their exclusive use and, as happened in 1993, it was used for terrorist purposes, for receiving stolen goods, to claim the release of inmates belonging to the gangs and so on. There is even an art produced by the mafia.

Stealing and theft, accompanied by the indifference of many, every day risk dropping thousands of historical documents and monuments into eternal forgetfulness and, with them, knowledge of the origins of our country, its civilization and its genius. In addition to the destruction for ideological reasons or in war crimes or calamities, there is, however, another cause of the forgetting of the heritage and that is its loss of memory. And undoubtedly, a lack of knowledge of the monuments and the huge heritage of our past by the younger generations, their lack of rooting in the community and in its collective memory, constitute the greatest danger. For this reason, the multimedia museum Consentia Itinera has developed, together with the Commander of the Heritage Protection Unit in 2019, a first form of contrast to the destruction of heritage through a path of civic education and heritage education conceived in 2019 on the occasion of the Second Regional Day of the Museums of Calabria (Figs. 11 and 12).

5.1 Agenda 2030, Goal 4: «TO ensure a Quality Educational, Equus and Inclusive"

On that occasion, Villa Rendano ideated with the Commander of the Heritage Protection Unit of Cosenza Cap. Bartolo Taglietti the educational project "Museums and legacy" to tell citizens (in meetings for both children and adults) about the operations that this

Fig. 11. In 2019 the Multimedia Museum created with the Command TPC of Carabinieri the project Museum and legality. Moments of the first meeting with schools and citizens carried out by the museum director Anna Cipparrone and the Commander of Carabinieri Cap. Bartolo Taglietti

Fig. 12. The project became, during the pandemic period, an educational project in blended learning about care and protection of the cultural heritage. Moment of the online lessons by the museum director and the Commander of Carabinieri Ten. Geloso

special section of the Carabinieri carries out every day. Calabria - land abundantly raped by grave robbers and other traffickers - in the direction of sensitizing people to the care of the heritage and denouncing any disrespectful actions towards the environment and cultural heritage. Since a few days the TPC Command of Cosenza had concluded an important investigative operation named "Achei"[5], that became occasion to talk with the citizens about the violences suffered by our land thanks to the illicit escavations. The

---

[5] https://www.quotidianodelsud.it/tags/operazione-achei/.

conference was also the opportunity to open an interesting debats about the preventative measures to sensitize the community to have positive behaviors towards cultural heritage.

The focus of the interventions for adults was the database with the Object IDs as well as the theme of auctions and the illicit market, in order to inform citizens both of the risks they run in the purchase of cultural goods and in the methods of self-protection when in possession of works of art.

This is in line with the social commitment that museums have in the 21st century and, more specifically, with the commitment of the Giuliani Foundation to stimulate active citizenship and contribute to the knowledge and care of the heritage.

That activity of 2019 had highlighted the lack of knowledge of citizens towards such an important sector and had recorded positive feedback (we talked about the missing objects database, the art market, auctions etc.) from adults and children giving the way to an active and fruitful collaboration with the TPC General Command of Rome whose Commander, General Roberto Riccardi, was a guest of our headquarters in July 2020 and July 2021 to present two of his volumes. One of these "Detectives of art. From the monuments men to the carabinieri of culture" (Riccardi 2019) in which the prevention and repression action of this special sector of the weapon is described 50 years after its establishment, throws a beam of light on an Institute built in full compliance with the constitutional dictates of referred to in Article 9 which states: The Republic protects the landscape and the historical and artistic heritage of the Nation.

On the basis of these experiences, during the 2020 lockdown, the Consentia Itinera Museum project to raise awareness of legality and heritage care was perfected and, also following a survey for participatory programming proposed to teachers of the provincial school network (in the form Google Module) to better address the relationship between Museums and Schools in a pandemic, online initiatives have been carried out together with the Heritage Protection Unit of Cosenza and two other museums in the city (Galleria Nazionale and Museo dei Brettii ed Enotri).

To better understand the intentions of the project, I always like to quote a passage from the volume by General Riccardi, where we read about a carabiniere, this brigadier Paolo Maralla, good at stalking, difficult to sow on two wheels, who had been chosen to act as a hound in the case of the thefts of Van Gogh's The Gardener. After having passionately described the commitment made by this man, who found himself by chance, in his life as a carabiniere dealing with an art theft, and never moved away from this admirable world, the author of the volume declares that there is no trace of his work in schoolbooks or in the caption of the work returned to its place in the Museum. Of course, the General clarifies, that of the carabinieri of art is not a result destined for years but for centuries, not for judicial news but for eternity and yet - and here I am returning to a trigger factor of the project that I am presenting today - they are above all the Museums which, by virtue of their growing social role, have the duty to actively contribute to the dissemination of knowledge on these issues and to raise awareness of the communities in order to stimulate respectful and virtuous behavior towards the environment and cultural heritage.

5.2   Agenda 2030, Goal 11: "MAke Cities and Human Settlements Inclusive, Safe, Long-Lasting and Sustainable" and "To Reinforce the Commitment to Protect and Safeguard the World's Cultural and Natural Heritage"

The project is committed to strengthening the participation of the community towards the safeguarding of cultural and natural heritage in the world by spreading, in addition to knowledge about the Calabrian heritage, a new attitude towards cultural heritage in general. The 2021–22 edition of the PCTO project on Museums and legality, expanded even more to the themes of Citizenship and the Constitution, in addition to having compensated for the closure of the Museums during the highlight of the emergency, wanted to continue in mixed mode in order to sow new skills among young people and make them protagonists of a radical change of paradigm. The question we ask them is "what can I do to generate change?".

The project, structured in three parts (one with preparatory online seminars, one with visits to the Museums of Cosenza and in the places of the historic center and the last with the creation of a project work chosen from digital products, research, podcasts, artistic performances in the most degraded places of the old city for the sole purpose of restoring vitality to them, etc.) continues today thanks to the involvement of the current Commander of the TPC Unit Lieutenant Giacomo Geloso and all the Directors of the Cosenza museum network (Museo dei Brettii e degli Enotri, National Gallery, Museum of Comics, Diocesan Museum) involved not only for the online part but also for student visits; this in the spirit and in full view of a territorial strategic network. Students are working about this topic. Some of them are producing social campaign to improve the attention of the citizens at the situation of the historical center. Others thinking to play music in the most declined area of the historical center to bring life where there isn't. Some other is working to change, in digital, the depauperation of the cultural heritage transforming it and proposing new use of some places.

From the speech of Hans Martin Hinz we read: "Museums are assuming an increasingly vital role in contributing to the definition of sustainable development and implementation of related practices. Museums must be able to guarantee their role in safeguarding cultural heritage, given the growing precariousness of ecosystems, situations of political instability, and the human-caused environmental challenges that may arise. The work of the museum, through education and exhibitions, strives to create a sustainable society. We must do everything possible to ensure that museums are part of the cultural driving force for sustainable development in the world". The commitment of the Museums towards sustainability is part of that challenge of contemporary society aimed at creating the conditions for living according to the limits of nature.

So, the educational project was presented at the conference "Museums, schools and territories" in April 2021[6], soliciting the launch of an ICOM Italia call "Museums, legality and territories"[7] addressed to all Italian museums aimed at to map and promote good practices in the relationship between Museums and Carabinieri and to sensitize communities to the care and protection of cultural heritage. ICOM, which has always

---

[6] https://www.youtube.com/watch?v=wts-MCGGNsY.

[7] https://www.icom-italia.org/musei-legalita-e-territorio-un-sondaggio-per-mappare-le-buone-pratiche-e-diffonderle/.

been committed to the issue of offenses against cultural heritage (just to name a few, article 7 of the museum code of ethics, the active contribution in the international arena, the agreement already signed with the Carabinieri Command and the consequent drafting of the volume on anti-crime security in museums, etc.), in fact, intends to start a dedicated working group, aimed at stimulating Museums and Nuclei in shared planning, in the publication of dossiers and documents, in the permanent story of the rescue actions of the exhibited heritage and not exposed and in the stimulation of an increasingly cohesive active citizenship.

In this sense, the project is also in line with some of the goals of the 2030 agenda including that of "ensuring quality, equitable and inclusive education" according to which the objective of the Nations is to ensure that by 2030 all students acquire the knowledge and skills necessary to promote sustainable development and above all that all people have sustainable lifestyles that promote a culture of peace, non-violence and cultural diversity. For our purposes, goal 11 is important, that is "to make cities and human settlements inclusive, safe, long-lasting and sustainable" because to do so we are committed to strengthening our commitments to safeguard the cultural and natural heritage in the world.

In this sense, the project is in line with the indications provided by the *Declaration of the G20 Culture*[8], Rome July 2021 in which the role of the digital transition and the value of the alliance between Museums and Schools for the construction of concrete capacities has been further framed and sanctioned. Aimed at the protection of cultural heritage in future generations (in primis the articles 5.1, 4.2, 4.5 and 4.6).

The project won the H.E.L.P prize (Digital Projects for heritage education) of ICOM Italia, Portugal and Rep. Ceka and is realizing a digital environment in which talk about this topic[9]. Since February 2022 was born the professional group to mapping and promoting the best practices in the cooperation between Museums and TPC Command of Carabinieri and to improve the permanent storytelling of legacy into the Museums.

The prospects of the project are wide and the outputs numerous and I hope that more and more cultural institutes and TPC Commands can join them. I conclude by quoting the words of General Riccardi - "not loving art, in Italy, is equivalent to a crime: it is the premise for letting it be destroyed". Not defending art, if you are Italian, is turning your back on your history, dishonoring your father and mother "[10].

Sitografia di riferimento

https://www.youtube.com/watch?v=hZQoBtEchWc
http://thefakefactory.com
https://www.quotidianodelsud.it/tags/operazione-achei/
https://www.youtube.com/watch?v=wts-MCGGNsY
https://www.icom-italia.org/musei-legalita-e-territorio-un-sondaggio-per-mappare-le-buone-pra tiche-e-diffonderle/
https://cultura.gov.it/comunicato/21073
https://www.icom-italia.org/help-project-final-report/
https://www.beniculturali.it/comunicato/22375

---

[8] https://cultura.gov.it/comunicato/21073.

[9] https://www.icom-italia.org/help-project-final-report/.

[10] https://www.beniculturali.it/comunicato/22375.

Bibliografia di riferimento

Arnaldo, J.: Atmosfere: Esperienze immersive nell'arte e al museo. Bononia University, Bologna (2021)

Bataille, G.: Lascaux, ou la naissance de l'art, Skira (1992)

Bianco, A.: The next society. Sociologia del mutamento e dei processi digitali, Milano, Franco Angeli (2019)

Biscioni, R.: Fotografia e public history: patrimonio storico e comunicazione digitale, Ospedaletto (Pisa), Pacini Editore (2017)

Bodo, S.: Il museo relazionale. Riflessioni ed esperienze europee, Torino, Fondazione Giovanni Agnelli (2003)

Bonacini, E.: Digital storytelling nel marketing culturale e turisti-co, Palermo, D. Flaccovio (2021)

Bonacini, E.: I Musei e le forme dello storytelling digitale, Roma Aracne (2020)

Branchesi, L., Curzi, V., Mandarano, N. (a cura di): Comunicare il museo oggi. Dalle scelte museologiche al digitale, Atti del convegno internazionale di studi, Sapienza Università di Roma, Dipartimento di Storia dell'Arte e Spettacolo, 18–19 febbraio 2016, Milano, Skira (2016)

Cataldo, L.: Dal museum theatre al digi-tal storytelling. Nuove forme della comunicazione museale fra teatro, multimedialità e narra-zione, Milano, Angeli (2011)

Celant, G.: Lucio Fontana: ambienti spaziali: architecture, art, environments, Milano (2012)

Cipparrone, A.: Fonti antiche sui fiumi. Il racconto multimediale nel Museo Consentia Itinera tra ricerca scientifica e nuove forme di comunicazione e divulgazione. In: Il capitale Culturale, Rivista dell'Università di Macerata, N. 20 Dicembre 2019, pp. 271–296 (2019). ISSN 2039-2362

Cipparrone, A.: I Musei del XXI seco-lo. Luoghi di democrazia culturale. Sviluppi sul tema dell'accessibilità nel Museo multimedia-le Consentia Itinera. In: Fuori Quadro – Trimestrale sui Beni Culturali della Calabria, Marzo (2020a). ISSN 1826-154X

Cipparrone, A.: Il Museo multimediale Consentia itinera nel circuito dei Musei Emotivi. In: FuoriQuadro, trimestrale di informazione sui Beni Culturali della Calabria, numero doppio Giugno-Settembre (2021a). ISSN 1826-154X

Cipparrone, A.: Il Museo multimediale Consentia Itinera nella città di Cosenza in "Nuova Museologia" Giugno (2018). ISSN: 1828–1591

Cipparrone, A.: Musei, scuole e territo-rio. In: Fuori Quadro – Trimestrale sui Beni Culturali della Calabria, Marzo (2021b). ISSN 1826-154X

Cipparrone, A.: Musei, scuole e territorio. In: Fuori Quadro – Trimestrale sui Beni Culturali della Calabria, Marzo (2021). ISSN 1826-154X

Colombo, M.E.: Musei e cultura digitale. Fra narrativa, pratiche e testimonianze, Milano editrice bibliografica (2020)

D'Acunto, G.: Rigenerazione e valorizzazione digitale del patrimonio culturale: alcuni casi studio. Geometria e costruzione, pp. 107–118 (2020)

D'Orazio, S.: Museo reale e museo digitale. Il caso del Museo Archeologico Regionale Salinas un anno dopo la riapertura. In: Il capitale culturale, vol. 16, pp. 399–419 (2017)

Dal Maso, C.: Racconti da Museo, Bari (2018)

Damone, G.: Processi di registrazione e rielaborazione digitale. In: Antonio Canova-atelier, pp. 87–91 (2019)

Gambaro, P., Vannicola, P.: Design e open source for cultural heritage. Il design del patrimonio culturale fra storia, memorie e conoscenza: l'immateriale, il virtuale, l'interattivo come materia di progetto nel tempo della crisi, Firenze, Alinea editrice (2015)

Greco, C., Christillin, E.: Le memorie del futuro. Musei e ricerca, Tori-no (2021)

Greco, C.: La biografia degli oggetti. Rivoluzione digitale e umanesimo. In: Ciccopedi, C. (a cura di): Archeologia invisibile, Modena (2019)

Greco, C., Rossi, C., Della Torre, S.: Digitalizzazione e patrimonio culturale tra crisi e opportunità. L'esperienza del Museo Egizio di Torino. In: Il Capitale Culturale, supplementi, no. 11, pp. 197–2021 (2020)

Halbwachs, M.: La memoria collettiva (1950). Milano 2001 Unicopoli

Incerti, M., D'Amico, S., Giannetti, S., Lavoratti, G.,Velo, U.: Le Digital Humanities per lo studio e la comunicazione di beni culturali architettonici: il caso dei mausolei di Teodorico e Galla Placidia in Ravenna. In: Archeologia e Calcolatori, no. 29, 2018 Novembre, p. 297 e ss. (2018)

Kadoyama, M.: Museums involving Communities, Londra (2018)

L'arte di salvare l'arte: Frammenti di storia d'Italia, a cura di Francesco Buranelli, Roma (2019)

La Fondazione Attilio ed Elena Giuliani 2016–2020. Un progetto identitario, a cura di Anna Cipparrone, Luigi Pellegrini Editore, Aprile 2021

La tutela del patrimonio culturale: Il modello italiano 1969–2019, a cura di Simona Pasquinucci, Roma (2019)

Laval, L.: La caverne peinte de Lascaux, Montignac (1950)

Liebenwein, W.: Studiolo. Storia e tipologia di uno spazio architettonico, a cura di C. Cieri Via, Berlino (1977)

Lughi, G.: Creatività digitale. Come liberare il potenziale delle nuove tecnologie, Franco Angeli (2015a)

Lughi, G.: Di cosa parliamo quando parliamo di cultura digitale. Agenda Culturale, 6 aprile 2021

Lughi, G.: Digital media and contemporary art. Mimesis Journal (2015b)

Lughi, G.: Intelligenza artificiale, arte, cultura. Agenda Culturale, 2 otto-bre 2020a

Lughi, G.: Interactive storytelling. In: I media digitali e l'interazione uomo-macchina, a cura di S. Arcagni, Aracne editrice (2015c)

Lughi, G.: La corsa al digitale negli ambienti scientifici: entusiasmi e contraddizioni. Agenda Culturale, 2 ottobre 2020b

Lughi, G.: La visualizzazione di-gitale negli studi di cultural heritage. Sci. J. Digit. Cult. 4(2) (2019)

Lughi, G.: Mobile/Locative Paradigm: Embodiment and storytelling in Digital Media. In: Body Images in the Post-Cinematic Scenario. The Digitization of Bodies. Mimesis International (2018)

Mandarano, N.: Musei e media digitali, Carrocci editore (2019)

Mascheroni, S.: Dipingere a parole. Storie circolari del Chianti e del Valdarno, Masso delle Fate (2019)

Mascheroni, S.: Lascio in eredità me stesso alla terra. Fare memoria tra volontariato e patrimonio culturale, Masso delle Fate (2021)

Mascheroni, S.: Per l'educazione al patrimonio culturale. 22 tesi (con A. Borto-lotti, M. Calidoni e I. Mattozzi, FrancoAngeli (2008)

Mascheroni, S.: Un patrimonio di storie. La narrazione nei musei, una risorsa per la cittadinanza culturale, Edizioni (2016)

Mattei, M.G.: Correnti magnetiche: immagini virtuali e installazioni interattive, Perugia, Arnaud-Gramma (1996)

Miller, C.H.: Digital Storytelling: a Creator's Guide to Interactive Entertainment. Focal Press, New York (2014)

Parry, R.: Museums in a Digital Age. Londra, New York (2010)

Prinz, W.: La galleria. Storia e tipologia di uno spazio architettonico, a cura di C. Cieri Via, Modena (1988)

Riccardi, R.: Detective dell'arte. Dai monuments man ai carabinieri della cultura, Rizzoli (2019)
Salvarani, R.: Tecnologie digitale e catalogazione del patrimonio culturale. Metodologie, buone prassi e casi di studio. Per la valorizzazione del territorio, Milano, Vita e pensiero (2013)
Schachtner, C.: The Narrative Subject. Storytelling in the Age of the Internet, Palgrave Macmillan, Cham (2020)
Studio azzurro, ambienti sensibili: Esperienza tra interattività e narrazione, a cura di Fabio Cirifino, Milano (1992)

Virtual Museums and Virtual Tours

Polyptych in Saint George's Church, an Inclusive Virtual Tour

Mario Covarrubias[1]([✉])(iD), Carla Ayala[2], Sabrina Galli[3], Luigi Barazzetti[4](iD),
Fabio Roncoroni[5], and Mattia Previtali[4](iD)

[1] Mechanical Engineering Department, Politecnico di Milano, Lecco, Italy
mario.covarrubias@polimi.it
[2] School of Design, Politecnico di Milano, Lecco, Italy
[3] Gli amici di San Giorgio, Annone, Italy
[4] Department of Architecture, Built Environment and Construction Engineering,
Politecnico di Milano, Lecco, Italy
[5] Politecnico di Milano, Polo territoriale di Lecco, Lecco, Italy

Abstract. At Annone di Brianza (Italy) in the Church of St. George, it
is possible to admire the "ANCONA DELLA PASSIONE" (altarpiece of
the Passion), an altarpiece painted and gilded carved wood cabinets. The
great altarpiece adorned the right side chapel of Saint John the Baptist,
whose construction dates back to the first half of the century XVI at
the behest of Annoni, one of the most authoritative families of Milan
of the sixteenth and seventeenth century. Since 2019 the altarpiece has
been protected inside a special room in order to avoid damage caused
by the temperature and humidity. Access to this room is not allowed to
people who visited the church. In order to allow the user to admire and
explore each minimal detail of the polyptych altarpiece a totem has been
designed and it's located just outside of the special room. The totem in
fact is composed of a 32 in. touch screen with a PC embedded and the
Virtual tour application.

The Virtual tour application has been developed with Unity3D. The
interactive application has different virtual scenes with photos, videos,
an external digital twin of the polyptych with both, open and closed
doors.

Keywords: Virtual tour · Visual impairment users · Inclusive tour ·
Digital twin · Photogrammetry

1 Introduction

The first building of the church of St. George is attributed around the end of
the eleventh-century [1]. Period of the cult and the devotion to the saint by the
Benedictines which enjoyed the religious probably as a small oratory. This stood
on the charming hill, which overlooks the town and the landscape, surrounded by
fertile land; this was in fact, the costume monastic era: settle in a place inviting
to meditation and prayer. A second reconstruction took place at the end of the

R. Furferi et al. (Eds.): Florence Heri-Tech 2022, CCIS 1645, pp. 343–354, 2022.
https://doi.org/10.1007/978-3-031-20302-2_25

fifteenth century, probably between 1479 and 1481, with the construction of the church with a single nave with a quadrangular apse oriented to the east and the west entrance facade.

1.1 The Passion of Ancona

The Ancona of the Passion is a great altarpiece in carved and painted wood made in the mid-sixteenth century by a workshop Antwerp and commissioned by a nobleman Giovan Angelo Annoni for the family chapel. Alternate paintings and sculptures narrate the dramatic story of the Passion. Its structure is given by two distinct elements: the bridle and the ancona real. Since 2019 the altarpiece has been protected inside a special room in order to avoid damage caused by the temperature and humidity. Access to this room is not allowed to people who visited the church. In order to allow the user to admire and explore each minimal detail of the Polyptych altarpiece a totem has been designed and it is located just outside of the special room, in front of the Polyptych. The totem in fact is composed of a 32 in. touch screen with a PC embedded and the Virtual tour application.

1.2 State of the Art VR

Developing a virtual reality tour considering a cultural heritage should provide visually immersive experiences [2] and various information [3]. It's really important to effectively provide media related information to cultural heritage in a virtual tour scenario or to measure their effectiveness. There are many virtual tours which reproduces content through various media (movies, animation, etc.), called film-induced tourism [4], is one way of utilizing content related to tourist sites [5]. However, while film-induced tourism has mainly used fictional stories such as movies, previous studies [6, 7] have shown that cultural heritage sites need content that effectively in-forms tourists about historical facts in augmented and virtual environments; video clips provided based on spatial data such as location and orientation have been considered fragmented and meaningless to the delivery of proper and interesting information. In our application we have integrated media info as Detailed pictures, 360° videos and the digital twin of the Polyptych sculpture.

2 Virtual Tour (VT) App Design

As mentioned before, the application was developed with Unity 3D, which was designed to be displayed on a 32-inch touchscreen device, which will be placed in front of the Polyptych to enhance the contemplation of the physical opera and not to replace it. The Polyptych presented a series of challenges, but the major problem was the difficulty for the user to see and understand the number of details contained therein. This problem is derived from its size 296 × 220 cm (closed); 296 × 396 cm (opened) with 33.4 cm of thickness, and the significant distance that must be between it and the user. The application will offer the added benefit of giving a close view (zoom in) of all the elements with a determined sequence and order. It was created having in mind that people with visual disabilities (related to age or birth conditions such as vision impairment or vision loss) would be able to use it thanks to the inclusion of audios that read and describe the different scenes contained.

The app was designed since the beginning to be used principally by the church staff in guided tours as the first scenario, then by the user itself, or in the case of the people with a visual weakness, by the person accompanying them.

In the following lines, a breakdown of the main interface structure and the principal scenes of the application can be appreciated, with some buttons and indicators that the user will find through the use of the app.

1. **The first scene:** It is a picture of the same sight that the user will find once is in front of the Polyptych, the opera contained after a vitrine in a controlled environment, and it comes with the respective button to start the interaction.

2. **The information section:** It is divided into two parts:
   - **2.1 General information section:** It contains the history of the family who ordered the construction and the transportation of the opera, with the deed notary document that proves the provenance.
   - **2.2 "Ancona della passione" information section:** It describes the opera and mentions the different scenes that could be found in the Polypthyc both 2D and 3D. There are mentioned here also two more similar operas, one in Denmark and one in Belgium.

3. **The measuring section:** It is divided into two parts as well:
   - **3.1 Graphical Measures:** It gives the user the general dimensions of the opera, in meters, with the possibility of interacting and choosing from the closed or the opened version.
   - **3.2 Architectural Plans:** It is oriented to a more specialized kind of user. It shows all the general dimensions in a more detailed way including the names of the different scenes and where they could be found in the Polyptych.

4. **The restoration section:** It is divided into three parts:
   - **4.1 Constructive aspect:** This one shows the physical construction of the Polyptych and the different layers that conform a sculpted scene (3D).
   - **4.2 Decorative elements:** It shows and describes the gilding, graffiti, and punching processes, as well as the combination of these different decoration techniques found through the opera.
   - **4.3 Before and after:** This scene remarks the visual difference of the opera elements before and after the restoration intervention.

Fig. 1. App interface structure. 4. Restoration section: Before and after(4.3)

5. **The video section:** It gives the user the possibility to learn more about the context and the journey that the Polyptych passed for being in its current place.

6. **The timeline:** This is the main section to be used for discovering the opera, as it redirects the user to the first scene: the cover of the Polyptych, and from there goes through the chronological order of the scenes showing the last and dramatic episodes of Jesus' earthly life (that are not built in a specific order). Each representation of a scene gives two possibilities and one feedback:
   - **Option A: A guided zoom in/out** through the different details and particular aspects that make unique the specific scene.
   - **Option B: A free interactive zoom in/out** scene for exploration
   - **Feedback (I.P.):** Where the user is sited physically in the opera to see the actual scene

Table 1. Buttons and indicators glosary.

Initials	Meaning	Initials	Meaning	Initials	Meaning
B.A.	Audio button	**B.Option A**	Option A button	**I.I**	Interaction indicator
B.B.	Back button	**B.R**	Reset button	**I.P**	Position indicator
B.E.	Exit button	**I.A**	Area indicator	**I.R**	References indicator
B.N.	Next button	**I.G**	Gallery indicator		

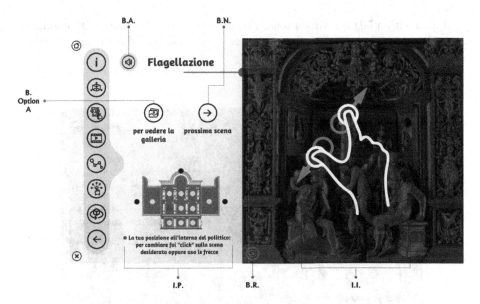

Fig. 2. 6. Timeline section: La Flagellazione (4. Option B: A free interactive zoom in/out)

7. **Interactive area:** This is a free exploration area that allows the user to navigate through the different scenes without following an order; it was developed for people who kept the attention of this opera previously or who want to see specific scenes.

   Each scene was thought to be presented with a milled representation as a supporting accessory; this way the user will have the chance to touch each scene in a real and 3D way, as well as to keep the attention for all of them, being him a visually impaired user or not. The Polyptych, as a piece of art and being closed in a controlled environment, will never be in contact with the people.

8. **Digital twin:** It shows the 3D digital version of the Polyptych in the open and close version with rotation and zoom in/out commands.

3   Polyptych Digital Twin

Digital recording was conducted using Structure from Motion Photogrammetry, which allows the generation of textured 3D models using a set of digital images. The geometry of the polyptych required the construction of a supporting device able to move the camera in both horizontal and vertical directions using two orthogonal sliders. Two different projects were conducted to create 3D models for two configurations of the polyptych: open and closed. In the case of the open configuration, more than 1,100 images were acquired with a Nikon D610 equipped with a 50 mm Nikkor lens. The camera was calibrated beforehand, and its calibration parameters were assumed as fixed quantities during the processing workflow.

Fig. 3. Detail of the open polyptych

Images were taken from about 1.7 m, resulting in a resolution of about 0.2 mm/pixel. Image configuration features both parallel captures (i.e., the optical axis of the camera directly oriented towards the polyptych) and oblique/convergent photographs in all directions (top-bottom-left-right). As the characters of the polyptych have a predominant 3D geometry, the use of convergent images allowed the reconstruction of 3D details with better geometric precision.

After orienting all images, a point cloud of about 21 million points was created. The textured mesh has about 4.2 million faces, and the digital orthophoto has a resolution of 0.2 mm/pixel. Processing time with Agisoft Metashape 1.7.1 took about 15 h. The workstation is an Intel(R) Core(TM) i7-6700 CPU @ 3.40 GHz, GPU(s) GeForce GTX 1070. The photogrammetric project was scaled and registered in a Cartesian reference system using some reference points measured with a total station Leica TS30. The textured mesh was exported and manually edited in Geomagic Wrap. Editing operations mainly required a manual correction of the edges, which were regularized, simplified, and straightened.

The reconstruction of the closed polyptych required fewer convergent images since the geometry of the upper part is more regular and relatively flat. The photogrammetric project was conducted with the same camera setup and about 300 images. The final point cloud has ca 11 million points and the textured mesh has ca 2.1 million faces. The digital orthophoto has a resolution of 0.2 mm/pixel. The use of a set of total station control points allowed the registration of the open polyptych into the same reference system. Data processing using the same workstation took about 3 h. Manual editing was also applied to refine the irregular edges of the final mesh, as described in the previous section.

Fig. 4. Detail of the closed polyptych

3.1 Testing Procedure and Results of the Virtual Tour App

The testing procedure is based on the standardized System Usability Scale (SUS) questionnaire [8] which features 10 statements to assess the Virtual Tour application. The questionnaire is based on the following procedure:

– The SUS questionnaire is based on a 1 to 5 Likert scale, where 1 means "strongly disagree" while 5 means "strongly agree"

- Each answer is normalized based on a 0 to 4 scale (Table 2)
- For positively-worded questions (Questions 1, 3, 5, 7, 9 in Table 2), the score contribution is the scale position minus 1. For negatively worded one, the contribution is 5 minus the scale position
- The final value is the sum of all contributions multiplied by 2.5, ranging therefore from 0 to 100

Table 2. SUS questionnaire results

	Statement	Likert scale (1:5)	Normal mean (0:4)	Std. Dev
1	I think that I would like to use this app frequently	4.45	3.45	0.93
2	I found the app unnecessarily complex	2.00	3.00	1.73
3	I thought the app was easy to use	4.73	3.73	0.65
4	I think that I would need the support of a technical person to be able to use this app	2.00	3.00	1.34
5	Found the various functions in this app were well integrated	4.64	3.64	0.50
6	I thought there was too much inconsistency in this app	1.45	3.55	0.69
7	I would imagine that most people would learn to use this app very quickly	4.64	3.64	0.50
8	I found the system very cumbersome to use	1.91	3.09	1.45
9	I felt very confident using the app	4.73	3.73	0.47
10	I needed to learn a lot of things before I could get going with this app	1.73	3.27	1.10
	Total (Sum*2.5)		**81.20**	**14.2**

As can be seen in Table 2, the outcome of the SUS questionnaires is 81.20 $\pm$ 14.2 points out of 100, giving a "good" usability result on the adjective-based rating of the SUS procedure.

4 Scene Milling for Blind People

The high-quality photos were introduced into an online and free software based on an algorithm that converts the different color tonalities to a gray scale, changing this feature the program is able to measure and recognize the different levels between pixels, and based on the brightness, the program will create a corresponding "3D" pixel where the height of the pixel is determined by the luminosity. A black pixel has a value that corresponds to height 0 mm, while a white pixel corresponds to the height specified [9], the composition of variations between these two specifications permits the height variation through the image, giving as a result of the transformation into a file in format.STL (stereolithography), this process allows having also from the paintings a 3d file for creating a prototype. Once the whole components are transformed into 3d models, the replication process can start; to reproduce this digital versions in a tangible objects.

4.1 The Process that Made It Possible: Milling

The process selected to realize the prototypes was milling, designed to recreate the shape through cuts using a rotating tool that moves in the different axes (x, y, and z). This process also allows the exploration through the materials that can be shaped, a HD polyurethane foam was proposed to "play" with the different densities (120, 450 and 600) and have feedback about the touch-sensitive responses.

The 3d files, independently if they there are from a 2d or a 3d scene, one by one, they need to be open in a parametric software like Fusion 360 from Autodesk and through a Computer-Aided Manufacturing feature (CAM) as in Fig. 5(a), and there a process can be selected to create the prototype as in Fig. 5(d). After selecting the corresponding process, the toolpaths trajectories have been created in order have two steps:

1. **Removing material** - to achieve this was necessary to mill with a rough tool of 5 mm diameter as in Fig. 5(b).
2. **Finishing** - for increase the quality finishing surface was necessary to mill with a 2 mm diameter tool as in Fig. 5(c).

This feature permits to visualize the paths while the milling machine is cutting. In the following Fig. 5 can be appreciated the whole process.

At the end, thanks to the "soft" material used and the 2 mm tool used in the second round, was discovered that for the plates which represent the 2d scenes or the paintings was not necessary to apply the 5 mm removing material step, the machine and tool were working together in a efficient way that permit to only do the second shaping process keeping the surface quality; what in terms of numbers reduced the manufacturing time.

The manufacturing time played an important roll while the replication process was being selected, and according to the two main prototype configuration, and the material selected; the times considered were the following:

- **For 2d scenes:** around 3.5 hrs - just second manufacturing step represented in the Fig. 5(c).
- **For 3d scenes:** around 5.5 hrs

Inside the software was needed to be defined few parameters to mill the material:

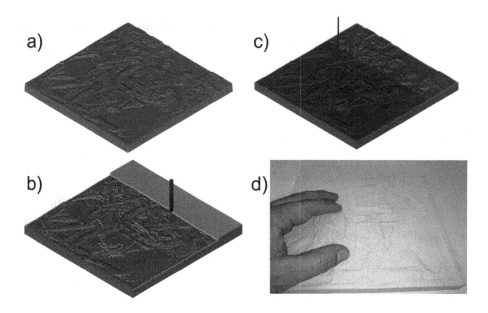

Fig. 5. 2D Scene milling process

- **Procedure**: parallel or additive.
  - **For the 2d scenes:** The proposal is to use a parallel procedure.
  - **For the 3d scenes:** A combination between additive and parallel procedures was needed, to take care about the material that needs to be removed and the tool access to the low levels. In the Fig. 5 can be appreciated the different procedures proposed for the 3d scenes and their respective preview.
- **Tool**: ball between 2 mm or 5 mm diameter.
- **Speed machine**: 10000 rpm for the densities used.
- **Step-over:** the half measure of the tool used.

4.2 But, Why Milling?

Inasmuch as the **prototypes are still in the modification phase**, the exploration in size, material, and parameters are a constant, the milling process grants this freedom unlike many other processes that are more rigid, like 3d printing, which in that case the material selection needed to remain in the commercial filaments like PLA, ABS, TPU, among others which not make the researched effect when this material is been touched, that also depends in which kind of printer is being used (If is a desktop 3d printer or a huge surfaces 3d printer); or the powder 3d printer that gives a good surface quality, but the relationship between benefit - cost - time invested is not optimal.

In the Fig. 6, could be appreciated the milling process inside the machine used "Charly 4U" to make a replication of a 3d scene in HD polyurethane of 120.

Fig. 6. 3D scene No. 5 - The crowning with thorns/milling process

5   Test with Vision Impairment User

This is a work in progress, we are enrolling some users which are part of the Blind National Institute Lecco Campus. The idea is related to mill different physical and scaled shapes of the polyptych in order to investigate some parameters related to the extrusion size, surface quality, cutting strategies, etc. Results will be reported in a few weeks.

6   Conclusions

This paper presents a virtual tour application in order to allow visitors to admire and explore each minimal detail of the polyptych altarpiece. A totem has been designed and it's located just outside of the special room in which the polyptych is preserved. The totem in fact is composed of a 32 in. touch screen with a PC embedded and the Virtual tour application.

The Virtual tour application has been developed with Unity3D. The interactive application has different virtual scenes with photos, videos, an external digital twin of the polyptych with both, open and closed doors.

The testing session with visual impairment users is in progress and the results will be presented in the next weeks.

References

1. di San Giorgio, A.: https://www.gliamicidisangiorgio.it/. Accessed 20 November 2021
2. Kenderdine, S.: Pure land: inhabiting the mogao caves at dunhuang, Curator: The Museum J. **56**(2), 199–218 (2013)
3. Kim, E., Kim, J., Kim, K., Hong, S., Lee, J., Park, N.-Y., et al.: Wearable AR platform for k-culture time machine. In: International Conference on Distributed Ambient and Pervasive Interactions, pp. 358–370 (2017)
4. Park, H., Kim, J., Bang, S., Woo, W.: The effect of applying film-induced tourism to virtual reality tours of cultural heritage sites. In: 2018 3rd Digital Heritage International Congress (DigitalHERITAGE) held Jointly with 2018 24th International Conference on Virtual Systems and Multimedia (VSMM 2018) 2018, pp. 1–4 (2018). https://doi.org/10.1109/DigitalHeritage.2018.8810089
5. Choi, Y.-M., Choi, H.-S., Choi, Y.-S.: Effects tourism storytelling on tourists attitude: Mt. Hanla on Jeju island. J. Korea Contents Assoc. **11**(12), 442–454 (2011)
6. Park, H., Woo, W.: Metadata design for AR spacetelling experience using movie clips. In: 2017 IEEE International Conference on Consumer Electronics (ICCE), pp. 388–391. IEEE (2017)
7. Park, H., et al.: K- culture time machine: a mobile AR experience platform for Korean cultural heritage sites. In: International Conference on Human Interface and the Management of Information, pp. 167–180. Springer (2018). https://doi.org/10.1007/978-3-319-92046-7_15
8. Bangor, A., Kortum, P., Miller, J.: Determining what individual SUS scores mean: adding an adjective rating scale. J. Usabil. Stud. **4**(3), 114–123 (2009)
9. Carfagni, M., Furferi, R., Governi, L., Volpe Y., Tennirelli, G.: Tactile representation of paintings: an early assessment of possible computer based strategies. EuroMed 2012: Progress in Cultural Heritage Preservation, pp. 261–270 (2012)

San Pietro Al Monte Abbey: An Inclusive Virtual Tour

Mario Covarrubias[1](✉)(iD), Beatrice Aruanno[2](iD), Laura Polo[3],
Luigi Barazzetti[4](iD), and Fabio Roncoroni[5]

[1] Mechanical Engineering Department, Politecnico di Milano, Via La Masa,
20156 Milano, Italy
mario.covarrubias@polimi.it
[2] Department of Civil and Industrial Engineering, University of Pisa,
Largo L. Lazzarino 1, 56122 Pisa, Italy
[3] Liceo Manzoni, Via Antonio Ghislanzoni, 7, 23900 Lecco, Italy
[4] Department of Architecture, Built Environment and Construction Engineering,
Politecnico di Milano, Piazza Leonardo da Vinci, 32, 20133 Milano, Italy
[5] Politecnico di Milano, Polo territoriale di Lecco, Via G. Previati,
1/C 23900 Lecco, Italy

Abstract. The "San Pietro al Monte Abbey project: a virtual tour for everyone" consists in the construction of a high-tech station that allows visitors with mobility limitations to be virtually accompanied by a guide to the Benedictine abbey of San Pietro al Monte along the ancient access route that can only be reached on foot with trekking equipment. The room with the virtual instrumentation is located in the Casa del Pellegrino in Civate (Lecco, Italy). It is a museum structure-based located in a media reception building. From its entrance, it is possible to see the final destination. The virtual tour preserves the dialogue between the environment, the monument, and the 'virtual pilgrim'. By also acting as an information database, it enhances the use of the basilica of San Pietro al Monte even for visitors equipped with tablets who reach the building on foot. The virtual tour application has been developed with Unity3D. The interactive application has different virtual scenes with photos, 360° videos, an external digital twin of the abbey, and some interesting internal digital twins of the most important monuments inside the abbey.

Keywords: Virtual tour · Photogrammetry · Digital twin

1 Introduction

According to historical and legendary sources [1], the origins of the complex of San Pietro al Monte date back to Desiderio, the last king of the Lombards. In their last completion, the current Romanesque buildings date to the 11th century. The housing parts of the monastery were probably destroyed during the 12th century for political reasons. Afterward, the monastic life continued in the monastery of San Calocero, in the town of Civate. The monks who had been living in Civate since the early Middle Ages were first the Benedictines and later the Olivetans. The history of the abbey ends in 1798 when Cisalpine Directory declared the abbey suppressed. The restoration and maintenance work started around 1930 thanks to Mons. Polvara and then to Don Vincenzo Gatti of the "Beato Angelico Family" . Their spirit still continues in the presence of the volunteers of the Association "Amici di San Pietro al Monte" [1]. The most important architectural places along the abbey are:

- **Main entrance:** A central staircase leads to the semi-circular pronaos, characterized by mullioned windows, up to the entrance to the Basilica of San Pietro
- **NAVE**: The structure of the central nave has a simple hall, closed at the top by a roof with an exposed truss ceiling. Originally the walls were completely frescoes and decorated with two bands of stuccoes.
- **CIBORIUM**: The Ciborium above the altar is of considerable artistic interest. The four external corners show the symbols of the four Evangelists, the eagle, the ox, the lion, and the man.
- **CRYPT**: The Crypt is the oldest part of the architectural construction. In ancient times, it was mainly decorated with stuccoes, now largely disappeared. Six granite columns support the cross vault.
- **S. BENEDETTO**: The oratory of San Benedetto stands in front of the Basilica of San Pietro. The building has a square plan with three semi-circular apses, decorated outside with continuous hanging bows and in the central apse, also with a band of dragon tail teeth.

San Pietro al Monte is located at 663 m above sea level and can be reached from the village of Civate (Lecco), going up a mule track accessible only on foot. It takes about an hour of medium difficulty walking to reach the monastery. Due to the medium-level difficult way, it could be particularly difficult to reach San Pietro al Monte abbey for people with limited motor abilities (e.g. using a wheelchair, lower limb motor limitations, etc.).

The "San Pietro al Monte Abbey project: a virtual tour for everyone" aims to allow visitors with mobility limitations to be virtually accompanied by a guide to the Benedictine abbey of San Pietro al Monte along the ancient access route that can only be reached on foot with trekking equipment. For this reason, a High-Tech station has been designed with the virtual tour application. The interactive application has different virtual scenes with photos, 360° videos, an external digital twin of the abbey, and some interesting internal digital twins of the most important monuments inside the abbey. The High-Tech station is located at "La casa del Pellegrino" [2], a museum-based building that hosts a dedicated room for the Virtual Tour of San Pietro al Monte.

1.1 Cultural Heritage Virtual Tour

Developing a virtual reality tour considering a cultural heritage should provide visually immersive experiences [3] and various information [4]. It's really important to effectively provide media-related information to cultural heritage in virtual reality or to measure their effectiveness. There are many virtual tours that reproduce content through various media (movies, animation, etc.), called film-induced tourism [5], which is one way of utilizing content related to tourist sites [6]. However, while film-induced tourism has mainly used fictional stories such as movies, previous studies [7,8] have shown that cultural heritage sites need content that effectively in-forms tourists about historical facts in augmented and virtual environments; video clips provided based on spatial data such as location and orientation have been considered fragmented and meaningless to the delivery of proper and interesting information. In our application, we have integrated media info as detailed pictures, 360° videos, and the external digital twin of San Pietro al Monte abbey and the main entrance internal architectural structure.

2   Virtual Tour App Design

The San Pietro al Monte project aims to be an interactive and inclusive tour that virtually accompanies the visitors from the starting point at "La Casa del Pellegrino" placed in the Civate Village to the "Basilica of San Pietro al Monte". The application has been developed using Unity3D. Unity3D is a game-engine software that allows to develop and deploy applications across multiple platforms [9], including the High-Tech station in Civate (LC), which includes a dedicated PC, screen, and connections for an external projector.

To guide the visitor into the discovery of the path to the abbey, the application is subdivided into eleven scenes (or pages), one for each most representative element of the tour. Figure 1 shows a screenshot of the application at the 7h stage (a).

The icons of the 11 scenes of the tour are listed at the top (e). The icons have been inspired by a symbol that best represents each stage of the real tour. The current location to visit is highlighted using brighter colors. In this example, the visitor is virtually located at stage n.6: "San Pietro esterno". At every moment, the user can visualize a map that shows the position of every scene of the virtual tour by clicking on the icon on the left (b).

In the real tour, it is necessary a certain amount of time to reach on foot the following stage. To improve the realism of the journey, and to mimic this aspect, the application shows with a progress bar (f) the time necessary to unlock the icon for the next location.

The application aims also to provide the sensation to actually walk on the path to the virtual pilgrim with motor disabilities. To reach this goal, each page of the virtual journey has a 360° video taken along the stage (g). Each step of the tour includes various elements to describe and show its main features. They can be explored by selecting them on the right side of the page.

Some stages of the tour to San Pietro al Monte have views or historical buildings that cannot be depicted completely with photographs. To provide a more engaging experience to the virtual tourist the application includes also some 3D reconstructions of the landscape captured using drones (c) and some exterior and internal rooms of the abbey (d). The following section will describe the techniques adopted for the 3D scanning and reconstruction of these models.

Fig. 1. Example of screenshot of the application when the visitors arrive at the 7th stage of the tour

The outputs of this methodology are 3D meshes (in the .fbx format) that have been imported in the Unity3D project. For each model, a new scene has been created. The model is placed in the middle of the scene and the user can rotate the camera, using a slider placed on the top of the page, to observe the mesh all around.

Furthermore, the user can go into detail about some aspects of the location (h). By clicking on the desired image, s/he moves to another page. As shown in the example in Fig. 2, on the left there is a collection of pictures including photographs, historical maps, and drawings that depict the subject. On the right, there is a scrolling text that narrates historical facts or myths and describes the images (with the reference numbers highlighted in purple).

3   San Pietro Al Monte Digital Twin

The creation of a digital twin of the complex was carried out using different digital recording tools following a multi-scale approach. The work was carried out considering the entire site at a cartographic level, a more detailed scale that includes the different buildings, and specific details such as the decorative elements.

UN UNICO MONASTERO

Nello stesso atto di consacrazione sono nominati San Pietro e San Calocero, pertanto, le due basiliche, quella a monte - dedicata all'apostolo - e quella a valle - dedicata al martire -, erano parte dell'unico monastero di Civate (1). L'atto di fondazione di un edificio sacro era collegato alla presenza di reliquie che venivano conservate in apposite capselle. Quattro di questi **contenitori di reliquie provenienti da Civate** vennero ritrovati nel 1516. Si tratta di piccoli contenitori, tra i 13 e i 17 cm. di lunghezza, con coperchio scorrevole nei due esemplari di pietra (marmo 2a e di marna 2b); nella capsella in lamina d'argento (2c) di forma ellittica è ancora presente all'interno una laminetta metallica incisa. A queste tre capselle di epoca tardoantica, conservate al Museo Diocesano di Milano, se ne aggiunge una quarta lunga 30 cm in stucco con due sigilli di epoca altomedievale (2d). Sempre il Trivulzio dice di aver ispezionato anche la tomba di San Calocero ritrovando un contenitore di profumo e dei resti di un velo di seta rosso. **La traslazione del corpo di San Calocero** da Alhanga a Civata potrahha assara avvanuta nalla

Fig. 2. Example of a deepening page

The digital survey was registered into the cartographic reference system UTM32-WGS84 ETRF2000-RDN, 2008.0 using a set of points measured with a GNSS receiver. A network of permanent GNSS stations (SPIN 3 GNSS) is available in the area to provide corrections and reach centimeter-level precision. A geodetic network was then measured with a total station and adjusted via least squares to obtain additional points all distributed around the site, including the interior of buildings.

Finally, laser scanning and photogrammetric data were collected to reconstruct the geometry of surfaces, including both consolidated methods and experimental solutions such as 360° and fisheye images as well as laser scans captured with low-cost mobile devices.

The next sections describe the procedure for acquisition and generation of only two products included in the virtual tour: the exterior of the Basilica and Baptistery as well as the topography of the site, and the main entrance of the Basilica.

3.1 3D Reconstruction of Topography and Building Exterior

The survey was conducted with a Parrot Anafi drone (320 g) that is equipped with a 1/2.4" CMOS sensor, 21 megapixels (5344 × 4016), and a focal length (35 mm format equivalent) 23–69 mm. A set of more than 200 images was captured in both automatic and manual ways.

The automatic flight was planned with Pix4Dcapture obtaining a set of pictures with regular frontal and side overlap, which is sufficient for the reconstruction of the roofs and the topography of the area. Additional convergent images were acquired all around the buildings using both automatic and manual

Fig. 3. Textured model and camera poses after photogrammetric processing

procedures. Finally, additional terrestrial images were acquired using a hand-held camera Nikon D610 and around the buildings. The set of convergent drone images has a tilting angle of about 45°, allowing the connection of the vertical (normal) drone images together with the terrestrial capture.

Data processing was carried out using Agisoft Metashape, which uses the structure from motion/photogrammetric processing workflow and is capable of generating 3D models. The final model consists of a texturized mesh georeferenced using GNSS points as can be seen from Fig. 3.

3.2   High-resolution Digital Model of the Entrance

The narthex at the entrance of the Basilica features rich and complex decorations and frescoes, which were captured with a workflow based on fisheye photogrammetry. Fisheye lenses provide images with a wide field of view and can be suitable for the digital reconstruction of small and narrow spaces. Indeed, a photogrammetric project with such images usually requires a reduced number of shots compared to traditional photogrammetry with frame (also called central perspective) images. However, fisheye images require a different camera model during photogrammetric processing which is currently supported by a limited number of commercial software packages. Data acquisition was carried out with a Nikon D610 equipped with an AF fisheye-Nikkor 16 mm f/2.8D featuring a 180° diagonal field of view. A set of 84 images was acquired with a photographic tripod to maximize the depth of field. The camera-lens system was calibrated with an independent photogrammetric project to estimate reliable calibration parameters, which were fixed during the photogrammetric reconstruction. The software used is Bentley ContextCapture, which delivers high-quality textured models.

Fig. 4. Textured 3D model of the entrance generated with fisheye photogrammetry

Data acquisition only took about 15 min, whereas processing was carried out in a few hours. No manual correction was carried on the resulting 3D models, except the manual refinements of the external edges using Geomagic Wrap as can be seen from Fig. 4.

4   User Test

Due to the ongoing Covid-19 pandemic, it was not possible to test the Virtual Tour application in the final location, at La Casa del Pellegrino in Civate, LC.

In order to have anyway a reliable feedback, it was decided to test the application with all the undergraduate and master thesis students that can frequent the Virtual Prototyping and Augmented Reality Laboratory at Politecnico di Milano - Lecco Campus and all the technical personnel that is present in the university also in these pandemic days. Basically, after a couple of days, 41 people were tested coming from completely different backgrounds, also the ASPOC Onlus Lab students have been included. ASPOC stands for Associazione per lo Sviluppo del Potenziale Cognitivo (Association for the Development of Cognitive Potential) and is an ONG foundation that help teenagers with disabilities and problems in cognitive development (Down Syndrome, Autism, mental retardation, etc.). ASPOC was founded by the parents of these teenagers [10].

Considering the ASPOC team, 13 students were tested. Basically, in this case to have a better learning outcome for the students it was decided to test the application first with the help of a projector guiding them to understand all the important aspects about the process and then, individually, the students had the possibility to play with the application. For a subjective point of view this activity was very interesting for all the scholars tested since they were really happy and interested in the application. All the students were excited about the possibility to see and interact with a virtual entity that clearly is not a common activity. Before having a quick look at the tests results it is important to highlight the some of the students that have tested the application do not have problems related to the input gestures, indeed some of them were able to interact with the virtual model much quicker and better compared to the engineering students or the technical staff.

4.1 Testing Procedure and Results

The testing procedure is based on the standardized System Usability Scale (SUS) questionnaire [11] which features 10 statements to assess the Virtual Tour application. The questionnaire is based on the following procedure:

- The SUS questionnaire is based on a 1 to 5 Likert scale, where 1 means "strongly disagree" while 5 means "strongly agree"
- Each answer is normalized based on a 0 to 4 scale (Table 1)
- For positively-worded questions (Questions 1, 3, 5, 7, 9 in Table 1), the score contribution is the scale position minus 1. For negatively worded one, the contribution is 5 minus the scale position
- The final value is the sum of all contributions multiplied by 2.5, ranging therefore from 0 to 100

As can be seen in Table 1, the outcome of the SUS questionnaires is 85.20 ± 17.8 points out of 100, giving a "good" usability result on the adjective-based rating of the SUS procedure.

5   Scene Milling for Blind People

The high-quality photos were introduced into an online and free software based on an algorithm that converts the different color tonalities to a gray scale, changing this feature the program is able to measure and recognize the different levels between pixels, and based on the brightness, the program will create a corresponding "3D" pixel where the height of the pixel is determined by the luminosity. A black pixel has a value that corresponds to height 0 mm, while a white pixel corresponds to the height specified, the composition of variations between these two specifications permits the height variation through the image, giving as a result of the transformation into a file in format.STL (stereolithography), this process allows having also from the paintings a 3d file for creating a prototype. Once the whole components are transformed into 3d models, the replication process can start; to reproduce this digital versions in a tangible objects.

Table 1. SUS questionnaire results

	Statement	Likert Scale (1:5)	Normal Mean (0:4)	Std. Dev
1	I think that I would like to use this app frequently	4.45	3.45	0.93
2	I found the app unnecessarily complex	2.00	3.00	1.73
3	I thought the app was easy to use	4.73	3.73	0.65
4	I think that I would need the support of a technical person to be able to use this app	2.00	3.00	1.34
5	found the various functions in this app were well integrated	4.64	3.64	0.50
6	I thought there was too much inconsistency in this app	1.45	3.55	0.69
7	I would imagine that most people would learn to use this app very quickly	4.64	3.64	0.50
8	I found the system very cumbersome to use	1.91	3.09	1.45
9	I felt very confident using the app	4.73	3.73	0.47
10	I needed to learn a lot of things before I could get going with this app	1.73	3.27	1.10
	Total (Sum*2.5)		85.20	17.8

5.1 The Process that Made It Possible: Milling

The process selected to realize the prototypes was milling, designed to recreate the shape through cuts using a rotating tool that moves in the different axes (x, y, and z). This process also allows the exploration through the materials that can be shaped, a HD polyurethane foam was proposed to "play" with the different densities (120, 450 and 600) and have feedback about the touch-sensitive responses.

The 3d files, independently if they there are from a 2d or a 3d scene, one by one, they need to be open in a parametric software like Fusion 360 from Autodesk and through a Computer-Aided Manufacturing feature (CAM) as in Figure 5 (a), and there a process can be selected to create the prototype as in Fig. 5 (d). After selecting the corresponding process, the toolpaths trajectories have been created in order to have two steps:

1. **Removing material** - to achieve this was necessary to mill with a rough tool of 5 mm diameter as in Figure 5 (b).
2. **Finishing** - for increase the quality finishing surface was necessary to mill with a 2 mm diameter tool as in Figure 5 (c).

This feature permits to visualize the paths while the milling machine is cutting. In the following Figure 5 can be appreciated the whole process.

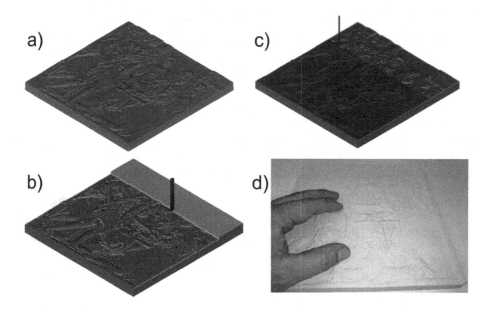

Fig. 5. 2D Scene milling process

At the end, thanks to the "soft" material used and the 2 mm tool used in the second round, was discovered that for the plates which represent the 2d scenes or the paintings was not necessary to apply the 5 mm removing material step, the machine and tool were working together in a efficient way that permit to only do the second shaping process keeping the surface quality; what in terms of numbers reduced the manufacturing time.

The manufacturing time played an important roll while the replication process was being selected, and according to the two main prototype configuration, and the material selected; the times considered were the following:

- **For 2d scenes:** around 3.5 hrs - just second manufacturing step represented in the Figure 5 (c).
- **For 3d scenes:** around 5.5 hrs

Inside the software was needed to be defined few parameters to mill the material:

- **Procedure**: parallel or additive.
    - **For the 2d scenes:** The proposal is to use a parallel procedure.
    - **For the 3d scenes:** A combination between additive and parallel procedures was needed, to take care about the material that needs to be removed and the tool access to the low levels.
    In the Figure 5 (d). can be appreciated the different procedures proposed for the 3d scenes and their respective preview.
- **Tool**: ball between 2 mm or 5 mm diameter.

- **Speed machine:** 10000 rpm for the densities used.
- **Step-over:** the half measure of the tool used.

5.2   But, Why Milling?

The milling process allow high surface quality unlike many other processes that are more rigid, like 3d printing, which in that case the material selection needed to remain in the commercial filaments like PLA, ABS, TPU, among others which not make the researched effect when this material is been touched, that also depends in which kind of printer is being used (If is a desktop 3d printer or a huge surfaces 3d printer); or the powder 3d printer that gives a good surface quality, but the relationship between benefit - cost - time invested is not optimal.

6   Test with Vision Impairment User

This is a work in progress, we are enrolling some users which are part of the Blind National Institute Lecco Campus. The idea is related to mill different physical and scaled shapes of the main entrance painting in order to investigate some parameters related to the extrusion size, surface quality, cutting strategies, etc. Results will be reported in a few weeks.

7   Conclusions

This paper presents a virtual tour application and allows visitors with mobility limitations to be virtually accompanied to the Benedictine abbey of San Pietro al Monte along the ancient access route that can only be reached on foot with trekking equipment. Such application has been developed with Unity3D. The interactive application has different virtual scenes with photos, 360° videos, an external digital twin of the abbey and some interesting internal digital twins of the most important monuments inside the abbey.

Acknowledgment. The authors would like to express their sincere gratitude to Monica Putzu, Corrado Albini, and Sarah Dominique Orlandi for their important contribution to the content and pictures of the Virtual Tour application.

References

1. Amici di San Pietro Homepage. https://www.amicidisanpietro.it/visit-to-san-pietro-al-monte/. Accessed 20 Nov 21
2. Luce Nascosta Homepage. https://www.lucenascosta.it/associazione/il-progetto/. Accessed 20 Nov 21
3. Kenderdine, S.: Pure land: Inhabiting the mogao caves at dunhuang. Curator Museum J. **56**(2), 199–218 (2013)
4. Kim, E., Kim, J., Kim, K., Hong, S., Lee, J., Park, N.-Y. et al.: Wearable AR platform for K-culture time machine. In: International Conference on Distributed Ambient and Pervasive Interactions, pp. 358–370 (2017)

5. Park, H., Kim, J., Bang S., Woo, W.: The effect of applying film-induced tourism to virtual reality tours of cultural heritage sites. In: 2018 3rd Digital Heritage International Congress (DigitalHERITAGE) held jointly with 2018 24th International Conference on Virtual Systems and Multimedia (VSMM 2018), pp. 1–4 (2018). https://doi.org/10.1109/DigitalHeritage.2018.8810089
6. Choi, Y.-M., Choi, H.-S., Choi, Y.-S.: Effects tourism storytelling on tourists attitude: Mt. Hanla on Jeju island. J. Korea Contents Assoc. **11**(12), 442–454 (2011)
7. Park, H., Woo, W.: Metadata design for AR spacetelling experience using movie clips. In: 2017 IEEE Inter- national Conference on Consumer Electronics (ICCE), pp. 388–391. IEEE (2017)
8. Park, H., et al.: K-culture time machine: a mobile AR experience platform for Korean cultural heritage sites. In: Yamamoto, Sakae, Mori, Hirohiko (eds.) HIMI 2018. LNCS, vol. 10905, pp. 167–180. Springer, Cham (2018). https://doi.org/10.1007/978-3-319-92046-7_15
9. Unity Technologies. https://unity.com/products/unity-platform. Accessed 30 Nov 21
10. Aspoc coleage. https://unity.com/products/unity-platform. Accessed 30 Nov 21
11. Bangor, A., Kortum, P., Miller, J.: Determining what individual SUS scores mean: adding an adjectiverating scale. J. Usability Stud. **4**(3), 114–123 (2009)

Fruition of Invisible Archaeological Knowledge Through Digital Technologies

Maria Laura Nappi$^{(\boxtimes)}$ ⓘ, Camelia Chivăran ⓘ, Sonia Capece ⓘ, and Mario Buono ⓘ

Department of Engineering, University of Campania "Luigi Vanvitelli", Aversa, CE, Italy
{marialaura.nappi,camelia.chivaran,sonia.capece,
mario.buono}@unicampania.it

Abstract. Digital technologies applied to archaeology have enabled the development of increasingly innovative methods in the phases of documentation, cataloguing, study and diagnosis of contexts and artefacts, leading to new possibilities of sharing "invisible" archaeological knowledge.

Although digital technologies have gained a prominent position in the methods of archaeological research, management, protection and valorization of the archaeological heritage, their potential in communicating, enjoying and using archaeological knowledge is not fully exploited. Dissemination to the public usually takes place after the interpretation and publication of data, and the digital access to archaeological contexts is often left to virtual reconstruction, while information on the processes and activities that characterize the research phases is lost.

The paper proposes an integrated approach to the dissemination of archaeological research to the audience through narrative strategies. Making archaeological excavation activities accessible implies a new mode of communication aimed to share the research process at the basis of stratigraphic investigations, archaeological methodologies, and analytical techniques. This might contribute to a greater involvement of the public in the process of knowledge construction and sharing.

Keywords: Archaeology · Digital heritage · Narration · Invisible knowledge

1 Introduction

Recently, the development and application of digital technologies have changed the way knowledge is produced and disseminated in archaeology. However, there is a clear separation between engaging, technology-mediated experiences and the actual transfer of scientific knowledge to the public. Only rarely are technologies used as mediating tools able to transform complex data and processes into accessible narrative products for users.

Museums have experimented with ways of using archaeological knowledge through new digital tools and multimedia forms that engage visitors in new cognitive experiences [1]. This process has not involved as effectively the open-air site, such as musealized archaeological sites, archaeological parks, and areas under excavation, which rely on few tools and a linear narrative to communicate archaeological research to the public.

R. Furferi et al. (Eds.): Florence Heri-Tech 2022, CCIS 1645, pp. 367–379, 2022.
https://doi.org/10.1007/978-3-031-20302-2_27

The development of theoretical reflections in archaeology and new participatory practices of Public Archaeology [2] in the field of communication, has opened the way for new forms of interaction between archaeologists and the non-specialist audience, changing the approach to archaeological excavation and research.

Public participation in archaeology transforms the perspective of archaeological communication [3] and implies the definition of new strategies of visitor involvement, made possible through the opportunities offered by digitization and by the new technologies for interactive and immersive use.

In this direction, the contribution explores current strategies for disseminating archaeological knowledge to the public and proposes an integrated approach combining methods and tools of archaeological research, models of interpretation and digital visualisation of Cultural Heritage, and multilinear narrative strategies through the use of advanced technologies.

2 Digital Technologies for Documenting and Sharing the Archaeological Record

Digital technologies applied to archaeology have enabled the development of increasingly innovative methods in the processes of documentation, cataloguing, study and diagnosis of artefacts, leading to new possibilities for sharing archaeological knowledge.

The documentation of archaeological excavations sees the increasing use of three-dimensional acquisition technologies (laser scanners, 3D scanners, 3D modelling techniques and digital photogrammetry, etc.) that allow the reconstruction of the archaeological context and the representation of its stratigraphy, for a complete visualisation of all chronological phases and their spatial location.

Increasingly precise digitised archaeological data populate GIS (Geographic Information System) and H-BIM (Heritage Building Information Modeling) projects, through which archaeological materials can be relocated within contexts, characterised with detailed information, and related to each other.

The large amount of digital data promotes a new "infrastructural" type of resource management, based on integrated systems of human resources and technologies [4] and on management strategies that go beyond the traditional concept of data storage to the sharing and "reuse" of information [5].

As research projects in this area have shown, it is possible to systematise the vast amount of information that archaeological excavation returns and create complex digitised archives that can be shared at various levels, from small groups of experts to non-specialist users.

The ARIADNE project – Advanced Research Infrastructure for Archaeological Dataset Networking in Europe [6] – envisaged the creation of an online searchable digital infrastructure to integrate knowledge contained in the various existing and non-communicating digital archives on a European level. The contents cover a time span from Palaeolithic to Industrial Archaeology and include data on sites, objects, areas, but also specific aspects such as metallurgy, palaeobotany and palaeoenvironment, geophysical and other data [7]. The user can consult these data in different ways and at different levels of detail and information.

3D models are often used by archaeologists to support conventional documentation, for the validation of results or for the identification of elements that two-dimensional, graphic and photographic documentation is unable to detect. Three-dimensional technologies allow the visualization of contexts and materials in three dimensions and in their spatial relationship, promoting a more reflexive approach to data and new interpretations [8, 9] and offering the possibility to experiment with new ways of fruition through representation.

In this direction, the Interactive Reporting System (IRS) [10] exploits the potential of web and 3D technologies for the creation of interactive digital reports of archaeological excavations. The project aims to obtain a digitised, interactive version of data, linking the three-dimensional documentation to the textual content of the archaeological reports written during the excavation. The result is a dynamic 3D spatial visualisation of the site containing the archaeological documentation and interpretations of the collected data. Within the platform, which is freely accessible online, the user can view, explore the interactive reports and consult the different interpretations of the archaeological contexts.

We can say that applying digital methods and tools to the archaeological documentation process generates a rich body of data that can be shared and made accessible at different levels of detail depending on the user (specialists, public).

However, the complexity and density of the information collected and managed by analysis and documentation tools are invisible at the end of the research process, as they contribute only minimally to the communication and dissemination phases of the results [11] in user experiences.

3   Dissemination in Archaeology: 3D Technologies and Representation

Nowadays, while a Public Archaeology at the service of the community is emerging, information technology plays a strategic role also for the communication and transmission of knowledge [5].

Technologies applied to archaeological heritage have led to the development of Virtual Archaeology, with forms of scientific visualization, simulation, and virtual representation of archaeological contexts [12] and Cyberarchaeology, through the processing of born-digital data [13]. Specifically, 3D technology is used not only for the representation and interpretation of physical reality but also for immersive visualisation of archaeological heritage [14].

With the increasing development of digital technologies for three-dimensional acquisition and restitution, the dissemination to the public has focused mainly on the 3D reconstruction of archaeological contexts and sites [15] by proposing reconstructive hypotheses to the public through virtual environments and the application of Augmented Reality (AR), Virtual Reality (VR) and Mixed Reality (MR) technologies.

Disclosure to the public usually takes place after the publication of data, the use and enjoyment is often entrusted to the simple three-dimensional visualization, while information on the processes and activities that have characterized the phases of research and interpretation are lost. In the long process of excavation, data recording, documentation, archiving and publication, there is a significant dispersion of information, and the interpretation does not consider a real critical and multivocal perspective [13].

Most virtual reconstructions in archaeology propose the presentation of a single interpretation of the site, which does not necessarily correspond to the real context. The presentation of a site or an archaeological context to the public by means of unreliable reconstructions creates a misperception of archaeology, both with regard to the archaeological research process and to the presented context.

The use of technologies for the spectacularization of projects and not for the real transfer of knowledge has highlighted some gaps in the correct use of digital dissemination in archaeology. This condition is caused by the lack of definition of guidelines and models of fruition for the transfer of knowledge in archaeology, in particular scientific knowledge.

The development of Virtual Archaeology has drawn attention to the need to advance new principles that address the requirements of emerging fields of scientific knowledge in archaeology [14]. The London Charter [16, 17] and the Seville Charter [18] responded to the urgent need for universally recognised standards, rules and principles to make virtual reconstruction a rigorous practice based on the authenticity and accuracy of simulated cultural content [12]. However, the scope of interpretation and public presentation of digital cultural and archaeological heritage has not been considered in the principles and objectives defined by the Charters.

Given the increasing development of projects for the virtual representation of archaeological contexts and sites, it is necessary to identify methods and guidelines for the dissemination of archaeology in a way that is transparent to the scientific community and accessible to the public.

One of the solutions adopted to meet this need is to combine 3D models with information on the contexts and related knowledge produced by archaeological investigations, intended both for the scientific community, and for the non-specialist public in a mediated form.

The European project INCEPTION - Inclusive Cultural Heritage in Europe through 3D semantic modelling [19], promotes accessibility of Europe's cultural heritage through: "enriched" 3D models; 3D digital reconstructions in an open standard format for Heritage Building Information Model (HBIM) which can be easily accessed and reused by researchers, experts and professionals; semantic integration of narratives through virtual and augmented reality to foster accurate perception and in-depth understanding for specialists and non-specialist users; applications that allow users to enrich the models by including their impressions.

For the Gabii Project's digital volumes, three-dimensional data obtained through Structure from Motion (SfM) techniques, the acquisition and digitisation of stratigraphic sequences, were combined with graphic and computerised data for the design of advanced graphic interfaces. Highly realistic 3D models and reconstructions of structures are associated with information elements through pop-ups, in an environment similar to an interactive game. The integration of data with the interpretations of archaeologists creates a customisable and adaptive experience with reflexive possibilities for the user [20].

Although technologies and tools such as multi-level virtual environments, haptic devices, augmented visualisations and immersive displays are used to amplify the user experience, technology alone can only provide partial interpretation [21]. New theoretical paradigms in heritage and archaeology have underlined the importance of multivocality and multiple perspectives, including those of the public [22]. There is a need to overcome linearity in the presentation of digital heritage and allow for multiplicity of interpretation, through multilinear adaptive narratives that engage users in understanding sites and artefacts.

4 The Narrative Dimension of Interpretation and Digital Visualization in Archaeology

The ICOMOS Charter for the Interpretation and Presentation of Cultural Heritage Sites defines the concept of Interpretation as the set of activities aimed at understanding the nature of an archaeological site, including research activities, as opposed to Presentation, which is "the carefully planned communication of interpretive content through the arrangement of interpretive information, physical access, and interpretative infrastructure at a cultural heritage site" [23].

A model that is still widespread today is the one defined by Grima [24] as the "ivory tower model", within which archaeologists, as "insiders", have privileged access to archaeological knowledge. This widens the gap between scientific knowledge and the public, which is excluded both in terms of physical access to the archaeological evidence subject of research, and in terms of access to knowledge. The alternative identified by the scholar is the "multiple perspective model" which acknowledges various perspectives, attitudes and needs according to different audiences. Within it, the whole public - thus not only archaeologists - has access to archaeological evidence and knowledge. In this model the involvement of the public promoted by Public Archaeology is fully developed (Fig. 1) [25].

In the field of digital visualisation of archaeological sites and contexts, the separation between the phases of research and public dissemination is even more evident, in the absence of specific methods and objectives for the interpretation of digital heritage.

Specifically, among the limitations deterring the process of creating a comprehensive method of interpretation for digital heritage by the public identified by Rahaman and Tan [26] is the "linear process of content development". On a first level, professionals (archaeologists, historians, etc.) examine and verify the available data to formulate the interpretation for the public. This receives information only at the second level, where there is no room for direct experience but only passive reception of information.

In fact, linear narrative forms of transmitting archaeological knowledge, linked to traditional media, are often used in projects of digital visualisation of archaeological contexts. Such narrative forms envisage a passive role of the user [27] and do not fully exploit the advantages of emerging digital technologies in terms of multisensory interaction and immersiveness.

According to Rahaman and Tan [26], the Interpretative process should consider three aspects, namely Embodiment, Cultural Learning, Presentation/Communication (Fig. 2).

The interconnection of these three aspects is useful to define the objectives for effective and engaging digital heritage interpretation: 1. Satisfaction: users should be fulfilled, and the interpretative process should aim to improve their enjoyment of the

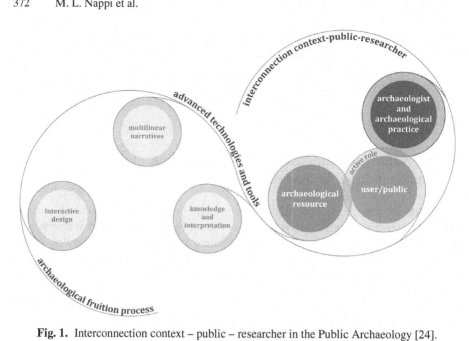

Fig. 1. Interconnection context – public – researcher in the Public Archaeology [24].

place and visit; 2. Provocation/Empathy: the process should upsurge their awareness of heritage; 3. Learning: the process should aim to impart knowledge to users; 4. Multiple perspectives of the past: the interpretative process should present the past from multiple perspectives [28].

In recent years new theoretical paradigms in archaeology have focused on aspects such as reflexivity, multivocality [29] and agency, changing the approach to archaeological documentation, the way data are recorded and transmitted to the expert community and to the public, with significant impacts also on archaeological communication.

The application of such theoretical approaches to the complex system of fruition of the archaeological heritage presupposes the adoption of new forms of narrative, multilinear and emergent nodal narratives, within which the user is an active participant in the process of producing and transferring knowledge [30]. "The power of multilinear narratives […] lies with the ability to facilitate multivocal explorations via multiple paths and to provide a platform by which the audience is afforded meaningful agency. Here the structure is able to facilitate forms that can tell a number of different stories about the past in a way that provides a powerful new dynamic between creator, media form, message and audience" [30].

Technologies enable the development of dynamic and polysemic content by encouraging the multiplicity of heritage interpretation and the active participation of the user in the creation, development, and dissemination of knowledge [26] through the narrative process (Fig. 3).

This process is defined by Ripanti and Osti [31] as multiverse, within which each "universe" has its own narrative structure, influenced more or less by the interaction between archaeologist and audience, with infinite possibilities of development.

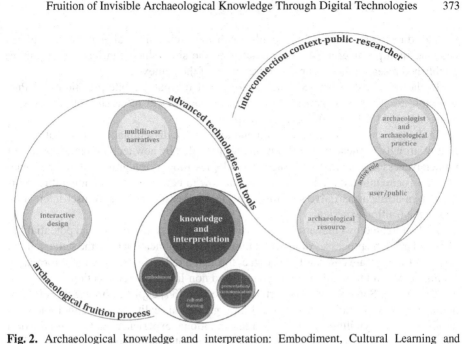

Fig. 2. Archaeological knowledge and interpretation: Embodiment, Cultural Learning and Presentation/Communication [26].

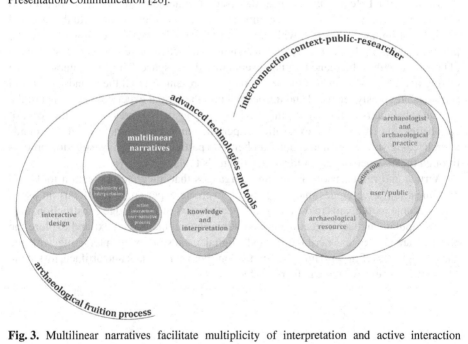

Fig. 3. Multilinear narratives facilitate multiplicity of interpretation and active interaction between users and the narrative process.

The direct interaction of the public with the archaeological material stimulates new and multiple interpretative approaches of the site, which can lead to rethinking established research themes and interpretations of the context.

In the relationship between archaeology and the public, Interpretation and Presentation are not two separate moments of archaeological research, but two closely interconnected [32] and often converging phases.

In the processes of communication and knowledge dissemination, this relationship is now strongly influenced by the advantages provided by new technologies in terms of immersiveness and interactivity. Such technologies allow storytelling within the archaeological context, and digital information can flow in new and ever-changing directions through multilinear narrative structures [30] that increase the levels of user interaction within the fruition experience [33].

As highlighted by Gunnarsson [33], within the process of creation and potential life of digital data, the processes of interpretation and communication have the same point of origin. Also, they are constantly in contact through a reflexive exchange of information leading to new interpretations in a dynamic and non-linear interconnection.

The project Sandby borg - A Virtual Connection [34] explored how archaeological heritage communication can be velated through virtual reality (VR) technologies and multisensory storytelling strategies to create emotional experiences in the virtual world and convey knowledge about the archaeological site of Sandby borg, in Sweden [35].

In the Virtual Reality experience, the user can interact with the environment and objects in different ways. Sound accompanies users in exploring the virtual space and is used to stimulate interaction with objects or to draw the user's attention to a specific point. In addition, the acoustic elements - music, effects, and recorded tracks - have a 3D position within the scene to guide users through the space. They can interact with a dual temporal register: that of the archaeologists present through the soundscape (field activities previously recorded and introduced into the virtual experience) and that of the ancient inhabitants of the site during the Iron Age, visually represented in the form of silhouettes. Specifically, the excavation experience immerses users through the sounds of archaeologists at work and enables audience to participate in the investigation process through the first-person use of the archaeologist's tools.

Virtual and multisensory forms and languages that integrate interaction tools and non-linear narrative modes make it possible to create experiences that focus on users. They become participants to the archaeological process of knowledge construction, they can manipulate archaeological materials within the simulated context and explore the physical archaeological heritage through digital means, actively interacting with the narrative process (Fig. 4). Thus, the connections between context and artifacts lost at the moment of the excavation can be recreated.

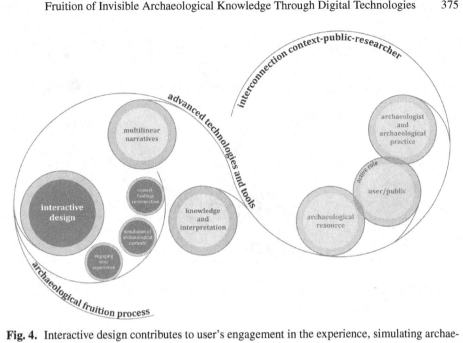

Fig. 4. Interactive design contributes to user's engagement in the experience, simulating archaeological contexts and aiming to reconnect context and findings.

5   New Approach for the Fruition of Archaeological Knowledge Through Technology

On the one hand, the potential of technologies, on the other hand, multilinear interactive storytelling strategies, represent the methodological basis for defining a new approach (Fig. 5) in the fruition of "invisible" archaeological knowledge that foresees an active role of the public in the interpretative process of archaeology [33, 36] and the definition of new models of user-archaeological context and user-artifacts fruition.

The aim is to make accessible the extraordinary complexity of Archaeology, normally not completely visible, if not totally hidden, to the public, which instead can become the protagonist of the digital story: to make accessible not only the conclusions of the research path, or the reconstructions, but also the stages of the process of knowledge acquisition itself [11]. It is a question of connecting the user with the process that is at the basis of stratigraphic archaeological research, the methodologies, and techniques of analysis in order to involve him more closely.

3D reconstruction and virtual simulation, as non-linear data visualisation systems, can be considered reflexive tools, both for the interpretation of archaeological documentation [37] and for the design of interactive user experiences.

In order to apply an approach aimed at user involvement with the interpretative process of archaeology, it is essential to define documentation methods that take into account the phases of use and dissemination to facilitate knowledge sharing.

The archaeological documentation produced for the archaeological site of Çatalhöyük exemplifies the methodological breakthrough that Digital Archaeology offers to produce, digitise, and communicate archaeological knowledge. The multivocal [29] and

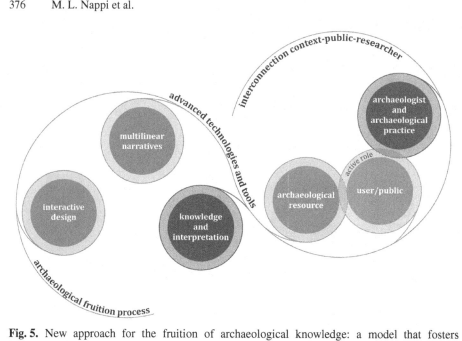

Fig. 5. New approach for the fruition of archaeological knowledge: a model that fosters interconnection between context-public-researcher through advanced technologies and tools.

interpretative approach "at the trowel's edge" and methods of "documenting the documentation process" such as the use of video cameras and multimedia tools enhance a reflexive and fluid methodology. Moreover, it promotes an "open" access to field research and to the archaeological knowledge produced, through which the public interacts with the interpretative process of archaeology [38]. Research on digital archaeological methods in Çatalhöyük has helped to underline the epistemic value of visualisation in archaeology by integrating 3D modelling, digital documentation, and virtual simulation into the daily activities of archaeologists [39].

Narrative plays a central role in defining new models for the use and enjoyment of archaeological knowledge. User interaction with the narrative process allows on the one hand to foster the multiplicity of interpretation. On the other hand, it promotes user engagement in the creation of digital contents, enabling the transmission of information and involving him/her in experiences that simulate archaeological contexts.

Making archaeological research activities accessible presupposes a new mode of communication, through a mediation of the technical language of archaeology for the public, which uses storytelling to make the complex process of excavation and related research activities easily accessible. "Artifacts and sites, as pieces of tangible cultural heritage, are gateways to a number of intangible, yet critically connected practices: the telling of a story, the recitation of a prayer, the research process the history of the exhibition, the relation to other objects, and so on" [38].

Recreating the connections between contexts and artifacts is possible through a valid use of technologies, as privileged tools for transferring the great and invisible heritage of knowledge inherent in the processes of documentation and analysis, making it an integral part of the users' fruition process [11].

6 Conclusion

The use of technology in the production and digitisation of archaeological knowledge has generated new possibilities for sharing data and processes with the public.

The application of three-dimensional acquisition and restitution technologies opens the way to new modes of interaction between archaeology and the public through narrative experiences.

The three-dimensional and immersive visualisation of archaeological contexts is a valuable cognitive tool and it can be used in the representation of the archaeological interpretation process to the public.

In order to narrate an archaeological context and the process of construction of interpretations in an engaging way, it is necessary to re-appropriate the specificities of the methodology and reaffirm the value of analytical research not only as a tool for the acquisition of knowledge but as an integral part of the content to be included in any communication project concerning archaeology [11].

The contribution has highlighted some aspects of fruition in archaeology, related to the interpretation of archaeological contexts and the engagement of users within narrative experiences mediated by digital technologies.

The user becomes a participant in the process of knowledge formation through inter-activity. Interactivity promotes multiplicity in visualizing the cultural heritage of the past. The centrality of the user experience requires a theoretical-methodological reflection, the definition of new models of use in the relationship between archaeology and the public, in physical and virtual spaces, the development of application projects and prototypes for the validation of methods [26].

The future of Digital Archaeology lies in the "interactive kinaesthetic process: enactive embodiments of data, models, users, human avatars" [13] and virtual performance represents a new digital framework within which archaeological interpretation can be generated and transmitted.

References

1. Greco, C.: La biografia degli oggetti. Rivoluzione digitale e Umanesimo. In: Ciccopiedi, C. (ed.) Archeologia Invisibile, Catalogo della Mostra. Franco Cosimo Panini, Piazzola sul Brenta (2019)
2. Volpe, G.: Archeologia pubblica. Metodi, tecniche, esperienze. Carocci, Milano (2020)
3. Forte, M.: Comunicazione archeologia. In: Manacorda, R., Francovich, D., Francovich R. (eds.) Dizionario di archeologia. Temi, concetti e metodi, pp. 75–80. Editori Laterza, Bari (2000)
4. Benardou, A., Champion, E., Dallas, C., Hughes, L. (eds.): Cultural Heritage Infrastructures in Digital Humanities. Routledge, London-New York (2018)
5. Moscati, P.: Informatica archeologica e archeologia digitale. Le risposte dalla rete. Archeologia e Calcolatori **30**, 21–38 (2019)
6. ARIADNE. https://ariadne-infrastructure.eu/. Accessed 09 Jan 2022

7. Nicolucci, F.: Un'infrastruttura di ricerca per l'archeologia: il progetto Ariadne. Archeologia e Calcolatori Suppl. **7**, 41–44 (2015)

8. Forte, M.: 3D archaeology: new perspectives and challenges— the example of Çatalhöyük. J. East. Mediterr. Archaeol. Herit. Stud. **1**, 1–29 (2014)

9. Dell'Unto, N.: Using 3D GIS platforms to analyse and interpret the past. In: Forte, M., Campana, S. (eds.) Digital Methods and Remote Sensing in Archaeology. QMHSS, pp. 305–322. Springer, Cham (2016). https://doi.org/10.1007/978-3-319-40658-9_14

10. Derudas, P., Dell'Unto, N. Callieri, M., Apel, J: Sharing archaeological knowledge: the interactive reporting system. J. Field Archaeol. **46**(5), 303–315 (2021). https://doi.org/10.1080/00934690.2021.1911132

11. De Felice, G.: Una macchina del tempo per l'archeologia. Metodologie e tecnologie per la ricerca e la fruizione virtuale del sito di Faragola. Edipuglia, Bari (2012)

12. Gabellone, F.: Archeologia Virtuale. Teoria, tecniche e casi di studio. Edizioni Grifo, Lecce (2019)

13. Forte, M.: Virtual reality, cyberarchaeology, teleimmersive archaeology. In: Remondino, F., Campana, S. (eds.) 3D Recording and Modelling in Archaeology and Cultural Heritage: Theory and best practices, pp. 113–127. Archaeopress, Oxford (2014)

14. López-Menchero Bendicho, V.M., Flores Gutiérrez, M., Vincent, M.L., Grande León, A.: Digital heritage and virtual archaeology: an approach through the framework of international recommendations. In: Ioannides, M., Magnenat-Thalmann, N., Papagiannakis, G. (eds.) Mixed Reality and Gamification for Cultural Heritage, pp. 3–26. Springer, Cham (2017). https://doi.org/10.1007/978-3-319-49607-8_1

15. Ferdani, D., Demetrescu, E., Cavalieri, M., Pace, G., Lenzi, S.: 3D modelling and visualization in field archaeology. From survey to interpretation of the past using digital technologies. Groma Doc. Archaeol. **4**, 1–21 (2020)

16. London Charter for the Computer-Based Visualisation of Cultural Heritage. https://www.londoncharter.org/. Accessed 09 Jan 2022

17. Hermon, S., Niccolucci, F.: Digital authenticity and the London Charter. In: Di Giuseppantonio Di Franco, P., Galeazzi, F., Vassallo, V., (eds.) Authenticity and Cultural Heritage in the Age of 3D Digital Reproductions, pp. 37–47. McDonald Institute for Archaeological Research, Cambridge (2018)

18. Gabellone, F.: La trasparenza scientifica in archeologia virtuale. Una lettura critica al Principio N.7 della Carta di Siviglia. CASPUR CIBER Publishing SCIRES-IT, SCIentific RESearch and Information Technology, 2 (2012). https://doi.org/10.2423/i22394303v2n2p99

19. INCEPTION PROJECT. https://www.inception-project.eu/en. Accessed 09 Jan 2022

20. Opitz, R.S., Johnson, T.D.: Interpretation at the controller's edge: designing graphical user interfaces for the digital publication of the excavations at Gabii (Italy). Open Archaeol. **1**(1), 274–290 (2016). https://doi.org/10.1515/opar-2015-0017

21. Rahaman, H., Tan, B.K.: Digital heritage interpretation: learning from the realm of real-world. J. Interpret. Res. **22**(2), 53–64 (2018)

22. Hodder, I., Hutson, S.: Reading the Past: Current Approaches to Interpretation in Archaeology, 3rd edn. Cambridge University Press, Cambridge (2003)

23. The ICOMOS Charter for the Interpretation and Presentation of Cultural Heritage Sites (2008). http://icip.icomos.org/downloads/ICOMOS_Interpretation_Charter_ENG_04_10_08.pdf. Accessed 09 Jan 2022

24. Grima, R.: But isn't all archaeology 'public' archaeology? Public Archaeol. (2016). https://doi.org/10.1080/14655187.2016.1200350

25. Schadla-Hall, T.: Public archaeology. Eur. J. Archaeol. **2**(2), 147–158 (1999)

26. Rahaman, H., Tan, B.K.: Interpreting digital heritage: a conceptual model with end-users'. Int. J. Archit. Comput. **9**(1), 99–114 (2011)

27. Copplestone, T-J.: Designing and developing a playful past in video games. In: Mol, A.A.A, Ariese-Vandemeulebroucke, C.E., Boom, K.H.J., Politopoulos, A. (eds.) The Interactive Past. Archaeology, Heritage and Video Games, pp. 85–98. Sidestone Press, Leiden (2017)
28. Rahaman, H.: Digital heritage interpretation: a conceptual framework. Digit. Creat. **29**(2–3), 208–234 (2018). https://doi.org/10.1080/14626268.2018.1511602
29. Hodder, I.: Archaeological reflexivity and the "local" voice'. Anthropol. Q. **76**, 55–69 (2003)
30. Copplestone, T., Dunne, D: Digital media, creativity, narrative structure and heritage. Internet Archaeol. **44** (2017). https://intarch.ac.uk/journal/issue44/2/toc.html. Accessed 09 Jan 2022
31. Ripanti, F., Osti, G.: The multiverse of fiction: exploring interpretation through community archaeology. In: Van Helden, D., Witcher, R. (eds.) Researching the Archaeological Past Through Imagined Narratives: A Necessary Fiction, pp. 128–147. Routledge, New York (2019)
32. Grima, R.: Presenting archaeological sites to the public. In: Moshenska, G. (ed.) Key Concepts in Public Archaeology, pp. 73–92. UCL Press, London (2017)
33. Gunnarsson, F.: Archaeological Challenges, Digital Possibilities: Digital Knowledge Development and Communication in Contract Archaeology. Linnaeus University Press, Diss (2018)
34. Gunnarsson, F., Kusoffsky, M., Sellin, D.: Sandby borg X. Sandby borg – a virtual connection. Creating a relevant dialogue through cultural heritage with virtual reality. The Swedish Foundation for Humanities and Social Sciences Communication Project 2017. Sandby borgs skrifter 10. Kalmar läns museum, Kalmar (2018). https://www.sandbyborg.se/wp-content/uploads/2018/10/SBS-X.pdf. Accessed 09 Jan 2022
35. SANDBY BORG PROJECT. https://www.sandbyborg.se/en/home/. Accessed 09 Jan 2022
36. Ask, C.: Interpreting in 3D - employing 3D modeling in field archaeology from research and public communication perspectives. Master's thesis in archaeology, Lund University (2012)
37. Lercari, N.: 3D visualization and reflexive archaeology: a virtual reconstruction of Çatalhöyük history houses. Digit. Appl. Archaeol. Cult. Herit. **6**, 10–17 (2017). https://doi.org/10.1016/j.daach.2017.03.001
38. Boast, R., Biehl, P.F.: Archaeological knowledge production and dissemination in the digital age. In: Kansa, E.C., Whitcher Kansa, S., Watrall, E. (eds.) Archaeology 2.0: New Approaches to Communication and Collaboration, Cotsen Digital Archaeology, vol. 1, pp. 119–156. Cotsen Institute of Archaeology Press, Los Angeles (2011)
39. Forte, M., Dell'Unto, N., Issavi, J., Onsurez, L., Lercari, N.: 3D archaeology at Çatalhöyük. Int. J. Herit. Digit. Era **1**, 351–378 (2012). https://doi.org/10.1260/2047-4970.1.3.351
40. Forte, M., Dell'Unto, N., Jonsson, K., Lercari, N.: Interpretation process at Çatalhöyük using 3D. In: Hodder, I., Marciniak, A. (eds.) Assembling Çatalhöyük, Themes in Contemporary Archaeology, pp. 43–57. Routledge (2015)
41. Boast, R., Bravo, M., Srinivasan, R.: Return to Babel: emergent diversity, digital resources, and local knowledge. Inf. Soc. **23**(5), 395–403 (2007)

Augmentation of a Virtual Exhibition of Paintings Through Sonification

Adriano Baratè$^{(\boxtimes)}$ ⓘ, Luca A. Ludovico ⓘ, Alessia Motola,
and Giorgio Presti ⓘ

Laboratorio di Informatica Musicale (LIM), Dipartimento di Informatica "Giovanni Degli Antoni", Università Degli Studi di Milano, Via G. Celoria 18, 20133 Milan, Italy
{adriano.barate,luca.ludovico,giorgio.presti}@unimi.it,
alessia.motola@studenti.unimi.it

Abstract. In this paper, we will take into consideration a virtual exhibition of paintings and focus on one of the possibilities offered by a virtual approach: the implementation of additional features aiming at the augmentation of users' experience. Specifically, we will propose a framework to sonify paintings by introducing virtual audio sources in the pictures. The reproduction of spatialized sound during the vision of the painting is expected to induce sensory enhancement. Audio materials can be introduced either to reinforce the experience, as for the natural sounds of a landscape, or to deliver new meanings, thus aiming at *Gesamtkunstwerk*, i.e. an all-embracing art form. After presenting the state of the art about virtual exhibitions and the use of sonification in virtual reality, this paper will introduce a publicly available prototype of sound-augmented experience. The project, implemented in Unity, represents a pilot study to be further developed with a back-end area to let the user configure her/his own exhibition space, showcase selected paintings, and add sound sources in custom positions of the artworks.

Keywords: Sonification · Visual arts · Virtual reality · Unity

1 Introduction

Online exhibitions are events whose venue is cyberspace. Advantages include the possibility to address a wider audience and attract a new category of visitors, the availability over a virtually infinite time, no timetables and closing dates, the reduction of production costs due to insurance, shipping, and installation, and easier management of conservation and preservation issues for fragile or rare artworks. These aspects turned to be particularly relevant during the COVID-19 pandemic, when online events let digitally equipped museums and institutions keep their cultural activities running despite the lockdown.

Concerning online exhibitions, *virtual exhibitions* rely on augmented reality (AR) and virtual reality (VR). The adoption of such technologies enables different audience categories, including the disabled and students of all ages, to access

R. Furferi et al. (Eds.): Florence Heri-Tech 2022, CCIS 1645, pp. 380–392, 2022.
https://doi.org/10.1007/978-3-031-20302-2_28

and interact with vast numbers of objects, potentially scattered among various localities, in a more engaging and informative way. In fact, in an AR/VR context, users should be able to interact with digital content as easily and naturally as they can with real-world objects.

In this work, we propose a Web platform to build and configure a gallery of digital paintings that can be enjoyed in a VR environment. Compared to similar initiatives, the key advancement is the possibility to augment artwork experience by adding sound sources to paintings, either to recreate the soundscape of their subject or to provide a soundtrack, also with aesthetic purposes.

The technological core of the proposal is represented by Unity, a cross-platform graphical environment and development platform largely used for 2D and 3D video games and employed in non-gaming environments as well, including film making and the automotive industry.

The rest of the paper is organized as follows: Sect. 2 will present the state of the art concerning the use of VR in visual art exhibitions, Sect. 3 will provide basic concepts about sonification, Sect. 4 will describe our proposal, and, finally, Sect. 5 will draw the conclusions and introduce future directions for further developments of the Web platform.

2 Virtual Reality and the Web for Virtual Museums

The two technological pillars of our proposal are: 1. VR for the experience of content, and 2. network technologies for the delivery to the end-user. Even if, at present, these two aspects are often coupled in virtual museums, they are not necessarily intertwined, and in scientific literature they have sometimes been discussed separately.

The idea of *virtual reality* refers to a computer-generated simulation of a real environment that can be interacted with in a seemingly real or physical way by using special devices, e.g. ad-hoc helmets or gloves fitted with sensors. VR has been explored in the scientific literature from multiple points of view – from technology to ergonomics, philosophy, and anthropology – and a general discussion of such a complex theme matter would be beyond the scope of this document. In this section, we will narrow the field to virtual museums, discussing the most noticeable results that emerge from the relationship between real life and the virtual world.

A *virtual museum* is a digitized version of a traditional one. In some cases, this is implemented in the form of virtual tours, which let the visitor "walk" through the museum and watch its artifacts and artworks in a way that recalls in-person visits. An example is provided in Fig. 1, which depicts the virtual tour of Musée d'Orsay, Paris presented by *Google Arts & Culture*.[1] In other cases, a virtual museum is an online selection of the art collections preserved in the real museum, with no reference to the metaphor of walking in a physical space. Both the former and the latter interpretation of what a virtual museum

---

[1] https://artsandculture.google.com/partner/musee-dorsay-paris.

is should start from key advice enunciated in [6]: "Do not try to re-create the traditional museum experience", since the Web is a different medium with its strengths and weaknesses, and it should be exploited to enhance the virtual visitor experience. Please note that such a principle is not automatically violated by the first interpretation, as the metaphor of moving in a re-created physical space could be accompanied by forms of storytelling that enhance the visit and foster user curiosity, understanding, and engagement, and is not automatically met by the second interpretation, as a mere online catalog of artworks could easily turn into a frustrating experience.

As demonstrated by a special issue of the *Museum International* journal published in 2000 [6], the subject was already studied at an early stage of Web and VR technologies as we know them now. In 2004, Lepouras and Vassilakis analyzed the enhancement of virtual museums thanks to 3D game-derived approaches in the context of edutainment [21]. In 2006, Hirose explored the relationship between museum exhibits and specific VR technologies, such as immersive projection, image-based world generation, and real-world VR supported by wearable computers [13]. A more recent comparative study of virtual museums is reported in [4], and an up-to-date interactive map of the most important virtual museums around the world is presented in [28].

Concerning weak points, Walczak *et al.* [29] listed some critical goals in adopting VR/AR technologies to enhance traditional museums, such as the efficient creation of 3D models of artifacts, the cost-effective implementation of virtual exhibitions containing these models, and the need to provide visitors with an intuitive human-computer interface based on well-known metaphors. In 2010, Carrozzino and Bergamasco [8] tried to understand why, despite their potential, immersive VR installations were quite uncommon to find in museums. They analyzed a series of examples, remarking their strengths and weak points, and identified the major issues which – at that time – were preventing VR technology from being widespread: costs, the need for an IT specialized team, space requirements for VR kiosks, user discomfort in wearing the equipment, the sense of loneliness and isolation, and the so-called "Guggenheim effect", i.e. the appeal of the container pushing into the background the essential element, namely the content. About 10 years later, we can observe that some critical issues have been (partially) solved. For example, the costs of the equipment for both the production and the fruition of VR materials have drastically lowered, the need for dedicated space has been overcome by the use of network technologies to deliver VR content, the isolation of users within a virtual environment has been addressed by making avatars interact in real time, and so on.

Focusing on the other pillar of our proposal, namely the remote experience of cultural heritage through network technologies, in an early work Bowen *et al.* discussed the opportunities for users who access museums via an Internet connection [7].

Current network technologies do not pose problems to content delivery, even in a highly-demanding field such as AR/VR. Baratè *et al.*, starting from the domains of music-related cultural heritage [2] and e-learning [3], have recently

Fig. 1. Virtual tour of Musée d'Orsay, Paris. Image taken from Google Arts & Culture.

conducted a detailed analysis of network requirements of multimedia applications, including interactive and immersive VR. The widespread diffusion of 5G networks should solve any potential issue, bringing significant improvements in terms of larger bandwidth, more reliable service, very low latency, and higher density of devices.

Nowadays, bringing the experience of a museum visit to the Web is not a technological problem. Rather, the scientific community has focused on the change in the communication paradigm. For example, the relationship between presence and enjoyment in a virtual museum has been explored in [26]. The study reported in [17] aims to understand the factors affecting visitor communication and their influences on virtual exhibitions, broadly dividing such factors into personal, social, content, and environmental ones.

Finally, it is worth mentioning some examples that get close to our proposal to some extent. Corcoran *et al.* in [9] introduce *Inuit 3D*, an interactive exhibition in which visitors navigate through three exhibition halls and interactively examine twelve 3D models of objects from the museum's collection. The kind of experience of our proposal recalls the metaphor adopted in *Inuit 3D* and many other later initiatives. Kiourt *et al.* report the experience of *DynaMus*, a fully dynamic 3D virtual museum framework that relies on the exploitation of distributed Web resources [18]. In this proposal, content retrieved from online repositories, such as Europeana and Google, can be employed by users to create their own virtual exhibitions. Finally, Giangreco *et al.* in [11] present *VIRTUE*, a system that allows curators to easily set up virtual museum exhibitions of static and dynamic 2D and 3D artifacts. Visitors can navigate through the virtual space to enjoy the artifacts and interact with them. As a noticeable aspect, the engine in use for the VR experience is Unity, like in our proposal. With respect to the mentioned works, the main novelty of our work is the fundamental role played by sonification in the augmentation of the experience. This concept will be better explained in the next sections.

As a final remark, some scholars and experts argue that the global trend is to emphasize the visual over other media, also in VR approaches [19]. This proposal, which gives new importance to the sense of hearing in the experience of visual artworks, tries to partially re-balance such an unevenness.

3   Sonification

According to the definition provided in [20], sonification is the use of non-speech audio to convey information, namely a way to represent data as sound. Sonification techniques are commonly in use to deliver information in several real-life contexts, from the audio feedback of medical equipment [1] to accessible pedestrian signals and traffic lights [24]. Other applications rely on the sense of hearing to monitor data evolution in real time and/or convey information too complex to be represented in numerical or graphical format [12]. Finally, sonification (and musification, namely the conversion of data into organized music events) can be employed for aesthetic purposes, too [5].

In an artistic context, data visualization and sonification are not limited to simply conveying information to users. For instance, artists can use data to control specific elements of their works (e.g., musical or visual parameters), reinterpret the data, and create awareness and engagement. As explained in [27], in doing so, the artists transform abstract data into an aesthetic experience. For instance, combined use of visualization and sonification techniques aiming to expand aesthetic dimensions of artworks has been reported in [14], where the generative gestures of an artist during his creation process have been tracked in terms of body movements and physiological biosignals (respiration, heart rate, etc.) and finally translated into visualization and sonification.

The relationship between sonification and visual art can be established by the artist, thus constituting an all-embracing art form, but also created a posteriori by a curator, acting on either the physical or the virtual space where the artworks are exhibited. For example, the use of *movement sonification* as a tool for engagement with artworks and the augmentation of the aesthetic experience in galleries and museums has been discussed in [15].

Addressing the digital domain, Nadri *et al.* have recently proposed an algorithmic approach to sonify paintings so as to reflect their art style and genre [25]. This study also offers some preliminary guidelines on the sonification of visual artworks by linking music & visual arts. Another relevant and very recent initiative is *SOVIA*, an interactive system aiming to enhance Claude Monet's art experience with responsive auditory performances [10]. The idea is to take users into the painting when they interact with a digital version of its landscape by mapping mouse positions onto sounds that artistically represent the pointed objects. Sonification strategies for artwork digital images can be manifold, as reported in [22].

In the present proposal, sonification consists in adding either coherent or non-coherent audio sources to the subject of each painting contained in the virtual museum. Audio sources are positioned in suitable locations of artworks as if each scene depicted were an independent virtual environment within the more general container represented by the virtual museum. Sonification is not intended here as a transformation of data into sound, rather as a sensory augmentation in the experience of artworks.

4   Case Study

In this section we will describe the Web platform we have designed to let visitors enjoy a sound-augmented virtual painting exhibition. We will discuss the project from different points of view:

1. Section 4.1 will provide the developer's perspective, giving technical details and discussing design choices;
2. Section 4.2 will address the visitor's point of view, providing some examples of user experience;
3. finally, Sect. 4.3 will present the curator's angle, showing the key back-office features to prepare and customize digital content.

A test virtual gallery is publicly available at http://virtualmuseum.lim.di.unimi.it/.

4.1   Technical Details and Design Choices

The project was implemented in *Unity*, with C♯ and additional *Unity* engine commands for scripting. *Unity* is a cross-platform game engine that can be used to create 3D interactive environments. Originally conceived for desktop computers and video-game consoles, it is compatible since version 5 with Web browsers, too.

To make the virtual-museum project available over the Web, it was exported in Web Graphics Library (WebGL) format. WebGL is a JavaScript API originally developed by the Mozilla Foundation for rendering interactive 2D and 3D graphics within any compatible Web browser without the use of plug-ins.

In this early prototype, the architectural design of the virtual museum is fixed, concerning the floor plan, the position and height of external and internal walls, the number and location of frames containing paintings, the choice of colors and materials, and the position of lights. All these aspects have been set in the design phase within *Unity* (Fig. 2).

The list of paintings and the corresponding sound sources can be easily customized outside the *Unity* environment, thanks to an ad-hoc Comma Separated Values (CSV) document that contains a list of files to be retrieved from the project's special folders.

The strategy to realize the sonification of each picture consists in dividing the content of the frame into a 3×3 grid and allowing one point-like sound source

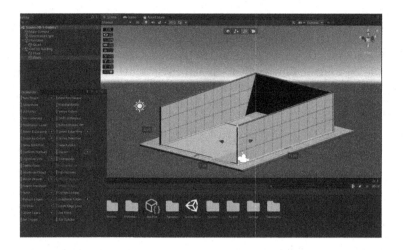

Fig. 2. A setup phase of the virtual museum in *Unity*.

per area. The grid element provides a rough position (width and height) of the sound source in the 2D environment represented by the painting, while the third dimension (depth) is managed through volume. All sounds in the grid are played simultaneously and mixed in the final audio performance, but they keep an independent spatial position within the 3D environment. The spatialized effect can be enjoyed, e.g., via binaural sound delivered by headphones. The approach based on a 3×3 grid is not particularly sophisticated, but it turned to be effective for final users and easy enough to be managed by non-expert curators. Once sound sources are positioned, their correct audio rendering within the scene is left to the 3D engine. The only precautions, from this point of view, concern the sound's range of action, which must be limited in order not to overlap the sonification of the other paintings, and the presence of architectural elements (in particular, the walls) that must prevent sound propagation across them. A complete example of painting sonification will be discussed in Sect. 4.3.

4.2   User Experience

For the user, entering the gallery is intended to be a Gestalt experience. The interaction with visual artworks is immediate and the audio effects are expected to amplify the sense of involvement. A suitable combination of sound and music can improve the immersive experience by creating a coherent soundscape for the scene depicted in the painting, or, alternatively, constitute an additional sensory channel to achieve a unique artistic goal. Concerning the latter scenario, some test users have found particularly interesting the sonification of paintings from Futurism and Surrealism, where the soundscape could hardly be a realistic one.

Visitors can experience the virtual gallery as a standard website, using mouse and keyboard controls to navigate it. Anyway, to obtain a fully immersive effect, users are invited to wear suitable equipment, i.e., a VR visor and headphones.

Fig. 3. The virtual museum.

Please note that, in our proposal, sonification is mainly applied to single artworks rather than to the virtual environment in general. Nevertheless, from a technical point of view, the two approaches can be easily combined. For example, the presence of other avatars during the virtual visit could be sonified as well, in order to overcome the sense of isolation mentioned in Sect. 2.

4.3   Customization of Painting Sonification

The activities listed in this section are typically demanded to the virtual museum's curator, who decides the collection to exhibit and how to augment artworks through sonification. Please note that the association between sound sources and picture subjects is an arbitrary operation that can also respond to aesthetic and communication goals.

Currently, the data structure to identify an art collection and assign up to a maximum of 9 sounds to each painting is very simple. A single CSV file contains as many lines as the number of paintings to exhibit, where each line starts with the file name of the digital artwork and subsequent fields list the audio files for any grid position. Empty fields denote the absence of sound in a given location.

For the sake of clarity, please consider Fig. 4, that shows the painting "La Gare Saint-Lazare" by Claude Monet. The number and type of sound sources to assign, and, more in general, the sonification strategy itself are up to the content creator. A possible solution to recreate a coherent soundscape could be: $2 \rightarrow$ distant birds, $4 \rightarrow$ steam sound, $5 \rightarrow$ train whistle, $6 \rightarrow$ station bell, $7 \rightarrow$ railroad switches, $8 \rightarrow$ faraway moving trains, $9 \rightarrow$ crowd. In a more creative approach, the left and the right channel of a stereo recording of "Gymnopédies" by Erik Satie could fit into positions 1 and 3, respectively.

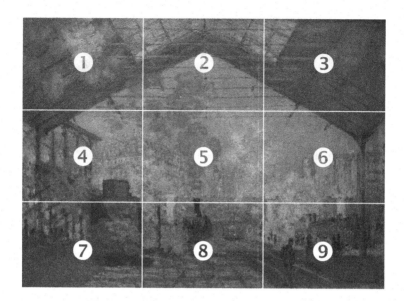

Fig. 4. The grid for the placement of sound sources in a painting.

4.4 Some Remarks

Since the release of the application is very recent, an assessment of its features with users has not been conducted so far. Together with the generalization and customization of some aspects that are currently fixed, this will be the subject of future work. However, it is possible to conduct an evaluation of the experience by referring to some methods presented in the literature.

First, we will refer to the classification of VR installations for cultural heritage proposed in [8]. Such a classification, shown in Fig. 5, is based on the evaluation of features along two axes: interaction and immersion. Concerning the former dimension, our web platform is intended to be experienced via dedicated equipment, such as a VR visor; consequently, the interaction has to be considered device-based. Since the response to the user's head movements goes in the direction of natural interaction, we decided to place the marker on the right side of the "device-based interaction" segment. Concerning the latter dimension, namely immersion, this proposal aims to be highly immersive. Such a goal has not been completely achieved so far, since several characteristics of the virtual museum cannot be customized, thus affecting the realism of the experience. In other words, the user currently feels immersed in a virtual space, but such a space is far from both the digital re-creation of a physical space and a realistic and believable synthetic environment [16]. Anyway, in our opinion the experience falls in the high-immersion category since it supports (even if it does not require) the use of VR visors. In conclusion, with respect to the classification of VR installations for cultural heritage, the proposed application scores low in the "high immersion" segment of the classification.

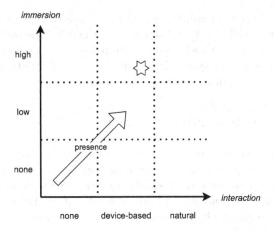

Fig. 5. The classification of VR museum installations along the interaction and immersion axes, as proposed in [8]. The star represents the coordinates of our proposal.

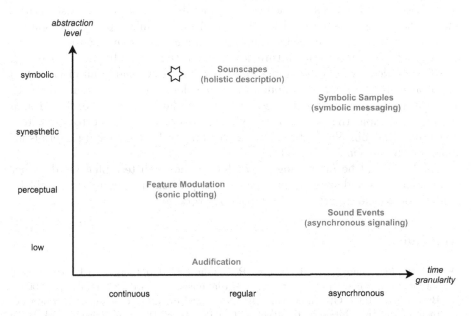

Fig. 6. The sonification space proposed in [23]. The star represents the coordinates of our proposal.

Now, let us focus on the sonification of single paintings. In the so-called *sonification space*, proposed in [23] and reported in Fig. 6 for the sake of convenience, the sonification of each artwork has a continuous time granularity, whereas the abstraction level is highly symbolic (as in the case of artistic sonification and musification, or the use of complex soundscapes).

5   Conclusions and Future Work

In this paper, we have presented an approach to augment the virtual experience of pictures through sonification. This process does not address the soundscape of the environment where the virtual exhibition takes place, but the content itself of artworks, namely the possible soundscape related to the subject of pictures. Moreover, sonification can be applied either realistically or creatively, using not only real sounds but also music and synthetic sounds.

The work proposed here can be extended in a number of ways. First, the sonification of single paintings could be improved and refined. As explained in Sect. 4, this early prototype has been realized by creating a 3 × 3 grid that supports single sound sources for each cell. A generalization both in data structures and in the *Unity* parser would let the exhibition organizer put sound sources at each pair of coordinates inside the frame. In addition, sound sources are currently point-like, whereas in a future development they could be also distributed, as for a crowded street or birds in a forest (from a theoretical point of view, this situation could be seen as a point-like source located at an infinite distance from the viewer). From the *Unity* development platform or the back-end area of the application, the layout of the virtual gallery could be customized, too, concerning the floor plan, internal walls, visitors' paths, colors and materials for architectural elements, lights, etc.

Finally, it will be interesting to conduct a thorough test phase and gather users' comments and suggestions about the improvement (possibly) brought by sonification to the experience of a virtual artwork gallery.

References

1. Ballora, M., Pennycook, B., Ivanov, P.C., Glass, L., Goldberger, A.L.: Heart rate sonification: a new approach to medical diagnosis. Leonardo **37**(1), 41–46 (2004)
2. Baratè, A., Haus, G., Ludovico, L.A.: Advanced experience of music through 5G technology. In: Florence Heri-Tech - The Future of Heritage Science and Technologies, 16–18 May 2018, Florence, Italy. IOP Conference Series: Materials Science and Engineering, vol. 364, pp. 012021.1–012021.13 (2018). https://doi.org/10.1088/1757-899X/364/1/012021
3. Baratè, A., Haus, G., Ludovico, L.A., Pagani, E., Scarabottolo, N.: 5G technology and its application to e-learning. In: Candel Torres, I., Gómez Chova, L., López Martínez, A. (eds.) EDULEARN19 Proceedings, pp. 3457–3466. IATED Academy (2019). https://doi.org/10.21125/edulearn.2019.0918
4. Barbieri, L., Bruno, F., Muzzupappa, M.: Virtual museum system evaluation through user studies. J. Cult. Herit. **26**, 101–108 (2017)

5. Bardelli, S., Ferretti, C., Ludovico, L.A., Presti, G., Rinaldi, M.: A sonification of the zCOSMOS galaxy dataset. In: Rauterberg, M. (ed.) HCII 2021. LNCS, vol. 12794, pp. 171–188. Springer, Cham (2021). https://doi.org/10.1007/978-3-030-77411-0_12

6. Bowen, J.P.: The virtual museum. Museum Int. **52**(1), 4–7 (2000)

7. Bowen, J.P., Bennett, J., Johnson, J.: Virtual visits to virtual museums. In: Museums and the Web, vol. 98 (1998)

8. Carrozzino, M., Bergamasco, M.: Beyond virtual museums: experiencing immersive virtual reality in real museums. J. Cult. Herit. **11**(4), 452–458 (2010)

9. Corcoran, F., Demaine, J., Picard, M., Dicaire, L.G., Taylor, J.: Inuit3D: an interactive virtual 3D web exhibition. In: Museums and the Web, pp. 18–20. Citeseer (2002)

10. Gayhardt, L., Ackerman, M.: SOVIA: sonification of visual interactive art. In: Proceedings of the 12th International Conference on Computational Creativity (ICCC 2021), pp. 391–394 (2021)

11. Giangreco, I., et.al.: VIRTUE: a virtual reality museum experience. In: Proceedings of the 24th International Conference on Intelligent User Interfaces: Companion, pp. 119–120 (2019)

12. Hermann, T., Hunt, A., Neuhoff, J.G.: The Sonification Handbook. Logos Verlag Berlin (2011)

13. Hirose, M.: Virtual reality technology and museum exhibit. Int. J. virtual reality **5**(2), 31–36 (2006)

14. Jeon, M., Landry, S., Ryan, J.D., Walker, J.W.: Technologies expand aesthetic dimensions: visualization and sonification of embodied penwald drawings. In: Brooks, A.L., Ayiter, E., Yazicigil, O. (eds.) ArtsIT 2014. LNICST, vol. 145, pp. 69–76. Springer, Cham (2014). https://doi.org/10.1007/978-3-319-18836-2_9

15. Kapsali, M.: Sonic bodies: sonification and the hybridization of aesthetic experience. Perform. Res. **25**(4), 45–53 (2020)

16. Kim, H., Giacomo, T.d., Egges, A., Lyard, L., Garchery, S., Magnenat-Thalmann, N.: Believable virtual environment: sensory and perceptual believability (2004). https://dspace.library.uu.nl/handle/1874/31244. Accessed 17 Dec 21

17. Kim, S.: Virtual exhibitions and communication factors. Mus. Manage. Curatorship **33**(3), 243–260 (2018)

18. Kiourt, C., Koutsoudis, A., Pavlidis, G.: DynaMus: a fully dynamic 3D virtual museum framework. J. Cult. Herit. **22**, 984–991 (2016)

19. Kiss, F., Mayer, S., Schwind, V.: Audio VR: did video kill the radio star? Interactions **27**(3), 46–51 (2020)

20. Kramer, G., Walker, B., Bargar, R., for Auditory Display, I.C.: Sonification Report: Status of the Field and Research Agenda. International Community for Auditory Display (1999)

21. Lepouras, G., Vassilakis, C.: Virtual museums for all: employing game technology for edutainment. Virtual Reality **8**(2), 96–106 (2004)

22. Lucioni, S.: Digital image sonification (2019). https://www.sarahlucioni.com/documents/1080FinalProjectReport.pdf. Accessed 12 Dec 12

23. Ludovico, L.A., Presti, G.: The sonification space: a reference system for sonification tasks. Int. J. Hum. Comput. Stud. **85**, 72–77 (2016). https://doi.org/10.1016/j.ijhcs.2015.08.008

24. Mascetti, S., Picinali, L., Gerino, A., Ahmetovic, D., Bernareggi, C.: Sonification of guidance data during road crossing for people with visual impairments or blindness. Int. J. Hum. Comput. Stud. **85**, 16–26 (2016)

25. Nadri, C., Anaya, C., Yuan, S., Jeon, M.: Preliminary guidelines on the sonification of visual artworks: linking music, sonification & visual arts. In: Proceedings of the 25th International Conference on Auditory Display (ICAD 2019). Georgia Institute of Technology (2019)

26. Sylaiou, S., Mania, K., Karoulis, A., White, M.: Exploring the relationship between presence and enjoyment in a virtual museum. Int. J. Hum. Comput. Stud. **68**(5), 243–253 (2010)

27. Ransbeeck, S.: Sonification in an artistic context. In: Cermak-Sassenrath, D. (ed.) Playful Disruption of Digital Media. GMSE, pp. 151–166. Springer, Singapore (2018). https://doi.org/10.1007/978-981-10-1891-6_10

28. Virtual Museums: Interactive map of the world's virtual museums. https://virtualmuseums.io/. Accessed 12 Dec 12

29. Walczak, K., Cellary, W., White, M.: Virtual museum exhibitions. Computer **39**(3), 93–95 (2006)

Mapping the History

An Intermedia Design for a Coastal Town in East China

Chenxi Qi(✉) ⓘ, Weijia Zhu ⓘ, Danni Zhou ⓘ, Sitong Liu ⓘ, Suyao Liu ⓘ,
and Yang Liu ⓘ

Institute of International Collaboration, China Academy of Art, Hangzhou, China
qicx@caa.edu.cn

Abstract. This article presents an intermedia design of the *East Sea Frontier* project, part of a design project commissioned by Xiangshan County for its cultural tourism and travel applications in the coastal area of Zhejiang province, east China. The concept is inspired by the coastal defense history of Changguo Wei, an ancient town in the county in the Ming and Qing dynasty. The *East Sea Frontier* project consists of four interactive installations: *Light Belt*, *Virtual Armor*, *Mapping Ancient Xiangshan County*, and an indoor intermedia exhibition, *Meta Space Tour* of Changguo Wei. Each part allows tourists to experience an aspect of the local history by applying visual and historical elements from relevant maps and paintings. The design integrated storytelling and interaction. The narration simulated the historical scene of a sea battle; the installations applied Touch Designer to realize the interaction between viewers and the design. The implementation of interactive installations and immersive experience design gives another positive solution as a tourism strategy aims to attract a broader class of visitors. Furthermore, this project delivers a cultural identity of the *East Sea Frontier* that embodies the intangible value of the area and would become a benchmark.

Keywords: Xiangshan County · East Sea Frontier · Changguowei · Mapping · Intermedia design · Interactive installation · Coastal defense · Virtual experience · Cultural tourism

1 Introduction

The intermedia design of the *East Sea Frontier* is part of a design proposal for a commission by Xiangshan County for its cultural tourism and travel applications in the coastal area of Zhejiang province, east China.[1] The concept is inspired by the coastal defense history of Changguo Wei, an ancient town in the county since the Ming dynasty.[2] It consists of four interactive installations, *Light Belt* leading from the main entrance to the

---

[1] This paper presents the academic research in this design project. The project remains as a proposal. The parts of the interaction design are realized in a laboratory circumstance.

[2] *Wei-Suo* (卫所制) is the basic unit of the military system in the Ming dynasty. It includes one guard town and several independent battalions. The soldiers operated military farms on a part-time schedule to provide their own supplies. Changguo Wei was one of the guard towns during the period.

© The Author(s), under exclusive license to Springer Nature Switzerland AG 2022
R. Furferi et al. (Eds.): Florence Heri-Tech 2022, CCIS 1645, pp. 393–403, 2022.
https://doi.org/10.1007/978-3-031-20302-2_29

central plaza, *Mapping Ancient Xiangshan County* on the wall of a building in the central plaza, *Virtual Armor* on an opera stage in the central plaza, and an indoor intermedia exhibition, *Meta Space Tour* of Changguo Wei, on the north side of the plaza. Each part allows tourists to experience an aspect of the coastal defense history of Changguo Wei. The *Light Belt* installation demonstrates how the watchtowers transmitted the signals of upcoming battles during wartime. The *Virtual Armor* allows the tourists to virtually dress up in a suit of lamellar armor in Ming style. The *Mapping Ancient Xiangshan County* is a projection of a digitalized ancient map of the county in the Ming and Qing dynasty. Finally, the intermedia exhibition shows the local history, an interactive wheel map of Changguo Wei, and an interactive installation of a virtual navy battle.

The parts of mapping projection and the intermedia exhibition revive the historical scene of the invasion of Japanese pirate ships and battles between the Ming army and the invaders nearly six centuries ago. Technically the project takes reference to many important ancient documents such as county maps, poems, paintings, and choreography from that time. Together these form a virtual visual system of the *East Sea Frontier*, which could be perceived as a specific cultural identity of Xiangshan County. The ideal location for the design project is a local theme park. *East Sea Frontier* would allow the tourists to enjoy an immersive exhibition with rich cultural content and living narration (See Fig. 1).

Fig. 1. Simulation of the *Mapping Ancient Xiangshan county* in the central plaza. Image © Institute of International Collaboration, China Academy of Art.

2 The History of Changguo Wei and Intermedia Design for Cultural Tourism

Xiangshan County was established officially in 708 ADS in the Tang dynasty, located in the middle area on the east coast of Zhejiang province, east China. As one of the most important ports of Zhejiang province at the outermost edge of the seaboard, Xiangshan County was famous for trading and as a safeguard for the coastal area. Since the early Ming Dynasty, this area was invaded annually by Japanese pirates. The Ming court decided to build sea defense to pacify the area. In Xiangshan, the system of "*Five Citadels and Nine Battalions*" (五卫九所) *Wei-Suo* was constructed and supplemented by military facilities such as inspectors, beacons, and piers. Changguo Wei was built as part of the system during this period (Zhang 2012). Overall, Changguo Wei consisted of one main citadel and four independent battalions connected by courier route.[3] (See Table

---

[3] Unless specified, the term *Changguo Wei* mentioned in the paper refers to an overall system.

1) The main citadel of Changguo Wei covered an area of approximately 1.1 km² with a garrison of over 4800 troops at maximum. There were offices, arsenals, temples, and barracks inside, walls with towers around, and training fields outside the citadel. (Tang 和He 2017) (See Fig. 2).

Table 1. The analysis of the urban plan of Changguo Wei in the Ming dynasty

Wei-Suo		Changguo Wei Citadel	Shipu Battalion	Juexi Battalion	Qiancang Battalion
Military facilities	Command centers	Dukun Office	Fensi Office	/	/
	Other military facilities	Qidao Temple, Military Office, Pharmacy, Lotus Pond, Training Fields, Barracks	Traning Fields, Martial Arts Hall, Barracks	Barracks	Traning Fields, Barracks
Civic facilities		14 temples, 1 palace, 1 hall	9 temples, 3 palaces, 1 hall, 1 pavilion	7 temples, 1 pavilion, 2 halls, 2 Palaces	2 temples

清 · 昌 国 卫 城 图

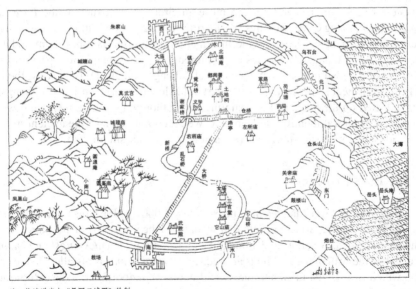

注：依清道光志《昌国卫城图》绘制

Fig. 2. *The Map of Changguo Wei Citadel* (昌国卫城图). In *Daoguang Chronicle of Xiangshan County* (清道光象山县志), Reprinted in the *Military Chronicle of Xiangshan*, 2011.

Initially, it functioned exclusively as a military fortress. Gradually the army became self-sufficient and increasingly involved in civic service due to the military farm system, like most of the garrisons did in the Ming regime (Frederick et al. 2007). To strengthen the control over the area, *Atlas of Coastal Defense* (筹海图编), an authoritative coastal defense document was edited by Hu Zongxian in 1562 in which the offshore areas, bays, tidal river-mouth, mountains, ports, watchtowers, camps, and main cities were all carefully recorded. Several paintings also depicted the history of sea battles against constant invasion. One is *Wako-Zukan* (倭寇图卷), probably produced in the early 17th century. The images, scenes, and narration in the maps and the paintings provided significant information for historians as well as our team.

Even though it was the birthplace of history, few cultural monuments remained in Changguo Wei at present and no other forms of displaying them. Due to rapid urban development during the last 40 years in the province, Changguo Wei faced a disequilibrium between economic demand and cultural inheritance, as many small towns did in China (Jian and Huang 2011). Developing tourism is a common strategy in such circumstances. The theme park, an ideal location for the project, was constructed in 2021. It is part of a more prominent tourist attraction by sea, Half Mountain, famous for its natural scenery. Changguo Wei's original location is only a few kilometers from the theme park. However, most visitors find the park lacks cultural attractions. People are no longer easily attracted by traditional sightseeing, and few come here except in summer. A new strategy is needed. Digitalization of cultural heritages might be a solution to this challenge.

There are design projects that transformed cultural heritages into artwork such as the project *Namban Byōbu the Tenshō Boys Embassy* by teamLab. Some works are more valuable for academic research or in a museum circumstance, such as the *Pure Land* projects of Dunhuang Cave Paintings (Kenderdine et al. 2014). In China, the usual digital products for tourism services provide information on transportation, accommodation, ticket sales, etc. Media technologies are commonly used for entertaining performances or virtual tours mostly on an elementary level (Zheng et al. 2021). Relatively, the East Sea Frontier project is more suitable as a part of the local cultural tourism for Xiangshan County. Based on the maps and the painting, the author and the team recreate *East Sea Frontier* as a cultural identity of Changguo Wei, a combination of the ancient military force and civic conditions. It symbolizes a new sort of tourism product.

3   The East Frontier

The whole project covers an area of approximately 3,000 m^2. Each installation occupies different spaces in the park. The *Light Belt* would lead the visitors from the main entrance to the central plaza. An enormous immersive of *Mapping Ancient Xiangshan County* is projected on the wall of the buildings around. The *Virtual Armor* is installed on the opera stage, which is modeled in an antique style. Finally, an indoor intermedia exhibition of Changguo Wei, *Meta Space Tour* of Changguo Wei is installed inside the building on the backside of the stage.

3.1 The Light Belt

According to *Sequel Research on Coastal Defense History in Zhejiang* (两浙海防类考续编) and ancient maps documented in the *Daoguang Chronicle of Xiangshan County* (道光象山县志), there were beacon towers or watchtowers all along the coast of Xiangshan in the Ming and Qing dynasty (Gong 2015). Five of these were constructed in the Changguo Wei area. The main body of the beacon tower was usually built of bricks with a granite base. It was narrower on the top and wider at the bottom. The towers were located on hills (Han 2001). Therefore, soldiers would light up fire or smoke to transmit signals when pirate ships were spotted. A communication system was rapidly put into operation.

The *Light Belt* installation simulates the beacon towers both in form and function. It is designed to be installed between the entrance and the central plaza of the theme park. It has three parts, two war drums with sound sensors, two LED light strips installed along the path from the entrance to the plaza, and several beacon lights attached to the wall of the building along the path. The LED strip is made of IP68-rated plastic and customized lightweight skeletonized aluminum and a light source with a color temperature of 3000K. The configuration of the beacon light embodies the key features of the ancient beacon tower—a frustum cone-like hollow lamp with incandescent light. The shell is made of cast copper coloring in bronze. The name of each beacon light is projected on the wall through the hollowed-out sections symbolizing the original beacon tower.

When visitors beat the war drums, the sensors capture the sound signals and trigger the light strips and the beacon. The LED strips would create a flowing light imitating the signal transmission in ancient times. The flowing light reaches the beacon and turns it on. The more the war drums are beaten, the brighter the 'fire' becomes. The concept is to recreate the battlefield atmosphere as transmitting a war message. Therefore, it not only corresponds to the historical reality but also allows the visitors to immerse themselves in the wartime scenario, thus recreating the atmosphere and spirit of Changguo Wei's coastal defense.

3.2 *Mapping Ancient Xiangshan County* **and** *Virtual Armor*

The *Light Belt* leads the visitors to the central plaza of the park. An interactive projection, the *Mapping Ancient Xiangshan County*, could be seen on the wall of a building on the south side of the plaza, showing Xiangshan County and Changguo Wei in the Qing dynasty. A virtual courier route that overlaps the map spreads out gradually when visitors approach. Alongside, multiple scenes reveal, such as fishers working with fishing nets, native people performing drama, beacon towers sending signals by lighting up a smoke, and soldiers training outside the barrack. Selected ancient poems and names of the mountains are also displayed during the process. The animated scenery provides an immersive experience for the visitors to the plaza (See Fig. 3).

The design combines two historical maps. The first one is a map of Xiangshan County documented in *The Atlas of Zhejiang* (浙江全图), whose author remains anonymous. This precious manuscript is in the collection of Département des Manuscrits, Bibliothèque Nationale de France currently. The complete set contains 88 maps of 11 counties in Zhejiang Province in the Qing Dynasty, including Xiangshan County. The

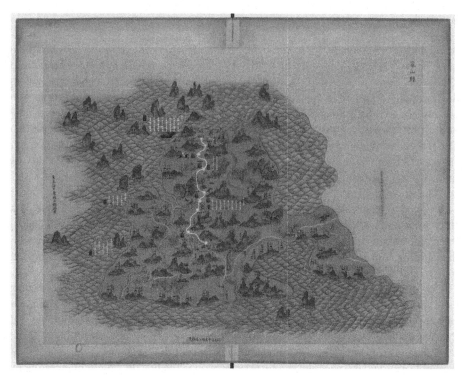

Fig. 3. The digital map of Xiangshan county in *Mapping Ancient Xiangshan County*. Image © Institute of International Collaboration, China Academy of Art.

map charts its geographical features and Changguo Wei's location along with the coastline. The other one is a roadmap from *A Brief Chronicle of Ningbo* (宁波府简要志) and reprinted in the *Military Chronicle of Xiangshan* (象山军事志). (Editorial Committee of Military Chronicle of Xiangshan 2011) (See Fig. 4) The map outlined the courier route from Xiangshan County to Changguo Wei, with each courier station inscribed. A courier route was an essential part of the ancient communication system, both for military purposes and civic services. Additionally, the design occupies specific ancient poems of Xiangshan to convey a cultural richness. Eighteen poems written by local poets in the Ming and Qing dynasty were documented in the *Chronicle of Changguo Wei* (昌国卫志), describing the landscapes and coastal defense history (Zhu et al.2018). We excerpted five of these poems and visualized the texts (See Table 2).

Table 2. Five poems excerpted from the Chronicle of Changguo Wei

Poets' names	Poem titles	Topic
Yu Zhaoyuan 俞兆元	*Mount Jin in Twilight* (金山暮望)	Landscape
Guo Zhiwen 郭志文	*Half Mount* (半爿山)	Landscape
Bao Zhijiao 鲍之交	*Bird Singing on the Mount* (鸡鸣高岭)	Landscape
Hu Jiangshu 胡姜述	*Bird Singing on the Mount* (鸡鸣高岭)	Landscape
Pan Dongya 潘东崖	*Tiding view from Mount Jiwan* (登鸡湾山观潮)	Landscape

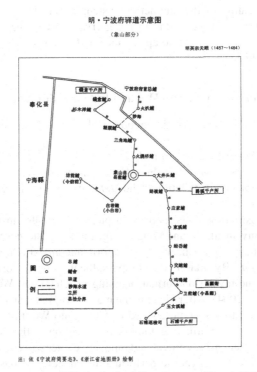

Fig. 4. *The courier route map of Ningbo* in the Ming dynasty (明·宁波府驿道示意图). In the *Daoguang Chronicle of Xiangshan County*, Qing dynasty. Reprinted in the *Military Chronicle of Xiangshan*, 2011.

We implemented the original map as the background layer and included additional visual elements, such as inhabitants, mountains, trees, poems, beacon towers, and the courier route. They were extracted, segmented into multiple layers, and added to the background layer. Subsequently, the augmented map was animated into a video. In the video, our team also created scenes, including fishers cleaning with nets, locals performing drama, smoke rising from the beacons, and soldiers training shooting arrows. Some images were redrawn after a similar style as *Wako Zukan*. The dynamic effect of the projection of *The Mapping Ancient Xiangshan County* visualized manifold information of Xiangshan and provided an aesthetics and interpretative experience.

After experiencing the digital map, the visitors could visit an opera stage across the plaza. The *Virtual Armor* is installed on the stage. It includes a display screen, a Kinect motion detect system, and backend processor. When a visitor's body movement is detected, the visitor's image is created on a screen attached to the stage wall. Rendered by Touch Designer, the human figure would appear as wearing a suit of lamellar armor.

In the Ming dynasty, lamellar armor for navy was made of iron, calabash, or leather (Yi 2021). We rendered the virtual armor with an iron texture and applied a suit pattern for higher rank officers. Therefore, it dressed the visitor as a navy officer from six centuries years ago. The virtual figures could move their limbs and interact if several visitors were detected. The application of the interaction system could ideally combine the visual effects with the historical background of the garrison in Changguo Wei. The *Virtual Armor* recreates the warrior's heroic appearance and enhances visitors' experience as participants in real history.

3.3 *Meta Space Tour* of Changguo Wei and Indoor Exhibition

The final part of *East Sea Frontier*, the indoor exhibition includes three sections:

- a chronological document exhibition
- a compass wheel carved with the urban map of Changguo Wei
- an immersive interaction installation of the *Meta Space Tour* of Changguo Wei (MST)

The document exhibition consists of eight pieces of scrolls introducing the history of Xiangshan County in the Yuan, Ming, Qing, modern, and contemporary periods. The compass wheel applies a concentric circle form and an extra translucent overlay of printed *Qimen Dunjia*.[4] By rotating the compass, the urban map corresponds to *Qimen Dunjia*, indicating the mysterious urban planning of Changguo Wei was devised for military tactics (Yoke 2004). After viewing the massive digital map of the whole county, visitors move forward to a specific context of Changguo Wei through the documents and compass (See Fig. 5). Further, as the essential section of the exhibition, the MST conveys a more comprehensive content and innovative interactive installation structure.

The MST uses Touch Designer to perform a mixed story of coastal defense. Physically it utilizes a vast screen and Kinect. Walking toward the screen, visitors can view a simulated space in which the 2D map of Xiangshan County is transformed into a 3D virtual world. The peninsula of Xiangshan County is morphed into a sphere—like a planet Xiangshan in a meta space. The sphere sits in the center of this space and rotates continuously. The space, a metaphor for the battlefield, is scattered with numerous images--mountains, villages, natives, ships, pirates, and soldiers dashing forward to

---

[4] *Qimen Dunjia* (奇门遁甲) could be interpreted as 'Strange Gates Escaping Techniques'. It was an arcade form of divination to form military tactics developed from the period of Warring states in China.

Fig. 5. Simulation of the compass wheel carved with the city map of Changguo Wei along with an extra translucent layer of printed *Qimen Dunjia* in *East Sea Frontier.* Image © Institute of International Collaboration, China Academy of Art.

the viewers endlessly. A virtual courier route in a linear form extends into the distancing space. When body motion is detected, the virtual courier route automatically stretches into deeper space and speeds up, enlarging the view.

In addition to the two maps mentioned above, the reconstitution of MST's narration employs a particular ancient picture scroll, the *Wako-Zukan.* It is a work that came to Japan from China in the early 20th and now is in the archive in the Historiography Institute, Tokyo University. The picture depicted a battle between the Ming army and Japanese pirates on the coast. In 2010, an infrared analysis of the scroll was conducted by Historiography Institute, and researchers discovered some characters beneath a painted flag on one of the ships. It indicates that the scroll was depicted as a story that possibly happened in 1558 (Makiko, Peng H. trans 2011). Compared with all the battles recorded in *Atlas of Coastal Defense,* several of these occurred in the Zhejiang province. The MST integrates the visual elements from this painting with its historical facts from the document into a symbolic battle scene in virtuality. We attempt to break the reality's timeline and geographic structure to create an imaginary space journey (See Fig. 6).

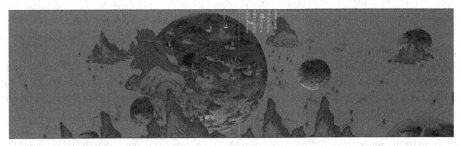

Fig. 6. The 2D visualization of *Meta Space Tour* of Changguo Wei. Image © Institute of International Collaboration, China Academy of Art.

Likewise, MST uses Kinect as an optical tracking device. Equipped with orientation sensors, an advanced 1-Megapixel depth camera, an array of 360° microphones, the tracking system is suitable for computational image process. With the reflective marker technology, the visitor's body movement is followed by infrared light sources built into each camera. A semi-enveloping 3D virtual scene is created to map the actual body movement. For example, in a valid visual field of 3 to 5 m^2, the distance between viewers and the screen would be detected precisely and transferred into Touch Designer. By analyzing the movement obtained by the tracker at different angles, the computer in the tracking system can identify and calculate the visitor's position in real-time. The movements are measured accurately at millimeter level that is essential for the smooth transformation in the visualization. After processing the data, Touch Designer broadcasts the data information to the electronic screen by the Virtual Reality Peripheral Network (VRPN) protocol via Ethernet. The numeral value of the distance maps the corresponding parameter in Touch Designer, initiating changes in the visual elements and rendering real-time images.

MST includes approximately three hundred polygonal shapes and various textures effects. The software translates the signals from the preset frequency bands into the spatial data of the corresponding graphics to initiate the movements. Graphics in MST are superimposed on the specific frequency bands, so a variable speed effect on the y-axis can be achieved. The LED screen is 6 m long and 4 m wide with a resolution of 3840 × 1088 pixels and a dot pitch of 3 mm. A black matte surface and corrugated light-absorbing masks enable the viewer to identify the screen clearly in bright environmental light. It is also furnished with an automatic brightness adjustment function that enhances a better user experience.

Inspired by ancient visual materials and historical facts, MST developed from a simple visual reconstruction to a multi-layered interactive narration. Digitalization has become a valuable tool for mapping history. The virtual tour provided an experience throughout space and time.

4 Conclusion

Altogether, the *Light Belt*, *Virtual Armor*, *Mapping Ancient Xiangshan County*, and *Meta Space Tour* of Changguo Wei consist of the whole project of the *East Sea Frontier*. Xiangshan county bears a crucial historical memory of the coastal defense of the East China Sea. Changguo Wei is the core figure in this memory. Utilizing ancient maps, paintings, poems, and other written records, the *East Sea Frontier* project created a cultural identity that embodied intangible cultural value. Implementing interactive installations and immersive experience design gives another positive solution as a tourism strategy aims to attract a broader class of visitors. The practice of the project expanded the reconstruction of a piece of history both in form and content.

Acknowledgements. Prof. Jeffrey Shaw provided great support to our research and design. The technical part of the *East Sea Frontier* was managed by Mr. Zhang Yifan and realized in Oasis Media Lab, Hangzhou, China.

References

Editorial Committee of Military Chronicle of Xiangshan: Military Chronicle of Xiangshan, pp. 705–2005 象山县军事志编纂委员会. 象山军事志, 705–2005 (2011)

Frederick, W.M., Twitchett, D.C., Fairbank, J.K. 编: The Ming Dynasty, Part 1, pp. 1368–1644. Cambridge Univ. Press, Cambridge (2007)

Gong, Y.Y.: A study of the maps in chronicles of Xiangshan. 龚缨晏. 象山旧方志上的地图研究. 浙江大学出版社, 杭州(2015)

Han, R.C.: A research on beacon towers. 韩若春.烽燧考辨. 咸阳师范学院学报., pp. 35–36 (2001)

Yoke, H.P.: Chinese Mathematical Astrology. Routledge, Milton Park (2004)

Jian, X.H., Huang, K.: An empirical analysis and forecast of the level and speed of urbanization in China. 中国特色社会主义研究.2, 60–71 (2011)

Kenderdine, S., Chan Leith, K.Y., Shaw, J.: Pure land: futures for embodied museography. J. Comput. Cult. Herit. 7, 1–15 (2014). https://doi.org/10.1145/2614567

Makiko, S.: Reconsideration of the Wako-Zukan 须田牧子, 彭浩（译）《倭寇图卷》再考. 中国国家博物馆馆刊., pp. 34–46 (2011)

Tang, S., He, Y.: Soldier city to civil city: a study of the spatial evolution of Ming dynasty coastal guard towns: Changguo Wei Cheng as an example. 唐爽, 何依. 兵城到民城:明代海防卫所城镇空间演变研究——以昌国卫城为例. 发表于 (2017)

Yi, H.Y.: A research on the armor style in the Ming dynasty: departure herald and return clearing and Wako-Zukan as examples 易弘扬.明代札甲形制考——以《出警入跸图》和《倭寇图卷》为例. 文物鉴定与鉴赏., pp. 66–68 (2021)

Zhang, W.: The establishment and evolution of Zhejiang DuSi changguo guard in the early Ming dynasty张维. 明初浙江都司昌国卫的建置及变迁. 浙江海洋学院学报(人文科学版29, 58–61 (2012)

Zheng, Z.R., Tao, L.K., Sun, L., Xu, J.: Research on the design of digital cultural tourism products in ancient villages based on augmented reality Technology.郑喆人, 陶林康,孙力,徐俊. 基于增强现实技术的传统村落文旅产品数字化设计研究. 建筑与文化., pp. 156–158 (2021). https://doi.org/10.19875/j.cnki.jzywh.2021.05.060

Zhu, G.L., et al.: Chronicle of Changguo Wei 竺桂良等.昌国卫志., 宁波(2018)

Hu, Z. (ed.): Atlas of coastal defense, vol. 1–8 胡宗宪. 筹海图编. 卷01至08.明天启四年新安胡维极重刊本 (1562). https://www.shuge.org/ebook/chou-hai-tu-bian/

Kenderdine, S., Shaw, J.: Archives in motion: motion as meaning. In: Grau, O. (eds.) Museum and Archive on the Move: Changing Cultural Institutions in the Digital Era, pp. 211–233. De Gruyter, Berlin (2017). https://doi.org/10.1515/9783110529630-014

Anon: Atlas of Zhejiang. Bibliothèque nationale de France, Département des Manuscrits. 佚名. 浙江全图https://gallica.bnf.fr/ark:/12148/btv1b52510472z. https://gallica.bnf.fr/ark:/12148/btv1b52510473d

Fan, L.: Sequel research on coastal defense history in Zhejiang, vol. 1&2 范涞. 两浙海防类考续编(1602)

teamLab: Project Namban Byōbu the Tenshō Boys Embassy. Nagasaki (2019). https://www.team-lab.com/nambanbyobu/

A Model to Integrate ICH Inventories and Open Data

Maria Teresa Artese(✉) ⓘ and Isabella Gagliardi ⓘ

IMATI - CNR (National Research Council), Milan, Italy
{teresa,isabella}@mi.imati.cnr.it

Abstract. Using the "ICH Light" metadata model created for the QueryLab portal, we sought to collect data from different archives, harvesting and storing it from a minimal set of information, with the goal of designing a discovery section to facilitate data search and retrieval.

This paper will describe the activities and problems faced while modeling the common data structure implemented aimed to design a new and extensible one, defining a format that also opens towards the Linked Open Data environment. Starting from the analysis of similar experiences applied to museum data, we studied how to apply the Europeana Data Model (EDM) classes and focused on the specific entities designed to express the intangible cultural heritage described by the CHDE model (Cultural Heritage in Digital Environments), which provides a solution using the concept of Instantiation.

Keywords: Inventory integration · Opening data · Common metadata model · ICH ontology

1 Introduction

Based on UNESCO guidelines, cultural mapping of the world's tangible, intangible and natural heritage is an important step in safeguarding human heritage. Several inventories are available online, sometimes as information systems other times just as simple lists, containing intangible assets recognized as part of the culture of a country or place.

But whatever the form, digital inventories or simple lists, these datasets need to be disseminated to make them known to as many people as possible, so the development of specific technological tools can enable stakeholders and communities to protect and preserve their heritage, promoting knowledge and disseminating it.

Thanks to dynamic websites and web services it is possible to integrate data and information collected from different archives, offering a digital place where cultures and traditions can be compared and shared. To integrate and query several archives at the same time it is necessary to share the same data model and to overcome the problem of data silos, so we studied and tested the ICH light model, created specifically for intangible heritage, based on standards, able to store information at different levels and always keeping a link to the original resource. The developed model is also useful for storing and preserving information stored on simple web pages and asset lists: the data model can host and structure the collected information, allowing a more advanced and dynamic visualization.

R. Furferi et al. (Eds.): Florence Heri-Tech 2022, CCIS 1645, pp. 404–417, 2022.
https://doi.org/10.1007/978-3-031-20302-2_30

2   Related Works

Many cultural heritage collections are on the web with the aim of making museum content available to users. As shown by the work in [10, 11], several features are appreciated by virtual visitors in their use of digital collections. Among the most appreciated ones are the availability of search and navigation tools to interact with the data and the integration of data from different sources.

There are several sites that serve as repositories for museum or tangible cultural heritage content, the best-known being Europeana [7], the European digital cultural platform. It includes the records of more than 10 million cultural and scientific artefacts, collected in a single inventory and presented in a variety of ways appealing to today's users.

For intangible heritage field, there is the UNESCO website [17] that offers interactive and innovative tools to query, navigate and visualize data related to objects included in the Intangible Cultural Heritage Lists and the Register of Good Preservation Practices.

To enhance the search for specific intangible heritage inventories and online catalogues, we used the Map of e-Inventories of ICH [15], developed by Memória Imaterial, a UNESCO-accredited non-governmental organization that in its updated version also allows for search options regarding the collected archives.

3   The QueryLab Project

QueryLab [13] is a web-based platform designed to explore multiple and different inventories all over the world, at the same time, in a transparent and simplified way.

The platform has been developed starting from the need to access different archives in an integrated way, so that the user provides a single query to search and retrieve data coming from all the inventories made available, which can be local inventories and online inventories at the same time.

3.1   Developed Tools

Different types of users have different interactions with the data, related to information needed and knowledges they have about the topics: they can be Experts, Communities, Tourists and Web Users. That's' why the platform offers different tools to search and show the data coming from the different sources, to simplify the interaction even when users aren't experts of the field, or aren't familiar with the content or language in which the terms are expressed. The tools developed so far are: Themed Routes, Semantic Query Expansion, Visual Suggestions and ICH Discovery, which are better detailed in [1, 2].

Whatever tool is chosen for the data search, the system propagate the same query to all inventories integrated so far, regardless of whether they are reached via web services or available locally.

3.2   Online Inventories

Online inventories are selected from those that offer RestApi Web Services, made available directly by inventory developers, which enables the access to their data through HTTP-based API services.

QueryLab implements this interaction for each inventory involved, making the process transparent and easy for users. The chosen online archives integrated into the platform till now are: Europeana[1], the Victoria & Albert Museum[2], the Cooper-Hewitt[3], Réunion des Musées Nationaux - Grand Palais[4], which collects the works of the most important French museums, the Auckland War Memorial Museum[5] dedicated to the history of New Zealand and the Maori people, and finally the Digital Public Library of America[6], containing materials from libraries, archives, museums and cultural institutions from all over America. The user can perform a query using different approaches and have results directly from all these big inventories, the system will translate the query applying the specific protocols.

3.3   Local Inventories and Intangible Heritage

The contents of the online inventories integrated within QueryLab are mostly related to tangible heritage and even in those cases when intangible heritage is part of the catalogued assets they are still managed as documents, instead as "living goods", memory of people and communities, evolving over time. We studied how to improve the section dedicated to intangible heritage and how to integrate this kind of assets with the inventories already reached, to give them a specific identity and a dedicated section.

The main problem has been the harvesting of intangible heritage inventories available on the web. Starting from the UNESCO site it is possible to have good hints, but unfortunately the information about the link to the inventory website, holding the heritage items found, is not available. As an effective search tool, we used the Map of e-Inventories of ICH, developed by Memória Imaterial[7]. The Map has also a tool for the search and retrieve of the catalogued inventories combining different keywords, related to inventory descriptions, and the results are points on the map reporting those inventories responding to the query applied.

We studied how to enlarge the search to the data contained in the archives themselves. The main idea is to collect data within a general index based on a data model specifically developed, allowing the navigation with the simple and attractive query tools developed within the QueryLab portal. Moreover, an index modelled considering the approach of web services could be easily combined with the portal, integrating the new inventory with the others. To define the data model, we started analyzing different ICH archives

---

[1] https://www.europeana.eu/en.

[2] https://www.vam.ac.uk/.

[3] https://www.cooperhewitt.org/.

[4] http://www.photo.rmn.fr/.

[5] https://www.aucklandmuseum.com/.

[6] https://dp.la/.

[7] https://review.memoriamedia.net/index.php/map-of-e-inventories-of-intangible-cultural-heritage.

available online, selected using the Map: some have a dedicated website, but many others are static, made up of simple lists and HTML flat pages that do not allow dynamic querying. The inventories analyzed so far are:

- ACCU Data Bank. Is the Asia Pacific Database on Intangible Cultural Heritage, that offers data on flat html pages compiled by experts from the Asia-Pacific region, including Australia, Cambodia, Fiji, Kyrgyzstan, Tajikistan, Tonga and Vanuatu (was at http://www.accu.or.jp/ich/en/arts/arts1.html, now available only thanks to WayBackMachine)
- Sahapedia (https://www.sahapedia.org/), an open online resource on the arts, cultures, and heritage of India
- the German Nationwide Inventory of Intangible Cultural Heritage (https://www.une sco.de/en/kultur/immaterielles-kulturerbe/german-inventory.html)
- IntangibleSearch, the online collection of "living good" of Lombardy Region and Alp territories, collecting oral traditions, languages, performing arts, technical knowledge, social practices, rituals and festive events (http://www.intangiblesearch.eu)

3.4 The ICH-Light Data Model

Data silos web sites are inventories in which data are strictly closed and structured with owner metadata. All the archives analyzed so far, and many others visited, includes practices and knowledges, rituals and traditions of the past to be safeguarded and defended, but they are closed withing their boundaries, cannot be integrated with others of the same type and often require specific skills and know-how to understand and access the contents.

A lot of problems have been faced while creating a common model to allow the opening and indexing of such different archives, in particular:

- different languages which make it difficult to understand and find the contents
- lack of web services to extract and access data
- different points of view and approaches in cataloguing and preservation
- different categories used for classification that do not reflect the 5 indicated by UNESCO.

We tried to focus on different challenges while creating the model, such as:

1. to implement search tools which are independent from different content languages,
2. to derive keywords useful to create guided tours,
3. to implement an interchange format or a participatory system for uploading data,
4. to study a metadata classification by analyzing the most suitable ontologies for this type of content.

After a testing phase with various data samples and through successive revisions and refinements, we developed a multilevel ICH Light data model, organized on three levels to allow different stages of content storage:

Index Level: contains the minimal set of data for the ICH asset, useful to create the basic indexing and integrated query. It provides the minimal set of information that can be expressed in the native language or in English, in detail the metadata of this level are archive of provenance, one or more domains of pertinence, place, representative image, denomination, brief description, link to the original resource and a set of keywords.

Catalog Level: is an expansion of the metadata defined by Level 1, to detail and preserve the catalogued intangible heritage, this level can be used especially by archives that currently keep their heritage as simple unsearchable lists.

Instantiation Level: is dedicated to the different instances of the catalogued ICH, a collection of data, images, audio, video, and other multimedia contents that witness the evolution and adaptions of the ICH entity over time.

The model has been tested using a subset of the data extracted from the archives described in the previous section, currently the data from German Nationwide Inventory and Sahapedia are inserted using the Index Level, while IntangibleSearch and AsiaPacific Databank are inserted using the Catalog Level. Asia Pacific Databank, in particular, was made by static html pages and is currently no longer available online, so data have been retrieved from WayBack Machine and stored to preserve their contents. The inventory created and integrated into the QueryLab Portal is named "IntangibleHeritage", it is a local archive and can be navigated using the tools already developed, together with the others reached via Web Services.

Figures 1 and 2 shows details of the three levels of the model. The Catalog Level is based on the Index Level and add new properties and classes, which are represented by the blue indications and the green boxes.

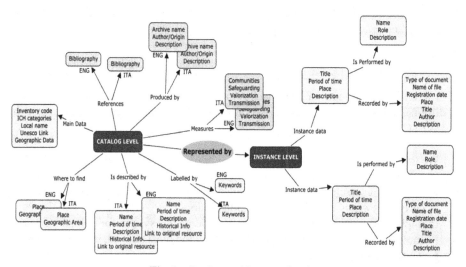

Fig. 1. Catalog and instance levels

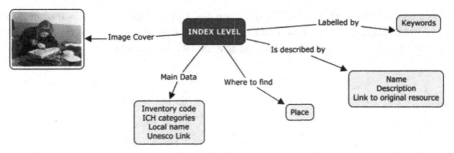

Fig. 2. Index level

4   An Ontology for ICH-Light Model

The modeling of an ontology describing the ICH-Light metadata is based on the work of Szekely et al. [16], where the activities and problems faced while mapping the Smithsonian American Art Museum in Linked Open Data format are reported. The reference model used here is the Europeana Data Model (EDM) and a new ontology (called SAAM) which extend EDM has been introduced. It is a significative example of how database-to-RDF process can be implemented for tangible heritage.

The work of Wijesundara and Sugimoto [18] and Wijesundara et al. [19], on the other hand, reports that "neither EDM nor CIDOC-CRM (the model by the International Council of Museums) has specific entities designed for expressing intangible cultural heritage". They purpose a new model, called CHDE (Cultural Heritage in Digital Environments) able to give a solution introducing *Instantiation*, they refer "an intangible cultural heritage is not an item physically collectable by memory institutions and the item-centric resource aggregation is not suitable. Instantiation acts as a bridge to aggregate those resources related to intangible cultural heritage". For this model "a traditional dance performance is an Instantiation of the corresponding intangible cultural heritage entity, performed in a specific place and time". By the CHDE model all digital resources related to a specific moment or occasion are collected into one instance, which will be transformed into a digital archive record according to the One-to-One Principle of Metadata [12], necessary to distinguish digital copies and their physical source.

The ICH Light model has been implemented having the *Instantiation* concept in mind, it provides a contextual and historical description of the ICH entity and also a set of different instances necessary to link the documentation collected during the diverse representations involving different people in different times and if represented using a timeline they can witness how the living good experiences changes and adaptations over time.

The modeling steps for the new ontology starts from the study and analysis of the available ontologies related to museums. For the ICH-Light model we referred to the Europeana Data Model (EDM) [6] and to the CHDE Model (Cultural Heritage in Digital Environments) [19] observing which classes and properties can be mapped and if a specific extension is needed. As shown by Fig. 3 a single ICH object coming from the IntangibleHeritage inventory can produce an EDM instance formed by the core classes of EDM: the class edm:EuropeanaAggregation is used to describe the EDM instance which is formed by edm:ProvidedCHO for the main description and by the class Instantiation (to be created as new), which is used to describe the digital resources of the ICH asset. The two classes are referred by edm:aggregatedCHO and edm:hasView properties.

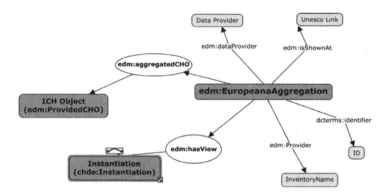

Fig. 3. Main EDM instances

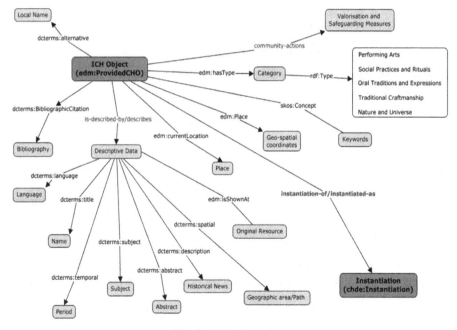

Fig. 4. ICH object class

Figure 4 and 5 shows all the classes and properties matched with the EDM model while in red there are the new properties to be defined: *is-described-by, community-actions, instantiation-of, aggregated, is performed by, has skill, etc.....*

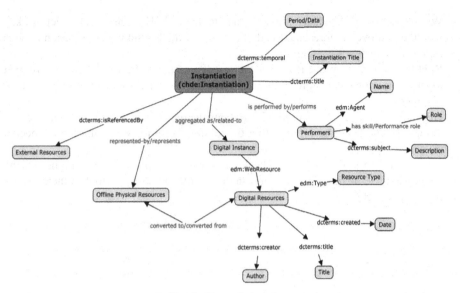

Fig. 5. Instantiation class

Instantiation class is defined as "chde:Instantiation" in CHDE Model, which suggests also to be a part (dcterms:hasPart) of the class "edm:Event".

5   ICH Discovery: Index Level Application

The ICH discovery section of QueryLab has been developed specifically as test use and application of the ICH-Light model developed. This section is dedicated to the visualization of ICH data collected by the model and is based on multi-step refinement queries based on the metadata available at the Index Level of the model [3]. The ICH assets collected from the inventories previously described can be browsed using mainly the themed routes, which are created using a tag structure built from keywords, but users can also apply subsequent refinements using free text, country keys, categories, content source or other tags. Beside the traditional layout of the results, showing a mosaic of images extracted from the query, the system purpose new and different visualization styles, based on different type of graphs, giving immediate feedback on the type of distribution of the results, focusing on the main keys: inventory source, category, country or domain.

The six different graphs made available by QueryLab are:

- Sunburst: a three-level interactive circle, where each section can be explored in detail by clicking on it.
- Force Graph: each ICH asset retrieved is linked to his domain, country or inventory, the graph is interactive so objects can be dragged and dropped to better investigate the links.

- Wind Rose: shows the distributions of the number of ICH assets with respect to a key pair, the first one is represented with the colors of the legend while the second one is represented inside the circle.
- Bubbles: similar to Wind Rose but the distributions are shown as bubbles grouped together in containers representing the country, the category or the inventory they belong to.
- Dependency Wheel: the outer circle contains the query keys which are connected by strings with a thickness representing the number of objects meeting the connected criteria.
- Sankey: similar to Dependency Wheel but drawn on the plane, it better highlights the connections of the main key, which is in the middle, with respect to the others two on the left and right.

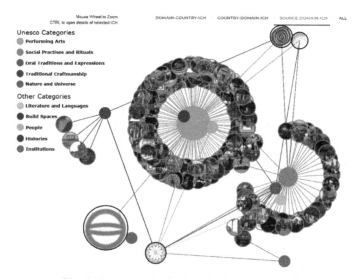

Fig. 6. Query results displayed using Force Graph

In Fig. 6 the ICH items concerning the theme "Traditional dances" are represented by Force-graph. On the left side the legend shows how each color is linked to a category/domain and this color is used also to draw the connections between domain and country or sources. ICH asset is identified using the representative image, the countries are identified by their flags while for inventory sources the available logo is used.

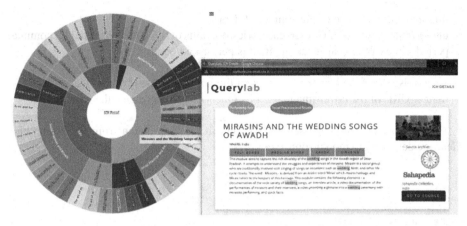

Fig. 7. Sunburst graph and ICH details

Figure 7 show the ICH items concerning the theme "Wedding" represented by Sunburst-graph. The main key is on the inner circle, followed by the domain in the middle circle and finally the ICH items in the outer circle. In this example we have the countries, categories for each country and ICH assets corresponding to the couple category/country below. On the right side the details of an item selected from the graph are shown, where the words used to perform the query are highlighted with yellow color.

5.1 Markup Systems: A Proposal

The Index Level metadata model is simple and light, so we studied how to use this model to develop a schema markup useful to improve the way search engines read and represent ICH assets pages. Schema.org is a semantic vocabulary of tags that can be added to the HTML pages created when ICH details are opened. These schema helps to provide information to search engines, such as Google, Bing, Yahoo and Yandex, to understand the content page and provide the best search results, it also improves the appearance of the page through rich snippets that are displayed when the page is retrieved by search engines.

Schema.org [14] has specified schema types, each of them having more specific sub-types and properties, but none of them is completely suitable to describe ICH contents. Considering metadata of Index Level we can imagine and purpose a new type for the schema, called "ICH Item" with the following properties:

- type: ICH Item
- identifier: containing the unique ID of the ICH assets in the QueryLab database
- sourceInventory: name of the source inventory of the item
- mainEntityOfPage: URL of the original resource in the source inventory
- sameAs: URL of the ICH item in the Unesco lists (if any)
- name: definition or title of the ICH item
- alternateName: another name or local name of the item
- location: the place where the ICH item is located/performed

- inLanguage: language of the content of data
- unescoCategory: list of Unesco categories/domains of the item, separated by commas
- period: time of the year when the item is performed/occurs
- description: short description of the ICH item
- keywords: list of the keywords or tags of the item, separated by commas
- image: URL of the cover image used by QueryLab to represents the item

We applied the purposed schema to some ICH assets taken from the Intangible-Heritage database, to model some examples:

```
<script type="application/ld+json">
{
  "@context": "https://schema.org",
  "@type": "ICH Item",
  "identifier": "ICHL-004",
  "sourceInventory": "IntangibleSearch",
  "mainEntityOfPage": "http://www.intangblesearch.eu/search/show_ich_de-
tail.php?db_name=intangible_search&lingua=inglese&idk=ICH-ACO01-
0000000645",
  "sameAs": "https://ich.unesco.org/en/RL/traditional-violin-
craftsmanship-in-cremona-00719",
  "name": "CREMONA LUTHIERY",
  "location": {
    "@type": "Place",
    "addressCountry": "Italy",
    "addressLocality": "Lombardia, Cremona (CR)"
  },
  "inLanguage": "English",
  "unescoCategory": "Traditional Craftmanship",
  "description": "The background knowledge and expertise of a tradi-
tional luthier from Cremona treasures the ability to make bowed string
instruments such as violins, …….",
  "keywords": "Luthiery, String Instruments, School, Violin/Fiddle, Mu-
sical Instruments",
  "image": "http://arm.mi.imati.cnr.it/querylab/multimedia/Intangible-
Search/TKD-64769.jpg",
}
</script>
```

[Example of the ICH Item "Cremona Liuthery", from IntangibleSearch, available at the address https://arm.mi.imati.cnr.it/querylab/ichl_detail.php?id=4].

```
<script type="application/ld+json">
{
  "@context": "https://schema.org",
  "@type": "ICH Item",
  "identifier": "ICHL-941",
  "sourceInventory": "German Nationwide Inventory of ICH",
  "mainEntityOfPage": "https://www.unesco.de/en/eisenachs-summer-gain",
  "name": "EISENACH'S SUMMER GAIN",
  "alternateName": "Eisenacher Sommergewinn",
  "location": {
    "@type": "Place",
    "addressCountry": "Germany",
    "addressLocality": "Eisenach (Thuringia)"
  },
  "inLanguage": "English",
  "unescoCategory": "Performing Arts, Social Practices and Rituals",
  "period": {
    "@type": "Schedule",
    "repeatFrequency": "a week before Laetere Sunday",
  },
  "description": "The 'Eisenacher Sommergewinn' is a spring tradition
which prepares for Laetere Sunday with a diverse festival program. Cen-
tral to it is the victory of summer over winter …….",
  "image": "http://arm.mi.imati.cnr.it/querylab/multimedia/GermanNation-
Wide/1_003_EISENACH_C_Torsten_Daut.jpg",
}
</script>
```

[Example of the ICH Item "EISENACH'S SUMMER GAIN", from German Nation-Wide Inventory, available at the address https://arm.mi.imati.cnr.it/querylab/ichl_detail.php?id=941].

6   Conclusions

The purpose of defining a specific metadata model and ontology for intangible cultural heritage is a real complex challenge, mainly due to different ways to describe data. Standards developed so far, such as EDM and CIDOC-CRM, do not cover the specific peculiarities of this type of data. Europeana's EDM format has been used by important American museums and libraries to describe tangible heritage, such as the Smithsonian and DPLA, but is possible to observe that neither EDM nor CIDOC-CRM are suitable to describe intangible entities and the relationship between digital objects and the entities they refer to, whether tangible or intangible. We started from the model presented by Wijesundara and Sugimoto in [18] to improve and update the ICH Light metadata in order to obtain a flexible and customizable structure, able to be applied to the different inventories involved so far.

The first level of the model has been used to create a new section specifically dedicated to the intangible heritage, where new ways to show query results has been experimented. The model has been mapped into the classes and properties of the recommended ontologies, EDM and CHDE, even if some of them need to be defined as new. Finally, a new markup type for schema.org has been studied and purposed.

References

1. Artese, M.T., Gagliardi, I.: Language independent searching tools for cultural heritage on the QueryLab platform. In: Euromed 2020: International Conference on Digital Heritage, Cyprus, 2–5 November 2020
2. Artese, M.T., Gagliardi, I.: A platform for safeguarding cultural memory: the QueryLab prototype. Memoriamedia Rev. **4**. Article no. 2. (2019). https://review.memoriamedia.net/index.php/querylab-prototype
3. Artese, M.T., Gagliardi, I.: ICH discovery: tools to integrate and share ICH archives with QueryLab. In: Sahapedia Conference 2021, #CultureForAll Conference on Cultural Mapping, Winner of the 1st Award in Mapping Technologies, Tools and Approaches Session (2021)
4. Beck, J., Büchner, M., Bartholmei, S., Knepper, M.: Performing entity facts. Datenbank-Spektrum **17**(1), 47–52 (2017)
5. Carboni, N., De Luca, L.: Towards a conceptual foundation for documenting tangible and intangible elements of a cultural object. Digit. Appl. Archaeol. Cult. Herit. **3**, 108–116 (2016)
6. Europeana Data Model. https://pro.europeana.eu/page/edm-documentation. Accessed 10 Jan 2022
7. Europeana Collections. https://www.europeana.eu/en/collections. Accessed 10 Jan 2022
8. Fink, E.E., Szekely, P., Knoblock, C.A.: How linked open data can help in locating stolen or looted cultural property. In: Ioannides, M., Magnenat-Thalmann, N., Fink, E., Žarnić, R., Yen, AY., Quak, E. (eds.) EuroMed 2014. LNCS, vol. 8740, pp. 228–237. Springer, Cham (2014). https://doi.org/10.1007/978-3-319-13695-0_22
9. Knoblock, C.A., et al.: Semi-automatically mapping structured sources into the semantic web. In: Simperl, E., Cimiano, P., Polleres, A., Corcho, O., Presutti, V. (eds.) ESWC 2012. LNCS, vol. 7295, pp. 375–390. Springer, Heidelberg (2012). https://doi.org/10.1007/978-3-642-30284-8_32
10. Lopatovska, I., Bierlein, I., Lember, H., Meyer, E.: Exploring requirements for online art collections. Proc. Am. Soc. Inf. Sci. Technol. **50**, 1–4 (2013). https://doi.org/10.1002/meet.14505001109
11. Lopatovska, I.: Museum website features, aesthetics, and visitors' impressions: a case study of four museums. Mus. Manag. Curators. **30**, 191–207 (2015). https://doi.org/10.1080/09647775.2015.1042511
12. Miller, S.J.: The one-to-one principle: challenges in current practice. In: International Conference on Dublin Core and Metadata Applications, pp. 150–164 (2010)
13. QueryLab. https://arm.mi.imati.cnr.it/querylab. Accessed 10 Jan 2022
14. Schema.org documentation. https://schema.org/docs/schemas.html. Accessed 10 Jan 2022
15. Sousa, F., Imaterial, I.R.: Map of e-inventories of intangible cultural heritage. Memoriamedia Rev. (2017)
16. Szekely, P., et al.: Connecting the smithsonian american art museum to the linked data cloud. In: Cimiano, P., Corcho, O., Presutti, V., Hollink, L., Rudolph, S. (eds.) ESWC 2013. LNCS, vol. 7882, pp. 593–607. Springer, Heidelberg (2013). https://doi.org/10.1007/978-3-642-38288-8_40
17. Unesco Archives. https://digital.archives.unesco.org/en/. Accessed 10 Jan 2022

18. Wijesundara, C., Sugimoto, S.: Metadata model for organizing digital archives of tangible and intangible cultural heritage, and linking cultural heritage information in digital space. LIBRES: Libr. Inf. Sci. Res. Electron. J., 58–80 (2018)
19. Wijesundara, C., Monika, W., Sugimoto, S.: A metadata model to organize cultural heritage resources in heterogeneous information environments. In: Choemprayong, S., Crestani, F., Cunningham, S. (eds.) ICADL 2017. LNCS, vol. 10647, pp. 81–94. Springer, Cham (2017). https://doi.org/10.1007/978-3-319-70232-2_7
20. Ziku, M.: Digital cultural heritage and linked data: semantically-informed conceptualisations and practices with a focus on intangible cultural heritage. LIBER Q., 1–16 (2020). https://doi.org/10.18352/lq.10315

VIEd'ARTE

A Web Publication Environment for the Digital Dissemination of the Cultural Heritage Knowledge

Andrea Ferrato[1], Antonella Gioli[1], Sonia Lazzari[1], Caterina Romagnoli[1],
Elena Scaravella[3], and Andrea Tomasi[2(✉)]

[1] Department of Civilisation and Forms of Knowledge, University of Pisa, Pisa, Italy
antonella.gioli@unipi.it, s.lazzari@live.it,
caterina.romagnoli@cfs.unipi.it
[2] Department of Information Engineering, University of Pisa, Pisa, Italy
andrea.tomasi@unipi.it
[3] Cultural Heritage Office of the Diocese of Massa Carrara Pontremoli, Massa, Italy
bbcc.elena@virgilio.it

Abstract. The fruition of the cultural heritage in the pandemic era has been stressed even more towards online and virtual environments. Usually the web site publishing process involves many competences, or the ability of the single cultural operator, which needs to become expert in many complex techniques. In the paper we present the VIEd'ARTE Project, an experience of implementation of a web publication framework supporting the work of cultural operators with tools for the data access to repositories and for the page design of the web applications. An example is shown using the VIEd'ARTE framework for the design of the virtual tour "On the trail of the Renaissance". The publication framework of VIEd'ARTE manages different types of cultural objects and many types of presentations. The front-end side features include templates and predefined layouts, supporting a presentation model for a large public. The back-end side offers access capabilities to SQL databases, in particular to BeWEB archives, which contain data of different types of cultural heritage assets. The metadata layer of the BeWeb Portal allows the integration of the various data fonts. The data access model will move in the next future to allow also no-SQL databases and OAI (Open Archives Initiative) or Linked Open Data protocols to access databases.

Keywords: Cultural heritage fruition · Virtual visit · Data integration · Integrated presentation framework · Online publication schemas

1 Introduction

Since year 2000, with the growing diffusion of digital communication technology in the Internet environment, many projects tried to achieve an effective online dissemination of knowledge about cultural heritage. The knowledge data source are usually contained in many databases, geographically distributed, owned by different proprietary entities. The objects relevant in cultural heritage are of different types (artworks and artistic objects, paintings, books and archival documents, historical buildings) and have different models of data description, according with the specific disciplinary standard applied.

The access to heterogeneous, distributed data has to face two main problems: the first at the data level, i.e. the collection of query results over the network, due to the distribution, the second one at the application level, i.e. the specification of the queries and the presentation of the results homogeneously, starting from heterogeneous data.

The main approach adopted in the early 2000s is based on Web Information Systems (WIS) [1], able to expose large amount of data in a well structured, accurate way to an ever increasing community of users. The architecture of a WIS follows the 3-tier model: the front-end or presentation level with the user interface, the functional logic level with the application software and the system processes, the back-end or data level with the data repositories and the Data Base management System (DBMS) functions. One of the main problems to be solved in order to make WIS effective is the development of a suitable model of data representation.

We are not concerned here with the problems related to the distributed system architecture, neither to the goals of performance of the network system or of database management, but only with the aims of integration of data representation: the solution given to such a problem affects the design of applications, in particular in the case of the web publication framework for cultural heritage knowledge. The data dissemination and fruition need in fact two different activities on data: the data access to the distributed data sources and the storytelling to the world of users. The two aspects are strictly related, in order to give to the user a comprehensive and consistent view of all the information pertaining a specific set of knowledge about single cultural heritage objects or about collections.

First of all we discuss in Sect. 1.1 the access to heterogeneous, distributed data, focusing on cultural heritage data and showing the different solution approach of some project to the interoperability or to the integration of data representation. The portal BeWeB, based on the approach of Ecumene Project [2], is briefly presented in Sect. 2 because it constitutes the back-end component of our web publication framework.

The web publication of cultural heritage information is presented in Sect. 1.2. When a cultural operator wishes to publish a web site with the aim of reaching a large public, he can use various tools for the publication, with various degrees of use complexity and different characteristics with respect to the phases of the publishing process: to get the data, to prepare text and images, to design the page layout, and so on. There are many Content Management Systems (CMS) proposal – the most popular being Drupal, Joomla and WordPress - with a lot of extensions for different types of presentations. Moreover there are specific products for particular types of presentations, for example for virtual exhibitions. The available frameworks differ from each other for the characteristics of data access and of metadata supported, or because they focus on the presentation of the web pages leaving to the user the research of data. The approach of the VIEd'ARTE Project offers to the operators a comprehensive framework able to give in the same environment the features of the publication tools and of the data access. The originality of the approach will be discussed in Sect. 3.

1.1   The Data Representation in Case of Heterogeneous, Distributed Data Sources

The data representation has to face the different levels of data repositories:

- The Database level, resident in the peripheral sites. At this level data are constituted by the description of specific types of cultural objects, i.e. artistic objects, like paintings, manufacts and others, archival documents, books, historical buildings and so on; each data type has been defined according to the particular disciplinary sector, either international or national: for example, ISAD (G) - General International Standard Archival Description [3] and ISAAR (CPF) - International Standard Archival Authority Records for Corporate Bodies, Persons and Families [4], or OA form for Art Objects [5] and A form for Architectural heritage [6], defined by ICCD – Istituto Centrale per il Catalogo e la Documentazione.
- The metadata level, implemented at the functional logic level in the Data Access Server. At this level should be implemented the interoperability and/or the integration of the heterogeneous, distributed data sources. The widely used Dublin Core metadata model [7] supports the interoperability of databases of the same type having different implementation details. The metadata are designed to meet the function requirements of different applications, so that Dublin Core model has been enriched by metadata models for specific cultural sectors and for the support of various activities [8]. The interoperability among metadata repositories is achieved by data access protocols such as Z39.50 [9] or by the Open Archives Initiative (OAI) [10]. The use of metadata for integrating heterogeneous data is nevertheless recognized insufficient [11], especially because it can hide semantic aspects of data sources interesting for knowledge dissemination. Hence a way to preserve at most the data semantic value should be found, as it is proposed with the definition of a semantic layer [12].
- The user presentation level. The growing interest for new approaches to cultural heritage fruition starting from the large diffusion of digital data sources enforces the need for a unified data representation and for metadata models allowing the integration of the various representations in a consistent way for the communication and the dissemination. XML [13] has become the data description language more widely adopted for metadata representation. At the presentation level web pages and structured data are all represented with XML, so XML can be seen at the various levels as the standard also for data exchange. XML can support not only interoperability, but also data integration, through mapping functions of the data and metadata representation to XML descriptions.

Many projects has faced the problem of data access in the case of heterogeneous, distributed cultural heritage data sources, with different approaches, stressing more interoperability solutions (Minerva, Aquarell, Perseus, LEAF, DELOS) rather than integration ones (Ecumene).

Minerva Europe Project (2002–2011) [14] was an effort of many public institutions in Europe to establish a network of coordinated initiatives, mainly to support the digitization and quality of web sites through best practices and guidelines, and to perform data access using interoperability tools and standards [15–17].

Ecumene Project (2001–2005) [18–20] chose a different approach, working on an integrated framework for data access and for presentation. The Ecumene approach is significant here because of its conceptual model for metadata, integrating different data sources and preserving their rich semantic (see Sect. 2.1), so we discuss it with more details in Sect. 2.

Other projects focused on specific sectors: Aquarell [21] for museums, which adopted the Z39.50 profile developed by CIMI (Consortium for Computer Interchange of Museum Information) [22], MALVINE and LEAF for documents and libraries, through the collection of authority files [23]. The Project Perseus [24] investigated the field of the so called digital libraries.

The main acquisitions of the projects in that period were the definition of protocols for interoperability based on metadata and the use of XML as the unifying description language, so that some disciplinary description standards mapped on XML, as in the case of EAD (Encoded Archival Description) [25]. Unfortunately some projects did not continue the activities after the deadline and their web sites were abandoned.

1.2   The Web Presentation Framework

The work on data representation and on data access can be seen at now as already established, as stated in the previous section. It constitutes the technological ground for the development of ever more sophisticated presentation tools.

The focus of research studies and of development moves now to the online diffusion of the cultural heritage knowledge to a large public. The audience interested in cultural heritage can access information of any kind and it can visit virtually any museum or gallery over the world. Hence the people may have different knowledge, different cultural bases and different interests towards the fruition. As a consequence, the presentation environment may use different presentation models and it may have different user interfaces according to the target public segmented in groups, having different views and privileges on data. Some basic models can be considered: geographic visiting tours, museum and exhibition visiting tours, virtual exhibitions.

The presentation environment can be structured in three layers:

- the data access layer offers to the application of knowledge dissemination the functions of data access and of mapping of data representation at the database level to the metadata used at the presentation level; as stated, XML is widely used for data description and for mapping;
- the composition layer support the development of the online presentation application; ready-made templates can help the developer and can reduce the effort of designing the pages layout;
- the user interface layer is the front-end application exposing cultural heritage knowledge to the final user with various presentation models.

Each one of the layers corresponds to a phase of the web publishing process, which is supported by many software environments. Usually the web publication software is independent from the particular knowledge content and it can have limitations on the graphical design and on the management of the page layout.

We therefore examine only some products specifically addressed to the web publication of contents related to cultural heritage information. They differ for the destination to the front-end or to the back-end features, the model of metadata supported, the characteristics of the framework for the support of the cultural operators in the work of web publishing. When using a publication framework, the operator should be careful: he should not only examine the characteristics of the framework compared with the publication needs, but he should also evaluate if there is an organization supporting the product for a long time into the future. The verification of the existence of a good staff in charge of maintenance, of technical and user assistance and the availability of satisfying documentation are mandatory to make a successful choice.

The web presentation of collections of data from various sources is the goal of Europeana [26], which includes a portal of cultural heritage objects [27]. Other initiatives focus on specific sectors, as Phaidra for archives [28].

The publication of web sites and online virtual exhibitions for museums and small cultural institution is the target of Movio [29], an open source software distributed by Italian Istituto Centrale per il Catalogo Unico - Central Institute for the Union Catalogue of Italian Libraries and Bibliographic Information (ICCU). All the information published by means of Movio tools must be contained in the inner Content Management System (CMS) of Movio and no access to external data is provided. The project appears to be not updated since a few years.

The lesson of the past experiences shows that the web presentation of a collection of data and the online virtual visits and virtual exhibitions are managed by different sets of framework, whether the cultural operators often need to have both at the same time. This is the aim of VIEd'ARTE, which composes its web publishing framework "on the top" of the BeWeB Portal.

2 The Ecumene Project and the Portal BeWeB.

The Ecumene Project [18, 19] was performed in the context of Parnaso Initiative funded by the Italian Ministry of University and Scientific Research. The aims of the project were the implementation of ICT tools addressing the fruition via Internet of knowledge on cultural heritage objects of different type. The knowledge base was extracted from many existing databases with data about artistic, architectural, bibliographic and archival assets. In particular were referenced the assets owned by entities of the Italian Catholic Church, the main cultural heritage property in Italy. Since 1996 the Italian Catholic Church invested a great effort in a long-term project of inventory and cataloguing of its cultural heritage assets. The Ecumene Project offered the technological ground and tools to the wide fruition online of the collected data. As a result of Ecumene Project it was implemented the BeWeb portal [2, 30, 31].

2.1 The Conceptual Data Model

The services offered by the Ecumene Web Information System strongly rely on the collection of a consistent view of the different objects involved in a particular search. A fundamental step is the design of the conceptual data model: this methodological phase is often referred to as the definition of the *semantic layer*, emphasizing the importance of semantic interoperability in systems that gather information from heterogeneous sources [12]. In particular, the definition of a *mediated schema* (or *global schema*, i.e. a purely logical schema for the purpose of issuing queries) is the central activity for the data integration within the web information system.

The approach of Ecumene [18, 32, 33] is the adoption of mediated schemas for the generic item representation and the introduction of metadata exploiting the semantic interconnections between the different domains. Metadata model is based on context information, entities and roles. Ecumene makes an extensive use of XML for the data description according to the main standards of sectors: the mediated schema is EAD compliant and XML support the mapping functions between the data source representation and the mediated schema, and between mediated schema and metadata [19].

2.2   The System Architecture

In Fig. 1 it is possible to recognize different system layers, containing the basic functional blocks to manage cultural heritage information.

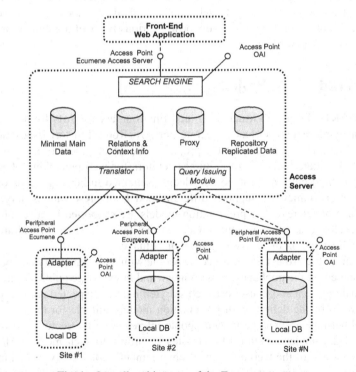

Fig. 1. Overall architecture of the Ecumene system.

The data source layer, the data access layer, and the data presentation layer give access to information with different characteristics, format, and accuracy. Queries can be issued to each functional block (indicated with a dotted line boundary) through proper endpoints, which are in charge of providing back the retrieved data/metadata. The front-end module constitutes the user interface of the web application, so that most of the usability issues have to be addressed at this level, conforming to quality design issues (see for example the quality recommendations of Minerva project [15, 34]).

2.3 The Beweb Portal

BeWeB Portal allows the web access to the catalogues of the cultural heritage assets of the italian catholic Church [31]. As today, BeWeb data repositories contain the description of 4.135.442 artistic manufacts, 7.084.780 books, 204.242 archival holdings, 66.395 architectural units. Although the user interface of BeWeb allows a lot of cross-queries on data, it should be noted that the cataloging data are often oriented to the fruition from disciplinary experts more than to the large public of people with generic interest in cultural heritage, so that it remains open the need for a web publication environment which makes a "mediation" between the content of data repositories and the web pages presented to the users.

Because of the large amount of heterogeneous data contained and thanks to characteristics of the data access server, BeWeb represents an ideal testbed for the development of an online publication framework supporting various types of dissemination tools on cultural heritage knowledge.

3   The VIEd'ARTE Project

The VIEd'ARTE Project (Virtual Integrated Environment for Arts Routes Territories Exhibitions/Esplorazioni Virtuali Integrate per Arti Rotte Territori Esposizioni) [35] started in 2020. The main goal of the project is the development of a software environment to facilitate the work of cultural operators for web publishing of integrated information about cultural heritage knowledge contained in heterogeneous databases. The publication framework supports different models of presentations, targeting different groups of interest. The presentation models are supported by a set of template layouts, developed according to the advices of the Italian Ministry of Culture on web site quality [36] and on the implementation of virtual exhibitions [37].

The team of the Project is composed by people with complementary competences in the development of the publication environment and in web page publishing, in cultural heritage management and in user oriented storytelling. The expected project results are the assessment of the definition of presentation models suitable for the dissemination of cultural heritage knowledge toward people interested in the sector, although if not skilled, and the implementation of web sites according to such models. The testbed for the assessment of the web publication environment is BeWeb. As stated in 2.3, the availability of a great amount of different data is a good data source for the dissemination. The integrated presentation environment of VIEd'ARTE supports the cultural operators in the access to data and metadata and in the composition of proper web page presentation within the same environment.

The adoption of BeWeB as the back-end data repository of VIEd'ARTE allows to use the data access model of BeWeB as the metadata layer integrating the different types of cultural heritage objects contained in the BeWeB databases. At the same level can be connected further data sources, adding the proper XML mapping functions.

3.1 The Presentation Framework

The page development is based on WordPress [38] extended with ad hoc plugins for data access and layout management. The WordPress CMS contains the pages and the authorization data for the developers. The data repositories are that of BeWeb databases, containing the inventory and cataloging data. During the phase of page composition the operator can store in CMS additional data to adapt the presentation to a wider audience, composed not only by experts, but also by people just curious about.

The published pages are the user interface of various types of applications: virtual geographic tours, virtual exhibitions and virtual museum, web versions of real exhibitions, virtual visit of historic buildings and churches. For each application it is developed a proper set of templates, including optional features for the main layouts of web pages.

The original characteristics of the front-end applications in VIEd'ARTE Project are the access functions to the BeWeB databases included in the presentation framework and the presentation schemas offered by the environment, supporting the cultural operators in the development of their own pages.

3.2 The Presentation Layout

The first presentation schema implemented by VIEd'ARTE is named "Routes" and support virtual geographic tours and physical site visits to cultural heritage assets.

The Route schema is structured in three levels, with three corresponding different page layouts:

- The Home Page includes a general description of the site content and of the presentation aims. The left side menu introduces a set of "Paths" crossing the works and the sites linked by the Route.
- The "Path" page allows a specific knowledge key of interpretation of the Route content. The different views of the presentation can be guided by the historic, artistic, technical characteristics of the asset, or they can give a particular cultural or religious reading. Additional views and further readings can be added to a Route simply inserting a new Path.
- The detail sheets are contained in the third level of the schema. The pages illustrate the data contained in the data repositories, e.g. inventory form of Art Objects or Architectural heritage (OA form or A form) in a way suitable for non-expert users, i.e. adding more information on the history of the heritage asset, of the author or of the content, or substituting the specialistic terms used by the inventory form with a description which uses the current language. The detail sheets can be cross-referenced by each Path. The third level layout can have nested pages of the same type, so that more specification levels can be added.

The work of cultural operators producing the site is supported by the developed publishing environment and by the included templates for the three layouts. A certain degree of customization is allowed to meet specific presentation needs, such as the inserting of image galleries and sliders, tagged maps and tagged images, administrative notices, bibliography sections, and others.

The "Routes" schema is described in Sect. 4 via the case study "On the trail of the Renaissance". The enrichment of the schema with the implementation of "Virtual Tours" allows to enter in a building and to visit its rooms with 360° panoramic views. In Virtual Tours the "Path" schemas may be implemented as sequential visits of the rooms in their physical order or as "Thematic Paths", in which the visit is accomplished following a specific interest. The Virtual Tour feature has been used in the case study of Archbishop's palace of Pisa [39].

4 The Case Study "On the Trail of the Renaissance"

The first step of the VIEd'ARTE Project has been the implementation of the web publication framework and its application to the development of the web site for a tour in the north of Tuscany, named Lunigiana, virtual visiting the places in which are preserved altarpieces of the Renaissance period. In Fig. 2 is shown the Home Page.

Fig. 2. HomePage of "On the trail of the Renaissance".

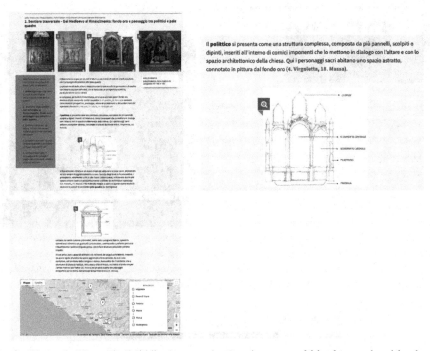

Fig. 3. The path "From the Middle Ages to the Renaissance: gold background and landscape between polyptychs and square blades"

The site contains five paths, structured as in Fig. 3. The body of the page may contains links to the detail sheets. The images in the page can be enlarged, as seen on the right of Fig. 3. An information box can be opened through the tag "i". The map on the low end of the page refers to the sites mentioned in the page.

An example of detail sheet is illustrated in Fig. 4 for a specific paint. The page contains information extracted from catalog card stored in the BeWeb database and enriched with the information added by the operator. The image of the paint enlarged on the bottom of the page has been tagged; tags open information boxes about the figures in the paint. The BeWeB database makes accessible to the experts the OA forms and many searching options, as shown in Fig. 5.

Fig. 4. Detail sheet. On the left is the upper part of the page, the lower on the right.

Fig. 5. The OA form and the search engine of BeWeB.

5   Conclusion

The online dissemination of cultural heritage knowledge is a valuable means not only for giving visibility to less known artistic works but also for the increase of touristic flows toward museums, churches and historical sites located outside the mainstream touristic circuits [40].

VIEd'ARTE Project has implemented a framework supporting cultural operators for the web publishing activities. So far it has been implemented the publication framework, extending the Wordpress engine with plugins for the main presentation schemas: Routes through geographic locations and Paths with specific interpretation keys, as discussed in the present work, and Virtual visits of buildings [24]. The Project is now continuing its research and development work on the implementation of data access tools and on the definition of more presentation schemas. The current activities concern the development of further extensions of the basic environment: on the publication side it is under development the application for virtual exhibitions, on the data access side it is being defined the extraction of information from databases compliant with the OAI protocol and with the Linked Open Data (LOD) model.

Acknowledgments. The work has been funded by Regione Toscana, under the grant "Assegni di ricerca in ambito culturale 2019 finanziati con le risorse del POR FSE TOSCANA 2014–2020 e rientranti nell'ambito di Giovanisì (www.giovanisi.it), progetto di Regione Toscana per l'autonomia dei giovani". (Research grants in the cultural field 2019 funded with resources of POR FSE TOSCANA 2014–2020 and falling within the scope of Giovanisì - www.giovanisi.it - initiative of Regione Toscana for the autonomy of young people).

The work is co-funded by Università di Pisa-Dipartimento di Civiltà e Forme del Sapere, Diocesi di Massa Carrara-Pontremoli, Associazione Firmafede di Sarzana, IDS&Unitelm S.r.l., WECA WebCattolici Italiani.

Partners of the Project are Università di Pisa-Dipartimento di Civiltà e Forme del Sapere e Università di Pisa-Dipartimento di Ingegneria dell'Informazione; Soprintendenze Archeologia, Belle Arti e Paesaggio per le province di Lucca e Massa Carrara e per le province di Pisa e Livorno; Archivi di Stato di Massa, di Lucca, di Pisa e di Livorno; Biblioteca Statale di Lucca e Bibli-oteca Universitaria di Pisa; Associazione Firmafede Sarzana; Diocesi di Massa Carrara-Pontremoli, Arcidiocesi di Pisa, Conferenza Episcopale Italiana; WECA Associazione Web Cattolici Italiani; IDS&Unitelm S.r.l.

References

1. Special issue on Web Information Systems. Commun. ACM **41**(7) (1998)
2. D'Agnelli, F.M.: Di nuovo BeWeB...BeWeB nuovo. In: Storie fuori serie. Gli archivi storici ecclesiastici in una nuova prospettiva condivisa. Proc. Online, Roma (2017). https://www.beweb.chiesacattolica.it/UI/attachments/Dinuovo_BeWeB_Dagnelli.pdf
3. ISAD (G): General International Standard Archival Description, 2nd edn. https://www.ica.org/en/isadg-general-international-standard-archival-description-second-edition
4. ISAAR (CPF): International Standard Archival Authority Record for Corporate Bodies, Persons and Families, 2nd edn. https://www.ica.org/en/isaar-cpf-international-standard-archival-authority-record-corporate-bodies-persons-and-families-2nd

5. ICCD: Beni artistici e storici - Schede OA. http://www.iccd.beniculturali.it/getFile.php?id=7508
6. ICCD: Beni architettonici e ambientali, Edifici e manufatti - Scheda A. http://www.iccd.beniculturali.it/getFile.php?id=4528
7. Dublin Core Metadata Initiative: Metadata Terms Documentation. http://dublincore.org/documents/dcmi-terms/
8. Metadata, Standards and Resource Discovery. In: Technical Guidelines for Digital Cultural Content Creation Programmes, pp. 47–62. https://www.minervaeurope.org/publications/MINERVA%20TG%202.0.pdf
9. Z39.50 Maintenance Agency. http://www.loc.gov/z3950/agency/
10. Open Archive Initiative. http://www.openarchives.org/
11. Parent, C., Spaccapietra, S.: Issues and approaches of database integration. Commun. ACM **41**(5), 166–178 (1998)
12. Vdovjak, R., Houben, G.-J.: Providing the semantic layer for WIS design. In: Pidduck, A.B., Ozsu, M.T., Mylopoulos, J., Woo, C.C. (eds.) CAiSE 2002. LNCS, vol. 2348, pp. 584–599. Springer, Heidelberg (2002). https://doi.org/10.1007/3-540-47961-9_40
13. Extensible Markup Language XML. https://www.w3.org/XML/
14. The Minerva Project. http://www.minervaeurope.org
15. MINERVA Quality Principles. https://www.minervaeurope.org/qau/qualityprinciples.htm
16. Handbook for quality in cultural Web sites: improving quality for citizens. http://www.minervaeurope.org/publications/qualitycriteria.htm
17. Technical Guidelines for Digital Cultural Content Creation Programmes. https://www.minervaeurope.org/publications/MINERVA%20TG%202.0.pdf
18. Bechini, A., Tomasi, A., Ceccarelli, G.: The *Ecumene* experience to data integration in cultural heritage web information systems. In: Proceedings of the International Workshop on Web Information Systems Modeling – WISM 2004, vol. 1, pp. 49–59. Riga Technical University, Riga (2004)
19. Bechini, A., Floridia, C., Tomasi, A.: Il Portale Ecumene: un Web Information System per i Beni Culturali. In: Atti del XLII Congresso Annuale AICA, pp. 675–688. AICA, Milano (2004)
20. Progetto Ecumene - Experience acquired from the development of technological instruments for the transmission of knowledge on Italian cultural heritage. Poster in: Conferenza Europea di MINERVA - Qualità del Web per la cultura. Il patrimonio culturale in rete per la ricerca, per la didattica, per il turismo culturale, Parma (2003). http://www.minervaeurope.org/events/parma/poster/ecumene.pdf
21. Aquarell Project. https://www.ercim.eu/publication/Ercim_News/enw33/michard1.html
22. Aquarell – CIMI Z39.50 Profile. https://www.ercim.eu/publication/Ercim_News/enw33/signore.html
23. LEAF Project. http://xml.coverpages.org/leaf.html
24. Crane, G.: Cultural heritage digital libraries: needs and components. In: Agosti, M., Thanos, C. (eds.) ECDL 2002. LNCS, vol. 2458, pp. 626–637. Springer, Heidelberg (2002). https://doi.org/10.1007/3-540-45747-X_47
25. EAD, Encoded Archival Description. http://www.loc.gov/ead/
26. Europeana. https://pro.europeana.eu/
27. Europeana Portal. https://www.europeana.eu/it
28. Andreoli, L., et al.: Phaidra, un archivio digitale FAIR per la disseminazione e l'accesso integrato a testi, testimonianze, immagini e storie del patrimonio culturale. Digitalia, Anno XIV, N. 1 (2019). http://digitalia.sbn.it/article/view/2281/1552
29. Movio. Mostre virtuali online. https://www.movio.beniculturali.it/index.php?en/1/home
30. BeWeb. Beni ecclesiastici in web. https://beweb.chiesacattolica.it/?l=it_IT. (partially available an english version)

31. BEWEB. Ecclesiastical Property on the Web. Poster in: Conferenza Europea MINERVA - Qualità del Web per la cultura. Il patrimonio culturale in rete per la ricerca, per la didattica, per il turismo culturale. Parma (2003). http://www.minervaeurope.org/events/parma/poster/beweb1.pdf

32. Caputo, G., Poggetti, C., Tomasi, A.: Il progetto Ecumene. In: Archivi & Computer, vol. 14, no. 1, Carocci, Roma, pp. 62–76 (2004)

33. Caputo, G., et al.: Il Progetto Ecumene: strumenti descrittivi per beni culturali di ambito archivistico e storico artistico. In: Archivi & Computer, vol. 12, no. 2, Carocci, Roma, pp. 96–102 (2003)

34. Minerva. Handbook on cultural web user interaction. https://www.minervaeurope.org/publications/Handbookwebuserinteraction.pdf

35. VIEd'ARTE Project. https://museia.cfs.unipi.it/Progetti/progetto-viedarte-virtual-integrated-environment-for-arts-routes-territories-exhibitions-esplorazioni-virtuali-integrate-per-arti-rotte-territori-esposizioni/

36. Manuale per la qualità dei siti web pubblici culturali. https://www.minervaeurope.org/publications/qualitycriteria-i.htm

37. Mostre virtuali online. Linee guida per la realizzazione vers. 1.0, sett. (2011). http://www.otebac.it/index.php?it/320/mostre-virtuali-online-linee-guida-per-la-realizzazione

38. WordPress. https://wordpress.org/

39. Barsotti, F., Baudo, V., Ferrato, A., Gioli, A., Romagnoli, C., Tomasi, A.: VIEd'ARTE: a web publication environment for cultural heritage knowledge. The case study of Archbishop's palace of Pisa. In: Proceedings of Congreso Internacional VIII Centenario Catedral de Burgos. El mundo de las catedrales, Burgos (2022, to be published))

40. Morvillo, A., Becheri, E.: (a cura di): Dalla crisi alle opportunità per il futuro del turismo in Italia. Supplemento alla XXIII Edizione del Rapporto sul Turismo Italiano. Rogiosi editore, Napoli (2020)

Innovative Technologies for Virtual Museums: An Overview

Rocco Furferi[✉] [iD]

Department of Industrial Engineering, University of Florence, Florence, Italy
rocco.furferi@unifi.it

Abstract. The ongoing cultural heritage transition process, in which elaborate digitization plans for cultural artifacts are developed to overcome concerns about the objects' long-term preservation and storage, is now addressing issues for improving and expanding access to digital objects. As a result, new techniques and cutting-edge tools are needed for galleries, libraries, archives, and museums players to deploy and distribute the richness of knowledge housed inside cultural property.

Accordingly, the present work provides an overview of the most significant studies addressing the use of innovative technologies for virtual museums and develops some thoughts on how the state of the art is improving as technology progresses. Following a discussion of the most current and significant research on this topic, the article drafts a number of proposals on how the state of the art might be overcome in the near future.

Keywords: 3D acquisition · Virtual museums · Augmented reality · Annotated models

1 Introduction

The ongoing cultural heritage transition process, in which extensive digitization plans for cultural artifacts are introduced mostly out of concern for the objects' long-term preservation and storage, is now addressing the concerns of improving and extending access to the digital objects. In this light, new methodologies and cutting-edge tools are required for galleries, libraries, archives, and museums (GLAM) players to deploy and distribute the wealth of information contained inside cultural heritage. To be valorized, digitized items must draw the attention on a general or more expert audience by providing educational and exhaustive material to capture the interest of "digital audience" and, at the same time, to enhance the visibility of cultural heritage.

Virtual Museums (VMs) creators are the most suitable mediator for this cultural content, as the user experience derived by new applications and tools is to be guided and customized depending on the kind of user to create a satisfying experience for visitors [1]. Virtual museums can be either as a sort of "digital footprint" of a physical museum, or they can work maintaining the authoritative character bestowed by the Inter-national Council of Museums (ICOM) in its definition [2]. Therefore, a virtual museum should not

R. Furferi et al. (Eds.): Florence Heri-Tech 2022, CCIS 1645, pp. 432–444, 2022.
https://doi.org/10.1007/978-3-031-20302-2_32

only represent existing exhibitions, or repositories of collections or archives [3]. Rather, it should serve as a framework for storytelling and learning tools that explain the context of the displayed items or collections by utilizing modern communication technologies and interacting with the user through personalization based on his experience and intentions, as well as his level of understanding.

As a result, the introduction of new tools and media on the one hand, and the spread of ICT literacy on the other, prepared the way for and compelled the use of digital technologies. In this context, VMs may improve access to the wealth of information contained in a collection by making available a greater number of documents and items than a traditional museum can display, as well as the ability to view parts and details of works that would not be visible through direct observation of the original. Moreover, they are required to remain accessible over time, and from all over the word.

Furthermore, a VM makes valuable works and information available to the public without putting them at danger. From the perspective of the curator, they also have the advantage of being dynamic in terms of both planning and activities and contents [4]. They can even be developed on a shoestring budget, are less expensive than live exhibitions, and can serve as an online repository for material show information. Researchers in the field of Cultural Heritage developed a variety of methodologies and tools to carry out the aforementioned critical procedures. Using such methodologies, the VM curator will be able to combine historical and cultural information about an artwork with other features such as its physical properties (e.g. 3D shape, visible colour), hidden data revealed by IR and X-ray imaging, augmented or virtual itineraries, and storytelling by implementing technology-based tools and software platforms. Not by chance, there is a lot of study going on in the scientific literature right now geared towards enriching and harmonizing the experience provided by virtual museums. Accordingly, the present paper proposes an overview of most relevant studies addressing the use of novel technologies for VMs and drafts some considerations on how the state of the art is evolving with technology progress.

2   State of the Art

The present work provide a bird eye view on the following methods and tools used to enhance the VMs design: 2D and 3D imaging technologies, 3D models from 2D artwork, annotated 3D models to support metadata, watermarking, creation and virtual/augmented reality techniques and methods. For each of the aforementioned method, the main literature studies are discussed. Furthermore, the paper drafts a number of considerations on how the state of the art might be overcome in the near future.

2.1   2D Imaging Technologies

Virtual museums require high-resolution photographs to transfer information about virtual exhibitions. As widely recognized, the level of detail of digital images is determined by their resolution. In the recent past, the high-resolution images were difficult to be maintained and sent across networks due to their reliance on bandwidth availability. For this reason, image servers used a imaging architecture able to provide the user with scalability and interactivity opportunities by storing different resolutions of an image in a single file [2]. This architecture is still used, even though internet connections are nowadays faster and more reliable. One of the most relevant cases of this kind of architecture is the Google Art Project; it was born out of a collaboration with some of the world's most prestigious art institutions to enable people to discover and view works of art online at a high level of detail. More than 45,000 artworks have been scanned utilizing *gigapixel* technology in partnership with over 250 institutes. [5]. *Gigapixel* photographs enable accurate documentation and analysis of artworks, which is valuable for art scholars and curators. Furthermore, the virtual representations that can be made from this type of image make the artwork accessible to anyone have an Internet access. Observers will be able to immerse themselves in the art in such a way that they will notice many details that would otherwise go unnoticed by the naked eye during a visit.

Due of the technical complexity and specialized equipment, there are very few companies specialized in obtaining *gigapixel* photographs of artworks outside than Google. Some examples include the French state organization *Centre de Recherche et de Restauration des Musées de France* CR2MF [6], the Italian firm *Haltadefinizione* [7] and the *Spanish Madpixel* [8].

2.2   3D Imaging Technologies

Because of its capacity to digitize items with high resolution and record exact surface data and distance information in a relatively quick and straightforward manner, 3D imaging/scanning is one of the greatest technologies for reality documenting. This is particularly true when the artwork consists of a sculpture, a bas-relief or an architectural piece. In fact, 3D recording can create detailed archives of important artefacts and allow for digital reconstruction of the above-mentioned artworks.

The fundamental advantage of 3D scanning in the sphere of cultural and historical heritage preservation is the possibility of high-precision fixation of dimensions and volumetric depiction of scanned objects.

As widely recognized, many methods for retrieving a 3D model of a three-dimensional artwork are available. Most important are photogrammetry, structured light scanning, laser scanning, RGB-D-based and computerized tomography. Photogrammetry is a technique for creating 3D models from many pictures of an object taken from various perspectives [9]. The earliest steps in photogrammetry were taken in the field of surveying to simulate geographical topography [10]. Structured-light 3D scanning is a way of acquiring the 3D geometry of an item by projecting structured patterns of light onto it. When a narrow band of light is projected onto a three-dimensionally constructed surface, it produces a line of illumination that appears distorted from viewpoints other than the projector's, and it can be used to geometrically reconstruct the surface shape. Pattern projection, which consists of numerous stripes at once or of arbitrary fringes, is a faster and more adaptive method since it allows for the capture of a large number of samples at once. The basic principle of laser scanning is the emission of a light signal (laser) by an emitter and the reception of the return signal by a receiver. During the reception phase, the scanner employs various distance-calculating procedures that distinguish the type of equipment. The 3D laser scanners are classified as based on "time of flight" (TOF) when the distance is calculated based on the time elapsed between the laser's emission and the reception of the return signal, or based on 'phase difference' (Phase shift based) when the calculation is performed by comparing the phases of the emitted signal and the return signal. The movement of the body and the mirror occurs at extremely high speeds, allowing data acquisition at rates of up to a million points per second.

Regardless of the approach employed, the result is a 3D point cloud of the scanned object that may be further processed using specialised software packages capable of reconstructing the 3D geometry of the scanned object in terms of surfaces. Another essential consideration when dealing with 3D reconstruction of artworks is the possibility of 3D printing replicas to be accessed by a visitor, or even to replace original artworks, for example, when the latter is damaged or destroyed. Just to cite a ew, replicas of statues were realized in the case of Michelangelo's David, presented at the Dubai Expo in 2021 and for the reconstruction of the ruined Nimrud Lion (see Fig. 1) in Iraq.

Fig. 1. 3D printed replica of the Nimrud Lion.

In scientific literature, there is a huge number of works proposing 3D reconstruction of artworks to be used for VM or for populating virtual collections [11]. Not by chance, 3D digitization of the cultural heritage has become a standard process in recent years, as demonstrated by the work within the Europeana Tech community on 3D digitization workflows and publishing pipelines.

2.3 From 2D Artworks to 3D Models

The topic of 3D reconstruction from a single 2D image has a long history in computer vision scientific literature, and it stems from studies aimed at recovering 3D information from 2D photos, photographs, or paintings. Two important papers dealing with this topic are [12] and [13]. Authors in [19] propose a methodology for retrieving a 3D representation of a painted scene with single point perspective using vanishing point identification, foreground from background segmentation, and scene polygonal reconstruction. Authors in [20] automatically generates a rough, scaled 3D model from a single photograph by classifying each image pixel as ground, vertical, or sky and predicts the location of the horizon. These remarkable contributions, as well as comparable approaches, aim to create a 3D virtual representation of the scene when elements are virtually isolated from one another. A more interesting approach for a transition from 2D artworks to 3D models, is to create digital bas-reliefs, especially when the 3D content can be made available to visually impaired people in the form of a 3D printed prototype. Some important studies dealing directly with relief reconstruction from single images may be found in the literature, particularly those concerning coinage and commemorative medals (see for instance references [14] and [15]). The input image, which frequently depicts logos, stemmas, human faces, and figures protruding from the image background, is converted into a flat bas-relief by adding volume. Commercial tools such as ArtCAM and JDPaint [16] have also been developed with bas-relief reconstruction functions from photos.

Users must employ a vector representation of the item to be reconstructed and "inflate" the surface delimited by the object outlines to use these software tools. The aforementioned method is useful for producing models in which the subjects are volumetrically isolated from the background but have compressed depth, such as figures created by embossing a metallic plate.

A significant interaction is required to obtain a faithful surface reconstruction; in particular, for sophisticated structures such as faces, vectorizing the subject's contours is insufficient; each part to be inflated must be both outlined and vectorized. Lips, cheeks, nose, eyes, brows, and other facial features must be drawn by hand.

When working with paintings, this is a time-consuming operation because they are often characterized by a variety of themes blended into the background (or by a

Fig. 2. Bas-relief reconstruction of artwork "The Healing of the Cripple and the Raising of Tabitha" fresco by Masolino da Panicale in the Brancacci Chapel (Church of Santa Maria del Carmine in Florence, Italy) [20].

background drawing attention from the main subjects). Several ways have been devised so far to address these challenges and build models that visually resemble sculptor-made bas-relief from paintings. Most relevant methods are described in [17–20] where different methods such as Shape From Shading, perspective and volume-based scene reconstruction and rapid prototyping are used to create tactile bas-relief (Fig. 2).

2.4 Annotated 3D Models

Current museum content management systems, such as Adlib Museum [21], MuseumPlus [22], and Museumindex [23], are primarily text-centric and are utilized with vast collections (e.g. State Museums of Berlin, Europeana, British Film Institute, Louvre, Victoria and Albert Museum,). A number of metadata, including CIDOC CRM, LIDO, METS are supported. Nonetheless, native 3D format for annotating, storing, and presenting virtual 3D/4D models is restricted, particularly for viewing and analyzing 3D/4D data.

The most common solution is to save the 3D data and then link to external tools to open, visualize, and manipulate it. This implies that the data "is not natively integrated in the museum content management system" [24]. The Collectionstrust, UK [24], provides an excellent summary of current content management systems. Other examples include the Smithsonian Explorer, a partnership between the Smithsonian Institution and Autodesk that uses proprietary technology to display goods in 3D on the web but is not integrated into their database backend. It enables the exploration and measurement of items, as well as the presentation of narrative storytelling centered on the 3D artefact. With the advent of 3D mass digitization, annotation with provenance and metadata is centered on the 3D Model, with the ability to create annotations by dragging and dropping them onto the surface of an object, or marking surface areas or regions of interest and connecting them to documents, pictures, or other 3D models. The IVB (Integrated Viewer Browser) [25] serves as the frontend, and the backend includes a CIDOC-CRM [26] and CRMdig [27] compliant metadata repository [28, 29] as well as object data repositories at the associated museums.

2.5 Watermarking

In the CH world, copyright protection is inextricably linked to access to digital contents resembling artworks. The use of multimedia watermarking as a vehicle to link copyright information on the new proposed type of cultural data (visible and invisible annotated 3D representations of artworks) is a true innovation in this field because it allows for the agile circulation of valuable data to facilitate access to and sharing of European cultural knowledge. To access such hidden information, a detector is required, whereas protected data can be imported, read, and processed by a software platform without the use of any special tools.

According to scientific literature [30], the main requirements of a generic watermarking system are transparency, robustness, and capacity. The first one implies that the embedded watermark should not corrupt the original image. Robustness defines the capability of the watermark in reacting to various attacks, either unplanned (e.g. cropping, compression or scaling) or planned (i.e. aimed at destroying the watermark).

The maximum quantity of information that can be kept in digital data to ensure proper watermark recovery is defined as capacity.

Each kind of data has its own peculiarity and requires specific algorithms and implementations to be developed. Audio, Video, Stereoscopic Video, Images and 3D data have been deeply investigated in literature [31, 32].

2.6 Virtual and Augmented Visualization Techniques

Integration into a VR-Environment, such as VR Museums, is used to add information layers over static content, such as printouts, or real-life surroundings, such as authentic places, but it can also function as a steering device, generating an interface for navigating around VR Applications. There have been many applications displaying the power of this VR Technique, and it was well incorporated in the market and the existing editor's api's. Not by chance, in CH, a lot of attention was drawn on VR Headsets whose principle is based on devices allowing immersive and augmented viewer experiences but follows the rule of user-tracked displays combined with stereo vision. Because these equipment will have a considerable impact on computer and mobile interfaces, their implementation for the optional viewing mode of Virtual Museums must be considered. Companies like Oculus Rift, Sony's Project Morpheus, HTC Valve, Vove VR, Avegant Glyph and Razer OSVR carried out beta-tests over the past years and released consumer versions to the market a few years ago. Other technologies, such as *Samsung Gear*, *Google Cardboard* and *Zeiss VR One* have already released hardware and are widely recognized on the market. Other wearable systems use mini-displays in front of special eyeglasses to augment and display content that merges real world and virtual settings. Some of the competitors are Google Glass, Microsoft Hololens, Sony Smarteyeglasses, Epson Moverio and VUZIX M100 and Optivent Oral and many others. It has to be mentioned that most of these solutions are still in beta state and are quite costly now, which prevents a wide usage these products, but will like the VR Headsets, reach a state of maturity and distribution. In addition to these techniques, a combination of tracked 3D glasses and a tracked input device (stylus pen) provides the most full 3D experience for this type of VR vision. While some of these techniques seem to be outdated it is likely that they will experience an uplift with mentioned solutions of auto-stereo and tracked stereoscopic devices and is still a vital cost-effective way to present VR 3D Content.

3   Advances Beyond the State of the Art

The methodologies and related technologies described in Sect. 2 embody the current state of the art in the field of 2D and 3D modeling and geometry retrieval for CH.

Based on the relevant work done by researchers all over the world, a number of potential future developments of these methodologies can be hinted at.

3.1   2D Imaging Technologies

Digital picture capture with *gigapixel* resolution is a demanding operation, and major challenges may develop owing to physical issues such as light diffraction, which operates as a barrier, limiting the sharpness that an optical device and a digital sensor can achieve. As a result, advancements in digital sensor resolution have already surpassed the limit set by light diffraction and the optical resolution provided by lenses [33], which cannot compete with the resolution of today's best digital sensors. Going beyond this would not actually take advantage of the sensor's effective resolution unless the size of the optical-sensor assembly is increased, which is not conceivable for the foreseeable development of traditional cameras.

Multi-shot panorama capture is a viable approach for overcoming diffraction and achieving *gigapixel* images with conventional cameras. It requires taking a series of shots from the same angle, with enough overlap between them to allow them to be merged to create a higher-resolution image using image-stitching software.

A panoramic head is required to fix the optical center or no-parallax point of the lens while spinning the camera to gather the various photos that will comprise the final image in order to make a perfect stitch between images and minimize parallax errors.

Unfortunately, various disadvantages limit image sharpness when recording artworks of moderate size due to the shallow depth of field supplied by long focal length lenses.

3.2 3D Imaging Technologies

Despite the use of 3D technologies is becoming more and more common in the CH field, the use of 3D devices has some drawbacks to be considered during their use.

When there is insufficient illumination, photogrammetry applications are limited by the difficulty in matching points between images with low-contrast, especially for uniformly textured surfaces. Furthermore, where there are canopy covers, the measurement's precision decreases, mostly due to light ray blockages and the inability to project its own light source.

The main challenge with structured light devices is specular reflections and ambient light. Because the volumetric 3D image is generated with grey levels, the ambient light must be low. Furthermore, the light projector must be of high quality, as projector defocusing (unless binary coded patterns are employed) can often damage the results. The projector must be properly calibrated, adjusted, and focused on the entire scene. It should also be noted that any vibration or movement can result in distorted 3D representations with incorrect geometric measurements. 3D reconstruction will eventually necessitate powerful processing units for extensive calculations.

Referring to laser-camera devices, the acquisition system is largely dependent on sensor characteristics: the sensor is one of the most limiting parts for speed limitations and overall performance. Moreover, inherent noise generated by the laser speckle reduces the resolution of systems.

The adoption of RGB-D cameras for 3D scanning has grown at a rapid pace, owing to their low cost and improving performance. Despite the fact that a number of studies [34] on the performance of RGB-D cameras indicated a certain reliability in utilizing such devices as 3D scanners, they were not designed for this purpose. For this reason, the main limits in using this technology for 3D acquisition of artworks is their low resolution. Future advancements on this technology, presumably by Intel (which leads the market) will allow a more accurate reconstruction in the future.

Shifting the focus from digital 3D models to physical, 3D-printed models, it is possible to state that 3D printing technology still has certain limitations in the application of sculpture. Many aspects, such as print size and materials, influence its close relationship with sculpture art. This means that visitors can get closer to the artefacts than ever before, but will the essence of the art is somehow lost in the translation of the actual statue and the replica. Moreover, costs and times for creating the 3D prototypes are still an issue to be considered.

Future advancements of this technology will allow increasing the availability of printed materials and to speed-up the process of 3D printing. This will help Museums curators to increase the number of printed replicas, thus helping with education, conservation and research.

Referring to the availability of datasets of 3D models, currently the information offered is highly variable. Frequently, consumers are unable to distinguish between 3D items that can be directly modified and basic images or movies of 3D models.

As a result, experts are currently attempting to develop better criteria for data producers and aggregators. This will aid in the appropriate labeling of 3D material and will promote the availability of more useful 3D content for consumers to discover and enjoy. Not by coincidence, a task force within Europeana is currently striving to strengthen support for 3D cultural heritage as well as the availability of this content for use in education, research, and the creative industries.

Future works in this field will be addressed to the development of FAQs and recommendations for 3D creators and CH institutions about posting 3D media online (both in the context of Europeana and in other databases). Moreover, ways for identifying viewers and 3D media formats suggested for inclusion in collections, as well as methods for linking and embedding 3D material are required for the future.

3.3   From 2D Artworks to 3D Models

The 3D model retrieval from paintings is subject to a number of limitations both referring to tasks than cannot be performed automatically (e.g. scene segmentation) and in terms of "interpretation" of the scene, (e.g. self-occlusions in the painted scene give rise to missing information in the 3D reconstruction). As a result, scientific literature should improve existing techniques by creating an interactive and specialized tool capable of (1) fast image segmentation, (2) building a consistent scene in which segmented objects are modelled and placed (e.g., according to perspective, if any), (3) reconstructing hidden parts (with consistent geometry), and (4) providing color and texture information for 3D reconstructed surfaces. Another important aspect to be considered [35] is the development of 3D scanning-based methods for assisting the exploration of bas-reliefs. This noble goal remains unfulfilled in scientific literature, not simply due to technical constraints. In fact, guiding a user through the exploration of an artwork, such as a visually impaired person, cannot be limited to a description of an artwork scene and/or touched areas, but rather a gradual aid in acquiring information and organizing it into a "mental scheme" that becomes progressively more complete and detailed. As a result, the development of a system capable of automatically providing spoken information about touched locations should be regarded as a step forward in this field. The introduction of such an automatic verbal guide could increase the user's autonomy during the exploration, allowing him to lead the experience (e.g., automatically establishing the time required for a full appreciation, moving the hands freely, taking time to think, etc.), achieving greater freedom in exploring the artworks.

3.4 Annotated 3D Models

Because many artefacts, once obtained, disappear in archives for an average of 14–15 years, there is a need for a multi-modular scanning technique to record surface and volumetric data, as well as extra information about them, in the best possible quality. This will open up a plethora of new avenues for exploration and experience, in addition to the ability to derive scientific conclusions from those models (such as devised in this project). Capturing the reflectance model of an artifact, for example, will allow perfect recreation of its look.

It will be possible to learn more about the conservation state or the processes used to make that work of art by using infrared or ultraviolet imaging. It will be easier to establish collaboratively and concurrently establish cross-relationships, retrieve related provenance data, find similar artefacts across collections, and demonstrate access to cultural heritage at large by fusing this data in web-based 3D-centered annotation, analysis, and exploration tools. By merging, investigating, and analyzing all of this rich information, we became able to consolidate 3D models in web-based 3D-centered annotation tools rather than cutting-edge but text-centric and platform-dependent museum software. Long-term goals include developing 3D consolidated data models that combine results from numerous scanning methods and enable for their exploration, annotation, and analysis via 3D web-based interfaces. In this context, 3D web-based annotation and analysis tools will be platform independent and provide museums with quick access to their data while requiring minimal gear.

3.5 Watermarking

Literature points out, for the future, the necessity of studying and implementing more robust algorithms able to fuse the existing watermarking techniques designed for the possible kind of raw data (2D/3D/audio/video) in a blind and robust watermarking schema for the annotated multi-textured 3D model. Having watermarks embedded in the novel kind of data will then allow fruition for everybody, from anywhere at any time, but in a controlled way, ensuring the possibility of a trusted distribution, publishing and distribution of such models.

3.6 Virtual and Augmented Visualization Techniques

WebGL technology have lately been used in the field of cultural heritage for 3D depiction of cultural artifacts on the web. Some of the recently funded EU projects in this regard are 3DCOFORM, 3DICONS and RE@CT. The 3DCOFORM project proposes and implements an open standard of 3D model annotation based on X3D for a variety of digital cultural artifacts. They demonstrated on the internet as well as in live displays. The virtual navigation interface can leverage the 3D model's metadata to focus on specific locations of interest on the cultural artifact. The 3DICONS project expanded on the success of 3DCOFORM by digitizing larger environments such as archaeological sites and structures. The goal of this study was to achieve accurate 3D reconstruction and texture estimate of real-world models. The virtual models could be navigated using a perspective camera that can be manipulated with the mouse and arrow keys. RE@CT introduces a new production approach for creating film-quality interactive characters by capturing actor performance in 3D video. Prior projects in cultural heritage had a key shortcoming in that the virtual navigation algorithms do not combine cinemato-graphic camera techniques and carefully created camera tracks. Some computer games and virtual reality interfaces now include such navigation techniques [36].

However, this has yet to be accomplished for data formats intended to store cultural assets. Accordingly, future works should be addressed to deal with this issue. Another item to examine is 3D hyperlink navigation and communication between users in a virtual world to bridge the gap between recreation, education, and scientific study [37, 38].

4 Conclusions

New techniques and cutting-edge tools are becoming more and more integrated in gal-leries, libraries, archives, and museums to deploy and spread the richness of knowledge housed inside cultural heritage. Not by chance, there is a lot of research going on right now in the scientific literature aimed at expanding and harmonizing the experience provided by virtual museums. The current study presented an overview of the most sig-nificant studies addressing the use of innovative technologies for VMs and developed some thoughts on how the state of the art is improving as technology progresses. The main aim of this work paper was to stimulate the discussion with experts in the CH field, which can increase the awareness of technology-based methods for improving the excellence of researchers in this area.

References

1. Sundar, S.S., Go, E., Kim, H.S., Zhang, B.: Communicating art, virtually! Psychological effects of technological affordances in a virtual museum. Int. J. Hum. Comput. Interact. **31**(6), 385–401 (2015)
2. Styliani, S., Fotis, L., Kostas, K., Petros, P.: Virtual museums, a survey and some issues for consideration. J. Cult. Herit. **10**(4), 520–528 (2009)
3. Lester, P.: Is the virtual exhibition the natural successor to the physical? J. Soc. Arch. **27**(1), 85–101 (2006)
4. Bowen, J.P., Filippini-Fantoni, S.: Personalization and the web from a museum perspective. In: Museums and the Web, vol. 4. Archives & Museum Informatics, Toronto, Canada (2004)
5. Cossairt, O.S., Miau, D., Nayar, S.K.: Gigapixel computational imaging. In: 2011 IEEE International Conference on Computational Photography (ICCP), pp. 1–8 (2011)
6. C2RMF. https://c2rmf.fr. Accessed 12 Jan 2022
7. Haltadefinizione. https://www.haltadefinizione.com. Accessed 21 Jan 2022
8. Madpixel. https://www.madpixel.es. Accessed 20 Nov 2021
9. Gruen, A.: Development and status of image matching in photogrammetry. Photogram. Rec. **27**(137), 36–57 (2012)

10. Luhmann, T.: A historical review on panorama photogrammetry. Int. Arch. Photogramm. Remote Sens. Spat. Inf. Sci. **34**(5/W16), 8 (2004)
11. Kalra, P., Kumar, S., Banerjee, S.: Acquisition, representation, processing and display of digital heritage sites. In: Mallik, A., Chaudhury, S., Chandru, V., Srinivasan, S. (eds.) Digital Hampi: Preserving Indian Cultural Heritage, pp. 71–90. Springer, Singapore (2017). https://doi.org/10.1007/978-981-10-5738-0_6
12. Horry, Y., Anjyo, K., Arai, K.: Tour into the picture: using a spidery mesh interface to make animation from a single image. In: Proceedings of the 24th Annual Conference on Computer Graphics and Interactive Techniques. ACM Press/Addison-Wesley (1997)
13. Hoiem, D., Efros, A.A., Hebert, M.: Automatic photo pop-up. In ACM SIGGRAPH 2005 Papers, pp. 577–584 (2005)
14. Wu, J., et al.: Use of non-photorealistic rendering and photometric stereo in making bas-reliefs from photographs. Graph. Models **76**(4), 202–213 (2014)
15. Wu, J., et al.: Making bas-reliefs from photographs of human faces. Comput. Aided Des. **45**(3), 671–682 (2013)
16. Governi, L., Furferi, R., Puggelli, L., Volpe, Y.: Improving surface re-construction in shape from shading using easy-to-set boundary conditions. Int. J. Comput. Vis. Robot. **3**(3), 225–247 (2013)
17. Reichinger, A., Maierhofer, S., Purgathofer, W.: High-quality tactile paintings. J. Comput. Cult. Herit. **4**(2), 1–13 (2011)
18. Carfagni, M., Furferi, R., Governi, L., Volpe, Y., Tennirelli, G.: Tactile representation of paintings: an early assessment of possible computer based strategies. In: Ioannides, M., Fritsch, D., Leissner, J., Davies, R., Remondino, F., Caffo, R. (eds.) EuroMed 2012. LNCS, vol. 7616, pp. 261–270. Springer, Heidelberg (2012). https://doi.org/10.1007/978-3-642-34234-9_26
19. Volpe, Y., Furferi, R., Governi, L., Tennirelli, G.: Computer-based methodologies for semi-automatic 3D model generation from paintings. Int. J. Comput. Aided Eng. Technol. **6**(1), 88–112 (2014)
20. Furferi, R., Governi, L., Volpe, Y., Puggelli, L., Vanni, N., Carfagni, M.: From 2D to 2.5 D i.e. from painting to tactile model. Graph. Models **76**(6), 706–723 (2014)
21. Adlib Museum – Website. http://www.adlibsoft.com. Accessed 01 Dec 2021
22. Zetcom Ltd. – Website. http://www.zetcom.com. Accessed 01 Dec 2021
23. System Simulation – Website. http://www.ssl.co.uk. Accessed 01 Dec 2021
24. Collections Trust UK – Website.: http://www.collectionstrust.org.uk/collections-link/collections-management/spectrum/choose-a-cms. Accessed 01 Dec 2021
25. Serna, S.P., Schmedt, H., Ritz, M., Stork, A.: Interactive semantic enrichment of 3D cultural heritage collections. In: Proceedings of International Symposium on Virtual Reality, Archaeology and Cultural Heritage (VAST), pp. 33–40 (2012)
26. Crofts, N.; Doerr, M.; Gill, T.; Stead, S., Stiff, M.: Definition of the CIDOC Conceptual Reference Model, ICOM/CIDOC CRM Special Interest Group (2006)
27. Doerr, M., Theodoridou, M.: CRMdig: a generic digital provenance model for scientific observation. TaPP **11**, 20–21 (2011)
28. Doerr, M., et al.: A repository for 3D model production and interpretation in culture and beyond. In: Proceedings of International Symposium on Virtual Reality, Archaeology and Cultural Heritage (VAST), vol. 11, pp. 97–104 (2010)
29. Pan, X., et al.: A repository infrastructure for working with 3D assets in cultural heritage. Int. J. Herit. Digit. Era **1**, 143–166 (2013)
30. Li, L., Wang, S., Zhang, S., Luo, T., Chang, C.C.: Homomorphic encryption-based robust reversible watermarking for 3D model. Symmetry **12**(3), 347 (2020)
31. Lopez, C.: Watermarking of digital geospatial datasets: a review of technical, legal and copyright issues. Int. J. Geogr. Inf. Sci. **16**(6), 589–607 (2002)

32. Delmotte, A., Tanaka, K., Kubo, H., Funatomi, T., Mukaigawa, Y.: Blind watermarking for 3-D printed objects using surface norm distribution. In: 2018 Joint 7th International Conference on Informatics, Electronics & Vision (ICIEV) and 2018 2nd International Conference on Imaging, Vision & Pattern Recognition (icIVPR), pp. 282–288. IEEE (2018)
33. Cabezos-Bernal, P.M., Rodriguez-Navarro, P., Gil-Piqueras, T.: Documenting paintings with gigapixel photography. J. Imaging **7**(8), 156 (2021)
34. Carfagni, M., et al.: Metrological and critical characterization of the Intel D415 stereo depth camera. Sensors **19**(3), 489 (2019)
35. Buonamici, F., Carfagni, M., Furferi, R., Governi, L., Volpe, Y.: are we ready to build a system for assisting blind people in tactile exploration of bas-reliefs? Sensors **16**(9), 1361 (2016)
36. Gherardini, F., Santachiara, M., Leali, F., Enhancing heritage fruition through 3D virtual models and augmented reality: an application to Roman artefacts. Virtual Archaeol. Rev. **10**(21), pp. 67–79 (2019)
37. Vlahakis, V., et al.: Archeoguide: an augmented reality guide for archaeological sites. IEEE Comput. Graph. Appl. **22**(5), 52–60 (2002)
38. Gherardini, F., Santachiara, M., Leali, F. 3D Virtual Reconstruction and Augmented Reality Visualization of Damaged Stone Sculptures. IOP Conf. Ser. Mater. Sci. Eng. **364**(1), 012018 (2018)

Author Index

Printed in the United States
by Baker & Taylor Publisher Services

Printed in the United States
by Baker & Taylor Publisher Services